THE POLARISATION OF ELIZABETHAN POLITICS
The Political Career of Robert Devereux, 2nd Earl of Essex,
1585–1597

The final decades of the reign of Elizabeth I were marked by the meteoric career of her last great favourite, Robert Devereux, 2nd earl of Essex (1566–1601), and the outbreak of bitter political divisions at Court and across the realm. This revisionist study challenges the traditional 'romantic' image of Essex as a military incompetent and political dabbler.

Studying his career between his arrival at Court in 1585 and his appointment as earl marshal at the end of 1597, the book casts Essex in a new light and re-examines his role in the outbreak of factionalism in Elizabethan politics. Using an unparalleled range of manuscript and printed sources it reveals Essex as an intellectual rather than as an instinctive politician, who sought to pursue honour and a sense of divinely ordained destiny through war with Spain. Rejecting the isolationist tendencies of Elizabeth and Burghley, Essex believed passionately that England must be fully engaged in European affairs. His pursuit of this Continental commitment ultimately led to conflict with the Cecils and with the queen herself.

This study explores the forces which drove Essex's career, why true political success remained frustratingly beyond his grasp, and how his efforts to achieve this success helped to fuel the polarisation of Elizabethan politics.

PAUL E. J. HAMMER is Senior Lecturer in History, University of New England, Australia.

Cambridge Studies in Early Modern British History

Series editors

ANTHONY FLETCHER
Professor of History, University of Essex

JOHN GUY
Professor of Modern History, University of St Andrews

JOHN MORRILL
*Professor of British and Irish History, University of Cambridge,
and Vice-Master of Selwyn College*

This is a series of monographs and studies covering many aspects of the history of the British Isles between the late fifteenth century and the early eighteenth century. It includes the work of established scholars and pioneering work by a new generation of scholars. It includes both reviews and revisions of major topics and books, which open up new historical terrain or which reveal startling new perspectives on familiar subjects. All the volumes set detailed research into broader perspectives and the books are intended for the use of students as well as of their teachers.

For a list of titles in the series, see end of book.

THE POLARISATION OF ELIZABETHAN POLITICS

The Political Career of Robert Devereux, 2nd Earl of Essex, 1585–1597

PAUL E. J. HAMMER

CAMBRIDGE
UNIVERSITY PRESS

PUBLISHED BY THE PRESS SYNDICATE OF THE UNIVERSITY OF CAMBRIDGE
The Pitt Building, Trumpington Street, Cambridge CB2 1RP United Kingdom

CAMBRIDGE UNIVERSITY PRESS
The Edinburgh Building, Cambridge CB2 2RU, UK   http://www.cup.cam.ac.uk
40 West 20th Street, New York, NY 10011–4211,   USA http://www.cup.org
10 Stamford Road, Oakleigh, Melbourne 3166, Australia

© Cambridge University Press 1999

First published 1999

Printed in the United Kingdom at the University Press, Cambridge

Typeset in 10/12 Sabon   [ce]

A catalogue record for this book is available from the British Library

Library of Congress cataloguing in publication data
Hammer, Paul E. J.
The polarisation of Elizabeth politics: the political career of Robert Devereux,
2nd Earl of Essex, 1585–1597 / Paul E. J. Hammer.
p.   cm. – (Cambridge studies in early modern British history)
Includes bibliographical references and index.
ISBN 0 521 43485 8 (hb)
1. Essex, Robert Devereux, Earl of, 1566–1601.
2. Great Britain – History – Elizabeth, 1558–1603 – Biography.
3. Great Britain – Politics and government – 1558–1603.
4. Great Britain – Court and courtiers – Biography.
5. Politicians – Great Britain – Biography.
I. Title.   II. Series.
DA358.E8H28   1999   942.05′5′092–dc21   98–35139   CIP
[B]

ISBN 0521 43485 8 hardback

This book is dedicated to my parents,
for their love of history, and to the late Geoffrey Elton,
for his practice of history.

CONTENTS

ILLUSTRATIONS

PREFACE

A little over a decade ago, when I first began graduate study, I looked around for a suitable topic for my Master's dissertation. Based upon my reading of Elizabethan historiography, I had two basic criteria: to avoid the 1590s, which seemed dark and labyrinthine, and to eschew the earl of Essex at all costs. Although I achieved this ambition for my first venture into historical research, it is one of life's little ironies that I have spent most of the time since then working on these very topics which I sought so earnestly to avoid.

Influenced by the books which I had read, I thought that Essex was a kind of political butterfly – colourful and dynamic, but a lightweight compared to the sober government practised by Lord Burghley and his son and political successor, Sir Robert Cecil. To my naive eyes, I think, such a flighty favourite did not really constitute a 'proper' topic for serious research. Like most observers, my views of Essex were based on impressionistic evidence and received opinion – every book seemed to sing a similar tune, so this impression of Essex must be correct. Once I began to delve into the manuscript evidence, however, I soon realised that this traditional view of Essex was profoundly wrong – and, with it, much of our understanding of late Elizabethan politics.

This book is the product of that realisation. It is an attempt to reconstruct the actions and intentions of Essex by using the fullest possible range of surviving evidence and, in the light of this new interpretation, to re-contour our understanding of Elizabethan political life – and, in particular, to explain why politics became so bitterly polarised in the 1590s. I argue that Essex was a far more substantial and significant figure, and that ideas and ideology played a far greater role in late Elizabethan politics, than conventional accounts allow. The latter theme may seem strange when discussing an age which saw the creative outpourings of politically aware writers such as Shakespeare, Marlowe, Spenser and Sidney, and which witnessed bitter and complex struggles over theology. However, it is no great exaggeration to say that modern historiography has largely squeezed ideas and ideology out of the grand narrative of Elizabethan politics, boiling conflict down to matters of personality and rivalry over patronage. Literary works were long ago consigned to the margins of 'history' as ornaments, rather than serious expressions of political ideas. The burst of 'new historicism' among literary scholars in the 1980s did little to change this. With G. R. Elton's attack on J. E. Neale's notion of a 'puritan choir' in Elizabethan parliaments, even religion began to seem a topic which was somehow distinct from 'political history'. Following the lead of scholars such as Patrick Collinson, this book seeks to escape from this intellectual strait-jacket and to put the mind back into our understanding of Elizabethan political culture. By recognising the power of ideas and eroding the artificially narrow conventions about what constitutes 'political' activity, it seeks to contribute to a broader rethinking and (hopefully) renaissance of Elizabethan studies.

No historian can work without access to relevant sources and I am indebted for permission to cite from manuscripts owned or controlled by: the earl of Aylesford; the marquess of Bath; the trustees of the Berkeley Castle Muniments; the keeper of Western Manuscripts at the Bodleian Library, Oxford; the dean and students of Christ Church, Oxford; the president and fellows of Corpus Christi College, Oxford; Viscount De L'Isle; the Henry E. Huntington Library, San Marino, California; the provost and fellows of King's College, Cambridge; the trustees of Lambeth Palace Library; the duke of Northumberland; the master and fellows of Peterhouse, Cambridge; the marquess of Salisbury; the marquess of Tavistock and the trustees of the Bedford Estates; the Robert H. Taylor Collection, Princeton University Libraries; the master and fellows of Trinity College, Cambridge; the University of Cambridge; and the keeper of the University Archives, Oxford. I am also grateful to staff at the Bayersiche Staastbibliothek, Munich; the Berkshire Record Office, Reading; the British Library, especially the Manuscripts Department; Scott H. Duvall, chair of the Special Collections and Manuscripts Department, the Harold B. Lee Library, Brigham Young University, Utah; the Institute of Historical Research, London; the University Library, Cambridge, especially the manuscripts and official publications departments; the Cathedral Library, Canterbury; the Centre for Kentish Studies, Maidstone; Mr R. C. Yorke of the College of Arms, London; Durham University Library; the Folger Shakespeare Library, Washington D.C.; the Guildhall Library, London; Robin Harcourt Williams, librarian and archivist to the marquess of Salisbury; Kate Harris, librarian and archivist to the marquess of Bath; Arthur Owen, archivist of King's College, Cambridge; Dr R. W. Lovatt, Perne Librarian, Peterhouse, Cambridge; Fr Thomas McCoog, archivist for the Jesuit Provincial Archives, London; Dr R. Moravec of the Osterreichische

Nationalbibliothek, Vienna; the Public Record Office, London; the Sheffield Central Library, Sheffield; the Society of Antiquaries, London; University College, London; the University of London Library; and the staff of the Dixson Library, Armidale, Australia.

I am glad to record my gratitude for the funding which has been so vital to my work. I am indebted to the Australian Academy of the Humanities for a travelling fellowship; to the Australian Research Council Small Grants Scheme for a series of awards; to the Leverhulme Trust for awarding me a visiting fellowship which allowed me the privilege of working with the Department of History at Birkbeck College, London; and to the Faculty of Arts at the University of New England for several small but invaluable grants which enabled my work to continue through some difficult times.

Historical research is a largely solitary occupation. There is no substitute for the slow and often tedious process of slogging through books and manuscripts, which can be a profoundly isolating experience. However, communicating the fruits of this research, and even making sense of it, is best done in a communal way, by interacting with other scholars, often from other disciplines. I have been vastly fortunate in all the advice and constructive criticism which I have received over the last few years and I wish to record my sincere gratitude for it. I am deeply indebted to my former supervisors, Michael Graves and the late Sir Geoffrey Elton, who taught me what it means to be an historian. I also owe a great deal to John Morrill, who has been a mentor and a source of acute scholarly advice for a decade. Pauline Croft, Simon Adams and Lisa Jardine offered encouragement when it was needed and made invaluable comments on my work, often telling me what I was saying when I was too obtuse to realise it for myself. Many other scholars have also helped me in many ways, including Bill Acres, Peter Beal, Susan Cerasano, Patrick Collinson, David Crankshaw, Steve Ellis, Doris Fletcher, John Guy, Simon Healy, Chris Kyle, Peter Lake, Wallace MacCaffrey, Thomas McCoog, Charlotte Merton, Helen Payne, Kathy Prior, Michael Questier, Conrad Russell, David Starkey, Bill Sherman, Alan Stewart, Andrew Thrush, Bill Tighe, Bob Tittler, Gustav Ungerer and my friends at Birkbeck. Their advice has made this a far better book than it would otherwise have been: all the defects which remain must be attributed solely to me. I am grateful to Judith Pollman, Ewoud Karelse and Corrie Theilman, who helped me at various times by translating Dutch sources for me. I am also profoundly indebted to my parents for their support and to my sister, Dr Margaret Hammer, for tracking down obscure articles for me when she was still in the midst of her own research on a very different topic. I wish to thank my various friends and colleagues in Armidale and London for all the fun along the way. Finally, I am indebted to Sandra for simply being Sybilline, in more ways than one.

ABBREVIATIONS

Add.	Additional (Manuscript(s))
Al. Oxon.	J. Foster (ed.), *Alumni Oxonienses: the members of the University of Oxford, 1500–1714* (4 vols., Oxford, 1891– 92)
APC	*Acts of the privy council of England, new series,* (eds. J. R. Dasent, E. G. Atkinson, *et al.*, 46 vols., London, 1890– 1964)
Apologie	[Robert Devereux, 2nd earl of Essex], *An apologie of the earle of Essex, against those which jealously, and maliciously, tax him to be the hinderer of the peace and quiet of his country* (London, 1603, *STC* no. 6788)
BIHR	*Bulletin of the Institute of Historical Research*
Birch, *Memoirs*	T. Birch, *Memoirs of the reign of Queen Elizabeth, from the year 1581 till her death, from the original papers of ... Anthony Bacon* (2 vols., London, 1754)
BL	British Library
BLO	Bodleian Library, Oxford
BRO	Berkshire Record Office, Reading
Camden, *Elizabeth*	William Camden, *The history of the most renowned and victorious Princess Elizabeth, late queen of England* (4th edn, London, 1688, Wing no. C 363)
'Career'	P. E. J. Hammer, '"The bright shininge sparke": the political career of Robert Devereux, *c.*1585–*c.*1597' (unpub. Ph.D. thesis, University of Cambridge, 1991)
Cecil MS(S)	Cecil MS(S), Hatfield House, Hertfordshire
CKS	Centre for Kentish Studies, Maidstone, Kent
Collins, *Sidney papers*	A. Collins, *Letters and memorials of state ... [of*

	the Sidney family] ... from the originals at Penshurst Place in Kent (2 vols., London, 1746)
Commons	P. W. Hasler (ed.), *The history of parliament. The House of Commons 1558–1603* (3 vols., London, 1981)
CSPD	*Calendar of state papers, domestic series, preserved in Her Majesty's Public Record Office, Edward VI, Mary I, Elizabeth, James I* (eds. R. Lemon, M. A. E. Green, 12 vols., London, 1865–72)
CSPF	*Calendar of state papers, foreign series, of the reign of Elizabeth* (eds. J. Stevenson, A. J. Crosby, et al., 23 vols. in 26, London, 1863–1950)
CSPIre	*Calendar of state papers relating to Ireland, of the reign of Elizabeth* (eds. H. C. Hamilton, E. G. Atkinson et al., 11 vols., London, 1860–1912)
CSPScot	*Calendar of the state papers relating to Scotland and Mary, Queen of Scots, 1547–1603, preserved in the Public Record Office, and elsewhere in England* (eds. J. Bain, W. K. Boyd, et al., 13 vols. in 14, Edinburgh and Glasgow, 1898–1969)
CSPSpan	*Calendar of letters and state papers, relating to English affairs, preserved principally in the archives of Simancas, Elizabeth* (ed. M. A. S. Hume, 4 vols., London, 1896–99)
CSPVen	*Calendar of state papers and muniments, relating to English affairs, existing in the archives and collections of Venice, and in other libraries of northern Italy* (eds. R. Brown, G. Cavendish-Bentick, et al., 38 vols., London, 1864–1947)
CUL	Cambridge University Library
Devereux, *Lives*	W. B. Devereux, *Lives and letters of the Devereux, earls of Essex, in the reigns of Elizabeth, James I and Charles I, 1540–1646* (2 vols., London, 1853)
Devereux MS(S)	Devereux MS(S), Longleat House, Wiltshire
DLB	*Dictionary of literary biography* (continuing series, Detroit, 1978–)
DNB	*Dictionary of national biography* (eds. L. Stephen and S. Lee, London, 1885–1900, 22 vols., 1908–9 edn).
DUL	Durham University Library

DWB	*Dictionary of Welsh biography down to 1940* (produced under the auspices of the Honourable Society of Cymmrodorion, London, 1959)
EHR	*English Historical Review*
ELR	*English Literary Renaissance*
FSL	Folger Shakespeare Library, Washington D.C., USA
GL	Guildhall Library, London
HBL	Harold B. Lee Library, Brigham Young University, Provo, Utah, USA
HEH	Henry E. Huntington Library, San Marino, California, USA
HJ	*Historical Journal*
HLQ	*Huntington Library Quarterly*
HMC	Historical Manuscripts Commission
HMCA	HMC. *Report on the manuscripts of the earl of Ancaster, preserved at Grimsthorpe* (Dublin, 1907)
HMCD	HMC. *Report on the manuscripts of Lord De L'Isle and Dudley preserved at Penshurst Place* (London, 6 vols., 1925–66)
HMCR	HMC *Twelfth report, appendix, part iv. The manuscripts of His Grace the duke of Rutland, GDC, preserved at Belvoir Castle* (London, 1888)
HMCS	HMC. *A calendar of the manuscripts of the Most Hon. the marquis of Salisbury, KG, &c, preserved at Hatfield House, Hertfordshire* (24 vols., London, 1883–1976)
L&A	*List and analysis of state papers, foreign series, Elizabeth I, preserved in the Public Record Office* (ed. R. B. Wernham, 6 vols., London, 1964–94)
Leycester corr.	J. Bruce (ed.), *Correspondence of Robert Dudley, earl of Leycester, during his government of the Low Countries, in the years 1585 and 1586* (Camden Society, 27, 1844)
LPL	Lambeth Palace Library, London
Murdin	W. Murdin, *A collection of state papers relating to affairs in the reign of Queen Elizabeth, from the year 1571 to 1596 …* (London, 1759)
Nichols, *Progresses*	J. Nichols, *The progresses and public processions of Queen Elizabeth* (3 vols., London, 1823)
N&Q	*Notes and Queries*

n.s.	new series
pr.	Printed or calendared in
PRO	Public Record Office, London
SA	Society of Antiquaries, Burlington House, London
SC	Sale catalogue(s) issued by Sotheby's of London
Spedding, *Bacon letters*	J. Spedding (ed.), *The letters and the life of Francis Bacon, including all his occasional works* (7 vols., London, 1861–74)
STC	*A short-title catalogue of books printed in England, Scotland and Ireland, and of English books printed abroad 1475–1640* (eds. A. W. Pollard and G. R. Redgrave, revised by W. A. Jackson, F. S. Ferguson and K. F. Pantzer, 3 vols., London, 1976–91)
Stow	John Stow, *The annales of England, faithfully collected out of the most autenticall authors, records and other monuments of antiquitie, from the first inhabitation untill this present yeere 1601* (London, 1601, *STC* no. 23336)
TCP	G. E. C[okayne] *The complete peerage of England Ireland Great Britain and the United Kingdom extant extinct or dormant* (eds. V. Gibbs, *et al.*, 13 vols. in 14, London, 1910–59)
Tenison	E. M. Tenison, *Elizabethan England: being the history of this country "in relation to all foreign princes"* (12 vols. in 13, pr. for subscribers, Leamington Spa, 1933–61)
TRHS	*Transactions of the Royal Historical Society*
UCL	University College, London
ULL	University of London Library
unfol.	lacking foliation or other forms of numbering
Ungerer	G. Ungerer (ed.), *A Spaniard in Elizabethan England: the correspondence of Antonio Perez's exile* (2 vols., London, 1974–76)
Unton corr.	R. J. Stevenson (ed.), *Correspondence of Sir Henry Unton, knt, ambassador from Queen Elizabeth to Henry IV king of France, in the years MDXCI and MDXCII* (Roxburghe Club, London, 1847)
VCH	*The Victoria history of the counties of England* (continuing series, London and elsewhere, 1900–)
Wing	*Short title catalogue of books printed in England,*

	Scotland, Ireland, Wales and British America, and of English books printed in other countries, 1641–1700 (ed. D. Wing, 3 vols., 1945–51, 2nd edn, New York, 1972– 88)
Wood	A. A. Wood, *Athenae Oxonienses: an exact history of all the writers and bishops who have had their education in the University of Oxford. To which are added the fasti, or annals, of the said university* (ed. P. Bliss, 4 vols., Oxford, 1891–92)
Wotton, *Parallel*	Sir Henry Wotton, *A parallel betweene Robert, late earle of Essex, and George late duke of Buckingham* (London, 1641, Wing no. W 3647)
WRO	Warwick County Record Office, Warwick

TECHNICAL NOTE

All dates are Old Style but the year is taken as beginning on 1 January, rather than 25 March.

Abbreviations have been expanded in quotations and the usage of 'u' and 'v' and 'i' and 'j' has been modernised. Punctuation and capitalisation have also been modernised where necessary.

In the footnotes and bibliography, the names of those authors who were contemporaries of Essex have been given in full. The forenames of all other authors have been reduced to abbreviations.

INTRODUCTION
'A playboy of the western world'?

The last decade or so of the sixteenth century has long been considered a distinct, almost autonomous, period in the reign of Elizabeth I. Compared to the glories of the 'high Elizabethan' age of the 1570s and early 1580s, the 1590s seem bleak and dark. These 'twilight years' of the reign are characterised by war and the heavy burdens which it imposed on the realm, the growing senescence of the queen and her councillors, and bitter factional discord which tore at the very heart of the regime. Patrick Collinson has recently described the decade as the 'nasty nineties',[1] while John Guy has suggested that the character of English government changed so much after 1585 that this period constitutes a genuine 'second reign' of Elizabeth I.[2] Although the latter claim may be somewhat exaggerated, there is a clear historiographical consensus that these years were markedly different from the earlier part of Elizabeth's reign.[3]

Historians are equally agreed about the prime characteristic of high politics in the 1590s: factional strife between Robert Devereux, 2nd earl of Essex, and a coalition of rivals led by the diminutive secretary of state, Sir Robert Cecil. This bitter rivalry turned the Elizabethan regime against itself and ultimately resulted in the destruction of Essex. As Lord Grey complained in a much-quoted letter to Lord Cobham of July 1598, 'my lord of Essix ... hath forced mee to declere myself either his only or frend to Mr Secretary and his enimy, protesting that ther could bee noe neutrality'.[4] Blessed with such explicit evidence, historians have had no difficulty in establishing a broad consensus about political events in the 1590s. Even

---

[1] P. Collinson, 'Ecclesiastical vitriol: religious satire in the 1590s and the invention of puritanism', in J. Guy (ed.), *The reign of Elizabeth I: Court and culture in the last decade* (Cambridge, 1995), pp. 150–70.

[2] J. Guy, 'The 1590s: the second reign of Elizabeth I?', in *ibid.*, pp. 1–19.

[3] The main area of disagreement seems to be when this turning-point actually occurred – 1585, as J. R. Seeley argued, or 1588, as Wallace T. MacCaffrey urges: Seeley, *The growth of British policy* (2 vols., London, 1895), I, pp. 168ff, esp. p. 175; MacCaffrey, *Elizabeth I: war and politics, 1588–1603* (Princeton, 1992), p. 3.

[4] Cecil MS 62/71 (pr. *HMCS*, VIII, p. 269).

Simon Adams, who has done so much to reinterpret notions of faction and patronage for the earlier years of Elizabeth's reign, argues that 'there is no need to dissent from the general agreement' about the nature of factionalism in the queen's final decade.[5] Nevertheless, there is room for fresh thought about the politics of the 1590s.

Recent historiography has laid great stress upon co-operation and collegiality in Elizabethan politics, particularly in the 1570s and 1580s. Great councillors such as Burghley, Leicester, Hatton and Walsingham now appear as old friends and business partners, rather than the factional rivals which they were once considered to be.[6] This revisionism may have gone too far in playing down conflict in Court and the privy council, but it has underlined even more starkly than before how much the politics of the 1590s differed from those of preceding decades. For Wallace MacCaffrey, the politics of the 1590s represent a return to the factionalism of the 1560s, whilst Simon Adams argues that such naked political rivalry had not been seen since the reign of Edward VI.[7] Such a curious phenomenon clearly demands explanation. The case for re-examining these years becomes even stronger when attention is paid to the evidence which historians have adduced to illustrate and explain politics in the 'nasty nineties'. In part, the reappraisal of faction and patronage in the 1570s and 1580s has been spurred by a recognition that earlier analyses were based upon the spurious use of evidence from the 1590s, which was then read backwards into these earlier decades. The same problem can be observed in comments upon the politics of the 1590s. Although evidence about factional politics derives overwhelmingly from the later 1590s, scholars have consistently projected ideas from these years back to the early part of the decade.

This tendency is perhaps especially marked because so much of the historiography of late Elizabethan politics is highly impressionistic or is restricted to article length. There have been only three substantial modern studies of late Elizabethan politics. Although it retains some value, E. P. Cheyney's two-volume study of the 1590s belongs to the early years of this

[5] S. Adams, 'The patronage of the crown in Elizabethan politics: the 1590s in perspective', in Guy, *Court and culture*, p. 24.
[6] See, for example, S. Adams, 'Eliza enthroned? The Court and its politics', in C. Haigh (ed.), *The reign of Elizabeth I* (Basingstoke and London, 1984), pp. 55–77; J. Guy, *Tudor England* (Oxford, 1988), pp. 257–8. For a more general perspective on the co-operative nature of Elizabethan government in these years, see P. Collinson, 'The monarchical republic of Queen Elizabeth I', *Bulletin of the John Rylands Library* 69 (1987), pp. 394–424. Recent historiography on this subject, as well as the older conception of factional rivalries amongst the council, is briefly surveyed in P. E. J. Hammer, 'Faction, patronage at Court and the earl of Essex', in Guy, *Court and culture*, pp. 65–7.
[7] MacCaffrey, *War and politics*, p. 13; S. Adams, 'Faction, clientage and party: English politics, 1550–1603', *History Today* 22 (1982), pp. 33–9.

century and has now been effectively superseded.[8] More recently, R. B. Wernham has devoted two volumes to exploring England's relations with foreign powers during the 1590s.[9] These are important studies, although the second of these volumes is broader-ranging and more satisfying than the first. However, foreign relations provide only a limited means for understanding politics in these years. More comprehensive is the final volume of Wallace MacCaffrey's trilogy on Elizabethan politics and government.[10] This is considered and elegantly written, and must be considered the magisterial work on the subject. Even so, the sources for this book are relatively narrow and it consequently excludes much information which can illuminate our understanding of Elizabethan politics.

In trying to explain how the politics of the 1590s could be so different from those of the preceding decades, much stress has been placed upon England's involvement in war after 1585, the ageing of Elizabeth, and deaths among her leading councillors. However, the most conspicuous new element in the politics of the 1590s was the emergence of a controversial royal favourite, the earl of Essex. All scholars agree that Essex must play a central role in any explanation of late Elizabethan politics. As John Guy puts it, 'Essex's relationship with the Cecils soon became the motor of political strife.'[11] In MacCaffrey's book, the whole concluding section on 'the revival of faction' is explicitly structured around Essex's career. Given his central importance to understanding the 1590s, it is not surprising that Essex has been commented upon frequently by historians – so much so that he seems a very familiar figure. Essex gains mention in almost every book concerning Elizabethan England and has been the subject of numerous biographical studies in his own right.[12]

The traditional and still-pervasive image of Essex apparently explains

---

[8] E. P. Cheyney, *A history of England from the defeat of the Armada to the death of Elizabeth* (2 vols., London, 1914–26).

[9] R. B. Wernham, *After the Armada: Elizabethan England and the struggle for Western Europe, 1588–1595* (Oxford, 1984); also his *The return of the Armadas: the last years of the Elizabethan war against Spain* (Oxford, 1994).

[10] MacCaffrey, *War and politics*. An abbreviated version of MacCaffrey's trilogy is his *Elizabeth I* (London, 1993).

[11] Guy, 'The 1590s' in his *Court and culture*, p. 6.

[12] W. B. Devereux, *Lives and letters of the Devereux, earls of Essex, in the reigns of Elizabeth, James I, and Charles I, 1540–1646* (2 vols., London, 1853); E. A. Abbott, *Bacon and Essex: a sketch of Bacon's earlier life* (London, 1877); L. H. Cadwallader, *The career of the earl of Essex from the Islands voyage to his execution in 1601* (published Ph.D. thesis, University of Pennsylvania, 1923); L. Strachey, *Elizabeth and Essex: a tragic history* (London, 1928, 1968 edn); G. B. Harrison, *The life and death of Robert Devereux, earl of Essex* (London, 1937); R. Lacey, *Robert, earl of Essex: an Elizabethan Icarus* (London, 1970). Essex has also been the subject of at least one major Hollywood film: 'The private lives of Elizabeth and Essex' (Warner Brothers, 1939), directed by Michael Curtiz and produced by Hal Wallis. Errol Flynn starred as Essex and Bette Davis as Elizabeth.

why Elizabethan politics went so badly awry in the 1590s. Essex was the ill-fated favourite of Elizabeth, the man who alternately enchanted and infuriated her until, in the end, he lost his head, both metaphorically and literally. Historians have consistently analysed Essex's career in terms of turbulent romance and tragic hubris. Essex was 'the romantic, high-spirited' earl,[13] the proud 'thoroughbred' whom Elizabeth needed to tame,[14] an individual with 'the most admirable qualities that can adorn a man, with the most fiery passions, and the most startling weaknesses';[15] 'gifted, headstrong, the darling of fortune, with no real judgment';[16] 'devoid of nearly every quality of which statesmen are made … impulsive as a schoolboy, he had no control whatever over his feelings'.[17] In his dealings with Elizabeth, he allegedly displayed 'matchless folly',[18] showing himself 'impatient, quarrelsome, swinging wildly between over-confidence and despair':[19] 'seldom did a royal favourite stand more in need of wise and righteous counsel'.[20] In spite of such alleged deficiencies in his character, or perhaps precisely because of them, Essex has routinely been described as a mere creature of the Court. His great martial aspirations, for example, have usually been dismissed as entirely unrealistic. Indeed, Essex's various appointments to military command have often been derided by historians: 'his practical ineptitude might be matched only by the lack of experience that had first qualified him for the job';[21] he was 'entirely without the gifts of a statesman or general';[22] he displayed 'instability and levity of purpose in execution';[23] 'Essex was not cut out to be a general'.[24]

Although it offered an easy explanation for the political problems of the

[13] Cadwallader, *The career of the earl of Essex*, unpaginated preface.
[14] J. E. Neale, *Queen Elizabeth I* (Harmondsworth, 1934, 1971 edn), p. 310.
[15] Devereux, *Lives*, I, 164.
[16] A. L. Rowse and G. B. Harrison, *Queen Elizabeth and her subjects* (London, 1935), p. 56.
[17] *DNB*, V, p. 889.
[18] Neale, *Elizabeth I*, p. 334. Neale's analysis of Essex's 'folly' is closely followed by P. Johnson, *Elizabeth I: a study of power and intellect* (London, 1974, 1988 edn), p. 370.
[19] J. Hurstfield, *Elizabeth I and the unity of England* (London, 1960), p. 188.
[20] Abbott, *Bacon and Essex*, p. 30. Abbott continues: 'outwardly brilliant and promising, his position was in reality so insecure that almost any dispassionate observer (so one now thinks) might have pronounced his ruin a near certainty, a mere matter of time'! (*ibid.*, pp. 30–1).
[21] Lacey, *Elizabethan Icarus*, p. 91.
[22] Cheyney, *History of England*, I, p. 27.
[23] J. S. Corbett, *The successors of Drake* (London, 1900), p. 304. Note, however, the concession which Corbett makes in the remainder of the sentence: 'his broad understanding of naval problems was conspicuous and undeniable, nor after a close examination of his career is it easy to deny him his romantic fancy that it was upon him above all others that Drake's cloak fell'. Clearly, Corbett's research suggested to him that there were real problems with the prevailing conceptions about Essex, although, understandably, he was not prepared to extend this recognition beyond the sphere of war.
[24] Strachey, *Elizabeth and Essex*, p. 117.

1590s, this consistent historical image of Essex is an awkward construc-
tion. If his character were as fickle and shallow as many writers claimed, it
seems hard to understand how Essex could have held such undoubted
importance for his contemporaries. Essex certainly underwent a breakdown
in the final years of his life and there are intermittent signs of strain
throughout his career. To this extent, talk of 'instability' and moodiness are
legitimate. However, the traditional image of Essex depends heavily upon
viewing Essex's earlier career from the perspective of these final years and
ignoring evidence which casts him in a different mould. These dismissive
judgements about Essex have also clearly been encouraged by a common
desire to cast Elizabeth's own actions in the best possible light. By
exaggerating Essex's positive and negative characteristics, historians have
legitimised both her impulse to make him a favourite and her later
willingness to destroy him. Estimates of Essex have also been bedevilled by
a priori assumptions about the nature of a 'favourite', which had powerful
connotations of dandyism and of temporary political importance unwar-
ranted by any talents except those required to catch and hold the
sovereign's affection. This prejudice against Essex has been reinforced by
drawing contrasts with his factional rivals, Lord Burghley and Sir Robert
Cecil, who seem the embodiment of measured statesmanship. Such a
contrast is all the more easily drawn because Cecilian archives – and hence
Cecilian perspectives – constitute the main evidential base for any study of
this period.

Clearly, the traditional image of Essex is a caricature. It is little wonder
that J. B. Black was moved to complain in 1959 that 'there is a manifest
tendency today to present this notable Elizabethan as a kind of "playboy of
the western world", who misbehaved himself and met the fate he
deserved'.[25] Yet, despite this observation and the fruits of subsequent
research, the 'playboy' image of Essex still stubbornly lingers. In the steady
flow of publications which touch upon the reign of Gloriana, Essex often
remains pictured as merely an incompetent lightweight.[26]

Even before Black complained about the simplistic treatment of Essex,
this traditional view was being attacked. In an idiosyncratic multi-volume
commentary on Elizabethan history, E. M. Tenison crusaded over a period

[25] J. B. Black, The reign of Elizabeth 1558–1603 (2nd edn, Oxford, 1959), p. iii.
[26] Thus, for Stephen Coote, Essex's behaviour was constantly blighted by 'the same blazing, all or nothing fury, the same political ineptitude' (A play of passion: the life of Sir Walter Ralegh (London and Basingstoke, 1993), p. 256), whilst M. M. Reese simply describes Essex as 'the rotten apple of her [i.e. Elizabeth's] declining years' (The royal office of master of the horse (London, 1976), p. 164). L. B. Smith dismissively terms Essex 'one of history's best documented butterflies' (Treason in Tudor England: politics and paranoia (London, 1986), p. 191). See also C. R. N. Routh, Who's who in Tudor England, revised by Peter Holmes (2nd edn, London, 1990), pp. 231–2 .

of three decades to resurrect Essex's modern reputation. Diligently researched, Tenison's work revealed much about Essex that had been ignored or misinterpreted, but her endeavours were undermined by the note of tabloid sensationalism with which she constantly hailed her 'discoveries'.[27] More seriously, she showed an inability properly to weigh evidence which did not fit with her hagiographical reappraisal of Essex.[28] Conyers Read perhaps typified the reaction to her work among professional historians when he cuttingly commended it as 'valuable for the illustrations'.[29]

Although Tenison's discoveries slowly began to filter into mainstream historical debate, there was no full-scale reappraisal of Essex and his part in late Elizabethan politics. J. E. Neale planned to undertake such a study but, like Joel Hurstfield's later work on Sir Robert Cecil, nothing substantial resulted from these intentions. Instead, reconsideration of Essex has proceeded piece-meal. L. W. Henry revealed that Essex was a serious strategist and a highly capable military organiser.[30] Simon Adams placed Essex's views on war and foreign policy in a broader intellectual framework.[31] More recently, Mervyn James explored the *mentalité* of those men who remained with Essex until his fall, emphasising their cultivation of martial honour and classical learning.[32] Major contributions have also

[27] E. M. Tenison, *Elizabethan England: being the history of this country 'in relation to all foreign princes'* (12 vols. in 13, pr. for subscribers, Leamington Spa, 1933–61). The constant implication of her heralding of new 'discoveries' is that previous historians had deliberately conspired to conceal the truth about Essex. Tenison's work on Essex was also summarised and published as M. Barrington, 'The Mercury of peace, the Mars of war', *Essex Review 59* (1950), pp. 165–81; *ibid.* 60 (1951), pp. 7–11, 76–80, 116–23, 169–78; *ibid.* 61 (1952), pp. 1–10.

[28] For example, Tenison seems highly sensitive about Essex's infidelity to his wife and even fiddles with evidence in order to exculpate him – by adding the word 'first' to a sentence in Essex's letter to Lady Bacon of December 1596, she argues that he had no extra-marital sexual liaisons between 1589 and the end of 1596 and hence that he had not committed adultery at all (Tenison, X, 162–9). This claim is all the more extraordinary because Tenison must have been aware of a land settlement of 1595 which includes explicit provision for Essex's 'base and reputed son' (PRO, SP 12/253, fol. 36r).

[29] C. Read (ed.), *Bibliography of British history: Tudor period, 1485–1603* (2nd edn, Oxford, 1959), p. 64 (no. 780).

[30] L. W. Henry, 'The earl of Essex as strategist and military organiser, 1596–7', *EHR* 68 (1953), pp. 363–93. Henry subsequently discussed Essex's disastrous Irish command in two articles which are still seldom cited: 'The earl of Essex and Ireland, 1599', *BIHR* 32 (1959), pp. 1–23, and 'Contemporary sources for Essex's lieutenancy in Ireland, 1599', *Irish Historical Studies* 11 (1958–9), pp. 8–17.

[31] S. L. Adams, 'The Protestant cause: religious alliance with the west European Calvinist communities as a political issue in England, 1585–1630' (unpub. D.Phil. thesis, University of Oxford, 1973).

[32] M. James, 'At a crossroads of the political culture: the Essex revolt, 1601', in his *Society, politics and culture: studies in early modern England* (Cambridge, 1986), pp. 416–65. James had previously touched upon Essex in his landmark essay, 'English politics and the concept of honour, 1485–1642' (*ibid.*, pp. 308–415), which was first published as a supplement to *Past and Present* in 1978.

been made by scholars from other disciplines. New insights into political culture have been revealed by exploration of the portraiture of Essex[33] and his association with music.[34] Scholars of English literature have long been interested in Essex because of his links with Sidney and Spenser,[35] but recent years have seen renewed interest in his chivalric image[36] and in his poetry.[37] Taken together, this growing body of scholarship projects a strikingly different image of Essex – that of an intelligent and highly cultivated aristocrat whose commitment to martial affairs was both passionate and reasoned. Although many parts still remain missing, a new picture is clearly emerging of Essex as a truly substantial political figure.

The consequence of these various historiographical developments is that interpretations of the 1590s are now in a state of flux. The recent emphasis upon collegiality and co-operation in the politics of the 1570s and 1580s makes events in the 1590s appear even more dramatic than before. Interdisciplinary studies have encouraged the use of new kinds of evidence and a broader appreciation of what constitutes significant political activity. Essex, the acknowledged key to factional rivalry whose actions have been simply described as those of a bull in a china shop, has also begun to emerge as a much more complex and interesting figure. However, much of the stimulating new work on Essex – especially by non-historians – has necessarily rested upon old-style historiography, creating a curious tension between new ideas and the factual errors and out-dated interpretations which blight many of these older works. Insights of the

[33] D. Piper, 'The 1590 Lumley inventory: Hilliard, Segar and the earl of Essex' (2 parts), *Burlington Magazine* 99 (1957), pp. 224–31, 299–303; R. Strong, 'The courtier: Hilliard's Young man amongst roses', in his *The cult of Elizabeth: Elizabethan portraiture and pageantry* (London, 1977), pp. 56–83; R. Strong, 'Queen Elizabeth, the earl of Essex and Nicholas Hilliard', *Burlington Magazine* 101 (1959), pp. 145–9; R. Strong, 'My weeping stagg I crowne: the Persian Lady reconsidered' in his *The Tudor and Stuart monarchy: pageantry, painting, iconography II. Elizabethan* (London, 1996), pp. 303–24.
[34] L. M. Ruff and D. A. Wilson, 'The madrigal, the lute song and Elizabethan politics', *Past and Present* 44 (1969), pp. 3–51; also their 'Allusion to the Essex downfall in lute song lyrics', *Lute Society Journal* 12 (1970), pp. 31–6.
[35] See especially R. Heffner, 'Essex the ideal courtier', *English Literary History* I (1934), pp. 7–36.
[36] R. McCoy, '"A dangerous image": the earl of Essex and Elizabethan chivalry', *Journal of Medieval and Renaissance Studies* 13 (1983), pp. 313–29. This article is published in a slightly revised form as his *The rites of knighthood: the literature and politics of Elizabethan chivalry* (Berkeley, Los Angeles and London, 1989), ch. 4. Essex also features heavily in A. Young, *Tudor and Jacobean tournaments* (London, 1987).
[37] S. W. May (ed.), 'The poems of Edward DeVere, seventeenth earl of Oxford, and of Robert Devereux, second earl of Essex', *Studies in Philology* 77 Texts and Studies issue (1980). Essex's poetry is contextualised in May, *The Elizabethan courtier poets: the poems and their contexts* (Columbia, Mo., and London, 1991). Note also E. Doughtie, 'The earl of Essex and occasions for contemplative verse', *English Literary Renaissance* 9 (1979), pp. 355–63.

1980s and 1990s jostle uncomfortably with narratives sketched out in the 1940s and 1950s.

This book seeks to encourage a new understanding of late Elizabethan politics. Building upon the work of historians such as MacCaffrey and Wernham, it also draws upon the work of scholars in other disciplines to help explain how English high politics became so polarised by the middle years of the 1590s. However, this book is not simply a synthesis of earlier studies. Unlike previous studies of the period (with the exception of Wernham's work), this work is heavily based upon manuscript sources rather than calendars and printed works. This solid base of evidence is profoundly important. The experience of writing this book has shown that there is simply no substitute for ploughing through manuscripts in order to understand the period and to avoid the many errors which printed sources have encouraged in successive generations of scholars.

The chief focus for this study is a reassessment of the earl of Essex, the complex and problematical figure whose ideas and actions were so central to the polarisation of politics. Following Essex's career from his formative years until his zenith in 1597, this study charts the emergence of political divisions and the part which he – and others – played in fostering them. Although it follows his career in close detail, this book should not be seen as a biography of Essex. In seeking to explain the polarisation of politics, its focus is not restricted to his actions alone. Nor does it attempt to follow the earl's career beyond the point where the process of polarisation was obvious to all. In contrast to previous works, which have been so strongly influenced by events in the final years of the decade, this book deliberately excludes these years from its analysis.

Opening with an account of Essex's adolescence, this study of Elizabethan politics begins about 1585, when England openly entered war against Spain. This was also the year in which Essex first ventured to Court, before leaving to begin his military career in the Netherlands. The book closes with Essex's appointment to the lofty post of earl marshal at the very end of 1597. For English politics and Essex's own career, the close of 1597 marked a decisive break. This year saw the last great action in Essex's scheme to carry the war to Spain and the permanent entrenching of factionalism at Court. Both of these phenomena were reflected in the earl's struggle to become earl marshal. By contrast, the dynamics of politics changed dramatically during 1598. Essex, in particular, found himself on the defensive. Instead of being the forthright advocate of new action against Spain, he was now forced into the negative role of trying to prevent peace. Within a few short months, the whole political landscape was also profoundly reshaped by the cessation of hostilities between France and Spain, military disasters in Ireland, the death of Burghley and Essex's own loss of royal favour. In this new world, the thrust of events was not the polarisation of politics – that was already an established fact – but the consolidation of factions, the undermining of Essex's position and the ultimate triumph of Cecil. These events after 1597 reflect a story which is quite different from the subject of this book and require a separate study in their own right.

The years covered by this work constitute the most expansive phase of the war against Spain. England's dispatch in 1585 of an army to the Netherlands and a fleet to the West Indies was answered by the unleashing of Spain's *Gran Armada* in 1588. This attempted invasion was matched in kind by an English expedition to Spain and Portugal in the following year. England continued large-scale naval operations in the Atlantic until 1592, when further offensive action was effectively delegated to privateers. On land, thousands of English troops continued to serve in the Low Countries and Ireland, while many more fought in France between 1589 and 1595. In the latter year, as the commitment to France drained away, England again returned to the offensive at sea. A substantial fleet went to the Caribbean, while much larger forces attacked Spain in 1596 and the Azores in 1597, prompting abortive Spanish retaliation. These years also saw a new army go to France and the steady increase of troops in Ireland as English control there crumbled. By the end of 1597, the demands of war seemed never-ending and the realm's ability to meet them appeared increasingly uncertain.

The years between 1585 and 1597 also saw Elizabeth's regime afflicted by the ravages of time. The privy council (the body of advisers and senior office-holders who ran the government under the queen's supervision) was decimated. By 1597, only one of the leading councillors from 1585 still survived – Lord Burghley, the ageing lord treasurer. As his old colleagues and friends died, even Burghley's prodigious appetite for work and control struggled to sustain the new burdens which Elizabeth thrust upon him. Although he continued to stagger on, Burghley's decline became more obvious every year. As Burghley tottered on, the stakes mounted in the struggle to succeed him as the queen's chief councillor between his younger son, Sir Robert Cecil, and his former ward, the earl of Essex. It was entirely characteristic of Elizabeth's regime that this struggle was a family affair, and all the more bitter and tragic for it.

Time also took its toll on the queen herself. By 1585, Elizabeth was over fifty and it was obvious that she would never marry or bear children. Image-makers cast her as the Virgin Queen, but the reality was that she was an ageing woman who ruled through an ageing privy council and whose realm had now entered a war which she had long sought to avoid. Age and the exigencies of war conspired together to undermine her personal authority. Historians once viewed Elizabeth as if she were set upon a pedestal, praising her every action – even her 'masterly inactivity' in the face of demands for urgent action.[38] More recently, scholars have taken a more critical view of Elizabeth.[39] Above all, modern studies have explored the difficulties which faced her as a female ruler.[40] For all her formidable talents, Elizabeth was a prince who could not even marry for fear of the political consequences.[41] This book presents an image of Elizabeth which conforms to this modern trend. Although she remained at the centre of political activity, her actions were remarkably constrained by circumstance and her gender. In many ways, this is a study of the decline of Elizabeth's authority over her own Court.

In keeping with its primary focus on the earl of Essex, the book is divided into two main parts, roughly corresponding to the periods of his career before and after his appointment to the privy council in 1593. Part I deals with Essex's formative years and his meteoric rise to royal favour. The second and larger section comprises six chapters which are chronologically parallel to each other, each exploring a different aspect of his bid for greatness between 1592 and 1597. This structure has been adopted to disentangle the many elements of Essex's career which would otherwise become obscured in a straightforward narrative. To some degree, the first five chapters of Part II build towards the final chapter in this section, which explores in detail Essex's relationship with the Cecils and the emergence of factionalism. Taken together, the information and analysis contained in these chapters seek to sketch a richer, more sensitive and more accurate picture of Essex himself and of the polarisation of Elizabethan politics.

[38] The *locus classicus* for this interpretation remains J. E. Neale, *Queen Elizabeth (I)* (London, 1934). A more moderate, but essentially similar, view can be seen in Wallace MacCaffrey's trilogy on Elizabethan politics and his subsequent biography of the queen, *Elizabeth I*.

[39] See, for example, C. Erickson, *The first Elizabeth* (London, 1983); C. Haigh, *Elizabeth I* (London and New York, 1988); and C. H. Wilson, *Queen Elizabeth and the revolt of the Netherlands* (London, 1970).

[40] See, for example, S. Frye, *Elizabeth I: the competition for representation* (Oxford, 1993) and C. Levin, *The heart and stomach of a king: Elizabeth I and the politics of sex and power* (Philadelphia, 1994).

[41] S. Doran, *Monarchy and matrimony: the courtships of Elizabeth I* (London and New York, 1996).

Part I

INTO THE FATEFUL CIRCLE: 1585–1592

'My lord of Essex'

Like any aristocrat of the sixteenth century, Robert Devereux was, in a sense, born into politics. As the eldest son of a member of the high nobility, he was almost inevitably destined to take a part in the government of the realm. However, precisely what role Robert Devereux would play in politics would depend upon circumstance and his own capabilities. The crucial arena of Elizabethan politics – the place where careers were made or marred – was the Court. As the scholar Gabriel Harvey put it, the Court was 'the only mart of preferment and honour'.[1] Here the queen consulted and spent time with her leading subjects, and decisions were taken about government and patronage which affected the realm as a whole. As a boy, Robert Devereux was taken on brief visits to the Court to prepare him for his future career.[2] This preparation had its first serious test when he began a prolonged stay at Court in late 1585 – in a sense, the young man's first, tentative steps on to the national stage. At the time, he was nearly twenty years of age and had already been earl of Essex for almost nine years.[3] It is perhaps significant that there is precious little evidence about his debut. In stark contrast to his spectacular success there in later years, it seems that Essex caused barely a ripple at Court in 1585.

The only direct account of Essex's entry into Court life comes from Henry Wotton, who became one of the earl's secretaries in the mid-1590s.

---

[1] Cited in G. Waller, *Edmund Spenser: a literary life* (London, 1994), p. 43.
[2] One such visit has spawned an erroneous impression of the young Essex. In February 1579, he went to Court to watch the grand reception for the German prince John Casimir. Essex seems to have been merely a spectator and took no part in the events held in Casimir's honour (FSL, L.a.37, p. 243). The story that the young earl sullenly refused to receive a kiss from the queen (repeated, for example, in R. Lacey, *Robert, earl of Essex: an Elizabethan Icarus* (London, 1970), p. 19) is based on a misreading of an account of Casimir's actions on this occasion.
[3] Essex was born on 10 November 1565: S. W. May, 'The poems of Edward De Vere, seventeenth earl of Oxford, and Robert Devereux, second earl of Essex', *Studies in Philology* 77, Texts and Studies issue (1980) p. 15; also May, correspondence in *N&Q* 235 (1990), p. 318; M. Margetts, 'The birth date of Robert Devereux, 2nd earl of Essex', *N&Q* 233 (1988), pp. 34–5.

According to Wotton, it was the earl of Leicester and Essex's mother – by then countess of Leicester – who persuaded the young earl to forsake a comfortable life on his Welsh estates and move to Court.[4] Wotton's account must be treated with caution, for it was written almost fifty years later and concerns events which occurred almost a decade before he himself entered Essex's circle.[5] The description of an impressionable young Essex being manoeuvred into becoming a courtier against his own better judgement also smacks of a tradition of political commentary in the early seventeenth century, which sought to caricature the earl of Leicester as the quintessential Machiavellian courtier.[6] Nevertheless, the broad outlines of Wotton's 'certain' report seem to be correct. Leicester undeniably played a central role in introducing Essex into national politics. A single surviving letter from this period also suggests that relations between Essex and his mother became rather strained during his time in Wales. Moreover, the bone of contention seems to have been the future direction of Essex's career. Responding to his mother's charges of 'undutifulnes as a sonne', Essex was moved to protest that 'my purposed course to do well I hope shall deliver me from the suspicion of carelesnes of mine owne estate'.[7] However, despite this sharp exchange, Essex was perhaps less unwilling to take his place at Court than Wotton allows. Given his rank and the scale of his debts to the queen, the central question was really not whether Essex would enter the world of national politics, but when he would do so.

The precise timing of Essex's move to Court has caused much confusion. The universal consensus among modern commentators is that Essex arrived there by late 1584.[8] However, Essex was clearly still living away from Court during most of 1585. He remained in his house of Llanfydd in Pembrokeshire until late April and then moved to Chartley, the chief family

---

[4] Wotton, *Parallel*, p. 1. Sir Robert Naunton's account of Essex explicitly relies on Wotton for his discussion of this point: Sir Robert Naunton, *Fragmenta regalia or observations on Queen Elizabeth, her times & favourites*, (ed. J. S. Cerovski, Washington, London and Toronto, 1985), pp. 26, 74–5.

[5] Wotton's *Parallel* was circulated in manuscript by 1634, although it was not published until after his death in 1641 (L. P. Smith, *The life and letters of Sir Henry Wotton* (2 vols., Oxford, 1907), I, p. 206). Wotton did not enter Essex's service until 1594.

[6] S. Adams, 'Favourites and factions at the Elizabethan Court', in R. Asch and A. Birke (eds.), *Princes, patronage and the nobility: the Court at the beginning of the modern age* (Oxford, 1991), pp. 265–87.

[7] BL, Add. MS 32092, fol. 48ʳ.

[8] This idea may have been encouraged by the fact that Essex first exchanged New Year's gifts with Elizabeth at the start of 1584, probably at the urging of his mother and stepfather: BL, Egerton MS 3052, m. 1 (a roll). The exchange of gifts did not require the donor to be present at Court – gifts were often presented by a third party. However, it does indicate that the donor was known to the queen and recognised as (or aspired to be) a frequenter of her Court. Perhaps significantly, Essex did not repeat the exercise at the start of 1585: FSL, Z.d.16.

estate in Staffordshire.[9] Despite a spectacular visit to Shrewsbury School at the end of May, where he was greeted by the scholars 'standing in battle raye with bowes and arrowes',[10] he remained at Chartley until at least mid-August.[11] Essex finally departed for Kenilworth Castle, Leicester's seat in Warwickshire, about the third week of that month.[12] Leicester was himself already in residence there, enjoying a summertime break from the pressures of the Court. Leicester was not only Essex's stepfather, but one of Elizabeth's oldest friends and her chief favourite. When he headed back to the royal presence, Essex travelled with him. If rewards to his servants are any guide, Essex arrived at Court at Nonsuch by early September.[13] He was certainly there by 20 September, when Leicester gave him £20 in cash.[14] This gift may indicate that Essex was short of money at Court. Alternatively, it might relate to his survival of a near-fatal hunting accident during this month.[15] Whatever the reason, the gift underlines Essex's dependence on his stepfather during this period. Leicester's importance in introducing Essex into the 'fatal circle', as Wotton terms the Court,[16] can hardly be doubted.

If the timing of Essex's arrival at Court can be plotted with some precision, other evidence about this early period of his career is frustratingly scanty. Many years later, Essex himself claimed that, when he first arrived there, 'in Court I had small grace and few friends'.[17] This statement must be treated with suspicion, for it is perhaps mainly indicative of Essex's subsequent distancing of himself from his late stepfather and of his own later standards of success at Court. Nevertheless, the claim does have some foundation. William Camden, the best known and best informed contemporary commentator on the reign of Elizabeth, wrote later that the young Essex initially 'had much adoe to get into' the queen's favour

---

[9] Devereux MS 5, fol. 69^r. Essex's letter to his mother (cited above) was written from Llanfydd on 12 April 1585.

[10] G. W. Fisher, *Annals of Shrewsbury School* (London, 1899), p. 77.

[11] A reward of sixteen shillings was paid there to a messenger who brought Essex news of the death of Sir Edward Mansell, who died on 15 August (Devereux MS 5, fol. 69^r).

[12] This is suggested by payment of a 20s reward to Essex's servant, William Trew, for carrying letters for Leicester from Kenilworth to Court: Christ Church, Oxford, Evelyn MS 258b, unfol., entry for 21 August 1585. This is printed in S. Adams (ed.), *Household accounts and disbursement books of Robert Dudley, earl of Leicester, 1558–1561, 1584–1586* (Camden Society, 5th series, VI, Cambridge, 1996), p. 294.

[13] Christ Church, Oxford, Evelyn MS 258b, unfol., entries for 6 and 7 September 1585 (pr. Adams, *Accounts of Leicester*, pp. 305–6). Leicester returned to Court on 8 September (Adams, *Accounts of Leicester*, p. 387).

[14] Christ Church, Oxford, Evelyn MS 258b, unfol., entry for 20 September 1585 (pr. Adams, *Accounts of Leicester*, p. 310).

[15] This event is recorded in a note on Essex's horoscope: '1585. He fell into a ditche & was almost drownd in going a hunting in September' (BL, Sloane MS 1697, fol. 54^v).

[16] Wotton, *Parallel*, p. 1.   [17] *Apologie*, sig. A2^v.

because she 'did not well affect his mother'.[18] After the death of her first husband, Essex's mother had been bold enough to marry Elizabeth's greatest favourite and the queen never fully forgave her for it. According to the Spanish ambassador, Elizabeth called the countess of Leicester 'a she-wolf'.[19]

Essex's assertion about the coldness of his first sojourn at Court, although undoubtedly somewhat exaggerated,[20] is also supported by an episode which occurred towards the end of 1585. In September of that year, it was decided to shift Mary Stuart from Tutbury to a more secure place of detention.[21] Although exiled and deposed from her throne in Scotland, Mary's presence encouraged plots against Elizabeth and constituted a major threat to English security. The new gaol chosen for Mary was none other than Chartley, Essex's principal estate in Staffordshire and virtually the only family property which had not been mortgaged to meet his late father's debts. Essex himself was probably still resident when the decision was first mooted, no doubt giving a special edge to his anger. Faced with the prospect of having his most important possession ravaged to supply fuel and food over the winter for the two households that surrounded the captive queen – one her own, the other that of her gaoler – Essex did his best to forestall the move. He deliberately obstructed the overseer of Mary's captivity, Sir Amias Paulet.[22] He also sought the aid of Leicester and of his maternal grandfather, Sir Francis Knollys, who was treasurer of the queen's household.[23] Ultimately, some measure of protection for Essex's estate was agreed, but Mary's transfer to Chartley went ahead in late December.[24] In the larger scheme of things, Essex's complaints could not be allowed to disrupt a vital matter of state security. The requisitioning of Chartley was not a hostile act against Essex, but a salutary reminder of how much Elizabeth might require of her nobility when occasion demanded it.

[18] Camden, *Elizabeth*, p. 623.
[19] *CSPSpan*, III, *1580–1586*, p. 477.
[20] One apparent piece of evidence about Essex's disenchantment during 1585 is a letter from William Sterrell to William Waad (Cecil MS 14/11 (pr. *HMCS*, III, p. 112)). This must be discounted. Despite the dating given in the HMC calendar, this letter was actually written on 15 October 1594, not 1585. This is quite clear when the contents of the letter are compared to P. Caraman, *John Gerard: the autobiography of an Elizabethan* (2nd edn, London, 1956), pp. 64–5.
[21] *CSPScot*, VIII, *1585–1586*, p. 102; J. Le Laboureur (ed.), *Les memoires de Messire Michel de Castelneau, seigneur de Mauvissiere* (3 vols., Brussels, 1731), I, p. 640.
[22] *CSPScot*, VIII, *1585–1586*, p. 125. Paulet made matters worse by asking Essex to leave his hangings and bedding at Chartley for Mary's use: J. Morris (ed.), *The letter-books of Sir Amias Poulet keeper of Mary Queen of Scots* (London, 1874), p. 95.
[23] BL, Harleian MS 285, fol. 133^{r-v}; BLO, Tanner MS 78, fol. 7^r.
[24] C. Read, *Mr Secretary Walsingham and the policy of Queen Elizabeth* (3 vols., Oxford, 1925), III, p. 7.

Like his introduction into courtly life, the Chartley episode shows that Essex began his initiation in high politics firmly under the wing of the earl of Leicester. Leicester was the last, and probably the most influential, of the three father-figures who guided Essex's formative years – his father, his guardians and Leicester. Of Essex's relations with his own father, Walter Devereux, the first earl of Essex of this creation (and the eighteenth since the title was first bestowed), almost nothing definitive can be said.[25] Henry Wotton reports 'constant information' that Essex's father 'died with a very cold conceit of him' and had a preference for Robert's younger brother, also named Walter.[26] Although this opens up intriguing possibilities about Essex's career embodying an urge to prove himself to the shade of his dead father, Wotton remains a somewhat uncertain source for these early years of the earl's life. Nevertheless, a number of facts about Earl Walter clearly did have a major impact upon the young Robert Devereux. Perhaps above all, Earl Walter ensured that his heir grew up in a strongly Protestant environment and had a deep pride in his aristocratic lineage.

Walter, 1st earl of Essex, was only thirty-five when he died in Dublin on 22 September 1576, leaving his son Robert aged only ten. Earl Walter died while embarking on his second major attempt to carve out a great new domain for his family across the Irish Sea. Although the queen provided a fig leaf for this attempted conquest by creating him earl marshal of Ireland,[27] Walter Devereux's efforts to create a miniature principality in County Antrim brought much brutality and precious little success.[28] His dismal and lingering death from chronic dysentery epitomised the suffering and emptiness wrought by his endeavours. Earl Walter's abortive campaigns merely destroyed his family's finances and left his young heir with massive debts to the crown, for he had mortgaged his estates in return for loans from the queen. His territorial ambition had brought the Devereux earldom of Essex to a low ebb within only four years of its creation.[29] Ironically, Earl Walter's unheroic death soon became the stuff of Protestant legend, thanks to the posthumous myth-making of some of his close servants. Edward Waterhouse, in particular, transformed the late earl's

[25] For Walter Devereux, 1st earl of Essex, see *TCP*, V, pp. 140–1; *DNB*, V, pp. 893–97; Devereux, *Lives*, I, chs. 1–6.

[26] Wotton, *Parallel*, p. 8.

[27] FSL, L.a.237; BL, Harleian MS 6992, fol. 54ᵛ. Earl Walter had originally asked for this to be made an hereditary office for the Devereux family (PRO, SP 12/45, fol. 45ᵛ).

[28] T. W. Moody, F. X. Martin and F. J. Byrne (eds.), *A new history of Ireland. III. Early modern Ireland 1534–1691* (Oxford, 1976), pp. 96–9; S. G. Ellis, *Tudor Ireland: crown, community and the conflict of cultures 1470–1603* (Harlow, 1985), pp. 267–8; R. Bagwell, *Ireland under the Tudors* (3 vols., London, 1885–90), II, chs. 30–3; N. P. Canny, *The Elizabethan conquest of Ireland: a pattern established 1565–76* (Hassocks, Sussex, 1976).

[29] H. A. Lloyd, 'The Devereux inheritance', *Welsh History Review* 7 (1974), pp. 27–31. The earl's debts were at least £18,000 at the time of his death (*ibid.*, p. 31).

demise into a model of Protestant piety by writing an account of his last days – complete with the words of the godly song that the earl allegedly sang as he lay dying – which was soon widely disseminated.[30] It was a desperate attempt to salvage family honour from a disastrous venture which had left the earldom to a minor and encumbered him with ruinous debts.

The conscious myth-making which surrounded his father's death bequeathed to the young Essex a store of sympathy and created a strong public association – albeit a highly romanticised one – between the Devereux family and staunch Protestantism. This was also a stance which Earl Walter had sought to instil in his son during his own lifetime. At the time of his father's death, one of Robert Devereux's companions was Gabriel, the son of the late French Protestant leader, the Count Montgomery.[31] Earl Walter also pointedly left Gabriel a bequest in his will.[32] From the beginning, Essex was encouraged to think of himself and his family as part of an international community of Protestants. These early years help to explain Essex's fascination with Continental Europe and his life-long francophilia.

Essex's father also bequeathed to his heir a fierce pride in his aristocratic heritage. At the time of Earl Walter's death, the Devereux family coat of arms contained no less than fifty-five quarterings. Walter Devereux's elevation to the earldom of Essex in 1572 demonstrated the practical importance of being aware of family lineage. After the death of the marquess of Northampton, who died without a male heir in 1571, Walter Devereux was able to establish a direct link through female descent to the Bourchier earls of Essex and thus to claim those lands owned by the late marquess which had once been part of the Bourchier estate. It was on the basis of acquiring these lands that Elizabeth elevated Walter Devereux from

---

[30] *HMCD*, II, p. 48. In addition to the sources noted in *DNB*, V, p. 897, manuscript copies of the account of Earl Walter's death and/or his final song are: *CSPIre, 1574–1585*, p. 99; H. E. Malden (ed.), 'Devereux papers, with Richard Broughton's memoranda (1575–1601)', *Camden Miscellany*, n.s., XIII (1923), pp. 6–11; HEH, EL 1205a, fols. 40^r–42^v (formerly EL 6162); BL, Cotton MS Vitellius C XVII, fols. 367^r–76^r, 380^r; BL, Add. MS 5845, fols. 337–349; BLO, MS Top.Oxon.e.5, pp. 138–48. Among the State Papers Ireland (PRO, SP 63) there is also a genealogical epitaph for Earl Walter, tracing his lineage back to Richard Strongbow, earl of Pembroke, and Eve, daughter of the king of Leinster (noted in *CSPIre, 1601–1603*, 353), although this may have been composed as late as 1602 (*ibid.*, *1574–1585*, 101). At least two ballads were also published to commemorate his death (E. Arber (ed.), *A transcript of the registers of the Company of Stationers of London, 1554–1640 AD* (5 vols., priv. pr., London, 1875–94), II, pp. 311, 314). For Waterhouse, see *DNB*, XX, pp. 899–901.

[31] 'Meus Gabrielus', as Essex called him, figures frequently in the accounts for Essex's minority until his return to France in May 1579. His father, Gabriel, Count Montgomery, had been executed in France in June 1574.

[32] Devereux MSS, box 4, no. 59.

Viscount Hereford to earl of Essex in 1572.[33] In turn, the new earl began to celebrate the Bourchier link by assuming the extended style of 'earl of Essex and Ewe', a practice which his son consistently followed. The earldom of Ewe (or Eu) had been granted to William Bourchier by Henry V but was lost when the English were driven out of Normandy in the mid-fifteenth century.[34] By Elizabeth's reign, the title of Ewe was little more than an affectation. Nevertheless its use sent a conspicuous signal about the desire of the Devereux to be included among the ancient nobility – in this period, those whose titles pre-dated the great upheavals of the peerage under Henry VIII. Essex himself testified to the continuing force of this desire when, despite the extremities of his financial position, he sought to buy lands in 1589 'which were of the possessions of my auncestors earles of Essex'.[35]

This claim to high nobility was perhaps all the more important because the Devereux had never been one of the great aristocratic families. Although they traced their line of descent back to the Conquest, they had only been Lords Ferrers since 1451 and Viscounts Hereford since 1550.[36] Like a number of the other noble families which attained high rank under the Tudors, the lineage of the Devereux was more impressive for its female Bourchier and Bohun connections than its direct male line. While far from being nouveaux, the Devereux had never played a major political role in the grand manner of the Talbots and Percies. In this light, Walter Devereux's success in winning an earldom was a major advance for the family, but his son's ability to recover from his father's disaster and to push the family to the very pinnacle of the English aristocracy was little short of remarkable.

Over the course of the sixteenth century, the view increasingly gained force across Europe that a nobleman should be distinguished not only by his birth but also by his actions. The highest form of nobility was a combination of ancient noble blood with the exhibition of 'noble virtues'. Broadly speaking, this cult of 'virtue' embraced a mixture of the traditional aristocratic values – concerning justice, generosity and, above all, war –

---

[33] Lloyd, 'Devereux inheritance', pp. 22–7; BL, Lansdowne MS 109, fol. 147ʳ. Walter Devereux's patent of creation as earl of Essex (but not of Ewe) is PRO, C 66/1090, m. 1.

[34] Devereux, *Lives*, I, p. 9. According to *The compleat peerage*, the title of Ewe actually remained with the Bourchier earls of Bath until the extinction of that line in 1654 (*TCP*, V, pp. 141, 159). However, there is no evidence of any complaint by the earl of Bath about this apparent usurpation of one of his family's distinctions.

[35] BL, Lansdowne MS 60, fol. 205ʳ.

[36] Although the Devereux family lost the earldom of Essex after the death of Robert, 3rd earl of Essex, in 1646, they retain the title of Viscount Hereford (now the senior viscountcy in Britain) to the present day. The current head of the family is the 18th Viscount Hereford. The rise of the Devereux family in the fifteenth and sixteenth centuries is traced in Lloyd, 'Devereux inheritance', pp. 13–20.

with more modern cultural and intellectual qualities.[37] Together with the proud exaltation of his lineage, these notions formed an ideal of nobility which Essex conscientiously and conspicuously tried to fulfil throughout his life. The feeling of being a great aristocrat was crucial to Essex's public image and his more private sense of self. His choice of personal motto – *Invidia virtutis comes* – was a powerful statement of identity and purpose: he would pursue virtue even though he knew that this must expose him to the malice of others.[38]

It would be no exaggeration to claim that Essex constructed his whole life around the conspicuous cultivation of 'virtue'.[39] This was not simply a reflection of Essex's innate idealism. For him, the pursuit of virtue was a moral, indeed religious, imperative. By seeking to act in accordance with virtue, Essex acknowledged the divine providence by which he had been born an aristocrat and sought to give that life a meaning which transcended the fatuousness of mere existence. This was an eternally active process, a constant struggle to defeat the 'idleness' which always threatens to make life empty and purposeless. This struggle was also played out in the community at large. Since a nobleman was a public person, aristocratic virtue had a direct impact on the state. By undertaking virtuous actions and by drawing others to imitate him through the power of his personal example, a nobleman could – and should – change the world for the better. For Essex, as for many of his contemporaries, virtue was what made an aristocrat's life worth living, what defined being an aristocrat.

At a less conscious level, Essex may also have felt the need constantly to emphasise his virtue in order to reinforce the claims about the high nobility of his blood: aristocratic behaviour was as much a signal to the world as ancient titles and heraldic display. This emphasis on aristocratic status was practical as well as highly congenial. When he came to enter national

---

[37] M. James, 'English politics and the concept of honour' in his *Society, politics and culture: studies in early modern England* (Cambridge, 1986), pp. 375ff; J. P. Cooper, 'Ideas of gentility in early-modern England', in his *Land, men and beliefs: studies in early-modern history* (eds. G. E. Aylmer and J. S. Morrill, London, 1983), pp. 43–77.

[38] Essex also made other telling statements of his commitment to virtue. A pocket dial which was made for him in 1593 was engraved: 'He that to his noble linnage addeth vertu and good condisions is to be praysed: they that be perfectli wise despise worldli honor: where riches are honored good men are despised' (J. Bruce, 'Description of a pocket dial made in 1593 for Robert Devereux, earl of Essex', *Archaeologia* 90 (1866), p. 343). See Plate 8. Essex also gave Giovanni Battista Basadonna a portrait of himself bearing the legend '*Conscium en age diem*' – suggesting that one must always seek to act virtuously, as if one is in the bright light of day (Smith, *Life and letters of Wotton*, II, p. 494: note that the recipient of the portrait has here been wrongly identified as Zuane Basadonna). Especially in his later years, Essex also used the motto *Basis virtutum constantia* – the foundation of (all) virtue is constancy.

[39] For an elegant discussion of Elizabethan 'virtue', see B. Worden, *The sound of virtue: Philip Sidney's Arcadia and Elizabethan politics* (New Haven and London, 1996), esp. ch. 2.

politics, Essex's rank was almost the only card he had to play. Thanks to his father's debts and his own youth, he could not trade upon his wealth or influence, while others had family connections no less important than his. Unlike other young courtiers, however, Essex was an earl and his stance as an exemplar of aristocratic virtues ensured that he took full advantage of this distinction.

Essex was always deeply conscious of his rank and of the validating effect upon it of displaying noble virtues. These ideas made Essex see himself as a public person, superior to other men because his actions had ramifications for the good of the commonwealth. Inevitably, this exalted self-image sometimes manifested itself in enormous arrogance. In 1586, Essex all too readily adopted a lofty tone in his letter to Serjeant Puckering on behalf of a servant in Wales. This did the servant little good and merely irritated Puckering, whom Essex subsequently had to approach with more respect.[40] A more positive consequence of Essex's inculcation of aristocratic virtue was a genuine streak of altruism, which made him dedicated to pursuing what he later termed 'the publike use for which wee are all borne'.[41]

Essex's early education in the attributes of an aristocrat and the public ends to which he should devote his career was perhaps best demonstrated by the funeral sermon given for his late father in 1577.[42] Like the hagiographical account of Earl Walter's death, this sermon was widely disseminated in an apparent attempt to win renown for the Devereux name and buttress its faltering claims to be reckoned as part of the nobility's élite. As well as being printed for sale, copies of the work were specially distributed among members of the peerage and, in cheaper form, among members of the Devereux affinity.[43] Essex himself presented copies as gifts during his first few months at Cambridge in 1577, including one to the well-known academic Gabriel Harvey.[44]

The printed version of Bishop Davies's sermon contains not only the

[40] BL, Harleian MS 6994, fols. 3ʳ, 11ʳ, 12ʳ, 15ʳ, 23ʳ–24ᵛ, 48ʳ⁻ᵛ, 62ʳ.
[41] LPL, MS 653, fol. 210r. See also *ibid.*, MS 657, fol. 136r.
[42] Richard Davies (bishop of St David's), *A funerall sermon preached the xxvi day of November in the yeare of Our Lord MDLXXVI in the parishe church of Caermerthyn … at the buriall of the right honourable Walter earle of Essex and Ewe …* (London, 1577, STC no. 6364). For identification of the authors of the various parts of this work, see E. J. Jones, 'The death and the burial of Walter Devereux, earl of Essex, 1576', *The Carmarthen Antiquary* 1 (1941), pp. 186–8.
[43] FSL, L.a.239; BLO, Douce MS 171, fol. 7ʳ. The sermon and Edward Waterhouse's accompanying epistle and poem were also printed in full in the 1577 edition of Holinshed's *Chronicles* ([Raphael] Holinshed, *Chronicles of England, Scotland and Ireland* (6 vols., London, 1807–8 edn), IV, pp. 331–9).
[44] V. F. Stern, *Gabriel Harvey: his life, marginalia and library* (Oxford, 1979), p. 208. While at Cambridge, Essex gave away copies worth at least £6 (BL, Lansdowne MS 25, fol. 113ʳ).

sermon itself but also an epistle directed to the young earl. Written by Edward Waterhouse, a former close servant of Earl Walter, this address undoubtedly reflects the kind of teachings which were drilled into Essex from his boyhood. One sample of Waterhouse's advice typifies the constant emphasis upon demonstrating noble virtues and serving the crown:

> to deserve well (as your father dyd) of your soveraigne and countrey in matters appertayning to hir Majestie's obedience, rather throw the helve after the hatchet, and leave your ruynes to be repayred by your prince then any thing to degenerate from honorable liberalitie.[45]

As his subsequent actions were to demonstrate, this was advice which Essex consistently followed. Another quotation casts an interesting light upon the frenetic quality of Essex's career by its description of the recent history of his family:

> Lastly, my lord, have always before your eyes the feare of God, and the counsell of the earle your father at his death: namely, that you shoulde ever be mindefull of the moment of tyme, assigned both to your father and grandfather, the eldest having attayned but to sixe and thirtie yeares, to the ende that upon consideration of the short course of lyfe that you in nature are to looke for, you might so imploy your tender yeares in vertuous studies and exercises, as you might *in the prime of your youth* become a man well accomplished to serve hir Majestie and your countrey aswell in warre as peace.[46]

Essex was barely eleven years old when he received this advice.

At the time of his father's death, Robert Devereux was living at Chartley with his older sisters, Penelope and Dorothy, and his younger brother, Walter.[47] Like all peers who succeeded to their titles as minors, the new earl of Essex now became a ward of the crown. As a result, Essex came under the influence of the second group of father-figures who were to shape his adolescence – his guardians. As he lay dying in Dublin, Earl Walter had nominated three noblemen to guide and protect his children: Thomas, earl of Sussex, the lord chamberlain; Henry, earl of Huntingdon, the lord president of the council of the north; and William, baron of Burghley, the lord treasurer. Earl Walter wished Huntingdon to supervise his younger children, while Sussex was to serve his heir as an exemplar for 'all the actions of his life tending either to the warre or to the institution of a noble

---

[45] Davies, *A funerall sermon … at the buriall of … Walter earle of Essex and Ewe*, epistle dedicatory, fol. 1ᵛ.
[46] *Ibid.*, epistle dedicatory, fol. 2ʳ⁻ᵛ (emphasis added).
[47] Essex remained at Chartley until 12 January 1577, when he set out for London (BL, Lansdowne MS 25, fol. 96ʳ). Penelope was born in January 1563 (M. Margetts, 'A christening date for Lady Penelope Rich', *N&Q* 238 (1993), pp. 153–4), whilst Dorothy was presumably born in 1564. Walter was not born until 1569.

man'. Burghley was to be the young Essex's pattern 'for your wisdom and gravity, and [to] lay up your counsells and advises in the treasury of his hart'.[48]

When Edward Waterhouse went to advise the young earl of his new circumstances in November 1576, he found a precocious and rather weak boy who seemed earnestly attentive to the admonitions of his elders. As Waterhouse reported to Burghley, the young Essex listened to his advice and read a letter from the lord treasurer several times:

> Uppon this, he wrote the letter which your lordship shall receive herewith without help or correcting of one word or sillable. He desired farder of me to knowe the names of his father's principall freendes in Wales, which I gave hym. Imediatly, he wrote ij lettres of like effect but in contrary wordes to those gentlemen, excusing his absence and taking knowledge of their good wills to his father & promising, with your lordship's licence, to visit them within a yere or two. He can express his mind in Latin & French as well as in Englishe, verie curteus and modest, rather disposed to heare then to aunswer, given greatly to lerning, weake & tender but very comly & bewtifull. I think your lordship will as well like of him as of eny that ever came within your charge.[49]

Although Waterhouse was predisposed to speak well of the new head of the Devereux family, this description captures many of the features which would emerge in Essex's future career.

Of the three guardians who helped to shape the young Essex by the choices which they made for him, Sussex's role was perhaps less significant than that of Huntingdon or Burghley. Sussex kept an eye on his charge's finances and the proceedings of his servants,[50] but there is no evidence about his personal dealings with the young earl. Huntingdon's influence on Essex was strong in the early 1580s. However, Burghley undoubtedly played the greatest part among the guardians.

Burghley had been a special friend to Earl Walter. Essex's father had even, at one point hoped to marry Essex to Burghley's younger daughter.[51] Further connections between Devereux and Cecil can be seen in the fact that one of Essex's childhood playmates was the son of Nicholas White, a

---

[48] BL, Harleian MS 6992, fol. 52ʳ.

[49] BL, Lansdowne MS 23, fol. 190ʳ. The 'absence' for which Essex apologised was his father's funeral in Carmarthen. Because of 'the tendernes of his body', Waterhouse claimed that he 'durst not consent to take him from hence [Chartley] in this extreeme cold wether to so long a journey' (*ibid.*).

[50] For example, FSL, L.a.301, 565; Devereux MS 5, fol. 55ᵛ; C. W. Foster (ed.), *Lincoln episcopal records in the time of Thomas Cooper, bishop of Lincoln AD 1571 to AD 1584* (Canterbury and York Society, XI, 1913), p. 51. (I am grateful to Dr Charlotte Merton for the latter reference.) Sussex died in 1583.

[51] BL, Lansdowne MS 17, fol. 47ʳ. Earl Walter was one of several fathers who sought the hand of Elizabeth Cecil for their sons. Another earl, Shrewsbury, was also politely rebuffed by Burghley (C. Read, *Lord Burghley and Queen Elizabeth* (London, 1960), pp. 149–50).

government official in Ireland who was then very much the lord treasurer's man.[52] Yet Burghley's involvement with Essex depended upon more than sentiment. Among his other offices, Burghley was master of the court of wards and he routinely acted as guardian for members of the high nobility who succeeded to their titles while underage. Essex was only one of a series of young earls whom Burghley sought to bring up as future servants for the queen and her realm.

Like Rutland, Oxford and Arundel before him, and Southampton afterwards,[53] the young Essex was soon separated from his siblings and summoned to London. There, he spent a brief time in Burghley's household at Cecil House. Although Burghley himself was usually away at Court, Essex dined regularly with Lady Burghley and with the countess of Oxford, Burghley's favourite daughter, who acted as a kind of aristocratic governess for her father's extended family. Judging by the surviving accounts, Essex's most regular dining partners during the ten weeks of his stay were the countess of Oxford and 'the children' of the household. Among this group was presumably Robert Cecil, Burghley's second son, who was only two years older than Essex.[54] This initial contact marked the beginning of a turbulent, complex and ultimately antagonistic relationship between them, which did much to shape the politics of the 1590s.[55]

After several visits to Court in the company of Burghley's wife,[56] Essex went up to Trinity College, Cambridge, in early May 1577.[57] Essex did not finally leave Trinity until mid-November 1581,[58] twice as long, for example, as Anthony and Francis Bacon spent at Trinity when they were there a few years earlier.[59] In many ways, this time was an immensely

[52] Strype, *Annals*, II, p. 465. The son was Thomas White, who accompanied Essex to Cambridge as a servant and died in 1586. For Nicholas White, see *DNB*, XXI, pp. 68–70; Leimon, 'Walsingham', pp. 78ff. Several letters to White from Burghley for the period 1569–77 survive as BL, Lansdowne MS 102, fols. 143^{r-v}, 152^r, 154^{r-v}, 162^r, 166^{r-v}.

[53] Read, *Burghley*, pp. 125–6.

[54] Cecil later emphasised to James VI the 'mutuall affections' between himself and Essex 'in our tender yeares' (J. Bruce (ed.), *Correspondence of James VI of Scotland with Sir Robert Cecil and others in England, during the reign of Queen Elizabeth* ... (Camden Soc., 78, 1861), p. 6).

[55] Cecil MS 226, unfol., entries between 28 February and 10 May 1577; C. Read, 'Lord Burghley's household accounts', *Economic History Review*, 2nd ser., 9 (1956–7), pp. 347–8.

[56] Cecil MS 226, entries for 8, 21, 24 and 30 April.

[57] Essex last dined with Burghley's family at Theobalds on 10 May 1577 (*ibid.*). Officially, he may not have matriculated at Trinity until 1579: W. W. Rouse Ball and J. A. Venn, *Admissions to Trinity College, Cambridge. II. 1546–1700* (London, 1913), p. 125.

[58] Essex left Trinity immediately after the celebration of the queen's Accession Day on 17 November 1581 (Trinity College, Cambridge, College Archives, Upper Commons Book, 1580–5, fol. 61^v).

[59] P. Gaskell, 'Books bought by Whitgift's pupils in the 1570s', *Transactions of the Cambridge Bibliographical Society* 7 (1977–80), p. 290.

formative period for Essex, and an experience whose importance has been insufficiently appreciated by subsequent commentators. These were crucial years in Essex's development – he arrived at Trinity aged eleven-and-a-half and left aged sixteen. At the time of his father's death, Essex had already begun to show a scholarly disposition, as the comments of Edward Water-house attest. Cambridge nurtured these qualities and instilled in him a passion for the intellectual life and the company of those who pursued learning. Unusually for a member of the nobility, he himself performed the prescribed public exercises in logic and ethics[60] and actually took an MA degree in 1581.[61] It was not merely youthful extravagance which led Essex to write of the university in 1578 as 'Ithacam meam'.[62] By the time he left Cambridge, this delight in intellectual endeavour had been fixed as a crucial part of his personality. In later years, as subsequent actions were to demonstrate, this disposition towards things academic had a major impact upon his political behaviour.

During his time at Cambridge, Essex made many important, long-term contacts. His tutor was Robert Wright, a fellow of Trinity, who had orginally been chosen as Essex's schoolmaster by Earl Walter, with the approval of the master of the college, Dr John Whitgift.[63] A product of Shrewsbury School,[64] Wright undoubtedly won this post through the good offices of Thomas Ashton, the school's headmaster and a close friend of Earl Walter.[65] Wright later became a personal servant of Essex and won advancement through him to an office in the queen's stables.[66] Essex's

---

[60] Richard Harvey, *Ephemeron, sive paean, in gratiam perpurgatae reformataeque dialecticae* (London, 1583, STC no. 12912), sig, A3ʳ; Wotton, *Parallel*, p. 8.

[61] Cambridge University Archives, Grace Book D, fol. 133ʳ; J. and J. A. Venn, *Alumni Cantabrigienses: a biographical list of all known students, graduates and holders of office at the University of Cambridge from the earliest times to 1900. Part I: From the earliest times to 1751* (4 vols., Cambridge, 1922–7), II, p. 38. For the rarity of a nobleman taking any kind of degree from a university (as opposed to being given an honorary degree), see L. Stone, *The crisis of the aristocracy* (Oxford, 1965), pp. 688–90. It is perhaps a measure of Burghley's belief in education that most of his charges received degrees (Read, *Burghley*, p. 125).

[62] HMCS, II, p. 207.

[63] Wright, *Queen Elizabeth and her times*, II, p. 44.

[64] Fisher, *Annals of Shrewsbury*, p. 24. Wright's time at Shrewsbury (he was in the 3rd class in 1562) would probably have overlapped with Philip Sidney and Fulke Greville, who entered the school together on 17 October 1564 (*ibid.*, p. 8).

[65] Ashton was closely involved in Earl Walter's Irish activities and twice visited him there on official business. On one occasion, in late 1574, he helped to defuse serious tensions between Earl Walter and the earl of Leicester. Ashton also apparently tutored Essex before the appointment of Robert Wright. In his will, Earl Walter left him a substantial pension of £40 and made him a feoffee of the Devereux estates during Essex's minority (*ibid.*, pp. 23–9). For Ashton, see DNB, I, p. 652.

[66] Wright was paid an annuity of £20 for his services to Essex (Devereux MS 5, fols. 35ʳ, 49ᵛ, 64ʳ, 72ʳ; BL, Lansdowne MS 25, fols. 107ʳ, 108ʳ). Note that Lloyd incorrectly identifies Wright with the puritan pastor of Lord Rich's household ('Essex inheritance', pp. 35–6).

association with Whitgift, the future archbishop of Canterbury and ultimately one of his colleagues on the privy council, had a less auspicious beginning. Whitgift was nominated to the see of Worcester before Essex arrived and he left Trinity soon after, in June 1577.[67] These circumstances perhaps explain why the initial arrangements for Essex's lodgings in college were the responsibility of another fellow of Trinity, Gervase Babington.[68] He later became a tutor to the family of Essex's relative by marriage, the earl of Pembroke, and then, successively, bishop of Llandaff, Exeter and Worcester. Among the earl's fellow students at Trinity were Robert Naunton, who later served as Essex's agent at the French Court,[69] John Overall, who later became regius professor of theology and bishop of Norwich,[70] and Gelly Meyrick, a Welshman and a son of the late bishop of Bangor.[71] Meyrick afterwards became the earl's steward and ultimately shared his fate as a co-conspirator in the abortive rising of 1601. Other early contacts included Andrew Downes, a former classmate of Robert Wright at Shrewsbury who later became regius professor of Greek,[72] and

The entry for Wright in *DNB* (XXI, pp. 1039–40) erroneously gives his date of death as 1596. In fact, he survived into the reign of James I, from whom he received a knighthood. By 1609, in addition to other his legacies, he was able to bequeath to his wife lands worth no less than £1,600 a year. Wright's will was proved on 27 March 1610 (PRO, PROB 11/115, fols. 206ʳ–207ʳ).

[67] *DNB*, XXI, p. 131. Whitgift was succeeded as master of Trinity by Dr John Still, hitherto master of neighbouring St John's College (*ibid.*, XVIII, p. 1258). Still was a chaplain of Leicester and a friend and former tutor of Gabriel Harvey (Longleat, Dudley MS 2, fol. 202ʳ). As master of St John's, Still also enjoyed close dealings with Burghley, who chose him as vice-chancellor of Cambridge in 1575 (BL, Harleian MS 7031, fol. 98ʳ). Wotton's claim that Essex spent time at Trinity 'under the oversight of Doctor Whitgift' seems erroneous (*Parallel*, p. 8).

[68] BL, Lansdowne MS 25, fol. 98ʳ. For Babington, see *DNB*, I, pp. 785–6; M. G. Brennan, *Literary patronage in the English Renaissance: the Pembroke family* (London and New York, 1988), pp. 12, 74, 88–91, 159.

[69] *DNB*, XIV, pp. 126–7.

[70] *DNB*, XIV, pp. 1269–70. The later claim by Godfrey Goodman (writing in the 1640s) that Overall was a tutor of the earl must be wrong – Overall was a year behind Essex at Trinity (J. S. Brewer (ed.), *The Court of James the First; by Godfrey Goodman, bishop of Gloucester* (2 vols., London, 1839), I, p. 145).

[71] Named in honour of his maternal grandfather's estate of Gelliwisc in Pembrokeshire, Meyrick became a servant of Essex in October 1579 (*DWB*, p. 630; Malden, 'Devereux papers', p. 21). Meyrick's father died when he was about nine years old and he was thereafter brought up at his mother's manor of Hascard, near Llanfydd in Pembrokeshire. Meyrick initially entered service with Essex's uncle, Sir George Devereux, who took him up as a favour because his late father's estate did not provide adequate means to support him (*HMCS*, XIII, 584). A further connection to the Devereux family was Meyrick's uncle, Dr Edmund Meyrick, who was successively a chaplain to Earl Walter and Essex himself. For Gelly Meyrick, see *DNB*, XIII, pp. 318–19; *Commons*, III, pp. 44–5.

[72] Lysias (edited by Downes), *Eratosthenes, hoc est, brevis et luculenta defensio Lysiae pro caede Eratosthenis* (Cambridge, 1593, STC no. 17121), sig. *3ʳ; Fisher, *Annals of Shrewsbury*, pp. 11–12. For Downes, see *DNB*, V, pp. 1297–8.

Gabriel and Richard Harvey, two brothers who were well-known person-
alities on the Cambridge scene.[73] It is almost certain that Essex also came
across William Temple during this time. A fellow of King's, Temple made
an international name for himself in the early 1580s as an ardent
proponent of the new Ramist logic, in which Essex was himself instructed.[74] He later became one of the earl's secretaries. Essex also clearly
had contacts with some of the hotter sort of Protestants who still flourished
in Cambridge in the late 1570s and early 1580s. Such men courted him as
both the son and heir of the godly Earl Walter and the stepson of their
chief protector, the earl of Leicester. These contacts certainly included
William Whitaker, who became regius professor of divinity in 1580,[75]
Andrew Willet, who became an anti-Catholic polemicist,[76] and Hugh
Broughton, the controversial hebraist of Christ's College who later went
into exile in Germany.[77] In 1579, Essex asked for Hugh Broughton to be
appointed his tutor in Greek and theology, and unsuccessfully tried to
prevent him losing his fellowship.[78] Essex also met students from his own
social class, including Maximilian Brooke, heir to Lord Cobham, whose
arrival at King's coincided with Essex's at Trinity.[79] Brooke's younger

[73] (Richard Harvey), *A theological discourse of the Lamb* (London, 1590, STC no. 12915),
sig. A2ʳ. For the Harvey brothers, see *DNB*, IX, pp. 83–5, 91–2. Gabriel Harvey's notoriety
within Cambridge was such that the audience had no doubt who was being satirised in the
play 'Pedantius', which was performed at Trinity on 6 February 1581. Richard Harvey was
also ridiculed in Cambridge during the 1580s (Stern, *Harvey*, pp. 69–70).

[74] On Ramus (Pierre La Ramée) and Ramism, see W. J. Ong, *Ramus: method and the decay of
dialogue* (Cambridge, Mass. and London, 1958); D. R. Kelley, *The beginning of ideology:
consciousness and society in the French Reformation* (Cambridge, 1981), pp. 131–50; D.
K. McKim, 'The function of Ramism in William Perkins' theology', *Sixteenth Century
Journal* 16 (1985), pp. 503–17. For Temple, see below, pp. 300–1.

[75] T. Baker, *History of the College of St John the Evangelist, Cambridge* (ed. J. E. B. Major, 2
vols., Cambridge, 1869), II, p. 604. For Whitaker, see *DNB*, XXI, pp. 21–3 and P. Lake,
Moderate puritans and the Elizabethan Church (Cambridge, 1982), esp. chs. 6–9.

[76] (Andrew Willet), *Sacrorum emblematum centuria una* (Cambridge, 1592?, STC no.
25695), sig. A2ʳ–3ʳ. On Willet's career, see *DNB*, XXI, pp. 288–92.

[77] Hugh Broughton, *Moses his sights on Sinai* (n.pl. [1592], STC no. 3873), unpag. dedication.
Hugh was the brother of Richard Broughton, who had been a servant of Earl Walter and
now acted as the business manager for the Devereux estates while they remained in
wardship. On Hugh Broughton, see *DNB*, II, pp. 1367–70.

[78] BL, Lansdowne MS 28, fol. 132ʳ; Malden, 'Devereux papers', pp. 20–1. Broughton was
reinstated in 1581 by order of Burghley as chancellor of the university, after solicitation by
Essex, Huntingdon and the bishop of Durham (*DNB*, II, p. 1368).

[79] Venn, *Alumni Cantabrigienses*, I, p. 227. Maximilian Brooke was five years older than
Essex (born 4 December 1560) but they may well have met at Burghley's house because
Cobham and his wife were old friends of the Cecils. He died while visiting Naples on 5
December 1583 (*TCP*, III, p. 349; D. McKeen, *A memory of honour: the life of William
Brooke, Lord Cobham* (2 vols., Salzburg Studies in English Literature CVIII, Salzburg,
1986), I, pp. 149–50; *ibid.*, II, pp. 431–2).

brother Henry, who was to become such a bitter rival of Essex, arrived at King's three years later.[80]

Essex's education at Cambridge was carefully monitored by Burghley. No doubt encouraged and guided by his tutor, Essex sometimes wrote to his chief guardian to profess his constant gratitude and show off his steadily improving skills in Latin composition. These letters are striking for their decidedly earnest tone and for demonstrating a powerful appreciation of the responsibilities attendant upon high rank. Although they were primarily intended to please Burghley, there seems to be genuine sincerity in these expressions of youthful idealism.[81] Essex's progress also seems to have been the subject of frequent letters to Burghley from Robert Wright. From those letters which have survived, it seems that these reports concerned expenditure on the young earl, as well as his academic achievements.[82] Some guide to Burghley's own views on education can be seen in a letter which he wrote to the young John Harington in 1578, who was then studying at Christ's College. Burghley's views on reading are entirely conventional, but he is insistent that Harington should 'sytte not in your studie reading, when you shoulde be in the hall hearinge ... you shall reache more discerninge of trothe in an howre's reasoninge with others, then a week's wrytinge by yourself; thoe I knowe nothinge I woulde have you more use then wrytinge'.[83]

Further indications of Essex's education can be glimpsed through the purchases of books. The accounts which Wright sent to Burghley during Essex's first year or so at Cambridge often record only the cost of books, but some titles are clearly identified. Such works include two books of Ramus, Sturmius on rhetoric, Grimalius's *De optime senatore*, and 'Isocrates in Greeke'.[84] These books indicate that Essex received the heavy

---

[80] Venn, *Alumni Cantabrigienses*, I, 225. Henry Brooke was born on 22 November 1564 (*TCP*, III, p. 349). As a youth and young man, Henry was outshone by both his older brother Maximilian and his younger brother William. After he became heir to the family title, Henry was cosseted by his father and encouraged to eschew all martial activities (McKeen, *Brooke*, II, pp. 433ff.).

[81] BL, Lansdowne MS 25, fols. 40^r, 52^r, 54^r; BL, Lansdowne MS 27, fols. 2^r, 16^r; BL, Lansdowne MS 28, fols. 132^r, 134^r; BL, Lansdowne MS 30, fol. 131^r; *HMCS*, vol. II, pp. 142–3, 207–8.

[82] BL, Lansdowne MS 25, fol. 105^r; BL, Lansdowne MS 30, fols. 164^r, 170^r; *HMCS*, vol. II, 215. Wright received new instructions from Burghley in August 1578 as a result of problems among Essex's entourage (*HMCS*, XIII, 156–7).

[83] T. Park (ed.), *Nugae antiquae: being a miscellaneous collection of original papers ... by Sir John Harington Knt* (2 vols., London, 1804), I, pp. 132–3.

[84] BL, Lansdowne MS 25, fol. 107^r. The books of Ramus were 'Ramus logique with a commentarie' and 'Ramus on Tullie's [i.e. Cicero's] orations'. Sturmius was Johann Sturm (1507–89), whose *De universa ratione elocutionis rhetoricae* was first published in 1575. Grimalius was Wawrzyniec Goslicki (d. 1607). His *De optimo senatore duo libri* was first published in Venice in 1568.

dose of rhetoric which was typical of first-year studies at university in this period.[85] Essex also received a good measure of Continental Protestant theology, for another purchase was the 'Questiones' of Theodor Beza, Calvin's successor at Geneva.[86] The last title among these first-year purchases was Gerard Legh's *The accedens of armory*, a manual on heraldry. Together with an accompanying bill for a representation of the earl's own coat of arms, this suggests that Essex received detailed instruction in his heraldic birthright.[87] Books named in his last year of study, 1580–1,[88] show that Essex continued to receive the traditional solid grounding in the classics (the works of Cicero 'faire bounde' for the decidedly upmarket price of £6, and four volumes of Plutarch) and more Calvinist theology (the complete works of Beza). Perhaps less expected was Richard Mulcaster's manual on education, *Positions wherin those primitive circumstances be examined necessarie for the training up of children*, hot off the press in 1581.[89] Other expenses indicate that a French servant was hired in 1579 'to parle French' with Essex after Gabriel Montgomery returned to France. Some fairly menial servant was also employed as a 'reader' for the earl.[90]

The reason for the obvious concern of Burghley and Wright about money becomes clear from many other entries in Essex's Cambridge accounts. Despite the rich academic environment which he enjoyed, Essex's time at Cambridge was no isolated, ivory-tower existence. For a start, he was frequently away from Cambridge. In 1578, he and young Montgomery spent no less than twenty-six weeks based at Keyston,[91] a manor which Essex owned in nearby Huntingdonshire. This figure was inflated by the

---

[85] The reformed arts course at Cambridge after 1549 is described in J. Simon, *Education and society in Tudor England* (Cambridge, 1966), pp. 252–4. For comments more specifically related to teaching at Trinity College under Whitgift, see D. M. McKitterick, *A history of Cambridge University Press I: printing and the book trade in Cambridge 1534–1698* (Cambridge, 1992), pp. 69–70. See also Gaskell, 'Books bought by Whitgift's pupils'.

[86] Theodor Beza, *Quaestionum et responsionum Christianarum libellus* (1571) (BL, Lansdowne MS 25, fol. 107^r).

[87] BL, Lansdowne MS 25, fol. 96^r. Legh's book was published in London in 1562 (STC no. 15392).

[88] Devereux MS 5, fols. 53^v, 54^r.

[89] Published London, 1581, STC no. 18253. For Mulcaster's views on education, see Simon, *Education and society*, pp. 119 n. 3, 259, 353–4; R. L. De Molen, *Richard Mulcaster (c.1531–1611) and educational reform in the Renaissance* (Nieuwkoop, 1991).

[90] Devereux MS 5, fols. 47^v, 53^r, 54^r. In the second instance, the Frenchman is referred to as the 'French reader'. The bills for both 'readers' are consistently included with those for the laundress, suggesting some kind of basic and intermittent service.

[91] *Ibid.*, fol. 39^r; BL, Lansdowne MS 25, fol. 111^r; BL, Lansdowne MS 27, fol. 59^r. When at Keyston, Essex came under the general oversight of his uncle by marriage, Henry Clifford. Clifford had married Earl Walter's sister Anne. Their son Nicholas was to become an intimate of Essex, before dying on the fatal voyage of Drake and Hawkins in 1595 (*Commons*, I, p. 617).

need to escape several outbreaks of plague in Cambridge during the year, but he also briefly returned home to Staffordshire in August and received the stewardship of Tamworth in person.[92] In his last year at Cambridge, Essex went to meet visiting French noblemen in London, travelled to Leicester's seat of Kenilworth in Warwickshire and made another visit to Staffordshire. He also attended his sister Penelope's wedding to Lord Rich on 1 November and attended the Newmarket horse-fair.[93] Although only a student, Essex clearly cut a conspicuous figure. He was already dispensing livery coats liberally and receiving substantial presents, including geldings from his brother-in-law Rich, Lord Berkeley and Mr Edward Littleton.[94]

Like other young noblemen under wardship, Essex was expected to live on a fixed allowance. Throughout his adolescence, Essex struggled with the inadequate value of this allowance, which he regularly exceeded, despite small economies. Soon after his arrival at Cambridge, Wright wrote in alarm to Burghley that the young earl would soon 'not only be thrid bare but ragged'.[95] However, the longer Essex stayed at Cambridge, the more comfortable he felt there – and the more freely he spent. By 1581, Essex was clearly very comfortable indeed because he exceeded his allowance by £634.[96] Essex seems to have been granted a certain indulgence from his elders over his expenditure during that year's Commencement, when his sharply increased bill for food and drink suggests that he celebrated his MA degree in ways not unfamiliar to students of more modern times.[97] Rather less acceptable were the much greater amounts spent on clothes, which testified to Essex's growing appetite for display and his desire to be a model of taste. On May Day 1581, he spent £12 9s 1d on 'tawney velvet hose & cloke laid on with flames of fiery gold & [a] dublet of tawney saten & ii pair of velvet pantafles'. Two sets of clothes for Penelope's wedding cost him over £40.[98] Such expenditure was to be an enduring feature of Essex's career. Three years later, when Essex paid a tailor 50s 7d, the keeper of his accounts was moved to comment that this merely 'a petie bill' for the earl.[99]

---

[92] Devereux MS 5, fols. 35ʳ, 38ʳ; *HMCS*, II, 207–8. See below, pp. 33, 271.

[93] Devereux MS 5, fols. 53ʳ, 54ʳ, 55ʳ. For the date of Lady Penelope's wedding, see *HMCR*, I, 128.

[94] Devereux MS 5, fol. 54ʳ⁻ᵛ. The appearance of bills for livery coats after mid-1580 seems to reflect a deliberate move by Essex to assert his status as a lord. The chief agent for the Devereux estates, Richard Broughton, wrote on 2 May 1580: 'I have sent blue coates & liveryes for my lord of Essex men. They shall not be gentlemen in clokes no more. It is my lord of Essex especiall request to have it thus' (FSL, L.a.248).

[95] BL, Lansdowne MS 25, fol. 103ʳ.

[96] Devereux MS 5, fol. 55ᵛ.

[97] *Ibid.*, fol. 53ʳ; Trinity College, Upper Commons Book, 1580–5, fol. 43ᵛ; Malden, 'Devereux papers', p. 21.

[98] Devereux MS 5, fol. 54ᵛ.   [99] *Ibid.*, fol. 68ᵛ.

In light of such expenditure, Essex's guardians, together with his maternal grandfather, old Sir Francis Knollys, decided that the young man should leave Cambridge. 'To reduce the saide earle from excessive expences', he was ordered to join the household of the earl of Huntingdon, lord president of the council of the north, based in York.[100] No doubt the city's distance from the bright lights of the Court and London helped to recommend this choice. Before then, however, Essex had to spend the winter under the austere regime of his reproving grandfather.[101] Not until late February 1582 did he depart for York and the household of Huntingdon.[102]

The earl of Huntingdon was a relative of the Devereux and renowned as an exemplar of godly nobility.[103] As the dying Earl Walter wished, he and his wife acted as guardians for Essex's younger brother and his two older sisters – Penelope and Dorothy Devereux staying with Lady Huntingdon in Leicestershire, while Walter spent time both there and at York.[104] Huntingdon was instrumental in arranging Penelope's (unhappy) marriage to Lord Rich[105] and later helped to marry off Walter Devereux to a Yorkshire heiress.[106] Essex spent some eighteen months with Huntingdon, still accompanied by Robert Wright, and now also by a growing band of servant friends including Gelly Meyrick, his Welsh friend from Trinity, and Anthony Bagot, whose family had long served the Devereux in Staffordshire.[107]

---

[100] *Ibid.*, fol. 55ᵛ. The idea of Essex moving to join Huntingdon had been mooted a year earlier but was deferred until he had finished his MA (Malden, 'Devereux papers', pp. 21–2).

[101] For Knollys's attitude towards Essex's extravagance, see his oft-quoted letter of 14 November 1585 (FSL, L.a.566; printed in G. B. Harrison, *The life and death of Robert Devereux, earl of Essex* (London, 1937), pp. 9–10, from Devereux, *Lives*, I, p. 178).

[102] Essex stayed with Sir Francis Knollys from 20 November 1581 until 20 February 1582 (Devereux MS 5, fols. 55ᵛ, 59ᵛ).

[103] For Huntingdon, see C. Cross, *The puritan earl: the life of Henry Hastings, third earl of Huntingdon 1536–1595* (London and New York, 1966). Huntingdon was a first cousin to Essex's father: Earl Walter's mother, Dorothy Hastings, was an aunt of Huntingdon (*ibid.*, p. 54).

[104] W. A. Ringler, *The poems of Sir Philip Sidney* (Oxford, 1962), pp. 437–8. Regular payments of £50 per annum were made to Huntingdon for Walter Devereux's maintenance between 1577 and 1584, when he went to Oxford (Devereux MS 5, fols. 31ʳ, 36ᵛ, 40ᵛ, 45ᵛ, 50ᵛ, 57ᵛ, 61ᵛ).

[105] BL, Lansdowne MS 31, fol. 98ʳ.

[106] Cross, *Puritan earl*, pp. 55–6. Walter Devereux's future wife, Margaret Dakins, better known by her later name of Lady Margaret Hoby, left a diary which described the godly upbringing she received with Huntingdon and his wife and the circumstances of her marriage to Devereux (D. M. Meads (ed.), *The diary of Lady Margaret Hoby* (London, 1930), pp. 3–5, 8–11).

[107] Bagot joined Essex at Trinity by February 1579 (FSL, L.a.37) and became one of his servants in the middle of that year (FSL, L.a.246; BL, Lansdowne MS 28, fol. 134r). He finally ceased attending on Essex after the earl arranged a suitable bride for him in mid-1594 (FSL, L.a.473).

Beside these facts, however, very little evidence survives about Essex's activities during this period. From his accounts, it is clear that his allowance remained inadequate – despite being increased by 50 per cent – and was often late in being paid.[108] Judging by a contrite letter to Burghley in December 1582, it seems that Essex's passion for sartorial display still drew reproofs from his guardians.[109] Little other information survives about Essex's sojourn in the north. A ballad, possibly written in 1582, describes how 'the noble earle of Essex' and 'the good earle of Cumberlande' each backed rival contestants in a good-natured archery contest at York on the occasion of a visit there by three emissaries from Russia.[110] Cumberland was slightly older than Essex and had been at Trinity a few years before him.[111] This event probably marked the first time that they competed against each other, inaugurating a friendly rivalry which was to be renewed many times in the years ahead. A fleeting reference in a poem also records a visit to Durham in late 1583 at which, accompanying Huntingdon, Essex joined a gathering of leading gentlemen from across the north to greet Sir Francis Walsingham on his return from a mission to Scotland and to discuss security along the border.[112] Many of these men would have close dealings with Essex later in his career.

The third, and perhaps the most influential, of the father-figures who shaped Essex's early years was Robert Dudley, earl of Leicester. Urbane, tough, but long restrained from starting a family because of his hopes of marrying the queen, Leicester was both Essex's stepfather (from September 1578) and his godfather. Robert Devereux was named in his honour. Despite these ties, however, Essex seems to have regarded Leicester with

---

108 Devereux MS 5, fols. 59ᵛ, 62ᵛ; BL, Lansdowne MS 50, fol. 183ʳ. When he was sent to York, Essex's allowance was increased from £140 a year to £210.
109 BL, Lansdowne MS 34, fol. 37ʳ.
110 'A new Yorkshyre song, intituled: Yorke, Yorke, for my monie … ', originally published by Richard Jones in London, 1584, printed in W. Chappell (ed.), *The Roxburghe ballads* (The Ballad Society, London, 1869, reprinted 1877 as first of 8 vols., 1877–95), pp. 4–9; R. T. Spence, *The privateering earl: George Clifford, 3rd earl of Cumberland, 1558–1605* (Stroud, 1995), p. 55. Essex himself was taught how to shoot a bow, perhaps because of the influence of Roger Ascham's paean to archery, *Toxophilus* (first published London, 1545, STC no. 837). Among Essex's bills at Cambridge in 1577–8 was one for 2s 6d 'for arrowes for my lord' (BL, Lansdowne MS 25, fol. 107ʳ).
111 Spence, *Privateering earl*, pp. 24–5. Like Essex, Cumberland was a royal ward, albeit in the custody of the earl of Bedford (*ibid.*, ch. 2).
112 BL, Add. MS 30352, fol. 8ᵛ. The poem is 'Musae Boreales', written by Richard Eedes (later a chaplain to the queen). It consists of some 600 Latin hexameters. Those present at this meeting in late September 1583 included Lord Scrope and Sir John Forster, wardens of the marches, Lord Russell, Sir Walter Mildmay, the bishop of Durham, Toby Matthew (the dean of Durham), and members of leading nothern families such as the Musgraves, Selbys and Fenwicks.

dutiful respect rather than genuine affection. There were certainly difficulties between them early on. Gossip had it that Leicester and Essex's mother had cuckolded his father and even alleged that Walter's painful death in Ireland was the result of a plot by them to poison him.[113] In his last years, Earl Walter had not been on good terms with Leicester. Sir Henry Sidney suggested to Leicester that 'if Essex had lived, you should have found him as violent an enemy as his heart would have served him'.[114] Lord Henry Howard later remarked of Essex's career that 'the greatest enemie to his father was his meane to rise'.[115] Immediately after Earl Walter's death, several servants of Leicester tried to pre-empt his heir from succeeding to the stewardship of Tamworth – only to be forestalled by the intervention of Essex's guardians.[116]

The marriage between his mother and Leicester early in the morning of 21 September 1578 may also have been confusing for the young Essex because it was conducted without his presence and in secret.[117] The revelation of the match during the following year caused a sensation. The queen made the new countess of Leicester *persona non grata* at Court and almost ordered her husband to be imprisoned in the Tower.[118] Essex's mother, born Lettice Knollys, was a cousin of the queen and looked remarkably like her. This similarity of appearance may well have given a

---

[113] A. Kendall, *Robert Dudley, earl of Leicester* (London, 1980), pp. 150, 163–4, 168; D. Wilson, *Sweet Robin: a biography of Robert Dudley, earl of Leicester 1533–1588* (London, 1981), pp. 225, 257.

[114] *HMCD*, II, 51.

[115] DUL, Howard MS 2, fol. 117[r].

[116] Devereux MS 5, fol. 25[v]; APC, X, *1577–1578*, pp. 200–1, 214, 333. In 1578, Essex visited Tamworth personally to receive the public submission of the chief culprit, Humfrey Ferrers. The question of the stewardship was a complex matter because Ferrers' family had held the office for several generations and he claimed to have a grant of the office under the exchequer seal and an offer of the post from the town corporation. In the event, Essex's tenure was reconfirmed (and granted to his heirs male in perpetuity) by a new patent of incorporation to Tamworth on 10 October 1588. Ferrers considered protesting this action but was advised by Burghley 'not to oppose my self agaynst the said earle for an office of so little value' (C. F. Palmer, *The history of the town and castle of Tamworth, in the counties of Stafford & Warwick* (Tamworth, 1845), pp. 105, 111–14, Appendix pp. xiv–xv).

[117] Leicester and Lettice (or Laetitia) Knollys were married about 8 a.m. on 21 September 1578 at Wanstead – two days before the queen herself arrived there for a visit. The witnesses were Lettice's father, Sir Francis Knollys, her brother Richard, the earls of Warwick (Leicester's brother) and Pembroke (Leicester's brother-in-law), and Lord North (Longleat, Dudley MS 3, fol. 61[r–v]). Leicester had bought the manor of Wanstead in Essex during the previous year and its proximity to London meant that the countess subsequently spent much of her time there. She also lived at Drayton Bassett in Staffordshire, which Leicester purchased in 1579.

[118] S. Adams, 'Queen Elizabeth's Eyes in Court', in D. Starkey, *Rivals in power: lives and letters of the great Tudor dynasties* (New York, 1990), p. 168; Wilson, *Sweet Robin*, p. 228; Kendall, *Leicester*, pp. 181–2.

sharper edge to Elizabeth's anger.[119] Not only had her special favourite secretly married another woman, but his choice of bride was a close relative, whose looks, temper and taste for display were uncomfortably like a younger version of the queen herself. Elizabeth found this so galling that she could never forgive Lettice, even when she remarried after Leicester's death.[120] Essex campaigned for her readmission to royal favour to the end of his life, without success.

In the years immediately after his marriage to Essex's mother, during the young earl's time at Cambridge, Leicester's contact with his eldest stepson was somewhat sporadic. Nevertheless, Leicester kept a close eye on Essex's interests. In May 1580, he was reported as being 'much greaved' at rumours which were circulating about the young man.[121] Perhaps about the same time, Leicester summoned Richard Broughton, who was responsible for administering Essex's possessions during his time in wardship, and gave him a severe reprimand for allowing a man to become a liveried servant of Essex without his knowledge.[122] Leicester's interest in Essex was also apparent when Dr John Still, the master of Trinity, wrote to Burghley for approval for 'Mr Gylford' to study with the earl's tutor and frequent his chamber: 'my lord of Lecester hath a good lykinge & my lord of Essex desyreth the same'.[123] Personal contacts between Leicester and his stepson seem to have stepped up towards the end of Essex's stay at Cambridge. In late summer 1581, Essex travelled with Leicester from London to visit

[119] Elizabeth's notorious dislike of Lettice Knollys may also have been strengthened by knowledge of her ill-judged attempt ('by some froward advise') to reject the jointure which her late husband had provided for her and instead to claim a full widow's third of his estate – prejudicial though this was to her son's financial interests. This resulted in legal action between the countess and the feoffees of her late husband's will before a compromise was finally agreed (Devereux MS 5, fol. 24ʳ).

[120] She married Sir Christopher Blount, Leicester's former gentleman of the horse, in July 1589. Essex termed this an 'unhappy choyse' (BL, Lansdowne MS 62, fol. 78ʳ) because Blount had been a servant to her late husband and because he was some sixteen years younger than her. For Blount, see _Commons_, I, pp. 446–7.

[121] FSL, L.a.248. The nature of these rumours is unknown, but may have related to Earl Walter's death.

[122] Devereux MS 5, fol. 24ᵛ. The man in question was Thomas Baskerville, the illegitimate son of a Devereux servant of the same name (d. 1578) and a relative of Essex's later comrade in arms, Sir Thomas Baskerville.

[123] CUL, MS Mm.2.22, p. 48. The original letter is BL, Lansdowne MS 30, no. 64. Henry Guldeford (or Guildford) of Hempstead, Kent, was a relative of Leicester and a ward of Burghley. He and his sisters were suspected of lapsing into popery because of the influence of their Catholic mother – hence Still thought that Essex and Wright would serve as a 'good example of well doing, both for religion, learning & good behaviour'. Guildford was knighted in 1591 and married Elizabeth, daughter of the earl of Worcester, in the great double wedding celebrated at Essex House in late 1596: BL, Lansdowne MS 36, fol. 199ʳ; R. C. Jenkins, 'The family of Guldeford', _Archaeologia Cantiana_ 14 (1882), pp. 1–17; J. Burke and J. B. Burke, _A genealogical and heraldic history of the extinct and dormant baronetcies of England, Ireland and Scotland_ (2nd edn, London, 1844), p. 231.

Kenilworth,[124] and met up with him again at Penelope's wedding on 1 November. At the end of 1583, after his return from York, Essex visited Leicester House in London.[125] In the following summer, Essex joined his stepfather's party in an elaborate progress across the Midlands, visiting some of Leicester's estates and various towns which looked to his patronage. Essex was present when Leicester visited Shrewsbury on 26 May 1584[126] and also at visits to Kenilworth, Denbigh, Chester[127] and Buxton, where Leicester went to take the waters. After Buxton, Leicester moved on to a welcome at Essex's own seat of Chartley.[128]

Although Leicester's association with his stepson became increasingly conspicuous in the early 1580s, this was by no means the primary focus of his familial attentions. Above all, he and his countess concentrated on bringing up the long-awaited heir to his own earldom. After remaining unmarried for so many years, Leicester was overjoyed when his wife bore what was to be his only legitimate offspring, Robert Lord Denbigh, on 6 June 1581.[129] However, Leicester's plans for securing the descent of his title ended in tragedy. Even as Leicester made his triumphal progress across the west Midlands, his 'noble impe' – Essex's half-brother – died on 19 July 1584.[130] Despite her anger at the marriage, even Elizabeth was sad at the news. The death of this child meant that both earldoms held by the Dudley family now faced the prospect of extinction, for the marriage of Leicester's elder brother, Ambrose, earl of Warwick, was also childless. Leicester did have an illegitimate son, Robert Dudley, who was able to inherit his father's lands, but he could never succeed to his father's title or position at

---

[124] Devereux MS 5, fols. 53ʳ, 54ʳ.

[125] Ibid., fol. 67ʳ.

[126] John Tomkys, *A sermon preached the 26 day of May 1584 in S. Maries Church in Shreswesbury* (London, 1586, STC no. 24110). Lord North was also present at this sermon, as were 'diverse knights' and all the municipal dignitaries. Leicester and his entourage had visited Shrewsbury School on the previous day, where the speeches of welcome included one by Thomas Sidney, a younger brother of Philip (Fisher, *Annals of Shrewsbury*, pp. 75–6).

[127] BL, Harleian MS 2125, fol. 42ʳ; BL, Add. MS 11335, fol. 23ʳ. These accounts date the visit to Chester of Leicester, Essex and the other aristocrats and gentlemen in their cavalcade to early June 1583. This seems to be an error for 1584. Essex apparently did not leave York until November 1583 (Devereux MS 5, fols. 62ᵛ, 67ʳ).

[128] Devereux MS 5, fol. 64ʳ.

[129] S. Adams, 'The papers of Robert Dudley, earl of Leicester. III. The countess of Leicester's collection', *Archives* 22 (1996), p. 3. According to the chaplain who performed the service, Essex's mother had married Leicester in 1578 wearing a 'loose gowne' (Longleat, Dudley MS 3, fol. 61ʳ). It is possible that she wore this informal attire because she was pregnant. If this were the case, the silence about any subsequent birth suggests that she miscarried. However, this interpretation must remain highly speculative. The countess's choice of wedding dress may be explained simply by the early hour at which she was married.

[130] TCP, VII, p. 552; Stow, *Annales*, p. 1177. Lord Denbigh died at Wanstead but his body was taken from there after the funeral for burial at Warwick.

Court.[131] If his political interests were to survive his death and pass down to another generation, Leicester now had to look to his nephews, Philip and Robert Sidney, and his stepson, Essex.

In the immediate aftermath of Denbigh's death, Essex ceased his close attendance on the grief-stricken Leicester. After attending his half-brother's funeral, Essex rode up to see Huntingdon at York, before returning to enjoy life at Chartley and then at Llanfydd in Pembrokeshire.[132] Life at Llanfydd proved especially enjoyable. Essex revelled in playing the role of local magnate there. At Michaelmas 1584, when rental payments were due, he 'did verie honorablie and bountifullie kepe house with many servantes in liverie and the repaire of most gentlemen in those partes to attend his lordship'.[133] Many years later, Essex looked back on 'my contemplative retirednesse in Wales' as a halcyon period in his life.[134] Yet such comments must be treated with caution, for they belong to an older, wearied Essex, filled with nostalgic yearning for an escape from the hurly-burly of courtly politics which had come to dominate his career. In late 1584, life at Court still lay ahead of him. However, as Wotton suggests, Leicester and his wife were probably already urging him to move there.

As he hesitated about finally moving to Court, Essex would have been confronted at some point during the autumn of 1584 or early 1585 by a copy of *Leicester's commonwealth*, a devastating Catholic attack on Leicester's career and character.[135] This pamphlet was printed overseas and banned in England, but enjoyed a wide currency in manuscript form.[136]

---

[131] By his will of 1587, Leicester left the bulk of his goods and possessions to this illegitimate son, Robert Dudley. Essex and Sir Robert Sidney were to inherit only if young Dudley died without an heir (PRO, PROB 11/73, fols. 2ʳ–4ʳ). Robert Dudley's long and extraordinary life is detailed in A. G. Lee, *The son of Leicester: the story of Robert Dudley, titular earl of Warwick, earl of Leicester and duke of Northumberland* (London, 1964).

[132] *Devereux MS 5*, fol. 64ʳ.

[133] *Ibid.*, fol. 63ᵛ. Llanfydd was actually the home of Essex's uncle, George Devereux. He lived in the house during Essex's 'pleasure' (*ibid.*, fol. 71ʳ). According to Earl Walter's will, George Devereux was to be allowed this privilege until Essex was able to grant him a pension of £40 a year (BL, Lansdowne MS 23, fol. 154ʳ).

[134] *Apologie*, sig. A1ᵛ. Cf. Wotton, *Parallel*, p. 1.

[135] D. C. Peck (ed.), *Leicester's commonwealth: the copy of a letter written by a Master of Art of Cambridge (1584) and related documents* (Athens, Ohio and London, 1985). This pamphlet was probably written by Robert Persons, utilising information supplied by Charles Arundel and (perhaps) Sir Edward Stafford, Elizabeth's ambassador to France (M. Leimon and G. Parker, 'Treason and plot in Elizabethan diplomacy: the "fame of Sir Edward Stafford" revisited', *EHR* 111 (1996), pp. 1142–3). *Leicester's commonwealth* also inspired other attacks on Leicester by Catholic exiles using similar material (e.g. D. C. Peck, '"News from heaven and hell": a defamatory narrative of the earl of Leicester', *ELR* 8 (1978), pp. 141–58). The story of Leicester poisoning Essex's father lingered on and was recycled, for example, by Thomas Nashe in his satire *Pierce Pennilesse* of 1592 (C. Nicholl, *A cup of news: the life of Thomas Nashe* (London, 1984), pp. 112–14).

[136] H. R. Woudhuysen, *Sir Philip Sidney and the circulation of manuscripts, 1558–1640* (Oxford, 1996), pp. 148–9, 389.

This vitriolic work would not only again have tested Essex's feelings for his mother and stepfather, but also perhaps his feelings about the political world he was about to enter. Among the key accusations in this libellous pamphlet was the old story of Leicester's illicit affair with Essex's mother and the alleged poisoning of his father, albeit now set in a broader context of alleged personal and factional vendettas.[137] No evidence survives about how Essex reacted to this work but its ultimate effect was to strengthen his bond with Leicester. Essex must have felt outraged at the way the work attacked the earl and his mother alike, and no doubt shared their sense of being done a mortal injustice. Sir Philip Sidney's violent riposte to the pamphlet suggests that this was a burden shared and resented by the extended Dudley family as a whole.[138]

Essex finally arrived at Court in September 1585 and joined Leicester's entourage there. Leicester gave him rooms in his London mansion, Leicester House.[139] Initially, Essex made little immediate impression at Court. This was not simply because Essex had 'smal grace & few friends', as he later claimed. In fact, Essex could hardly have picked a worse time to enter upon the political stage. After decades of uneasy peace, England was now on the verge of war with Spain. During the last months of 1585, even the arrival of a young earl at Court was lost amid the frenzy of diplomacy and martial preparations. Leicester himself was furiously busy seeking to secure command of the queen's forces being sent to the Low Countries.[140] For Essex, looking on as this frantic activity took place all around him, these must have been difficult times indeed – disappointed of any hopes of success at Court and desperate to be part of the great crusade which was about to be launched across the Channel.[141]

How long Essex was left on the margins of these martial preparations is unclear. It is even possible that he only agreed to come to Court in the first place if Leicester and his mother promised to support his participation in whatever military venture was launched in the coming months.[142] A promise of this sort might not have been easy to fulfil. As an aristocrat and ward of the crown, Essex's participation would have required the approval

---

[137] For a rebuttal of the charge that Leicester poisoned Essex's father, see E. St J. Brooks, 'The death of Alice Draycott', *County Louth Archaeological Journal* 13 (1954), pp. 179–89.

[138] Peck, *Leicester's commonwealth*, pp. 249–64.

[139] BL, Harleian Roll D.35, mm. 5–6. For letters written by Essex from Leicester House in October and November 1585, see BL, Harleian MS 6993, fols. 112^r, 116^r.

[140] Adams, *Accounts of Leicester*, pp. 385–95.

[141] *Apologie*, sig. A2^v.

[142] The probability of English troops going to the Low Countries had grown steadily since mid-1584 and Leicester's appointment as commander of such an army was firmly in prospect by 22–3 August 1585 (Adams, *Accounts of Leicester*, p. 386). This was about the time that Essex finally left Chartley to join his stepfather, who was then anxiously waiting on events at Kenilworth.

of Burghley, and probably also of Elizabeth herself. Whatever the process involved, by early November at the very latest[143] Essex received the news he most wanted to hear – that he would soon be leaving Court and accompanying his stepfather to war in the Low Countries. This decision not only reaffirmed Essex's connection with Leicester but had a decisive impact on his subsequent career. Essex was not a Dudley, but a Devereux, and extremely proud of it. Nevertheless, it was with Leicester that Essex underwent his military and political apprenticeship, and from Leicester's circle that he imbibed many of the ideas and perceptions which influenced his later actions. The year which Essex spent campaigning with Leicester – his first experience of war and service to the queen – was enormously important in this process. Essex returned from the war with a knighthood and freed from his status as a royal ward, while Leicester at last began to put his full weight behind his stepson's advancement at Court. The Dutch campaign in 1586 and the months which followed his return proved to be the real launching-pad for Essex's political career.

[143] FSL, L.a.566. There are no references to Essex, or to any earl other than Leicester, in the paperwork which accompanied the preparations for the campaign during September and October (e.g. *CSPF*, XX, *Sept. 1585–May 1586*, pp. 8, 53, 112, 126–7; Longleat, Dudley MS 3, 63^r).

2

'Yowr sonne most ready to doe yowr service'

The war to which Essex and his stepfather sailed in December 1585 dominated, and indeed transformed, English politics over the course of the next two decades. As so often in the history of warfare, few of the participants ever imagined the conflict could drag on for so long. For many English Protestants, England's intervention in the Netherlands was nothing less than a national crusade. All around them, the forces of the Counter-Reformation seemed to be mustering in a great international conspiracy to destroy them and their co-religionists on the Continent. In the Low Countries, the Spanish army was systematically crushing the Dutch Protestants, whilst the forces of Catholic reaction were increasingly aggressive in their opposition to Protestantism in France. At home, the endlessly restive Irish offered a back-door into England for foreign invaders, all too often linking up with the equally untrustworthy Scots. Even within England itself, Catholic missionaries roused hostility to the Protestant regime and stirred support for invasion and fresh attempts against the queen's life. Perhaps worst of all, if the queen should die, the strongest claimant to the English throne was a Franco-Scottish Catholic, Mary Stuart – better known as Mary Queen of Scots. Faced with such a terrifying range of threats, many Englishmen judged that it was time – and, indeed, well past time – for Elizabeth to take an open stand against the king of Spain and his coadjutors.

If the course of national policy seemed both obvious and urgent to internationally minded English Protestants, the move to war proved slow and painful for Elizabeth's government. While some councillors, such as Leicester and Sir Francis Walsingham, the sharp and industrious secretary of state, urged the queen to intervene in the Low Countries throughout the 1570s, other advisers argued strongly against any such action. They believed that England should not fight a superpower like Spain and feared that the old enemy, France, might find a way to take advantage of the situation. Elizabeth herself disliked the idea of intervention and anxiously sought to avoid entanglement in the messy conflict across the Narrow Sea.

Her aim was to solve the conflict in the Low Countries by negotiation rather than by force of arms. Elizabeth's chief tactic was to invite French involvement in a way which would counterbalance Spanish military power in the Low Countries and yet also allow her to limit French influence there. This was one of the reasons why Elizabeth came close to marrying the brother of the king of France, the undersized duke of Anjou, during 1579–80. Yet the idea of a French marriage proved even more divisive than the prospect of war and Elizabeth had to abandon the venture.[1]

Despite this bruising experience, Elizabeth doggedly persisted with her hopes of an Anglo-French alliance for several more years. To her, almost any alternative seemed more appealing than war against Spain. Memories of the ruinous wars of the 1540s and 1550s, and the humiliating defeat of the Newhaven expedition at the start of her own reign, had taught her that war was enormously expensive and yielded unpredictable – and often unpalatable – results.[2] Bitter experience in bankrolling mercenaries to aid the Dutch over the past decade only reinforced this point. Lobbying from commercial pressure groups also reminded her that war with Spain would mean a painful blow to her own customs revenue and financial loss for powerful merchants, many of whom regularly lent money to the crown.[3] Although she had no desire to see fellow Protestants crushed into conformity with the Roman Church, Elizabeth believed that the Dutch were rebels against their lawful sovereign. As a prince who had a high opinion of her own regality, she viewed the Dutch cause without enthusiasm, and with not a little distaste. Above all, however, Elizabeth feared that war would severely restrict her own political freedom of action. Instead of making choices, she would be confronted by the inexorable logic of war, and be forced to bow before it. War meant delegating genuine authority to men whom she knew were desperately eager for power and glory. For a queen who had spent her whole reign dodging the demands of her leading male subjects, this was a distinctly unpleasant thought.

By 1584, Elizabeth's options were running out and pressure was building for her to act. The death of Anjou in early June weakened relations with France, whilst the subsequent assassination of the Dutch leader, William of Orange, left the Low Countries in disarray. In the past, Elizabeth had been

---

[1] W. T. MacCaffrey, 'The Anjou Match and the making of Elizabethan foreign policy', in P. Clark *et al.* (eds.), *The English commonwealth 1547–1640* (Leicester, 1979), pp. 59–75; S. Doran, *Monarchy and matrimony: the courtships of Elizabeth I* (London and New York, 1996), ch. 7; B. Worden, *The sound of virtue: Philip Sidney's Arcadia and Elizabethan politics* (New Haven and London, 1996).
[2] W. T. MacCaffrey, 'The Newhaven expedition, 1562–1563', *HJ* 90 (1997), pp. 1–21.
[3] P. Croft, *The Spanish Company* (London, Record Society, IX, 1973), pp. ix–xxix; G. D. Ramsay, *The queen's merchants and the Revolt of the Netherlands: the end of the Antwerp mart*, II (Manchester, 1986).

able to stall demands for military action by playing upon the diversity of opinion and sense of caution in her privy council – the select body of men whom she had chosen to be responsible for the day-to-day running of government and for offering her policy advice. However, the march of events and the deaths of conservative members such as the earl of Sussex increasingly narrowed the range of opinion. The news of Orange's murder, in particular, sent a collective shiver around the council board. Not only did his demise create an immediate crisis in the Low Countries but the manner of his death reinforced their fears of new Catholic plots against the life of Elizabeth and the prospect of Mary Stuart's succession to the throne. In dramatic fashion, Orange's death demonstrated the intimate linkage between events at home and abroad.

After some months of informal debate,[4] the privy council finally met to consider the situation in the Netherlands in a direct manner in October 1584. Despite 'very many [arguments] on either side', the councillors decided that the queen must act to save the Dutch from defeat, unless she wanted a victorious Spain which could within a few years threaten her realm with overwhelming power. In the collective opinion of the council, the international situation simply left England with no safe alternative. If the French could not be brought to act against Spain, Elizabeth would have to intervene without them, or risk facing a war without even the meagre support which the Dutch might provide.[5] Not surprisingly, this advice prompted the queen to make one last diplomatic overture to the king of France.[6]

Even before the question of England's parlous international position came before them, the council sought to tackle the threat posed by Catholic conspiracies and the presence of Mary Queen of Scots by sponsoring the Bond of Association. This extraordinary document, which was signed by the leading gentlemen of every county, was a commitment to virtual lynch law in the event of Elizabeth's assassination.[7] Although not specified, it was clear that the target of this wholesale retribution would be the supporters of Mary. Members of the council and most of the leading clergy of southern

---

[4] *CSPF*, XVIII, *July 1583–July 1584*, p. 622.
[5] *CSPF*, XIX, *August 1584–August 1585*, pp. 95–9; *HMCS*, III, 67–70.
[6] W. T. MacCaffrey, *Queen Elizabeth and the making of policy, 1572–1588* (Princeton, 1981), pp. 305–10; R. B. Wernham, *Before the Armada: the growth of English foreign policy 1485–1588* (London, 1966), pp. 369–70.
[7] D. Cressy, 'Binding the nation: the Bonds of Association, 1584 and 1696', in D. J. Guth and J. W. McKenna (eds.), *Tudor rule and revolution* (Cambridge, 1982), pp. 217–34; P. Collinson, 'The monarchical republic of Queen Elizabeth I', *Bulletin of the John Rylands Library*, 69 (1986–7), pp. 413ff. The Bond was regularised by an act of parliament in 1585 (J. E. Neale, *Elizabeth I and her parliaments 1584–1601* (London, 1957), pp. 33–6, 44, 51–3, 114–16).

England signed the document in a great ceremony at Hampton Court on 19 October, a scene repeated on a smaller scale at gatherings across the realm.[8] At one such ceremony, Essex put his name to the Bond at the head of the gentlemen of Pembrokeshire.[9]

The remarkable nature of the Bond illustrates the depth of fear which Mary's claim to the throne evoked in the Protestant élite which governed England.[10] For them, Mary's succession represented a nightmare prospect, threatening them with the loss of their political predominance and conjuring up images of interference in English affairs by foreign powers, a return to the persecution of Protestants and perhaps also the confiscation of those private lands which had once been ecclesiastical property. The fear of such an eventuality drove some members of parliament and privy councillors repeatedly to urge Elizabeth to protect their mutual interests by executing Mary for treason. Until the early 1580s, when she became too old, similar pressures were applied to make Elizabeth choose a husband, in the hope that she would produce a child of her own and thereby cut Mary out of the succession. These urgings consistently failed, but the very existence of Mary's claim to the English throne had a powerful moderating effect on English politics during the 1570s and 1580s. While she remained alive, a common fear of the consequences of her succession acted as a brake upon real dissension, especially among members of the privy council. In other circumstances, despite the many things that bound them together, the senior members of this body might well have fought among themselves to ensure the primacy of their own influence, as had happened in earlier times. However, the presence of Mary within the realm was a constant reminder to councillors that their administration depended upon the single thread of the queen's life.

If the privy council were united in their concern for the safety of the queen, they remained divided over the Low Countries. Sir James Croft, the comptroller of the queen's household and a well-known sympathiser with Spain,[11] opposed any intervention. More importantly, opinions were mixed among the four men who now dominated the council, each of whom had varying degrees of influence with the queen: Burghley, Leicester, Walsingham and Sir Christopher Hatton, the smooth and politically adept vice-chamberlain. Leicester and Walsingham were strongly in favour of

---

[8]   Collinson, 'Monarchical republic', p. 414.
[9]   PRO, SP 12/174, fol. 41ʳ. Essex was then resident at Llanfydd. His signature was immediately followed by that of his brother-in-law, Thomas Perrot.
[10] For a broad-ranging discussion of this subject, see P. Collinson, 'The Elizabethan exclusion crisis and the Elizabethan polity', *Proceedings of the British Academy* 84 (1994), pp. 51–92.
[11] For Croft, see *DNB*, V, pp. 110–12; *Commons*, I, 672–4; R. E. Ham, 'The autobiography of Sir James Croft', *BIHR* 50 (1977), pp. 48–57.

intervention in the Netherlands. They shared a belief that England's best response to the Spanish threat was to protect its Protestant co-religionists in the Netherlands, ideally as the leading force in a multi-national Protestant league. Both men had invested a great deal of time and political capital in the Dutch cause over many years. Leicester had been expected to lead an English force to the Netherlands in 1577 and had been bitterly disappointed when the queen changed her mind.[12]

For Leicester and Walsingham, and the many Englishmen who thought like them, the queen's policy towards the Netherlands had a greater significance than merely the fate of the Dutch, important though that was. In their eyes, the Low Countries represented the crucial test-case for the notion of a broader international 'Protestant cause'.[13] This view was based upon the idea that the Protestant communities of northern Europe must act together against the forces of the Counter-Reformation. Aside from strong Protestantism, support for this cause was characterised by a rich intellectual culture and an internationalist conception of political and military action. Each of these characteristics struck a chord with Essex, who had been brought up with the son of a former French Protestant leader and gone up to Cambridge under the shadow of his father's godly reputation. From his subsequent contacts with Leicester, Essex clearly also heard much about the many glittering European connections of Leicester's eldest nephew, Sir Philip Sidney, and of his endeavours to advance a Protestant league.[14] Although far removed from the inner workings of policy, Essex undoubt-edly shared something of his stepfather's despair about the Netherlands in late 1584 and early 1585.

The frustration of Leicester and Walsingham over the queen's prevarica-tion was also felt by their conciliar colleagues. Although always conscious that his political influence depended entirely upon the queen's favour, Sir Christopher Hatton had often sided with Leicester and Walsingham in matters of foreign policy in the past and he recognised the dangers of this continued drift. Burghley must have seen the same problem but he was profoundly affected by his sovereign's unwillingness to intervene. Since his elevation to the office of lord treasurer in 1572, Burghley had become increasingly cautious on matters of state, often to the point of

---

[12] MacCaffrey, *Elizabeth and the making of policy*, pp. 226, 228–9.

[13] Essential for an understanding of this phenomenon and its relevance to Leicester's expeditions to the Netherlands is S. L. Adams, 'The Protestant cause: religious alliance with the West European Calvinist communities as a political issue in England, 1585–1603' (unpub. D.Phil. thesis, University of Oxford, 1973), chs. 1–3. See also Worden, *Sound of virtue*, esp. chs. 3–4.

[14] R. Howell, 'The Sidney circle and the Protestant cause in Elizabethan foreign policy', *Renaissance and Modern Studies* 19 (1975), 31–46; Worden, *Sound of virtue*, pp. 43–5, 51–7, 60–1, 79.

indecision.[15] His papers are full of notes in his hand which carefully tally up the pros and cons of an issue and only point to his desired outcome by implication. At the meeting of the council in October 1584, Burghley probably argued against intervention in the Netherlands but, as so often, his memoranda on the issue are rather opaque. Although he recognised the need to ensure that the Dutch Protestants were allowed some form of religious toleration, Burghley never had much sympathy for the idea that they might be good allies. If anything, he tended to view the Dutch as liabilities.[16] As lord treasurer, Burghley was also concerned about the costs of war and the danger that the scale of English involvement might expand to an unexpected and unsupportable degree. Above all, his doubts about intervening in the Low Countries were fuelled by Elizabeth's own reluctance and his desire to seem conformable to the royal will. Taking his cue from his sovereign's unwillingness, he remained unenthusiastic about the council's hard-won consensus about the inevitability of war. Like the chancellor of the exchequer, Sir Walter Mildmay, Burghley may well have voiced concerns about open involvement in Dutch affairs early in 1585.[17]

The lord treasurer's equivocal position irritated the interventionists because it reinforced Elizabeth's own determination not to send an army to aid the Dutch. However, open disagreement was something which the leading councillors always tried to avoid – especially when there was no chance of the queen taking their side. Instead, urged on by the increasingly alarming news across the Narrow Sea, unidentified advocates of the Dutch cause – perhaps including Leicester and Walsingham themselves – began to criticise Burghley's conduct. This criticism seems like the venting of pent-up frustrations, but it is conceivable that it was a deliberate attempt to make Burghley shift his ground. At times, the talk threatened to strain good relations between the leading councillors. During July, Burghley felt compelled to respond to stories being circulated about him which suggested that he was more concerned with his own private interests than the good of the realm. The news of these rumours, and Burghley's wounded response to them, came in his correspondence with one William Herle, who had once acted as an *agent provocateur* for Burghley and who also had contacts with Walsingham and Leicester. The length and tone of Burghley's letters to

[15] M. M. Leimon, 'Sir Francis Walsingham and the Anjou marriage plan, 1574–1581' (unpub. Ph.D. thesis, University of Cambridge, 1989), p. 177.
[16] *HMCS*, III, p. 69. Burghley's disregard for the Dutch (or, for that matter, the Huguenots) as allies was also apparent in his dealings over the proposed marriage between Elizabeth and Anjou in 1579 (Leimon, 'Walsingham', pp. 117, 137).
[17] F. G. Oosterhoff (*Leicester and the Netherlands, 1586–1587* (Utrecht, 1988), p. 40) points to the difficulty of categorising Burghley's behaviour at this juncture. Oosterhoff claims that an anti-interventionist paper of 18 March 1585 (BL, Harleian MS 168, fol. 102^r), which Conyers Read attributed to Burghley, was in fact written by Mildmay.

Herle make it clear that they were really directed at his fellow councillors rather than Herle himself.[18] By August, Burghley felt no happier and he wrote directly to Leicester, protesting that he was neither his enemy nor opposed to aid for the Dutch.[19] In reply, Leicester professed innocence of any action against Burghley and reminded him of how they both suffered from envy and slanders because of their high political importance.[20] This was true, but also perhaps somewhat disingenuous.

By the time Burghley was corresponding with Herle, the decision to intervene in the Netherlands had in fact already been taken. The continuing advance of Spanish forces under the duke of Parma had made matters there ever more urgent, especially when the city of Antwerp came under siege. From France came news at the beginning of March that the king had refused once and for all to co-operate with Elizabeth.[21] A few weeks later, the French Catholic League demanded instead that their monarch turn against the Protestants in his own country.[22] On 22 March, Walsingham first received reports about a secret alliance between the Catholic League and the Spanish.[23] By this agreement, Spain promised to support the Catholic cause in France with money and troops, opening up the terrifying prospect of a combined Spanish and French threat just across the Channel.[24] Two months afterwards came the final blow: the Spanish began seizing English ships which were anchored in their ports.[25] All of this seemed to prove that there was indeed a vast Catholic plan to destroy England and that it was already well underway. England therefore had to act promptly – before the Dutch were defeated and the front line of this conflict moved from the Low Countries to England itself.

In the light of these events, any pressure applied to Burghley in mid-1585 must be seen less as an attempt to remove his opposition to the war than to

---

[18] C. Read, *Lord Burghley and Queen Elizabeth* (London, 1960), pp. 314–16. Note that Read also suggests that there was some exchange between Burghley and Walsingham in early 1585. Further light is shed on Herle's character and career in D. L. Jones, 'William Herle and the office of Rhaglaw in Elizabethan Cardiganshire', *National Library of Wales Journal* 17 (1971–2), pp. 161–79.

[19] BL, Lansdowne MS 102, fol. 230[r–v].   [20] BL, Lansdowne MS 45, fols. 79[r]–81[r].

[21] *CSPF*, XIX, *August 1584–August 1585*, p. 315.   [22] *Ibid.*, pp. 361–2.

[23] *Ibid.*, p. 370.

[24] *Ibid.*, p. 370. This was the Treaty of Joinville, which was concluded in late December 1584.

[25] Simon Adams emphasises that the news of Spain's action against English shipping only confirmed, and did not initiate, the move towards alliance with the Dutch ('The outbreak of the Elizabethan naval war against the Spanish empire: the embargo of May 1585 and Sir Francis Drake's West Indies voyage', in M. J. Rodriguez-Salgado and S. Adams (eds.), *England, Spain and the Gran Armada 1585–1604* (Edinburgh, 1991), p. 63). Ironically, the Spanish action (which also affected Dutch and German vessels) was driven by a need to obtain ships which could be used to help protect shipments of American silver. The Spanish knew that Sir Francis Drake was preparing a fleet and believed that Elizabeth would soon let him use it against the treasure ships.

goad him into putting his full weight behind it. This was important because Burghley became closely involved in the negotiations with the Dutch for a treaty of assistance in July and August.[26] Moreover, Leicester and Walsingham were conscious of how fragile Elizabeth's commitment to intervention remained.[27] When Dutch envoys offered her the sovereignty of the rebel provinces in June 1585, she rejected it outright.[28] By doing so, she eschewed an open provocation to the king of Spain but she also kept her options open for a unilateral withdrawal from the Netherlands at some later date. The tensions between Burghley and Leicester must therefore be placed in the context of the Leicester's very real fears that, unless her leading councillors maintained a common front, Elizabeth might find some way to renege on her new commitment to protect the Dutch. These doubts received further confirmation during September, when Elizabeth dithered over Leicester's appointment as commander of the army going to the Low Countries,[29] and then again in early December, when she quibbled over granting him a mortgage to help meet the costs of being her general.[30] No wonder, then, Leicester finally left England with a plea to Burghley to continue his now vigorous support for the venture and 'have this cause even to your hart ... for this I must say to you, yf hir Majesty fayle with such suplye and maintenance as shalbe fytt, all she hath donn hetherto wylbe utterly lost and cast away, and wee hir pore subiectes no better than abjectes'.[31]

After months of haggling and anxiety, Leicester finally left England at the beginning of December 1585, and Essex sailed with him.[32] After his short stay at Court, Essex departed for his first experience of war with obvious

---

[26] *CSPF*, XIX, *August 1584–August 1585*, pp. 703–9.
[27] For example, PRO, SP 12/183, fol. 176ʳ.   [28] Wernham, *Before the Armada*, p. 371.
[29] S. Adams (ed.), *Household accounts and disbursement books of Robert Dudley, earl of Leicester, 1558–1561, 1584–1586* (Camden Society, 5th series, VI, Cambridge, 1996), pp. 385–95. Walsingham reported that one reason for Elizabeth's hesitancy about confirming Leicester as general was her continuing jealousy of Essex's mother: 'there is great offence taken in the carrying down of his lady' (*CSPF*, XX, *September 1585–May 1586*, p. 8. Cf. BL, Cotton MS Galba C IX, fol. 79ʳ). Leicester himself claimed that 'she [the queen] doth take every occasion by my mariage to withdrawe any good from me' (PRO, SP 12/182, fol. 1ʳ).
[30] *Leycester corr.*, p. 21; *CSPF*, XX, *September 1585–May 1586*, pp. 196–7. Leicester's commission as general was dated 2 October 1585 and enrolled as PRO, C 66/1255, mm. 42–3. It was actually signed on 21 October, along with a separate commission allowing him to levy 500 of his tenants for service in the Netherlands (*ibid.*, SO 3/1, fol. 41ᵛ). For the delay in approving his mortgage, see Adams, *Accounts of Leicester*, p. 394.
[31] *Leycester corr.*, p. 23.
[32] Leicester and his immediate entourage sailed from Harwich on 8 December 1585 aboard the *Amity*. They arrived at Flushing two days later. For the subsequent trip to Middleburgh, Essex boarded the *Signet*, while Leicester travelled separately on a hoy (*ibid.*, pp. 461, 464).

glee. His enthusiasm for the great adventure was reflected in an expenditure on outfitting himself which utterly appalled his grandfather Knollys.[33] Essex's steward later estimated that he spent £4,000 'at the leste' during the eleven months which he spent in the Low Countries.[34] Yet this expenditure could hardly be avoided. Going to war cost everyone a great deal of money. Leicester had to strain his finances almost to breaking point, while Lord North spent almost £2,400 on his year's service[35] and Lord Willoughby's three years in the Netherlands left him over £4,000 in debt, even after mortgaging his estates.[36] Things were made worse by the fact that none of the expedition's senior officers were to receive any pay until they were reimbursed by the Dutch. Yet, in a sense, Essex's expenditure was to prove money well spent. The year which Essex spent at war in the Netherlands represented his equivalent of the Continental tour with which young gentlemen were now frequently rounding off their formal education. Unlike the majority of its equivalents, however, Essex's 'tour' gave him experiences which patently had an enduring influence on his later career and attitudes; it constituted the start of his apprenticeship as a soldier. Essex's experiences in the Low Countries also gave a specific and distinctive political shape to the ideas about nobility and religion with which he had been brought up.

Essex's military apprenticeship can be summarised fairly quickly because the year he spent at war witnessed very little actual fighting. In December 1585, Essex left England to take part in the greatest military expedition that Elizabeth's reign had yet seen. Spurring him on were the excitement of the venture and the sense of religious mission with which it was trumpeted, for this was intended to be a Protestant crusade against the Spanish forces of the Antichrist.[37] As he had during Leicester's visits to the Midlands, Essex initially travelled in his stepfather's entourage, witnessing the ceremonial welcomes and the expressions of public expectation which accompanied the expedition's start.[38] On 10 January 1586, when the English cavalry was first mustered, Essex was named to the coveted position of colonel-general of the horse.[39] As he was barely twenty and completely

---

[33] FSL, L.a.566 (pr. Devereux, *Lives*, I, pp. 178–9).   [34] Devereux MS 2, fol. 82[r].

[35] BL, Stowe MS 774(ii), fol. 107[r–v].

[36] G. Bertie, *Five generations of a loyal house. Part I: Containing the lives of Richard Bertie, and his son, Peregrine, Lord Willoughby* (London, 1845), pp. 253–4, 525–8.

[37] Adams, 'Protestant cause', ch. 2. For additional discussion of the expedition and its problems, see Oosterhoff, *Leicester and the Netherlands*. Important light is thrown upon the creation of Leicester's army in S. Adams, 'The gentry of North Wales and the earl of Leicester's expedition to the Netherlands, 1585–1586', *Welsh History Review* 7 (1974), pp. 129–47.

[38] BL, Harleian MS 6845, fol. 26[v]; BL, Add. MS 48014, fol. 153[r–v].

[39] PRO, SP 15/29, fol. 161[r]; *Apologie*, sig. A2[v]; Stow, *Annales*, p. 1193. See also S. Adams, 'Gentry of North Wales', pp. 137–9. About 400 cavalrymen had initially been mustered

inexperienced, the real work attached to this command was performed by Sir William Russell, a younger son of the late earl of Bedford.[40] This appointment was also a potent political signal for the future. Since the cavalry consisted primarily of Leicester's own followers and servants,[41] the appointment of Essex to lead them was a conspicuous sign that the young earl might one day succeed Leicester as their political leader.

At the end of March, having demonstrated the effects of his military training in public exercises, Essex left his stepfather's entourage and began his service with the cavalry in the field.[42] Thereafter, he enjoyed precious little action: in April, he was involved in a minor skirmish near Nie-kerken;[43] in June, he sat as a commissioner for a court martial;[44] at the fall of Doesburg, at the beginning of September, he and some of the other gentlemen officers were forced to beat back their own soldiers to prevent them despoiling women who were fleeing the town.[45] The predominant experience of Essex, as for the rest of Leicester's officers, was one of frustration and a growing impatience to perform some gallant deed.

Greatly aggravating these feelings were the many political, logistic and strategic problems which rapidly turned the whole expedition sour.[46] When the great crusade began, much emphasis was placed upon unity and ensuring broad support among English and Dutch alike. In a conscious act of political balancing, the command of the two Dutch towns which were placed under English control was divided between Sir Philip Sidney and Burghley's heir, Sir Thomas Cecil.[47] Symbolic representations of unity were also prominent in the propaganda which accompanied the English intervention, including such works as Geffrey Whitney's *A choice of emblemes and other devises* (published at Leiden in 1586).[48] However, such appeals to a

near Westminster at the start of December 1585, before accompanying Leicester to the Low Countries as part of his train.

[40] PRO, SP 15/29, fol. 161ʳ. For Russell, see *Commons*, III, pp. 310–12; *DNB*, XVII, pp. 476–9; J. H. Wiffen, *Historical memoirs of the house of Russell; from the time of the Norman Conquest* (2 vols., London [1833]), II, pp. 1–5. Before his death in August 1585, Bedford seems to have been a vigorous supporter of Leicester's expedition: S. Adams, 'A puritan crusade? The composition of the earl of Leicester's expedition to the Netherlands, 1585–1586', in P. Hoftijzer (ed.), *The Dutch in crisis, 1585–1588: people and politics in Leicester's time* (Leiden, 1988), pp. 20–1.

[41] Adams, 'A puritan crusade', pp. 7–34 (esp. pp. 7–8, 13, 23–4).

[42] Stow, *Annales*, p. 1197.   [43] *CSPF*, XX, *September 1585–May 1586*, p. 557.

[44] *Ibid.*, XXI(II), *June 1586–March 1587*, pp. 173–4.   [45] Stow, *Annales*, pp. 1230–1.

[46] J. E. Neale, 'Elizabeth and the Netherlands, 1586–7', *EHR* 45 (1930), pp. 373–96 (reprinted in his *Essays in Elizabethan history* (London, 1958), pp. 170–201); Oosterhoff, *Leicester and the Netherlands*.

[47] Sidney was appointed governor of Flushing and Cecil governor of Brill (PRO, C 66/1266, mm. 8, 10, 11).

[48] *STC* no. 25438. See also R. C. Strong and J. A. van Dorsten, *Leicester's triumph* (Leiden and London, 1964).

common cause could not remove the inherent contradictions of the expedition. Leicester's instructions ordered him to adopt a passive mission: 'rather to make a defensive then an offensyve warr, and not in any sort to hazard a battaile without great advantage'.[49] In terms of strategy, his task was merely to prevent a Dutch defeat, while the real pressure was applied to the king of Spain by offensive naval operations.[50] Such a negative role is very difficult to perform, even in the best of circumstances. Yet these were far from ideal circumstances. The size of the English force and the need to co-ordinate matters with the Dutch meant that there were constant problems in ensuring an adequate supply of provisions, pay and reinforcements. Moreover, Leicester's own status relative to the Dutch authorities was unclear. He himself clearly saw his part as being that of another William of Orange – the valiant leader of international Protestantism's opposition to the 'tyrannical' power of Spain.[51] In seeking to pursue this ambition, Leicester undermined his support among the Dutch by supporting Calvinists at the expense of regional sensitivities[52] and infuriated Elizabeth by accepting the office of governor-general without her permission.

This latter act, at the beginning of 1586, had particularly unsettling consequences for the English political scene. Always unhappy about her commitment in the Low Countries, Elizabeth perceived Leicester's action as not merely an endeavour to clarify his authority but an attempt to force upon her a responsibility for the Dutch which she had rejected in the previous year. Elizabeth made her feelings quite clear in a series of letters to the earl which were full of scathing reproaches.[53] In the end, Leicester was forced to surrender his new title, but not before bitter recriminations had passed among the queen's ministers. Like every commander of an overseas expedition during Elizabeth's reign, Leicester blamed the councillors who stayed at home for not giving him adequate support. Elizabeth's dispatch of commissioners to investigate affairs in the Netherlands made matters worse. Leicester felt that he was to be the victim of a witch-hunt. He responded with expressions of self-pity to Burghley, Walsingham and Hatton, and vitriol to lesser men. In fact, Leicester's doubts about his colleagues were unfair: the driving force in this affair was Elizabeth herself, while her ministers constantly tried to deflect the force of her anger away

---

[49] *Leycester corr.*, p. 12.
[50] S. Adams, 'The lurch into war', *History Today* 38 (May 1988), pp. 18–25; G. Parker, 'Why the Armada failed', *History Today* 38 (May 1988), pp. 26–33.
[51] *CSPF*, XX, *September 1585–May 1586*, p. 67; *Leycester corr.*, p. 20.
[52] J. Israel, *The Dutch Republic: its rise, greatness and fall, 1477–1806* (Oxford, 1995), pp. 220–30; G. Parker, *The Dutch Revolt* (London, 1977), pp. 220–1, 241, 245; MacCaffrey, *Elizabeth and making of policy*, pp. 372–4; Oosterhoff, *Leicester and the Netherlands*, esp. chs. 4–5, 7.
[53] *CSPF*, XX, *September 1585–May 1586*, p. 510; *Leycester corr.*, pp. 95ff.

from Leicester.[54] As in other cases, this episode suggests that the natural instinct of the council was to protect one of its own number, so long as this remained consonant with their duty to the queen and the realm. Time and again during her reign, Elizabeth's councillors seem to have decided that they needed to moderate the force of her desires in order to protect what they perceived to be the queen's own best interests. In this instance, Leicester's colleagues judged that these best interests depended upon his position in the Netherlands being weakened as little as possible, lest it bring a collapse in English authority there.

At the same time that heated messages passed back and forth between Leicester and the Court over matters of high politics, bitter divisions also began to appear within Leicester's army. Sharp frictions grew between the officers who were associated with Leicester, among whom Essex was inevitably numbered,[55] and those who looked to Sir John Norris, the colonel-general of the foot. Norris had originally been designated to lead an English force to relieve Antwerp in August 1585[56] and resented being relegated to a subordinate position under Leicester, especially when he and the earl fell out over matters of operational control and the way in which patronage seemed to be monopolised by Leicester's friends and relatives. In turn, Leicester regarded Norris as a former client who had now ungratefully rejected his old patron.[57] Essex was caught in the middle of the worst incident caused by this rivalry, when Norris's brother Edward was assaulted at a drunken dinner at Gertruydenburgh in early August 1586 and had to flee in fear of his life.[58] Essex felt moved to warn Leicester that that such antagonism encouraged 'our owne private warres, which ... I must needs think ... more dangerous then the annoyaunce of any enemy'.[59] Such experiences helped to shape Essex's own actions as a general in the following decade.

The events of Essex's year in the Low Countries also helped to give his subsequent political career much of its distinctive character. At heart, his political ambitions were essentially those of a soldier: he wanted to be a great captain. Essex's first taste of war whetted these martial ambitions. To some degree, he was perhaps influenced by the splendour and glory which attended upon his stepfather as commander-in-chief in the Netherlands. 'His excellency', the earl of Leicester, was attended by 100 red-coated

[54] See, for example, *Leycester corr.*, pp. 104, 113, 143, 189, 196–9.
[55] *CSPF*, XXI(II), *June 1586–March 1587*, 173–4.
[56] PRO, C 66/1266, mm. 6–7; Murdin, p. 783.
[57] MacCaffrey, *Elizabeth and making of policy*, pp. 369–71; BL, Add. MS 48014, fol. 160[r]; BL, Cotton MS Galba D I, fol. 43[v].
[58] PRO, SP 84/9, fols. 68[r]–69[r]; *Leycester corr.*, pp. 391–5; Longleat, Thynne MS 40, fol. 1[r].
[59] PRO, SP 84/9, fol. 241[r].

bodyguards and his celebration of St George's Day at Utrecht was 'most princelike'.[60] These heady experiences were perhaps counterbalanced by the privations which he observed among the common soldiers and by familiarity with his stepfather's growing despair as his dreams of being another William of Orange dissolved into ashes. However, despite all this suffering, or perhaps because of it, Leicester's expedition drove home for Essex those notions of a Protestant cause and ideal noble virtues with which he had been raised. As the campaign stuttered and hostile missives came from the queen, Leicester and the other members of his circle could only cling tenaciously to their belief in the rightness of their cause and pray for the chance to vindicate themselves by fulfilling the highest ideals of martial excellence. In the face of adversity grew a partisan solidarity and an even greater belief in the importance of their godly purpose. As the general's dutiful stepson, and an enthusiastic apprentice of war, Essex inevitably imbibed and shared these views.

Essex finally got his chance to fight the Spanish in a relatively major battle at the end of September. Near Zutphen, along with other eager young captains, including Peregrine Lord Willoughby and Henry Unton, he took part in a cavalry charge against a greatly superior Spanish force which was trying to re-provision the town. The whole engagement was a confusing mêlée in thick mist and failed to stop the Spanish completing their manoeuvre. Nevertheless, Essex and the other English horsemen pressed the attack with a recklessness which gave full vent to their long-frustrated desire to live up to the ideals of knightly conduct.[61] This proved to be the decisive event of Essex's time in the Netherlands. For his gallantry in the engagement, Essex was one of four men made a knight banneret, the highest rank of knighthood conferred on the battlefield.[62] Lesser knighthoods were also conferred on a number of other men who shared in the action, including several who were to be close comrades of Essex in the years ahead, such as Sir William Knollys, Sir Robert Sidney, Sir Philip Butler, Sir Henry Unton and Sir Roger Williams.[63] Above all, Zutphen

[60] V. von Klarwill (ed.), *The Fugger letters, second series, being a further selection from the Fugger papers specially relating to Queen Elizabeth and matters relating to England during the years 1565–1605* (trans. L. S. Byrne, London, 1926), p. 100; Nichols, *Progresses*, II, pp. 455–7; Stow, *Annales*, p. 1199; J. L. Motley, *History of the united Netherlands; from the death of William the Silent to the Twelve Years' Truce – 1609* (4 vols., London, 1875), II, pp. 14–15.
[61] PRO, SP 12/194, fol. 61ʳ; BL, Harleian MS 305, fol. 151ʳ; Stow, *Annales*, pp. 1232–4; Motley, II, 45–53.
[62] H. Leonard, 'Knights and knighthood in Tudor England' (unpub. Ph.D. thesis, University of London, 1970), pp. 217ff; M. Keen, *Chivalry* (New Haven and London, 1984), p. 168. The other knights banneret were Lords Willoughby, Audley and North (Stow, *Annales*, p. 1236).
[63] There are a number of lists of the knights made by Leicester on this occasion, not all of

cemented Essex's special association with Sir Philip Sidney, for the battle which saw Essex come of age as a soldier, and as a man, also cost Sidney his life.

Sidney was some eleven years older than Essex and, as Leicester's eldest nephew, a cousin by marriage. At one time, Sidney had been destined to marry Essex's favourite sister, Penelope.[64] Although that plan collapsed with the death of Essex's father, Sidney subsequently made her the focus of a sonnet sequence, the 'Stella' to his 'Astrophil'.[65] In 1581, Leicester apparently hoped that Sidney would marry Penelope's younger sister, Dorothy, but that too fell through.[66] Evidence about the early association between Sidney and Essex himself remains elusive.[67] Nevertheless, it seems probable that Sidney was idolised by the adolescent Essex. Sidney was widely travelled, sophisticated and in touch with a glittering range of contacts across Protestant Europe: the embodiment of what Protestant knights should seek to be. Sidney's personal accomplishments and his consanguinity with Leicester made him seem a man certain to succeed, and he was accordingly fêted at home and abroad. Yet such expectations were too great a burden for Sidney to bear. Before the Netherlands campaign, his career was one of almost constant frustration.[68] Although his intellectual and physical prowess led him to be recognised as the leading figure of his generation, Elizabeth never took to Sidney, nor he to her.

Not until the end of 1585, when he went to the Low Countries with his uncle, did it seem that Sidney might come into his own on the political stage. By then, he had already played the role of 'front man' for the cause of a Protestant league for a decade. Now his vigour and European experience made him Leicester's right-hand man. By 1586, it seemed that Leicester was even hoping that Sidney would succeed him as the English commander in the Netherlands.[69] By contrast, Essex was still a young man learning his way, unproven either in battle or diplomacy. Essex's view of

which are identical: BL, Add. MS 48014, fol. 163ʳ; BL, Harleian MS 305, fol. 151ʳ; BL, Harleian MS 6063, fols. 45ʳ; BLO, Ashmolean MS 840, fol. 161ʳ, 163ʳ; Stow *Annales*, pp. 1232–4.

64 J. M. Osborn, *Young Philip Sidney 1572–1577* (New Haven and London, 1972), pp. 424, 443–4; K. Duncan-Jones, *Sir Philip Sidney: courtier poet* (London, 1991), pp. 196–201.

65 H. H. Hudson, 'Penelope Devereux as Sidney's Stella', *Huntington Library Bulletin* 7 (1935), pp. 89–129.

66 In his superseded will of 30 January 1582, Leicester bequeathed £2,000 to further the match between Sidney and Dorothy Devereux (Longleat, Dudley MSS, box 3, no. 56).

67 Most of the evidence for their friendship derives from works written in memory of Sidney, which sought to flatter Essex by emphasising the link with Sidney. See, for example, Thomas Moffet, *Nobilis or a view of the life and death of a Sidney* (ed. V. B. Heltzel and H. H. Hudson, San Marino, 1940), pp. 82–3, 94.

68 F. J. Levy, 'Philip Sidney reconsidered', *English Literary Renaissance* 2 (1972), pp. 5–18.

69 J. van Dorsten, 'The final year', in D. Baker-Smith and A. F. Kinney (eds.), *Sir Philip Sidney: the making of a legend* (Leiden, 1986); M. Poort, '"The desired and destined successor": a

Sidney, therefore, was one of a young man watching his idol performing the tasks and shouldering the responsibilities to which he himself could not yet aspire. Unlike Sidney, Essex was not part of that letter-writing network by which Leicester and his senior associates tried to maintain their friendly relations with the leading councillors at home, and was also a much less conspicuous member of Leicester's entourage than Sidney. Sidney figured prominently in Whitney's A choice of emblemes, but, in spite of the many names mentioned in the book, Essex was not mentioned even once.[70]

With the exception of the literature that he created, the greatest success of Sidney's life was in the manner of his dying. By his death after Zutphen, Sidney was elevated to the status of a Protestant martyr, aided by a deliberate propaganda campaign which sought to forge through him an indissoluble link between the knightly values of chivalry, the godly cause and nobility.[71] Far greater than the effort which followed the death of Essex's father, this campaign culminated in a highly elaborate funeral at St Paul's, which Essex attended along with Sidney's friend, Lord Willoughby, and most of the other leading members of the extended Dudley-Sidney-Devereux family, including the earls of Leicester, Huntingdon and Pembroke, and Lord Rich.[72] Like most posthumous legends, the public image of Sidney contained more fiction than fact, but, for Essex and others of a generation which still awaited their chance to perform great deeds, its significance and emotional resonance were enormous. For Essex, in particular, the Sidney legend immediately assumed a great personal importance. In witnessing the apotheosis of his friend, Essex saw how Sidney had made a 'conquest of death by fame in his life'.[73] Essex himself reinforced the truth of this observation by frequently invoking the memory of Sidney through his own subsequent actions. Having been bequeathed Sidney's 'best swoord', he earnestly sought to assert his claim to Sidney's mantle as the great exemplar of true knightly virtues.[74] In doing so, Essex aspired to

chronology of Sir Philip Sidney's activities 1585–1586' in ibid. (This collection is hereafter cited as Sidney legend.)
[70] For references to Sidney, see Whitney, Choice of emblemes, pp. 38, 109–10.
[71] D. Baker-Smith, '"Great expectations": Sidney's death and the poets', in Sidney legend, pp. 89ff. and C. A. Upton, '"Speaking sorrow": the English university anthologies of 1587 on the death of Philip Sidney in the Low Countries', in H. de Ridder-Symoens and J. M. Fletcher (eds.), Academic relations between the Low Countries and the British Isles, 1450–1700 (Ghent, 1989), pp. 131–41. See also R. Falco, 'Instant artifacts: vernacular elegies for Philip Sidney', Studies in Philology 89 (1992), pp. 1–19 and J. Buxton, 'The mourning for Sidney', Renaissance Studies 3 (1989), pp. 46–56.
[72] S. Bos, M. Lange-Meyers and J. Six, 'Sidney's funeral portrayed', in Sidney legend; Buxton, 'Mourning for Sidney', pp. 49–51.
[73] John Philip, The life and death of Sir Philip Sidney ... (London, 1587, STC no. 19871), sig. A2ᵛ. The phrase comes from the dedication, which was addressed to Essex himself.
[74] PRO, PROB 11/74, fol. 56ʳ. Peregrine Lord Willoughby was also bequeathed 'an other swoord the best I have'. It should be noted that, while Sidney had an exalted literary

be seen as the leader of the younger generation in the same way that Sidney had been. This sense of succession was dramatised by Essex's gift to Elizabeth for New Year 1587, when he gave her a jewel featuring a rainbow over two pillars.[75] One of the pillars was cracked, almost certainly in token of the dead Sidney. The other pillar probably stood for himself, as a symbolic declaration that he was assuming the chivalric burden left by his friend. Even more importantly, Essex secretly married Sidney's widow, apparently in 1590.[76] This was especially significant because Essex married Frances Sidney (née Walsingham) in clear preference to a bride who might have had bluer blood and a large dowry. According to Camden, much of the queen's anger about this match derived from her belief that 'by this affinity he had disparaged the dignity of the house of Essex'.[77] In choosing Frances Sidney, Essex fully committed himself both to the Sidneian pursuit of knightly honour and to the political cause which Sidney had espoused, of aggressively confronting Spanish power in defence of Protestantism on the Continent.

As well as being a mark of his association with Sidney, Essex's participation in the battle of Zutphen at the end of September 1586 had more immediately tangible effects. By his subsequent knighting, Essex not only passed the test of battle with high honour, but he also automatically ceased to be one of the queen's wards. He was now able to claim control over his own estates.[78] Moreover, he was able to do so without paying the usual fine to the crown, thereby giving him a windfall profit from his release from wardship.[79] Unfortunately, Essex needed every financial benefit he could

reputation among the élite, he was primarily known to the mass of his contemporaries as a heroic soldier: W. H. Bond, 'The reputation and influence of Sir Philip Sidney' (unpub. Ph.D. thesis, 2 vols., Harvard University, 1941), I, p. 57.

[75] BL, Add. MS 8159, m. 1 (a roll); *ibid.*, Sloane MS 814, fol. 33^{r-v}.

[76] The only solid evidence about the date of Essex's marriage to Sidney's widow, Frances, the daughter of Sir Francis Walsingham, is that she bore Essex a son at the very beginning of 1591 (FSL, L.a.258). The child, later 3rd earl of Essex, was baptised by Lancelot Andrewes on 22 January 1591 (W. B. Bannerman, *The registers of St Olave, Hart Street, London, 1563–1700* (Harleian Society, XLVI, 1916), p. 14). This merely suggests that the marriage is likely to have taken place before Walsingham's death in April 1590.

[77] *Elizabeth*, p. 624. Elizabeth had been unenthusiastic even about Frances Walsingham's original marriage to Sidney in 1583 (*HMC. Twelfth report, appendix pt iv. The manuscripts of His Grace the duke of Rutland, GCB, preserved at Belvoir Castle*, I (London, 1888), p. 149).

[78] A copy of Essex's petition to the court of wards is BLO, Ashmolean MS 862, pp. 86–7. The formal release from wardship was granted in Easter term 1587 (Devereux MSS, box 5, no. 68). Essex's licence of entry on to his father's possessions was finally enrolled on 27 November 1587 (PRO, C 66/1304, mm. 1–2).

[79] J. Hurstfield, *The queen's wards: wardship and marriage under Elizabeth I* (London, New York and Toronto, 1958), pp. 164ff. Between 1586 and 1588, Essex received almost £6,000 in entry fines from his tenants, most of which was immediately used to pay off

obtain, for the inheritance to which he now succeeded was a very slender and encumbered estate indeed.

Thanks to the enormous costs of his failed conquests in Ireland, the considerable landed wealth with which Walter Devereux was made an earl in 1572 had been greatly dissipated by the time of his death in 1576. By the time Robert attained his majority ten years later, the estate to which he succeeded was saddled with a debt of £11,000 (although this was down from £18,000 at the time of his father's death) and had a gross annual income of only about £1,400.[80] If he was not 'the poorest earle in Yngland',[81] he was not far from it. Having spent his adolescence under constant pressure from his guardians about his expenditure, Essex was well aware of the weakness of his position. Such was the magnitude of his problem that he must have realised that there was only one means by which he could salvage his finances: by winning the favour of the queen, to whom over half his debt was owed. Acute financial need therefore provided a hard practical edge to Essex's early ambitions of glory and public service.

After his return to England at the end of October 1586,[82] Essex made spectacularly rapid progress towards obtaining the royal favour which he needed so much. Unlike his previous spell at Court, Essex now arrived having attained his majority and as a war hero. The latter distinction, in particular, he was able to emphasise by making his first appearance at the annual tilts which celebrated Elizabeth's Accession Day on 17 November.[83] Essex had jousted in public for the first time earlier in the year, at Leicester's St George's Day celebrations in Utrecht,[84] but this was his debut before the queen and the assembled Court. The Accession Day tournament at White-hall was one of the most important and spectacular fixtures on the courtly calendar. By the time Essex first appeared in it, the occasion was already well established as a chance for virile young courtiers to catch Elizabeth's eye and to impress the other members of Court (female as well as male) by their martial prowess and the magnificence of their appearance. Adding to the drama and ingenuity of the spectacle were the *imprese*, or chivalric mottoes, with which participants emblazoned their shields. Sidney had

outstanding debts (Cecil MSS, Accounts 4/21). After his coming of age, Essex was also able to take possession of certain lands held by his mother during his minority as part of an agreement over her jointure in 1577 (Devereux MS 5, fol. 24ʳ).
80 H. A. Lloyd, 'The Essex inheritance', *Welsh History Review* 7 (1974), pp. 13–39, esp. pp. 35, 31, 32.
81 FSL, L.a.566.
82 Together with Sir Thomas Perrot, Sir Philip Butler and Sir Thomas Cooke, Essex was waiting for passage back to England from Middleburgh by 22 October 1586, only five days after Sidney's death (*Leycester corr.*, p. 444).
83 A. Young, *Tudor and Jacobean tournaments* (London, 1987), p. 170.
84 Nichols, *Progresses*, II, 455–7; Stow, *Annales*, p. 1199.

been reputed a master at this specialised art-form.[85] Appropriately enough, Essex's first public foray into the tilt-yard may well have evoked a deliberate tribute to Sidney: *Par nulla figura dolori* (Nothing can represent [my] sorrow).[86]

Within a few months of this public display, Essex began to be described as the queen's new favourite. The significance of this development can hardly be overstated. Royal favour was the very linchpin of all that followed in Essex's career. Unfortunately, like so much else in his early years, detailed evidence about the process by which Essex attained this vital status is often more tantalising than conclusive. As historians of the early modern Court know only too well, the business which passed there was essentially personal and ephemeral – small-talk, arguments, passing compliments, cutting deals and striking poses. Many of the most important events at Court were purely verbal exchanges which have left no written trace.[87] The rise of Essex must therefore be charted by a combination of explicit evidence and logical inference.

If there is any truth to Sir Robert Naunton's observation that it was part of Elizabeth's 'natural propension' to grace soldiers and members of the ancient nobility,[88] Essex was a natural candidate for her attentions by the end of 1586. As a newly fledged knight, he now qualified on both counts. Essex's intellectual cultivation also appealed to Elizabeth. As his 'fantasticall' letters to his sister Penelope demonstrate, he possessed a sophisticated wit and considerable personal charm.[89] On one occasion, the queen felt able to tease Essex about the prospect of learning Russian.[90] Whatever the precise nature of their rapport, Elizabeth had certainly made Essex a frequent companion by May 1587. By then, one of his servants felt able to boast that 'when she [the queen] is abroade, noboddy [is] neere but my lord of Essex. At night my lord is at cardes or one game or an other with her,

[85] A. R. Young, 'Sir Philip Sidney's tournament impresas', *Sidney Newsletter* 6 (1985), pp. 6–24; also his *The English tournament imprese* (New York, 1988), pp. 5–6; R. W. Parker, 'The art of Sidney's heroic impresas', *English Literary Renaissance* 20 (1990), pp. 408–30.

[86] Young, *Tudor and Jacobean tournaments*, pp. 133, 138. It is unclear whether this *impresa* was used by Essex in 1586 or in 1590 (also Young, *English tournament imprese*, p. 101).

[87] See, for example, D. Loades, *The Tudor Court* (London, 1986); D. Starkey (ed.), *The English Court from the Wars of the Roses to the Civil War* (Harlow, 1987); S. W. May, *The Elizabethan courtier poets: the poems and their contexts* (Columbia, Mo., 1991), ch. 1.

[88] Naunton, *Fragmenta regalia*, pp. 56, 69.

[89] BL, Add. MS 64081 (pr. A. Freeman, 'Essex to Stella: two letters from the earl of Essex to Penelope Rich', *English Literary Renaissance* 3 (1973), pp. 248ff.); BLO, MS Don.c.188 (pr. in K. Duncan-Jones, 'Notable accessions: Western Manuscripts', *Bodleian Library Record* 15 (1996), pp. 308–14). See also R. Heffner, 'Essex the ideal courtier', *A Journal of English Literary History* 1 (1934), pp. 7–36.

[90] The occasion was the return of Sir Jerome Horsey from Russia in October 1587: BL, Harleian MS 1813, fol. 46v (pr. E. A. Bond (ed.), *Russia at the end of the sixteenth century* (Hakluyt Society, 1st series, XX, London, 1856), p. 233).

[so] that he commeth not to his owne lodginge tyll the birdes singe in the morninge.'[91] By the end of 1587, Essex was able to dramatise his new status with his New Year's gift for Elizabeth: a jewel which featured a naked man inside a flower of gold.[92] This was an altogether courtier-like motif, at once expressive of a golden fortune and of total dependence upon royal favour.

Although Essex became the queen's newest favourite during 1587, he was by no means her only favourite. Over the course of her reign, Elizabeth had at various times shown special grace to a large number of courtiers. Although most had not lasted long in her favour, the attempt to catch the queen's eye by gallant behaviour was a well-worn path to courtly advancement. This was not simply a matter of Elizabeth's personal tastes but a reflection of the structure of the Court. The fact that Elizabeth was a female sovereign meant that, during her reign, the status and rewards traditionally to be obtained by physical intimacy with the monarch could not be sought through membership of the privy chamber.[93] Instead, such intimacy was expressed through the convention of expressing romantic love for the queen, with the result that ambitious young men at Elizabeth's Court literally became suitors for her favour. As the queen grew older, this phenomenon became an increasingly bizarre, almost schizophrenic, game for the courtiers. For all their pretence of being in amorous pursuit of her, each passing year made it more obvious that none of these suitors could ever consummate their quest by actually marrying Elizabeth. Publicly, ambitious young courtiers conformed themselves to this elaborate charade in the hope of winning the only gratification available from the queen: material reward. Privately, these same men resented the hold which Elizabeth had over them and felt demeaned by the poses which she made them strike. Behind the obsequious façade, many of the younger generation of courtiers viewed their time at Court as a trial to be endured and muttered scornful comments about their royal mistress.[94]

Essex returned from the Netherlands with a new confidence that enabled him to take to this extraordinary game with a vengeance. To place his success in establishing himself as a favourite in perspective, it is perhaps useful to distinguish two distinct generations of royal favourites. On the one hand, there were Leicester and Hatton, both of whom were long

---

[91] FSL, L.a.39.   [92] BL, Egerton MS 3052, m. 1 (a roll).

[93] P. Wright, 'A change in direction: the ramifications of a female household, 1558–1603', in Starkey (ed.), *English Court*, pp. 147–72.

[94] Sidney, for example, was not untypical of many courtiers in his dislike of Court and his private disdain for the ageing Elizabeth (Duncan-Jones, *Sidney*, pp. xi, 106, 264). The escapism of pastoral poetry written by many Elizabethan courtiers should also be seen in this light (*ibid.*, p. 140).

established in the queen's favour and formal participants in government for many years through their membership of the privy council.[95] Leicester, at least, had once seemed a possible consort for Elizabeth.[96] Over time, these senior favourites had become an integral part of the queen's immediate physical and psychological environment. She trusted them for advice and rewarded their intimacy with important offices and lavish grants. Ironically, the very success of Leicester and Hatton as royal favourites created a need for the queen to seek new, younger companions to share her idle hours. Advancing age and the growing demands of government business increasingly reduced the amount of time which they spent which their mistress. Indeed, they began to have more and more in common with Burghley, who had earned a similar degree of trust from Elizabeth by his work as an administrator.[97] This gradual change may perhaps have been another reason for the relative stability and solidarity among the leading councillors by the 1580s. In contrast to the early years of the reign, the potential for dissension because of a favourite's use of courtly wiles to 'interfere' in matters best known to bureaucrats, or vice versa, now seemed remote. Although they remained courtiers first and foremost, Leicester and Hatton spent much of their time on matters of administration, while experience had proven that Burghley (but less so Walsingham) had a genuine place of his own in Elizabeth's affections.

Beside these established confidants of the queen were a younger generation of favourites, principally represented by Sir Walter Ralegh and Essex himself. Far younger than the queen, they were not credible suitors but were, in effect, royal protégés. For them, Elizabeth's favour was the launching pad for careers and reputations still to be made. While Leicester and Hatton could usually rest secure in their favour with the queen, there was no such luxury for these younger favourites. They had to stand the strain of spending long hours keeping the queen amused, and glory in it. They also had to be aware that the appearance of any new rival for the queen's affections might imperil their own hopes of future fame and fortune.

In this contest for royal favour, Essex had a special advantage over and above his own personal qualities. Unquestionably, the celerity of Essex's

---

[95] Leicester joined the council in early 1563 and Hatton in December 1577.

[96] Doran, *Monarchy and matrimony*, ch. 3. Leicester may have floated the idea of marriage to the queen as late as the summer of 1575 (also her 'Juno versus Diana: the treatment of Elizabeth I's marriage in plays and entertainments, 1561–1581', *Historical Journal* 38 (1995), p. 266).

[97] See, for example, Elizabeth's warm and playful letter addressed to Burghley as 'Sir Spiritt' (e.g. BL, Harleian MS 787, fol. 66ʳ; BL, RP 2895). Elizabeth called Leicester her 'eyes' and Hatton her 'mutton' and 'lids'. Walsingham (who cannot be classed as a favourite) was nicknamed her 'Moor', which suggests a certain royal ambivalence towards him.

rise to become the queen's frequent companion had much to do with his special bond with Leicester, Elizabeth's oldest and dearest favourite. Although Leicester seems to have done little to advance his stepson at Court in late 1585, he behaved quite differently after his return to England in late November 1586.[98] In part, this was another result of Zutphen. With Sidney and his own 'noble impe' both dead, any plans which Leicester might make for a political successor now had to revolve around Essex. Such thoughts were essential if the noble leadership of the Protestant cause were to be maintained in England beyond the time of Leicester's own death. Accordingly, Leicester helped to clarify his stepson's tangled financial position by instigating a detailed scrutiny of Essex's finances,[99] and also began to help the young earl to push himself forward at Court.

In this task, Leicester and Essex were assisted by the political storm which was caused by the execution of Mary Queen of Scots in February 1587. Despite all the tensions during 1586 which had grown out of Leicester's command in the Low Countries, the privy council had remained united in their determination to remove the threat posed by Mary. After years of trying, the council finally gained the necessary lever to achieve this end when Walsingham exposed the Babington Plot, and Mary's involvement in it, at the beginning of August 1586.[100] This put Elizabeth under enormous pressure to have done with Mary, both from the council and from the members of a hastily called parliament. After a trial, Elizabeth finally signed Mary's death warrant in February 1587, only to order its suspension. At this point, the council decided to take matters into their own hands. Meeting together (with the exception of Walsingham, who was fortuitously ill), they decided to put the warrant into effect. In an extraordinary act of group solidarity, they chose to act in what they considered to be the queen's higher interests, in defiance of her own express command.[101] When she heard the news of Mary's death, Elizabeth's exploded. To the council's horror, she wanted to hang William Davison, the junior secretary of state to whom she had entrusted the warrant.[102] Elizabeth also turned her anger against Hatton and, above all, Burghley

---

[98] Leicester reached London on 23 November and went to Court that very evening (Stow, *Annales*, p. 1239).

[99] *HMCS*, V, p. 218.

[100] C. Read, *Mr Secretary Walsingham and the policy of Queen Elizabeth* (3 vols., Oxford, 1925), III, pp. 1–70.

[101] Read, *Burghley*, pp. 366ff.

[102] BL, Lansdowne MS 108, fols. 90ʳ–91ʳ; BL, Add. MS 48116, fols. 151ʳ–152ʳ; Sheffield Central Library, Bacon Frank MS 5, item 4 (loose, enclosed in a pocket at the end of the volume). Davison was ultimately fined and imprisoned at the queen's pleasure (PRO, SP 12/199, fols. 137ʳ–139ʳ; BL, Harleian MS 290, fols. 225ʳ–239ᵛ). Interestingly, Davison had previously been made the scapegoat over Leicester's acceptance of the governor-generalship of the Netherlands in the previous year.

himself. In spite of a series of pleading letters, Burghley was barred from her presence for several months.[103] This experience was all the more traumatic and humbling for him because Leicester escaped unscathed; indeed, Burghley began to fear that Leicester was deliberately turning the queen against him.[104] In reality, Elizabeth's special viciousness towards the old lord treasurer had the same source as her blistering letters to Leicester a year before. Just as she had lashed out against what she considered to be Leicester's betrayal of her trust in the Netherlands, she now turned against Burghley for failing to exercise that customary caution which she had come to rely upon as a buttress for her own hesitations. Elizabeth felt such betrayals keenly and made sure that those who exposed her vulnerability in this way experienced pain of their own.

As the clouds of royal anger hung heavily over the Court, Essex had the advantage of being a fresh and wholly innocent companion for the queen. Essex's naive attempts to defend Davison merely emphasised his blamelessness in the whole affair.[105] At the end of April, Leicester was even able to get Elizabeth to agree that Essex should take his place as master of the horse.[106] Besides an estimated value of some £1,500 a year,[107] this appointment greatly reinforced Essex's status as a favourite because it entailed close attendance upon the queen, both at grand ceremonial occasions and in the more informal circumstances of travel and hunting. This appointment accorded with the normal pattern of her dealings with favourites. Once a male courtier had won a firm place in her affections,

---

[103] BL, Lansdowne MS 102, fols. 8^{r-v}, 10^{r-v}; BL, Lansdowne MS 115, fols. 48^{r-v}, 89^r. See also Read, *Burghley*, pp. 370ff.

[104] BL, Lansdowne MS 102, fol. 10^r.

[105] Essex was the not the only man to defend Davison but he was probably the most fervent of Davison's supporters because many councillors and other close servants of the queen felt compromised by their own involvement in the affair. For Essex's efforts on Davison's behalf, see BL, Harleian MS 290, fols. 240^{r-v}, 244^r; BL, Cotton MS Vespasian C XIII(ii), fol. 288^r; BL, Stowe MS 145, fols. 132^r–134^r; BL, Hargrave MS 225, fols. 38^v–39^r; BLO, Tanner MS 79, fols. 46^r, 50^r, 89^r, 99^r; BL, Tanner MS 82, fol. 43^{r-v}. Some of these documents (most of which are undated) probably refer to Essex's renewed attempt to secure his rehabilitation in 1590.

[106] FSL, L.a.39. Essex was ultimately appointed master of the horse on 18 June 1587 (Stow, *Annales*, p. 1243). However, his patent was dated 23 December and he was paid from 21 July (PRO, C 66/1321, m. 35). Significantly, Essex kept this office to the very end, after he had lost everything else. He was paid for the last time as master of the horse on 3 January 1601 (PRO, E 403/2363, unfol., account of Sir Henry Killigrew).

[107] This is evidently a figure given to Essex by Leicester (FSL, L.a.39). Much of this income would have come from the master's oversight of the stables at the royal palaces and of the royal studs at Tutbury and Malmesbury. On the latter, see C. M. Prior, *The royal studs in the sixteenth and seventeenth centuries* (London, 1925). Only fragmentary evidence about the stables seems to survive for the late Elizabethan period (e.g. PRO, E 101/107/33), but total expenditure in the last year before Essex took over as master of the horse was running at about £5,200, including £1,732 for wages (PRO, SP 12/205, no. 26).

Elizabeth invariably granted him some chamber or closely related house-hold post, in order to regularise his access to her in the privy chamber. Hatton and Ralegh, for example, were successive captains of the queen's guard. Essex's appointment was even more significant because the master-ship of the horse had been Leicester's special preserve since the beginning of the reign.[108] According to the Spanish ambassador, Leicester had refused to give up this post when he was offered the much higher office of lord steward in 1585. Now it seems that Leicester had another chance at this promotion, and took it.[109] In doing so, he was able to demonstrate to the world that Elizabeth's trust in him had fully recovered from the events of the previous year.[110] At the same time, by relinquishing the post of master of the horse to Essex, Leicester openly encouraged expectations that Essex was to be his chosen political heir.[111]

Despite this endorsement, Essex's rise to become the queen's newest favourite inevitably caused some friction at Court, especially after Leicester returned to the Low Countries at the end of June.[112] These problems were most spectacularly revealed in an explosive row which developed between Essex and Elizabeth during her visit to Northaw, the home of Leicester's brother, the earl of Warwick, during the last days of July. As Essex recounted the story to his friend Edward Dyer,[113] Elizabeth sought to

---

[108] Leicester's tenure had a profound effect upon the office. Before his appointment in 1558, it had not been an especially significant post in political terms. After Leicester, every succeeding master of the horse was a peer at the time of his appointment (M. M. Reese, *The royal office of the master of the horse* (London, 1976), p. 154).

[109] The whole question of Leicester's promotion to the lord stewardship is somewhat obscure. The report by the Spanish ambassador, Mendoza, merely states that Leicester had refused to give up the mastership of the horse in return for the lord stewardship and, in consequence, Elizabeth had suspended promotions to *other* men (*CSPSpan*, III, *1580–1586*, p. 537). Leicester's modern biographers claim that he was appointed lord steward in 1584 (e.g. A. Hayne, *The white bear: the Elizabethan earl of Leicester* (London, 1987), p. 141). However, Stow dates Leicester's appointment to the same time as Essex became master of the horse: 18 June 1587 (*Annales*, p. 1243). A sample of entries for Leicester in the Patent Rolls between 1584 and mid-1587 reveals no reference to the lord stewardship. Such entries are usually a good guide to the most important offices and titles of the person(s) being named, especially when the entries relate to commissions from the queen.

[110] Leicester's favour with the queen was also demonstrated by grants of a lease of lands in the lordship of Grafton, dated 1 March 1587 (PRO, C 66/1290, mm. 16–17), and of the lucrative 'queen's fines' in chancery, dated 21 June 1587 (*ibid.*, 1292, mm. 8–12).

[111] The former Spanish ambassador to England, Mendoza, therefore had some excuse for reporting that Essex had been made master of the horse as Leicester's 'eldest son' (*CSPSpan*, IV, *1587–1603*, p. 122).

[112] Although opinions of him in the Low Countries were sharply divided, the States-General requested Leicester's return there in a letter of 28 May 1587 (7 June n.s.). He reported his willingness to return on 31 May (HBL, Beale-Walsingham Papers, nos. 37–8). Leicester finally sailed from Margate on 25 June (Stow, *Annales*, p. 1243).

[113] BLO, Tanner MSS 76, fol 29ʳ⁻ᵛ; 77, fol. 178ʳ (pr. Devereux, *Lives*, I, pp. 186–9). Further information on this incident comes from *HMCA*, p. 49 and F. H. Mares (ed.), *The*

exclude one of his sisters from the Court, despite the fact that she was already staying at the house, and he felt moved to protest strongly. To his surprise, his progressively more angry expostulations were answered in kind by the queen. Wounded and confused by this rebuff, Essex immediately ordered his sister to leave the house and stormed off into the night himself. Soon after, he tried to board a ship at Sandwich to go and join the defence of the besieged Dutch town of Sluys, only to be stopped on the queen's orders by Robert Carey.

This is a revealing incident. When discomforted at Court, it seems that Essex's instinctive response was to flee the scene and hearken after the certainties of war and service to his stepfather. This was to prove a recurring pattern in Essex's career when confronted by humiliating reverses at Court – escape into solitude, followed by a new effort to recover his honour by some bold act. Yet there was another, more calculated level to his actions in this instance which was also characteristic of his subsequent courtly career. After fleeing from Northaw, Essex stopped and took the time to write to Dyer, who had been one of Sidney's closest friends,[114] which suggests that Essex's decision to set out for Sluys was not simply taken on the spur of the moment. Furthermore, this melodramatic action seems very similar to Sidney's own thwarted departure for the West Indies in September 1585, when it seemed that Elizabeth had dashed his hopes of serving in the Netherlands.[115] It is also interesting that Carey was actually able to find and stop Essex, despite his head start. Essex may have tried to recover from his initial, rash departure from Court by making a show of bold martial action, perhaps in imitation of Sidney, but with the principal aim of pressuring the queen into calling him back to Court.

Essex's argument with Elizabeth, which preceded his flight, is equally illuminating. It demonstrated that Essex's noble pride could lead him to berate even his anointed sovereign when he felt 'me and my house disgraced'.[116] The immediate cause of this 'disgrace' was Essex's feeling that his sister's exclusion was the work of Sir Walter Ralegh, who had

---

memoirs of Robert Carey (Oxford, 1972), p. 5. For Dyer, see R. M. Sargent, *At the Court of Elizabeth: the life and lyrics of Sir Edward Dyer* (Oxford, 1935).

[114] Essex actually spent some time trying to see Dyer in person and only resorted to writing a letter when this proved impossible: 'I wold have given a thousand poundes to have had one houre's speech with yow' (BLO, Tanner MS 76, fol. 29ʳ). Essex mentioned his decision to go to Sluys in the letter to Dyer.

[115] Poort, '"Desired and destined successor"', pp. 27–8. Some mystery is added to this affair by the mysterious dealings of Drake (W. H. Bond, 'The reputation and influence of Sir Philip Sidney', (unpub. Ph.D. thesis, Harvard University, 2 vols., 1944), I, 23; Howell, 'Sidney circle and Protestant cause', p. 45). For Fulke Greville's gloss on this incident, see J. Gouws (ed.), *The prose works of Fulke Greville, Lord Brooke* (Oxford, 1986), pp. 42–5.

[116] BLO, Tanner MS 76, fol. 29ᵛ.

become his bitter rival for royal favour. Essex's summary of the incident suggests that his antipathy to Ralegh was based on two fundamental grounds. By his charges about 'what he had bene and whose he was',[117] Essex indicated that he shared the view that Ralegh was a follower of Leicester who had turned traitor to his master.[118] Yet he did not vent his spleen against Ralegh merely out of partisanship for his stepfather. Essex also believed that his new status of favourite entitled him to a monopoly of the queen's favour, or at least to exclude from it the 'unworthy' Ralegh. Hence he interpreted any grace which Elizabeth showed to Ralegh as a derogation of his own special claims: 'I saw she was resolved to defend him and to crosse me.'[119] For the young Essex, so eager to prove the pre-eminence of his nobility and virtues, the one action was tantamount to the other.

Essex's rivalry with Ralegh needs to be seen in the context of Ralegh's own career and the general political situation of mid-1587. Ralegh had initially begun his career at Court in the late 1570s as a follower of the earl of Oxford. Like Oxford, Ralegh had mixed with a group of Catholic courtiers who supported Elizabeth's marriage to the French duke of Anjou, in violent opposition to Leicester, Walsingham and Sidney. When Oxford turned against this Catholic party and denounced them as traitors, Ralegh followed suit and attached himself instead to Leicester.[120] This abrupt *volte-face* secured him a military command in Ireland but perhaps also contributed to his life-long reputation for possessing dubious religious beliefs.[121] Ralegh's service in Ireland proved to be the springboard for his return to Court at the end of 1581, when he came to Elizabeth's attention as the bearer of urgent news from the lord deputy of Ireland. Offering expert advice on Irish affairs (although it was counter to that of his superior, the lord deputy) and trading on his recent heroism in fighting the Irish, Ralegh quickly became a favourite of Elizabeth.[122] All of this seems remarkably similar to the pattern of events with Essex some five years later. However, Ralegh lacked the social rank, political contacts and wealth which Essex enjoyed. The growing importance of Ralegh in his native West Country and the money which came to him from a series of lucrative grants

---

[117] *Ibid.*
[118] For Ralegh's earlier devotion to Leicester, see E. Edwards, *The life and letters of Sir Walter Ralegh* (2 vols., London, 1868), II, p. 17; Wotton, *Parallel*, pp. 1–2.
[119] BLO, Tanner MS 76, fol. 29ᵛ.
[120] D. C. Peck, 'Raleigh, Sidney, Oxford and the Catholics, 1579', *N&Q* 223 (1978) pp. 427–31.
[121] P. Lefranc, *Sir Walter Ralegh écrivain: l'œuvre et les idées* (Paris, 1968), ch. 12. Ralegh's alleged religious heterodoxy provoked a formal enquiry in Dorset in 1594 (*ibid.*, pp. 379ff).
[122] S. W. May, *Sir Walter Ralegh* (Boston, 1989), pp. 4–6.

in the mid-1580s[123] depended entirely upon Elizabeth's generosity. This made the rise of any new rival a serious threat. Moreover, the jealousies which these rewards aroused won Ralegh new enemies at Court and made him more dependent than ever upon royal favour. One of his grants even cut across 'the queen's expresse covenant' in an earlier patent issued to Lord Hunsdon, the lord chamberlain and the queen's closest male relative.[124] The anger provoked by this grant may explain why Ralegh almost came to blows at the tennis court with Robert Carey, one of Hunsdon's younger sons, in April 1587.[125] Yet the rivalry behind this confrontation was soon far outweighed by the challenge to Ralegh's position offered by Essex.

Essex's bid for royal favour ensured that Ralegh was faced not only with formidable competition from Essex himself but also direct hostility from Leicester. Thanks to his special bond with the queen, his sprawling family connections and notorious willingness to pursue a vendetta, Leicester was probably the worst possible enemy to have at Court – a reputation which added another, less obvious dimension to his support of Essex. For Ralegh, this political muscle was all the more threatening because his early ties to Leicester had gradually turned sour. By 1585, Leicester was openly hostile towards him.[126] In early 1586, when the issue of the governor-generalship of the Netherlands was dominating affairs, Leicester complained that Ralegh was 'back-biting' him at Court. Ralegh himself wrote to Leicester in March and protested that he was no 'drawer-bake' of the war effort, and attributed the rumour to some 'poeticall scribe'.[127] However, the bad feelings persisted and a month later Elizabeth herself felt it necessary to instruct Walsingham to reassure Leicester about Ralegh.[128]

By the spring of 1587, when Leicester's efforts had helped to make Essex the queen's new favourite, and hence a direct threat to Ralegh, the circumstances for Leicester's relations with Ralegh were even less

[123] J. H. Adamson and H. F. Folland, *The shepherd of the sea: an account of Sir Walter Ralegh and his times* (Boston, 1969), pp. 100–3.
[124] PRO, SP 46/20, fol. 229ᵛ.
[125] BL, Lansdowne MS 96, fol. 69ʳ. Ralegh's fiery character had been evident as early as February 1580, when he was called before the privy council to explain his quarrel with Thomas Perrot, Essex's future brother-in-law (Edwards, *Ralegh*, I, p. 50). A month later, Ralegh was again imprisoned for duelling, this time with a member of the Wingfield family (Adamson and Folland, *Shepherd of the Sea*, p. 46).
[126] For example, CSPSpan, III, *1580–1586*, p. 538. Close followers of Leicester, such as the notorious Sir William Stanley, echoed their patron's views. Stanley called Ralegh 'the blacke man' and one of his associates had a horse named 'Reud Rawley' (Thomas Heywood (ed.), *Cardinal Allen's defence of Sir William Stanley's surrender of Deventer, January 29, 1586–7*, (Chetham Society, XXV, 1851), p. xlii; PRO, SP 12/206, fol. 84ᵛ).
[127] *Leycester corr.*, pp. 193–4 (also pr. Edwards, *Ralegh*, II, p. 33–4).
[128] *Leycester corr.*, p. 207.

propitious.[129] Although Leicester was able to prevail with Elizabeth for his own promotion and the advancement of Essex, things were going from bad to worse in the Netherlands and the queen still blamed him for the huge cost of the 1586 campaign. For his part, Leicester blamed Sir John Norris, Thomas Wilkes and Lord Buckhurst for undermining his authority in the Low Countries.[130] This added another layer of personal bitterness to Court politics in 1587, as Leicester sought vindication and the victims of his enmity sought assistance from other courtiers, including Ralegh. At the same time, Elizabeth was becoming genuinely enthusiastic about the prospects of arranging a peace treaty with Spain. Low-key negotiations had been going on with the Spanish through various intermediaries since 1585 but now things seemed to be changing.[131] Much to the despair of Leicester and Walsingham, Elizabeth grasped at what she hoped would be an honourable means of escaping from her commitment in the Low Countries.[132] Ralegh had played a part in the contacts with Spain during the previous autumn and, at Elizabeth's command, he was again involved in this new peace offensive.[133] Ralegh's rivalry with Essex was therefore intimately connected with the larger question of English foreign policy. In other circumstances, Ralegh was a bitter enemy of Spain, but his desire to maintain royal favour, preferably at the expense of Leicester and Essex, overcame any sympathy which he might otherwise have had for the Protestant cause in 1587.

In light of this background, it can be seen that Essex's outburst at Northaw was both an expression of personal rivalry with Ralegh and of his profound commitment to the absent Leicester. Remarkably, the incident had no lasting consequences for Essex. Undoubtedly, soothing words from

[129] Perhaps significantly, Leicester intervened against Ralegh at the end of February 1587 in the latter's long-running dispute about the licensing of wine-sellers in Cambridge, using his post as high steward of the university (Cambridge University Archives, MS Lett.9, B.20f). In the wake of this, the poet Thomas Churchyard wrote a verse entertainment for Ralegh and several other courtiers which was probably performed at Court in April 1587 and dramatised 'the whole service of my lord of Lester' (*Churchyards challenge* (London, 1593, STC no. 5220), sig. A5ʳ). Churchyard's tone about Leicester's actions seems to be decidedly sarcastic but it is not clear whether this means that the performance itself was an attack on Leicester, or this is merely Churchyard's own later gloss on an entertainment which was meant to encourage reconciliation between Ralegh and Leicester.

[130] For the background to this, see Oosterhoff, *Leicester and the Netherlands*, chs. 10–12. After their return to England, Norris and Buckhurst were briefly ordered into house arrest during July. Norris made his peace with Leicester in December (*HMCR*, I, 234), while Buckhurst was reconciled with the earl during August through the good offices of the lord admiral (BL, Cotton MS Titus C VI, fol. 66ʳ). The unfortunate Thomas Wilkes was sent to the Fleet prison (BL., Cotton MS Galba D I, fols. 43ʳ–45ʳ; BL, Harleian MS 287, fol. 32ʳ⁻ᵛ). He remained in detention until after Leicester's death.

[131] These early contacts are summarised in *CSPF*, XX, *September 1585–May 1586*, pp. xxxiii–xlviii.

[132] BL, Cotton MS Galba C XI, fol. 294ᵛ.   [133] Lefranc, *Ralegh*, pp. 357–9.

the countess of Warwick, who had invited Essex's sister to Northaw and who had witnessed the shouting match, did much to lessen the queen's anger against him.[134] Although he had dared to question whether he could 'give myself over to the service of a mistress that was in awe of such a man',[135] Elizabeth received her erring young favourite back at Court within a few days. Ironically, the first occasion on which he called upon his freshly renewed favour was in urging the queen not to blame Leicester for the fall of Sluys, the very town to which he had attempted to sail only days before.[136] This illustrates the new role which Essex was now playing for his absent stepfather, that of a defender of his interests who had ready access to the queen's person. As he boasted in a letter to Leicester, 'I will watch with the best diligence I can that yowr enemies may not take advantage of yowr absence.' Significantly, he signed this letter as 'yowr sonne most ready to doe yowr service'.[137] Essex seems to have taken to his new responsibility with enthusiasm. He lobbied Elizabeth on Leicester's behalf and even tried to win royal approval for the suits of some of his stepfather's followers.[138] Although he had little success with the latter, it is clear that Essex had now assumed a greater importance in Leicester's political plans. He was graduating towards the kind of right-hand man status which Sidney had enjoyed in 1585–6.

Essex's staunch support for Leicester in the privy chamber was complemented by a continual cut-and-thrust with Ralegh. This running battle was fought out with increasing bitterness and ingenuity over a period of months. Perhaps trying to counter Essex's support from Leicester, Ralegh struck out at his rival in the first half of the year by sending Elizabeth the poem 'Fortune hath taken thee away my love'. This was the opening shot of a series of poetic exchanges between them which would last, off and on, until Essex's fall in 1601. Elizabeth replied to Ralegh with a poem of her own:

> Ah silly pugg, wert thou so sore afrayd?
> Mourne not my Wat, nor be thou so dismaid . . . [139]

Such poetic reassurances received more concrete expression in March 1587 when Elizabeth granted Ralegh various lands which had belonged to the traitor Anthony Babington.[140] A few months later, there was also some

---

[134] Lady Leighton, Essex's aunt and a lady of the privy chamber, may also have aided him here. She was attending the queen at this point and Essex had already used her to warn the queen of his sister's presence at Northaw even before the Court moved there from Theobalds (BLO, Tanner MS 76, fol. 29ʳ).
[135] *Ibid.*, fol. 29ᵛ.   [136] BL, Cotton MS Galba D I, fol. 141ʳ.   [137] *Ibid.*
[138] BL, Cotton MS Galba D II, fols. 4ʳ, 139ʳ; BL, Lansdowne MS 53, fol. 132ʳ.
[139] May, *Elizabethan courtier poets*, pp. 119–22. For the text of these poems, see *ibid.*, pp. 318–21.
[140] Ralegh was also granted all of Babington's personal and movable posessions (PRO, SO

expectation that Ralegh would be made captain of the guard,[141] thereby balancing Essex's appointment as master of the horse. This seemed logical because Elizabeth chose to fill the void left by the death of the lord keeper, Sir Thomas Bromley, by appointing the incumbent captain, Sir Christopher Hatton, as lord chancellor.[142] Ralegh was also treated with signal favour by Elizabeth in July.[143] However, Tudor politicians almost never surrendered an office voluntarily – a fact which makes Leicester's surrender of the mastership of the horse all the more extraordinary. Despite his promotion, Hatton continued as captain of the guard until his death in late 1591 and Ralegh remained without a household post.[144]

Hatton's unprecedented co-tenure of these positions suggests how extraordinary was his appointment to this great office of state. Although he proved to be an adequate chancellor, he was clearly a royal favourite, not a career lawyer. Nevertheless, there was a certain logic in Elizabeth's decision, for Hatton's elevation confirmed that he was effectively co-equal in her government with Leicester, now lord steward, and Burghley, the lord treasurer. Walsingham, the fourth key figure in government, was a full step below this newly formed triumvirate. More significantly for Essex and Ralegh, the demands of Hatton's new office meant that he spent less and less time with Elizabeth, increasing the opportunities for the younger men to spend time with the queen, intensifying the competition between them.

Ralegh's poetic gambit in attacking Essex as 'fortune base' was a stinging blow. Ralegh thereby suggested that Essex had caught the queen's attention merely because of his birth and connections. This strategy had the obvious aim of disqualifying Essex's inherent advantages over Ralegh, whilst proclaiming that his own vulnerabilty made him a worthier and truer suitor for royal favour. However, Ralegh's attack also had a sharper, even more personal edge. By dwelling on the 'fortune' of his birth, Ralegh shrewdly hit Essex at a particularly tender point. Like Sidney before him,[145] Essex

---

3/1, fol. 88ᵛ; PRO, C 66/1301, mm. 38–41). These grants passed the signet on 9 March and were enrolled on 17 March 1587.

[141] BL, Lansdowne MS 96, fol. 69ʳ.

[142] Bromley died on 12 April 1587. Hatton was appointed lord chancellor on 25 April and took the oaths of office on 3 May (*DNB*, IX, p. 161). Further grants consequent upon this office were issued on 21 May 1587 (PRO, C 66/1292, mm. 19–20).

[143] *HMCA*, p. 49.

[144] Hatton's continuation as captain of the guard is demonstrated by his approval of the payment of wages to the guard for 1587–8 (PRO, E 351/542, fol. 122ʳ). For the office of captain of the guard, see R. Hennell, *The history of the king's body guard of the yeomen of the guard* (Westminster, 1904).

[145] Sidney's favourite motto was allegedly *Vix ea nostra voco* ('I scarcely call those things my own') (Duncan-Jones, *Sidney*, p. 135). See also Sidney's letter to Edward Denny of 1580 ('since the unnoble constitution of our tyme doth keepe us from fitte imployments ...', printed in J. M. Osborn, *Young Philip Sidney 1572–1577* (New Haven and London, 1972), pp. 535–40).

had been brought up to believe passionately that his life would only have purpose if he performed great deeds in his own right. The accusation that he merely traded on the 'fortune' of his birth was anathema to Essex – as Ralegh well knew – and touched upon those fundamental assumptions which underlay the earl's life-long preoccupation with the display of noble virtues and the pursuit of fame. It is little wonder that Essex was so vehement against Ralegh in the episode at Northaw.

The rivalry of Essex and Ralegh continued unabated during the late summer and autumn of 1587. According to reports passed on by the Spanish ambassador in Paris, Essex actually hit Ralegh during August, prompting the queen to intervene by commanding them to make up.[146] Whether this story is true or not, the intensity of the rivalry seems to have been undiminished. In September, Ralegh pointedly came out in support of Sir John Norris, who had been recalled from the Netherlands to face charges for his conduct towards Leicester. In the opinion of William Herle, who was reporting on developments at Court for Leicester, Ralegh did so 'ether of his ill nature or of emulation to the erlle of Essex, for that he doth good offices with her Majestie for your excellencie'.[147] Perhaps in response to this competition, Essex made a special effort to create a bold impression at the Accession Day tilts in November.[148] Either during this period, or in 1588, Essex also had himself painted by Hilliard as *The young man among the roses*.[149] This miniature was a kind of visual equivalent to Ralegh's poetic appeal to the queen, full of allusions to love, virtue and Elizabeth herself, albeit tinged with a subtle complaint about the queen's refusal to let him fulfill his dreams of martial glory.[150] Whether independently or in direct response to this image, Ralegh posed in 1588 for the well-known portrait which displays him in a sumptuous black and white suit of clothes.[151] Essex's image of the love-lorn young man framed by eglantine (a symbol of Elizabeth) was matched by that of Ralegh dressed in the queen's own colours, reinforced by the appearance of the crescent moon device of Cynthia/Elizabeth in the upper-left corner.

In mid-December 1587, Essex's position at Court received a major boost

[146] *CSPSpan*, IV, *1587–1603*, p. 127.   [147] BL, Cotton MS Galba D II, fol. 27ᵛ.

[148] J. W. Stoye, 'An early letter from John Chamberlain', *EHR* 62 (1947), p. 529; I. H. Jeayes (ed.), *Letters of Philip Gawdy of West Harling, Norfolk, and of London to various members of his family 1579–1616* (Roxburghe Club, London, 1906), p. 25.

[149] See Plate 1. For detailed discussion of the work and its identification as an image of Essex, see R. Strong, *The cult of Elizabeth: Elizabethan portraiture and pageantry* (London, 1977), ch. 2. For a somewhat different reading of this image, emphasising notions of friendship over romantic connotations, see M. Edmond, *Hilliard and Oliver: the lives and works of two great miniaturists* (London, 1983), pp. 87–91.

[150] See below, p. 208.

[151] Now at the National Portrait Gallery, London. It is featured, for example, in the books on Ralegh by May and Lefranc.

1   'Young man among the roses', showing Essex as the jealous young favourite.
Miniature by Nicholas Hilliard, *c.* 1588.

when Leicester returned from the Netherlands for good.[152] Leicester relinquished his command there with a mixture of relief and bitterness, his hopes of being another William of Orange completely shattered. Even before his return, Ralegh left the Court, allegedly out of fear of facing Leicester in person.[153] Left in possession of the field, Essex's identification with his stepfather increased still further. Over the winter of 1587–8, Essex acted in support of Leicester's efforts to forestall the formal opening of peace talks with the Spanish, the first instance of his life-long aversion to such discussions.[154] In April 1588, Essex and a group of friends were incorporated Master of Arts of the University of Oxford.[155] Leicester was chancellor of Oxford and clearly arranged this honour. Among the other honorands in this ceremony were Sir John Norris and his brother Henry, a sign that Norris had now regained Leicester's favour.[156] A few days after this occasion, along with Hatton and the earl of Ormonde, Essex was elected a knight of the garter, at the precocious age of twenty-two.[157] Again, there can be little doubt that Leicester, as a senior member of this élite order, had helped to arrange the honour for his stepson. Leicester had actually first nominated Essex for the order on St George's Day 1587.[158] In August of that year, while he was still in the Netherlands, Leicester had also included provision in his will for Essex to receive a bequest of 'a George and garter, in hope he shall weare it shortly'.[159]

While Essex continued to consolidate his position at Court, the broader

---

[152] Leicester returned to London on 13 December 1587 (Stoye, 'Chamberlain', p. 526). His instrument of resignation from his command in the Netherlands was dated 17 December (BL, Add. MS 48129, fol. 58ʳ).

[153] *HMCR*, I, p. 234. Ralegh had written a letter to Leicester in early October in an attempt to soothe the earl's anger towards him (BLO, Tanner MS 79, fol. 117ʳ).

[154] [Francis H. Egerton, 8th earl of Bridgewater], *The life of Thomas Egerton lord chancellor of England* (Paris [1816]), p. 132.

[155] BLO, Oxford University Archives, NEP/Supra/Register L, fol. 292ʳ; *Athenae Oxon.*, V, cols. 244, 247–8.

[156] Norris was also friendly with Essex. When Thomas Wilkes again sought 'my pacification withe my lord stuard' in July, Norris pre-empted his approach to Leicester and instead 'imbarked my lord of Essex, who hathe promised to deale therein effectually' (HBL, Beale-Walsingham Papers, no. 48). Essex was perhaps a little too eager to gratify Norris's request – despite his intervention, Leicester apparently remained unmoved in his hostility towards Wilkes.

[157] Nichols, *Progresses*, III, p. 23. Essex was elected with the votes of Leicester, Howard, Burghley, Worcester and Huntingdon (BL, Add. MS 36768, fols. 28ᵛ–29ʳ). The ceremony for his installation took place a month later (BLO, Ashmolean MS 1113, fol. 199ʳ; *ibid.*, vol. 1115, fols. 69ʳ–70ᵛ). In a further sign of his francophilia, Essex apparently introduced into England the French habit of wearing knightly devices on a ribbon, rather than on a chain (A. MacGregor (ed.), *The late king's goods: collections, possessions and patronage of Charles I in the light of the Commonwealth sale inventories* (London and Oxford, 1989), p. 271). Many portraits show Essex wearing his George (the badge of a knight of the garter) on a ribbon.

[158] BL, Add. MS 36768, fol. 28ʳ.   [159] PRO, PROB 11/73, fol. 4ʳ.

political scene was becomingly increasingly schizophrenic. Elizabeth's innate enthusiasm for a peace with Spain had been strengthened in mid-1587 by the loss of Sluys. Encouraged by the hispanophile Croft, she ordered Burghley to step up contacts with the duke of Parma. Burghley did so, but with little enthusiasm. By February 1588, despite the opposition of Leicester and Walsingham (and Essex), peace commissioners, including the earl of Derby, Lord Cobham, Croft and Sir Amias Paulet, were ready to set out for a meeting with their Spanish counterparts. However, with the exception of Croft, all of the commissioners were pessimistic about the nature of their mission and worried by the news of Spanish naval preparations.[160] Reports of these preparations had been reaching England for some time.[161] In consequence, the privy council spent much of its time trying to improve the defences of the realm in anticipation of the worst, even as it grudgingly carried out the queen's commands about peace talks. By mid-1588, despite the dispatch of the peace commissioners, the Spanish naval threat seemed imminent. As Leicester and the rest of the council became increasingly preoccupied with overseeing national defence, Essex correspondingly fell heir to requests for his stepfather's courtly patronage. Essex joined with Leicester in writing to the chief baron of the exchequer on behalf of Cambridge University[162] and received requests for favours in Leicester's stead from Huntingdon and Francis Bacon.[163] By late August, Elizabeth even asked Essex to move into Leicester's now-vacant lodgings at Court.[164] In all quarters, Essex was recognised as his stepfather's surrogate at Court. Yet, despite this success, the air of national emergency and the appointment of Leicester as commander of the main anti-invasion army exerted a greater pull on him, for Essex passionately craved the opportunity to win further martial glory. As he wrote from London on the eve of the Armada campaign, 'yt is not now fitt for me to tary heere'.[165]

---

[160] For these peace contacts in 1587–8, see Read, *Burghley*, pp. 396–407; MacCaffrey, *Elizabeth and making of policy*, pp. 391–9; D. McKeen, *A memory of honour: the life of William Brooke, Lord Cobham* (2 vols., Salzburg Studies in English Literature CVIII, Salzburg, 1986), II, ch. 19. The commissioners were still talking at Ostend when the Spanish fleet arrived in the Channel.
[161] De L. Jensen, 'The Spanish Armada: the worst-kept secret in Europe', *Sixteenth Century Journal* 18 (1988), pp. 621–42; G. Parker, 'The worst-kept secret in Europe? The European intelligence community and the Spanish Armada of 1588', in K. Neilson and B. J. C. McKercher (eds.), *Go spy the land: military intelligence in history* (Westport, Conn., and London, 1992), pp. 49–72.
[162] CUL, University Archives, Collect. Admin.5, fols. 197v, 198r.
[163] Longleat, Dudley MS 2, fols. 232r, 234r; PRO, SP 12/209, fol. 101r. Thomas Wilkes, still paying for his rift with Leicester, also looked for Essex's help in these months (PRO, SP12/212, fols. 61r, 124r).
[164] Longleat, Dudley MS 2, fol. 265r.
[165] *A select collection of interesting autograph letters of celebrated persons, English and foreign ... engraved in exact facsimile of the originals* (Stuttgart, 1849), no. 204. No

By the time the Spanish fleet sailed for England, Essex was an established figure at Elizabeth's Court. Unlike 1585, when the realm was last galvanised by a military emergency, Essex was far from being in 'smal grace' at Court. Even 'a burning ague' in March and a painful fall from his horse in early June did little to slow his rise.[166] With Leicester's support, he had got the upper hand over Ralegh and was beginning to feel the benefits of this success as Elizabeth bestowed substantial material rewards upon him – windfalls which his finances desperately needed. In October 1587, Elizabeth had granted him parsonages and tithes notionally worth £300 a year, in return for him assuring to her lands worth £150 a year.[167] By early 1588, Essex was allowed use of York House, one of the great mansions which lined the Strand. This gave him a London base independent of his stepfather, but conveniently close to Leicester House.[168] In June, Essex also gained a warrant for a lucrative grant of lands from the attainted estate of Sir Francis Englefield.[169] Such was Essex's favour with Elizabeth by the summer of 1588 that, when he asked for his familiar post of general of the horse, she responded that 'she wold not have me discontented', even though the command had already been bestowed elsewhere.[170] Accordingly, Essex was designated as supreme commander of the cavalry, over the heads of those who had already been appointed.[171]

---

author or editor is given for this publication. The letter is in Essex's holograph, written from York House at midnight on 29 July 1588.

[166] BL, Sloane MS 1697, fol. 54ᵛ. The fall from the horse gave Essex 'a swelling in the face' and injured his leg.

[167] PRO, SO 3/1, fol. 122ᵛ; Murdin, p. 786. Essex later sold these parsonages for almost £1,000 (L. Stone, *The crisis of the aristocracy 1558–1641* (Oxford, 1965), p. 409).

[168] During Elizabeth's reign, York House was normally occupied by the lord chancellor or lord keeper (B. M. Ward, *The seventeenth earl of Oxford* (London, 1928), p. 383, n. 1). However, Hatton already had a grand town-house when he was appointed lord chancellor in mid-1587 (Ely Place at Holborn). This may explain why Essex was able to obtain a lease of York House. Essex sold this interest to Lord Keeper Puckering by June 1593 (BL, Harleian MS 6996, fol. 13ʳ).

[169] PRO, SO 3/1, fol. 160ʳ; Murdin, p. 788; *VCH, Berkshire*, III, pp. 407–8. By September 1588, this grant seems to have been changed to embrace most of the estate (PRO, SO 3/1, fol. 167ᵛ; PRO, C 66/1321, mm. 12–15). Sir Francis Englefield was attainted in 1585 but these lands had hitherto been protected against seizure. According to John Manningham, Essex was able to obtain this grant because Andrew Blundell, a lawyer of the Inner Temple, found a flaw in Englefield's legal arrangements and informed Essex as an act of revenge against the family: G. de C. Parmiter, 'Plowden, Englefield and Sandford: I', *Recusant History*, 13 (1975–6), pp. 168–9; also his 'Plowden, Englefield and Sandford: II', *Recusant History* 14 (1977–8), pp. 10–21; R. P. Sorlien (ed.), *The diary of John Manningham of the Middle Temple, 1602–1603* (Hanover, New Hampshire, 1976), pp. 89–90.

[170] BL, Harleian MS 286, fol. 144ʳ.

[171] BL, Royal MS 18.C.xxi, fols. 22ʳ, 31ʳ; S. P. Haak (ed.), *Johan van Oldenbarnevelt: bescheiden betreffende zijn staat-kundig beleid en zijn familie, 1570–1601* ('S-Gravenhage, 1934), p. 136.

Like his time in the Low Countries, Essex's experience during the Armada campaign of 1588 was characterised by equal measures of enthusiasm and frustration. Because he did not participate in the great naval engagements of the summer, Essex missed out on the chance for any new glory in battle. Instead, he could only report the deeds of others. At the end of July, he and Sir Thomas Gorges galloped to Court with urgent news from Dover.[172] As master of the horse, Essex also joined in the rallying of forces under Leicester at Tilbury.[173] Although apparently unpaid for his command,[174] he provided the largest contingent of soldiers set out by any nobleman.[175] According to a later claim by his steward, this action cost Essex some £3,500.[176] This was an impressive sign of where his priorities lay, and all the more so when it is recognised that, despite having received some generous grants, he had to borrow money from his friends to pay for this display of martial zeal.[177] In part, Essex was motivated to make this kind of commitment by a combination of patriotic fervour and the desire to join Leicester and many of his old colleagues from the Low Countries. Yet a more fundamental and signifi- cant reason for his eagerness to serve in the field was that Essex also nourished a genuine 'ambition of warr'.[178]

Despite the golden fortune which his meteoric rise to royal favour entailed, Essex's desire to prove himself as the new Sidney constantly pricked him with the urge to return to war. Indeed, his thwarted ambition to serve against the Spanish Armada in 1588 was only one of many attempts which he made to return to the fighting during the period when he was becoming established as a favourite. Throughout most of 1587, Essex nominally remained general of the horse in the Low Countries, as if his return to Court were to be merely temporary.[179] In January 1587, he

---

[172] *HMC. Seventh report, appendix* (London, 1879), p. 645 (Loseley MSS).

[173] *Cabala, sive scrinia sacra: mysteries of state and government in letters of illustrious persons and great ministers of state* (2nd edn, London, 1691, Wing no. C 186), p. 343. See also S. Frye, 'The myth of Elizabeth at Tilbury', *Sixteenth Century Journal* 23 (1992), pp. 95–114.

[174] PRO, E 351/242; cf. PRO, SP 12/215, fols. 159^r–161^v.

[175] *HMC. Fifteenth report, appendix v* (London, 1897), p. 40 (Foljambe MSS). See also Princeton University Library, Robert H. Taylor Collection, no. 48470, Essex to Richard Bagot, 20 August 1588.

[176] Devereux MS 2, fol. 82^r.

[177] Essex apparently pressed his friends to loan him parcels of £300, or to stand surety for the same amount on his behalf (BL, Add. MS 12097, fol. 4^r). Essex's debt of £50 to Henry Lord Compton, outstanding in 1589, may have been contracted during this time (PRO, PROB 11/74, fol. 292^v). Essex also sought the loan of horses, including one from Sir John Spencer (SC, 21 July 1916, p. 24, lot 136, Essex to Spencer, 30 July 1588).

[178] The phrase is that of Sir Roger Williams, describing Essex (PRO, SP 78/24, fol. 112^r).

[179] Clearly, there were also financial motives for maintaining this position so long. Essex was paid as general of the horse in the Low Countries until 11 November 1587, a full year

and two of his Netherlands comrades, Sir William Russell and Sir Roger Williams, volunteered their willingness to join Viscount Turenne in the service of Henri of Navarre, the Protestant heir-apparent to the throne of France.[180] This initial contact with Turenne, and with the cause of Henri himself, was the first sign of Essex's active connection with French affairs, which would ultimately shape his political aspirations in the same way that the Netherlands had shaped those of Leicester. In April 1587, an alternative outlet for Essex's martial aspirations was suggested by Edward Waterhouse, Earl Walter's old servant, who proposed that Essex should be given command of a garrison in Ireland.[181] Waterhouse's own interests were very much focused on that kingdom and he undoubtedly hoped to profit by playing upon the young earl's ardour to revive the Devereux presence there. However, Essex's ambitions to emulate Sidney's role as a Protestant chivalric hero pointed him firmly away from any thoughts of Ireland. Instead, it was to the stage of Continental Europe that Essex looked, as his attempt to join the defence of Sluys at the end of July showed.

Although his departure for Sluys proved abortive (and perhaps deliberately so), Essex continued to display a hankering for war. By early 1588, if not before, he was engaged in secret dealings with Sir Francis Drake about a naval venture. Once again, there are echoes of Sidney in this affair, for it was with Drake that Sidney had intended to sail away at the end of 1585. After his successful 'singeing of the king of Spain's beard' in the previous year, Drake was preparing a fleet to convey the pretender to the throne of Portugal, Dom Antonio, back to his native land and to help him foment a rebellion against the Spanish forces of occupation there.[182] Essex was certainly an investor in this scheme, and very probably intended to sail with Drake, whether the queen approved or not. In mid-February 1588, Drake reassured Essex that 'there is some greate parte to be played in the churche of God by [your] honour and my self, if we cann hold this secrett ... there is nothinge [can] hurte us but the knowledge of your

---

after he left there (*CSPF*, XXI[II], *April–December 1587*, p. 363). He also remained as captain (in effect, absentee owner) of a company of cavalry there until some time in 1588 (*ibid.*, XXII, *July–December 1587*, p. 411).

[180] LPL, MS 647, fol. 207ʳ. Essex and his friends made their offer through the person of Arthur Champernowne, the quartermaster of Leicester's army in the Netherlands. Champernowne was not only a relative by marriage to Essex's childhood companion, Gabriel Montgomery (Gabriel's older sister had married Gawen Champernowne), but also a cousin of Sir Walter Ralegh (*Commons*, I, p. 592; May, *Ralegh*, p. 2). For his part, Turenne's first wife, and the mother of his heir, was a daughter of the late William of the Orange (*Leycester corr.*, p. 14).

[181] PRO, SP 63/129, fol. 4ʳ.

[182] J. Corbett, *Sir Francis Drake* (London and New York, 1890, reprinted Westport, Conn., 1970), pp. 132–9.

lordship's purpose'.[183] In the event, Elizabeth's desire for peace with Spain stalled the venture, before the approach of the Armada finally transformed the whole purpose of Drake's preparations. Once again, Essex was frustrated, but the thrust of his ambitions was clear. Royal companion though he had become, Essex remained dedicated to the martial display of his noble and knightly virtues.

[183] *SC*, 12 and 13 June 1911 (Sale of the library of Henry and Alfred H. Huth), lot 62. A photograph of this letter from Drake to Essex, dated 16 February 1587[8], is provided at the end of the cat?·ogue, from which it has been possible to make a full transcription. The original manuscri¡ was bought at the Sotheby's sale by the bookseller Bernard Quaritch for £100 but its p ·sent whereabouts are a mystery. None of the records deposited by Quaritch in the Br ish Library (Add. MSS 64132–415) seems to shed any light on the subsequent purchaser of the document. Part of the letter is printed in J. S. Corbett, *Drake and the Tudor navy* (2 vols., London, New York and Bombay, 1898), II, pp. 127–8.

'To whom muche is geven ... '

In early September 1588, Essex's political career received an unexpected blow when news arrived that Leicester, his stepfather and mentor, had died in Oxfordshire.[1] The implications of this event were enormous. Leicester's death suddenly deprived Essex of the patronage which had advanced him in almost every aspect of his career to date. Leicester's demise also now loaded Essex with a heavy burden of expectation, for the lord steward had very publicly groomed him as his political heir.[2] The leading men of Maldon therefore soon called upon Essex to take Leicester's place as the high recorder of their town.[3] The Inner Temple also quickly invited him to join their society in Leicester's stead.[4] However, despite these pregnant courtesies, Essex did not simply inherit his stepfather's mantle – Leicester's death had come too soon for that. With Leicester gone, Lord Chancellor Hatton now stood alone as the queen's senior favourite, while Essex was left to fight off a fierce new challenge from Ralegh. Leicester's political leadership passed to another old stager. Although increasingly burdened by illness, Sir Francis Walsingham became the leading advocate of the Protestant cause in English politics. Secretary of state since 1573, Walsingham had been a long-time ally of Leicester, although in recent years relations between them had become somewhat strained.[5] By contrast,

---

[1] Leicester died of a fever at his country house at Cornbury Park on 4 September 1588. He was travelling in the countryside to recuperate after the rigours of the Armada campaign. At the time of his death, he was aged about 55 or 56.

[2] Essex's link with Leicester was publicly reaffirmed when he served as chief mourner at his funeral on 10 October 1588 (BLO, Ashmolean MS 818, fol. 38^r). For further information on this event, see S. Adams (ed.), *Household accounts and disbursement books of Robert Dudley, earl of Leicester, 1558–1561, 1584–1586* (Camden Society, 5th ser., VI, Cambridge, 1996), pp. 450–9.

[3] Devereux MSS, box 5, no. 70.

[4] F. A. Inderwicke (ed.), *A calendar of the Inner Temple records* (5 vols., London, 1896–1936), I, p. 354. Hatton was also a prominent member of the Inner Temple, having been admitted in 1562 (*ibid.*, p. 220).

[5] BL, Lansdowne MS 96, fol. 69^{r-v}. Perhaps the best evidence of this estrangement lies in the consistent frankness with which Thomas Wilkes and Buckhurst wrote to him of their frustration and anger about their treatment by 'Themistocles' (i.e. Leicester). See F. G.

Leicester's status as Elizabeth's *de facto* military commander-in-chief had no obvious claimant, principally because his successor in the Low Countries, Lord Willoughby, lacked the political stature and ambition of Leicester.

In 1588, Essex did not – and could not – inherit the political weight which his stepfather had built up over three decades of service to the queen. Nevertheless, he did begin to follow in Leicester's footsteps in less taxing ways – aided, no doubt, by Elizabeth's profound affection for Leicester's memory.[6] Essex assumed his late stepfather's role as the queen's chief host to visiting foreign dignitaries. With Leicester's office of lord steward now defunct, Essex qualified for this function by virtue of his earl's rank and his post as the master of the horse. Essex's steward later claimed that 'intertayninge of strangers' cost his master £400 or £500 a year 'since my lord of Lester dyed'.[7] Such expenditure became affordable because Essex also quickly succeeded to Leicester's lucrative farm of the customs on sweet wines. This had been surrendered to the queen in part payment of Leicester's large debts to the crown.[8] On 12 January 1589, Elizabeth granted this crucially important customs farm to Essex for a term of five years.[9] Twice later renewed, this was to provide a vital support for Essex's finances throughout the next decade.

Oosterhoff, *Leicester and the Netherlands, 1586–1587* (Utrecht, 1988), p. 173 and the sources cited there. See also HBL, Beale–Walsingham Papers, nos. 23–5, 28, 31, 34, 38–41, 48.

[6] Elizabeth's attitude towards Leicester's memory can be seen in her endorsement on a letter written by Leicester on 29 August 1588: 'His last letter' (formerly PRO, SP 12/215, no. 65, now BL, Wall Case III, no. 9). A Spanish agent reported that Elizabeth was so upset by the news that she locked herself away for several days, until Burghley and other councillors ordered the doors broken open (*CSPSpan*, IV, *1587–1603*, p. 431).

[7] Devereux MS 2, fol. 82ʳ. The first mention of Essex's performance of this function seems to be his entertainment of Viscount Turenne at the end of 1590 (see below).

[8] BL, Harleian Roll D.35.1, m. 54. The farm was mortgaged to the queen in return for a loan which was due to be repaid on 25 February 1589 (BL., Harleian MS 61, fol. 206ʳ). For a brief discussion of Leicester's sweet wines farm, see A. L. Merson, *The third book of remembrance of Southampton 1514–1602*, III, 1573–1589 (Southampton Records Series, VIII, 1965), appendix v.

[9] PRO, C 54/1332, unfol., noted in enrollment of a subsequent indenture between the queen and Thomas Crompton, Robert Wright and Gelly Meyrick of 2 April 1589. The grant may have been changed to a four-and-a-half year lease (ending on 25 September 1593) on 4 April (F. C. Dietz, *English public finance 1558–1641* (New York and London, 1932), p. 316). Subsequent to negotiating this grant with the queen, Essex also obtained the parallel grant formerly held by Leicester for the port of Southampton (*HMC. Eleventh report, appendix iii* (London, 1887), p. 127; Merson, *Third book of remembrance*, p. 76). As well as taking over these customs farms, Essex paid £3,000 towards Leicester's debt to the queen on 29 September 1590 (PRO, E 163/16/15, unfol.). Apparently in return for clearing this debt, Elizabeth granted Essex a loan of precisely £3,000 by a privy seal of 13 October 1590, £2,000 of which was paid over to Essex on 16 October (BLO, MS Eng.hist.c.477, fols. 106ʳ, 262ʳ).

Rather more of a mixed blessing were expectations which Essex's association with Leicester had built up among his stepfather's followers. After his death, the large and diverse body of clients which Leicester had established over several decades began to look for new patrons. Some of these, but by no means all, turned to Essex. This posed a problem for him. Although it was flattering to be the subject of praise and the object of men's attentions, Essex lacked the political standing and an appropriate royal office which would allow him to consolidate this support into a genuine political power-base. This was to remain a constant problem in Essex's career. Accordingly, he always had to rely upon conjuring a personal bond with his followers and exploiting every possible opportunity to reward them. Because he lacked adequate means to gratify his following through institutional channels, Essex was perhaps also more susceptible to the efforts of his supporters to manipulate him for their own particular ends.[10]

Although many of Leicester's servants and courtly followers felt little need to seek the patronage of Essex,[11] soldier clients of the late earl did. So, too, did the more forward Protestants, often called puritans.[12] Theirs was perhaps the most striking example of followers of Leicester who sought to mould Essex to fit their own need for a new patron. It seems clear, for example, that puritans spearheaded the abortive bid to have Essex succeed Leicester as chancellor of Oxford University in September 1588. Allegedly, this initiative was encouraged by Essex's incorporation as an Oxford MA earlier in the year, which was seen as having been undertaken 'the better to capacitate him' eventually to succeed Leicester as chancellor.[13] In the face of Hatton's candidacy for the post, the nomination of Essex had no chance of success.[14] The move was a desperate attempt by radical Protestant academics to find a new bulwark against the pressures for religious conformity which were then being exerted by Hatton and Archbishop

---

[10] The nature of Essex's following is discussed in detail in Chapter 7.

[11] W. J. Tighe, 'The Gentlemen Pensioners in Elizabethan politics and government' (unpub. Ph.D. thesis, University of Cambridge, 1984), p. 158. The same lack of continuity can be observed in the careers of many of Leicester's household servants (Adams, *Accounts of Leicester*, pp. 461–88). However, the latter evidence can only be advanced on a very tentative basis. Since Essex already had his own household staff in 1588, he may not have been able to employ many of Leicester's old household servants even if he (and they) had wished to do so (I am grateful to Dr Adams for advice on this point).

[12] Fundamental to the subject of Essex's relationship with the puritans is P. Collinson, *The Elizabethan puritan movement* (London, 1967), pp. 444–7. The most recent discussion of Leicester's association with the godly is S. Adams, 'A godly peer? Leicester and the puritans', *History Today* 40 (January 1990), pp. 14–19.

[13] Wood, V, col. 244.

[14] Hatton was formally invited to be chancellor by the university authorities on 20 September 1588 and his election was declared on 3 October (Oxford University Archives, NEP/Supra/ Register L, fol. 294^r–v; LPL, MS 178, fol. 46^r).

Whitgift.[15] Essex himself was flattered but also embarrassed by the incident, not least because Hatton was a powerful friend. Despite the risk to Oxford puritans, he very quickly disavowed his candidacy in favour of the lord chancellor.[16]

A similar desire to manipulate Essex is obvious in the plea which Sir Francis Hastings addressed to him only days after Leicester's death: 'to whom muche is geven, from him muche is required'.[17] With Leicester dead, Hastings argued, it was now time for Essex to show his commitment to the cause of God and the further reformation of the Church by taking up where his stepfather had left off. This appeal clearly had a particular resonance for Essex. Hastings's plea was at once a call to him as the heir of Leicester and as an aristocrat who was dedicated to the public pursuit of virtue. It was also an appeal to the godly creed in which he had been brought up – a point which was all the more telling because Francis Hastings, like Essex, was a member of the extended Dudley-Sidney-Devereux family network.[18]

Beginning under his father, and then with Leicester and Sidney while fighting for 'God's cause' in the Low Countries, Essex had consistently been associated with a strong brand of Protestantism. To the end of his days, he remained loyal to this heritage, sometimes to the amusement of his friends.[19] He also made sure that his son and heir was brought under godly instruction.[20] On the other hand, Essex's Protestantism did not make him

---

[15] According to Wood, Essex's candidacy for the chancellorship was advanced by 'the puritanical party' in the university but was defeated by the intervention of Archbishop Whitgift on behalf of Hatton (Wood, V, col. 241). On the so-called 'little faction' of Whitgift and Hatton, see Collinson, *Puritan movement*, pp. 387–8 and Sir George Paule, *The life of the most reverend and religious prelate John Whitgift lord archbishop of Canterbury* (London, 1612, STC no. 19484), p. 36.

[16] Oxford University Archives, NEP/Supra/Register L, fols. 293ᵛ–294ʳ. A copy of this document, incorrectly dated 4 September (no year), is BLO, Tanner MS 338, fol. 215ʳ.

[17] HEH, Huntingdon Correspondence, box 3, HA 5090.

[18] Francis Hastings was a younger brother of the earl of Huntingdon, the former guardian of Essex and his siblings. Huntingdon's wife was Catherine Dudley, a sister of Leicester, who ultimately survived her husband by a quarter of a century. As noted above, the Hastings family were also relatives of the Devereux.

[19] The French general Marshal Biron, for example, 'derided this his piety as rather becoming some silly minister than a stout soldier' (Camden, *Elizabeth*, p. 623). In 1596, Antonio Perez joked with Essex that, by dealing with Essex, he would be making his confession 'non cum Romano, sed cum purissimo puritano' (Ungerer, I, p. 437). After Essex's death, several of his friends bemoaned the fact that he had always been too susceptible to appeals made upon the basis of religion (e.g. BLO, Rawlinson MS D 1175, pp. 199, 202). For Essex's own affirmation of the life-long constancy of his profession, see *ibid.*, pp. 203–4.

[20] V. F. Snow, *Essex the rebel: the life of Robert Devereux, third earl of Essex 1591–1646* (Lincoln, Nebr., 1970), p. 12.

personally anti-Catholic,[21] and nor did it prevent him from maintaining friendships both with the puritan Thomas Cartwright and his persecutor, Archbishop Whitgift.[22] Essex's Protestantism did not extend to making windows into other men's souls.

For a few years after the death of Leicester, Essex responded to the appeals of Hastings and others by taking up the godly cause in domestic politics. In consequence, a succession of religious books and treatises appeared with dedications which lauded Essex and urged him to still greater commitment.[23] In November 1588, religious radicals felt sure enough of Essex's sympathy to show him a draft bill, perhaps prepared in anticipation of a new session of parliament, which attacked the clergy's tenure of glebe lands.[24] During the uproar over the Marprelate tracts, Essex's name was apparently linked with that mysterious propagandist.[25] In 1590, after the death of Walsingham (by then his father-in-law), Essex

21 According to Camden, Essex was 'a man who never approved the putting of people to death merely for their religion' (*Elizabeth*, p. 482). Essex's dealings with Catholics are discussed in Chapter 5.
22 Wotton, *Parallel*, p. 9. On Essex's relations with Whitgift, see Paule, *Life of Whitgift*, pp. 55–7. Only a single letter has survived to illuminate Essex's dealings with Cartwright. Dated in September 1598, this is clearly only one of a series of letters written by Cartwright to Essex (A. F. Scott Pearson, *Thomas Cartwright and Elizabethan puritanism* (Cambridge, 1925), pp. 384–6). It is also possible that Essex had a part in Cartwright's appointment as chaplain to Cornet Castle in 1595 (*ibid.*, p. 373). Sir Thomas Leighton, the governor of Guernsey, who appointed Cartwright, was married to Essex's aunt, Lady Elizabeth Leighton, *née* Knollys. For Leighton, see A. J. Eagleston, 'Guernsey under Sir Thomas Leighton (1570–1610)', *La Société Guernsiaise: Report and Transactions* 13 (1937–1945), pp. 72–108.
23 Although the authors reflect various shades of godly opinion, the following dedications may be noted in the years up to 1593: [Henry Holland], *A treatise against witchcraft* ... (Cambridge, 1590, STC no. 13590), sig. A2ᵛ. On Holland see *DNB*, IX, pp. 1034–5; [Richard Harvey], *A theologicall discourse of the Lamb of God and his enemies* ... (London, 1590, STC no. 12915), sig. A2ʳ–3ᵛ. On Harvey see *DNB*, IX, pp. 91–2; Andrew Willet, *Synopsis papismi* ... (London, 1592, STC no. 25696), unpag. dedication to Essex between pp. 278–91; also Willet, *Sacrorum emblematum centuria una* ... (Cambridge (1592), STC no. 25695), sig. A2ʳ–3ʳ. On Willet see *DNB*, XXI, pp. 288–92; Hugh Broughton, *Moses his sights on Sinai* (n. pl., 1592, STC no. 3873), unpag. dedication to Essex. On Broughton see *DNB*, II, pp. 1367–70; Matthew Sutcliffe, *de Catholica orthodoxa et vera Christi ecclesia* (London, 1592, STC no. 23455), sig. A2ʳ–3ᵛ. On Sutcliffe see *DNB*, XIX, pp. 175–7. Virtually unique in eschewing extravagant praise in its dedication to Essex was John Phillips, *The perfect path to paradice* ... (London, 1588, STC no. 19872), sig. A3ʳ–6ʳ.
24 Perhaps worried by its contents, Essex showed this bill to Whitgift. The archbishop in turn wrote to Burghley, 'hartely praying your lordship to stay the same, being in my judgement the most unresonable suite that was ever moved, and tendinge to the overthrowe, or at least the generall molestation, of all the clergie in England' (LPL, MS 3470, fol. 96ʳ).
25 A. Peel (ed.), *The notebook of John Penry 1593* (Camden Society, 3rd ser., LXVII, 1944), p. 70. Peel thinks that Essex may perhaps have promised protection to the writer of these tracts (*ibid.*, p. xvi). L. H. Carlson argues that 'Martin Marprelate' was Job Throckmorton: *Martin Marprelate, gentleman: Master Job Throkmorton laid open in his colours* (San Marino, Calif., 1981).

continued the funding of theological lectures given at Oxford by John Rainoldes.[26]

During the following year, Essex also co-operated at Court with Burghley and Ralegh in defending the puritans from Whitgift.[27] However, even this pooling of political strength proved inadequate to stall the drive for conformity within the Church of England which began in early 1589.[28] Whitgift had tried, and failed, to launch a similar campaign soon after his appointment as archbishop of Canterbury in 1583. Since then, the growing stridency of radical presbyterians had served to strengthen the forces of reaction against them, whilst the outbreak of open war with Spain made the claim that puritans were 'the most diligent barkers against the popish wolf' seem increasingly irrelevant.[29] Whitgift was supported in his campaign not only by Elizabeth herself but also by Hatton and Buckhurst. By contrast, the puritan cause sorely lacked Leicester's political weight and soon also lost Mildmay and Walsingham. For all his influence, Burghley could not hold the line against manoeuvres which he viewed as 'too much savouring of the Romish inquisition'.[30] The climax of the struggle came in May 1591, when Cartwright and other radicals were prosecuted for sedition in Star Chamber. Although this trial never reached a verdict, their indictment and temporary imprisonment marked the political defeat of radical puritanism and the affirmation of a distinctly elevated view of ecclesiastical – and royal – authority.[31] This decision, and the intellectual arguments which were arrayed to support it, laid the foundations for a political milieu in the 1590s which was very different from the environment in which Leicester had operated. It is not surprising that Essex therefore began to drift away from any outright espousal of the puritan cause in domestic politics.[32] With the very notion of puritanism open to question

26 [John Rainoldes], *De Romanae ecclesiae idolatria* ... (Oxford, 1596, STC no. 20606), sig. *3ʳ; J. McConica (ed.), *The history of the University of Oxford. Vol. III: The Collegiate University* (Oxford, 1986), p. 312. Walsingham had founded this temporary lectureship to counter Catholic polemics in 1586 (J. W. Binns, *Intellectual culture in Elizabethan and Jacobean England: the Latin writings of the age* (Leeds, 1990), p. 327).
27 PRO, SP 12/238, fol. 118ᵛ; PRO, SP 12/239, fol. 123ʳ; PRO, SP 15/32, fol. 10ʳ. Cf. BL, Add. MS 4125, fol. 14ʳ.
28 The new mood was heralded by the anti-presbyterian sermon delivered by Richard Bancroft, a protégé of Hatton and Whitgift, at Paul's Cross on 9 February 1589: M. Maclure, *The Paul's Cross sermons, 1534–1642* (Toronto, 1958), pp. 73–4.
29 The phrase is that of Sir Francis Knollys (cited in Collinson, *Puritan movement*, p. 247).
30 C. Read, *Lord Burghley and Queen Elizabeth* (London, 1960), p. 295.
31 J. Guy, 'The Elizabethan establishment and the ecclesiastical polity', in Guy (ed.), *The reign of Elizabeth I: Court and culture in the last decade* (Cambridge, 1995), pp. 129–49.
32 Essex's weakening support for the puritan cause may help to explain John Penry's desperate attempt to entice his support for radical religious reform by arguing that ecclesiastical lands should pass into lay hands: Peel, *Notebook of Penry*, pp. 85–95.

after this defeat, Essex's support was increasingly limited to protecting individual puritans.[33]

Despite the gradual toning down of his support for the so-called puritans at home, Essex remained strongly committed to the cause of defending Protestantism abroad, as Sidney and Leicester had been. On 3 April 1589, Essex made a spectacular restatement of his commitment to this cause, when he defied Elizabeth by joining the expedition to Spain and Portugal led by Sir John Norris and Sir Francis Drake.[34] The strongly Protestant character of this expedition – reinforced by the presence of a Dutch contingent – coincided neatly with his concurrent domestic association with the puritan cause.[35] However, Essex's participation in the Portugal venture was influenced by more than mere godliness.

Despite the Dutch involvement, the Portugal venture embodied a national English desire, which Essex shared, to strike back after the Spanish naval attack of the previous year.[36] Indeed, the Portugal expedition was seen by its leading proponents – in contrast to Elizabeth's more limited aims – as actually offering England the chance of decisive victory over Spain. By installing Dom Antonio as king of Portugal, success in this scheme would not only have challenged Spanish power at its very heart, but cut Spain off from all the resources of its vast transmarine empire. With such a victory, the costly war in the Low Countries which had so frustrated and debilitated Leicester could be rendered irrelevant.[37] In the light of his

---

[33] Collinson, *Puritan movement*, pp. 445–7. See also, for example, Cecil MS 203/120 (pr. *HMCS*, XIII, p. 460); LPL, MS 3470, fol. 217ʳ; PRO, SP 12/244, fol. 123ʳ; [W. H. and H. C. Overall (eds.)], *Analytical index to the series of records known as the Remembrancia preserved among the archives of the City of London. AD 1579–1664* (London, 1878), p. 367.

[34] The most convenient discussion of this expedition is R. B. Wernham, *The expedition of Sir John Norris and Sir Francis Drake to Spain and Portugal, 1589* (Navy Records Society, CXXVII, 1988). The queen commanded that no noblemen should take part in the expedition, which caused the earl of Northumberland to withdraw his investment of £2,000 (*HMCS*, III, p. 233: note that this memorandum has been dated as 1586 by the editors of this calendar, although it very clearly relates to 1589). For Essex's secret departure to join the fleet, see Wernham, *Expedition of Norris and Drake*, pp. xxxiv–xxxv, 133–8.

[35] While the expedition was being prepared, a disputation was held among certain ministers in London during November 1588 to justify giving assistance to a Catholic king (CUL, MS Hh.vi.10). Godly meditations concerning 'martiall matters' were also sent to Sir Francis Drake by Oliver Pigge in February 1589 (CUL, MS Dd.xi.76, fol. 2ᵛ and *passim*). The godly underpinning of the expedition is discussed in detail by Adams, 'The Protestant cause', pp. 104–7. More generally, the religious dimension of the venture also made Archbishop Whitgift willing to browbeat the clergy into contributing towards the expedition at the beginning of November 1588 (BLO, Dugdale MS 32, fol. 18ʳ).

[36] *Apologie*, sig. A3ʳ.

[37] S. Adams, 'The lurch into war', *History Today* 38 (May 1988), pp. 18–25; Wernham, *Expedition of Norris and Drake*, pp. xv.

secret dealings with Drake during 1588, there can be little doubt that Essex was an eager supporter of this bold strategy. As he secretly assured William Davison before his departure, it was 'my resolute purpose to perfourme' in this matter.[38] Nevertheless, like the other leading participants in the venture, Essex also had more immediately personal reasons for his desperate eagerness to take part. Thanks to the extravagant (and entirely unrealistic) promises of Dom Antonio, the expedition was also intended to bring a healthy profit to those who invested in it.[39] This was a worldly motive which Essex could not disregard, for he claimed that he was now at least £22,000 in debt.[40] Among the forty or so letters which he left behind when he stole away to join the expedition[41] was one to Sir Thomas Heneage which explained his departure with the promise that 'I will adventure to be rich.'[42] Beyond this, Essex saw the campaign as an irresistibly attractive stage upon which he could again display his martial virtues.

Essex's desire to prove himself as a warrior was perhaps especially strong after his stepfather's death.[43] Deprived of Leicester's support, he clearly felt the need to demonstrate to the world that he was in charge of his own destiny. In this sense, the Portugal expedition was profoundly important, for it offered him the chance to prove his commitment to war and to distance himself from the courtliness of his late stepfather. Here was his great opportunity to break free from the golden fetters of royal favour in which Leicester had helped to bind him and to shake off the frustrations of being able to observe war only from the distance of Court. Essex's willingness to risk royal anger was not simply rash exuberance, but a calculated risk which involved 'many monethes' of planning.[44] Seen in a broader context, Essex's secret departure for sea in April 1589 marked the opening act of a protracted struggle to show Elizabeth that he was no longer merely a youthful royal favourite, but a rapidly maturing man of action. In effect, Essex now sought to break the mould in which his life was being shaped.

If Essex hoped to transform himself by martial endeavour, he remained jealous of royal favour at home and fiercely competitive with Ralegh.

---

[38] BLO, Tanner MS 79, fol. 46ʳ.

[39] Tenison, VIII, pp. 7–13.

[40] Cecil MS 18/82 (pr. *HMCS*, III, pp. 458–9; also pr. Murdin, p. 635).

[41] FSL, L.a.40.

[42] Murdin, pp. 634–5. Only one other of these letters – that to William Davison – is still extant.

[43] It is possible that the (admittedly partisan) sentiment expressed by Spenser in *The ruines of time* (published in 1591) may have begun to emerge soon after Leicester's death: 'He now is dead and all his glories gone/And all his greatness vapourèd to naught' (ll. 218–19).

[44] Essex emphasised that he was well aware of the implications of his action: 'yf yow call yt rashness, I will better allow yt to be heresy then error' (BLO, Tanner MS 79, fol. 46ʳ).

Indeed, he may have been more willing to gamble on the Portugal expedition because Ralegh was an investor, and apparently also a participant, in the venture.[45] For most of 1588, owing to Ralegh's prolonged absence from Court, the old enmity between Essex and Ralegh had remained in abeyance. After the death of Leicester, however, Ralegh was emboldened to return to Court.[46] Thereupon, the former rivalry between the two men was renewed with fresh force. By Christmas, Elizabeth reportedly had to travel from Greenwich to Richmond in order to pacify them.[47] Despite this, a few days later, Essex challenged Ralegh to a duel. In order to spare the queen further anguish about her two favourites, the privy council sought to have this fact 'repressed and ... bureed in silence'.[48] However, the quarrel still smouldered in February.[49] The violence of this renewed rivalry between Essex and Ralegh, and especially the resort to challenges,[50] marked a dangerous escalation in the struggle for royal favour which was almost unprecedented. In the previous years of Elizabeth's reign, the intensity of this rivalry was perhaps equalled during the controversy over the queen's projected marriage to the duke of Anjou in late 1579, and then only briefly.[51]

Essex's aggressive attitude was reflected not merely in his rivalry with Ralegh, but also in another quarrel which he entered into during these months. Observing that the queen had given a token of favour to Sir Charles Blount, Essex insulted him and ended up fighting a duel.[52] Clearly,

---

[45] Despite some errors of detail (such as the erroneous claim that Essex challenged Ralegh to a duel after the return of the Portugal fleet, based upon a misreading of the cited source), the argument advanced by C. E. Mounts suggests very strongly that Ralegh did actually sail with the fleet (C. E. Mounts, 'The Raleigh–Essex rivalry and *Mother Hubberd's Tale*', *Modern Language Notes* 65 (1950), pp. 509–13).

[46] Ralegh was at Court by 13 December 1588, when he wrote from there to Sir Humphrey Gilbert offering dubious advice about how to obtain the maximum financial benefit from a prize cargo (PRO, SP 9/55, item 12, no. 3).

[47] *CSPSpan*, IV, *1587–1603*, p. 504. Some support for this claim comes from the fact that neither Essex nor Ralegh are noted among those who exchanged New Year's gifts with the queen on 1 January 1589 (BL, Lansdowne Charter 17, mm. 1–2, 4^d–5^d).

[48] PRO, SP 12/219, fol. 115^r.

[49] *CSPSpan*, IV, *1587–1603*, p. 513.

[50] It is conceivable that Essex's willingness to engage in duels was encouraged by his francophilia. François Billacois has argued that duelling was a custom which had peculiarly strong connotations with France (*The duel: its rise and fall in early modern France* (trans. T. Selous, New Haven and London, 1990), esp. ch. 4). Although French behaviour may possibly have helped to legitimise duelling in Essex's mind, Billacois certainly underestimates the native traditions of fighting for personal honour in England and elsewhere. See, for example, V. G. Kiernan, *The duel in European history: honour and the reign of aristocracy* (Oxford, 1988), chs. 4–5.

[51] For the famous (but short-lived) outburst during this time between Sir Philip Sidney and the earl of Oxford, see K. Duncan-Jones, *Sir Philip Sidney: courtier poet* (London, 1991), ch. 7.

[52] Essex lost the duel but he and Blount subsequently became friends (Naunton, *Fragmenta regalia*, p. 76).

the earl's noble pride had led him to believe that, excepting Hatton, he should now brook no competition for the queen's favour. Elizabeth resented this behaviour and took pains to reward both Ralegh and Blount in early 1589.[53] However, other members of Court were perhaps rather less concerned, especially when Ralegh was the target of Essex's anger. Ralegh was always a deeply unpopular figure[54] and many at Court were only too willing to support a young nobleman of such conspicuous virtues against a man whom they considered an upstart.[55]

This was especially important when Essex came to return from his illicit adventure in Portugal. Although Elizabeth's own thunderous anger at his secret departure soon faded, her change of temper was undoubtedly encouraged by the pleading on Essex's behalf of leading councillors such as Walsingham, Hatton and Burghley.[56] As one contemporary observer explained, although he now lacked Leicester's protection, Essex was 'mightelie backt by the greatest in opposition to Sir Walter Ralegh, who had offended manie and was maligned of most'.[57] In addition to the three councillors, Essex's cause was undoubtedly sustained by influential courtiers such as Lord Hunsdon, his mother's maternal uncle, Sir Francis Knollys, his maternal grandfather, and the countess of Warwick, the late Leicester's sister-in-law. Working upon Elizabeth's own profound affection for him, such powerful supporters helped Essex to regain his position of royal favour very quickly after his return.[58] Within six weeks, Essex's followers were even able to crow that the earl 'hath chassed Mr Rauly from

---

[53] Elizabeth gave Ralegh a gold chain upon his return from Portugal, whilst pointedly denying any such award to Essex and his followers (Mounts, 'The Raleigh–Essex rivalry and *Mother Hubberds Tale*', pp. 509, 511). In May 1589, she also renewed his extremely favourable grant of export rights to broadcloths, even though it was prejudicial to a similar grant awarded to Lord Hunsdon (PRO, SO 3/1, fol. 192^r; PRO, SP 46/20, fol. 229^r). In late February, Blount was appointed keeper of the New Forest (PRO, SO 3/1, fol. 181^r; PRO, C 66/1324, mm. 6–7). The timing of this grant suggests a *terminus ante quem* for Blount's duel with Essex.

[54] See, for example, John Clapham, *Elizabeth of England: certain observations concerning the life and reign of Queen Elizabeth* (eds. E. P. and C. Read, Philadelphia, 1951), p. 93; BL, Harleian MS 1629, fol. 34^v; BL, Add. MS 12510, fol. 8^r; LPL, MS 650, fol. 52^v; FSL. L.a.39.

[55] Hence Ralegh was often contemptuously referred to in courtly poems as 'Fortune' (S. W. May, 'The poems of Edward de Vere, seventeenth earl of Oxford and of Robert Devereux, second earl of Essex', *Studies in Philology* 77, special fifth no. (1980), p. 87).

[56] For example, when Elizabeth raged in her characteristic manner about hanging Sir Roger Williams, Essex's chief accomplice in his furtive departure (PRO, SP 12/224, fol. 14^r), Walsingham seems to have done his very best to mollify her (*ibid.*, fol. 9^r).

[57] BL, Egerton MS 2026, fol. 32^r.

[58] Essex returned to Court at Nonsuch on 9 July, having sent his brother Walter ahead to test the water (BL, Egerton MS 2598, fol. 12^r; Murdin, p. 793; *CSPSpan*, IV, *1587–1603*, p. 550).

the Coart and hath confined him in to Irland'.[59] Ralegh himself protested that he had genuine reasons for travelling to Ireland[60] and he certainly retained sufficient favour with the queen to introduce the poet Edmund Spenser to Court later in the year.[61] Nevertheless, Ralegh's departure gave Essex the upper hand in their great rivalry. Although Ralegh boasted to Sir George Carew about his continuing favour, 'which still I injoy, and never more',[62] it was Essex who was 'in all the favor wythe her Majestie' at the end of 1589.[63]

Ralegh's growing insecurity about his position with the queen may explain why his battle with Essex saw a new outpouring of partisan verse during 1590. Here again their rivalry strained the limits of accepted courtly behaviour. In the past, courtiers had used poetry to praise the queen and to contemplate their own misfortunes, as Ralegh had done in 1587. Now Essex and Ralegh began to write verse specifically to attack each other.[64] Ralegh's friend Spenser lauded him at Essex's expense in new revisions to *Mother Hubberd's tale*.[65] Ralegh himself poured scorn on Essex as a 'meaner wit' and a 'cuckoe' in his commendatory verses to Spenser's the *Faerie Queene*.[66] In response, Essex turned Ralegh's verse around and cast his rival as ' … that cursed cuckowe … that hath crost sweete Philomela's note … that parrate-like can never cease to prate'.[67] Quite possibly, this poem ('Muses no more but mazes be your names') was written by Essex after the revelation of his secret marriage to Sir Philip Sidney's widow in late 1590, when Elizabeth's anger briefly drove him from Court. It is conceivable that Essex's scorn towards Ralegh in this poem arose from the fact that it was Ralegh himself who had told the queen about the earl's

[59] LPL, MS 647, fol. 247ʳ.

[60] Edwards, *Ralegh*, II, p. 41.

[61] S. W. May, *Sir Walter Ralegh* (Boston, 1989), p. 11.

[62] This letter is dated 27 December 1589 (E. Greenlaw, C. G. Osgood, F. M. Padelford *et al.* (eds.), *The works of Edmund Spenser: avariorum edition* (10 vols., Baltimore, 1932–57), VII, 457).

[63] LPL, MS 3200, fol. 102ʳ.

[64] S. W. May, *The Elizabethan courtier poets: the poems and their contexts* (Columbia and London, 1991), pp. 123–6, 138–9.

[65] Mounts, 'The Raleigh–Essex rivalry and *Mother Hubberd's Tale*'. Spenser indulged in this attack despite including Essex among the sixteen courtly recipients of dedicatory sonnets which accompanied the publication of the first half of the *Faerie Queene* (for the sonnet to Essex, see *Works of Spenser*, III, p. 192). Despite the glancing blow at Essex, Spenser's prime target in *Mother Hubberd's tale* was the political dominance of Lord Burghley, who was represented as a fox, and the aspirations of Sir Robert Cecil, who was cast as an ape. The work appeared at the start of 1591 and was immediately banned. Spenser was soon forced to retreat to Ireland (R. S. Peterson, 'Spurting froth upon courtiers', *Times Literary Supplement*, 16 May 1997, pp. 14–15).

[66] Ralegh here seems to be suggesting that Essex was trying to win Spenser away from his patronage: May, *The Elizabethan courtier poets*, p. 124.

[67] May, 'The poems of Oxford and Essex', pp. 43, 84–8.

marriage.[68] At the very least, Ralegh must have tried to make capital out of Essex's disfavour.

While the rivalry with Ralegh rumbled on for all to see, it is more difficult to observe Essex's relations with the queen's leading councillors during this period. Sir Francis Walsingham became Essex's father-in-law before his death in April 1590, but evidence about their dealings is frustratingly thin.[69] Nevertheless, there is no reason to doubt that Walsingham looked on Essex with favour. Both of them were ardent proponents of the international Protestant cause and the marriage link between them confirmed this bond in the strongest possible terms. Sir Christopher Hatton, the lord chancellor, was of a rather different political hue, but he also seems to have regarded the thrusting young earl with a somewhat fatherly eye. Essex was highly complimentary of Hatton in his letter disavowing his candidacy for the chancellorship of Oxford in 1588 and named him as a feoffee in his will of 1591.[70] This mutual affection between Essex and the queen's senior favourite was subsequently borne out by Hatton's actions during the crisis over Essex's command in Normandy.

Far more can be said about Essex's relations with Lord Burghley, whose influence on the privy council after Leicester's death was approached only by Hatton. Although Essex became increasingly closely identified with Leicester over the course of the 1580s, he retained a special bond with his former guardian. This is evident in the surviving correspondence between them during these years, in which Essex shows a filial respect for the lord treasurer, as well as an awareness of the necessity of his help in financial matters.[71] Like Hatton, Burghley proved to be a crucial political ally in 1591. However, their relationship was not entirely grounded upon Essex's emotional and practical ties to Burghley. At the end of 1587, when Essex was still cementing himself in royal favour, Robert Cecil, Burghley's younger son, sought the earl's help in obtaining from the queen the reversion of his father's offices in Hertfordshire. After some kind of initial

---

[68] *Ibid.*, pp. 86–7; May, *The Elizabethan courtier poets*, p. 124.

[69] Godfrey Goodman, a controversial bishop of Gloucester (1625–40), recounted a story about Essex's early dealings with Walsingham which had been told to him by Henry Savile, who had, in turn, heard it from Dr John Overall after Essex's death. Overall had spoken with Essex about it in the last years of the earl's life, ten years or so after the events concerned. Goodman himself probably did not write his recollections until the 1640s: J. S. Brewer (ed.), *The Court of James the First; by Godfrey Goodman, bishop of Gloucester* (2 vols., London, 1839), I, pp. 145–6. For Goodman, see *ibid.*, pp. vii–xvii.

[70] PRO, PROB 11/128, fol. 22ᵛ. This, Essex's only valid will, was dated 26 July 1591. It was finally proven on 17 June 1616.

[71] A considerable number of Essex's letters to Burghley are to be found among the Lansdowne MSS at the British Library. For other correspondence between them before 1591, see *HMCS*, II, pp. 207–8, 508; *CSPF*, XX, *Sept. 1585–May 1586*, p. 332.

hiccup, Essex's advocacy proved successful.[72] Clearly, Essex and Cecil were on good terms at the end of the 1580s.[73] Yet there is also a wider significance to this episode. Given the importance of the matter, it seems unlikely that Cecil would have approached Essex about this suit without his father's approval, if not his active encouragement.[74] It seems very likely that Burghley used this suit to accustom his son and Essex to the idea of mutual co-operation. Indeed, Burghley may well have pursued this intention for some time. When Essex received his MA at Cambridge in July 1581, Burghley sent his son to observe the ceremonies and soak up the university atmosphere. To the vice-chancellor and others, this seemed like a clear indication that the two young men should be regarded, not as equals, but closely linked nevertheless: 'I wolde have wisshid him to have bene made a Master of Arte with my lord of Essexe, yf it had bene yowr pleasure [but] withowt the knowledg wherof, nayther he nor we durst attempt any thinge at this tyme.'[75]

Essex's involvement in the Portugal expedition demonstrated that he wished to be seen as a very different kind of favourite from his stepfather. Unlike Leicester, who had learned by long experience that he must ultimately accept the queen's restrictions upon his martial and political aspirations,[76] Essex rejected such constraints when he went to Portugal and challenged Elizabeth in a way that Leicester would never have done. This action greatly delighted military men,[77] but it left his supporters at home 'in desperate suspence what would become of him'. By flagrantly defying the queen in this way, they feared, 'all his hopes of advancement had like to be strangled in the very cradle'.[78]

---

[72] *HMCS*, III, p. 276; BL, Cotton MS Titus B VII, fol. 57[r]. It may be significant that this occurred when Leicester, with whom Burghley had recently had uneasy dealings, was in the Low Countries. Burghley himself was still under a cloud because of the Mary Queen of Scots episode.

[73] For further evidence of this, see Cecil's friendly letter to Essex concerning a point of awkwardness between two of their servants in January 1588 (BL, Cotton Charter iii.10).

[74] The importance of these offices lay in the fact that Burghley intended that Robert should inherit his estates and influence in Hertfordshire, centring on the mansion of Theobalds, while his elder son, Sir Thomas Cecil, inherited the baronial estate of Burghley and his lands in Northamptonshire and Lincolnshire. This division is quite clear in Burghley's frequently altered will (PRO, PROB 11/92, fols. 241[v]–245[v], esp. fol. 242[v]).

[75] PRO, SP 12/149, fol. 152[r–v].

[76] R. C. McCoy, *The rites of knighthood: the literature and politics of Elizabethan chivalry* (Berkeley, Los Angeles and London, 1989), ch. 2.

[77] [Anthony Wingfield], *A true coppie of a discourse written by a gentleman, employed in the late voyage of Spaine and Portingale* (London, 1589, STC no. 6790), p. 26; anon., *Ephemeris expditionis Norreysii & Draki in Lusitaniam* (London, 1589, STC no. 18653), p. 10.

[78] Wotton, *Parallel*, p. 3.

These differing reactions to Essex's departure are instructive, for they point to a bifurcation within the following which Essex attracted and a divergence in how these followers perceived his political actions. In broad terms, Essex attracted a following after Leicester's death which consisted of a domestic, civilian group and a military group which was concerned with fighting the land war overseas. The latter group were men who had previously been associated with Leicester – often quite loosely – in the Low Countries and the Armada campaign. After Walsingham's death, many soldiers associated with the secretary also turned to Essex. The concerns of such men lay with action and the material rewards which flowed from military command. Essex himself had served with some of these men and was eager to succeed Leicester as the natural patron of officers. His involvement in the Portugal venture, and the generosity which he displayed there, proved a decisive first step in this process.

Essex's domestic following was more diverse. In addition to the godly, as noted above, it also included a core of Devereux family dependants. Unlike the soldiers, these civilian followers were primarily interested in Essex's activities at home. Although they lauded the defence of Protestantism abroad, the godly were most pressingly concerned with the earl's defence of their own weakening position within England. Essex's old family supporters had rather different priorities. Their consistent concern was that Essex should reinforce the family position in the Welsh marches and unburden his estate of its heavy debts. As Essex began to back away from overt support for the godly, and after he had established himself securely as the queen's prime young favourite, a new, more Court-based group of clients also began to look to him. These were men like Francis Bacon, who saw Essex's rising fortunes as their ticket to crown appointments.[79]

Although perhaps less true of the Devereux family dependants, the primary element which linked these diverse civilian followers together was the widespread belief that Essex's career would proceed along the model of Leicester's. According to this view, Essex would use his special grace with Elizabeth to influence royal policy and to win and dispense liberally the sweet fruits of patronage. He would also protect his friends, such as the godly, when they were in trouble. Essex's position of favour with the queen was the touchstone of his future prospects – and those of his followers – and anything which threatened it was a cause of concern. Not understanding – or perhaps fearing – the significance of his participation in the Portugal expedition, Essex's domestic supporters therefore looked for reassurance after his return that their image of him as a younger Leicester was correct. When Essex's secret marriage to Sidney's widow was revealed

[79] For Francis Bacon's early cultivation of Essex, see below at pp. 153ff.

during October 1590,[80] they seized upon the obvious parallels. Although Elizabeth was initially furious at this match (perhaps incited by Ralegh's meddling), within a few short months Essex was fully restored to her favour, just as Leicester had been after the revelation of his marriage. Thomas Phelippes undoubtedly expressed a widely held view when he opined that Essex was 'likelye enough, if he had a few more yeares, to cary Lecester's creditt & sway with men'.[81] A more pressing cause of comparison between Essex and Leicester arose in 1591 with Essex's determination to secure command of the army being sent to Normandy. Because it entailed his lengthy absence from the queen, the prospect of this appointment dismayed Essex's civilian followers. Former associates of Leicester, in particular, had good cause to remember the deep anguish which service in the Low Countries had caused their late master. Until the very moment of Essex's nomination as general, 'his frendes here ... advized him to the contrary, wishing him rather to seke a domesticall greatnesse like to his father's in law [i.e. stepfather's]'.[82] Even as he was about to depart, friends continued to urge him against this costly endeavour.[83]

Such anxieties typified the reaction of Essex's domestic supporters, and especially those based at Court, whenever he ventured abroad on military expeditions during his career. With good reason, they feared that Essex's pursuit of military glory would endanger the continuity of domestic political influence which they needed to prosper. Yet Essex never really fitted this model of a Leicester-like 'domesticall greatnesse' – a fact of which his courtly followers gradually became uncomfortably aware.[84] Despite his developing appreciation of political means and ends, Essex was unwilling merely to await his future destiny at Court. To be sure, he attempted to make certain that he had as tight a hold as possible on the queen's favour, even to the extent of bullying rivals such as Ralegh and Blount.[85] Nevertheless, the years which immediately followed his step-

---

[80] Essex was openly treating his wife as a countess by the end of October 1590, although she remained at the house of her mother, Lady Walsingham (LPL, MS 3199, p. 116). Anticipating the queen's anger over the match, Essex remained philosophical in the face of her wrath and simply waited for it to abate (LPL, MS 3201, fol. 208[r]).

[81] PRO, SP 15/32, fol. 10[r].

[82] PRO, SP 12/239, fol. 93[r].   [83] *Ibid.*, fol. 123[r].

[84] The best example of this tension is perhaps Francis Bacon's famous letter to Essex of 4 October 1596 (pr. Spedding, *Bacon letters*, II, pp. 40–5), which is discussed below, pp. 317, 324ff., 336.

[85] In April 1591, Essex was also called before the privy council to explain 'some unkindnes and fallinge out' with the earl of Kildare in the presence chamber. It is quite possible that this was another incidence of Essex's extreme jealousy over displays of the queen's favour during these years (*APC*, XXI, *1590*, p. 53). It is also likely that this incident contributed to the sharp animosity between Essex and Kildare's wife, Frances (née Howard), a daughter of the lord admiral.

father's death saw Essex deliberately trying to break out of the Leicestrian mould, as he grew up – and away – from a youth that had seen him playing cards with an ageing queen 'tyll the birdes singe in the morninge'.[86]

Within days of his return from Portugal, Essex again sought to take charge of his own destiny by making secret overtures to James VI of Scotland, Elizabeth's most likely successor.[87] Although James had sent letters to him immediately after the death of Leicester,[88] only now did Essex seek to cultivate the king. Like many of his actions during this painful period of reshaping his political career, Essex's approach to James proved clumsy and naive. Together with his sister, Lady Rich, Essex sent letters to the king with Jean Hotman, one of Leicester's former secretaries, who acted as their emissary.[89] Lord Rich and the countesses of Warwick and Cumberland also supported the initiative with verbal messages to the king.[90] However, Essex's choice of intermediary, Richard Douglas, proved indiscreet and inadequate. Despite the arresting qualities of Lady Rich's letters and various bold assurances, James's interest in the correspondence rapidly cooled, not least because of Douglas's inability to inspire trust.[91] By early October, the whole business had been reported to Burghley.[92] It is not clear how many of these details were passed on to Elizabeth, but Essex apparently received a sharp reprimand for meddling in matters concerning the succession.[93]

Despite its humiliating end, the nature of Essex's approach to James is

---

[86] FSL, L.a.39.

[87] Essex's agents arrived in Edinburgh by 29 July 1589 (Cecil MS 18/37 (pr. *HMCS*, III, p. 426)). For details of this episode, see Cecil MS 18/50–1, 55–6, 59–60 (pr. *HMCS*, III, pp. 435–6, 438–9, 443).

[88] *HMCS*, III, p. 360; PRO, SP 59/26, fol. 133ʳ.

[89] D. B. Smith, 'Jean de Villiers Hotman', *Scottish Historical Review* 14 (1916–17), esp. pp. 153–5. In addition to the letters which passed between the two parties, a portrait of Lady Rich, apparently painted by Nicholas Hilliard, was carried to James by Henry Constable (*HMCS*, III, p. 438; R. C. Strong, 'Queen Elizabeth, the earl of Essex and Nicholas Hilliard', *Burlington Magazine* 101 (1959), pp. 145–6).

[90] Cecil MS 18/55.

[91] From the start, Douglas himself had 'not so muche credit with the kinge' and his efforts to increase it compromised the endeavour (Cecil MS 18/51). By early November 1589, James was thoroughly disenchanted with this overture and Douglas was left in limbo after returning to London (Cecil MS 18/59–60).

[92] The reports on the matter which Burghley received from Thomas Fowler, his agent in Edinburgh, bear annotations in Burghley's own hand. One such document is also endorsed: 'L. Burghley spectator. Mr Fowler fidelis' (Cecil MS 18/51).

[93] This is suggested by the opening of James's letter to Essex of 13 April 1594: 'allthoch I have this long tyme forborne the writting unto you because of the vronge ye receavid thairthrouch, suppose not in my default, but in thaime that vaire emploied betuixt us' (pr. Birch, *Memoirs*, I, p. 175). James did send at least one letter to Essex between 1589 and 1594, in October 1592. Nevertheless, it is unlikely that James would have recalled signing it, for the letter was merely a minor request for Essex to aid the bearer in a piracy suit (*CSPScot*, X, *1589–1593*, pp. 799–800).

illuminating. Judging by the reports sent to Burghley, Essex's sudden eagerness to win favour with James was driven by a belief that Elizabeth would soon die. He and his collaborators assured 'the poore kinge to hoope for hap shortly, and that hir Majeste cowld not lyve above a yere or ii by reson of sum imperfeccion'.[94] For Essex, who was still only twenty-four and anxious to build a glittering career in the decades which seemed to lie ahead of him, Elizabeth's time was rapidly running out and, with it, the end of his current frustrated existence. Essex made sure that James was well aware of his impatience with Elizabeth. One of Penelope Rich's letters described her brother as 'the wery knight': 'he is excedinge wery, accomptinge it a thrale he lyves nowe in and wysshes the change'.[95] Undoubtedly, Essex's sense of thraldom implied not only frustration at the courtly duties which detained him from service in war but also the demeaning nature of these duties because they were demanded of him by an ageing woman. By contrast, Essex expected to be liberated from his thraldom by the imminent new Jacobean age and reinvigorated as a soldier by serving a king in his prime.

Despite the failure of his bid to bind himself to James, Essex remained impatient with life at Court and driven by the feeling that he must make his mark soon if the great events of the world were not to leave him behind. Although the Portugal venture had reduced his finances to a shambles,[96] he remained desperate to play a part in the great struggle of armies and nations. Above all, these internationalist yearnings pulled Essex in the direction of France and its embattled Protestant king, Henri IV.[97] In contrast to Leicester, whose beliefs and ambitions had been shaped by events in the Low Countries in the 1570s and 1580s, Essex was increasingly absorbed by events in France. Where Leicester looked to the example of William of Orange, Essex found inspiration in the cause and friendship of the embattled French king. This concern with France was largely the result of developments in international politics. Henri's succession to the French crown as a Protestant in August 1589 hardened the religious divisions within that realm and opened the way for full-scale civil war and invasion by Spain. In consequence, as Essex himself declared, France became 'at thys daye the theater and stage wheron the greatest

---

[94] Cecil MS 18/51.   [95] Cecil MS 18/50.

[96] According to a later estimate, Essex's participation in the Portugal voyage, far from bringing any profit, cost him about £7,000 (Devereux MS 2, fol. 82[r]). Despite the agreement to lease the farm of sweet wines made earlier in the year, and the continuing struggle of Richard Broughton to ease the debt problem (FSL, L.a.253), the expenses of going to Portugal brought Essex's finances to a state of crisis by September 1589. At that point, hearing that Essex was on the verge of alienating almost his entire estate, Elizabeth ordered Burghley to stop the sales and sought to aid the earl with a favourable exchange of lands (BL, Lansdowne MS 61, fol. 165[r]).

[97] For an overview of Essex's relations with France, see Adams, 'The Protestant cause', ch. 4.

actions are acted'.[98] For a man who desired to prove himself a great captain against the forces of the Counter-Reformation, the pull of French affairs was obvious. Essex's commitment to Henri was further reinforced by more personal links. Essex had been exposed to French affairs, and French Protestantism in particular, during his childhood years with Gabriel Montgomery. Huguenot culture and contacts had also figured very prominently in the cultural activities of Sidney and Walsingham, despite the concern which they shared with Leicester for the Low Countries. French affairs therefore saw a conjunction of Essex's cultural and martial aspirations, and for many years made his support for Henri almost instinctive.

Essex's passionate interest in the developments in France began to stir even before the death of Leicester. In January 1587, he and two friends offered to fight for Henri under his general, Viscount Turenne.[99] Although nothing came of this offer, one of these comrades, Sir Roger Williams, took his younger brother, Walter Devereux, to fight with Henri a year later.[100] Essex himself started to cultivate the French ambassador to England, Beauvoir la Nocle, by regularly feeding him information.[101] He also began to correspond with Henri himself.[102] For his part, the French king replied in terms which were calculated to inflame Essex's desire to campaign in France.[103] This tactic proved remarkably successful. In one letter, Essex assured the king that 'there is nobody in the world who hates the name of unfruitful more than I, or who feels more envious of those who can be more forward in your service'.[104] By June 1590, Essex was sufficiently encouraged to request that Henri stand as a godfather to the child to which his sister, Lady Rich, was about to give birth.[105] This friendship with the king gave Essex an emotional focus for his commitment to French affairs,

---

[98] ULL, MS 187, fol. 14^r (pr. P. E. J. Hammer, 'Essex and Europe: evidence from confidential instructions by the earl of Essex, 1595–6', *EHR* 111 (1996), p. 379).

[99] See above, p. 74.

[100] Williams took Walter Devereux to Navarre as early as April 1588, as part of his military apprenticeship (BL, Add. MS 35841, fol. 43^v). Devereux and Williams both returned to Henri's service after taking part in the Portugal expedition (LPL, MS 647, fol. 247^v). They also fought in France again in 1590 (BL, Egerton MS 6, fol. 71^r).

[101] This is most easily seen in those despatches of Beauvoir for 1590 and 1591 which are printed in [Egerton, Francis H., 8th earl of Bridgewater], *The Life of Thomas Egerton lord chancellor of England* (Paris [1816]), pp. 317–92. Essex also gave special encouragement to the envoy [Charles de] Saldaigne, [sieur d'Incarvile] (BL, Egerton MS 8, fol. 48^r).

[102] For example, *HMCS*, IV, pp. 30, 32; BL, Egerton MS 6, fols. 144^{r-v}, 146^{r-v}; [J.] Berger de Xivrey (ed.), *Recueil des lettres missives de Henri IV* (9 vols., Paris, 1843–76), III, p. 281.

[103] For example, *HMCS*, IV, pp. 30, 32. Henri's cultivation of Essex probably began in response to advice from Beauvoir la Nocle, who urged the king to write to Essex frequently in order to encourage him (BL, Egerton MS 6, fol. 69^v).

[104] Tenison, VIII, p. 335. This letter was written in June 1590 or 1591.

[105] BL, Egerton MS 6, fol. 71^r; Egerton, *Life of Egerton*, p. 359. Lady Rich was churched after the birth of this child on 6 September 1590 (Cathedral Archives, Canterbury, 'Diary of Arthur Throckmorton', II, fol. 83^v).

just as Leicester and Walsingham had had similar personal focal points for their commitment to the defence of the Dutch Protestants a decade or more earlier.[106]

Essex constantly sought the chance to demonstrate his commitment to Henri IV by military action. When Lord Willoughby d'Eresby was nominated to lead an English army to Normandy in late 1589, Essex 'was most opposite against' him in the hope of gaining the command himself.[107] This agitation brought no success. Early in 1590, Beauvoir reported that Essex was reduced to begging Elizabeth for permission to fight in France for a month or two as a gentleman volunteer.[108] Essex reiterated his frustration in a letter intended for transmission to the Huguenot general, François de la Noue: 'si je suis un fois libre de ce place ici, je me hasterai bientost de me trouver en sa trouppe ou la vie me sera bien plus plaisant qu'en la court d'Angleterre'.[109] Perhaps in expectation that it might aid his plans for service in France, Essex purchased the Channel Island of Alderney.[110] Later

---

[106] For Leicester and Walsingham, see S. Adams, 'The queen embattled: Elizabeth I and the conduct of foreign policy' in Adams (ed.), *Queen Elizabeth I, most politick princess* (London, 1986), pp. 40–1.

[107] G. Bertie, *Five generations of a loyal house. Part I: containing the lives of Richard Bertie, and his son Peregrine, Lord Willoughby* (London, 1845), p. 406. On this expedition, see R. B. Wernham, *After the Armada: Elizabethan England and the struggle for western Europe 1588–1595* (Oxford, 1984), chs. 7–8. Willoughby received his final discharge from his command in the Netherlands on 20 August 1589 (PRO, SO 3/1, fol. 204) and was appointed as general of the army going to Normandy by 15 September (*APC*, XVIII, 1589–1590, pp. 113–14).

[108] BL, Egerton MS 6, fol. 41r. The queen's reaction to this appeal was cool (*ibid.*, fol. 52ʳ). If he had obtained leave for this very brief spell, Essex actually intended 'quand il aura l'honneur d'estre pres de vostre Majesté, qu'il en empruntera bien quatres [mois]' (*ibid.*, fol. 41ʳ).

[109] SC, sale of 25 April 1912, lot 46, transcript on pp. 13–14 (Essex to Jean Hotman, 30 June [1590]).

[110] This is a puzzling transaction. Despite the chronic state of his finances, Essex apparently paid £1,600 to John Chamberlain for a 1,000–year lease of the whole island, including its dilapidated castle and all the weapons and munitions it contained (PRO, C 54/1341, unfol., indenture of 26 March 1590). Conceivably, Lord Rich (who was another party to the agreement) provided Essex with the money. A. H. Ewin suggests that Chamberlain sold the island to Essex in connection with a contract to supply victuals to English troops in France ('Essex Castle and the Chamberlain family', *La Société Guernsiaise: Report and Transactions* 16 (1955–9), p. 249). If so, this presumably related to the expeditions led by Willoughby or Norris, rather than the Rouen campaign of the following year. For a more romantic, but improbable, local tradition about Essex's plans for the island, see A. N. Symons (ed.), 'History of Alderney from two manuscripts', *La Société Guernsiaise: Report and Transactions* 13 (1937–45), pp. 42, 52. Essex subsequently leased the island to William Chamberlain for £100 per annum (Devereux MS 3, fol. 113ʳ). During 1595, as part of the general reorganisation of his finances, Essex planned to sell his interest in Alderney, but it apparently failed to sell. Essex's connection with Alderney was subsequently celebrated by the building of Fort Essex (or Essex Castle) in the 1810s: R. Lemprière, *Buildings and memorials of the Channel Islands* (London, 1980), pp. 127–8.

in 1590, when it became apparent that a force would have to be sent to Brittany, he made a private arrangement with Sir John Norris, the former commander of the Portugal expedition. By this agreement, Norris promised to seek only the position of second-in-command of the Brittany army, leaving the post of general available for Essex.[111] Inevitably, this unrealistic deal soon broke down. Norris was the obvious choice to lead the force and Elizabeth appointed him as its commander. However, Essex was so desperate to play his part at a time when Henri was perilously close to losing his throne that he furiously tried to reverse this appointment, almost until the time of Norris's departure in the spring of 1591.[112] Three times he urged her to let him take Norris's place, on one occasion spending two hours on his knees.[113] In Elizabeth's mind, Essex still seemed a young courtier, not a credible general.

Essex's cause was not helped by conduct at Court which only seemed to confirm this impression. Perhaps in reaction to the constraints imposed on his behaviour by the requirement to attend upon an ageing queen, Essex became the leading light in the Court's 'rat pack' of young aristocrats. When Essex and many of his friends departed for the war in 1591, one of his companions who remained behind lamented that 'love heare is almost banyshed'.[114] Although he had only recently concluded his secret marriage, Essex and his friends pursued 'love' with several of the queen's maids of honour – a sign that his romantic match with Sidney's widow was a matter of politics rather than love. One of the maids, Elizabeth Southwell, even became pregnant by Essex in 1591.[115] However, he was, for the moment,

[111] BL, Egerton MS 6, fol. 81[r].
[112] *Ibid.*, fols. 81[r], 86[r-v]; Egerton, *Life of Egerton*, p. 389; HMCD, II, p. 113.
[113] BL, Egerton MS 6, fol. 81. This incident is usually cited, incorrectly, as evidence of Essex's eagerness to win the Rouen command later in 1591.
[114] Cecil MS 168/53 (pr. HMCS, IV, p. 142).
[115] Camden, *Elizabeth*, p. 624. Elizabeth Southwell was the daughter of Sir Thomas Southwell of Woodrising, Norfolk (W. Rye (ed.), *The visitacion of Norfolk made and taken (in)* ... *1563 ... and also ... 1613* ... (Harleian Society, XXXII, London, 1891), p. 261). This made her the half-sister of Sir Robert Southwell, who was son-in-law to the lord admiral (*Commons*, III, p. 422). Elizabeth Southwell's mother, Nazareth Newton, was a member of the privy chamber in the 1560s and later made an unfortunate marriage to Thomas, 3rd Lord Paget (*DNB*, XV, p. 59). She was a sister of Frances Lady Cobham, making Elizabeth Southwell first cousin to Henry Brooke, who succeeded as Lord Cobham in 1597 (D. McKeen, *A memory of honour: the life of William Brooke, Lord Cobham* (2 vols., Salzburg Studies in English Literature, CVIII, Salzburg, 1986), I, p. 144; TCP, III, p. 348). Elizabeth Southwell ultimately married Sir Barentine Moleyns in 1600, when she was aged thirty, after a long and turbulent courtship. Moleyns was apparently notorious for his ugliness. He was also 'allmost bereaft of his sight and very weake of body' because of wounds received in the queen's service overseas (W. H. Rylands (ed.), *The four visitations of Berkshire made and taken (in)* ... *1532 ... 1566 ... 1623 and ... 1665–66* (2 vols., Harleian Society, LVI–LVII, London, 1907–8), I, p. 112; A. L. Rowse, *Simon Forman: sex and society in Shakespeare's age* (London, 1974), pp. 194–5; PRO, SP 14/89, fol. 4[r]). The

shielded from the potentially disastrous consequences of his amorous pursuits. Thomas Vavasour took the blame for 'Mrs Southwell['s] lamnes in her legg', enduring the queen's anger and a brief spell of imprisonment for his alleged misconduct.[116] Nevertheless, this affair would return to haunt Essex later in his career.

Despite such youthful frolics, Essex remained profoundly committed to the cause of Henri IV and made regular displays of his eagerness to serve in France. Perhaps the most important of these was his sumptuous entertainment[117] of Viscount Turenne,[118] who visited England in November 1590 before going on to seek soldiers for Henri in Germany.[119] In his capacity as chief host for visiting dignitaries, Essex kept close attendance on Turenne and entertained his entourage at

child, whom Essex acknowledged and named Walter, was apparently born at the end of 1591 (*Al. Oxon.*, I, p. 399). He was given over to the care of Essex's mother, the countess of Leicester, at Drayton Bassett. He died about 1641 (J. G. Wedgwood, *Staffordshire parliamentary history from the earliest times to the present day* (3 vols., Collections for a history of Staffordshire, 1919–33), II, p. 52). Essex made provision for Walter in a financial rearrangement in July 1595 (PRO, SP 12/253, fol. 36^r).

116 Cecil MS 168/55, 20/65 (pr. *HMCS*, IV, p. 153). Vavasour was probably the gentleman pensioner of this name, who had served with Essex in the Netherlands. It is possible – but not certain – that he was subsequently knighted by Essex in 1597: *Commons*, III, pp. 553–4; Tighe, 'Gentleman pensioners', pp. 463–4.

117 For Turenne's reception in England, see LPL, MS 3199, p. 127; LPL, MS 3201, fol. 208^r; FSL, L.a.256. Among the surviving papers relating to Essex's finances, there is a later document which includes the statement that £2200 was spent entertaining 'the vydam and the French one moneth at York House, & the French geven to understand thatt her Majestie would paye for it . . . besydes pryvatt gyftes' (Devereux MS 2, fol. 82^r). Since the details of this visit accord with that of Turenne (but not with the vidame de Chartres in 1593), it seems that 'vydam' may have been a slip of the pen for 'vicomte'. Regarding the additional expenditure on 'pryvatt gyftes', there is a list of jewels purchased by Essex during 1590. Many of these items seem to have been intended as gifts for the time of Turenne's visit (Devereux MS 3, fol. 47^r). These include five diamonds worth £160 which were presented on 17 November, when Turenne and his entourage attended the Accession Day celebrations (Segar, *Honor military and civill*, p. 197), and two large jewels in the form of the 'flower de luce', worth some £940.

118 Henri de la Tour de l'Auvergne, 4th vicomte de Turenne (created duke of Bouillon after his marriage to Charlotte de la Marck in 1591), was ten years older than Essex and had a convert's commitment to the Huguenot cause. Formerly a follower of Francis, duke of Anjou, he became a Protestant in 1575 and entered the service of Henri of Navarre. He soon became chief gentleman of bedchamber and lieutenant-general to the king: F. Delteil, 'Henri de la Tour, vicomte de Turenne humaniste et protestant', *Bulletin de la Société de l'Histoire du Protestantisme Français* 115 (1969), pp. 230–54.

119 For copies of Turenne's instructions on this mission, see BL Add. MS 5455, fols. 308^r–17^r and PRO 31/3, vol. 29, fols. 1^r–5^v. He arrived in England at the very beginning of November 1590 (LPL, MS 3199, p. 127) and left for Germany from Harwich on 4 December (Cathedral Archives, Canterbury, 'Throckmorton diary', II, fol. 87^r). The diplomatic significance of Turenne's mission is discussed in Wernham, *After the Armada*, ch. 12 and H. A. Lloyd, *The Rouen campaign 1590–1592: politics, warfare and the early-modern state* (Oxford, 1973), ch. 2.

York House.[120] The lavishness of this hospitality may have been partly intended to appease Elizabeth after the recent disclosure of his marriage, demonstrating his renewed commitment to royal service. However, Essex's reception of Turenne was principally a demonstration of his personal commitment to the cause of Henri IV. Strongly encouraged in this by Turenne,[121] who soon became a fast friend, Essex re-emphasised his support for the king by offering to contribute about £1,000 towards the costs of hiring German troops for him[122] – even though debts were forcing him to sell lands which had been held by his family for 150 years.[123]

Essex's chance to take to the field on behalf of Henri IV finally came later in 1591, when Elizabeth sent another army to France, in order to assist in the besieging of Rouen.[124] This had all the prospects of being a plum appointment for Essex. The size of the army, at 4,000 men, was as big as that which Willoughby had taken to Normandy at the end of 1589. In addition, Elizabeth, for once, was strongly in favour of the venture. External circumstances also aided his cause. Because the army was intended to operate in conjunction with Henri's own force, a nobleman of high status was required to lead it. With Willoughby worn out and ill,[125] the appointment of the general for Rouen also opened the way for the successful peer to take up Leicester's mantle as England's leading noble soldier. This was a status which Essex desperately wanted. As he described it in subsequent years, to have failed to win this command would have condemned him to 'have seene my *puisnes* leape over my head'.[126]

---

[120] LPL, MS 3199, pp. 127, 473(5)-4(6) (the pagination of this volume is in error at this point); *HMCA*, p. 307.

[121] PRO 31/3, vol. 29, fols. 4ᵛ–5ʳ. It is significant that Essex was listed first in Turenne's instructions among the Englishmen whom the viscount should lobby on the king's behalf.

[122] This aid to the French king was co-ordinated by Sir Horatio Palavicino (L. Stone, *An Elizabethan: Sir Horatio Palavicino* (Oxford, 1956), pp. 157ff). Palavicino complained regularly that Essex's zeal to aid Henri was not matched by his payment of the promised 5,000 florins (*L&A*, II, *July 1590–May 1591*, pp. 227, 229, 420, 428, 434, 435). In the end, it was not paid over until mid-1591 and then only after Burghley had intervened to help Essex meet his obligation (*L&A*, III, *June 1591–April 1592*, p. 459). The sum in question may have originated as part of Essex's debt to Palavicino (Devereux MSS, box 5, nos. 71a and 71b), a portion of which Palavicino assigned to the queen's use in early 1590 (Devereux MS 2, fol. 29ʳ).

[123] Among the properties which Essex was forced to sell about this time was the manor of Cotesbach in Leicestershire, which was alienated to Sir Thomas Sherley. The Devereux family had been remarkably benevolent lords of this manor since 1436, but this sale initiated an 'agrarian revolution' which soon had sweeping effects upon its inhabitants: L. A. Parker, 'The agrarian revolution at Cotesbach, 1501–1612', *Transactions of the Leicestershire Archaeological Society* 24 (1948), pp. 41–76.

[124] The essential work on this expedition is Lloyd, *Rouen campaign*. The specifically military aspects of Essex's involvement in this campaign will be discussed in Chapter 6.

[125] Willoughby therefore seems to have supported Essex's bid for the Rouen command (*HMCA*, p. 313; *HMCS*, IV, p. 131).

[126] *Apologie*, sig. A3ᵛ.

Essex finally won this important command, but it required several months of hard lobbying.[127] A number of causes contributed to this landmark appointment – a recognition, at last, that he was more than merely a favourite. With the possible exception of Lord Burgh,[128] there was no obvious rival for the post. Essex was also able to bring into play his genuine personal influence with Elizabeth. Although he had met with a series of refusals in his previous efforts to go to France, his special power over the queen had become steadily more obvious, as demonstrated by his rapid return to favour after the revelation of his marriage. Being 'fully bent to parforme' at Rouen, Essex now spared no effort to convince her of his fitness for the post.[129] Essex's own suasions were reinforced by the fruit of his zealous cultivation of Henri IV and Beauvoir. At first, the king merely authorised the ambassador and a special envoy, de Reau, to support Essex's appointment very delicately.[130] Nevertheless, perhaps partly as a result of Essex's rich hospitality to the two French representatives,[131] they soon began to lobby the queen rather more strongly, and even brought Henri himself to write to Elizabeth on the earl's behalf.[132] Perhaps most crucially, Essex's candidacy also won the active support of Burghley and Hatton.

As the two senior members of the privy council and the men most trusted by Elizabeth, Burghley and Hatton played a decisive role in advising the queen on all matters of importance, especially after Walsingham's death in April 1590.[133] Despite Elizabeth's instinctive reluctance to commit her resources abroad, both men had come to the conclusion that urgent aid to Henri IV was necessary if England were to be spared greater danger and expense in the future, and urged the queen accordingly.[134] In their eyes,

---

[127] Essex's appointment as general was formally agreed on 25 June 1591 (Murdin, p. 797) but he was assured of the post by 20 June, when he began the mobilisation of his friends and tenantry (Devereux, *Lives*, I, p. 215). His instructions were dated 20 July (BL, Lansdowne MS 103, fols. 200ʳ–203ᵛ) and his patent as lieutenant-general of the queen's army being sent to Normandy was dated 22 July (Devereux MSS, box 5, no. 74).

[128] LPL, MS 3199, p. 322. The tension between Essex and Burgh was evident in the latter's complaint to Burghley in August that the withdrawal of men from his command at Brill for service in France was the result of Essex's 'ill disposition' towards him (PRO, SP 84/42, fol. 276ʳ). For his part, Essex pointedly reported that the force sent from Brill was 'the weakest in the army' (PRO, SP 78/25, fol. 170ʳ). It is not clear how seriously Burgh was considered for this command. The ill-will between Burgh and Essex did not last long.

[129] LPL, MS 3199, p. 322.

[130] PRO, SP 78/24, fols. 214ᵛ, 244ʳ.

[131] Essex apparently entertained Beauvoir and de Reau at Wanstead in April (Devereux MS 2, fol. 72ʳ). Loose accounts for some of the provisions used in this feast are bound between folios 64 and 65 of this manuscript.

[132] LPL, MS 3199, p. 322; BL, Cotton MS Caligula E VII, fol. 364ʳ⁻ᵛ (pr. [J.] Berger de Xivrey (ed.), *Recueil des lettres missives de Henri IV*, III, pp. 399–400).

[133] See, for example, PRO, SP 12/234, fol. 5ʳ.

[134] For notes on aid to France by Burghley and Hatton respectively, see PRO, SP 12/234, fols. 14ʳ–15ʳ, 26ʳ.

although not in Elizabeth's, the salvation of Henri embodied a genuine 'common cause'. As Robert Cecil put it to Hatton: 'yf this occasion overpass, halfe a million next yeare will not much helpe him for, togeather with her Majestie's withdrawinge, all his parte will grow cold and desperate'.[135] Hatton and Burghley therefore took the lead in ensuring that the Rouen expedition would go forward, and that Essex would command it.

Hatton's part in the Rouen venture can be seen in the nomination of his protégé, Sir Henry Unton, as the ambassador who would accompany Essex to France and offer him guidance and support.[136] Burghley's role in the dispatch of Essex was even more obvious. Burghley himself claimed that he had been 'the principal furtherer in this voyage'.[137] Essex later praised him as his 'pylote' in the expedition.[138] In the light of later events, Burghley's support for the earl has sometimes been seen as decidedly disingenuous – a Machiavellian ploy to clear the way for Robert Cecil's elevation to the privy council.[139] However, this seems unlikely. Essex's own statement that he sought the Rouen command as a response to 'strong & dangerous opposition'[140] must also be treated with suspicion, especially as it was made seven years after the event – this claim should be seen as a reflection of Essex's position in 1598, rather than that of 1591.

During 1591, as before, Essex and his former guardian seem to have been on reasonably good terms.[141] Both men were greatly concerned about Archbishop Whitgift's actions against the more enthusiastic members of the godly.[142] Although the lord treasurer's concern about balancing the queen's books contrasted with the passionateness of the earl, they were both very

---

[135] UCL, Ogden MS 7/41, fol. 31[v].

[136] For Unton, see *DNB*, XX, pp. 32–4; *Commons*, III, pp. 542–3; R. Strong, *The cult of Elizabeth: Elizabethan portraiture and pageantry* (London, 1977), ch. 3; J. G. Nichols (ed.), *The Unton inventories* (Berkshire Ashmolean Society, London, 1841), pp. l–lxvii. Unton's nomination was regarded as certain by 21 June: LPL, MS 3199, p. 320. His letter of credence to Henri IV, dated 16 July 1591, is PRO, SP 78/25, fol. 45[r]. Much of his surviving correspondence for this mission is printed in R. J. Stevenson (ed.), *Correspondence of Sir Henry Unton, knt, ambassador from Queen Elizabeth to Henri IV king of France, in the years MDXCI and MDXCII* (Roxburghe Club, London, 1847). It is cited hereafter as *Unton corr.*

[137] *Unton corr.*, p. 60. This is why Elizabeth blamed Burghley as soon as events in Normandy failed to run according to her expectations (*ibid.*, p. 36).

[138] PRO, SP 78/26, fol. 278[r].

[139] This view is, for example, at least implicit in one near-contemporary account (BL, Egerton MS 2026, fol. 32[r]) and is explicit in Read, *Lord Burghley and Queen Elizabeth*, p. 477.

[140] *Apologie*, sig. A3[v].

[141] Like Hatton, Burghley and Robert Cecil were named among the feoffees in Essex's will of 26 July 1591 (PRO, PROB 11/128, fol. 22[v]).

[142] See above, p. 81.

anxious about events in France and co-operated in 'the common cause'.[143] Nevertheless, there was occasional friction between Essex and 'old Saturnus'.[144] Above all, this centred around Burghley's efforts to secure the political future of his younger son, Robert.

By 1591, Burghley was becoming increasingly anxious about the future of Robert Cecil, who was now twenty-eight years old. Lacking the kind of rapport with the queen and high birth which Essex enjoyed, Cecil's future depended upon his father's efforts to place him where his talents could assure his survival and promotion. To this end, Burghley applied pressure to Elizabeth by staging a number of withdrawals from Court, pleading age and weariness.[145] At one such retirement, during a royal visit to his house at Theobalds in May 1591, she responded by composing a mock charter recalling 'the hermytte of Tybott ... too yoor olld cave'.[146] While playing upon the queen's affection for him in this way, Burghley sought to demonstrate his special devotion to her service by pointedly refusing to plead for his son's advancement.[147] Instead, this was left to Hatton, whom Cecil had been cultivating – with his father's encouragement – since at least the time of Hatton's appointment as lord chancellor.[148]

This coordination between Burghley and Hatton during 1590–1 is a unique phenomenon in Elizabeth's reign. Agreed on major policies (except in matters of religion) and no longer troubled by old rivals like Leicester, they were the last active members of the group of men who had filled the privy council and dominated national affairs since the 1570s. In recent years, a string of deaths had decimated the ranks of their colleagues – Leicester in 1588, Mildmay in 1589, and Walsingham, Croft and Warwick in 1590. With these deaths in mind, Burghley and Hatton consciously sought to regulate the transfer of power to a new generation, led by Essex and Cecil. This would enable Burghley and Hatton to shed some of the

[143] Essex assured Beauvoir at the end of 1590 that Burghley was now 'tout resolu d'embrasser entièrement les affaires de France' (BL, Egerton MS 6, fol. 83ʳ). Essex also passed on to Burghley information from Sir Roger Williams in France which, Williams informed the lord treasurer, 'I durst not comitt unto my boye's writing' (PRO, SP 78/24, fol. 122ʳ).

[144] *HMCD*, II, p. 122.

[145] W. D. Acres, 'The early political career of Sir Robert Cecil *c*.1582–1597: some aspects of late Elizabethan secretarial administration' (unpub. Ph.D. thesis, University of Cambridge, 1992), pp. 9–10.

[146] BL, RP 2895, charter dated 10 May 1591. The strange spelling in this document is probably intended to enhance the comic effect. For Burghley's elaborate entertainment of Elizabeth on this occasion, see Nichols, *Progresses*, II, pp. 76–8 and BL, Egerton MS 2623, fols. 15ʳ–18ᵛ.

[147] UCL, Ogden MS 7/41, fol. 3ʳ. Despite this, Burghley's hopes for his son were patently clear. In a letter to Hatton after Cecil's promotion to the privy council, Burghley termed him 'a vicar her(e) servyng as a curat under me. He is as yet hable for no gretar cure, but I hope he will in that behalf dischardg me of my cure' (BL, Cotton MS Titus C VII, fol. 16ʳ).

[148] Murdin, pp. 588–9.

killing burden of work which they now had to bear. The larger, unspoken agenda behind their actions was to ensure stability when Elizabeth herself finally died and the uncertain matter of the succession had to be settled. Ralegh apparently had no place in this grand scheme. Quite what Elizabeth herself thought of this co-operation between her two old warhorses is unclear. Throughout her reign, Elizabeth's greatest fear was being dictated to by her leading male subjects. Judging by the hiccups and delays in making appointments during these months, this was a worry which remained just below the surface of things, despite her great affection for her 'mutton' and 'Sir Spirit'.

For Essex, the support of Hatton and Burghley for his future advancement was reassuring, but also somewhat frustrating: it 'is plotted but ... the erle is impatient of so slow a progresse as it must needes have during the life of the 2 old figures, the chancellor & tresorer'. Yet, despite Essex's impatience, 'the tresorer semeth to encline to him'.[149] Although he may have had doubts about the the military ambitions of this young 'Cyrus',[150] Burghley recognised the potential importance of Essex for the realm as a whole, as well as for the future prospects of his own son. Nevertheless, Essex himself was less enamoured of this longer-term perspective and caused much confusion by forgetting the script, as it were, in early 1591. When Burghley raised the urgency of appointing a new secretary of state and Hatton put forward Cecil as a candidate, Essex responded by urging Elizabeth to recall William Davison, the secretary who had been disgraced for his part in the execution of Mary Queen of Scots.[151] This was certainly unhelpful to Cecil and irritating to his father. Nevertheless, it was probably not an act of deliberate resistance to Cecil, as it has often been seen. Instead, it was a token of Essex's continuing personal commitment to Davison, pursued as a matter of honour regardless of its political consequences.[152]

---

[149] PRO, SP 12/239, fol. 93^r.

[150] 'Cyrus' was the codename which Burghley assigned to Essex in the cipher which he sent for the use of Sir Henry Unton and Sir John Norris. Burghley chose the name 'Aurelius' for himself, which itself has interesting connotations (PRO, SP 78/25, fols. 88^v, 99^v; PRO, SP 106/2, fol. 141^r).

[151] PRO, SP 15/32, fol. 9^v; PRO, SP 12/239, fol. 244^r; BLO, Tanner MS 82, fol. 42^v–43^r. Burghley's pressing concern about Robert's future was perhaps encouraged by the birth of Robert's own heir on 28 March 1591 (*HMCS*, V, p. 71). Regarding Davison, it should be noted that, although fined and imprisoned in 1587, he continued to receive his salary as a secretary of state (R. B. Wernham, 'The disgrace of William Davison', *EHR* 46 (1931), pp. 632–6). For a while at least, Davison also continued to do some work for the queen's service. Before he was released from the Tower in October 1588 (BL, Add. MS 48027, fol. 402^r), he wrote a discourse on Ireland to accompany maps in Walsingham's possession (*HMCS*, V, p. 427).

[152] In one letter Essex promised Davison: 'I will not be forgetfull [of you] like Pharo's butler' (BLO, Tanner MS 79, fol. 99^r).

Essex's support for Davison had no decisive effect on Cecil's failure to win the secretaryship in 1591. Elizabeth clearly thought him too inexperienced for so vital a post, especially as there were a number of alternative candidates.[153] Elizabeth may also have refused Cecil the secretaryship as a sign of resistance to the co-ordinated efforts of the lord treasurer and lord chancellor. While Burghley's entertainment of the queen at Theobalds won Cecil a knighthood on 20 May,[154] Hatton's direct lobbying as Cecil's 'chiefest undertaker'[155] initially made little headway. Using Unton as his 'often instrument', Hatton could only send repeated messages of reassurance to Cecil and his father.[156] However, only a week after Unton's departure for France, Hatton's actions had their reward: on 2 August, his pressure won Cecil an all-important seat on the privy council.[157] Judging by the tone of their correspondence, it seems very likely that Unton himself also expected to join Cecil on the council once he had completed his service in France.[158]

While Hatton lobbied for Cecil, Burghley himself came out in support of Essex's candidacy for the Rouen command.[159] Quite apart from his noble rank and enthusiasm for 'the common cause', Essex must have appealed to Burghley (and also Hatton) as the ideal candidate for this command precisely because of his youth and inexperience. Because it was his first taste of over-all command, Essex could be controlled in this delicate mission more readily than an experienced general. Almost certainly, this kind of argument helped to sway Elizabeth, who was determined to

---

[153] Among the others named as contenders for the post, and manoeuvring to win it, were Thomas Wilkes, Sir Edward Stafford, Edward Dyer and Edward Wotton (FSL, L.a.258; LPL, MS 3199, p. 159; *HMCD*, II, p. 120; PRO, SP 12/239, fol. 244^r; BL, Cotton MS Caligula E VIII, fol. 126^r). In the face of this intense competition, Cecil complained to Hatton in April 1591 that 'my case hath a long tyme bynn tossed ... like a tennis ball' (UCL, Ogden MS 7/41, fol. 6^r).

[154] Murdin, p. 796.

[155] PRO, SP 78/25, fol. 107^r.

[156] *Ibid.*, fols. 99^v, 107^r; *Unton corr.*, p. 439.

[157] Murdin, p. 797. For Cecil's own account of this appointment, and of Hatton's part in it, see his letter to Unton of 5 August 1591: BL, Cotton MS Caligula E VIII, fol. 128^{r-v}.

[158] This can only be speculation because of the guarded, almost conspiratorial, nature of their exchanges. In the margin of a letter to Unton of 3 October, Cecil wrote: 'Yow know me and I yow. From henceforth towch in your lettres owr trew loves no more so largely, for I dare never shew your lettres for that, which otherwise I would do to take occasion to speake of yow to the queen, which shold do yow no harme, thogh little good' (BL, Cotton MS Caligula E VIII, fol. 116^r). Antonio Perez was still suspicious of the relationship between Cecil and Unton five years later (Ungerer, I, p. 420).

[159] This support was symbolised by the fact that, before his departure for France, Essex paraded his cavalry for Elizabeth at Burghley's house in Covent Garden (BL, Cotton MS Titus B VI, fol. 34^r; Murdin, p. 797). Essex and Burghley also co-operated closely over the choice of captains: one list of officers drawn up in June bears the hands of Burghley, Essex and Cecil (PRO, SP 12/239, fols. 43^r, 44^r).

maintain complete control of the action in Normandy – and of her young favourite. Essex was therefore given strict instructions and a short commission.[160] Elizabeth and Burghley also surrounded the fledgling general with a number of hand-picked advisers.[161] As well as ensuring a check upon any youthful excesses,[162] these men offered a useful hedge against the French king simply using the army according to his own purposes, as he had in 1589.[163] Extra money was also spent on trying to improve communications with France.[164] From the outset, Essex's command and, indeed, the whole campaign were conceived of by Elizabeth and Burghley as being conducted on a short leash.[165]

Although Essex understood these limitations and respected them in his actions,[166] his own ambitions in this venture were far grander. Above all, he wanted to prove himself as a captain of men, as the epitome of martial virtue. This quest for honour was all the more important and the stakes all the greater because Henri's weak hold on the French crown threatened the whole Protestant cause with crisis. Essex was 'infinitely inflamed' by the knowledge that he fought 'for the good of all Christendom and ... the

[160] Essex's commission initially extended for only two months. For the detailed instructions given to him, see PRO, SP 78/25, fols. 70ʳ–73ʳ. Burghley's draft of them is BL, Lansdowne MS 103, fols. 200ʳ–203ᵛ.
[161] Apart from Sir Henry Unton, who went as the queen's ambassador, Essex's advisers were Sir Thomas Leighton (PRO, SP 15/32, fols. 29ʳ–30ʳ; Murdin, p. 797) and Henry Killigrew (PRO, SP 12/239, fol. 123ʳ). Sir Thomas Sherley, already treasurer for English forces in the Low Countries, was also appointed treasurer for this expedition (HMCD, II, p. 119; APC, XX, 1590–1591, pp. 317–18). Thomas Wilkes, unlike Sherley, managed to avoid being sent to France with Essex (HMCD, II, p. 119).
[162] Unton's instructions from the queen, written in Burghley's hand but probably drafted according to the Elizabeth's own directions, included the warning that 'comenly yong noble men at the first do not embrace advertisementes of thynges to be reformed, but we charge yow upon your duty not for any such respect to forbeare to deale playnly in honorable sort with the sayd erle' (BL, Lansdowne 103, fol. 289ʳ).
[163] Wernham, *After the Armada*, ch. 8. Elizabeth's subsequent attitude to Henri IV was epitomised in a letter from Burghley about the forces being sent to Brittany in April 1591: 'her Majestie will thinke her cost evill bestowed in the aideing of the king yf he shold reject her so good councell and advise in a matter of so great importance' (LPL, MS 647, fol. 266ʳ: the original is LPL, MS 648, fol. 29ʳ⁻ᵛ).
[164] PRO, E 351/542, fol. 158ʳ.
[165] Essex and Unton were expected to send back full reports on their actions at least once a week (*Unton corr.*, p. 35), although in early September Burghley seems to have increased this demand to 'daylie letters' from Unton (PRO, SP 78/25, fol. 285ʳ). Part of the diary which Unton maintained in order to keep track of this correspondence and of the coming and going of messengers survives as BRO, TA 13/2. Burghley also seems to have kept a special journal for matters relating to the expedition, part of which survives as BL, Cotton MS Titus B VI, fols. 34ʳ–35ᵛ.
[166] Essex himself thanked Burghley for 'your wyse, favorable and fatherly instructions, of which your lordship's lettres are very full. I confesse myself bound infinitely for them and I will with all duty and service deserve your lordship's precious favour' (PRO, SP 78/25, fol. 105ᵛ).

honor of our nation'.[167] In political terms, Essex hoped to win conspicuous honour on the battlefield to commit Elizabeth to new and greater efforts in France – and also to boost his own career. As he explained it in later years, 'the greatnesse of her Majestie's favor must grow out of the greatnesse of her servants' merits: & I saw no way of merit lye so open as by service in her wars'.[168] Along with Essex's 'ambition of warr', therefore, went a belief in the political efficacy of military renown. This was the natural product of Essex's intimate association of martial honour with nobility and virtue. It was also a conclusion to be drawn from his own experiences, which the aftermath of Zutphen had seemed to demonstrate and which the sequel to his Portugal journey had failed to disprove. As Essex crossed to France, there was 'great expectacion of this erle, & if he returne with honor from this viage, he is like to be a great man in this state'.[169]

Inevitably, neither the hopes of Essex nor those of the queen and her advisers survived the test of events. Militarily, the campaign proved a failure. Worse, Elizabeth's dwindling enthusiasm for the venture began, almost at once, to turn to bitter anger. Finding herself unable to exert the unrealistic degree of control over Essex and the king which she had expected, despite footing the bills, she lashed out with furious missives.[170] As a result, although he did his best to observe his instructions,[171] Essex received a series of sharp reproaches which made him complain to Burghley that 'all my actions [are] construed to the worst part'.[172] Similar anger was also directed at anyone else whom Elizabeth suspected of excusing Essex's actions, including Unton, the earl's advisers, and even Burghley and Hatton themselves. Acting as an intermediary for his father, Cecil sympathised with Hatton that 'yt is very hard for the Embassador . . . to avoide her Majestie's blame except he doe eyther pull my lord [of Essex] on his head or not deliver his minde for the cause, though his heart thinketh yt'.[173] Cecil also reported his own bewilderment at the queen's temperamental behaviour: 'I find that att some time good is bad and, another time, worse is not so ill taken.'[174] Characteristically, Elizabeth's grudging involvement in Continental warfare soon turned to a feeling of being trapped, which spawned recrimination and anger.

If the bitter letters which Essex received from Elizabeth in 1591 seemed painfully reminiscent of the experiences of Leicester in the Netherlands, the altered political balance at Court prevented the kind of mistrust which had

---

[167] PRO, SP 78/26, fols. 115^r, 116^r.   [168] *Apologie*, sig. A3^v.
[169] PRO, SP 12/239, fol. 123^r. Cf *HMCD*, II, p. 120.
[170] For example, *Unton corr.*, pp. 35–6, 38–41; *HMCS*, IV, pp. 143–4, 145–6.
[171] Lloyd, *Rouen campaign*, pp. 106–23.
[172] PRO, SP 78/25, fol. 299^r.
[173] UCL, Ogden MS 7/41, fol. 4^r.   [174] *Ibid.*, fol. 23^r.

seen Leicester turn against Norris, Wilkes and Buckhurst. Although Elizabeth wanted to withdraw from Normandy, the privy council recognised that the military situation in France made this impossible. Despite their sharp differences over domestic religious policy, Hatton and Burghley remained united in supporting Essex, and they were supported in this stand by Hunsdon and the lord admiral. None of these councillors doubted that Elizabeth's criticism of Essex, Unton and the others in France was often unjustified. Nevertheless, for the sake of the larger cause, the councillors urged those in France to make a show of obedience to the queen, even if they disgreed with her.[175] On occasion, they also opposed Elizabeth. In one instance, Burghley exploded over her constant criticism of events: 'God, madam, I would have written as hee did & so done also, except you meant to make him stand for a cypher.'[176] Absent from the Court because of ill-health and official duties in London, Hatton resorted to more subtle techniques. Using Cecil as his messenger, Hatton sent Elizabeth a jewel with the plea 'that to the distressed earle yt might be sent . . . to shew her gratious disposicion in comforting of him'.[177] In this case, Elizabeth responded with words of affection, but on other occasions she bridled at Hatton's interventions: 'the queen saith your lordship is one that hath ever cockered the earle and would not suffer her to chasten him'.[178]

From Essex's perspective, Elizabeth's chastisements seemed like persecution and were hard to bear. However, in early September, the force of these rebukes was vastly compounded by the death of his brother Walter, 'the halfe arch of my house'.[179] Pursuing an enemy force in apparent retreat, he was caught in an ambush and cut down with a musket shot.[180] With that blow, Essex collapsed physically and mentally. For a time, many even feared for his life.[181] To make matters worse, Elizabeth resolutely

[175] For their encouragement to Essex, see, for example, Murdin, pp. 646–8. Messages of a more intimate tone were sent by Sir Robert Cecil (for example, PRO, SP 78/25, fol. 390[r–v]; PRO, SP78/26, fol. 337[r]).

[176] UCL, Ogden MS 7/41, fol. 22[r]. This outburst arose from Burghley's unwillingness to pen a rebuke to Sir Henry Unton in the bitter terms which Elizabeth desired. The report is by Cecil to Hatton, and reflects the concern of Burghley that Hatton should know how diligently he is trying to protect the lord chancellor's client.

[177] *Ibid.*, fol. 34v. Cf. *Unton corr.*, p. 143.

[178] UCL, Ogden MS 7/41, fol. 19[r].

[179] *Apologie*, sig. A1[v]. Significantly, Essex gave the name of Walter to the son which his wife bore in January 1592 (Bannerman, *The registers of St Olave*, p. 15). The child died only a month later.

[180] BLO, MS Eng.hist.c.61, fol. 6[r] (printed in R. Poole, 'A journal of the siege of Rouen in 1591', *EHR* 17 (1902), p. 530). At Court, there was an unsuccessful attempt to keep the news from Elizabeth for fear it would still further weaken her support for the expedition (UCL, Ogden MS 7/41, fols. 28[v], 31[r]).

[181] *Unton corr.*, pp. 69, 77, 79, 81; PRO, SP 78/25, fols. 275[r], 285[r], 294[r], 297[r–v], 312[r], 390[r].

demanded that he abandon his command and return home.[182] Together, these shocks had a shatteringly visceral impact upon Essex. Henry Killigrew reported that the arrival of the queen's latest letter 'put his honour in suche an extreme agony and passion that he sownded often and did so swell that, castyng hem selfe upon his bed, all his bottons of his doblett brake away as thoth they had ben cut with a kneffe'.[183] Apart from grief at the death of his brother, the prospect of his humiliating recall let loose upon Essex all the emotional energy which he had invested in the success of the expedition.[184] These few days of despair reveal something of the gloom to which Essex was so prone when faced with crisis, and which came to hang like a pall over the last years of his career. By striking at his martial ambition and his acute sense of noble honour, these twin blows undercut nothing less than the primary manifestations of his sense of self-identity. For a few days, he felt that he had nothing left to him but 'to curse my birth day and to long for my grave'.[185]

Although Essex soon recovered from this black despair, the true resurrection of his hopes came with Elizabeth's decision to extend his command.[186] This ultimately did little for Essex's pursuit of military renown. The belief that he might snatch some glory from the fag-end of a dwindling campaign proved no more than a mirage, and by early in the New Year he was glad to return home.[187] The true importance of the continuation of his command was political. By reversing her decision to call Essex home, Elizabeth accepted the arguments put forward by the earl and his advisers in France, thereby tacitly recognising that she and Burghley could no longer try entirely to control operations from afar. In itself, this opened the way for Essex to exercise more independence in his command. However, because he returned to England as he was ordered and put his case in person, Essex also made Elizabeth accept him as a true general in a more direct manner.[188] Thereafter, the demeaning and abusive comments in the queen's correspondence with him ceased.[189] Upon his return to France, Elizabeth

---

[182] PRO, SP 78/25, fols. 348^r, 352^r, 388^{r-v}. The postscript to the last letter scolds Essex that he should understand the queen's reasons for his recall, 'if yow be not senseless'. Although the hand is Burghley's, the words are clearly those of Elizabeth.

[183] *Ibid.*, fol. 294^r.

[184] For Essex's reaction to these blows, see the Hulton MS (formerly BL, Loan 23), fols. 19^r–20^r, 22^r, 25^r; PRO, SP 78/25, fols. 299^r–300^r, 365^r–6^v, 390^{r-v}.

[185] Hulton MS (formerly BL, Loan 23), fol. 20^r.

[186] *Unton corr.*, p. 186.   [187] *Ibid.*, p. 260.

[188] Essex left for England on the evening of 8 October and returned to Dieppe eleven days later. He also made a second trip home to procure more supplies and to renew his command again between 19 November and 10 December.

[189] For all this, see Lloyd, *Rouen campaign*, pp. 124–5; Wernham, *After the Armada*, pp. 354–6.

also accepted and acted upon his military advice about the necessity of sending reinforcements.[190] Essex's new importance was further underlined by the poor state into which the army had fallen in his absence. Reportedly, only his return prevented a mutiny.[191]

Seen in a larger context, the confirmation of Essex's command at Rouen in October 1591 opened a new phase in his career. By forcing Elizabeth to treat him as a real soldier, Essex made a giant step in his 'ambition of warr' at Rouen. No longer was he merely a grand gentleman adventurer, as he had been in Portugal, or a hobbled commander, as he had been at the outset in Normandy. From being a kind of glorified pawn, he had graduated to become a genuine knight, a true general. As a result, Essex could legitimately aspire to Leicester's mantle as the realm's chief aristocratic commander, 'the generall hope of al souldiors'.[192] Essex's political stature also increased. After this, he could never again be considered at Court as merely the queen's favourite. Although he had needed the support of senior councillors to do so, he had faced the queen's determined efforts to recall him and defeated them. Essex's command in Normandy also swelled his reputation on the international scene. In France, in particular, his aristocratic bearing and martial zeal had a powerful impact and firmly cemented his friendship with Henri IV.[193] Essex could now genuinely lay claim to the role of Walsingham – and of Leicester before him – as the leading advocate of the overseas Protestant cause in English politics.

Despite these advances, Essex was profoundly disappointed by the Rouen campaign. He won no great victory in Normandy. The impatient hopes of glory – and consequent political influence – which he had harboured before his departure came to nothing. Elizabeth's recognition of him as a responsible commander could not disguise the fact that she had become thoroughly hostile to the Rouen expedition, and Essex with it. When the chancellorship of Oxford again fell vacant after Hatton's death

---

[190] PRO, SP 78/26, fols. 142[r]–143[r].

[191] Ibid., fols. 52[r], 54[r], 58[r–v], 72[r]–73[r], 74[v]. For Essex's vigorous measures to restore order to the army, see ibid., fols. 121[r], 148[r]; Sir Thomas Coningsby, 'Journal of the siege of Rouen, 1591', J. G. Nichols (ed.), Camden Miscellany 1 (1847), p. 30.

[192] Matthew Sutcliffe, The practice, procedings and lawes of armes ... (London, 1593, STC no. 23468), sig. B2[v].

[193] Essex was praised, for example, for the lavishness of his train when he met Henri IV near Noyon in August. Accompanied by sixty gentlemen attendants, he went to meet the king preceded by six trumpeters and six pages on great horses with rich harnesses and wearing Devereux orange with gold embroidery. A French observer reckoned the value of Essex's own attire and the harness of his horse alone as worth at least 60,000 crowns ([Pierre Cayet], Chronologie novenaire, contenant l'histoire de la guerre, sous le regne du tres chrestien roy de France & de Navarre Henry IIII (3 vols., Paris, 1608), II, book 3, fols. 464[v]–465[r]).

in late November, Elizabeth made sure that Essex did not win the post.[194] Essex was now on the threshold of attaining a new weight and significance in politics but, ironically, his position when he returned from Rouen at the start of 1592 was all the more difficult because of that. How Essex managed to cross this threshold, and to advance himself beyond it in pursuit of his high ambitions, is the subject of the succeeding chapters.

[194] BL, Add. MS 6177, fol. 14ʳ. Du Plessis, the French king's special envoy, claimed that Elizabeth deliberately denied Essex the chancellorship in order to punish him for his continuing unwillingness to give up his command in France (Philippe de Mornay, sieur du Plessis, *Mémoires et correspondance pour servir à l'histoire de la Réformation* ... *édition complète* ... (12 vols., Paris, 1824–5), V, p. 170). For the lobbying of Essex's servants on his behalf in Oxford, see *HMCS*, IV, pp. 162–3. Encouraged by the queen, Whitgift weighed in against Essex's candidacy, which caused some difficulties between the two men for a period (LPL, MS 2004, fol. 7ʳ; Paule, *Life of Whitgift*, pp. 55–6).

Part II

THE QUEST FOR GREATNESS: 1593–1597

'One of her Majestie's privy councillors'

At the beginning of 1592, after his final return from France,[1] Essex reached a crucial turning-point in his political career. Essex returned from his first overseas command with his personal status enhanced in subtle but significant ways. Now that Elizabeth had been forced to accept him as a fully-fledged general, he was no longer merely an aspiring soldier and her special favourite. However, Rouen had also proved a hard lesson. Essex's aristocratic pride was deeply bruised by the failure of the campaign to achieve its objectives and by the finality of his departure. As he wrote to the French king, 'I am very ashamed that we English have so soon quitted your Majesty's service.'[2] Despite his best efforts and huge expenditure, the painful experiences in Normandy had dashed his hopes that he might be able to advance himself – and promote the cause of large-scale assistance to Henri IV – by soldiering alone. For all the conscious bravado of his final farewell to his troops,[3] Essex's departure from his command acknowledged the truth of the advice which had bombarded him from every quarter. He now had to accept that, in the short term at least, the place where he could do the greatest good to the Protestant cause, to Henri IV and to his own fortunes was not in the field, but back at Court.

In the weeks immediately after his return, Essex's thoughts remained with the siege at Rouen and his heart with the cause of the French king.[4] Anxious for the latest news, he maintained a weekly correspondence with Sir Henry Unton, who remained as ambassador there.[5] He also pressed

---

[1] Accompanied by Sir Thomas Leighton, Essex returned to Court on 14 January 1592 (*HMCS*, XIII, p. 464).

[2] Tenison, VIII, p. 573.

[3] 'Ce seigneur, en s'embarquant pour l'Angleterre, tira l'epée et en baissa la lame' (quoted without reference in Devereux, *Lives*, I, p. 275).

[4] Essex's letter to Henri of 10 January 1592, on the eve of his return, is highly instructive: 'next after my conscience to God and loyalty to her Majesty my sovereign, there is nothing I hold so dear as the favour of your Majesty ... I hope your Majesty believes that a nobleman, having given his faith to a Prince with so much affection as I have often shown, will not be inconstant in his profession nor fail of his word' (Tenison, VIII, pp. 573–4).

[5] *Unton corr.*, p. 372.

Elizabeth to reinforce her troops in Normandy. Ultimately, she agreed to send more men, but this was not the work of Essex alone. Recognising the force of circumstances and the urgings which assailed her from all sides, Elizabeth finally made up her own mind that action was needed.[6] When it came to the point, Essex's personal urging of the French cause, for all its passion, did Henri IV no great good. As Essex confessed to Unton: 'the queen sayth [I] am too partiall and doth not beleeve me'.[7] Although she welcomed his return to Court and allowed him the intimacy through which he was able to press her for aid to France, Elizabeth still could not really accept Essex as a responsible adviser on foreign affairs.

This put Essex in an awkward position. At Rouen, he had tried to promote both himself and the policy of large-scale military aid to the French king by endeavour on the battlefield, and had failed. Now all Essex's hopes of influencing the queen's foreign policy – and of winning opportunities to pursue his 'ambition of warr' in the future – rested entirely upon his ability to convince her by direct personal argument. In the past, he had had some success in this. As the French ambassador informed his master in 1590, Essex was 'infiniment affectioné; il ne laisse de donner les bons coups, et bien à propos, quant il peut'.[8] Such good turns by Essex included expediting the dispatch of powder across the Channel and helping the French ambassador press Elizabeth to send troops to Brittany.[9] Yet, in light of the huge scale of ambition which he had displayed at Rouen, it is clear that Essex could no longer afford to be content with such a marginal role in the queen's affairs. As a result, Essex now began a major effort to win over his sovereign by presenting himself in a new light: he 'resolved to give this satisfaction to the queen, as to desist for a tyme from his cowrse of the warrs and to intend matters of state'.[10]

At one level, this new resolution was simply good sense. In seeking to give 'satisfaction', Essex sought to reinforce his special personal relationship with Elizabeth, which had been severely strained by mutual recriminations during his time in Normandy. By showing a new willingness to accommodate himself to royal desires, Essex offered a clear contrast with the wilfulness of which she had so sharply accused him when he served in France. As such, he could demonstrate that he had learned a lesson from his time abroad and increase the likelihood that Elizabeth might listen to his arguments with favour. At another level, however, this new pose of

[6] R. B. Wernham, *After the Armada: Elizabethan England and the struggle for western Europe 1588-1595* (Oxford, 1984), pp. 379–81.
[7] BL, Cotton MS Caligula E VIII, fol. 176ʳ.
[8] [Francis H. Egerton, 8th earl of Bridgewater], *The life of Thomas Egerton lord chancellor of England* (Paris, [1816]), p. 354.
[9] *Ibid.*, pp. 355, 385.   [10] LPL, MS 653, fol. 3ʳ.

moderation and self-control embodied a major turning-point in Essex's career. Significantly, it was about this time that he began to alter his signature to reflect this refashioning: instead of 'R. Essex', he became plain 'Essex'.

Since the start of his political career, Essex had always shown himself to be remarkably single-minded in his efforts to follow his 'ambition of warr'. Now, for the first time, he recognised that he had to step aside from this 'cowrse of the warrs' in favour of a new ambition, 'to intend matters of state'. Of course, the intentions behind this change ultimately still reflected his martial aspirations: Essex hoped to please Elizabeth and to encourage her to pursue policies which would eventually allow him the chance to campaign again. Nevertheless, he was now thinking in the longer term. His previous frustrations about conforming himself to the desires of an old woman and his impatience for her demise were put aside – 'for a tyme' at least. This new perspective had far-reaching effects. Rather than merely refurbishing his relations with the queen, Essex's new resolution laid the basis for a remodelling of his whole political stance – a more gradual but ultimately far more dramatic development than his previous struggle to be recognised as more than a courtly ornament. To his growing reputation as a soldier and favourite, Essex now added the objective of becoming a formal participant in state affairs as a member of the privy council. By winning a place on the council he would gain formal endorsement of his right to advise the queen and open recognition that he had an important part to play in public affairs.

Although he had not previously signalled his intentions so clearly, Essex had undoubtedly been looking towards a place on the council well before early 1592. In June 1590, the French ambassador had reported of Essex to his king that 'il faict ce qu'il peut. Mais n'estant que du conseil privé, et non de celuy d'estat, il ne peut pas beaucoup.'[11] Essex and his friends were all too aware of his lack of conciliar status. Since the late 1530s, a seat on the privy council had been a virtual prerequisite for involvement in politics at the highest level.[12] Essex undoubtedly hoped to gain a closer association with council affairs when he secretly married Lady Sidney, but these hopes were thwarted when Secretary Walsingham died before the marriage could

[11] BL, Egerton MS 6, fol. 69ᵛ. This analysis reflects the French pattern of a separate 'privy' council, which kept close attendance upon the sovereign, and a distinct council of state, which included all the great aristocratic office-holders (R. Dallington, *The view of France* (London, 1604, STC no. 6202), sig. Q4ʳ⁻ᵛ). The Elizabethan privy council combined both of these roles. Essex remained in close attendance on the queen and offered her advice whenever she seemed receptive, but, because he was not a councillor, his actions were completely informal.
[12] D. Starkey (ed.), *Rivals in power: lives and letters of the great Tudor dynasties* (London, 1990), p. 16.

even be made public.[13] Nevertheless, the direction of Essex's ambition was obvious. Essex's reported impatience at the continuing sway of Burghley and Hatton in 1591 clearly implied that he wished to supplant them as the dominant influences on the council. Almost certainly, he had hoped a place at the council board would be one of the rewards which he would gain for winning glory in Normandy.

After Essex's return from France, the importance of his attaining conciliar status grew. Apart from his own burning desire to convince Elizabeth that he offered responsible advice on foreign matters, Essex learned that he had been denied the chancellorship of Oxford partly because he lacked conciliar status. This news added salt to the wound of this disappointment.[14] Winning a place at the council board also seemed more urgently necessary – and perhaps more rapidly attainable – because of Hatton's death in November 1591.[15] With his passing, Essex again lost a senior figure who had helped to push forward his career and cushion the impact of his mistakes. Nevertheless, Essex clearly hoped that this latest death among the council would accelerate the transfer of political power to younger men like himself.

Hatton's passing radically changed the political balance at the heart of the Elizabethan regime. The old collegiality of the privy council – the familiar, occasionally awkward, co-operation among men who had long become accustomed to working together for the queen's service – was dead. As the last fully active survivor of his generation, old Lord Burghley no longer had any equals. No lord steward was ever appointed to replace Leicester and no lord chancellor was chosen to take the place of Hatton.[16] As lord treasurer, master of the court of wards, acting secretary of state, confidant of the queen for nearly forty years and long-time patron of many of the men who filled bureaucratic posts at Court and across the realm, Burghley's dominance of government in the early 1590s was unequalled. According to the Florentine Petruccio Ubaldini, other members of the privy council consistently looked to Burghley's guidance – so much so that he was, in effect, the driving force behind all matters and the determiner of every perplexity.[17]

---

13 G. Goodman, *The Court of James the First* (ed. J. S. Brewer, 2 vols., London, 1839), I, pp. 147–8.
14 Sir George Paule, *The life of the most reverend and religious prelate John Whitgift Lord Archbishop of Canterbury* (London, 1612, STC no. 19484), p. 56.
15 Hatton died at his London house, Ely Place, on 20 November 1591. For a drawing of the elaborate procession which accompanied his coffin to burial in St Paul's Cathedral on 16 December, see FSL, MS Z.e.3 (a roll).
16 Hatton's successor as head of the legal system, Sir John Puckering, was a career lawyer. He received the lesser office of keeper of the privy seal. For Puckering, see below, p. 290.
17 '... esendo egli in effetto il motore delle cose et lo deffinitore d'ogni perplessità' (A. M.

Ironically, Burghley's unprecedented dominance in the queen's counsels opened up possibilities for Essex. After so many deaths among the old councillors, new appointments were needed to sustain the burden of work. With Sir Robert Cecil's appointment to the council in the previous August and Ralegh still anathema to 'the greatest' at Court, Essex was the obvious candidate from the younger generation who might be advanced to fill this place. Soon after Essex's return from France, Cecil opined to Unton that the earl might yet 'shortely receave some apparent marke [of royal favour] ... in the eye of the world'.[18] From Unton's reaction to this letter, it seems probable that he, at least, envisaged 'my lord of Essex advancement' in terms of appointment to the council.[19] For the time being, however, these speculations proved to be unfounded.

Over the course of 1592, Essex's promotion to the council became increasingly likely, and indeed inevitable. One reason was that he finally put an end to his long-running feud with Ralegh. This pleased the queen and suggested that Essex was putting his youthful excesses behind him. In the wake of his recovery from the revelation of his marriage and his successful quest to lead the Rouen expedition, Essex could afford to be magnanimous to his old rival. For his part, Ralegh had realised for some time that he could no longer compete with Essex and his powerful backers. Apart from occasional sniping, all he could do was wait for occasions when Essex angered the queen and quietly try to encourage her feelings of indignation. This is precisely what Ralegh did when he learned of the wholesale dubbing of knights by Essex in Normandy in October 1591. It is not hard to imagine the glee with which Ralegh imparted this news to Elizabeth, carefully delaying his intervention until Hatton had left the royal presence.[20] Yet even this indiscretion was not enough to weaken Essex's hold on favour for long. After Hatton's death in November, Ralegh finally obtained an office at Court, succeeding to the post of captain of the guard.[21] Soon after, he was granted the manor of Sherborne in Dorset which he had coveted for years.[22] However, this success swiftly became a

Crino, 'Avvisi di Londra di Petruccio Ubaldini, fiorentino, relativi agli anni 1579–1594, con notizie sulla guerra di Flandra', *Archivio Storico Italiano* 127 (1969), p. 502). This report is dated 15 February 1592. Ubaldini had long experience of England and was very well connected: F. Bugliani, 'Petruccio Ubaldini's *Accounts of England*', *Renaissance Studies* 8 (1994), pp. 175–97.

[18] *Unton corr.*, p. 287.
[19] *Ibid.*, pp. 328–9. For Unton's comments on this matter, see also *ibid.*, pp. 329–30, 398–9.
[20] UCL, Ogden MS 7/41, fol. 24ʳ, Cecil to Hatton, 27 October 1591.
[21] The first evidence of Ralegh's tenure as captain of the guard is a warrant for the guard's liveries, dated 7 April 1592 (BL, Add. MS 5750, fol. 114ʳ).
[22] J. H. Adamson and H. F. Folland, *The shepherd of the oceans: an account of Sir Walter Ralegh and his times* (Boston, 1969), 199; P. A. Howe, 'The Ralegh papers at Sherborne Castle', *History Today* 21 (March 1971), pp. 213–14. This manor belonged to the see of

hostage to fortune. Ralegh himself became critically vulnerable to royal displeasure when he secretly married Elizabeth Throckmorton, one of the queen's maids of honour. Although this may have occurred as early as February 1588, it seems more likely that Ralegh did not marry until November 1591, when his wife was already several months pregnant.[23]

By early 1592, Essex's desire to please the queen and Ralegh's urgent need to win Essex's support produced an extraordinary rapprochement between the two men, who were once such bitter rivals.[24] Like Sir Charles Blount before him, Ralegh now saw the emnity of Essex transformed into generous friendship. On 10 April, Arthur Throckmorton, Ralegh's brother-in-law, recorded that 'Damerei Raelly was baptyzed by Robert Earlle of Essesxes and Ar[thur] Throkemorton and Anna Throkemorton.'[25] A fortnight later, at the St George's Day celebrations, Essex nominated Ralegh as a possible knight of the garter – the most exclusive social group in the realm.[26] However, Ralegh's secret life caught up with him. Having denied rumours that he was married, Ralegh soon stood revealed as a bare-faced liar and suffered a more complete exclusion from Court than any other favourite of the reign. Imprisoned at the end of May, he was sequestered from his captaincy of the guard and banned from the Court indefinitely.[27] Ralegh's shattering fall left Essex unchallenged as Elizabeth's only favourite and enabled him to set about transforming himself with a new sense of security about his relationship with the queen.

Essex's efforts to cultivate a more mature and sober image in Elizabeth's

---

Salisbury. For Ralegh's long and unscrupulous campaign to strip it from the bishop, see the comments of Sir John Harington in his 'A briefe view of the state of the Church of England as it stood in Q. Elizabeth's and king James his reigne to the yeere 1608', in T. Park (ed.), *Nugae antiquae: being a miscellaneous collection of original papers … by Sir John Harington* (2 vols., London, 1804), II, pp. 124–7, 129.

23 A. L. Rowse, *Ralegh and the Throckmortons* (London, 1962), p. 160. The earlier date is advanced, on the basis of a legal document relating to the transfer of property, in P. Lefranc, 'La date du mariage de Sir Walter Ralegh: un document inédit', *Etudes Anglaises* 9 (1956), pp. 192–211. It seems more likely that a legal document could be deliberately deceptive about the date of Ralegh's marriage than that Elizabeth Throckmorton could have deceived her brother (to whom she was very close) for so long.

24 One public sign of this reconciliation was a positive reference to Essex's participation in the Portugal expedition in Ralegh's account of the loss of the *Revenge*, published anonymously in late 1591: *A report of the truth of the fight about the Iles of the Acores* (London, 1591, *STC* no. 20651), sig. A4ᵛ.

25 Cathedral Archives, Canterbury, 'Diary of Arthur Throckmorton', II, fol. 104ʳ. Damerei Ralegh had been born on 29 March. For the historical, indeed aristocratic, pretensions behind this choice of name, see S. W. May, *Sir Walter Ralegh* (Boston, 1989), p. 12.

26 BL, Add. MS 36768, fol. 31ᵛ. Essex was the only knight to advance Ralegh's name.

27 Rowse, *Ralegh and the Throckmortons*, pp. 160–4. Charles Nicholl speculates that news of Ralegh's marriage was reported to Elizabeth by the lord chamberlain, Lord Hunsdon, or by his son, Sir George Carey, the knight marshal. Nicholl suggests that they may have heard the story from one Charles Chester (*A cup of news: the life of Thomas Nashe* (London, 1984), pp. 104–6).

eyes were also demonstrated by other gestures of moderation. Acting upon hints from the queen, Essex entered into closer friendship with Archbishop Whitgift[28] and toned down his previously open support of puritans during this period. Essex underlined his concern with national security by presenting Elizabeth with a growing stream of intelligence gathered by agents in his employment.[29] Despite his weak financial position after the enormous costs of the Rouen campaign, Essex also continued to correspond with leading men in allied nations and to offer hospitality to dignitaries who visited England, such as the heir to the duke of Württemberg, whom Essex welcomed on the queen's behalf in August 1592.[30]

In all this, Elizabeth clearly supported Essex. Her desire was always to encourage and channel his vigour for the benefit of her service. Yet, as she had shown over the Rouen expedition, Elizabeth never hesitated to criticise Essex when she felt that he might be disregarding her orders in pursuit of his own conception of what her service required. When she perceived that Essex's exalted view of war might be leading him to commit her too deeply to the 'common cause' of Henri IV or endangering his own life, the full corrective force of her anger was turned against him. Now that he was bent on giving the queen 'satisfaction', royal comments took a distinctly more positive tone. According to one report, Elizabeth even briefly considered appointing Essex to the council in July. Much to Essex's dismay, she accepted Burghley's advice that he be spared 'for a whyle, untill he hathe gotten more experience'.[31]

Despite this delay, Essex's promotion seemed increasingly urgent because of the obvious imbalance in the council. After so many deaths among its leading members, the council had declined precipitously both in numerical strength and in the 'quality', or social standing, of its membership. As Catholic propagandists eagerly observed and imputed to sinister purposes, the composition of the privy council at the beginning of the 1590s was striking for the absence of the higher nobility.[32] Whereas there had been four earls on the council in 1588, in 1591 there was only the old earl of

---

[28] Paule, *Life of Whitgift*, pp. 56–7.

[29] Essex's sponsorship of intelligence is discussed at length in the following chapter.

[30] W. B. Rye, *England as seen by foreigners in the days of Elizabeth and James the First. Comprising translations of the journals of the two dukes of Wirtemberg in 1592 and 1610* (London, 1865), pp. 11–13, 46.

[31] A. G. Petti (ed.), *The letters and despatches of Richard Verstegan (c. 1550-1640)* (Catholic Record Society, LII, 1959), p. 59.

[32] For Burghley's continuing sensitivity about such criticism from 'they that malitiously doe reprehend her [Majesty's] government', see his comments on the privy council in 'A medi[ta]tion of the state of England duringe the raigne [of t]he Quene Elizabeth', which was written in 1594–5 (PRO, SP 12/255, fols. 149^r–150^r).

Derby, who was a regular absentee.[33] By 1592, when Burghley was branded by 'John Philopatris' as a deliberate suppresser of the ancient nobility,[34] talk of impending noble appointments to the council was keeping some peers in anxious suspense.[35] When Essex was finally sworn to the council in February 1593, it was expected that the earl of Shrewsbury and other peers would also be appointed.[36] In the event, only Essex was so favoured. Shrewsbury had to wait until Elizabeth again felt the need of an aristocratic bolstering to her council – significantly enough, after the fall of Essex.[37]

The privy council of the early 1590s was also remarkably elderly. In February 1593, the average age of councillors was almost sixty.[38] Although Essex was just twenty-seven at the time of his appointment, his arrival only lowered the average age to fifty-six. Moreover, only three councillors were not born in the 1520s or 1530s – Essex, Cecil (then aged twenty-nine) and Lord Keeper Puckering, who was aged about fifty. All the other councillors had begun their careers by the 1550s, and some as far back as the late 1530s. This was clearly a body in desperate need of new blood.

Essex offered not only the prospect of youthful vigour for the privy council but also valuable political resources. His sponsorship of intelligence-gathering saved Elizabeth money and helped to sharpen her understanding of events overseas, whilst his increasingly weighty foreign correspondence indicated respect abroad for his zeal in the Protestant cause. Essex's special commitment to war and soldiers also coincided with the needs of a regime struggling to cope with a conflict which seemed to be sprawling out of control and straining resources beyond their limits. In the expeditions to Normandy and Portugal, Essex had demonstrated that he was the realm's most committed individual advocate of soldiers' fortunes and opinions. Simply in terms of personnel management, such a major patron of officers could not be divorced from the making of military policy for long. Essex's ardent 'ambition of warr' also provided a useful balance to Burghley's well-known sense of caution: adding Essex to the council would

---

[33] In 1590, for example, Derby only once signed a council letter (*APC*, XIX, *1590*, p. 8). In 1593, he was a regular participant in council affairs during the time of the parliament and for the following few weeks. However, he died on 25 September, aged sixty-two (*TCP*, IV, p. 212).

[34] BL, Add. MS 12510, esp. fols. 8ʳ, 22ʳ.   [35] Petti, *Verstegan letters*, pp. 58–9.

[36] LPL, MS 648, fol. 162ʳ; LPL, MS 701, p. 141; BL, Cotton MS Caligula E IX(i), fol. 181ʳ. Among the other expectant peers was probably Roger, Lord North. He had gone to Court in the hope of being appointed to the council, only to be disappointed, in June 1591 (LPL, MS 3199, p. 321). He was still trying in May 1596 (LPL, MS 657, fol. 108ᵛ). North finally succeeded in his quest in September 1596 (*APC*, XXVI, *1596–7*, p. 135).

[37] *APC*, XXXI, *1600–1*, p. 467.

[38] This calculation is approximate because the birth dates of some councillors remain somewhat uncertain.

enable Elizabeth to obtain policy advice which was contested, or at least thoroughly argued. Promoting Essex would also give formal voice to an important vein of political opinion – the supporters of the 'Protestant cause' – which had been missing from her regime since the death of Walsingham.

Although Essex's ultimate elevation to the privy council was probably inevitable once he set himself to achieving it, its precise timing depended upon the calling of a parliament for early 1593. By his vigorous efforts to secure the election of a significant number of his friends and followers,[39] Essex reminded Elizabeth that he had political weight within the realm and that he had a following which could be useful to her. Perhaps even more importantly, the main purpose for which this assembly was summoned – to raise further money for the conduct of the war[40] – matched Essex's own well-known political interests perfectly. What better sign could Elizabeth give to the parliament of her commitment to the effective military use of their taxes than by promoting the best-known military nobleman to her privy council?

The case for Essex's advancement was further strengthened by the demands of managing the parliament. During February, Burghley, the queen's chief parliamentary manager, was ill.[41] Given its declining noble membership, this meant that the privy council looked decidedly weak in the House of Lords. Essex's appointment would give the council a voice among the senior nobility and help to spread the load entailed in representing conciliar interests in the debates and committee work of the Upper House. At the same time, Essex's supporters in the Commons would be made available to support the council's demand for a large new subsidy.

Taken together, these reasons proved sufficient to persuade Elizabeth that the time had come to end Essex's political apprenticeship. About four o'clock in the afternoon of Sunday 25 February 1593, Essex took the oaths of supremacy and of a privy councillor.[42] At last, all his efforts to win a place at the council board had gained their reward. Officially and publicly, Essex was now recognised as one of the queen's advisers in matters of state.

---

[39] *Commons*, I, 63–5; J. E. Neale, *The Elizabethan House of Commons* (Harmondsworth, revised 1963 edn), pp. 56–7, 161–2, 227–8.

[40] J. E. Neale, *Elizabeth I and her parliaments 1584–1601* (London, 1957), pp. 241, 246–8.

[41] Petti, *Verstegan letters*, p. 104. Burghley had recovered sufficiently over the course of March and April to take up the full burden of government (*ibid.*, p. 126; BL, Cotton MS Caligula E IX(i), fol. 181ʳ), although he subsequently suffered a relapse in May which may have been the result of over-exertion (CUL, Ee.iii.56, no. 5). For Burghley's pivotal role in parliamentary management, see M. A. R. Graves, *The Tudor parliaments: Crown, Lords and Commons, 1485–1603* (Harlow, 1985), pp. 136, 137, 145–52.

[42] *APC*, XXIV, 1592–3, p. 78; FSL, L.a.45.

Essex, the soldier and favourite, had finally succeeded in making himself a genuine politician.

After his elevation to the privy council, Essex went through a brief period of trying to prove himself in his new role. Ever conscious of his public image and anxious to win favour with his new colleagues, Essex immediately sought to act like the ideal young councillor. 'Hys lordship is become a newe man', one of his followers reported, 'cleare forsakinge all hys former youthfull trickes, cariinge hym sealf with very honorable gravyty and singulerly lyked of, boath in parliament and at [the] counsayle table.'[43] Having successfully remodelled himself as a politician, Essex now sought to perfect his new image.

Essex threw himself into his new role with enormous energy and vigour. These qualities, indeed, were to become hallmarks of his career as a councillor up to the end of 1597. Throughout, Essex proved a dedicated politician, and one who worked hard at being a councillor. As he himself later advised the young earl of Rutland in 1596, 'the first thing your lordship must seeke in all this course is industrie, for as greate difference is betwixt it and idlenes ... as betwixt a lyving [man] and a dead'.[44] This was a moral as well as a political imperative, for 'industrie' was a sign of virtue and 'idlenes' its nemesis. While the parliament was in session, Essex attended sittings in the House of Lords. In the afternoon and early morning, he was busy 'upon comittees for the better pennyng & amendment of matter in bills of importance'.[45] Outside the parliament, membership of the council acquainted him with the sheer hard work of daily confronting 'a world of papers'.[46] At times, he had to cope with urgent papers being thrust into his hands even before he could get out of bed.[47] Although he was no bureaucrat, Essex remained fairly diligent in fighting this constant battle with paperwork. As his personal secretary reported on one occasion in late 1594, he 'hath bene much payned all this daye in his head, and yet [he] hath not spared hymself to peruse his dispatches, so carefull is he of her Majeste's service'.[48]

Quite how careful Essex was of the queen's service can be gauged from the surviving formal records of his activities as a member of the council board. These records throw light on two spheres of his conciliar activity: his participation in council meetings and in parliaments. Records of his attendance and behaviour in Star Chamber, where councillors most

---

[43] FSL, L.a.45. See also FSL, L.a.267; BL, Cotton MS Caligula E IX(i), fol. 181[r].
[44] Hulton MS (formerly BL, Loan 23), fol. 147[v].   [45] FSL, L.a.269.
[46] LPL, MS 653, fol. 293[r]. Essex complained that this mass of papers had built up during an absence from Court of only two days.
[47] PRO, SP 12/247, fol. 159[r].   [48] LPL, MS 648, fol. 100[r].

explicitly exercised a crucial judicial function, have not survived.[49] This problem of the survival of evidence also affects the most important single source for studying Essex's conciliar activities, the registers of the privy council. No registers survive for the period from the end of August 1593 until the beginning of October 1595. Unfortunately, this was the very period when Essex established himself as a truly influential politician.

Despite this hiatus, the council registers provide a quantifiable indication of Essex's involvement in council business. From the time of his appointment as a councillor at the end of February 1593 until 26 August 1593, when the record fails, he was recorded as being present at 71 per cent of the council's meetings.[50] This creditable attendance perhaps reflected his desire to establish himself as a member of the board. By late 1595, when the record is again available, his rate of attendance was down, perhaps because his energies had now become more dispersed in the very broad range of his activities. For the period from 2 October 1595 until the end of that year, he attended only 59 per cent of council meetings.

In 1596 and 1597, Essex's participation in meetings was disrupted by his departure to lead expeditionary forces for the queen. As might be expected, his involvement in the preparation of these forces ensured that he had a central role in the conciliar business during the months immediately preceding each expedition. However, despite this general similarity, the patterns of Essex's attendance at council meetings differed sharply between 1596 and 1597. During the period between 4 January and 9 April 1596, when he left to oversee the intended relief of Calais, Essex was noted as present at 84 per cent of meetings. After his return from Cadiz, when his actions abroad were the subject of intense scrutiny, he was even more active in council. From 9 August until the end of 1596, his attendance rate increased to 92 per cent. In the following year, however, despite the same pattern of a lengthy absence due to military service, Essex's attendance was strikingly down. In the period before his departure for Plymouth in the middle of June 1597, he was present at only 67 per cent of meetings. After his return from the Azores, his record was even worse: a mere 8 per cent.

---

[49] There is very little extant evidence about Essex's conduct in Star Chamber. Although Francis Bacon refers to the earl's 'diligence' there (Spedding, *Bacon letters*, II, pp. 43–4), the surviving sources throw little light on how regularly he attended Star Chamber. See 'Career', pp. 72, n. 35. Additional material on the meals consumed by councillors is equally unhelpful in this matter (PRO, E 407/53).

[50] This and the following percentages of recorded attendances are calculated from *APC*, vols. XXIV–XXVIII. These figures include only those occasions when the clerk of the council clearly records an actual meeting of the privy council. Occasions when councillors merely signed letters are excluded because, although they are indicate attendance at Court, they by no means indicate attendance at the council meeting itself. For further details of these figures, see 'Career', pp. 72–3.

The explanation for both sets of figures for 1597 lies in the changed political environment. By 1597, Essex and his supporters were becoming alienated from the politics at Court. Essex's attendance at council meetings in the months before the Azores expedition was reduced by his prolonged withdrawal from Court in March, allegedly on the grounds of sickness and a desire to visit his Welsh estates. After his return from that expedition, Essex's absence from the council amounted to a deliberate boycotting of the queen's business. This extraordinary episode exemplified in an extreme manner the tension between Essex's twin roles as favourite and councillor. By withdrawing from public service until he received satisfaction from the queen, he disrupted the proceedings of the council with the necessarily personal tactics of a favourite. Only after he had been promised the office of earl marshal did he return for virtually the last meeting of the year.

A similar pattern of general diligence marred by disenchantment in 1597 can be seen in Essex's record of attendance in parliaments. In 1593, when he was first appointed to the council, he was noted as being present for 91 per cent of the sittings for which the clerk recorded attendance in the Lords.[51] Even Burghley, at 88 per cent, did not quite manage to match this degree of assiduity. It was also a considerable change from Essex's own previous record. Having become eligible when his knighthood released him from wardship in October 1586, he took his seat in the House of Lords in the latter stages of the 1586–7 parliament, on 23 February 1587. From then until the end of the parliament, he attended only 31 per cent of the sittings. In 1589 his record was better, but still only reached 63 per cent of the sittings for which attendances were recorded. Clearly, elevation to the council did make him 'a newe man' in parliament, encouraging him to display a degree of diligence far beyond that of earlier years.

In late 1597, when a parliament next met, Essex kept himself aloof from the business of the realm, as he did from meetings of the council. Despite a motion suggested by Burghley to the Upper House which had the obvious purpose of forcing him to end his dereliction of duty, or to own up to it, Essex deliberately maintained his absence from parliament.[52] Not until his new appointment as earl marshal enabled him to take his place above the lord admiral did he finally appear in the Lords, on 11 January 1598. Thereafter, Essex attended each of the remaining twelve sittings of the House. Moreover, he was at once furiously busy with committee work. On

---

[51] The percentages for Essex's recorded attendances in the House of Lords are calculated from *Journals of the House of Lords*, II (London, 1846) [hereafter cited as *LJ*]. Instances where the clerk of the parliaments has failed to record attendances are, of course, excluded from the calculations. For further details of these figures, see 'Career', pp. 74–5.

[52] For Burghley's motion, see *LJ*, II, p. 196. Essex excused himself on the grounds of illness and the belated receipt of his summons to the parliament (*ibid.*, p. 198).

the day of his return, he was appointed to three separate committees and another on each of the following two days, as well as more in subsequent sittings.[53] Although the Lords' Journal for earlier parliaments makes it impossible to draw firm conclusions,[54] this flurry of work was probably also typical of his labours as a new councillor in 1593.

Beyond the formal records of attendance at council meetings and parliament, Essex's activities as a member of the privy council can overwhelmingly be seen to reflect his commitment to foreign and military matters. Burghley was scrupulously accurate when he described Essex, in an account of the council in 1595, as 'very well given, learned and adicted boath to warlike actions and to knowledg of all foraigne affaires'.[55] Although he was heavily involved in the overseeing of military expeditions and the provision of supplies for garrisons, Essex did not involve himself in the labyrinthine business of government finance. For all his 'addiction' to foreign and military affairs, there is also relatively little evidence that he was greatly occupied in these years with another staple of council business, events in Ireland.

Following his appointment as a councillor, Essex stuck to his resolution of 1592 to desist temporarily from seeking further military command overseas. Despite this, Essex's martial ambitions and following among soldiers were sustained by his involvement in a growing range of domestic military tasks. Such work naturally gravitated to Essex because of his passionate concern for war and because the council was critically short of men with military experience. Leicester had never been replaced and no new master of the ordnance was appointed after Warwick's death in 1590.[56] Besides Essex and the lord admiral (Lord Howard of Effingham), the only genuine soldier on the council was the lord chamberlain (Lord Hunsdon), who was old and increasingly unable to undertake vigorous activities. Ironically, this decline in martial leadership at the highest level came at a time when the demands of war were steadily expanding and when the privy council was exerting an ever-greater control over all aspects of the war effort. This trend had been evident for some time[57] but Essex's energy and enthusiasm for martial matters accentuated this process of centralisation and soon gave him an unprecedented – although not monopolistic –

[53] *Ibid.*, pp. 214ff.
[54] No lists of committee membership are recorded for the 1593 parliament and only a few for the 1588–9 parliament. Among the latter, Essex is recorded as a member of only one committee, that for the bill 'concerning captains and soldiers' (*ibid.*, pp. 148, 149).
[55] PRO, SP 12/255, fol. 150^r.
[56] R. W. Stewart, *The English ordnance office, 1585–1625: a case study in bureaucracy* (Woodbridge, 1996), p. 8.
[57] These developments are sketched in J. S. Nolan, 'The militarization of the Elizabethan state', *Journal of Military History* 58 (1994), pp. 391–420.

influence over war policy and military administration. Within only a few years, he made himself the chief political beneficiary of the war.

Of all his conciliar colleagues, Essex perhaps worked most regularly with the lord admiral. Now in his late fifties, Howard of Effingham was the only other active military leader on the council. In many ways, Essex gradually began to act in a similar capacity for land operations to that in which the lord admiral acted for the queen's sea forces, somewhere between a chief-of-staff and a commander-in-chief. The expertise and personal contacts of the two men also complemented each other. In times of crisis, they went to take joint charge of affairs on the coast, whence they reported back to Elizabeth and their conciliar colleagues who remained at Court. In October 1593, Essex and Howard were hastily ordered to Dover to supervise the defence of Ostend.[58] While Howard organised the shipping, Essex arranged for the despatch of ordnance to the town.[59] The same combination of earl and lord admiral was initially designated to lead an expedition to Brest in the following year.[60] However, Elizabeth decided that they were too valuable to risk overseas when the safety of the realm was not at stake and held them back from this command.[61] In 1596, Elizabeth grudgingly allowed Essex and Howard to serve as joint commanders of an expedition to Spain, but not before interrupting their preparations and ordering them to Dover in an abortive attempt to relieve the siege of Calais.[62]

As these actions suggest, Essex played an increasingly pre-eminent role in overseeing the defence of the realm. Shortly before hastening to Dover in 1593, he made a brief visit to Wiltshire and the Isle of Wight,[63] which was almost certainly a trip to inspect the defences along the south coast. In 1595, when it was feared that the Scilly Isles would be attacked, Essex oversaw the despatch of levies to defend them.[64] Soon afterwards, when Spanish ships actually raided Cornwall, Essex submitted written considerations to Elizabeth on how the realm should be defended against enemy attack, expressing his views in a dichotomous table, a means of structuring

---

[58] PRO, SP 84/47, fol. 126^r; BL, Cotton MS Caligula E IX(i), fol. 175^r. Essex's accounts indicate that the cost of his stay at Dover between 24 October and 1 November was £143 11s 6d (Devereux MS 3, fol. 77^v).

[59] PRO, SP 78/32, fol. 279^r.

[60] *HMC. Seventh report, Appendix* (London, 1879), p. 652. A warrant to the exchequer to release money to Sir Thomas Sherley, the queen's treasurer for her forces in France, described the expedition as 'under the charge of the erle of Essex and the lorde admirall' (PRO, SP 38/4, unfol., warrant of 20 July 1594).

[61] LPL, MS 650, fol. 227^{r-v}; *HMCS*, IV, p. 567.

[62] PRO, SP 12/257; *HMCS*, VI, pp. 141ff.

[63] LPL, MS 649, fol. 289^r. Essex's accounts record that this trip lasted from 16 to 20 September 1593 and cost him no less than £249 10s 2d (Devereux MS 3, fol. 77^v).

[64] CUL, Ee.iii.56, no. 54.

ideas which was associated with the Ramist logic he had learned at Cambridge.[65]

By 1595, Essex was widely recognised as playing a central role in military matters. In December 1595, Sir Ralph Lane claimed that 'the consultation of martial affairs doth particularly appertain' only to Essex and Burghley.[66] When a fresh rumour came during that month of a possible threat to Ostend, Essex felt confident enough of his position on the council to criticise his colleague, Lord Cobham, for not returning to Dover from his house in London.[67] The papers of Burghley also include notes which Essex wrote at this time about individual cavalry officers. These indicate Essex's deep familiarity with his nation's leading soldiers and a confident expectation that his judgements would be accepted. About Sir Nicholas Parker, for example, he wrote: 'he was in my time [in the Netherlands] lieutenant of Sir William Pelham's horse companie & hath since bin manie yeares captain & hath donne ever valiauntly in all incounters'. Sir John Wingfield had adequate cavalry experience '& was hurte at the incounter before Zutphen'.[68] Although almost a decade had passed, the experiences of his first military campaign and of that fateful clash at Zutphen were still fresh in his memory.

Essex's involvement in military administration reached its peak in 1596 and 1597, when he led naval expeditions against Spain and co-ordinated efforts to defend the realm against Spain's subsequent efforts at retaliation. Unlike previous years, his prominence in national defence in 1596 and 1597 depended upon his renewed status as an active general more than his dominance of military affairs on the council. In 1596, his victory at Cadiz made him England's most famous soldier and helped him to lead the *ad hoc* council of war which advised on how England should be defended.[69] As commander-in-chief, he embarked on a rapid tour of key coastal defences in mid-November.[70] In the emergency of October 1597, his appointment as

---

[65] LPL, MS 651, fol. 276[r–v]. This is a copy taken by Anthony Bacon.

[66] PRO, SP 63/185, fol. 45[r].   [67] *HMCS*, V, p. 492.

[68] BL, Lansdowne MS 78, fol. 138[r–v]. Essex also makes telling comments about incidents in the Portugal and Rouen expeditions. This document (endorsed with the date of 1 November 1595) is a secretarial copy, suggesting that it was only one of perhaps a number of copies made from Essex's notes. Burghley himself read this document because he endorsed it 'leaders of horse bandes'. Essex's own orginal notes are Cecil MS 47/85 (pr. *HMCS*, VI, pp. 570–1, where it is misdated as 1596).

[69] For this council's discussions according to the agenda set out by Essex, see PRO, SP 9/52, no. 23. The paper endorsed by Cecil as 'a concordance of opinions in the expectation of the Adelantado' was probably also a product of the views of this body (PRO, SP 12/260, fol. 142[r–v]). Burghley was the chairman of the committee (at Essex's insistence (*HMCS*, VI, p. 469)), but Essex clearly dominated the debate.

[70] PRO, SP12/261, fol. 39[r]; LPL, MS 660, fol. 103[r]. Essex also sent Sir Samuel Bagenal to help reinforce the defences on the Isle of Wight, where the 2nd Lord Hunsdon was in command

supreme commander of the realm's defences was even more clearly linked to his earlier appointment to lead an expeditionary force. The fleet with which Essex returned from the Azores was virtually the only force which could confront the Spanish in time[71] and his authority over that force was simply extended to embrace the whole of the area in which it might have to operate.[72]

Outside these short periods of crisis, Essex performed more routine military administration. In August 1593, Ralph Lane wrote to him about the methods employed in taking musters of the queen's forces in Ireland. Lane disagreed with the new system which had been instituted by the council and urged Essex to press for a revised procedure based upon the ancient Roman model, enclosing a paper on the subject to prove his point.[73] What Essex made of this request is unknown, although Lane's 'collecione and explicacione' based on reading and personal experience probably interested him greatly. A more mundane task was arranging for artillery and munitions to be sent to Brittany in July 1594, as he had done for Ostend in the preceding October.[74] In February 1595, he scrutinised the accounts for the new fortifications being built at Portsmouth with the lord treasurer and the lord admiral.[75] Seven months later, in the wake of the alarm caused by the raid on Cornwall, Essex combined with the lord admiral and the lord chamberlain to establish what stocks of munitions and ordnance remained available for defending the country.[76] The same three councillors also signed a contract with the armourers of London to provide new equipment.[77]

Essex's administrative abilities were most fully tested when he prepared his overseas expeditions in 1596 and 1597. These ventures demonstrated how fully, and competently,[78] Essex could master the administrative details of war. Indeed, his absorption in assembling and supplying these forces became almost total. As one of his servants complained in March 1596: 'he is in continewall labour. I thinke the husbandman endureth not more toyle. I wisshe it were the lesse, for it maketh hym the more hard to

(Gloucestershire Record Office, MF1161 (Berkeley MSS), fols. 85ʳ (Essex to Hunsdon, 11 November 1596), 93ʳ⁻ᵛ (Hunsdon to Cecil, 5 December 1596)).
[71] PRO, SP 12/264, fol. 228ʳ.   [72] *HMCS*, VII, 449–50.
[73] PRO, SP 63/171, fol. 101ʳ⁻ᵛ.   [74] PRO, SP 78/33, fol. 377ʳ.
[75] PRO, SP 12/251, fol. 74ʳ; PRO, SP 38/4, unfol., warrant of 9 March 1595. Essex had apparently been involved with overseeing the work at Portsmouth for at least a year by this time: H. M. Colvin (ed.), *The history of the king's works*, IV, *1485–1660*, part II (London, 1982), p. 526.
[76] PRO, SP 12/253, fol. 149ʳ; PRO, SP 12/254, no. 64.
[77] BL, Lansdowne MS 158, fol. 127ʳ.
[78] Aside from many favourable contemporary comments on Essex's competence as a military organiser, see also L. W. Henry, 'The earl of Essex as strategist and military organizer', *EHR* 78 (1953), pp. 363–93.

please in his service.'[79] Despite the discomfort it caused his servants, Essex knew that his hopes of success in these expeditions depended on attention to detail. Moreover, by showing his industry in this way, he was able to impress Elizabeth with his commitment to these ventures and remind her of his ability to shoulder further responsibilities upon his return, when his general's commission ceased. After Cadiz, at least, such diligence had its reward. In March 1597, Essex was finally appointed to the long-vacant mastership of the ordnance, the conciliar post for military administration *par excellence*.[80] In a tribute to his efficiency and probity, Essex was specifically ordered to put a broom through this notoriously corrupt organisation.[81] To strengthen his hand, the term of his appointment was for life, not simply during the queen's pleasure. Until 1599, Essex discharged this office with characteristic diligence, attending even to many routine administrative details, which runs counter to his traditional reputation.[82]

Although he regularly studied inventories and signed orders to move munitions, the real focus of Essex's activities as a councillor involved policy matters and dealings with foreign powers. Inevitably, Essex's administrative work often blurred into the field of policy. In early 1594, for example, he wrote to pass on instructions from the queen to Sir John Norris, her commander in Brittany, about when and how he should withdraw his troops.[83] These instructions had political as well as strategic implications, and Essex himself clearly had a part in formulating them. Political considerations also encouraged foreign powers to seek Essex's assistance in military matters. In a typical instance, the Dutch ambassador in England, Noël de Caron, asked Essex to support a proposal to strengthen the English

---

[79] LPL, MS 656, fol. 75[r]. The enormous volume of paperwork involved in launching the Cadiz expedition can be gauged by the various letters received by Sir John Wynn of Gwydir concerning the levying of troops in Caernarvonshire: *Calendar of the Wynn (of Gwydir) papers, 1515–1690, in the National Library of Wales and elsewhere* (Aberystwyth, Cardiff and London, 1926), pp. 31–33 (nos. 164, 166, 167, 169, 170). Significantly, only Essex wrote again after the expedition to express gratitude for the quality of the troops selected (*ibid.*, p. 33 (no. 176)).

[80] PRO, SO 3/1, fol. 638[v]. Essex's patent as master of the ordnance was dated 19 March 1597 (Devereux MSS, box 6, no. 85).

[81] PRO, SP 12/262, fols. 171[r]–173[r]. On corruption in the ordnance office, see LPL, MS 659, fols. 289[r]–290[v]; BL, Egerton MS 1943, fol. 78[v]; BL, Lansdowne MS 78, fols. 141[r], 143[r]; BL, Sloane MS 871, fols. 129[r]–132[v]; Stewart, *Ordnance office*, ch. 3; R. Ashley, 'Getting and spending: corruption in the Elizabethan Ordnance', *History Today* 40 (Nov. 1990), pp. 47–53; also his 'War in the Ordnance Office: the Essex connection and Sir John Davis', *Historical Research* 67 (1994), pp. 337–45.

[82] Stewart, *Ordnance office*, p. 8. On the work of the master of the ordnance and his subordinates, as well as the details of their administrative methods and problems, see *ibid.*, chs. 2 and 3.

[83] PRO, SP 78/33, fols. 189[r–v], 217[r–v].

companies in the Netherlands during February 1594.[84] Naturally enough, this reflected a hope that Essex would favour the Dutch petition, as indeed he did. However, Caron's approach also showed an appreciation that Essex had a particular mandate from the queen – as well as an ability to influence her – in foreign and military matters.

Given his own pressing personal interest, it is not surprising that Essex's involvement in foreign affairs as a councillor was wide-ranging and constant. Throughout, his primary aim was always to impress Elizabeth with the need to follow policies which aggressively confronted Spanish power and which gave strong support to England's Protestant allies. The constant reiteration of these views was crucial to Essex because Elizabeth and Burghley became more and more uncomfortable with England's Continental entanglements as the decade wore on. Burghley, in particular, had never put much trust in foreign allies and was constantly aware of England's limited resources. As he confided to Whitgift in early 1596, 'I am right sory to see so many extraordinarye charges, wherof I se no remedy untill it may please God to send us peace.'[85] Elizabeth herself became increasingly suspicious, even hostile, towards Henri IV, especially after he converted to Catholicism in 1593.[86] Taking his cue from his mistress, the lord treasurer prayed for 'some notable avendg upon the French kyng for his perfydie towards God and man'.[87] Both Elizabeth and Burghley also sought a reduction in support for the Dutch and the repayment of debts already contracted. By contrast, Essex remained a staunch advocate for Henri and protective of the Dutch. As he reassured Count Maurice of Nassau in December 1594, 'there is nothing more connected with the welfare of England than the prosperity of the United Provinces'.[88] Sir Francis Vere, the commander of the English field forces in the Low Countries, believed that Essex was instrumental in thwarting the queen's plan to call a regiment home in 1595.[89]

Essex was not always free to express his own views about foreign affairs. At times, he acted as the queen's mouthpiece in dealing with envoys or foreign correspondents, occasionally by himself, but more regularly in

---

[84] PRO, SP 84/48, fol. 65ʳ.

[85] LPL, MS 3470, fol. 179ʳ. The comment is made in a holograph postscript.

[86] Wernham, *After the Armada*, pp. 475–6, 492–7; J. B. Black, *Elizabeth and Henry IV: being a short study in Anglo-French relations, 1589–1603* (Oxford, 1914), pp. 67, 71–2. For Henri's conversion, see A. G. Williams, 'The abjuration of Henry of Navarre', *Journal of Modern History* 5 (1933), pp. 143–71. The French domestic context for Henri's action is discussed in M. Wolfe, *The conversion of Henri IV: politics, power and religious belief in early modern France* (Cambridge, Mass., 1993).

[87] CUL, MS Ee.iii.56, no. 26 (pr. Wright, *Elizabeth and her times*, II, p. 435).

[88] Tenison, X, p. 356.

[89] R. B. Wernham, *The return of the Armadas: the last years of the Elizabethan war against Spain, 1595–1603* (Oxford, 1994), p. 34.

combination with other councillors. When Elizabeth changed her mind and decided not to withdraw her troops from Brittany in 1594, she delegated Essex and Burghley to inform the French ambassador.[90] On another occasion, a few months later, Essex joined with Burghley, Howard, Hunsdon and Sir Robert Cecil in conveying the queen's wishes to the Dutch ambassador.[91] In November 1595, when Elizabeth was anxious publicly to vindicate Essex after the embarrassment of his receiving the dedication of a treasonous book on the succession, she pointedly relied on him alone to answer foreign correspondence on her behalf.[92]

Essex's own correspondence was another means by which he served the queen in her foreign relations. Even before he became a councillor, Essex had established a wide range of contacts with important political figures among allied and neutral states across Europe. This network of contacts expanded still further after his promotion. With the possible exception of Lord Burghley, until at least 1597 no other councillor could match the quality and range of Essex's correspondents.[93] This was a tribute both to his interest in European affairs and the political calculation of his many overseas contacts. Recognising his unequalled hold on royal favour and growing importance on the council, many foreigners viewed their dealings with Essex as a means of entering into indirect communication with Elizabeth herself or of wooing him to lobby the queen on their behalf. For her part, Elizabeth required that Essex keep her informed about his international connections. In reply to one correspondent, he declared: 'I receive nothinge but with my soveraigne's privity.'[94] This assertion was at once truthful and deliberately deceptive. Essex clearly informed Elizabeth about the identity of his correspondents and reported specific details contained in their letters. However, other information was undoubtedly kept private.[95] Certainly, the packets sent and received in these overseas correspondences sometimes contained separate papers which were kept secret from the queen.[96]

At times, Essex found the need to give frequent briefings on his post – and

---

[90] LPL, MS 653, fol. 234ʳ.   [91] PRO, SP 84/49, fol. 56ʳ.

[92] Collins, *Sidney papers*, I, p. 360.

[93] For comments on Essex's correspondence during this period, see *HMCS*, IV, p. viii; *ibid.*, V, pp. iv–v; *ibid.*, XIII, pp. xxxi–xxxiii; *ibid.*, XIV, p. xi.

[94] LPL, MS 651, fol. 312ʳ.

[95] For example, Elizabeth's farewell of the duke of Bouillon in May 1596 indicates that she was well aware of his close and long-running correspondence with Essex (LPL, MS 657, fol. 110ᵛ). In the letters which they exchanged, the two aristocrats were often very unguarded in their comments (many of those sent by Bouillon to Essex are in *HMCS*, vols. XIII–XIV). However, it is not at all clear how much of the personal content of these letters was edited out by Essex in his (presumably verbal) reports about them to the queen.

[96] See, for example, the practice of English officials abroad sending Essex 'general' and 'private' letters, which is discussed below (p. 196).

the editing process which this entailed – rather burdensome. As he sleepily complained to Francis Bacon late one evening: 'I am oppressed with [a] multitude of lettres that are come, of which I must give the queen some accompte to morowe morninge.'[97] However, the effort involved in reporting to the queen also provided important opportunities. Every occasion when Essex briefed Elizabeth on his latest letters and intelligence also gave him a valuable chance privately to argue matters of policy with her.

Essex also continued to act as the chief host for visiting foreign dignitaries. Essex not only succeeded Leicester in this role but took over two of Leicester's chief estates and made them his own. Essex began to make use of the great house and park at Wanstead by early 1591, although his tenure was not regularised for another eighteen months.[98] Wanstead was a country estate north of London but was ideally located for easy travel to and from Greenwich Palace.[99] It quickly became an important venue for Essex's entertainment of foreign guests and an escape from the pressures of Court. Essex also took over his stepfather's London base, Leicester House.[100] This was crucially important to Essex because its

---

[97] LPL, MS 650, fol. 147[r].

[98] The countess of Leicester took over Wanstead immediately after her husband's death and paid a fine of £10 for entering upon the estate without formal licence in October 1588 (PRO, C 66/1316, m. 20). However, Leicester's huge debts to the crown prompted the sequestration of the estate in 1590. The crown's 'seizur' of Wanstead lasted until November 1593 and was only lifted when the countess of Leicester succeeded in finding suitable alternative properties to guarantee the debt (PRO, SP 12/246, fol. 15[r]; VCH, *Essex*, VI, pp. 323–4). Prior to this agreement, Essex presumably had special permission to use the estate from Elizabeth. Thereafter, Essex leased Wanstead from his mother for £220 per year (e.g. Devereux MS 3, fol. 77[r]). Essex sold his interest in Wanstead to Lord Mountjoy for £4,300 at the end of 1598 (PRO, C 66/1503, m. 23; VCH, *Essex*, VI, pp. 323–4).

[99] S. Adams (ed.), *Household accounts and disbursement books of Robert Dudley, earl of Leicester, 1558–1561, 1584–1586* (Camden Society, 5th ser., VI, Cambridge, 1996), p. 26.

[100] Leicester House was also seized by the crown because of Leicester's debts. In mid-1590, all of Leicester's goods which still remained there were auctioned off (C. L. Kingsford, 'Essex House, formerly Leicester House and Exeter Inn', *Archaeologia* 73 (1923), p. 9). However, the property was leased back to the countess of Leicester only a few months later, on 11 August (S. Adams, 'The papers of Robert Dudley, earl of Leicester. III. The countess of Leicester's collection', *Archives* 22 (1996), p. 5, n. 23). Essex was able to rent Leicester House from his mother (Tenison, XI, p. 443, n. 3), although the property was included in the prolonged series of assurances and conveyances which were required to meet Leicester's debts until at least 1593 (e.g. PRO, SP 12/246, fol. 15[r]). According to Leicester's will, his widow was granted a life interest in Leicester House, with the remainder to Robert Dudley, his natural son. Dudley subsequently sold this reversionary interest to Essex for 1,000 marks (Devereux MS 3, fol. 170[r–v]). The countess of Warwick also had interests in the house and in the properties surrounding it. She conveyed the former to Essex on 20 July 1593 (Adams, 'Papers of Leicester. III', p. 5, n. 23) and sold the latter to him for 1,000 marks a year later (Devereux MS 3, fol. 170r; PRO, C 54/1479, unfol., indenture of 8 June 1594).

location on the Strand allowed ready access to all the palaces along the Thames, while Sir John Puckering's appointment as lord keeper in July 1592[101] undoubtedly put pressure on him to vacate York House. By 1593, Leicester House had become the heart of his domestic establishment and had gained a new name: Essex House. Bit by bit, Leicester's former presence was being erased from the English political scene.

Essex entertained many distinguished visitors at Wanstead, Essex House and at Court. In 1593, for example, he spent very heavily on entertaining the vidame de Chartres in June,[102] and somewhat less heavily on welcoming the earls of Emden in July.[103] In the following year, he played host to 'certayne Germaynes' in January,[104] the admiral of Zeeland in the middle of the year[105] and the brother of the prince of Anhalt in August.[106] In 1595, he welcomed an embassy from the duke of Württemberg in March and April[107] and the marquis of Baden in October.[108] He also helped the Dutch ambassador, Caron, to visit Oxford and Cambridge in May.[109] At the end of the year, he had the delicate task of entertaining an envoy from the late Dom Antonio, whilst deflecting any new request from the Portuguese exiles for further English aid.[110] In 1596, despite being preoccupied with his military activities, Essex had responsibility for overseeing the visit of the young baron von Zerotin between March and May.[111] He also entertained his friend the duke of Bouillon with a feast of enormous extravagance at the end of August.[112] Most expensive of all, however, was

---

[101] Murdin, p. 799.

[102] Essex's lavish entertainment of the vidame and the French ambassador at Wanstead included a highly successful hunt (Crino, 'Avvisi di Ubaldini', p. 535). Essex also lent £500 to the vidame (who was chronically short of money because Henri was unable to pay him properly), £200 of which he had to borrow from Capt Arthur Savage (Devereux MS 3, fol. 73ʳ). Essex was still waiting to be repaid at the end of 1597 (HMCS, VII, p. 548).

[103] The earls were entertained at a dinner at Hampton Court in July which cost £67 16s 9d (Devereux MS 3, fol. 73ʳ).

[104] LPL, MS 649, fol. 10ʳ.   [105] PRO, SP 84/48, fol. 266ʳ.

[106] I. H. Jeayes (ed.), Letters of Philip Gawdy of West Harling, Norfolk, and of London to various members of his family 1579–1616 (Roxburghe Club, London, 1906), p. 88.

[107] V. von Klarwill (ed.), Queen Elizabeth and some foreigners, being a further series of hitherto unpublished letters from the archives of the Hapsburg family (trans. T. H. Nash, London, 1928), pp. 355–414, esp. pp. 359–60, 362, 366–7, 380–1, 412–13.

[108] HMCS, V, p. 400.   [109] Devereux MS 3, fol. 93ᵛ.

[110] Tenison, IX, p. 465. Dom Antonio died at Paris in August 1595. Scipio Figueiredo de Vasconellos, who claimed the title of governor of Terceira, was delayed in presenting his master's death-bed letters because of his own ill-health. When he arrived in England, Elizabeth refused to see him and made it clear that she did not want a visit from Antonio's younger son, Dom Cristobal (HMCS, VI, pp. 33–4). This was especially embarrassing for Essex, whom the dying Dom Antonio had addressed as 'one of the truest and greatest [friends] I possess' (Tenison, IX, p. 456).

[111] LPL, MS 656, fols. 65ʳ, 75ʳ, 89ʳ, 91ʳ, 150ʳ, 217ʳ; O. Odlozilik, 'Karel of Zerotin and the English Court (1564–1636)', Slavonic Review 15 (1937), pp. 421–2.

[112] Anthony Bacon reported that the banquet for Bouillon and his train 'stoode him [the earl]

hospitality for Antonio Perez, the former secretary of Philip II who had fled to France and entered the service of Henri IV. He arrived in England with the vidame de Chartres and did not leave until July 1595. Essex paid him a stipend of £20 a month, in addition to meeting other expenses which ran into hundreds of pounds.[113]

From this selection of dignitaries, it is apparent that Essex continued to place much emphasis upon bolstering relations with France. Still true to 'the cause', he remained the French king's key supporter at the English Court.[114] This sample of visitors also suggests that Essex had contact with a considerable number of noblemen from Germany. This is significant because evidence of his correspondence surviving in British archives throws little light on his German contacts, even though it was reported that he 'greatly desires to make his name famous among the German princes'.[115] Almost certainly, this gap in Essex's correspondence is a result of the division of labour in his secretariat. Essex's central European correspondence went through the hands of one particular secretary, Henry Wotton. Since almost none of Wotton's own papers survive for the period of his service with Essex, it seems likely that all of these documents were lost or destroyed together, probably deliberately.[116]

The dangers of arguing *ex silentio* also counsel caution in assessing Essex's involvement in another major area of conciliar activity: Irish affairs. During the late sixteenth century, England's occupation of Ireland faced a succession of major challenges and spawned a staggering quantity of paperwork. However, very little of it shows any trace of Essex. This is

at the leaste a 1000 marks' [i.e. £666] (LPL, MS 659, fol. 160^r). Essex's extravagance was perhaps partly an attempt to make amends for the very brief welcome which he gave Bouillon during the duke's previous visit to England in April (LPL, MS 250, fol. 344^v; Birch, *Memoirs*, I, p. 466: note that Birch himself erroneously contradicts this evidence on the following page).

[113] Ungerer estimates that Essex spent about £400 on Perez's monthly 'entertainment' between November 1593 and mid-1595. He also identifies further expenditure worth £817 3s 5d, which surely underestimates the earl's support for Perez by a considerable margin (Ungerer, I, pp. 296–7). It is not clear if this figure includes the sum of £500 which Essex borrowed from the jeweller Peter Vanlore 'for the furnishing [of] Mons. Perez, &c' (Devereux MS 3, fol. 112^r). At Christmas 1594, Elizabeth gave Essex lands worth £130 per annum to help subsidise this heavy expenditure (Ungerer, I, p. 223), but it probably took him some time to start recouping his expenditure.

[114] See, for example, Crino, 'Avvisi di Ubaldini', p. 538. In his many letters to Henri IV, Essex termed himself 'vostre serviteur' and reiterated a constant theme: 'je ne manqueray jamais de m'acquitter de mon devoyr envers vostre Majestie' (BL, Add. MS 45359, fol. 5^r).

[115] von Klarwill, *Queen Elizabeth and some foreigners*, p. 413.

[116] P. E. J. Hammer, 'The uses of scholarship: the secretariat of Robert Devereux, 2nd earl of Essex, c.1585–1601', *EHR* 109 (1994), p. 37. L. P. Smith was able to trace only 11 of Wotton's letters for the years 1595–1600 (*The life and letters of Sir Henry Wotton* (2 vols., Oxford, 1907), I, pp. 30, 298ff.).

especially striking because Irish matters came to have an increasingly important impact on war policy in the 1590s and because Essex himself possessed an estate there.[117] Essex participated in council discussions on Ireland and received information about developments there. In December 1594, for example, he joined the lord admiral and Lord Buckhurst in meeting at Burghley's house 'for Ireland causes'.[118] Along with most of his colleagues, he also approved instructions for Sir John Norris and Geoffrey Fenton to negotiate with the rebellious earl of Tyrone in March 1596.[119] Yet this is hardly evidence of a pressing concern for developments in Ireland. Certainly, there is nothing in his papers to match the enormous concern about Ireland which Burghley and Sir Robert Cecil displayed in their correspondence.[120]

Most of the evidence about Essex's involvement in Irish matters relates to military patronage there. As the scale of operations against the rebels increased, Essex sought to extend his domination of military matters to include Ireland. This was inevitable because more and more of the officers being sent to Ireland had previously served with Essex. One of his earliest followers there was Sir Richard Bingham, the controversial and increasingly beleaguered governor of Connaught, who had served with Essex under Leicester.[121] As opportunities elsewhere contracted, commands in Ireland became increasingly appealing. In early 1594, Essex pushed for Sir Francis Aleyn to be made seneschal of Clandeboye, but the appointment was cancelled when Burghley had the position quashed to save money.[122] Eighteen months later, Essex clashed heatedly with Norris over the appointment of new officers for Ireland.[123] Perhaps as a result of this outburst, greater effort was made to clear sensitive appointments with Essex in advance. On a list of officers being considered for service in Ireland in August 1596, Cecil made a marginal note that Essex should 'be spoken

---

[117] Essex inherited from his father the 'countrey of Ferny', one of five baronies in County Monaghan. These lands had been granted to Essex's father 'in recompence for his title to the landes of Edmond Mortimer erle of Marche' (Devereux MS 3, fol. 127[r]). The location of these lands is clearly marked on a coloured map of the county which is dated December 1590 and bears notations in Burghley's hand: PRO, MPF/76. In 1592, Essex leased them to John Talbot for three years at £250 per annum (Devereux MS 3, fol. 128[r]). For details of this estate and its despoliation by Irish rebels in 1595, see 'Career', p. 83, n. 89.

[118] *HMCS*, XIII, p. 508.

[119] Woburn Abbey, Russell MSS, HMC 13, Journal of Sir William Russell, fol. 72[v].

[120] Although true of their paperwork in general, this can perhaps most readily be seen in Burghley's private letters to his son, such as CUL, MS Ee.iii.56.

[121] Bingham began seriously to cultivate Essex as a patron – and a protector – after Walsingham's death in 1590. He was recognised as having a 'speciall dependinsie upon therle of Essex' by 1593 (PRO, SP 63/170, fol. 132[r]). Bingham's desperate need for such support in 1596 is discussed below. For Bingham's career, see *DNB*, II, pp. 514–15.

[122] LPL, MS 649, fol. 388[r–v]; PRO, SP 63/173, fol. 38[r–v].

[123] Cecil MSS 35/63–5 (pr. *HMCS*, V, pp. 413–14); PRO, SP 63/186, fol. 211[r–v].

with' before including Sir Samuel Bagenal.[124] Four months later, Essex was
also delegated by the council to take charge of mustering fresh troops for
Ireland.[125] With his military involvement there growing steadily in the mid
1590s, it is little wonder that his followers in Ireland included the arms
supplier William Grosvenor of Bellport.[126]

Essex's dealings with successive lords deputy of Ireland were limited and
patchy. There is little evidence of contact with Sir William Fitzwilliam (lord
deputy for the last time between February 1588 and August 1594). As the
successor and bitter enemy of Sir John Perrot, the earl's relative by
marriage, Fitzwilliam's relations with Essex were probably very cold. It is
possible that Essex's stubborn refusal to compromise over his lands in
County Monaghan arose partly because Fitzwilliam supported the plan.[127]
Essex was far more comfortable with Lord Burgh, who was appointed at
the start of 1597.[128] A fellow military man, Burgh was a frequent
correspondent with Essex while governor of Brill during the first half of the
decade. As lord deputy, Burgh was anxious that Essex and Cecil would co-
operate to protect his interests back in England. Both men seem to have
been well disposed towards Burgh until his sudden death in October
1597.[129]

Essex may have had a hand in the naming of Lord Burgh as lord deputy
in 1597.[130] He certainly backed the appointment of Burgh's predecessor,
Sir William Russell – his old mentor from cavalry service in the Low
Countries – in 1594.[131] Nevertheless, although various requests for
patronage passed between the two men, relations do not seem to have been
very close. If a reference by his secretary in August 1595 to 'the yong Lord

[124] PRO, SP63/192, fol. 118^r.

[125] PRO, SP63/196, fol. 105^r. This task may explain notes by Essex about officers who might
be employed in Ireland, which seem to date from this period (*HMCS*, VI, pp. 558–9).

[126] R. Bagwell, *Ireland under the Tudors* (3 vols., London, 1885–1890), III, p. 248.

[127] H. Morgan, *Tyrone's rebellion: the outbreak of the Nine Years' War in Tudor Ireland*
(London, 1993), pp. 65–9.

[128] News of Burgh's appointment reached Ireland on 21 January 1597, but he did not arrive in
Dublin until 15 May (Woburn, Russell Journal, fols. 103^r, 110^r). Before his departure,
Burgh spent a day talking with Essex (Bagwell, *Ireland under the Tudors*, III, p. 281).

[129] PRO, SP 63/199, fol. 233^{r-v}; PRO, SP63/200, fols. 22^v, 42^r, 209^r, 262^r. For Cecil's efforts
to ease Burgh's anxiety about Essex's absence from England during the Azores expedition,
see PRO, SP63/200, fols. 187^v, 321^v–322^r.

[130] Sir Robert Naunton, *Fragmenta regalia or observations on Queen Elizabeth, her times &
favourites*, (ed. J. S. Cerovski, Washington, London and Toronto, 1985), p. 76.

[131] *HMCS*, IV, p. 499. Thus, Essex was one of the first people to whom Russell wrote after
setting out for Ireland in July 1594 (Woburn, Russell Journal, fol. 2^v). Francis Bacon also
later described Russell to Essex as the only lord deputy who was 'conceived yours, but
curbed' (BL, Lansdowne MS 238, fol. 244^r). Despite Essex's initial support for him,
Russell knew that approval from Burghley – whose followers now dominated the Irish
administration – was a *sine qua non* for any new lord deputy. When he lost the confidence
of the Cecils, Russell became a lame duck.

Essex' is any indication, Russell may have had some difficulty in adjusting to the fact that his former charge was now far more politically important than himself.[132] Rowland Whyte, Sir Robert Sidney's agent at Court, reported that Essex was openly dismissive of Russell by late 1595.[133] Even so, Russell's unhappy experiences as lord deputy led him to plead for Essex's support against a steadily growing chorus of critics, apparently with little success.[134]

The desperate appeals of Russell reflect a basic fact of life for English officials in Ireland. The relative ease with which wealth and land could be obtained (and monopolised), the extreme brutality of the occupation, and divided opinions about how to deal with the troublesome Irish all created ferocious competition within the English regime there. Worse, policy in Ireland – which set the rules by which rewards were fought for, often literally – was determined back in England. As a result, English officials in Ireland were constantly trying to win friends at the English Court, and to discredit their rivals. There was a constant flow of contradictory, partisan reports across the Irish Sea. As Sir Henry Sidney learned by painful experience, service in Ireland '(for the most part) was subject to the eare, and not object to the eie'.[135] After the death of Walsingham, English policies in Ireland were overwhelmingly dominated by Burghley and Sir Robert Cecil.[136] This meant that opponents of Cecil adherents in Ireland were always eager to lobby for new policies and to cultivate rival patrons who might serve as a counterweight to the Cecils. Essex was a prime target for such blandishments. Several times, suitors tried to draw him into taking an active part in Irish affairs. In mid-1593, for example, the earl of Tyrone sought Essex's help in clearing himself of charges of treason.[137] Almost

132 Woburn, Russell Journal, fol. 30ᵛ.   133 HMCD, II, p. 198.
134 The only evidence about Essex's reaction to these pleas consists of a single comment by Sir John Norris that, on one occasion, Russell felt relief at receiving a packet from the earl (PRO, SP 63/187, fol. 131ᵛ). This packet is probably the one sent by Essex from Court at Richmond late on the night of 17 March 1596 (ibid., fol. 126ʳ).
135 Raphael Holinshed, The chronicles of England, Scotlande and Irelande (3 vols., 1587, STC no. 13569), III, p. 1552.
136 This process was magnified and accelerated by the destruction of Sir John Perrot (who had been a client of Walsingham) during 1591–2 and the subsequent consolidation in power of his successor as lord deputy of Ireland, Sir William Fitzwilliam. A client and relative by marriage of Burghley, Fitzwilliam helped to make the English regime in Ireland an almost exclusively Cecilian preserve. For the demise of Perrot, which is discussed below, see H. Morgan, 'The fall of Sir John Perrot', in J. Guy (ed.), The reign of Elizabeth I: Court and culture in the last decade (Cambridge, 1995), pp. 109–25.
137 PRO, SP 63/170, fols. 41ʳ, 43ʳ⁻ᵛ. See also Morgan, Tyrone's rebellion, pp. 152ff. In 1596, Capt. Thomas Lee suggested making use of this previous good will between Essex and Tyrone to improve the chances of negotiating a cessation of arms (PRO, SP 63/188, fol. 3ᵛ). Nothing seems to have come of Lee's suggestion.

certainly, Tyrone looked to Essex because of his own former dependency on Leicester.[138]

Perhaps the most elaborate plea to Essex came from the poet Edmund Spenser, who held land and a government post in Munster. A friend and client of Sir Walter Ralegh, Spenser seems to have turned towards Essex by 1596. During a visit back to England, Spenser lauded Essex after his return from Cadiz as 'Great Englands glory and the Worlds wide wonder'.[139] It seems likely that Spenser also thought of Essex when he included the Burbon and Artegall episode in the new instalment of the *Faerie Queene* which was published in the first half of 1596. An apparent allegory of Essex's support for Henri IV (the first king of the new Bourbon dynasty), Artegall's rescue of Burbon seems intended to compliment Essex for championing the French king and to incite further acts of martial prowess in defence of Protestantism.[140] Although Spenser undoubtedly hoped for patronage from Essex in reward for his poetic skills,[141] he also harboured more political hopes for him. These can be seen in *A view of the present state of Ireland*, which he wrote – or at least revised – during this period. In this work, Spenser pressed for the all-out suppression of Irish resistance and the complete imposition of Protestant English culture in Ireland. To oversee this massive operation, Spenser envisaged the appointment of a lord lieutenant based at the English Court to support operations by a new lord deputy in Ireland. There can be little doubt that he had Essex in mind for this role of lord lieutenant – 'such an one I could name upon whom

---

[138] Morgan, *Tyrone's rebellion*, p. 97. Tyrone had also been on good terms with Hatton (*ibid.*).

[139] *Prothalamion*, l.146, printed in E. Greenlaw, C. G. Osgood *et al.* (eds.), *The works of Edmund Spenser: a variorum edition* (10 vols., Baltimore, 1932–57), VIII, p. 261. For discussion of Essex and this poem, see A. C. Hamilton (ed.), *The Spenser encyclopedia* (Toronto, Buffalo and London, 1990), pp. 254, 561–2; A. Fowler, *Conceitful thought: the interpretation of English Renaissance poems* (Edinburgh, 1975), ch. 4.

[140] *Faerie Queene*, Book V, Canto xi (pr. in *Works of Spenser*, V, pp. 134ff). There is considerable controversy about the identification of Artegall with Essex here. It is clear that the character of Artegall cannot be seen as consistently embodying one historical figure – in Canto xii he obviously reflects actions of Lord Grey of Wilton during the early 1580s. It has also been suggested that Artegall in the Burbon episode represents Sir John Norris (e.g. J. W. Bennett, *The evolution of the Faerie Queene* (Chicago, 1942, reprinted New York, 1960), pp. 191–4). Although possible, this seems much less likely than an identification with Essex: R. Heffner, 'Essex and Book Five of the *Faerie Queene*', *English Literary History* 3 (1936), pp. 67–82; *Works of Spenser*, V, pp. 324–35. David Norbrook has argued that the whole of Book V of the *Faerie Queene* endorses a distinctly Protestant view of recent history and is intended as a spur to Essex and his friends, in particular (*Poetry and politics in the English Renaissance* (London, 1984), pp. 124–39).

[141] As C. E. Mounts points out, there is no incontrovertible evidence that Spenser's pursuit of patronage from Essex ever brought reward. However, his argument that Spenser's efforts were, in effect, doomed to failure from the start is not very credible ('Spenser and the earl of Essex', in G. W. Williams (ed.), *Renaissance papers, 1958, 1959, 1960* (Durham, NC, 1961), pp. 12–19).

he ey of all Englande is fixed and our last hopes now rest'.[142] However, Essex's martial ambitions remained focused elsewhere. Artful as they were, the pleas of Spenser seemingly made little impact.

Essex was eager to establish dominance of military administration and patronage in Ireland, but he clearly sought to avoid more direct entanglement there. Given the central importance of war in Essex's world-view, it is instructive that he saw the Irish conflict as 'a miserable beggerly ... war'.[143] When it was bruited shortly after his return from Cadiz that he might be offered command in Ireland, Essex could only see it as a devious attempt to divert him from matters of real importance.[144] Because of this perception, Francis Bacon had little success with his proposal that Essex should take advantage of Cecil's absence from England in April 1598 to enter into Irish affairs. Significantly, Bacon couched his plan in terms which emphasise Essex's previous aloofness from Irish matters: the earl should have 'put your sickle in others' harvest'.[145] In Essex's eyes, Ireland was clearly no fit place for a man who aspired to play a part upon 'the stage of Christendom'.

In addition to bringing him into the business of government, Essex's promotion to the council provided a platform for his widely recognised sense of ambition. By gaining a seat on the council, Essex forever ceased to be merely the queen's favourite – he became an accepted and active player in the business of policy and government. As an earl who was renowned for his staunch and personally energetic commitment to the war against Spain, and as a man who already occupied a privileged place in the queen's affections, Essex was plainly no ordinary new councillor. Nor was he content to act like one by entering into a lengthy apprenticeship in the affairs of state, much to the irritation of his elders on the board. Essex's real and perceived political importance quickly swelled, both as a result of the status and delegated authority which he gained as a councillor and because of his own efforts at self-promotion. Abroad, Essex gained substance as a major international political figure, even a statesman. Within England itself, the 'newe man' of 1593 grew by 1596 into 'the great earl',[146] equally

---

142 *Works of Spenser*, IX, pp. 228–9, 428–9; R. B. Gottfried, 'Spenser's View and Essex', *Proceedings of the Modern Language Association* 52 (1937), pp. 645–51. Ray Heffner suggested that Essex may have commissioned Spenser to write the *View* ('Spenser's *View of Ireland*: some observations', *Modern Language Quarterly* 3 (1942), 509). This seems improbable and Heffner's case is weakened by factual errors.
143 *Apologie*, sig. E1ᵛ.
144 Ungerer, I, p. 446. Antonio Perez entirely agreed with Essex's distaste for the idea: 'ne te intra istum angustum orbem Hiberniae occludas' (*ibid.*, p. 449).
145 BL, Lansdowne MS 238, fol. 244ᵛ.   146 HMCA, p. 330.

able to deal with the queen's foreign correspondence and lead her forces to victory in war.

If any single incident truly signalled Essex's arrival as a politician whose views carried genuine weight with Elizabeth and his colleagues, it was the prosecution of the queen's physician, Dr Roderigo Lopez, at the start of 1594. By driving Lopez to the gallows, Essex not only demonstrated his mastery of intelligence, but exposed and triumphed over any remaining doubts about his capacity as a councillor. When he announced his claim that the doctor was a traitor, Burghley and Sir Robert Cecil poured scorn upon the idea.[147] Elizabeth herself rebuked him with a phrase which cuttingly revealed her most fundamental reservations about him, 'callinge [him a] rasshe & temerarious youthe'.[148] Yet Essex quickly managed to dispel these doubts about his case, and about himself. By the real (or threatened) use of torture, he mustered sufficient evidence to make his charges stick. Although Elizabeth delayed the execution until June,[149] the dismembered body of Lopez served as gruesome proof that Essex had learned to play political hard-ball. This grim lesson was all the more impressive because the charges against Lopez scuttled plans for renewed contact with Spain about peace talks, which Essex bitterly opposed.[150] Moreover, by destroying Lopez, who had important contacts in Constantinople, Essex delivered a devastating blow to any future diplomatic overtures whch might involve Elizabeth's mediation between the Emperor and his Turkish enemies.[151] As one astute observer put it, the earl 'hathe wunne the spurres, and sadle also, yf right be done hym'.[152]

With this success, Essex completed the transformation which had begun during the Rouen campaign, and conceived even earlier. After the Lopez case, Essex was clearly a councillor to reckon with, and his every

---

[147] LPL, MS 650, fols. 25ᵛ–26ʳ.   [148] *Ibid.*, fol. 26ʳ.

[149] Lopez and his co-conspirators had been scheduled to die on 19 April 1594. He finally died on 7 June. In a rare act of mercy, Elizabeth allowed the doctor's widow to retain his property (*HMCS*, IV, p. 601; PRO, C 66/1503, m.14). Traditionally, this action has been ascribed to Elizabeth's own doubts about Lopez's guilt. However, Ubaldini claims that Essex was instrumental in winning this favour for the widow (Crino, 'Avvisi di Ubaldini', p. 568).

[150] R. B. Wernham, 'Elizabeth I, the Emperor Rudolf II and the Archduke Ernest in 1593–94', in E. I. Kouri and T. Scott (eds.), *Politics and society in Reformation Europe*, pp. 437–51; also his *Return of the Armadas*, pp. 11–15; W. T. MacCaffrey, *Elizabeth I: war and politics 1588–1603* (Princeton, 1992), p. 194. Wernham suggests that the charges against Lopez may have been a deliberate effort by Essex to torpedo the planned peace talks.

[151] English mediation with the Turks was offered as a crucial enticement to the Emperor when Dr Christopher Parkins was sent to Prague in mid-1593 (Wernham, 'Elizabeth I, Rudolf II and the Archduke Ernest', pp. 438–9). For Lopez's contacts in Constantinople, and the damage done to English influence there by his fall, see D. S. Katz, *The Jews in the history of England, 1485–1850* (Oxford, 1994), pp. 52ff, 99–100.

[152] LPL, MS 650, fol. 136ʳ.

subsequent service for the queen further reinforced this impression. However, just as he was no ordinary new councillor when he was first appointed, so Essex could never be merely *a* leading councillor once he became established on the board. His public ambition for himself and for the conduct of the war demanded more. Essex patently aspired to political greatness. French observers believed that he might have the power to settle the succession after Elizabeth's death,[153] and 'R. Doleman' deliberately sought to embarrass him by stating as much in print: 'no man is in more high & eminent place or dignitie at this day in our realme then your selfe ... & consequenti no man like to have a greater part or sway in deciding of this great affair .[154] Equally malicious gossip even suggested that Essex might be aiming at the crown for himself.[155]

Underpinning this widespread reputation of Essex as 'a man of great designs'[156] were two distinct, but mutually reinforcing, influences: the qualities which marked him out as a person of special importance to his contemporaries and his own deliberate efforts at self-advertisement. After his promotion to the council, the concurrency of qualities which marked Essex out to his contemporaries took on a new importance and lustre. On the council board, his rank and his deliberate cultivation of 'noble virtues', at a time when the greatest noble houses were in eclipse, made him a figurehead for the higher nobility.[157] In combination with his youth and continuing hold on royal favour, this suggested that he would play a crucial part in England's future. Many observers were also impressed by the sheer momentum of his career. At the most crude level of political calculation, his youth and rank and energetic service for the queen all suggested that he would probably dominate the council – and perhaps in the not-too-distant future – when old Burghley died. Aged only twenty-seven at the time of his appointment, Essex was of a markedly different generation from all his conciliar colleagues except Cecil. Self-interest as well as admiration for virtue dictated that Essex should be accorded a special respect.

Essex's meteoric career could also be seen in religious terms. Since historical events were recognised as the manifestation of predestined divine

---

[153] PRO, PRO 31/3/29, fol. 102ʳ.
[154] R. Doleman, *A conference about the next succession to the crowne of Ingland* (n. pl., 1594, STC no. 19398), sig. *2ᵛ–*3ʳ. For discussion of the identity of 'Doleman', see P. Holmes, 'The authorship and early reception of *A conference about the next succession to the throne of England*', *HJ* 23 (1980), pp. 415–29.
[155] PRO, SP 12/248, fol. 125ʳ⁻ᵛ.
[156] [André Hurault, sieur] de Maisse, *A journal of all that was accomplished by Monsieur de Maisse, ambassador in England from Henri IV to Queen Elizabeth anno domini 1597* (eds. G. B. Harrison and R. A. Jones, London, 1931), p. 7.
[157] For example, Lord Henry Howard claimed that Essex's qualities were all the more precious 'in this barren age wherin nature is so scant in hir proportions to honorable howses' (DUL, Howard MS 2, fol. 117ʳ).

will, Essex's swift rise and intimate association with the anointed sovereign suggested that he was an instrument of God. Many of Essex's followers believed their lord to be a man of destiny. The soldier Sir Francis Aleyn wrote to Essex that 'I counte it [a] great happines to me that even I mett with the age wherein you livd, foorseing you ar borne to do particular good, sowell as generall.'[158] Puritans, who still hoped for Essex's further-ance of their cause, played upon this theme with some insistence. However, this view also had a far wider currency, especially at times when he enjoyed a signal success. In 'saving' Elizabeth from the machinations of Dr Lopez and storming Cadiz, for example, Essex seemed like God's gift to the English nation. Lord Henry Howard claimed that 'the verie time and manner of his advancement prove one argument of providence pro bono publico'.[159] William Waad, a clerk of the privy council, called him 'the hope of our aage'.[160] Nicholas Faunt, another royal servant, echoed this sentiment: 'I rejoyced greatly ... even for the common good, for that it seemeth the Lord by his meanes offreth grace yet to the synnes of this lande.'[161]

If Essex's contemporaries were generally disposed to expect him one day to become a great man, he also believed this himself, and he constantly worked to hasten the day when it would become a reality. After his promotion to the council, this sense of ambition caused some problems. More seasoned councillors – men who had once looked upon Essex with forbearance, even affection – now had to deal with him as a colleague. At times, this proved an irritating experience. According to Camden, Essex 'presently made it his business (as the wiser sort of courtiers complained) to goe beyond both his equals and superiors'.[162] Ironically, it was easy for Essex to demonstrate this characteristically thrusting and vigorous beha-viour because the privy council had evolved very settled rules of precedence and conduct. Despite his youth and inexperience, Essex immediately took precedence (by virtue of his earl's rank) over every councillor except the lord keeper and the lord treasurer. In a body whose very membership was determined by office-holding and rank, this was crucially important.[163]

In the eyes of his colleagues, and of Elizabeth, Essex sometimes offended against the rules of conduct for a councillor when he used the (necessarily)

---

[158] LPL, MS 650, fol. 344[r]. For a further example of this kind of fulsome praise, see Lord Henry Howard's comments to Essex of December 1596 (LPL, MS 660, fol. 275[r]).
[159] DUL, Howard MS 2, fol. 117[r].   [160] LPL, MS 650, fol. 114[r].   [161] *Ibid.*
[162] *Elizabeth*, p. 623.
[163] The importance of precedence and due order can be seen most clearly in the signing of council letters, a procedure which followed every meeting. Each councillor could only sign in the appropriate place and gaps were left when a member did not sign. Promotion to higher office was signalled by signing further to the left or closer to the text. The process is best observed over a substantial run of privy council letters, such as LPL, MS 3470.

personal tactics of a favourite in matters of government. The most famous example of this confusion of roles was his vigorous support for the suits of Francis Bacon during 1593–4, when he openly played upon Elizabeth's affection for him in the hope of making his friend attorney- or solicitor-general. However, Essex's lobbying proved an embarrassing failure and he soon adopted the more restrained methods of applying pressure to Elizabeth by reasoned argument and written submissions. Yet, despite bowing to the rules of the game in this matter, Essex sometimes still strained the limits of accepted behaviour in other ways. Perhaps the most consistently galling aspect of his conduct for his fellow councillors (as well as for many others at Court) were his constant efforts to proclaim his own personal pre-eminence, especially as these were intimately linked to support for policies which increasingly seemed contentious. As the decade wore on, annoyance at this consistent self-promotion gradually polarised opinions towards him.

As he showed by his actions in Portugal and Normandy, as well as in the tilt-yard, Essex was a man given to grand public gestures. After his appointment to the council, he continued to court public acclaim. Francis Bacon later warned him about the dangers of being seen to cultivate 'popular reputation'.[164] These dangers were all the more acute because Essex combined this thirst for popular adoration with an obvious and more directly political goal: to lay claim to becoming the queen's next helmsman for the ship of state.[165]

Driven by ambitions of greatness formed in his youth, by his mixed experiences at Court, and by close association with Leicester, Burghley and Hatton, Essex aspired to become his sovereign's chief confidant and adviser. Even in 1591, he was reportedly 'impatient' at the continuing sway of Hatton and Burghley and clearly desired to supplant them. This immense personal ambition formed an integral part of Essex's continual and public promotion of the policy of waging an all-out war against Spain. By associating himself so strongly with this policy, Essex not only sought to popularise the cause itself, but also implicitly asserted his own personal indispensability to it. To be fair, Essex genuinely saw himself as an instrument for this cause, as well as its beneficiary. As he told Anthony Bacon in May 1596, 'yf I be not tyed by the handes, I know God hath a greatt worke to worke by me'.[166] In simultaneously promoting an expansive war policy and his own special claims to oversee it, Essex was always

---

[164] Spedding, *Bacon letters*, II, p. 41. Essex's deliberate cultivation of his public image is discussed below in Chapter 6.

[165] For use of this image in reference to Essex, see for example *HMCS*, VI, p. 478 and LPL, MS 657, fol. 194[r].

[166] LPL, MS 657, fol. 134[r]. The notion of being an instrument of the greater good is a common theme in Essex's writings.

conscious that the elevation of his own political status would, in turn reinforce his ability to implement the policy itself. Such considerations indeed, underlay Essex's resolution to make himself into a councillor in 1592.

Once he became a councillor, Essex's political ambitions began to take on a new substance. Having gained his seat at the council board, the recognised political importance of that body gave Essex a new weight in the eyes of observers, both within the realm and without. His work as a councillor also gave him new opportunities which he exploited to advance his own private aspirations. This can be seen, for example, in his role in managing the country's war effort. By employing Essex in military matters, Elizabeth recognised that he had succeeded in establishing himself as England's leading soldier. The more work which he performed in this sphere and the more responsibility which was delegated to him, the greater his martial reputation became. Essex quite deliberately exploited this situation to reinforce his reputation with soldiers, by appointing as captains or muster-masters men whom he knew himself, or who were recommended to him by his friends. In April 1597, for example, he used his responsibility for overseeing the defence of the realm to nominate the officers for the reorganised militia forces of the maritime counties.[167] In turn, this political influence made it all the more necessary for military officers to cultivate his patronage.

A similar process can be observed in Essex's dealings in foreign affairs. Essex always cast himself in an internationalist mould and Elizabeth's willingness to take advantage of his foreign contacts helped to reinforce those contacts and to bring him new ones. In this process, as in his dealings with soldiers, Essex was especially diligent in taking advantage of the possibilities which the queen's service afforded him to advance his own reputation. His role as the host for visiting dignitaries, for instance, allowed him to demonstrate his own importance in English affairs to an audience both foreign and domestic. To the visitors, in particular, he sought to show himself a generous host and a willing friend for them about the queen. By bestowing gifts at their departure, sometimes of considerable value, he left the visitors with enduring tokens of his good will, which helped to advance his reputation in their home countries.[168] The success of such efforts was demonstrated by the subsequent efforts of the dignitaries,

[167] PRO, SP 12/262, fol. 227^{r-v}.

[168] In addition to the lavish gifts which he bestowed on Turenne in 1590, Essex also gave a horse to the future duke of Württemberg in 1592 (Rye, *England as seen by foreigners*, p. 46) and £300 to the vidame de Chartres in 1593 (Devereux MS 3, fol. 73^r). A 13oz chain worth £38 8s which was sent to Essex at Court in July 1593 may also have been bestowed on a foreign visitor (*ibid.*, fol. 75^r).

or the states which they represented, to ensure themselves of his support for the future.[169]

Essex also made his ambition for political pre-eminence under the queen obvious in other ways. By the middle of the decade, as the following chapter will show, Essex employed agents to represent his own interests in a number of friendly states. He also maintained, and expanded, a voluminous foreign correspondence. Through both of these channels, Essex sought to convince his audience abroad of two consistent ideas: that he alone in England was truly committed to affairs on the Continent and that he alone would soon hold sway under the queen. Sweeping though these claims were, Essex had begun making them even before he was appointed to the council. Indeed, Elizabeth had complained about this sort of boasting during Essex's time in Normandy: 'qu'il faisoit accroire au roy qu'il gouvernoit tout'.[170]

In later years he perhaps showed a little more discretion, for the clearest instances of such claims come in letters written, not by Essex himself, but by followers on his behalf. Anthony Bacon, for example, wrote to urge Marshal Matignon of the unique benefits of entering into regular correspondence with Essex. To that end, he instanced not only Essex's special favour with the queen but also 'his nobility and vertue of so great reputacion with all this realme, and therfore [he is] like to runne a fortune awnserable to so extraordinary and emynent a concurrencie'.[171] In 1596, another writer sought to assure Mons. Desdiguières of the special value of relying upon Essex: 'car ses genereuses parties vous declareront combien elles importent de mérite, estant en sa qualité *nostre seul gouvernail soubs nostre princesse*'.[172]

Essex's efforts to convince foreign statemen that he should be their prime contact in England were matched by deliberate efforts by foreigners to sustain his enthusiasm for Continental affairs. Although they also wooed Burghley, Cecil and sometimes other councillors as well, foreign diplomats and correspondents generally viewed Essex as more likely to support their various suits to Elizabeth and lauded him accordingly. Many suitors did this by playing upon his commitment to international Protestantism and the need to confront Spanish power. The heady compliments which these correspondents offered undoubtedly helped to strengthen Essex's own sense of honour and of mission. A not untypical example of these incitements comes in a letter from du Plessis, an envoy of the French king. In seeking Essex's support for further aid to France, he encouraged him as 'ung

---

[169] See, for example, von Klarwill, *Queen Elizabeth and some foreigners*, pp. 412–13.
[170] Philippe de Mornay, sieur du Plessis, *Mémoires et correspondance pour servir à l'histoire de la Réformation ... édition complete ...* (12 vols., Paris, 1824–5), V, p. 155.
[171] LPL, MS 653, fol. 3ʳ.   [172] PRO, SP 12/261, fol. 39ʳ. Emphasis added.

seigneur qui ne veult pas seulement estre né pour sa patrie, mais selon le
courage qui est digne de lui, pourt[sic] tout le monde'.[173]
    Essex also signalled his political ambitions very clearly to the domestic
audience. In contrast to his appeals to foreign observers, the thrust of his
domestic self-promotion was less to extol his present political importance
than to stake his special claim to be accorded political pre-eminence in the
near future, when Burghley died. In spite of a series of direct challenges
which he made to Burghley's authority in the months immediately after his
appointment to the council, Essex gradually seems to have recognised that
he could not replace the old lord treasurer as Elizabeth's most influential
adviser overnight – a recognition which paralleled his earlier decision to
restrain his impatience for the accession of King James. Accordingly, he
began to set himself for the long haul. Essex's consistent aim became to
establish himself as the obvious candidate to succeed Burghley as Elizabeth's next chief councillor, her next 'sine quo factum est nihil'.[174] Having
successfully remodelled himself as a politician, Essex now sought to style
himself as a statesman.
    In large measure, Essex's efforts to project himself as Burghley's successor
revolved around his work on the council board. Whenever he tendered
advice to Elizabeth, Essex consciously sought to appear grave and
thoughtful, and yet also more attuned than Burghley to the dangers and
opportunities created by the war. In his work as a councillor, he sought to
strike a clear contrast between his youth and energy and the lord treasurer's
aged caution. He built up his intelligence system still further, corresponded
directly with the queen's ambassadors abroad, and surrounded himself
with a range of high-powered advisers and servants. Nevertheless, it was
characteristic of Essex that he also sought to advertise his capabilities by
other, more public means. During late 1595, such actions clustered together
so closely and involved such elaborate preparation that it is hard not to
conclude that Essex launched a deliberate propaganda campaign.
    The biggest event during the year at Court was the anniversary of the
queen's succession, 17 November, which was marked by elaborate festivities and a great tournament of jousting. The whole of London and
Westminster was caught up in the occasion, with sermons and bonfires
across the City and thousands of spectators packing into the tilt-yard at
Whitehall palace. Because he was a superb jouster and helped to run such
competitions as master of the horse, Essex constantly made a bold showing
on these occasions.[175] In 1594, he ran six courses each against fifteen

---

[173] du Plessis, *Mémoires*, V, pp. 197–8.   [174] LPL, MS 649, fol. 388ᵛ.
[175] A. Young, *Tudor and Jacobean tournaments* (London, 1987), pp. 37, 50, 68, 102–3, 138,
    140, 170–6.

different challengers and broke fifty-seven lances in the process.[176] Although no record catalogues the details of his athletic performance in 1595, Essex clearly – and deliberately – stole the limelight on this great day. Not only did he star in the jousts but he also presented a dramatic set-piece which caught the attention of the audience and became the talk of London. Francis Bacon apparently played a major part in scripting this show, but the co-ordination and writing also involved a much larger effort from Essex's secretariat and circle of friends, even drawing upon actors from Oxford and Cambridge. Essex himself seems to have supervised the final production. Weeks, if not months, of planning went into the spectacle and the cost of the whole venture must have been enormous.[177]

Essex's entertainment was performed both before and after the supper break, and featured the characters of a hermit, a soldier and a secretary of state, each of whom tried to urge him to follow their particular profession. In the terms of the drama, these characters were representatives of the Lady Philautia, or Self-Love, for whom they sought to win the earl. Through his squire, Essex rejected their pleas and proclaimed 'that this knight wold never forsake his mistress's love'.[178] The show was thus a symbolic reaffirmation of Essex's devotion to Elizabeth. By this performance, Essex demonstrated to the queen, and to the public, that he remained her professed favourite, despite the recent embarrassment caused by the 'Doleman' book.[179] However, the deliberate transparency of the allegory suggested a further dimension to Essex's profession of 'love' to Elizabeth. It was readily apparent that the three representatives of Philautia each embodied qualities associated in real life with Essex himself – war, politics and learning. By spurning their advances, Essex asserted that he cultivated

[176] R. Strong, 'Elizabethan jousting cheques in the possession of the College of Arms', in his *The Tudor and Stuart monarchy: pageantry, painting, iconography. Vol. II: Elizabethan* (Woodbridge, 1995), p. 108.

[177] For all of this, see P. E. J. Hammer, 'Upstaging the queen: the earl of Essex, Francis Bacon and the Accession Day celebrations of 1595', in D. Bevington and P. Holbrook (eds.), *The politics of the Stuart Court masque* (Cambridge, 1998), pp. 41–66. Most of the extant remains of this entertainment are discussed and printed *in extenso* by Spedding (*Bacon letters*, I, pp. 375–91). A good eye-witness account of the occasion is given by Rowland Whyte (CKS, MS U 1475, C 12/26; pr. Collins, *Sidney papers*, I, pp. 362–3).

[178] CKS, MS U 1475, C 12/26.

[179] Elizabeth confronted Essex with this book at the start of November and the shock drove him to his sick bed. Despite a visit from the queen on 4 November, he did not fully recover until 12 November (*HMCD*, II, pp. 182–4). Essex undoubtedly knew about this book some months before it came to Elizabeth's attention because his follower Anthony Standen wrote directly to Robert Persons about it. Persons recapitulated the book's main arguments in his reply to Standen at the end of August (Farm St Church, London, MS 46/12/3, pp. 387–9).

these qualities only for the queen's service, and not for the sake of his own ambition, or 'self-love'.

Elizabeth herself was far from impressed by being upstaged on her Accession Day. According to Rowland Whyte, 'the queen sayd that, if she had thought their had bene so much sayd of her, she wold not have bene their that night, and soe went to bed'.[180] In her eyes, rather than denying the earl's personal ambition, the entertainment had almost the opposite effect. This would suggest that Essex's show was a costly failure. However, Whyte emphasised that 'my lord of Essex's devise is much commended in these late triumphes'. Henry Wotton also singled out the 'darling piece of love and self-love'[181] for special mention when he wrote about Essex many years later. These comments suggest that the Accession Day entertainment was indeed a success and that pleasing Elizabeth was not its main goal. In all probability, the performance was not intended to convince the queen about the merits of Essex and his ideas – after all, he had already been urging this case for years – but to appeal over her head to the assembled ranks of courtiers and citizens. By gaining their support, Essex could build up political momentum and exert pressure on Elizabeth to place more trust in him and his policies.

The audience certainly recognised that this was a drama about Essex, not about adoration for Elizabeth. However, rather than equating the three representatives of Philautia with qualities associated with Essex, they interpreted them as caricatures of men at Court. Whyte complained that 'the world makes many untrue constructions of these speaches, comparing the hermytt and the secretary to two of the lords [of the council] and the soldier to Sir Roger Williams'.[182] The two councillors were clearly Burghley (who had adopted the pose of an old hermit for his own entertainment for the queen at Theobalds in 1591) and Cecil, the man who most aspired to be secretary of state. Despite explicit claims in the show that Philautia's envoys embodied distinct personal qualities, many of the audience preferred to see Essex's production as a satirical attack on his two chief rivals, combined with some fun at the expense of his old comrade Williams. This misapprehension by the audience may not have been entirely unexpected by Essex, or unintended.

Having put so much time and energy into the Accession Day performance,

---

[180] CKS, MS U 1475, C 12/26.

[181] Wotton, *Parallel*, p. 8. Wotton here implies that the entertainment was peculiarly Essex's own work, although it is clear from surviving fragments that Francis Bacon composed some of the speeches (Spedding, *Bacon letters*, I, pp. 387ff; PRO, SP 12/254, fols. 139[r]–140[r]). Probably the most accurate way to view the work is as a project which was written under the earl's auspices by Bacon (and possibly also others), but which Essex himself ultimately shaped to suit his own fancy.

[182] CKS, MS U 1475, C 12/26.

Essex apparently sought to make further capital from his investment. A variety of contemporary manuscript copies survive of the text for the after-supper section of the show.[183] This strongly suggests that Essex deliberately circulated copies in manuscript form – effectively a kind of publication which restricted access to members of the social and political élite.[184] There is also a miniature of Essex in tournament garb by Nicholas Hilliard. Almost certainly, it was painted to commemorate this very occasion, perhaps to be given as a gift.[185] Several 'instant' ballads were published in the days after the event and it is possible that some of these were also quietly commissioned by friends of Essex.[186]

Even as he was still making capital out of his showing at the Accession Day celebrations, Essex gained an unexpected, but sorrowful, opportunity to stage another *coup de théâtre*. This was the funeral for Sir Roger Williams, the bluff Welsh soldier who was allegedly the butt of Essex's humour in the Accession Day show. Only weeks after returning from a diplomatic mission to Henri IV (during which he had also carried private messages for Essex[187]), Williams developed 'a burning ague' and died on 12 December.[188] A relative of Essex's steward, Gelly Meyrick, and flamboyant in his manner, Williams was one of the earl's dearest friends.[189]

[183] There are at least eight surviving fair manuscript copies of these speeches: P. Beal (ed.), *Index of English literary manuscripts. I: 1450–1625*, Part I (London and New York, 1980), pp. 51–2.

[184] On the circulation of manuscripts, see H. R. Woudhuysen, *Sir Philip Sidney and the circulation of manuscripts, 1558–1640* (Oxford, 1996), chs. 1–6 and H. Love, *Scribal publication in seventeenth-century England* (Oxford, 1993), chs. 1–2. See also A. F. Marotti, *Manuscript, print and the English Renaissance lyric* (Ithaca and London, 1995). This method of unofficial publication also avoided censorship laws and allowed the desired audience for a work to be precisely targeted.

[185] See plate 4. For discussion of this miniature and its connections with this occasion, see Hammer, 'Upstaging the queen', n. 10. Unlike scribal copies of a manuscript, a miniature was essentially a private token and not suitable for wide circulation.

[186] E. Arber (ed.), *A transcript of the registers of the Company of Stationers of London, 1554–1640 AD* (5 vols., priv. pr., London, 1875–94), III, p. 53. The evidence about political as well as financial motives prompting the publication of these works is inferential and this suggestion must remain entirely speculative. Nevertheless, there are some interesting coincidences involved. Several intimates of Essex, including Henry Cuffe, Sir Roger Williams, Sir Thomas Baskerville and Fulke Greville, had close dealings with various printers. I hope to discuss some of these ideas in a future paper on George Peele's *Anglorum Feriae*, a verse description of the Accession Day tournament. The poem is reprinted in D. H. Horne, *The life and minor works of George Peele* (New Haven and London, 1952), pp. 265–75. The uncertainties about its publication are discussed in *ibid.*, pp. 178–9.

[187] Ungerer, I, 353–4, 356–60; *ibid.*, II, p. 29. For this mission, see Wernham, *Return of the Armadas*, pp. 36–8. Williams was a frequent envoy to France: F. J. Weaver, 'Anglo-French diplomatic relations, 1558–1603 (pt. 2)', *BIHR* 7 (1929–30), p. 19.

[188] *HMCD*, II, p. 197. He died on 12 December 1595.

[189] For Williams, see *DNB*, XXI, pp. 441–5. He is frequently described as the likely model for Shakespeare's character of Fluellen in *Henry V*.

Like Essex, he was a veteran of the fateful charge at Zutphen and had been knighted by Leicester for his conspicuous bravery. Williams subsequently acted as an expert military adviser to Essex and shared adventures with him, including the Portugal expedition (when they plunged into the surf together at Peniche[190]) and the siege of Rouen. Their special bond lasted to the very end, when Essex 'indeed saved his sowle, for none but he cold make hym take a feeling of his end, but he died well and very repentant'.[191]

Although the circumstances were far from welcome, Essex sought to extract the maximum propaganda value from his comrade's funeral. At the time, Essex was still locked in dispute with Elizabeth and Burghley over new military aid to France, and a spectacular display of martial values offered the prospect of whipping up public support for an aggressive war strategy, and for himself. To this end, he used the £2,000 or so which Williams reportedly left him[192] to orchestrate a grand public spectacle which deliberately echoed another great funeral at St Paul's almost nine years earlier. As Rowland Whyte reported to Sir Robert Sidney, 'I hear that Sir Roger Williams shalbe buried at Sir Ph. Sidney's feete.'[193] Essex's preparations were disrupted by news of the death of the earl of Huntingdon, his former guardian, which required a rushed trip to York.[194] Nevertheless, the great event went ahead on 23 December, with Essex and 'all the warlike men of the city of London' as mourners.[195] Although the funeral certificate is incomplete,[196] it is very likely that the 'earles, barons, knights, esquires & gentlemen' who took part in the ceremony included many of Essex's friends who had competed with him in the tilt-yard on Accession Day – men like Cumberland, Sussex, Bedford, Southampton, Compton, Sir Francis Knollys Jr and Robert Dudley.[197] Whether by arrangement or for purely commercial motives, the printer John Danter registered a new ballad, *The deathe of Sir Roger Williams*, on the day before the funeral took place.[198]

[190] BL, Stowe MS 159, fol. 370[r].   [191] Collins, *Sydney papers*, I, p. 377.   [192] *Ibid.*
[193] *HMCD*, II, p. 201.
[194] *Ibid.* Like Essex's father, Huntingdon was subsequently eulogised by one of his former servants for the exemplary godliness of his death: M. C. Cross, 'The third earl of Huntingdon's death-bed: a Calvinist example of the *ars moriendi*', *Northern History* 21 (1985), pp. 80–107.
[195] Collins, *Sydney papers*, I, p. 377. The only detailed evidence about this event which seems to have survived is a bill for the painters (totalling £12 10s 8d) who provided rich materials for the heraldic items needed in an elaborate display, such as 'a creaste carvid & wrought' and 'a wreath of silke of his coullors' (College of Arms, London, Vincent MS 188, fol. 10[v]).
[196] College of Arms, London, Vincent MS 90, p. 311.
[197] All of these men are mentioned by Peele in *Anglorum Feriae* as participants in the Accession Day tournament.
[198] Arber, *Registers of the Company of Stationers*, III, p. 56. Unfortunately, no copies of this work seem to have survived.

The deaths of Williams and Huntingdon cast a pall over Essex's Christmas in 1595. Nevertheless, he remained very busy. In addition to all the consultations which accompanied the despatch of Sir Henry Unton as ambassador to France, Essex was occupied with another exercise in self-promotion. In October 1595, the young earl of Rutland left on an extended Continental tour.[199] As a mentor for the young earl, Essex wrote at least three detailed letters of instruction for him, the third of which was dated 16 October 1595.[200] During the Christmas holiday season of 1595–6, the opportunity was taken to polish up the first of these letters for circulation in manuscript. This was probably a joint effort between Essex himself and members of his secretariat, with the earl approving and revising the final

---

[199] Roger, 5th earl of Rutland received his licence to travel on 26 September (PRO, SO 3/1, fol. 551ᵛ; *HMCS*, V, p. 392) and took his leave from Court in late October (*HMCD*, II, pp. 174–6). Essex's cousin, Robert Vernon, was supposed to accompany Rutland on the first stage of his journey (*ibid.*, p. 169).

[200] Hulton MS (formerly BL, Loan 23), fol. 147ʳ⁻ᵛ. It is printed in *HMC. Twelfth report, appendix ix. The manuscripts of the duke of Beaufort, KG, the earl of Donoughmore, and others* (London, 1891), p. 173 and in *SC*, 14 December 1992 (Sale of the Hulton Papers), pp. 26–7. The original is written in the hand of Essex's personal secretary, Edward Reynoldes. Essex explains in a holograph postscript that the letter had originally been written on the previous evening (i.e. 15 October) 'butt so ill written as I was fayne to use my man's hand to copy yt owt bycause [of] the hasty writing and my indisposition after my jorney, which keepes me from correcting yt'. The dating of this letter – 1595, not 1596 – is explained in P. E. J. Hammer, 'Letters of travel advice from the earl of Essex to the earl of Rutland: some comments', *Philological Quarterly* 74 (1995), pp. 317–25. The date is important because it torpedoes claims that this third letter was written by Francis Bacon rather than Essex – a spurious notion which depends upon a tortured reading of Essex's postscript. Despite this, Bacon's authorship has recently been re-stated by Prof. Brian Vickers in his *Francis Bacon* ((Oxford, 1996), p. 540) and in his seriously misguided article 'The authenticity of Bacon's earliest writings', *Studies in Philology* 94 (1997), pp. 248–96. Vickers is presumably determined to defend the 1596 date for this letter – even though it makes no sense in the light of its contents and even though Essex was certainly not at St Albans in October 1596 – because accepting the correct date of 16 October 1595 would give the whole game away over Bacon's alleged authorship. In October 1595, Essex did not visit St Albans to see Bacon, as Vickers suggests. Bacon was actually resident at Twickenham Park, near Richmond Palace, as his letters of 11 and 14 of October to the lord keeper demonstrate (these are printed in Spedding *Bacon letters*, I, pp, 368–9). As he explained to the lord keeper: 'I am now at Twicknam Park, where I think to stay.' It was therefore physically impossible for Bacon to have written this letter to Rutland, which was clearly penned in some haste by Essex himself. The reason for Essex's visit to St Albans was not to see Bacon but, presumably, to visit the substantial royal stables there in his capacity as master of the horse. Essex may well have had some 'Baconian' ideas in mind when he wrote this letter, but the idea that Bacon was its author cannot be sustained. This information totally undermines the stylistic evidence which allegedly supports Vickers's contentions about this letter ('Authenticity', pp. 287–8. Cf. P. E. J. Hammer, 'The earl of Essex, Fulke Greville and the employment of scholars', *Studies in Philology* 91 (1994), p. 169). In fact, the methodology of Vickers's whole article is contrary to historical logic (in effect, *ante hoc, propter hoc*) and its reliance upon stylistic inferences is fraught with danger because we still lack proper scholarly editions of Bacon's works against which valid stylistic comparisons can be drawn.

text.[201] In the process, the letter was redated to 4 January 1596 and studded with apt Latin tags. It was also given some self-conscious touches which point both to its contrived nature and sophisticated target audience: 'if any curious scholar happening to see this discourse shall quarrel with my divisions of the gifts of the mind, because he findeth it not perhaps in his book ... '.[202] In this highly polished form, the Rutland letter was circulated in and around the Court, ultimately gaining a widespread currency.[203]

By giving Rutland detailed advice on how to extract the maximum personal benefit from his tour, Essex was able to expound upon matters which served to demonstrate his own intellect and judgement. The political nature of this exercise is signalled to the reader in the very first sentence: 'I hold it for a principle in the course of intelligence of state, not to discourage men of mean sufficiency from writing unto me ... '[204] At once, it is clear that Essex is writing as an experienced man of affairs and that he is willing to consider advice from all quarters. In discussing knowledge and the aims of education (in terms clearly designed to satisfy 'any curious scholar'), Essex was also able to state his own political and philosophical positions:

if it seem strange that I account no state flourishing but that which hath neither civil wars nor too long peace, I answer, that politic bodies are like our natural bodies, and must as well have some exercise to spend their humours, as to be kept from too violent or continual outrages which spend their best spirits.[205]

This view was hardly unique or original, but sincerely held all the same: in Essex's opinion, 'idlenes', the enemy of virtue, was as unhealthy for a state as it was for an individual. Another important message in this letter concerns the quality which Essex and Rutland share: their noble status. Essex urges the special importance of noblemen and the responsibility they have to equip themselves properly for government:

the most part of our noblemen and gentlemen of our time have no other use of their learning but their table-talk ... but God knows they have gotten little that have only this discoursing gift; for though, like empty casks, they sound loud when a man knocks upon their outside, yet if you pierce into them you shall find them full of nothing but wind.[206]

[201] See below, pp. 313–14.
[202] Spedding, *Bacon letters*, II, p. 15.
[203] For a very incomplete list of the many surviving manuscript copies of this document, see Hammer, 'Essex, Greville and the employment of scholars', p. 171, n. 20. The success of the letter (and the growing popularity of the genre of travel advice) ultimately led to its publication in print: *Profitable instructions: describing what speciall observations are to be taken by travellers in all nations. By Robert, late earle of Essex. Sir Philip Sidney. and Secretary Davison* (London, 1633, STC no. 6789).
[204] Spedding, *Bacon letters*, II, p. 6.   [205] *Ibid.*, p. 12   [206] *Ibid.*, p. 14.

The political implications of this are very obvious. The whole document sets up a powerful contrast between these ignorant blow-hards (whose rank and identity are kept deliberately vague) and Essex himself, whose copious talents are shown by his constant praise of applied learning and the whole tenor of the letter. Artfully constructed and shrewdly disseminated, this document is nothing less than a demonstration of Essex's credentials to helm the ship of state, and a testimonial to his vast ambition. However, the political resonance of this document was even greater than its contents suggest. Burghley had written a similar letter of advice for a previous earl of Rutland[207] and Essex's decision to circulate this letter could not fail to invite comparisons between the two documents and the two authors. Essex's letter to Rutland was not only a political manifesto, but also an implicit public challenge to the old lord treasurer.

---

[207] Burghley wrote a letter of travel advice for Edward, 3rd earl of Rutland in August 1571: C. Read, *Lord Burghley and Queen Elizabeth* (London, 1960), pp. 127–8; B. W. Beckingsale, *Burghley: Tudor statesman* (London, 1967), p. 248. I am indebted to Dr Pauline Croft for reminding me of this letter and its significance.

---- ⟪ **5** ⟫ ----

'Matters of intelligence'

When Essex joined the council in February 1593, Elizabeth gave special encouragement to his work in the gathering of foreign intelligence. In her eyes, this was a test of his abilities and a productive way to channel his enthusiasm for Continental affairs. For his part, Essex was eager to prove himself and gathering intelligence was a sphere of activity which appealed to him. There was a natural affinity between the role of favourite and intelligence, for both involved the sharing of secret confidences and a zealous concern for the queen's safety.[1] However, Essex's participation in this world of secrets and spies also opened new possibilities for influencing royal policies. The private audiences at which intelligence was imparted to the queen offered Essex the chance to impress her with his knowledge and judgement and to emphasise special subjects of concern without interjection from other councillors.[2] Intelligence therefore became a central feature in Essex's political endeavours and he invested a great deal of time and money in pursuit of fresh information.

Despite its importance (or perhaps because of it), exploring Essex's intelligence-gathering activities is a frustrating exercise. Ciphers and obscure language are a frequent (and intentional) barrier to understanding, while a great deal of evidence has been lost through the ravages of time and the deliberate culling of files. Although a fair number of reports from agents survive, there is little indication about how such reports were analysed and how they may have affected government actions. Like other goings-on at Court, many of the most important matters relating to intelligence were probably conducted only by word of mouth and have left no trace on paper. For reasons of security, government accounts also often disguised or concealed payments and other rewards to agents.[3] Essex may

---

[1] See, for example, DUL, Howard MS 2, fol. 127ʳ.
[2] For Essex's reporting of intelligence to Elizabeth, see 'Career', pp. 135–6.
[3] For example, spies were often paid as extraordinary messengers (e.g. E. de Kalb, 'Robert Poley's movements as a messenger of the Court, 1588 to 1601', *Review of English Studies* 9 (1933), pp. 13–18).

have used a similar strategy in his own financial records.[4] In a budget paper drawn up about 1593, his steward simply stated that 'intelygence ... is a matter of secrett & therfore I can make noe estymatt but leve itt'.[5]

These evidential problems inevitably restrict and shape the discussion which follows. Dispatches survive from some of Essex's agents, but by no means all of them. How many other sources of information Essex possessed can only be guessed at. Of those reports which do survive, some give a detailed impression of the activities and concerns of the agent who wrote them, at least for certain periods of time. Other dispatches give only a fleeting impression of their author and tantalising hints about the nature of his mission. Nevertheless, it is clear that most of the information which constituted 'intelligence' in this period was hardly 'top secret'. Although some spies were intent upon what was termed 'practice' – the deliberate misleading and subornment of the enemy, usually by acting as a double agent – most agents at this time were really just gatherers and reporters of current affairs. In an age without mass media, governments had to find their own ways of learning about events in foreign lands. Because England had few diplomatic posts overseas and much of Europe was under the control of her enemies, individual agents had to provide much of the basic information which the government needed. Despite its sometimes dark and dangerous secrets, the business of gathering intelligence was primarily a never-ending struggle for news.[6]

Essex's involvement in the world of spies began in the early months of 1591, when he was approached by Thomas Phelippes and Francis Bacon about employing an agent who could be used to 'practise' with English

---

[4] The only obvious reference to a spy in Essex's accounts – perhaps a slip – is a payment of £5 in 1595 to Thomas Cload, 'being a spie for Spaine' (Devereux MS 3, fol. 83ʳ). Cload seems to have left no other trace of his work. This suggests that either this name is an alias or that all the papers relating to his activities have been lost.

[5] Devereux MS 2, fol. 82ᵛ.

[6] Perhaps inevitably, published work on this subject tends to emphasise 'practice' rather than routine intelligence gathering. For a useful recent survey of this subject, see A. Haynes, *Invisible power: the Elizabethan secret services 1570–1603* (London, 1992). A. Plowden, *The Elizabethan secret service* (London, 1991) and J. M. Archer, *Sovereignty and intelligence: spying and Court culture in the English Renaissance* (Stanford, 1993) are poor. More specialist recent studies include J. Bossy, *Giordano Bruno and the embassy affair* (London, 1991); P. E. J. Hammer, 'An Elizabethan spy who came in from the cold: the return of Anthony Standen to England in 1593', *Historical Research* 65 (1992), pp. 277–95; M. Leimon and G. Parker, 'Treason and plot in Elizabethan diplomacy: the "fame of Sir Edward Stafford" revisited', *EHR* 111 (1996), pp. 1134–58; and M. Questier, 'Practical anti-papistry during the reign of Elizabeth I', *Journal of British Studies* 36 (1997), pp. 371–95. For relevant older works, see 'Career', p. 98, n. 1. There is also much useful information in C. Nicholl, *The reckoning: the murder of Christopher Marlowe* (London, 1992), but its central argument should be treated with great caution: P. E. J. Hammer, 'A reckoning reframed: the "murder" of Christopher Marlowe reconsidered', *English Literary Renaissance* 26 (1996), pp. 225–42.

Catholic exiles in Flanders.[7] Phelippes and Bacon were long-time associ-ates[8] and both had been involved in intelligence matters with Sir Francis Walsingham. Bacon had acted as an interrogator of suspects, while the bespectacled Phelippes had been Walsingham's chief decipherer and a controller for some of his key agents.[9] The spy whom Bacon and Phelippes sought to sponsor, William Sterrell (alias Henry St Main), was another veteran of the old secretary's time.[10] According to their plan, Sterrell would pose as an agent for the Catholic exiles in order to feed them false information and try to learn their secrets, especially any plots against Elizabeth. Essex would secure the queen's approval for Sterrell's actions and provide him with money (and also Phelippes and Bacon, no doubt). In return, Essex would be able to report all Sterrell's information to the queen, thereby demonstrating his concern for national security.[11]

Although Bacon probably saw this contact only as a stepping-stone to greater things, Phelippes and Sterrell were eager to win Essex's patronage because Walsingham's death had sharply reduced the possibilities of employment for spies. Over many years, Walsingham had used his position as secretary of state to dominate the gathering of intelligence for Eliza-beth.[12] In his zeal for information, he allegedly spent a great deal of his own money, as well as an official secretarial emolument for intelligence pur-poses.[13] After his death, no secretary was appointed to take Walsingham's

---

[7] William Sterrell advised Phelippes of his efforts to introduce himself to Essex in a letter dated 18 April (PRO, SP 12/238, fol. 184[r]). The supposition by the editor of *CSPD* that this document belongs to 1591 is borne out by comments in a later letter from Phelippes to Essex (*HMCS*, VI, p. 511).

[8] Bacon and Phelippes had had close dealings with each other since at least the early 1580s (University of Edinburgh Library, Laing MSS, division iii, no. 193, fol. 142[v]; J. O. Halliwell (ed.), *The private diary of Dr John Dee, and the catalogue of his library of manuscripts* (Camden Society, XIX, 1842), p. 16). A younger brother of Phelippes, possibly Stephen, was described in late 1586 as 'brought upp with Mr ffrances Bacon thes too or three yeares' (PRO, SP 12/194, fols. 13[r], 42[r]).

[9] J. Martin, *Francis Bacon, the state and the reform of natural philosophy* (Cambridge, 1992), pp. 35, 46, 97; C. Read, *Mr Secretary Walsingham and the policy of Queen Elizabeth*, (3 vols., Oxford, 1925), II, pp. 316, 335, 432–3; *ibid.*, III, ch. 12. The most succinct account of Phelippes's career is *Commons*, III, pp. 219–20.

[10] There is no adequate account of Sterrell. C. H. Carter, who discusses Sterrell's work in the Jacobean era, describes his career as 'unclassifiable' (*The secret diplomacy of the Habs-burgs, 1598–1625* (New York and London, 1964), ch. 12). After the accession of James I, Sterrell was granted a reward for his services during Elizabeth's reign by being appointed keeper of St John's (alias St John's of Jerusalem) in London (PRO, C 66/1608, unfol., privy seal bill of 19 May 1603).

[11] Cecil MSS 47/6 (pr. *HMCS*, VI, pp. 511–12), 103/151 (pr. *HMCS*, XVII, p. 39); BL, Cotton MSS Appendix, vol. 39, fols. 73[r]–74[v]; BL, Cotton MS Vitellius C XVII, fols. 377[r]–378[v]; PRO, SP 14/12, fol. 59[r–v].

[12] Leimon and Parker, 'Treason and plot', pp. 1136–9.

[13] This emolument was set at £2,000 per annum in mid-1588. Previously, grants of money for disbursement by the secretary on intelligence had been made in an *ad hoc* fashion.

place and control of the office, including intelligence, fell to Burghley.[14] As lord treasurer, Burghley was concerned about the ballooning costs of intelligence and the dubious book-keeping which it produced. Together with Sir Thomas Heneage, the vice-chamberlain, Burghley quickly implemented a process of retrenchment and rationalisation in intelligence matters. Many agents were removed from the royal pay-roll.[15] Burghley's use of the secretarial intelligence vote also ceased by mid-1591.[16]

This process of retrenchment had important consequences. Although it saved the queen money, it also restricted the amount of intelligence which she and her ministers received. Elizabeth always prided herself on being well informed about events abroad and expected her advisers to be able to brief her accordingly. Although Walsingham sought to centralise and dominate intelligence gathering, other members of the privy council had employed agents of their own as well. Burghley's cuts now placed an added burden on these councillors, especially those who held offices which had some affinity with intelligence matters. Elizabeth's expectations about being kept adequately informed and Burghley's determination to cut costs encouraged a kind of rough division of labour, even specialisation. As governor of Berwick, Hunsdon remained a leading expert on Scottish affairs, while the lord admiral concentrated on seeking information about Spanish shipping. Lord Cobham, as warden of the Cinque Ports, watched comings and goings across the Channel. Other councillors, such as Hatton, Heneage and Buckhurst, also paid for agents out of their own pockets, picking up former employees of Walsingham. However, reducing the queen's expenditure on intelligence – partial privatisation, as it were – was not without its negative effects. Among those agents whose services were discontinued, the cuts soured views of royal patronage, and of Burghley himself. In the scramble for new paymasters which followed, many exaggerated claims were also made which encouraged false expectations and outright lies.

In his dealings with Phelippes and Sterrell, Essex seems to have been a victim of such unrealistic expectations. During 1591, he was a complete neophyte in intelligence matters. The advice which Bacon gave Phelippes

---

Walsingham's official payments for the period 1585–9 were summarised after his death in PRO, SP 12/229, fol. 86^r.

[14] Hammer, 'Return of Standen', pp. 280, 283ff.

[15] Burghley and Heneage were hard at this task by May 1590, using Walsingham's own papers and abstracts prepared by his former employees (PRO, SP 12/231, fols. 19^r, 86^r; PRO, SP 12/232, fols. 20^v–21^r). This process was all the more urgent because news of Walsingham's death prompted a series of claims from agents for outstanding payments. For example, the Frenchman Henri Chateaumartin (real name Pierre d'Or) demanded no less than £1000 to meet his expenses (BL, Harleian MS 6995, fol. 6^r; PRO, SP 78/21, fol. 289^r).

[16] Burghley received this emolument only once, by a privy seal of 20 May 1590 (PRO, E 403/2427, unfol., listed under miscellaneous payments).

for dealing with Essex in 'this begynnyng of intelligence' is remarkable, not only for its image of Essex's eagerness to learn about espionage, but also for its typically Baconian didacticism: 'the more playnely and frankely yow shall deal with my lord, not onely in disclosing particulars but in gyving him caveats and admonishing him of any error which in this action he may comytt (such is his nature), the better he will take it'.[17] Such trust continued after Essex's return from Rouen, even though Bacon gradually distanced himself from Phelippes. Responding to an urgent request from Phelippes in May 1592, Essex replied 'take no pity of my purse'.[18] However, the constant exchanges of fraudulent letters and the comings and goings of Sterrell and other spies brought no spectacular results.[19] By June 1593, Essex's patience with Phelippes was wearing thin: 'this matter is nott to be playd withall, therfore I pray yow waken him, for besides the duty which wee all owe, my reputation is ingaged in yt and I will not indure thatt the negligence of such a fellow shold turne to her Majestie's unquiettnes and my disgrace'.[20]

As so often in these matters, it remains unclear on what venture Essex had staked his reputation in mid-1593. However, if the nature of this initiative remains mysterious, the identity of the agent being 'wakened' offers some interesting clues. Rather than Sterrell, this agent was one Roger Walton, a rogue of the first order who had dealings with several councillors during his chequered career.[21] Walton's speciality was acting as an *agent provocateur*, encouraging others to vow dangerous deeds and then reporting on them.[22] Whatever the precise nature of the service in question,

---

17 PRO, SP 12/238, fol. 206r.
18 PRO, SP 12/242, fol. 69ʳ.   19 'Career', pp. 103–6.
20 PRO, SP 12/245, fol. 57Aʳ. This hasty note is undated but has been endorsed 'June 1593' in Phelippes's hand.
21 Born about 1562 (*HMCS*, V, p. 341), Walton was a page to the 8th earl of Northumberland (d. 1585) and later acted as a spy for Walsingham in the household of his son, Henry, 9th earl of Northumberland (A. G. Petti (ed.), *The letters and despatches of Richard Verstegan (c.1550–1640)* (Catholic Record Society, LII, 1959), p. 204; Nicholl, *The reckoning*, p. 200). He was fingering men as traitors by October 1586, when he passed on the names of various individuals to the notorious Richard Topcliffe (P. J. Blok (ed.), *Correspondance inedite de Robert Dudley, comte de Leycester, et de François et Jean Hotman* (Haarlem, 1911), pp. 156–7). He received payments from the English government by 1588 (PRO, E 351/542, fol. 111ʳ). During 1593, in addition to his work for Essex, he also sent French intelligence to Cecil (*HMCS*, IV, p. 325; W. D. Acres, 'The early political career of Sir Robert Cecil c.1582–1597: some aspects of late Elizabethan secretarial administration' (unpub. Ph.D. thesis, University of Cambridge, 1992), p. 62). Essex clearly did not trust Walton. In August 1595 he had him shadowed and arrested (*HMCS*, V, p. 341). Walton was still in gaol a year later. In August 1596, he desperately offered his services to Sir John Stanhope and Cecil, complaining that he had spent 30 of the last 36 months in close confinement and that he had been racked three times (*HMCS*, VI, pp. 352–3).
22 The Catholic intelligence gatherer, Richard Verstegan, reported that 'by other letters it was signified that Walton did in England make an occupation of accusing men, and that he had broughte 5 or 6 to the gallowes' (Petti, *Verstegan letters*, p. 205).

Essex's employment of Walton is highly suggestive. Walton's gruesome record (of which Essex and Phelippes were clearly well aware) provides circumstantial evidence to support allegations by modern historians that Essex and other privy councillors used agents actually to foment conspiracies against the queen,[23] a technique sometimes termed 'projection'.[24] Such plots were exposed when the time seemed right and the participants were tried and executed with maximum publicity. By this means, Catholic exiles could be discredited and Elizabeth could be encouraged to maintain a hard line against Spain, whose support was blamed for each new conspiracy.

There seems little doubt that the English government did sometimes indulge in such conduct. The Babington Plot, for example, which ultimately brought death for Mary Queen of Scots, was largely driven by *agents provocateurs* employed by Walsingham.[25] Sir Robert Cecil may have taken a leaf from the late secretary's book in his prosecution of Richard Hesketh for trying to suborn the earl of Derby in late 1593.[26] The contact with Walton suggests that Essex may have been up to something similar. However, Thomas Phelippes was also well experienced in such matters (he had been Walsingham's right-hand man during the Babington Plot) and, through Sterrell, was in frequent contact with exile leaders who were consistently blamed for instigating these plots against the queen.[27]

[23] As the young Edward Hyde (later earl of Clarendon) wrote of Sir Robert Cecil: 'for whom (indeed) it seemed as necessary there should be treasons, as for the state that they should be prevented. Insomuch as it was then (how unjustly soever) conceived that though he created none, yet he fomented some conspiracies, that he might give frequent evidences of his loyalty, having no other advantage (as the earl and others had in person) to justifie him in an ordinary estimation, but by eminent services' ('The difference and disparity between the estates and conditions of George, duke of Buckingham, and Robert, earl of Essex' in Sir Henry Wotton, *Reliquiae Wottonianae, or a collection of lives, letters (and) poems with characters of sundry persons* (4th edn, London, 1685, Wing no. W 3651), pp. 187–8).
[24] The term (which is modern, not contemporary) is used, for example, by Nicholl. He describes it as 'a piece of political theatre, conjured up for reasons of cynical expediency' (*The reckoning*, p. 147; see also pp. 246, 248–9, 301). Catholic historians, eager to exculpate victims of Elizabethan justice, have long emphasised (and condemned) the same practice.
[25] The most recent accounts of this episode are Haynes, *Invisible power*, chs. 6–8, and Nicholl, *The reckoning*, ch. 17. See also A. G. Smith, *The Babington Plot* (London, 1936).
[26] C. Devlin, 'The earl and the alchemist', *The Month*, n.s., 9 (1953), pp. 23–38, 92–104, 153–66; Nicholl, *The reckoning*, pp. 247–8, 258–9, 320. Devlin's account ultimately hinges upon accepting the truth of Hesketh's claim that the evidence against him was planted. The Hesketh Plot won Cecil his spurs as an intelligence operator in the same way that the Lopez Plot marked Essex's maturity in this sphere: Acres, 'Early career of Cecil', pp. 27–9.
[27] One of Sterrell's key contacts, for example, was Hugh Owen (e.g. PRO, SP 12/241, fol. 4^r; PRO, SP 12/243, fol. 218^r; PRO, SP 14/12, fol. 59^r). Owen was regarded as the mastermind behind many plots against Elizabeth's life and was automatically blamed for instigating the Gunpowder Plot under James I (A. J. Loomie, *The Spanish Elizabethans: the English exiles at the Court of Philip II* (New York, 1963), ch. 3).

No explicit evidence survives to indicate that Essex used Phelippes and Sterrell (or even Walton) in this way, but this is hardly surprising. Nevertheless, it is interesting that a rash of plots against the queen were detected during 1593–4 and that Essex was instrumental in discovering several of them. Some of the details elicited during these investigations are highly suggestive. Manuel Luis Tinoco, one of the Portuguese executed for complicity with Dr Lopez, claimed that he had cleared his actions with Essex beforehand.[28] According to notes made by the lord admiral, John Annias, whose associate Patrick Cullen was executed in 1594 for allegedly trying to assassinate Elizabeth, 'had a juell to have presented to the e[arl] of Essex and so to have becomm his man'.[29] Edmund Yorke, who was arrested with Richard Williams for conspiring to kill Elizabeth in August 1594, also returned to England under cover of seeking to enter service with Essex.[30] It is conceivable that the capture of Yorke and Williams may have been part of a much broader penetration of the activities of the leader of the exiles, Sir William Stanley, by agents of Essex.[31] Such action may even have caused Essex some fleeting embarrassment, for he found himself 'falslie charged with that which he never intendyd' about this time.[32] It is also significant that Francis Bacon sought to make political capital out of

[28] J. Gwyer, 'The case of Dr Lopez', *Transactions of the Jewish Historical Society of England* 16 (1952), p. 173. Gwyer's supposition that Tinoco was an agent for Essex stretches this evidence a little too far. Perhaps coincidentally, Tinoco was the only one of the Lopez 'conspirators' to plead guilty at his trial (PRO, KB 8/52, m. 5).

[29] PRO, SP 12/247, fol. 59ʳ. Cullen (or Collen) claimed that his target was not the queen, but Antonio Perez. For his trial, see PRO, KB 8/51. Perez subsequently made a point of watching Cullen's head being placed above the city gates (G. Maranon, *Antonio Perez: 'Spanish traitor'* (trans. C. D. Ley, London, 1954), p. 319). By contrast, Annias escaped prosecution for his activities and sought release from the Tower in early 1596 (*CSPD, 1595–7*, IV, pp. 169–70).

[30] *CSPD, 1591–4*, III, pp. 522, 539. Essex himself played a leading part in this investigation. Interrogation notes survive in Essex's own hand (PRO, SP 12/249, fol. 122ʳ⁻ᵛ). Yorke and Williams were executed in February 1595.

[31] A. H. Dodd suggests that Owen Salusbury was involved in furthering Stanley's hopes of winning over the earl of Derby to the Spanish cause and of fomenting a rebellion in North Wales during 1593–4. Dodd speculates that Salusbury's name was never mentioned during the investigation of Yorke, Williams and others because he was protected by Essex ('North Wales in the Essex Revolt of 1601', *EHR* 59 (1944), pp. 357–9). Although this interpretation is clearly speculative, Salusbury's close friend, Peter Wynn, was certainly employed by Essex during this time (see below).

[32] This claim is made in an extraordinary letter to Thomas Phelippes from Hugh Owen – a frequent correspondent and Phelippes's opposite number, as it were, among the Catholic exiles in Flanders (PRO, SP 12/248, fols. 125ʳ-126ᵛ). Owen says that he has heard Essex is 'much moved' by these false allegations and writes to clear the earl (and himself) from these assertions. The stories in question seem to relate to manoeuvrings by Stanley, Owen and others to win over the earl of Derby during 1593 and claims made by agents of Essex about their master's willingness to support Derby. Owen's letter is open to a variety of interpretations, including that it is an attempt to undermine future 'projected' plots by reminding Essex of the dangers involved in such activities.

these plots, no doubt with Essex's encouragement. In a series of notes about ensuring the queen's safety, he urged 'the breaking of these fugitive traytors and filling them full of terror, dispayre, jalousy and revolt'.[33] By trumpeting intelligence successes, he claimed, 'the fugitives will grow into such a mutuall jalousy and suspicion one of another as they will not have the confydence to conspyre together'.[34]

The most intriguing evidence about Essex's possible use of agents to 'project' plots upon enemies of the state concerns Roger Walton and the earl's first and most spectacular counter-intelligence coup – the destruction of Dr Lopez in early 1594. The Lopez case has long been the subject of great controversy and most modern commentators argue that he was innocent of the charge of trying to poison Elizabeth.[35] Lopez certainly had compromising dealings with the Spanish[36] but these were twisted to fit the most extreme interpretation, while confessions of dubious value were extracted from his alleged accomplices by coercion. If the claims of a desperate man are to be believed, Tinoco was directly encouraged into fatally compromising actions by Essex himself. This claim seems plausible because there are fragmentary hints which suggest Essex may have used Roger Walton to push Lopez (and perhaps also Tinoco) into some of their fatally compromising actions, at least in the early stages of the operation.

Essex's note to Phelippes in June 1593 begins: 'I heare Walton is nott gone. Yow know how neere the day of the appointed meeting is. This matter is nott to be playd withall ...' The nature of Walton's meeting remains mysterious. However, Walton had alerted Essex to dubious activities by Lopez only a short while earlier. In a confession which is raised in none of the charges against Lopez, one Robert Draper (or Diapar) claims that he chanced upon incriminating evidence against the doctor during a trip to Antwerp soon after Easter. At the time, Draper was working as a courier for Walton, who took the material (a packet of letters addressed to Lopez from correspondents in Flanders) to give to Essex. Five or six weeks

---

[33] LPL, MS 936, no. 1.

[34] *Ibid.*, no. 2. Internal evidence suggests that this document was written about the middle of 1594. Both this fragment and the last are printed in Spedding, *Bacon letters*, I, 305–6.

[35] See, for example, S. L. Lee, 'The original of Shylock', *Gentleman's Magazine*, 246 (1880), pp. 185–200; A. Dimock, 'The conspiracy of Dr Lopez', *EHR* 9 (1894), 440–72; M. A. S. Hume, *Treason and plot: struggles for Catholic supremacy in the last years of Elizabeth* (London, 1901), pp. 116–53, 162–4; also his 'The so-called conspiracy of Dr Ruy Lopez', *Transactions of the Jewish Historical Society of England* 6 (1912), pp. 32–55; Gwyer, 'The case of Dr Lopez'; Tenison, IX, 247ff; Haynes, *Invisible power*, pp. 112–20. The best contemporary account of this episode, although hardly unbiased, is the full-length report by William Waad, one of the leading investigators (BL, Add. MS 48029, fols. 147ʳ-184ᵛ).

[36] These are well illustrated in the only substantial work which rejects the traditional line of Lopez's innocence: D. S. Katz, *The Jews in the history of England 1485–1850* (Oxford, 1994), ch. 2.

later, Draper saw Walton with Lopez beside the highway near Kingston, 'where they talked familiarly & privately together by the space of a quarter of an houre'.[37] Although the nature of his contact with Lopez is uncertain, the latter scene suggests an *agent provocateur* hard at work.[38] Lopez was clearly excited when he had a series of discussions with one of his co-conspirators, Esteban Ferreira da Gama. According to da Gama, these meetings took place during a visit to Wanstead in the summer of 1593.[39] Wanstead belonged to Essex and the occasion to which da Gama refers was almost certainly the earl's grand two-day reception for the vidame de Chartres, which occurred on 21–2 June.[40] It is tempting to suggest that Walton's meeting may have had some connection with da Gama's discussions with Lopez, although this cannot be proven. All that can be said for certain is that whatever service Walton promised to perform for Essex – and whatever his dealings with Lopez – collapsed at the start of September, when the spy was arrested on charges of conspiring to betray the Dutch port of Ostend to the Spanish.[41]

If Essex had tried to use Walton to lead on Lopez and his associates, the attempt failed. By October 1593, Essex's endeavours were directed towards more orthodox investigative techniques, intercepting letters and interrogating suspects.[42] This slow grind finally encouraged Essex to raise charges of treason against the old doctor in mid-January 1594, but Elizabeth and

---

[37] PRO, SP 12/247, fol. 64ʳ. Rough corroboration for the chronology of this testimony can be seen in payments authorised by Sir Thomas Heneage, which indicate that Walton left England after 25 March and made a brief visit back to England from Calais in the middle of May (PRO, E 351/542, fols. 181ʳ, 182ᵛ). Clearly, Walton was back in England again during June. The deponent here may be the 'Robert Daper' whom Essex committed to the custody of the knight marshal in 1595 (Devereux MS 3, fol. 75ᵛ).

[38] This incident seems to be open to at least two interpretations. Firstly, this meeting (by chance or planned?) could show Walton and Lopez genuinely working together in order to trick mutual contacts in Flanders (and/or Essex himself). Alternatively, Walton may have been working against Lopez, deliberately leading him on with talk about potential rewards for dangerous services. In this case, Walton would have been only posing as a friend and collaborator. According to either of these scenarios, Lopez was involved in dubious activities and laying himself open to action by Essex.

[39] BL, Add. MS 48029, fol. 155v. This was the occasion when Lopez allegedly declared how much money he wanted from the Spanish as a reward for his treason.

[40] Devereux MS 3, fol. 74ᵛ.

[41] PRO, SP 84/47, fols. 36ʳ–37ʳ, 38ʳ⁻ᵛ, 41ʳ, 46ʳ⁻ᵛ, 50ʳ, 60ᵛ–61ʳ, 62ʳ⁻ᵛ, 68ʳ, 81ʳ, 98ʳ, 129ʳ. Essex and the Dutch ambassador in England, Noël de Caron, had to intervene with the local authorities to save Walton's life (Petti, *Verstegan letters*, pp. 204–5).

[42] BL, Add. MS 48029, fol. 148ʳ. Essex told Lord Cobham in early November that this operation was to counter a plot for kidnapping Dom Antonio's two sons to Spain (*HMCS*, IV, p. 409). It is unclear whether this was a genuinely new investigation which later led back to Lopez by chance, or this surveillance of other Portuguese suspects was simply a change of tactics in Essex's pursuit of Lopez, brought about by Walton's failure. It is also conceivable that the explanation to Cobham was a ruse to veil Essex's interest in Lopez.

the Cecils dismissed them out of hand.[43] Their ridicule plunged Essex into another of those profound personal crises which occurred when his high expectations of success and reward were challenged by the sudden threat of failure. He shut himself up alone in his chamber for an hour and refused to speak with any councillor but the lord admiral for the next two days.[44] When he finally returned to the queen, Essex raised the political stakes by claiming new evidence that Lopez had actually planned to kill her.[45] Faced with these charges, Elizabeth was forced to open a full-scale investigation of Lopez. Men accused of treason rarely stood a chance in Tudor England and this was the beginning of the end for Lopez. This sudden change of fortunes was a very sweet moment for Essex. However grudgingly, Elizabeth was forced to recognise the value of his intelligence. For once, Burghley and Cecil were forced to dance according to his tune. Like the rest of the council, they had to demonstrate their concern for the queen's safety by throwing their full weight behind the investigation.[46]

Essex worked very hard to turn this political victory into a public triumph. Having convinced Elizabeth that his charges against Lopez should be pursued, Essex set himself to destroy Lopez with all the energy which he could muster. With that enormous dynamism which was so characteristic of his enthusiasm, he pursued the case relentlessly through February and March 1594, with almost daily interrogations or meetings to consider progress: 'by continuall labor, supinge, myninge, and hewinge out of hard rock, and approachinge by little and little, all there defences were taken

---

[43] Hume's explanation for the scepticism of the Cecils is probably correct (*Treason and plot*, p. 137). They were well aware of Lopez's past dealings with the Spanish ('Career', p. 123, n. 124) and assumed that there was nothing new in Essex's claims. Burghley's attitude is signalled in the holograph postscript of his letter to Cecil of 23 January 1594: 'in [name scrawled out but clearly "Lopez"] folly I se no poynt of treason intended to the queen but a redynes to make some gayn to the hurt of [two words scrawled out but probably meaning "the king of Spain"]' (CUL, MS Ee.iii.56, no. 15). Burghley believed that Lopez wanted only to trick the Spanish out of a large sum of money, no doubt to make up for the massive sum of 50,000 crowns which he apparently lost by investing in the Portugal expedition of 1589 (Haynes, *Invisible power*, p. 115). At his trial, it was alleged that Lopez was to have been paid exactly 50,000 crowns for killing Elizabeth (PRO, KB 8/52, mm. 17, 19).

[44] LPL, MS 650, fols. 25ʳ, 26ʳ.

[45] LPL, MS 653, fol. 312ʳ. Waad's account attributes this revelation to the fortuitous arrival of a letter which seemed to incriminate Lopez (BL, Add. MS 48029, fol. 154ʳ). It is also possible that Lopez and other prisoners were threatened with torture, since they were then being held at Essex House in the custody of Gelly Meyrick (*ibid.*, fol. 155ʳ; LPL, MS 650, fol. 26ʳ). Essex himself claimed that he had 'beene so tyred with examinations [over the last two days] as I had scarse leysure to eate' (LPL, MS 653, fol. 312ʳ).

[46] Hence Burghley instructed William Waad to write a 'short narration' of the plot and took personal charge of editing and amending it for publication (PRO, SP 12/248, fol. 8ʳ; C. Read, 'William Cecil and Elizabethan public relations', in S. T. Bindoff, J. Hurstfield and C. H. Williams (eds.), *Elizabethan government and society* (London, 1961), pp. 52–3).

awaye and a breache was made'.[47] Although Cecil and the lord admiral also played active roles,[48] the 'generall' in the case was clearly Essex.[49] Elizabeth was sufficiently impressed with his work to use him as an interrogator on several other important treason cases in the following years.[50] Once the sentence had been passed, Essex urged Elizabeth to cease delaying the grisly rituals of public execution.[51] Some of his friends may even have helped to encourage the wave of anti-semitism which swept London during 1594, playing upon Lopez's Jewish origins.[52] The case became so infamous that Essex was able to make political capital out of it even much later in his career.[53] In the short term, he gained public acclaim and had the satisfaction of seeing rumours of peace talks turn to ashes.[54]

Essex gained a great deal of political momentum out of the Lopez case and widespread recognition for the excellence of his intelligence. However it apparently did little good for Essex's relationship with Thomas Phelippes. Essex seems to have become increasingly disillusioned with Phelippes and ultimately transferred control of William Sterrell's activities to William Waad.[55] Essex enjoyed close dealings with Waad during the Lopez case and knew him as a clerk of the privy council and former servant of

[47] BL, Add. MS 48029, fol. 164ʳ.

[48] Cecil, for example, was reported as being so preoccupied by his involvement in the case that he 'passethe throughe the Presence lyke a blynde man not looking upon any' (LPL, MS 650, fol. 78ᵛ).

[49] BL, Add. MS 48029, fol. 167ʳ.

[50] Important interrogations were conducted by a team of privy councillors and other officials. Essex usually worked with Cecil and the lord admiral. Cases in which Essex took part included the investigation of Edmund Yorke, Richard Williams and Henry Young in August and September 1594 (PRO, SP 12/249, fols. 105ʳ–106ᵛ, 114ʳ⁻ᵛ, 118ʳ⁻ᵛ, 122ʳ⁻ᵛ, 134ʳ⁻ᵛ, 137ʳ, 162ʳ–163ᵛ, 164ʳ, 171ʳ–175ʳ, 186ʳ⁻ᵛ, 199ʳ), Nicholas Williamson in April 1595 (PRO, SP 12/251, fols. 152ʳ–155ʳ), an unnamed Italian in May 1595 (PRO, SP 12/252, fol. 64ʳ), the Jesuit Thomas Wright in June 1595 (ibid., fols. 150ʳ, 151ʳ) and Thomas Arundell in April 1597 (HMCS, VI, pp. 151–2 (apparently misdated); ibid., VII, p. 167).

[51] Essex himself penned one of the privy council's letters ordering the execution of Lopez and his associates in early June (BL, Harleian MS 6996, fol. 162ʳ).

[52] M. Hotine, 'The politics of anti-semitism: The Jew of Malta and The merchant of Venice', N&Q 236 (1991), p. 38.

[53] Apologie, sig. B4ʳ. Essex's success against Lopez was also emphasised in the 1596 edition of Lewis Lewknor's The estate of English fugitives under the king of Spaine and his ministers. Although the text was unchanged from the 1595 edition (STC no. 15564, sig. N4ʳ–O1ʳ), the 1596 version added a marginal note by the description of Lopez: 'The Earle of Essex' (STC no. 15565, sig. P2ᵛ). Essex is the only councillor singled out in this way.

[54] In fact, although the Lopez affair convinced the council of the impossibility of dealing with Spain, it seems that Elizabeth herself was not finally persuaded to abandon all hope of new peace talks until the discovery of the plot of Yorke and Williams in August 1594 (R. B. Wernham, 'Queen Elizabeth I, the Emperor Rudolph II and Archduke Ernest, 1593–94', in E. I. Kouri and T. Scott (eds.), Politics and society in Reformation Europe (Basingstoke, 1987), pp. 445–7). Perhaps significantly, this plot was another episode in which Essex had curious early dealings

[55] HMCS, VI, pp. 511–12.

Walsingham.[56] Possibly Essex was frustrated with Phelippes over the performance of Walton and the slow progress of Sterrell. He may even have discovered that Phelippes was also conducting another secret correspondence with Catholic exiles through another old hand at 'practice', Thomas Barnes.[57] Whatever the reason for Essex's action, Phelippes's stocks fell even further when he was imprisoned for large debts to the crown arising from his role as a customs official. Although Phelippes continued to perform work for members of the council, he often had to do so from a prison cell.[58]

Essex's growing disenchantment with the intelligence work of Phelippes was undoubtedly accentuated by his increasing reliance upon Anthony Bacon, the elder brother of Francis.[59] Anthony Bacon returned to England in early 1592 after spending a decade abroad, mostly in France – an experience which harmonised nicely with Essex's own ardent francophile tendencies. During his long sojourn, Bacon made a remarkable range of contacts, even to the point of almost being appointed 'one of the iiii chamberlayns in France abowt the king'.[60] In contrast to Thomas Phelippes, whose contacts were essentially restricted to English exiles in Flanders, Anthony Bacon brought to Essex's service a host of valuable connections with Frenchmen and Scots who travelled in France. Bacon's influence was crucial in expanding the scope of Essex's secret activities far beyond mere counter-intelligence work amongst Catholic exiles.

Anthony Bacon began to gravitate towards Essex soon after his return to England. This link sprang primarily from the close association with the earl of his brother Francis,[61] but Anthony Bacon also looked towards Essex because of disenchantment with the welcome afforded him by his uncle, Lord Burghley. During his stay abroad, Bacon had provided Burghley with intelligence about affairs in France. On his return, Bacon felt that the lord treasurer displayed callous ingratitude after having 'inned my ten yeares' harvest into his owne barne without anie halfpennie chardge': 'I founde nothinge but faire wordes which make fooles faine and yet, even in those,

56 For Waad, see *DNB*, XX, pp. 401–4; *Commons*, III, pp. 560–2.
57 'Career', p. 103, n. 19. Alan Haynes (*Invisible power*, p. 136) suggests that Barnes and Sterrell were actually the same man. Comparison of their handwriting suggests that this is highly unlikely.
58 Phelippes was imprisoned in late 1595 and released in June 1597. He was sent back to prison again soon after.
59 For Anthony Bacon, see D. du Maurier, *The golden lads: a study of Anthony Bacon, Francis and their friends* (London, 1975) and J. T. Freedman, 'Anthony Bacon and his world, 1558–1601' (unpub. Ph.D. thesis, Temple Univ., 1978). Neither work is very satisfactory.
60 LPL, MS 659, fol. 104ᵛ.
61 *Ibid.*, fol. 25ʳ⁻ᵛ; Sir Francis Bacon, *Apologie*, p. 11.

no offer or hopefull asseurance of reall kindenes, which I thought I might justlie expecte at his lordship's handes.'[62] Essex, by contrast, welcomed Anthony Bacon with open arms.

From the start, Anthony Bacon enjoyed a special relationship with Essex, who consistently treated him with a remarkable degree of respect.[63] Bacon's letters to Essex enjoyed a priority of access which even the earl's personal secretary envied.[64] Essex was lavish in his constant readiness to do him favours. Usually, these favours were for Bacon's friends or for suitors who 'not a little incombred' him in the hope of capitalising on his intimacy with Essex.[65] All this 'unspeakable kindnes'[66] demonstrated just how highly Essex valued the intelligence work which Bacon performed for him: such gratitude was fully justified by the results which Bacon achieved. Moreover, this conspicuous liberality served to aid his work. The knowledge that he was specially favoured by Essex made it far easier for Bacon to encourage men to open correspondence with him.

Although he began working for Essex during 1592, the results of Anthony Bacon's recruitment did not really make themselves felt until 1593. In that year, Bacon's efforts began to bear fruit both on the Continent and in Scotland. In the latter sphere, in particular, some of these early fruits of Anthony Bacon's work were profoundly important. Above all, after Essex's own abortive attempt to enter into communication with James VI in 1589, Bacon now provided Essex with the keys which unlocked the door to close and secret co-operation with the Scottish king – with all that this implied about the succession to the Elizabeth's throne.

During 1593 and early 1594, Anthony Bacon began correspondence with what were to be three very important Scottish agents for Essex. The first of these agents was Dr Thomas Moresin,[67] a physician whom Bacon had met in France[68] and with whom he shared various intellectual interests.[69] Following Moresin's return to Scotland, Bacon convinced him

---

[62] LPL, MS 659, fol. 25^{r-v}.

[63] See, for example, LPL, MS 650, fol. 139^r; LPL, MS 653, fols. 184^r, 214^r, 224^r.

[64] LPL, MS 655, fol. 64^r. Bacon was also able to send letters to Essex which his secretaries never read (LPL, MS 658, fol. 179^r (a copy is *ibid.*, fol. 15^r); LPL, MS 659, fol. 379^r).

[65] LPL, MS 656, fol. 132^r.

[66] LPL, MS 649, fol. 312^r.

[67] On Moresin, see *DNB*, XIII, pp. 960–1. Despite the claims made in some older books, this agent was definitely *not* Fynes Moryson.

[68] Hence Moresin sent Bacon news from France before he himself returned to Scotland (LPL, MS 649, fols. 485^r, 489^r, 497^r, 502^r, 503^r, 505^r).

[69] Moresin wrote to Bacon about the availability of certain learned books (*ibid.*, fols. 497^r, 501^r) and apparently lent him writings of his own composition (*ibid.*, fol. 505^r). Moresin also addressed Latin verses to Bacon as 'Monsieur de Gorambere (Gorhambury)' (*ibid.*, fols. 486^{r-v}, 487^r–488^r).

to become an agent for Essex by May 1593.[70] Contact with Moresin was initially conducted using the diplomatic postal system of Robert Bowes, the queen's ambassador in Scotland.[71] Despite some early doubts of Bacon and Bowes about the value of the doctor's information and contacts,[72] over the autumn and winter of 1593–4 Moresin briefly became Essex's most important agent.

During 1593, Elizabeth and her council were increasingly worried about Spanish attempts to win influence in Scotland. Although Elizabeth had always taken a special interest in the affairs of her northern neighbour,[73] this concern now took on a new urgency. At the very end of 1592, various papers were found aboard a Scottish ship which incriminated three Catholic earls in Scotland and seemed to hint at Spanish overtures to the king himself – the so-called 'Spanish blanks affair'.[74] Elizabeth urged James to take a hard line against the Catholic earls but found him consistently evasive. In response, Elizabeth initiated a secret policy to build up a pro-English Protestant party in Scotland, centring on the earl of Bothwell. This operation, which began in August 1593, was managed by the Cecils, who used Henry Lok as their intermediary with Bothwell.[75] However, during a trip to the north of Scotland in late June, Dr Moresin met and became friendly with the leader of the Catholic noblemen, the earl

---

[70] *Ibid.*, fol. 139[r]; LPL, MS 653, fol. 291[r].

[71] LPL, MS 649, fols. 139[r], 412[r]; LPL, MS 653, fols. 224[r], 232[r], 236[r]. Bowes was also sent £40 for distribution to Moresin in 1593 (Devereux MS 3, fol. 75[v]). At some point before July 1595, Moresin became Bowes' private physician, although this may not have been until after he ceased being an agent for Essex (*CSPScot*, XI, *1593–95*, p. 642).

[72] Bacon himself initially thought Moresin's main function would be to serve 'as a whetstone' for the endeavours of Bowes (LPL, MS 649, fol. 186[r]). For Bowes' doubts, see *ibid.*, fol. 139[r].

[73] The Jesuit Robert Persons explained Elizabeth's sensitivity to the secretary of the king of Spain: 'owing to Scotland's proximity to England, this is to touch the very pupil of her eye' (Persons to Don Juan de Idiaquez, 31 (21) August 1593, Jesuit Provincial Archives, Farm St Church, London, MS 46/12/3, transcript and translation by Fr Leo Hicks of Archivo General de Simancas, Estado 839, fol. 76. I am indebted to Fr Thomas McCoog for alerting me to the existence of these transcripts).

[74] H. G. Stafford, *James VI and the throne of England* (New York and London, 1940), ch. 3; T. G. Law, 'The Spanish blanks and the Catholic earls', in his *Collected essays and reviews* (ed. P. H. Brown, Edinburgh, 1904), pp. 244–76; F. de B. Medina, 'Intrigues of a Scottish Jesuit at the Spanish Court: unpublished letters of William Crichton to Claudio Acquaviva (Madrid 1590–1592)', in T. M. McCoog (ed.), *The reckoned expense: Edmund Campion and the early English Jesuits* (Woodbridge, 1996), pp. 215–45. The most succinct outline of Elizabeth's dealings with Scotland in this period is W. T. MacCaffrey, *Elizabeth I: war and politics 1588–1603* (Princeton, 1992), ch. 15.

[75] For Lok's instructions, see *CSPScot*, XI, *1593–5*, pp. 153–5. For the work of Burghley and Cecil in this matter, see Acres, 'Early career of Cecil', pp. 88–90. Lok himself was a poet as well as an agent: J. Doelman, 'Seeking "the fruit of favour": the dedicatory sonnets of Henry Lok's *Ecclesiastes*,' *English Literary History* 60 (1993), pp. 1–15.

of Huntly.[76] This opened up entirely new possibilities for English interests. Moresin was not only directed 'to ey the k[ing], Huntly and Bothwell' and to observe 'in them ther desire to deale with Spayne, with us, or one with another',[77] but also to negotiate with Huntly in the queen's name.[78] Several heavily ciphered copies of letters written to Moresin survive among the papers of Anthony Bacon and these indicate the kind of dealings which took place. Huntly was invited to send a representative to stay at Bacon's house at Twickenham Park, close to Richmond Palace.[79] There was also mention of arranging a compact between Elizabeth and James in order to guarantee Huntly's good behaviour towards both monarchs.[80] Moresin's reports delighted Essex: 'the queen did never take more satisfaction in any man's service'.[81] Caught up in the excitement of events, Essex chafed at the wait until new reports arrived from Moresin, sometimes himself tearing open letters in the hope that he could make some sense of them before they were deciphered.[82] On one occasion, Essex even ventured to send Moresin a £100 bonus, before reducing the amount to a more reasonable 100 crowns.[83] However, these heady days of intrigue came to an abrupt end when Essex received a 'suddayne countermand' from the queen. Elizabeth later reversed her decision and asked Essex 'to entertayne Huntly anew' at the end of October, but the excitement of the initial contacts was now replaced with cool wariness.[84] Essex had learned the lesson of not committing himself too far in secret dealings. This new-found caution proved to be well justified. The significance of Moresin's work faded over the early months of 1594, when it became clear that there could be no accommodation with Huntly and his friends, and the Lopez case took centre-stage.

Although communications with Dr Moresin seem to have tailed off,[85] this episode had significant consequences. Although brief, Moresin's activities were an intelligence coup for Essex. By opening contact with Huntly,

---

[76] LPL, MS 649, fol. 210[r]. Almost certainly, Huntly sought to use Moresin as a means of easing English suspicions, in the hope of reducing the pressures put on James to act against him.
[77] LPL, MS 653, fol. 295[r].   [78] *Ibid.*, fol. 180[r].
[79] LPL, MS 649, fol. 490[r]. I am deeply indebted to Prof. Eric Barnes, late of the University of Adelaide, for breaking these ciphers for me.
[80] *Ibid.*, fol. 494[r].   [81] *Ibid.*, fol. 180[r].
[82] *Ibid.*, fol. 301[r]; LPL, MS 653, fol. 214[r]. Cf. LPL, MS 649, fol. 398[r].
[83] LPL, MS 649, fols. 306[r], 310[r]; LPL, MS 653, fol. 182[r].   [84] SA, MS 444A, fol. 51[r].
[85] The latest correspondence which I have so far been able to find is a letter from Moresin to Bacon in March 1595, in which the doctor passes on news of the arrest of a Jesuit and a personal assurance from James about the exiling of Huntly and Errol (LPL, MS 651, fol. 101[r]). In July of that year Moresin became a minister (*CSPScot*, XI, *1593–5*, p. 642), having evinced strong Calvinist views in the subject matter and dedication of his 1594 book *Papatus, seu depravatae religionis origo et incrementum* … (Edinburgh, 1594, STC no. 18102), sig. A3[v] and *passim*. When James succeeded to the English throne, Francis Bacon wrote to Moresin 'to renew the ancient acquaintance which hath passed betwene us' and to beg him to use his influence with the king to further his career (Spedding, *Bacon letters*, III, p. 66).

Moresin gave Elizabeth a second and quite separate dimension to her efforts to pressure James over the 'Spansh blanks'. Because of the sensitivity of the operation, each part was carefully compartmentalised, with the Cecils dealing with Bothwell and Essex with Huntly. As Cecil noted, 'the queen would have her ministers doe that she will not avowe'.[86] Nevertheless, Elizabeth actively co-ordinated these activities. When Essex sent Moresin new instructions in mid-December 1593, the queen personally vetted them.[87] The compartmentalised structure meant that when the dealings with Bothwell blew up into a full-scale political disaster, James blamed Burghley and Cecil for this gross infringement of his sovereignty. This, in turn, opened the way for renewed and lasting contacts between James and Essex.

The Bothwell affair reconfirmed James's feelings of genuine suspicion towards Burghley and, by association, towards Cecil. James blamed Burghley for the death of his mother, Mary Queen of Scots, while over-looking the venomous hatred for her of his chief supporters in England at the time, Leicester and Walsingham.[88] Clearly, their agents in Scotland had heaped blame for the deed entirely upon Burghley and William Davison, the official scapegoat. This belief was still firmly planted in the king's mind when Lord Zouche was sent to Scotland in early 1594 to protest against his lenient treatment of the Catholic earls. James noted that Zouche was 'one of my mother's jurie and [an] enemy to my title, being Burlyi's dependar, who favouris the house of Hartforde'.[89] In reality, the Cecils were largely the victims of circumstance. As controllers of the vacant secretaryship of state, Burghley and Cecil were responsible for dispatching Elizabeth's condescending letters to James[90] and implementing her disruptive and contradictory policies towards Scotland. Although Elizabeth ordered a reduction in James's pension in September 1596, the king's agent in London instinctively blamed Burghley himself for this unexpected cut.[91] Such ingrained suspicions of the Cecils were not confined merely to the king and his servants. Distaste for Burghley was widespread among other Scots as

[86] Marginal notation in Cecil's hand on the instructions for Lord Zouche's mission to Scotland in late January 1594 (PRO, SP 52/52, p. 29).

[87] LPL, MS 649, fol. 440^r.

[88] The Catholic spy John Cecil (alias Snowdan alias James Cumyn) reported in October 1597 that James had an abiding hatred for all who bore the name Cecil because of his mother's fate (CSPIre, XI, 1601–3, p. 601). Sir Robert Cecil was still trying to combat this belief in December 1600, when the master of Gray (acting as his agent) urged James that 'thearle of Leicester or Sir Francis Walsinghame ver only the coutters of her throt and inducers of Davisone to do as he did' (Cecil MS 90/92 (pr. HMCS, X, p. 389)).

[89] A. I. Cameron (ed.), The Warrender letters, (2 vols., Edinburgh, 1931–2), II, p. 43. These are holograph notes by James, probably intended for an envoy travelling to Denmark.

[90] See, for example, Elizabeth's letter of August 1593, in which she lectured James about how he should deal with his own servants (BL, Add. MS 19401, fol. 164^r–165^r).

[91] LPL, MS 659, fol. 18^r.

well, aiding Essex in his dealings with them. One report from Soctland in 1594 claimed that 'the haill nobillitie heir speik honorablie and seem well affectit to the erle of Essex', but described Burghley's reputation there as 'bludie, cruell and conscienceles'.[92]

Even before the Bothwell fiasco, Anthony Bacon had been in touch with David Foulis, an 'ancient friend' who acted as a frequent envoy between James and Elizabeth.[93] As early as June 1593, Foulis put Bacon in contact with James Hudson, James VI's resident agent in London and Foulis' 'brother'.[94] As the king's principal agents for dealing with Elizabeth, Foulis and Hudson had close ties with the Cecils and made regular reports to them.[95] However, despite outward appearances, their feelings towards the Cecils were little warmer than their master's.[96] By early 1594, Bacon's contacts with Foulis had encouraged James to enter into 'une mutuelle intelligence' with him – and hence also with Essex.[97] According to this understanding, news of Scotland was sent south for Essex, initially by Foulis, while Bacon reported to Foulis about English affairs for James's benefit. By this means, Essex and James now entered into secret indirect communication. Because of the extreme political sensitivity of the succession issue, neither party could be seen to have dealings with the other, as their abortive previous contact had demonstrated.[98] Secrecy, deniability

---

[92] HMCS, XIV, p. 22. Another, undated report even made the remarkable claim that the 'l(ord) t(treasurer's) designs tend to the subversion of the nobility, and to establish a democracy' (*ibid.*, III, p. 385).

[93] LPL, MS 656, fol. 278ᵛ.

[94] BL, Add. MS 4125, fol. 38ʳ. Although English by birth, Hudson was a servant of James VI by the early 1580s, when he frequently carried confidential communications between John Colville and Sir Francis Walsingham (D. Laing, *Original letters of Mr John Colville 1582–1603. To which is added his palinode, 1600* (Bannatyne Club, CIV, Edinburgh, 1858), pp. 24, 27, 57, 87, 95, 223, 230, 239).

[95] These survive in the State Papers Scotland (PRO, SP 52), which is essentially a Cecilian archive during this period.

[96] For example, when James' pension was cut in 1596, Foulis sent Bacon a note about Cecil's conduct which, as Bacon informed Essex, 'made me blush all alone, in reading of it, to my soveraigne, as he well observed, so ill served and a king ... so absurdly scorned ... [with] dangerous and damnable insolency' (LPL, MS 659, fol. 244ʳ).

[97] BL, Add. MS 4125, fol. 38ʳ. In Foulis' correspondence with Bacon, Essex was 'Plato' or '28' and James was 'Tacitus' or '10'. Like Moresin, Foulis corresponded with Bacon in French.

[98] The concern for secrecy was perhaps heightened by the example of Peter Wentworth. In August 1591, Wentworth sought to present Essex with a copy of his *Pithie exhortation* on the succession through Dr Thomas Moffet. Wentworth's (unrealistic) hopes of having Essex present the work to Elizabeth were foiled when news of his intentions reached the privy council and he spent six months in varying degrees of confinement. Wentworth subsequently tried to raise his pamphlet in the 1593 parliament. Wentworth was sent to the Tower and, this time, there was no release. He ultimately died there in July 1597 (J. E. Neale, *Elizabeth I and her parliaments 1584–1601* (London, 1957), pp. 255–66). Moffet had been Sir Philip Sidney's physician and accompanied Essex to France in October 1591 (HMCS, IV, pp. 154–5, 174; Thomas Moffet, *Healths improvement* (London, 1655, Wing no. M2382), p. 60).

and reliance upon the pens of friends and servants therefore characterised the communications between Essex and James.

From the letters of Foulis, it is clear that Essex performed some secret act of kindness towards Foulis which much impressed the king.[99] The growing association between Essex and James was reinforced in April 1594, when the king sought the earl's assistance for envoys which he was sending to England to protest about Elizabeth's illicit support for Bothwell.[100] By the middle of 1594, Foulis was reporting that James likened Essex to another Sidney, a compliment which must have delighted the earl.[101] Although Foulis could not put his master's promises to Essex on paper, it is clear that Essex was intended to receive some special reward, in return for assisting James's succession to the English throne.[102] In effect, Essex was positioning himself for the next reign.

Although facilitated by the friendship of Foulis and Anthony Bacon, this gradual and secret growth of trust between Essex and James VI had a clear political logic to it. Essex was attracted to James's cause because he needed to secure himself against Elizabeth's inevitable demise and because he aspired to shape his nation's destiny. Moreover, James's principal external rival for the succession was the Spanish Infanta, an alternative which was totally repugnant to Essex. The idea of seeing some fellow subject rise above him as his future prince probably seemed equally odious.[103] Accordingly, he became the leading advocate of the Stuart succession, albeit in a rather guarded manner.[104] For his part, James needed a strong supporter in

[99] BL, Add. MS 4125, fol. 162ᵛ. Essex's kindness to Foulis was apparently counterpointed by scandalous disrespect towards him by Burghley and Cecil.

[100] G. P. V. Akrigg (ed.), *Letters of James VI & I* (Berkeley, Los Angeles and London, 1984), pp. 130–1. This was a diplomatically acceptable means for James to make contact with Essex. These envoys, the laird of Wemyss and Edward Bruce of Kinloss, presumably also carried some verbal message to Essex from the king (Birch, *Memoirs*, I, p. 175; J. M(aidment) (ed.), *Letters and state papers during the reign of King James the Sixth. Chiefly from the manuscript collections of Sir James Balfour of Denmyln* (Abbotsford Club, Edinburgh, 1838), pp. 7–8). Like David Foulis, Wemyss was an old friend of Anthony Bacon and corresponded through him with Essex by 1595 (LPL, MS 930, no. 157; LPL, MS 656, fols. 148ʳ⁻ᵛ, 353ʳ; LPL, MS 658, fol. 93ʳ⁻ᵛ; LPL, MS 661, fol. 177ʳ⁻ᵛ; Cecil MS 24, fol. 105ʳ⁻ᵛ).

[101] '... et qu'il est bien aise d'avoir recouvert en sa person Sire Philipe Sydnay' (BL, Add. MS 4125, fol. 164ʳ). In token of his association with Leicester and Walsingham in the 1580s, James had himself contributed a poem to one of the volumes published to commemorate Sidney's death (*Academiae Cantabrigensis lachrymae* (London, 1587, STC no. 4473), sig. K1ʳ⁻ᵛ).

[102] BL, Add. MS 4125, fol. 164ʳ.

[103] This is perhaps explains Essex's sharp antagonism towards Lord Beauchamp, the son and heir of the earl of Hertford, a possible English claimant to the throne, in August 1594 (*HMCA*, p. 315). James's note about Lord Zouche, quoted above, indicates that he thought Burghley supported Hertford's claim.

[104] Elizabeth's extreme sensitivity about James's claim to the throne, and Essex's interest in it, are demonstrated in the story which John Harington told about a controversial sermon on

England and, by 1594, he clearly judged that Essex was now influential enough to play this part. In cultivating Essex as his champion, James was undoubtedly conscious of Essex's kinship and political affinity with his previous chief supporters in England, Leicester and Walsingham.[105] Perhaps even more importantly, James viewed Essex as a counterweight to Burghley, as is shown by a letter which James wrote for conveyance to Essex in October 1595: 'I am also glad that he who rules there is begun to be loathed at by the best and greatest sort there, since he is my enemy (though undeserved, as God knows).'[106] Clearly, James's hatred of the Cecils remained undiminished and, by late 1595 at least, Essex traded upon and encouraged this emnity.

While Elizabeth remained healthy, the most conspicuous sign of James's trust in Essex was the flow of letters and papers which came to Anthony Bacon from Foulis and Hudson. From about the middle of 1594, Hudson began passing over to Bacon what he claimed was all of the correspondence he received from Scotland, which Bacon then digested for Essex's benefit.[107] Over the succeeding few years, this channel of communication produced great quantities of intelligence for Essex about affairs in Scotland, sometimes several times in a week.[108] Many of the letters which Hudson handed over came from intimate servants of the king, such as Roger Aston, Sir William Keith and Colonel Sir William Stewart of Houston, no doubt writing with their master's approval.[109] How much information flowed

this very topic by Matthew Hutton. Elizabeth's reaction was decidedly frosty (although less so than Court gossip anticipated), while Essex unsuccessfully used Harington to seek a written copy of the sermon ('A briefe view of the state of the Church of England', in T. Park (ed.), *Nugae antiquae: being a miscellaneous collection of original papers ... by Sir John Harington, knt.* (2 vols., London, 1804), II, pp. 248–53).

[105] The two letters which James sent to Essex in 1588 were part of the king's immediate response to the news of Leicester's death, as was a decision to reinforce his contacts with Walsingham (*HMCS*, III, pp. 359–60).

[106] Akrigg, *Letters of James VI & I*, pp. 142–3. This holograph letter is addressed to 'My goode friend SHB' but is clearly intended for Essex himself, or for a close friend of his, such as Anthony Bacon, who would then pass it on to the earl. In this letter, James also makes the point that 'I am sorry that ye have so much longed for my answer ... but, as I wrote to you in my last, I pray you think not that either sloth or negligence breeds my slowness in answering, but only the care I have that my letters be surely conveyed since there is so many Argus eyes that watches over me.'

[107] LPL, MS 652, fol. 296^r; LPL, MS 654, fols. 53^r, 291^r; LPL, MS 660, fol. 53^r.

[108] There are dozens of letters sent on from Hudson to Bacon in LPL, MSS 651–2, 654–61. Many of these are copies made by Bacon before returning the originals to Hudson. How many papers were not copied before being returned is uncertain.

[109] This is perhaps most obvious with Roger Aston, who was a groom of the bedchamber to James VI. Aston also corresponded very regularly with Robert Bowes and Cecil, passing on very similar information about events in Scotland (*CSPScot*, XI and XII). He seems to have been deputed to keep lines of communication open with the Cecils and the queen. His letters to Hudson allowed Hudson and Bacon to see what kinds of information Elizabeth and the Cecils were receiving by this means.

northwards in the direction of the Scottish Court remains unknown. Nevertheless, when Hudson briefly returned to Scotland in early 1596, he did take at least one paper from Bacon, which disappeared 'in a fume' after a private interview with James.[110]

At the same time as he maintained these secret, indirect contacts with James, Essex also cultivated certain links with men near to king – again through Anthony Bacon – which he made known to Elizabeth. These were links by which Essex openly sought to further her service in Scotland, just as he conducted intelligence activities on her behalf in other foreign countries. During 594, for example, Essex had some fleeting contact with the earl of Mar, th guardian of James's son and heir.[111] In mid-1595, this became more serious, when Essex was courted by the chancellor of Scotland, a rival of Mar in the king's council.[112] Knowing the tide of affairs in Scotland, Essex was distinctly cool to the chancellor[113] and, instead, began exchanging news with Mar. From the start, the terms of such correspondence were clear: 'I receive nothinge but with my souveraigne's privity, nor sende anie thing to yow but by her Majestie's direction.'[114] By early 1596, Mar was sending fairly regular letters for Essex to read to Elizabeth, by means of trusted followers around Berwick.[115]

Although Essex was intimately associated with James, he realised that he could not afford to rely entirely upon information provided by men anxious to portray the king in a flattering light. Essex also knew that James's desperate insecurity about his claim to the English throne led him

[110] LPL, MS 656, fol. 226^r. The meeting, although not the contents of the paper, is described in detail by Hudson in *ibid.*, fols. 231^r–232^r.

[111] LPL, MS 650, fol. 323(A)^r. For Mar's guardianship of the son of James, see LPL, MS 659, fol. 368^r; *HMC. Supplementary report on the manuscripts of the earl of Mar & Kellie preserved at Alloa House, Clacmannanshire* (London, 1930), pp. 35–6.

[112] LPL, MS 651, fol. 260^r. On Chancellor Maitland's rivalry with Mar during this period, see M. Lee, *John Maitland of Thirlestane and the foundation of Stewart despotism in Scotland* (Princeton, New Jersey, 1959), pp. 284ff.

[113] LPL, MS 651, fol. 312^r.

[114] This phrase is actually from Essex's reply to Maitland (*ibid.*) but expresses the spirit in which Essex now corresponded with Mar. Mar himself received a copy of the exchange of letters between Essex and Maitland, probably from Essex himself (*HMC. Mar & Kellie*, pp. 36–7). Proof that Essex showed Elizabeth his correspondence with Mar can be seen in Mar's lament to Essex in December 1595 that he had heard that 'hir Majestie vith sum jalosie aprehends my long silens' (LPL, MS 652, fol. 270^r) and in Anthony Bacon's attempt in October 1596 to send Mar a jewelled representation of the queen (LPL, MS 659, fol. 217^v).

[115] Letters were sent back and forth between Sir Alexander Hume and Capt. William Selby, respectively the agents of Mar and Essex on the Northumberland border (LPL, MS 656, fol. 106^r). Selby was gentleman porter at Berwick and had been a lieutenant in Essex's horse company in the Netherlands in 1586. He succeeded his brother in the post at Berwick through Essex's mediation with Hunsdon (LPL, MS 655, fol. 218^r). For further correspondence between Essex and Mar, see LPL, MS 654, fol. 298^{r-v}; LPL, MS 656, fol. 177^r; LPL, MS 659, fol. 171^r.

to make overtures to the pope and the king of Spain which were directly counter to English interests.[116] In consequence, he tried to gain intelligence on Scottish affairs from as many sources as possible, both from within Scotland and without. Much information, for example, came from the Netherlands, where there was a Scottish regiment in Dutch service.[117] Other snippets of information came from agents elsewhere.[118] Perhaps the most remarkable material was gathered by the double-dealing seminary John Cecil (alias Snowden),[119] who made some valuable reports during 1596 and 1597. Among other things, these described dealings at Rome and in Spain, not only by the Catholic earls who had been exiled from Scotland, but also by James himself.[120] However, the quality of this intelligence seems almost too good. Given his notorious shiftiness, it is conceivable that John Cecil deliberately leaked this information in the expectation that it would be passed on to Elizabeth and poison relations between her and the Scottish king.

There were also dangers associated with another important source of information about Scottish affairs, Presbyterian ministers and their sympathisers. Always suspicious of James's manoeuvrings, and correspondingly impressed by Essex's own Protestant reputation, they plied the earl with intelligence in the hope that he would encourage Elizabeth to strong-arm the king into throwing in his lot with them against the Catholics.[121] Inevitably, these reports had a strong tendency to alarmism and habitually put James in a poor light, but they did provide a balance to the royalist

[116] T. G. Law (ed.), 'Documents illustrating Catholic policy in the reign of James VI, 1596–1598', *Miscellany of the Scottish History Society* 1 (1893), pp. 3–70; Stafford, *James VI and the throne of England*, pp. 146ff.; J. D. Mackie, 'The secret diplomacy of King James VI in Italy prior to his accession to the English throne', *Scottish Historical Review* 21 (1923–4), pp. 267–82. For Essex's indulgent but reasoned view of such initiatives by James, see Cecil MS 135/224 (pr. *HMCS*, XIII, pp. 553–4).

[117] Scottish affairs figure prominently both in the letters which the English ambassador in the Netherlands sent to Essex and in the cipher which Essex, in turn, sent to the ambassador, probably during 1595 (BL, Cotton MS Galba D XI, fol. 238^{r-v}).

[118] For example, LPL, MS 658, fols. 69^r, 71^r. These reports are from Anthony Rolston.

[119] For comments on the mysterious career of Father Cecil, see Hume, *Treason and plot*, pp. 41–9, 69–74, 201–3, 210–15; Loomie, *The Spanish Elizabethans*, pp. 73–5; P. McGrath, 'Apostate and naughty priests in England under Elizabeth I', in D. A. Bellenger (ed.), *Opening the scrolls: essays in Catholic history in honour of Godfrey Anstruther* (Bath, 1987), pp. 71–2. Cecil first offered his service to Essex in March 1594 (PRO, SP 12/248. fol. 124r). For comment on his duplicitousness, see Sir Robert Cecil's letter to Robert Bowes of July 1596 (*CSPScot*, XII, *1595–97*, p. 267). For Burghley's feelings about this agent who shared his family name, see Hammer, 'Return of Standen', p. 288.

[120] LPL, MS 655, fol. 173^r; *HMCS*, VI, p. 382. John Cecil also betrayed to Essex a list of all the papers and letters of introduction which he carried into Scotland when he went there on a mission for Spain (LPL, MS 656, fol. 84^r; copy is LPL, MS 661, fol. 91^{r-v}).

[121] For example, LPL, MS 652, fols. 181^{r}–182^{v}; LPL, MS 660, fols. 165^{r-v}, 255^r–256^r, 257^{r-v}.

ntelligence which Essex received through Hudson. Nevertheless, James's deteriorating relations with the ministers increasingly threatened to place Essex in an embarrassing position. In January 1597, two ministers, Robert Bruz and Walter Balcanqual, asked Essex for passports to protect them from the king and allow them to flee into England.[122] Although full of sympathy for their plight, Essex declared himself unable to help.[123] Ultimately, whatever the merits of their individual cases, Essex was not prepared for their sake to compromise his special relationship with James.

Anthony Bacon also unlocked useful contacts for Essex on the Continent. One of his first blows for Essex was to recruit his close friend Anthony Standen. Standen had been an agent for Walsingham in Italy and Spain, and still remained active through partnership with Anthony Rolston, who was based on the Franco-Spanish border. In June 1593, Standen's cover was blown and he returned to England to find a cold reception from Burghley. At once, even before the lord treasurer made a final decision about what to do, Bacon prevailed upon Essex to take Standen into his protection. In the event, Standen's career as a spy was finished but his long experience proved a useful resource for the earl's service.[124]

This is a highly significant incident because Bacon and Essex both realised that taking up Standen would 'wrong' Burghley.[125] That they proceeded is testimony not only to Essex's trust in Bacon but also to his desire to build up a large intelligence system in emulation of his late father-in-law. In contrast to Burghley, who consistently resisted following the example of Walsingham,[126] Essex's attitude to intelligence was distinctly expansive. His scribbled response to Phelippes – 'take no pity of my purse' – is highly reminiscent of Walsingham's maxim: 'knowledge is never too dear'. Essex's appetite for intelligence was further whetted by the queen. Soon after his appointment to the privy council, Elizabeth required him to draft instructions for agents who might be sent to Rheims and Rome. Essex regarded this as an exercise 'to try my judgment', for the queen seemed 'willing now ... to use my service thatt way [i.e. in a 'matter of intelligence']'.[127] Successes with real agents, such as Dr Moresin, soon followed.

---

[122] LPL, MS 654, fol. 256[r]. For their offence, see LPL, MS 660, fol. 257[r]. It is not clear whether Robert Bruz is the same man as the Bruz who had become an important correspondent for Anthony Bacon in Edinburgh during the latter part of 1596 (LPL, MS 655, fol. 137[r]; LPL, MS 657, fol. 159[r]; LPL, MS 659, fols. 11[r], 217[r–v]; LPL, MS 660, fol. 131[r]).

[123] HMCS, VII, pp. 10–11; LPL, MS 655, fol. 60[r].

[124] For all of this, see Hammer, 'Return of Standen'.   [125] LPL, MS 653, fol. 242[r].

[126] Acres, 'Early career of Cecil', pp. 15, 18, 24, 33.

[127] LPL, MS 653, fol. 189[r]. Essex called upon Francis Bacon and Thomas Phelippes to assist him in this exercise.

By the end of 1593, Anthony Standen felt able to boast that 'all matters o intelligence are wholly in his handes, wherin the queene receyveth gret lykinge'.[128] Standen was guilty of exaggeration, but the dynamism o Essex's quest for intelligence was undeniable. In December, the earl eve began constructing new rooms in Essex House specifically to allow him t consult with 'frendes' at all hours.[129]

Although primarily focused on the queen, the new expansiveness o Essex's intelligence operations was also boosted by another consequence o Standen's return. Among English exiles abroad, it was believed tha Elizabeth's regime conducted an unfair and often brutal repression of he Catholic subjects. The treatment of captured priests and occasional crack downs seemed to confirm this belief. Essex was never comfortable witl such repression,[130] perhaps because his circle of relatives, friends an(acquaintances had always included almost as many Catholics as member: of the godly.[131] Although the public image that he cultivated for domesti(consumption always remained staunchly Protestant, and sometimes eve anti-Catholic,[132] Essex began to move towards supporting toleration fo loyal, anti-Spanish Catholics in the early 1590s. There may have been ar element of political calculation about this drift. Supporting toleration no only won Essex support among Catholic circles but also established another contrast between himself and Burghley, who was widely blamed b Catholics as the architect of their repression.[133] However, Essex's positior also reflected a broader mental shift away from simple anti-Catholicism

---

[128] LPL, MS 649, fol. 429v.   [129] *Ibid.*

[130] Camden, *Elizabeth*, p. 482. Christopher Devlin also suggests that the term 'Topcliffian' (meaning excessively brutal, after the notorious priest-hunter and torturer Richard Topcliffe) first surfaced among Essex's circle of friends (*The life of Richard Southwell, poet and martyr* (London, 1956), p. 232).

[131] According to Topcliffe, Essex's own 'country' of Staffordshire was a distinctly 'backwod shyre' in terms of Protestant religion (A. G. Petti (ed.), 'Roman Catholicism in Elizabethan and Jacobean Staffordshire: documents from the Bagot Papers', *Collections for a history of Staffordshire*, 4th ser., IX (1979), p. 43).

[132] For example, in his *Apologie*, Essex explicitly inveighed against not only the full restoration of the Catholic order in the Netherlands ('they banish God's true service, to bring in idolatrie . . .' (sig. C3r)) but even against toleration there ('where there is not unitie in the church, there can be no unitie nor order in the state, for as the mingling of poyson with wholesome liquor in one vessel, doth not corrupt that which is Letheal, but corrupteth that which is wholesome, so the poysoned doctrine of these espaniolized Jesuites once brought in, will quickly leave no one professour in al the united provinces' (*ibid.*)).

[133] See, for example, LPL, MS 648, fol. 140r; LPL, MS 659, fol. 393r–v; Petti, *Verstegan letters*, pp. 15–16, 39–40, 150; P. Caraman, *Henry Garnet, 1555–1606, and the Gunpowder Plot* (London, 1964), p. 58. In particular, Burghley was regarded as the inventor, or at least the chief defender, of the so-called 'bloody questions' used in the interrogation of Catholic suspects. (Cf. P. McGrath, 'The bloody questions reconsidered', *Recusant History* 20 (1990–1), pp. 305–19, esp. pp. 314–15.)

towards inclusive nationalism and anti-Spanish sentiment, which had been pioneered by Huguenot thinkers and began to take hold in England after the defeat of the Armada in 1588.[134]

Standen's arrival enabled Essex to make political capital out of his support of religious toleration.[135] The news that Standen was allowed to practise his Catholicism under Essex's protection was deliberately leaked abroad through the contacts of Anthony Bacon and Thomas Phelippes.[136] The shadowy Peter Wynn may also have spread the story when he mingled with English exiles at Venice in October 1593.[137] By March 1594, John Cecil reported that the news was 'wonderfull famous in Spayne', with all the details eagerly digested by the English community there.[138] The example of Standen was perhaps all the more convincing because Essex had quietly been demonstrating his support for Catholics at home in other ways. In April 1593, he sponsored the brief release from prison of the well-known recusant Sir Thomas Tresham.[139] Perhaps with some prompting on his own part, the story also circulated that Essex had praised Father John Gerard for his fortitude in the face of torture.[140] During the Cadiz expedition of 1596, despite his expressions of Protestant zeal, Essex sought to comport himself as an anti-Spanish crusader, not an anti-Catholic one.[141] A rather more subtle sign of Essex's good will towards Catholics was his crucial part in encouraging the new art-form of madrigals composed in English, which attained a considerable vogue during the

---

[134] J. Lock, '"How many tercios has the pope?" The Spanish war and the sublimation of Elizabethan anti-popery', History 81 (1996), pp. 197–214.

[135] Essex may have begun to dabble in this matter in late 1591. According to the Jesuit Henry Walpole, a number of officers from Essex's army in Normandy paid visits to Flanders, renewing their commitment to Catholicism and raising hopes of a more general improvement for Catholics in England (Stonyhurst MS Anglia A I, fol. 64[r], consulted at Jesuit Provincial Archives, Farm St Church, London).

[136] Hammer, 'Return of Standen', p. 291. Standen probably attended Mass at Essex House with Antonio Perez (Ungerer, I, p. 145).

[137] PRO, SP 85/1(ii), fol. 155[r].

[138] PRO, SP 12/255, fol. 28[v].

[139] PRO, SP 12/244, fol. 219[r]. The report also notes that Tresham's son had lately become a follower of Essex. Tresham's Catholicism and dealings with the state are discussed in S. Kaushik, 'Resistance, loyalty and recusant politics: Sir Thomas Tresham and the Elizabethan state', Midland History 21 (1996), pp. 37–72. For a similar intervention in 1595, when Essex asked Whitgift to permit the lawyer Richard Godfrey and his wife not to attend church, see LPL, MS 652, fol. 325[r–v].

[140] Caraman, Garnet and the Gunpowder Plot, p. 232. A similar story is told about Essex and William Weston (Caraman, William Weston: the autobiography of an Elizabethan (London, 1955), p. 228).

[141] HMCS, VI, p. 380. However, Essex's respect for the Church in Cadiz slipped somewhat in a curious incident with a Franciscan friar, whom the earl reviled as 'a dog ... All Spaniards, he said, worshipped gods of wood and paint, but God could not be in Heaven and earth as well' (cited in J. S. Corbett, The successors of Drake (London, 1900), p. 63).

1590s.[142] Many of the composers of these madrigals were Catholic, while the Italian origins of the genre helped to ensure that a Catholic association adhered to those written in English.[143] The musician John Mundy suggested something of Essex's role in such matters when he very pointedly compared 'your honourable patronage' with the 'priviledge of a religious sanctuarii'.[144]

Essex's semi-public support for toleration drew a variety of responses from Catholics, quite apart from Mundy's praise cloaked in the guise of metaphor. Many English Catholics who rejected association with Spain, both at home and abroad, came to see Essex as a friendly figure. Some moderate Catholics believed that Essex might actually be able to do them some concrete good. The poet exile Henry Constable, for example, was moved to correspond with Essex from France between 1595 and at least 1597. Constable's great hope was that Elizabeth might be brought to tolerate the religion of her Catholic subjects in return for their public disavowal of Spain's war against her, thereby depriving Spain's actions of any religious justification.[145] At some point in the 1590s, an anonymous petition was also directed to Essex to achieve this same goal, even specifying a Catholic oath of loyalty for the purpose.[146] Essex's reaction to these overtures is, unfortunately, unknown. Nevertheless, the duration of Constable's correspondence with him suggests that genuine negotiation occurred between them.[147] Almost certainly, Essex was moving towards the kind of policy later adopted by Sir Robert Cecil in his dealings with the so-called Appellants, deliberately seeking to undermine Spanish influence upon English Catholics by encouraging religious moderates.[148]

For pro-Spanish Catholics, Essex's support for toleration was a serious

---

[142] L. M. Ruff and D. A. Wilson, 'The madrigal, the lute song and Elizabethan politics', *Past and Present*, 44 (1969), pp. 3–51. Note also Ruff and Wilson, 'Allusion to the Essex downfall in lute song lyrics', *Lute Society Journal* 12 (1970), pp. 31–6.

[143] Ruff and Wilson, 'Madrigal and lute song', and D. C. Price, *Patrons and musicians of the English Renaissance* (Cambridge, 1981), ch. 4, esp. pp. 159, 177.

[144] John Mundy, *Songs and psalmes composed into 3 4 or 5 partes, for the use and delight of all such as either love or learne musicke* (London, 1594, STC no. 18284), unpaginated dedication to Essex.

[145] Son of Sir Robert Constable, former lieutenant of the ordnance, and a relative of the earls of Rutland, Constable had been a contemporary of Essex at Cambridge. In August 1591, Constable accompanied Essex's army to Normandy but declared himself a Catholic and went into exile in France. See G. Wickes, 'Henry Constable, poet and courtier', *Biographical Studies* 2 (1953–4), pp. 272–300, esp. pp. 279–81; J. Bossy, 'A propos of Henry Constable', *Recusant History* 6 (1961–2), pp. 228–37; *DLB*, CXXXVI, pp. 45–52.

[146] FSL, V.b.214, fols. 268ʳ–270ʳ (pr. A. J. Loomie, 'A Catholic petition to the earl of Essex', *Recusant History* 7 (1963), pp. 33–42).

[147] See, for example, Cecil MS 35/50–51 (pr. *HMCS*, V, p. 403).

[148] J. Hurstfield, 'The succession struggle in late Elizabethan England' in S. T. Bindoff, J. Hurstfield and C. H. Williams (eds.), *Elizabethan government and society: essays presented to Sir John Neale* (London and Toronto, 1961), pp. 379–89.

hreat because it weakened support for their objective of fully restoring the
old Catholic order in England by force of arms. According to John Cecil,
news of Standen's treatment made die-hard supporters of Spain like Sir
William Stanley 'haulf desperate' to stop defections from their cause.[149]
Such fears were justified by the example of the Jesuit Thomas Wright in
1595. As a result of contact with Anthony Rolston, Standen's old partner,
Wright surrendered himself to Anthony Bacon as soon as he arrived in
England, passing on intelligence about naval preparations in Spain to
ensure that he received a warm welcome.[150] Even before this disaster,
Essex's pro-toleration stance gave 'R. Doleman' a special incentive to
embarrass him with the dedication of his polemical tract on the succession.[151] Similar ideas of discrediting Essex in Elizabeth's eyes, rather than
genuine subornment, may also have been the ultimate intention behind
various clandestine attempts to win Essex over to the Spanish cause.
Rolston's visit to England in mid-1597, for example, was alleged to have
had the secret purpose of sounding out Essex on this subject.[152] This may

[149] PRO, SP 12/255, fol. 28ᵛ.
[150] HMCS, VI, p. 284. Thomas Wright arrived in London on 8 June 1595. His career is
discussed in T. A. Stroud, 'Father Thomas Wright: a test case for toleration', Biographical
Studies 1 (1951–2), pp. 189–219. For Wright's prior contact with Rolston, see PRO, SP
12/278, fol. 110ᵛ. Details of his reception by Essex were sent to Rolston by Standen within
a fortnight of his arrival (LPL, MS 651, fol. 232ʳ). As a reward for his services, Wright was
allowed to visit his family and friends in York, but he clashed with the ecclesiastical
authorities there and was recalled to London. By late October, he was required to lodge
with the dean of Westminster (Stroud, 'Father Thomas Wright', pp. 197–8). Wright
subsequently wrote a Latin treatise arguing that English Catholics could legitimately bear
arms to defend the realm against Spain (BL, Lansdowne MS 115, fols. 95ʳ–101ʳ. For
discussion of this document, see A. Pritchard, Catholic loyalism in Elizabethan England
(Chapel Hill, N.C., 1979), pp. 61–7; P. Holmes, Resistance and compromise: the political
thought of the Elizabethan Catholics (Cambridge, 1982), pp. 199–200). This paper was
apparently presented to Essex by the beginning of 1596 (LPL, MS 654, fols. 101ʳ, 109ʳ).
Wright also continued to inform Bacon and Essex of intelligence which he learned from
other Catholics in England (Birch, Memoirs, II, pp. 71–2, 179–80, 187–8). However,
Wright was dogged with suspicion, including the possibility that he was a Spanish plant
(PRO, SP 12/271, fol. 57ʳ⁻ᵛ). In 1597, he became notorious for converting William
Alabaster, one of Essex's chaplains. He may also have converted Ben Jonson in the
following year (G. M. Story and H. Gardner (eds.), The sonnets of William Alabaster
(London, 1959), p. xiii; T. A. Stroud, 'Ben Jonson and Thomas Wright', English Literary
History 14 (1947), pp. 274–82).
[151] 'Doleman' turned the knife by expressing mock gratitude to Essex partly for the 'good
turnes and benefites received by some frendes of myne at your lordship's handes'
(R. Doleman, A conference about the next succession to the crowne of Ingland (n.pl.,
1594, STC no. 19398), sig. *2ʳ).
[152] LPL, MS 656, fol. 83ʳ; Apologie, sig. B4ʳ⁻ᵛ. Cf HMCS, VI, p. 381; T. F. Knox (ed.),
Records of the English Catholics under the penal laws. Chiefly from the archives of the see
of Westminster. II. The letters and memorials of William Cardinal Allen (1532–1594)
(London, 1882), pp. 439–41. On the basis of information sent by John Cecil, Rolston was
arrested soon after his arrival in London on 18 April 1597 (LPL, MS 661, fol. 137ʳ), first
being committed to Mr Norman Hallyday's house (HMCS, VII, p. 188), then to the Tower.

also have been the thrust of queries about Essex directed at William Sterrel during 1594.[153]

Despite such feelers about his religious and political loyalties, Essex' support for toleration was not a sign of his secret Catholicism. Throughout he remained a devout Protestant.[154] Essex supported toleration *sub rosa* because he genuinely disliked religious persecution and because it was a natural concomitant of his desire to be a major figure in 'Christendom' – a term which Essex and his friends used frequently.[155] By allowing visitors to England to practise their Catholicism, Essex gained full access to the cultural and political life of all but the Spanish-dominated parts of the Continent.[156] As a result, he received visits from European fencing masters, horse-trainers and musicians.[157] Demonstrating that he was not anti Catholic also brought Essex many political benefits abroad. For a start, it enabled him to remain supportive of Henri IV, who abjured his Protes tantism for the sake of securing his hold on the French throne in July 1593. It also undoubtedly assisted him in developing links with moderate Catholic states in Italy.

Contact with Italy offered Essex great opportunities for gathering intelligence and new possibilities for fulfilling his desire of playing a part upon 'the stage of Christendom'. Quite apart from their great cultural allure, the various Italian states remained important as the meeting-point of the European and Mediterranean worlds, and key contributors to Spanish military power. Those Italian states which resisted Spanish influence, such

---

Rolston was still in the Tower at Christmas 1602 (J. H. Pollen, 'Tower bills 1595–1681, with Gatehouse certificates, 1592–1603' *Catholic Record Society Miscellanea* 4 (1907), p. 236). James I later awarded him a pension of £100 per annum (BL, Lansdowne MS 165, fol. 249v).

153 Cecil MS 14/11. This letter has been wrongly dated as 1585 in *HMCS*, III, p. 112.
154 However, Essex's sister, Penelope Lady Rich, did allegedly flirt with Catholicism at one time (P. Caraman (ed.), *John Gerard: the autobiography of an Elizabethan* (London, 1951, 2nd edn 1956), pp. 34–5).
155 P. E. J. Hammer, 'Essex and Europe: evidence from confidential instructions by the earl of Essex, 1595–6', *EHR* 106 (1996), pp. 368–9. Note also Essex's description of Italy as 'le jardin de la Chrestienté' (cited below). This sense of a broader European identity which transcended confessional divisions seems to have been quite common among internation-ally minded Protestants: Sir Philip Sidney and his friends had thought in terms of Christendom (B. Worden, *The sound of virtue: Philip Sidney's Arcadia and Elizabethan politics* (New Haven and London, 1996), pp. 54, 57, 62) and James VI even composed an epic poem about the battle of Lepanto (K. Sharpe, 'The king's writ: royal authors and royal authority in early modern England', in K. Sharpe and P. Lake (eds.), *Culture and politics in early Stuart England* (Stanford, 1993), p. 129).
156 According to Vincentio Saviolo, an Italian fencing master, Essex's 'benigne p(r)otection and provision for strangers maketh you reported off as theyr safe sanctuary' (Vincentio Saviolo, *Vincentio Saviolo his practise. In two bookes. The first entreating of the use of the rapier and dagger. The second, of honor and honorable quarrels* (London, 1595, STC no. 21788), sig. A3v).
157 For example, LPL, MS 661, fol. 181r; PRO, SP 46/125, fol. 248r.

as Venice and Florence, had appeal as potential allies for England. Despite the religious and political upheavals of recent decades, the old commercial links between England and northern Italy also remained. Indeed, these trade links were becoming increasingly important. Italy also provided crucial information about the growing tensions between pro- and anti-Spanish factions among English Catholic exiles.

For all of these reasons, Essex was happy to employ James Guicciardini as his agent at Florence in late 1593. Although his family were prominent Florentine merchants, Guicciardini was born in London and was the nephew of Edmund Spenser's close friend, Lodowick Bryskett. Following disputes over his father's will, Guicciardini travelled to Florence, where his uncle, Lorenzo, was a leading official under the grand duke of Tuscany.[158] During 1592 and early 1593, writing on his master's behalf, Lorenzo Guicciardini had tried to open communications with Burghley.[159] Although he wished to keep it secret, the duke was anxious that England should endorse Henri IV's conversion. However, Burghley was unenthusiastic and it seems that contact with Florence was passed over to Essex – clearly, with Elizabeth's approval. James Guicciardini arrived back in England during this period, and when he finally returned to Florence at the end of 1593, he did so under direction from Essex. Unfortunately, his uncle died before his return and he himself had to assume the role of secret contact between Essex and the duke.[160] Guicciardini seems to have performed this function well, sending useful intelligence on the duke's behalf about Spanish military intentions, papal overtures to Henri IV and Italian news, which Essex, in

---

[158] For the connection with Bryskett and family feuding, see D. Jones, 'Lodowick Bryskett and his family', in C. J. Sissons (ed.), *Thomas Lodge and other Elizabethans* (Cambridge, Mass., 1933), pp. 269–328. James was clearly in Florence by late 1591, when Henry Wotton and the visiting Lord Darcy both met him there (L. P. Smith (ed.), *The life and letters of Sir Henry Wotton* (2 vols., Oxford, 1907), I, p. 284; *L&A*, III, *June 1591–April 1592*, p. 441). He also gave five crowns to a destitute English Catholic in 1591 (*HMCS*, VI, p. 420).

[159] Lorenzo's initial letter to Burghley, together with a paper of related intelligence, was dated 6 June (i.e. 27 May in the English style) 1592. One copy of these papers was sent back via John Wroth at Venice (PRO, SP 98/1, fols. 79–81) and another copy was dispatched to England by Lord Darcy (*ibid.*, fols. 83–5). For subsequent contacts, see *L&A*, IV, *May 1592–June 1593*, pp. 364–7. The involvement of Lorenzo has led to much confusion about the respective roles of these two men. L. P. Smith, for example, conflated 'Mr Guicciardini' (ie James) and 'Lorenzo Guicciardini (one of the Forty-Eight)' (*Life and letters of Wotton*, I, pp. 284, 287). This error was perpetuated in Ungerer, I, p. 266 n. 1; *ibid.*, II, pp. 10, 171, 172 and 'Career', p. 124. The reverse mistake was made by Deborah Jones, who ascribed a letter of 'Le Chevalier Guicciardin' to James, instead of Lorenzo ('Bryskett', pp. 329–32). The account by Jones is the only substantial discussion of Guicciardini's activities (*ibid.*, pp. 332–45).

[160] *HMCS*, IV, pp. 447–8; Murdin, p. 669.

turn, reported to Elizabeth.[161] What information flowed in the other direction is uncertain. Nevertheless, it is clear that the bonds between Essex and the grand duke of Tuscany grew steadily stronger. When Guicciardini returned to Florence after another visit to England in late 1596,[162] Essex sent him back in the company of Sir Thomas Chaloner, who was to supplement Guicciardini's activities and act as the earl's own resident emissary in Florence.[163] In the latter part of 1597, Essex also sent one of his secretaries, Henry Cuffe, on a mission there which lasted several months.[164]

If there is much that is obscure about Essex's contacts with Florence, those with Venice are more straightforward. This is because, although Essex probably obtained a far greater volume of intelligence from Venice, he was never as politically well connected there as in Florence and hence there was little to hide. Essex's connection with Venice sprang from his contact with Antonio Perez, who proved to be as influential on the earl's Continental contacts as Anthony Bacon. As the former secretary of Philip II, Perez was himself a prize intelligence asset, offering for the first time an insight into the inner workings of Philip's empire. Sent to England by Henri IV with the vidame de Chartres in mid-1593, Perez was delighted with Essex's generous hospitality and managed to avoid being recalled to France for two years. In that time, he gave Elizabeth, Burghley and Essex detailed briefings on the strengths and weaknesses of the Spanish regime.[165] More importantly, Perez found that his grand talk about international statesmanship and his own professed 'proper function and vocation' of 'tempering Christiandome'[166] struck a chord with with Essex. Perez's enthusiasm whetted the earl's imagination, reinforcing his dreams of international fame

---

[161] For letters to Essex from Guicciardini, see *HMCS*, IV, pp. 472, 476; *ibid.*, V, pp. 402, 437–8, 502–3, 506–7, 510–11; *ibid.*, VI, pp. 154–6, 454, 518; *ibid.*, VII, pp. 95, 109–11, 235–6, 547–8; *ibid.*, VIII, p. 493. Guicciardini's 'case-officer' was Essex's personal secretary, Edward Reynoldes. The cipher used by Guicciardini can be found in Cecil MS 329/3, endorsed as 'Mr Guicciardini' in Reynoldes's hand.

[162] He was ready to leave London by 25 October 1596, having received from Reynoldes a letter from Essex for the grand duke, as well as gifts from the earl and various other papers and instructions (Cecil MS 45/108 (pr. *HMCS*, VI, p. 454)). Guicciardini also carried a letter to the grand duke from Elizabeth, dated 25 October (GL, MS 1752, p. 187).

[163] Chaloner and Guicciardini left London at the end of October and arrived in Florence in mid-December 1596 (LPL, MS 659, fol. 218ʳ). Chaloner usually communicated with Essex through Anthony Bacon. Chaloner's surviving dispatches include: LPL, MS 655, fols. 89ʳ⁻ᵛ, 102ʳ⁻ᵛ, 103ʳ, 105ʳ⁻ᵛ; LPL, MS 661, fols. 32ʳ, 103ʳ, 168ʳ, 170ʳ; *HMCS*, VII, pp. 10, 37–8. Letters from Bacon to Chaloner include: LPL, MS 655, fols. 88ʳ, 90ʳ, 104ʳ.

[164] P. E. J. Hammer, 'The uses of scholarship: the secretariat of Robert Devereux, 2nd earl of Essex, c. 1585–1601', *EHR* 109 (1994), p. 38. Cuffe's initial audience with the grand duke was arranged by Guicciardini (*HMCS*, VII, p. 424).

[165] Ungerer, I, pp. 72–4, 92–108; *ibid.*, II, pp. 233–5; PRO, SP 12/245, fols. 59ʳ, 113ʳ.

[166] Ungerer, II, p. 125.

and influence. Perez's knowledge also gave Essex new insights into European politics, while his contacts gave Essex (and Elizabeth) new sources of information about European affairs. Such information undoubtedly began to give Essex's aggressive policies more credibility in the queen's eyes.

Before he returned to France, Perez prevailed upon Elizabeth to let Essex employ a resident agent at Venice.[167] The function of this agent was to act as an unofficial diplomat for the queen and to collect intelligence from various Italian contacts of Perez. One source of information was to be Perez's former servant, Giacomo Marenco, who lived in Genoa and had secret contacts with a secretary of the Spanish ambassador there.[168] Elizabeth agreed to this arrangement but things went awry when Essex's agent, Peter Wroth, died in mid-1595 before even reaching Venice. Wroth's replacement, Dr Henry Hawkyns, did not reach there until the end of the year.[169] Worse, Hawkyns arrived without any letter of authority from Elizabeth or Essex and his early reports were deemed inadequate by the earl. Essex was so anxious to make a success of this venture that he even made provision for replacing Hawkyns with a new agent whom he was sending to Vienna, Mons. le Douz.[170] In the event, the reports of Hawkyns improved, but he remained too stiff a Protestant to be successful in the quasi-diplomatic side of his work.[171]

[167] Perez was discussing this matter with Elizabeth by late January 1595 (LPL, MS 650, fol. 41^r). For the whole venture, see Ungerer, II, ch. 7, and 'Career', pp. 128–31, 146–7. Perez's friend, Giovanni Battista Basadonna, the Venetian factor in London between 1593 and 1599, was also crucial to advancing this scheme. For Basadonna, see Ungerer, II, pp. 174–8.

[168] The importance of Marenco was reflected in the quasi-ambassadorial level of hospitality which Essex lavished on him during his visit to England in early 1597. Essex paid for his lodging and maintenance and at his departure gave him 100 crowns for expenses, a horse, and a jewel inset with the queen's portrait (LPL, MS 655, fols. 156^{r-v}; LPL, MS 656, fols. 33^r, 72^r, 118^r, 120^r).

[169] Hawkyns travelled to Italy with an agent for James VI, Sir William Keith – a further sign of Essex's intimacy with the Scottish king. Essex won Keith an audience with Elizabeth before his departure from England (LPL, MS 652, fol. 225^r). Once in Venice, like Hawkyns, Keith's correspondence was received by Anthony Bacon, who passed it on to James Hudson or David Foulis. Thomas Edmondes, Elizabeth's agent in France, reported that Keith's real mission was to lobby support in Italy for his master because of 'the greate hate she [i.e. Elizabeth] beareth him' (G. G. Butler, *The Edmondes papers* (Roxburghe Club, Westminster, 1913), pp. 292–3). For Hawkyns, see Hammer, 'Essex and Europe', pp. 361–2.

[170] A passport for le Douz to travel in the Netherlands and Germany 'for some necessarie busines' was drawn up and dated 10 February 1596 (LPL, MS 655, fol. 191^r). For le Douz, see Ungerer, I, 240–1; *ibid.*, II, p. 172.

[171] Hawkyns also occasionally indulged in some more covert activities. At the end of 1595, he managed to intercept some important letters sent from Spain (*HMCS*, V, pp. 448–9; LPL, MS 652, fol. 221^{r-v}; LPL, MS 654, fols. 264^r, 299^r). He also succeeded in recruiting a secret informer within the English College at Rome, Robert Markham (LPL, MS 655, fol.

Essex's concern with Hawkyns and Venice, and his subsequent repetition of the exercise with Chaloner at Florence a year later, indicates a great deal about his political priorities during the mid-1590s. Both ventures were extremely costly and focused resources on an area well away from England's immediate vicinity.[172] The weekly reports of Hawkyns, in particular, produced large amounts of intelligence but only a fraction of it related to the military threat which Spain posed to England or news of English Catholics at Rome. This was anticipated from the start, as the instructions which Essex gave Hawkyns make clear.[173] Essex wanted intelligence about Spanish activities but, above all, he wanted news about current events in Italy, the Ottoman Empire and southern Europe. Such information would allow him to place Spanish actions in a larger context, but it also fed his private craving for knowledge about Christendom. This personal desire is made explicit in his instructions to Mons. le Douz.[174] Like Hawkyns, le Douz was to gather information for detailed reports on each of the Italian states. Essex sought such reports 'pour mon propre contentement' because 'mon malheur a esté tel que Dieu n'aye jamais voulu permettre d'avoir veu l'Italie, le jardin de la Chrestienté'. This is a quite extraordinary turn of phrase for a strong Protestant like Essex and powerful testimony to his sense of being part of the great sweep of European history.

Essex was clearly thinking big when he undertook to retain an agent in Venice, and later also in Florence. The venture gave him an eye and a voice at the crossroads of Europe, both for the queen's service and for his own purposes. In the short term, Essex was able to capitalise on his monopoly of steady intelligence from Italy by doling out censored versions of Hawkyns's reports to friends like Lord Keeper Egerton.[175] However, Essex was also thinking on a far larger scale. His requirement that Hawkyns and le Douz produce substantial dossiers on each Italian state suggests a truly

239v; P. Renolds (ed.), *The Wisbech stirs (1595–1598)* (Catholic Record Society, LI, 1958), p. 244), as well as another correspondent at Milan (LPL, MS 657, fols. 248ʳ, 265ʳ; LPL, MS 658, fol. 64ʳ).

[172] Essex's payments to Dr Hawkyns alone amounted to £300 in the period from November 1595 to March 1597 (LPL, MS 652, fol. 180ʳ; LPL, MS 656, fols. 30ʳ, 71ʳ, 398ᵛ; LPL, MS 657, fol. 73ʳ; LPL, MS 659, fol. 238ʳ).

[173] ULL, MS 187, fols. 9ᵛ–11ʳ. Another copy is BLO, MS Eng.hist.c.121, fol. 9ʳ⁻ᵛ. These instructions are printed in Hammer, 'Essex and Europe', pp. 374–7.

[174] LPL, MS 656, fol. 186ʳ⁻ᵛ. See Hammer, 'Essex and Europe', pp. 380–1.

[175] Anthony Bacon took the initiative to show Egerton despatches from Hawkyns immediately after his appointment as lord keeper as a way of winning his support for the bid of Francis to become the master of the rolls (LPL, MS 657, fols. 22ʳ, 31ʳ⁻ᵛ, 105ʳ). Essex readily approved and continued this action. Bacon encouraged Hawkyns with the thought that Egerton's good will might one day win him a mastership in chancery (*ibid.*, fol. 154ᵛ). For further details, see 'Career', pp. 136–7.

massive information-gathering process. Moreover, this activity was not confined to these agents or focused exclusively on Italy. During a European tour largely funded and facilitated by Essex, Francis Davison, the son of the disgraced secretary of state, produced a survey of the German state of Saxony for the earl. Davison was only one of a series of young gentlemen whose trips around Europe were encouraged by Essex, including the earl's cousin Robert Vernon, Robert Naunton and the earl of Rutland. Essex, it seems, wanted his friends to experience life on the Continent, even if he could not. However, there was also a long-term political agenda behind Essex's support for travel. This was expressed most openly in the directions which he gave Dr Hawkyns: 'the cheife ende of my employinge yow be rather your inablynge hereafter then your present service'.[176] Rutland and Naunton received very similar advice and Chaloner, Vernon and Davison almost certainly did too. Quite clearly, Essex was anxious to do more than merely obtain information from the Continent: he sought to train men of his own choosing in the affairs of Europe for future royal service.[177]

Essex's lofty ambitions were most obvious in his Italian contacts but they were also expressed in other ways. Fragmentary evidence suggests that Essex's connections with Central Europe may also have been very significant. In 1596, Henry Wotton was described as having special responsibility for Essex's correspondences with 'Transilvania, Polonia, Italy [and] Germanye'.[178] Having spent several years in Germany and Austria, one of Wotton's first tasks for Essex involved compiling a list of acquaintances who might be suitable contacts for the earl.[179] How many of these men became suppliers of information for Essex is unknown because virtually all the papers handled by Wotton were later destroyed.

[176] ULL, MS 187, fol. 9ᵛ (pr. Hammer, 'Essex and Europe', 374).
[177] For all of this, see Hammer, 'Essex and Europe'. The 'inablynge' of these men seems to reflect advice given to Essex by Lord Henry Howard that he keep 'a seminar[y] of forward mindes and spirits to be recommended for places of importance' (DUL, Howard MS 2, fol. 126ʳ).
[178] LPL, MS 660, fol. 214ʳ.
[179] Smith, *Life and letters of Wotton*, I, pp. 299–301. Also printed HMCS, XIII, pp. 555–6. This discussion of 'advertisers of occurrences out of the parts where I have been' must have been one of Wotton's earliest services for Essex and was probably written in late 1594, as Smith surmises. It seems likely that Essex and Wotton acted on the contents of this document. One of the fifteen men whom Wotton had listed as a possible 'advertiser' was Scipione Lentulo. In October 1597, an urgent item of intelligence which Wotton reported to Essex came directly from a letter which Wotton had received from Dr Paolo Lentulo, a physician at Berne and son of Scipione (Smith, *Life and letters of Wotton*, I, pp. 304–5). Wotton probably also named English merchants who could support Essex's planned activities in Germany, including Edward Parvish: LPL, MS 661, fol. 253ʳ; L. A. Shapiro, 'Donne, the Parvishes and Munster's "Cosmography"', *N&Q*, n.s. 211(1966), pp. 243–8.

The same problem inhibits comment about agents whom Essex employed as full-time intelligence gatherers in the region, like Mons. le Douz. However, it is clear that George Hungerford served in this capacity for at least a year before his return to England in late 1596, visiting the imperial Court and travelling extensively in Central Europe.[180] Le Douz may well have been despatched as his replacement. Almost certainly, Hungerford joined Essex's service through the offices of his brother-in-law, Arthur Atey, a former secretary to Leicester and occasional consultant in intelligence and other matters for Essex.[181] During his time abroad, George Hungerford's activities demonstrated the same blurring of the line between service to the queen and advancing the interests of Essex himself that was evident in the work of Dr Hawkyns at Venice. In Germany, Hungerford literally sought to buy influence for Essex by distributing coins sent from England as medals among leading men of 'the cheife citties of the religion'. As Hungerford informed Essex, this would demonstrate 'your love & respect towardes them, who should be thought the onely councellor & worker of it, as allredy you are with the greatest matters, that is, with her [i.e. the queen's] order'.[182] Perhaps partly by similar means, Essex's reputation was also extolled during 1595 to the emperor in Prague.[183]

Hungerford continued his association with Essex even after his return to London. In 1597, he provided information about the use of cannon by

---

[180] In a letter of 20 December 1595, Hungerford refers to a letter from Essex dated 18 September responding to an earlier letter which he had written to the earl (LPL, MS 654, fol. 257[r–v]). This dates Hungerford's employment by Essex to at least August 1595 and probably before. It is also apparent that Wotton was responsible for paying and corresponding with Hungerford. Their means of contact was through Robert Granger at Nuremberg, who paid Hungerford £20 in December 1595 but reported to Essex that the agent demanded another 100 crowns at once (*ibid.*, fol. 250[r]). Granger was a London cloth merchant who became a 'denizen' of Nuremberg by 1593 and married a local woman there in October 1597 (W.-R. Baumann, *The Merchants Adventurers and the Continental cloth trade (1560s-1620s)* (Berlin and New York, 1990), pp. 176, 178, 343–4).
[181] The second wife of Atey (or Atye) was Judith, daughter of Walter Hungerford of Cadenham, Wiltshire (*Commons*, I, pp. 363–4). For Atey's work as secretary to Leicester, see E. Rosenberg, *Leicester, patron of letters* (New York, 1955), pp. 150–1; S. Adams, 'The papers of Robert Dudley, earl of Leicester. II. The Atye-Cotton collection', *Archives* 20 (1992–3), pp. 131–44, esp. 132–5. From the handful of letters which survive, it seems that the principal point of contact between Essex and Atey was William Downhall, the earl's gentleman of the horse and probably another former servant of Leicester. In one letter, probably written in early 1597, Atey described himself as Essex's 'cypher frend' and canvassed the possibility of Hungerford being sent back to Germany to inform the Count Palatine and the Landgrave of Hesse about Essex's new expedition against Spain (Cecil MS 179/105 (pr. *HMCS*, XIII, p. 570)). See also *HMCS*, VII, pp. 107–8.
[182] LPL, MS 654, fol. 257[r–v].
[183] LPL, MS 659, fol. 367[r].

imperial forces in their war against the Turks, at precisely the time when Essex was establishing himself as the master of the ordnance.[184] Hungerford also continued to exchange information with foreign friends like the Nuremberg physician Dr Joachim Camerarius. Reports of events in Central Europe from Camerarius were passed 'nostro comiti', while news heard in London and general information about English affairs were communicated back to the doctor.[185] Both correspondents were also always anxious for news of mutual friends, such as Lord Willoughby or John Wroth, the elder brother of Peter. Hungerford even assured Camerarius that he would look after the doctor's sons if he sent any of them to England.[186] Although few of their letters survive,[187] they demonstrate the kind of international networking that Essex was able to exploit and the way that much of the information which he received came from the correspondence of third parties rather than letters sent to him directly. The contents of these letters also reinforce the point that most intelligence was not 'top secret' information, but news of current affairs – the comings and goings of important men, rumours of war or new taxes, and reports of great events in other lands.

Given his concern for the affairs of France, it is not surprising that Essex received a great variety of intelligence from that country. Sources ranged from local governors who sought to keep good relations with a key figure in the English government to Huguenots who hoped that Essex's influence with Elizabeth would allow him to use diplomatic pressure on Henri IV to protect the interests of his Protestant subjects. The most important of Essex's Huguenot correspondents was his friend the duke of Bouillon, with whom he had an almost conspiratorial intimacy.[188] Essex also employed

---

184 LPL, MS MS 661, fols. 164ʳ–165ᵛ. This is an English summary of a report made to the Emperor by his master of artillery, Lord Zwartz, on 22 (12) Jan. 1596. The summary is endorsed 4 May 1597. It is unclear whether Hungerford had only recently obtained this document (through one of his foreign correspondents) or he had brought it back in the previous year and only now translated it.

185 Bayerische Staatsbibliothek, Munich, Clm 10364, nos. 669, 671, respectively, Hungerford to Camerarius, London, 19 (9) January and 20 (10) April 1597. For Camerarius and his connection with Sir Philip Sidney in the 1570s, see A. P. McMahon, 'Sir Philip Sidney's letter to the Camerarii', *Proceedings of the Modern Language Association* 62 (1947), pp. 83–95.

186 Bayerische Staatsbibliothek, Clm 10364, no. 678, same to same, Prague, 20 (10) May 1596.

187 Thirteen letters from Hungerford survive among Camerarius's papers (*ibid.*, nos. 668–80), dated between 1595 and 1598. There is also one letter from Hungerford to a Mons. de Laet at Amsterdam in 1596 (no. 667), and letters to Camerarius in 1596 from Lord Zouche (no. 681), Lord Willoughby (no. 682), Lord Grey (no. 683) and Edward Jordan (no. 684), all dated in 1596.

188 Some of their letters are printed in *HMCS*, XIII, pp. 518–19, 525–7, 528–9, 530–1, 533–5, 537, 539–44, 573–4, 580–1, 585, 590; *ibid.*, XIV, pp. 15, 26, 57–60, 62–3, 79, 83–4, 107. By late 1595, the main intermediary between Essex and Bouillon was Mons.

agents of his own in France, such as Anthony Ersfield in 1595–6[189] and William Lyly in 1596–8.[190] He also received great quantities of intelligence from Antonio Perez in France. When he was no longer able to send Essex information directly, Perez used Robert Naunton to convey his news.[191] Much to Naunton's dismay, Essex ordered him to abandon hopes of a Continental tour and become his resident agent with Perez, writing in his letters what Perez himself could not express. The volume and quality of Naunton's reports made Elizabeth 'everie daie more and more pleased with your lettres and [she] dothe promise me she will not let your syfre ruste'.[192] However, while Perez's consistently anti-Spanish line pleased Essex and no doubt allowed him to press Elizabeth about renewed intervention on the Continent, it was increasingly out of step with the needs of the French king. By late 1597, the Spaniard's influence was waning and the value of his information declined. With great relief, Naunton was released from his onerous charge by February 1598.

If Essex had the benefit of a multitude of contacts in France, this was certainly not the case for his attempts to obtain intelligence from Spain. For Essex, Spain was not only an enemy power but the source of a 'tyranny' which threatened all of Europe. England alone could not stand up to such a power, so common cause had to be made with allies like France, and good will and support had to be won from friendly powers like Florence or Venice. Exchanging intelligence – 'the true commerce of princes', as

---

de la Fontaine, the minister of the French Church in London. La Fontaine served as the French *chargé d'affaires* in England after Beauvoir la Nocle, Henri's long-serving ambassador, returned home in mid-March 1595 (PRO, SP 78/36, fol. 193^r; Ungerer, I, p. 153). For La Fontaine, see C. Littleton, 'The French Church of London in European Protestantism: the role of Robert le Maçon, dit de la Fontaine, 1574–1611', *Proceedings of the Huguenot Society* 36 (1994), pp. 45–57.

[189] Three copies of Essex's instructions (dated 25 October 1595) to Ersfield survive: LPL, MS 652, fol. 73^r; ULL, MS 187, fols. 11^r–12^r; BLO, MS Eng.hist.c.121, fol. 9^v. For further details about Ersfield, see Hammer, 'Essex and Europe', pp. 360–1, 371, 376–7.

[190] Between 1583 and 1590, Lyly had been a secretary to the English ambassador in France, Sir Edward Stafford. Like his master, he had secretly supported Mary Queen of Scots during the mid-1580s (Leimon and Parker, 'Treason and plot', p. 1143). About 1593, he became the second husband of Anne Donne, sister to the poet John Donne. About the same time, Lyly received £30 from Essex to equip himself to accompany Nicholas Clifford to France (Devereux MS 3, fol. 75^v). He returned to France in October 1596 as 'commissary of musters' for the English troops sent to Picardy under Sir Thomas Baskerville. It was in this capacity that he reported on the course of the war in France for Essex. His reports are printed in *HMCS*, VI–VIII. Lyly's life is discussed at length in R. C. Bald, *Donne and the Drurys* (Cambridge, 1959), ch. 6.

[191] For Naunton's association with Perez, see Ungerer, II, ch. 6. There are some additional details in Hammer, 'Essex and Europe'.

[192] Ungerer, II, p. 124.

Antonio Perez termed it[193] – was one important means by which such bonds of amity between states could be quietly nourished and the true dimensions of the Spanish threat defined. Essex's contacts with these states, and much of the intelligence which he received from them, must be seen in this quasi-diplomatic context. Although his enthusiasm for European affairs probably made him bolder in his secret promises than the cautious Elizabeth might have wished, Essex's contacts with the grand duke of Tuscany through James Guicciardini, for example, can be seen as a kind of extension of his role as the purveyor of royal hospitality for important visitors to England.

The intelligence about Spanish actions and intentions which Essex received from such arrangements was particularly important to him because, unlike Burghley or the lord admiral, he initially had few means of obtaining news directly from Spain itself. Essex's main source was Standen's old partner, Anthony Rolston, who sent news of shipping movements and the activities of English exiles from his base on the Franco-Spanish border.[194] Rolston scored a coup by obtaining an accurate list of Englishmen receiving Spanish pensions at the start of 1594[195] but thereafter the quality of his intelligence became increasingly poor.[196] The great bulk of Essex's Spanish intelligence came from other countries, and especially from Antonio Perez. If the scraps of evidence are an accurate guide, this situation changed dramatically in 1595. At the very time that he was establishing a post in Venice and seeking to find a safe means for Perez to continue providing intelligence after his return to France, Essex began to send agents to spy in Spain itself.

---

[193] The phrase comes from a paper which Perez used for briefing Elizabeth: 'el commerçio prinçipal de los Prinçipes' (*ibid.*, I, p. 99). Anthony Bacon's loose French version of this document translates it as 'le vray commerce des Princes' (LPL, MS 653, fol. 127ᵛ).

[194] Rolston's reports to Standen and Anthony Bacon survive in LPL, MSS 648–52, 656–60. These include both original dispatches in cipher and deciphered copies. Rolston remained at Fuenterrabīa and received money and letters through Joseph Jackson, who worked as the factor at St Jean de Luz for his brother Arthur, a London merchant (LPL, MS 650, fol. 239ʳ; LPL, MS 654, fol. 147ʳ). For further details of Rolston's work, see A. J. Loomie, 'Spain and the English Catholics, 1580–1604' (unpub. Ph.D. thesis, University of London, 1957), pp. 431–7.

[195] LPL, MS 650, fol. 65ʳ⁻ᵛ. Rolston also sent an account of the Spanish government at the same time (*ibid.*, fols. 66ʳ–67ᵛ). According to their endorsements, both documents were received by Anthony Bacon on 4 February 1594. Loomie claims that Rolston's list was the only accurate list of Spanish pensioners obtained by an English agent ('Spain and the English Catholics', p. 433).

[196] See, for example, LPL, MS 650, fol. 239ʳ. Like many Catholic exiles who passed information to the English government, Rolston was a double-agent (Hammer, 'Return of Standen', p. 284). It seems that after Standen's return to England, Rolston gradually became more anxious to please his Spanish paymasters than Bacon and Essex.

This move was related to Essex's changed appreciation of how England should fight the war.[197] While his hopes for large-scale intervention on the Continent remained unfulfilled, Essex became increasingly alarmed by reports about the growth of Spanish naval power and the threat which this posed to England and Ireland.[198] Instead of sending aid to France or the United Provinces, he now began to recognise that England's main effort might be directed at Spain and its ports. This reappraisal of strategy required detailed intelligence about Spain's land and sea defences, both in order to convince Elizabeth of the practicality of his arguments and to provide information about possible targets in the event that she should accept his advice. Moreover, the fact that Burghley and Cecil scornfully dismissed Thomas Wright's early report of a new Spanish Armada added extra urgency to Essex's efforts.[199] He now had to vindicate himself and prove that Spain was bent upon a re-run of 1588.

The easiest means of establishing agents at port cities in Spain was to employ foreign merchants, or at least Englishmen who could pass as foreigners. Accordingly, Essex financed a shipload of merchandise for Thomas Marchant in 1595, which enabled him to work as a trader in various Spanish ports before settling at San Sebastian.[200] The same tactic was adopted for Marchant's cousin, Nicholas Le Blanc, who based himself at Seville after an initial stay at Bilbao. Communicating through a merchant at Rouen, Alonse Faribault,[201] both men survived until 1597, when they were betrayed by the double-agent Edmund Palmer. At the time of their arrest, Palmer reported that a third man, Philip Scamps, was on his way to Lisbon with bills of exchange for 'a great sum of money'.[202] Whatever the purpose of the money carried by Scamps, there can be little doubt that this was a very expensive way to gather intelligence. When Sir

---

[197] See below, pp. 247ff.

[198] For the recovery of Spanish naval power in the mid-1590s and the creation of the *Armada del Mar Oceano*, see D. Goodman, *Spanish naval power, 1589–1665: reconstruction and defeat* (Cambridge, 1997), pp. 7–9, 14, 32–3, 114, 122.

[199] LPL, MS 652, fol. 87^r. Wright's intelligence continued for some time after his arrival in England. In October 1595, Anthony Bacon declared that 'by this preist his meanes I exspect daylye advertisementes out of Spayne'. The nature of Wright's 'meanes' is unclear.

[200] Loomie, *The Spanish Elizabethans*, p. 65. A Thomas Marchaunt, merchant of London, was restrained from trading with enemy territories (on pain of a £100 fine) by a warrant from the lord keeper in March 1594. The fact that Anthony Bacon kept a copy of this warrant (LPL, MS 650, fol. 159^r) suggests that this was same man who later became the agent for Essex.

[201] For correspondence between Faribault and Anthony Bacon in 1596–7, see LPL, MS 653, fols. 64^r–65^r; LPL, MS 656, fols. 10^r, 57^r, 263^r, 265^{r-v}, 271^{r-v}; LPL, MS 657, fol. 178^{r-v}; LPL, MS 658, fols. 32^r, 34^{r-v}, 39^r, 177^r, 182^{r-v}; LPL, MS 659, fols. 59^r, 275^r; LPL, MS 661, fol. 259^r. No reports from Marchant or Le Blanc seem to survive.

[202] Loomie, *The Spanish Elizabethans*, p. 65.

Robert Cecil tried the same tactic in 1597, it cost 1000 ducats (£275) for a single cargo of appropriate merchandise.[203] Essex also paid for at least one more resident agent at this time, Peter Tremble, who was based in Lisbon.[204]

Although the aggressive intentions which Essex and his agents attributed to the Spanish in 1595 were actually misplaced,[205] the pattern of ship movements and the strength of their flotillas suggested that England faced genuine danger. Spain's fleet had become stronger since 1589 and Essex sincerely believed that it would soon be turned against England. Nevertheless, he undoubtedly played up the danger of a new Armada when reporting intelligence to Elizabeth in order to dramatise the Spanish threat. Judging by their response to the news of Thomas Wright, Burghley and Cecil believed that Essex was guilty of exaggeration. These doubts about Spain's true intentions were well merited, but they soon proved irrelevant. In late July, Spanish ships launched a small raid on Cornwall, confirming the dangers of which Essex and others had warned.[206] Even if Spain's desire to invade England remained uncertain, there could be no doubt that Spanish ships again posed a direct threat to the realm. The growing rebellion in Ireland also suggested that a Spanish fleet might find a ready welcome there, with potentially disastrous consequences for Elizabeth's regime. Suddenly the danger seemed very real and all subsequent intelligence about Spanish activities was interpreted accordingly. As a result, defensive plans were reviewed, stocks of munitions were checked and increased, and preparations began for a pre-emptive strike against the enemy, which grew into the Cadiz expedition.

---

203 PRO, SP 12/265, fol. 204[r]. Cecil split the cost of this venture with the merchant-cum-intelligencer Thomas Honeyman. The agent in question was meant to spend only twenty days in Spain and was paid an additional sixty ducats for his pains. In the event, the venture proved a disaster. The ship and its cargo were seized by the Spanish authorities, the spy was tortured and garrotted, and the innocent Dutch master was sentenced to eight years as a galley-slave (L. Stone, 'The fruits of office: the case of Robert Cecil, first earl of Salisbury, 1596–1612', in F. J. Fisher (ed.), *Essays in the economic and social history of Tudor and Stuart England* (Cambridge, 1961), p. 93).

204 Only two reports from Tremble seem to survive: PRO, SP 12/263, fol. 185[r–v] (probably written in early 1598) and PRO, SP 12/265, fols. 150[r], 151[r] (seemingly written in 1597).

205 In fact, Spanish naval preparations in 1595 were primarily defensive measures aimed against the long-delayed new expedition of Drake and Hawkins, not the start of a new 'Enterprise of England': K. R. Andrews, *The last voyage of Drake & Hawkins* (Hakluyt Society, 2nd ser., CXLII, 1972), pp. 12–18; P. Pierson, *Commander of the Armada: the seventh duke of Medina Sidonia* (New Haven and London, 1989), pp. 194–5; A. J. Loomie, 'The Armadas and the Catholics of England', *Catholic Historical Review* 59 (1973), pp. 393–6.

206 PRO, SP 12/253, fols. 48[r], 49[r], 65[r], 66[r]. The Spanish raiding force consisted of four galleys from Blavet in Brittany.

Once the decision had been made to sail against Spain, intelligence obtained by Essex, Cecil and other councillors was pooled to support the operation.[207] Essex supplemented this information with specific naval intelligence secured by his own means. Edward Reynoldes was consequently indignant when he heard a 'mallitious suggestion' by Henry Brooke that the success at Cadiz 'was but a matter of chance: that your lordship went to seeke blowes at adventure without anie certen knowledge'.[208] In reality, Essex prepared the Cadiz operation with great care, personally collating intelligence about Spanish naval dispositions.[209] He also employed Captain Peter Wynn to gather information up to the very point of the fleet's departure. Wynn apparently scouted the coast of Spain, before returning with urgent news via Stade in Germany and London.[210] After briefing Essex at Plymouth, Wynn returned to sea, using a pinnace to seize vessels which had sailed from Spain and interrogating their masters about the latest ship movements in and around Cadiz.[211] This was certainly how Wynn was employed in 1597. Returning from Spain in March with news of the numbers of ships to be found in various ports,[212] he was given a vessel and three months' victuals by order of the privy council at the end of April.[213] Although much remains mysterious about Wynn's activities, it is

---

[207] Close co-operation and careful intelligence work prepared the way for the Cadiz expedition, as the activities of Capt. Peter Wynn (see below) and Capt. William Morgan demonstrate. There may have also been an element of good fortune at the last minute. Two men allegedly swam out to the fleet with intelligence about Cadiz on the day before the city was attacked. Their information seems to have been the basis for an assault map which still survives. It is not clear whether these swimmers acted by prior arrangement or (more likely) in the hope of winning reward. See P. E. J. Hammer, 'New light on the Cadiz expedition of 1596', *Historical Research* 70 (1997), pp. 188–91.

[208] LPL, MS 657, fol. 106ᵛ.

[209] HMCS, VI, p. 231.

[210] Wynn's return from Stade was arranged by Thomas Ferrers (LPL, MS 657, fol. 24ʳ), the agent for the Merchant Adventurers in that town and Essex's 'cousin'. Ahead of him came a letter, which Wynn addressed to Sir Edward Dyer, who in turn passed it to Reynoldes, who acted as Essex's agent at Court while he was absent on military service. Reynoldes arranged for Wynn to travel to Plymouth by procuring him a pass from Cecil under a false name (*ibid.*, fol. 108ʳ). Reynoldes took great care 'that Capt. Wyn's name not be used' in any open way (*ibid.*, fol. 45ʳ). Wynn's remarkable career is detailed in P. E. J. Hammer, 'A Welshman abroad: Captain Peter Wynn of Jamestown' (forthcoming).

[211] There is a report to this effect which looks very much like Wynn's work (Cecil MS 99/15–16 (pr. *HMCS*, VI, pp. 607–9)). Internal evidence indicates that it was compiled at the end of May or early June 1596.

[212] Rowland Whyte noted Wynn's return on 26 March 1597 (*HMCD*, II, p. 257). A report of the information which Wynn obtained on this voyage, written in secretarial hand and edited for clarity by Edward Reynoldes, is Cecil MS 49/90–91 (pr. *HMCS*, VII, pp. 136–8).

[213] The ship was the *Sunne*, a pinnace owned by Essex's follower Sir Thomas Gerard (*APC*, XXVIII, *1597*, p. 62). During the invasion scare later in the year, Wynn was designated to command a company of troops under Gerard (*ibid.*, p. 105).

clear that Essex spared no effort or expense to obtain the intelligence which he needed to make a success of his military operations against Spain.

In December 1593, Anthony Standen had boasted of Essex that 'all matters of intelligence are wholly in his handes'. This was an exaggeration, but an understandable one. Standen himself had become an aggressive partisan of the earl, while the scale and dynamism of Essex's pursuit of intelligence were increasingly impressive. By 1594, Essex undoubtedly had the greatest single intelligence apparatus in England and it continued to grow in the following years. Essex was able to receive news from an impressive range of contacts in Scotland and across Europe, many of them men whom he employed specifically for this purpose. However, by the end of 1597, Essex had clearly lost his position as Elizabeth's pre-eminent supplier of intelligence.

In part, this was a result of Essex's return to active campaigning in 1596 and 1597. In the desperate rush to prepare Essex's expeditions to Cadiz and the Azores, the routines of his secretaries were thrown into confusion. 'I doubt not my lord hath lost many lettres', declared Edward Reynoldes, 'for we have bene much out of our course by reason of this present service.'[214] Henry Wotton, the secretary responsible for correspondence with the Empire and Italy, sailed with Essex on both expeditions, putting him out of contact for months at a time. Anthony Bacon was spared disruption on this scale, but his work was nevertheless upset by his difficulties in dealing with the distracted and over-worked earl – a sign of how far Essex was himself personally involved in the daily managing of intelligence matters. Many of the newly arrived dispatches which Bacon needed remained lodged in Essex's sleeve or in his personal cabinet.[215] It took time to get Essex to make decisions, let alone actually to write the necessary letters.[216] Repeatedly, Bacon had to inform Dr Hawkyns that he was unable to reply to any specific points raised in the doctor's recent letters.[217] Even after Essex returned from his campaigns, there was little immediate let-up. One correspondent was moved to regret 'that he can heare no oftener from your lordship, and when it is, it is performed perfunctorily by Mr Reynoldes in waie of excuse of your lordship's infinite domesticall imploimentes, and no further'.[218] Essex's preoccupation with military matters and the politics of Court may also explain why he failed to deal with the fierce personal

[214] LPL, MS 656, fol. 268^r.
[215] For example, LPL, MS 654, fol. 29^r; LPL, MS 655, fols. 62^r, 66^r, 90^r; LPL, MS 656, fols. 268^r, 274^r.
[216] For example, LPL, MS 655, fol. 53^r; LPL, MS 656, fols. 14^r, 67^r, 69^r, 267^r, 343^r.
[217] For example, LPL, MS 654, fol. 104^r; LPL, MS 656, fols. 71^r, 273^r, 274^r, 305^r.
[218] LPL, MS 660, fol. 93^v.

rivalry which arose between Wotton and Bacon at the end of 1595, even when this helped to make a shambles of the first few months of Hawkyns' employment at Venice.[219]

The effects of this dislocation were all the more severe because Essex for the first time began to face serious competition in matters of intelligence following Sir Robert Cecil's appointment as secretary of state in July 1596. Under Walsingham, this post had been the focal point of intelligence-gathering for the queen,[220] but Burghley's concern for economy had allowed Essex and other members of the council to take up the slack by employing more agents themselves. As his father's assistant, Cecil had followed Burghley's lead in matters of intelligence during the first half of the decade. One agent described his attitude as 'sumwhat reserved, puntual & precise'.[221] Essex viewed this as a miserly and short-sighted approach.[222] However, once he became secretary of state, Cecil's attitude began to change. Cecil exhibited a new aggressiveness about intelligence and, at times, a thinly veiled sense of rivalry with Essex.

This new assertiveness of Cecil marked a reversal of previous behaviour. In the past, it had been Essex who had aggressively used his intelligence activities to further his ambition of succeeding Burghley as Elizabeth's next chief adviser. During his enthusiastic early months as a councillor, Essex sometimes clumsily allowed his competitive instinct to become obvious. His manoeuvring over Anthony Standen in June 1593 was an open affront to Burghley. On at least one occasion later in the year, he rushed off to see Elizabeth with a dispatch from Anthony Rolston in order to upstage the lord treasurer.[223] Essex may also have indulged in more subtle actions. During 1593, Burghley was involved in co-ordinating secret overtures to Rome over possible peace talks.[224] Ultimately, these feelers produced no concrete result. Cardinal Allen heard that they had failed because Burghley was opposed to further dealings in the matter, even though Essex wanted

[219] For all of this, and related tensions between Wotton and Edward Reynoldes, see Hammer, 'Uses of scholarship', pp. 35–7.

[220] BL, Cotton MS Julius F VI, fol. 154^r; Read, *Walsingham*, III, pp. 435–7; C. Hughes, 'Nicholas Faunt's discourse touching the office of principal secretary of estate, &c 1592', *EHR* 20 (1905), pp. 502–3.

[221] PRO, SP 12/248, fol. 124^r.   [222] LPL, MS 653, fol. 242^r.

[223] LPL, MS 649, fol. 475^r.

[224] There seem to have been two sets of contacts which may have been unconnected with each other. One involved Richard Hopkins, an English exile living in Antwerp, and Michael Moody, a former agent of Walsingham now run by the Cecils and Sir Thomas Heneage (M. Haile, *An Elizabethan cardinal: William Allen* (London, 1914), pp. 346–9; CUL, MS Ee.iii.56, no. 15). The other initative centred on the mission to Rome of John Arden, another agent run jointly by Burghley and Heneage (*L&A*, IV, *May 1592–June 1593*, pp. 373–9; R. B. Wernham, *The return of the Armadas: the last years of the Elizabethan war against Spain, 1595–1603* (Oxford, 1994), pp. 9–10). Burghley himself drafted instructions for Arden in April 1593 (PRO, SP 85/1(ii), fol. 132^{r-v}).

talks to continue.[225] Given Essex's life-long aversion to peace talks with Spain, Allen's comments invite suspicion that the cardinal may have been fed this information by agents of Essex, anxious to draw a contrast between their master and the aged lord treasurer. By blaming Burghley for the impasse and portraying Essex as enlightened and tolerant, such reports would not only reinforce hostility in Rome towards Burghley but further encourage English Catholics to believe that their only hope for the future lay in support for Essex.

Whether or not this supposition is accurate, the Cecils certainly faced a series of provocations from Essex in 1593. In response, they tried to maintain a mask of inscrutability. They quietly refused to share information with Essex,[226] excluded Standen from any royal preferment and concentrated on maintaining a flow of news to Elizabeth which kept her content and adequately informed. However, despite the tensions, there was also a degree of co-operation and acceptance between Essex and the Cecils in matters of intelligence. Their efforts in Scotland with Bothwell and Huntly, for example, were complementary and carefully co-ordinated by the queen herself. Elizabeth also seems to have deliberately encouraged a broader kind of specialisation in their intelligence, which not only reduced the potential for conflict over the next few years but enabled Essex and the Cecils to pursue their own, quite different views of policy.

As his acceptance of responsibility for communications with Florence and the exercise which the queen set him about sending an agent to France and Italy suggest, Essex's intelligence activities were primarily directed towards the Continent. This emphasis became increasingly pronounced as Essex employed new agents in Italy, Central Europe and Spain. Contacts in Scotland were also very important for Essex but neither Elizabeth nor the Cecils could be allowed to know how strong these were. The queen's sensitivity about the succession and tensions with the Cecils made these contacts politically explosive. Despite its importance as a source of information about Spain, Essex seems to have left Ireland to the Cecils. Although he claimed in 1595 that he 'would gyve any thinge to knowe the trouthe of the Spaniardes' arryvall in Ierlande', there is no evidence that he did anything to increase the paltry amount of information which he received from there.[227] By contrast, Ireland was vitally important to the Cecils and formed one side of an intelligence triangle which also embraced

[225] Haile, *Elizabethan cardinal*, p. 348.
[226] PRO, SP 12/244, fol. 167^r.
[227] LPL, MS 652, fol. 51^r. Sir William Russell urged Anthony Bacon to exchange intelligence with him in late 1595 (*ibid.*, fols. 70^r, 87^r) but there is no sign that this proposal had any effect.

Scotland and the Low Countries.[228] Outside these areas, the Cecils had relatively few agents.[229] Their innate suspicions about spies, and especially foreign ones, were reinforced by disastrous experiences with Manuel de Andrada[230] and Henri Chateaumartin.[231] They were apparently happy to see Essex pursue intelligence in expensive and glamorous locations such as Venice and Florence, while they concentrated on Flanders, Scotland and Ireland.

After the initial storm over Essex's charges against Dr Lopez, there was occasionally more active co-operation between Essex and the Cecils, as well as other councillors, in matters of intelligence.[232] They also sometimes shared the role of interrogating prisoners in important investigations. At times, Cecil sent Essex intelligence from Ireland,[233] and on one occasion at least, Elizabeth directed him to show Essex a new report from Scotland.[234] Cecil also provided much intelligence for the Cadiz and Azores

[228] Acres, 'Early career of Cecil', p. 24.
[229] This is most readily seen by the considerable gaps in many of the State Papers Foreign classes in the PRO, which are essentially Cecilian in their nature. For example, there are no regular reports in the State Papers, Venice (SP 99), between the departure of John Wroth in mid-1592 and the arrival of Thomas Wilson at the turn of the century. The State Papers, Italian States (SP 85), are also very thin for most of the 1590s.
[230] Manuel de Andrada was first exposed as an active agent for the Spanish in July 1591, when he was captured with compromising papers at Dieppe, including letters to Dr Lopez (PRO, SP 94/4(i), fols. 23^r, 33^{r-v}, 41^{r-v}). Despite this, he was re-employed by Burghley in mid-1593, with the support of Lopez (*HMCS*, XIII, pp. 483–4). De Andrada was out of England when Lopez was arrested in early 1594 and consequently evaded interrogation. George Gilpin offered Burghley the chance to seize him in the Low Countries in April 1594 but nothing seems to have come of this initiative (PRO, SP 84/48, fol. 133^r).
[231] Chateaumartin was probably Burghley's most important and expensive agent on the Continent. Upon Walsingham's death, he lodged a claim for payment of £1,000 (PRO, SP 78/21, fols. 289^r, 291^r) but this was settled by a 'gift' from the queen of £180 (PRO, E 403/2277, unfol., account of Richard Stonley). Thereafter, his salary was set at 1,000 crowns (£200) a year (Wernham, *After the Armada*, p. 449, n. 15). Chateaumartin acted as English consul for Bayonne and St Jean de Luz (LPL, MS 655, fol. 206^{r-v}; LPL, MS 656, fol. 194^r), which he used as cover for reporting on events in Spain and the Gironde (M. Wilkinson, 'The English on the Gironde, 1592–3', *EHR* 31 (1916), pp. 279–91; Ungerer, I, pp. 4–29). Chateaumartin was also highly regarded as an agent by Philip II, who paid him even more than Burghley (Loomie, 'Spain and the English Catholic exiles', pp. 410–11). Ultimately, Chateaumartin was charged with conspiring to betray Bayonne to Spain and was beheaded in July 1595 (PRO, SP 12/253, fol. 50^r).
[232] Perhaps the councillor least willing to co-operate in intelligence matters with Essex was Lord Cobham. He oversaw the vetting of post and travellers passing through the Cinque Ports and operated a network of agents across the Channel (D. McKeen, *A memory of honour: the life of William Brooke, Lord Cobham* (2 vols., Salzburg Studies in English Literature, CVIII, Salzburg, 1986), II, pp. 592ff.). Cobham felt that he had not been fully informed when Essex sought his help to intercept incriminating information about Dr Lopez. Cobham also resented Essex's frequent insinuations that his intelligence about Spanish intentions towards the French Channel ports was inadequate and underestimated the likelihood of Spanish aggression (*ibid.*, pp. 593–5, 601–3).
[233] See, for example, LPL, MS 654, fols. 74^r, 101^r, 109^r.
[234] *HMCS*, V, p. 485.

expeditions.[235] Both men regularly made use of the same subordinates for their operations. William Waad, for example, replaced Thomas Phelippes as Essex's 'case officer' for William Sterrell, but he also acted as one of Cecil's key assistants in intelligence matters.[236] Otwell Smith, an English merchant based at Dieppe, provided support for a whole range of confidential services by members of the privy council, including Essex and Cecil.[237]

The *modus vivendi* between Essex and the Cecils in matters of intelligence also extended to an acceptance of the queen's diplomats abroad supplying Essex with copies of the reports which they sent to Burghley. From Essex's point of view, this enabled him to see much of the information which Burghley and Cecil were reporting to Elizabeth and a principal ingredient in the formulation of their policy advice. Cultivating the queen's ambassadors also enabled him to seek their support for his covert operations abroad and accorded with his ambitions to be a true statesman. For their part, Elizabeth's ambassadors and other diplomatic agents were constantly in need of high-level support at home. Leave was difficult to obtain and diplomatic pay was usually well in arrears.[238] Having access to a man of Essex's standing also helped to give a diplomat political credibility in his place of residence. As far as the Cecils were concerned, the reporting by diplomats both to themselves and Essex was simply a fact of political life. They only became concerned if a diplomat seemed to be becoming a partisan of Essex, at the expense of their own influence.

Essex prevailed upon the queen's agent in France, Thomas Edmondes, to provide him with copies of his dispatches almost as soon as he won a place on the council.[239] A former secretary to Sir Henry Unton, ambassador to France in 1591-2,[240] Edmondes seems to have begun his contact with

---

235 The most explicit example of their co-operation in this regard is their joint approval of payment to Capt. John Legatt, who was employed to scout off the Spanish coast (BL, Lansdowne MS 84, fol. 27^r). It is unclear whether this document relates to Legatt's employment in 1596 or 1597 (*CSPD*, IV, *1595-1597*, pp. 302, 342, 546-7). On the latter occasion, he received payment of £78 10s by a privy seal of 24 December 1597 (PRO, E 403/2656, fol. 101^v).

236 Acres, 'Early career of Cecil', p. 34.

237 For his dealings with Essex, see, for example, Ungerer, I, p. 392, n. 11; *ibid.*, II, pp. 91, 128. Smith sent intelligence reports to Burghley from Dieppe and had extensive dealings with the lord admiral and Lord Cobham.

238 G. M. Bell, 'Elizabethan diplomatic compensation: its nature and variety', *Journal of British Studies* 20 (1981), pp. 1-25.

239 PRO, SP 12/244, fol. 144^r; BL, Cotton MS Caligula E IX(i), fol. 170^v. Edmondes's surviving letters to Essex can be found in the Cecil MSS and in LPL, MSS 650-2. Many of Edmondes's letters to Burghley and Cecil are printed in Butler (ed.), *The Edmondes papers*.

240 BRO, TA 13/2, fol. 1^r.

Essex through Unton's intercession.[241] Essex soon reinforced the link by providing Edmondes with substantial sums of money.[242] By 1595, Edmondes was no longer merely sending Essex copies of dispatches to Burghley but writing separate reports for Essex himself. At his request Essex sometimes showed these letters to Elizabeth, so Edmondes began to send him distinct 'private' letters which had a more personal character than the 'generall' ones.[243] A similar pattern can be seen in Essex's dealings with the queen's representatives in the Low Countries. Essex began receiving reports from the English agent there, Thomas Bodley, by May 1593, and later also from his deputy, George Gilpin.[244] Bodley was an old university colleague of Essex's friends Henry Savile and Arthur Atey.[245] When Bodley visited England in late 1594, Essex courted him and demanded regular reports,[246] and in consequence, Bodley began sending Essex letters almost weekly, enclosing with each a copy of his dispatch for Burghley.[247] Gilpin also markedly stepped up his correspondence with Essex.[248] Unfortunately for Bodley, Essex thought so well of his efforts (no doubt encouraged by their mutual friends at Oxford) that he began to put him forward as a rival candidate to Cecil for the secretaryship of state in 1595. This proved to be the kiss of death for Bodley's public career.[249]

---

[241] BL, Cotton MS Caligula E IX(i), fol. 170[v].

[242] For example, Essex sent Edmondes a gift of £30 in 1593 (Devereux MS 3, fol. 75[v]) and authorised Otwell Smith to advance him £180 beyond his official allowance in 1595 (LPL, MS 652, fol. 86[r]).

[243] This practice was explained by Sir Robert Sidney in a letter to Essex of November 1595: 'in this other letter ... I have added nothing but of publique matters, according to your direccion, because, if yow thinke it fitt, yow may showe it or, if yow do not shew it, there is no harme donne' (LPL, MS 652, fol. 166[v]). For the difference, see for example Edmondes's two letters to Essex of 21 May 1595 (LPL, MS 651, fols. 157[r]–158[r], 164[r]).

[244] Bodley first commended Gilpin to Essex as a correspondent in early May 1593 (HMCS, IV, p. 323).

[245] J. R. L. Highfield, 'An autograph manuscript commonplace book of Sir Henry Savile', Bodleian Library Record 7 (1962–7), p. 79.

[246] LPL, MS 650, fol. 163[r].

[247] Many of these letters are now in the Cecil MSS at Hatfield and are calendared in HMCS. Examination of the documents indicates that the letters there addressed to Burghley are copies which Bodley sent to Essex and not copies made by Cecilian clerks. Further copies of some of these letters, including some sent by Essex, were made by the earl's clerks and survive among the papers of Anthony Bacon (especially in LPL, MSS 650–2, 654, 656). From his complaints about receiving the news about Groeningen later than Essex, it is apparent that Burghley was aware of this duplication of correspondence by Bodley (PRO, SP 84/49, fols. 99[r–v], 111[r]).

[248] For the co-ordination between Bodley and Gilpin, see, for example, LPL, MS 654, fol. 251[r]. Again, the surviving letters are at Hatfield and Lambeth.

[249] (Sir Thomas Bodley), The life of Thomas Bodley ... written by himselfe (Oxford, 1647, Wing no. B 3392), pp. 9–12. Cecil later relented in his treatment of Bodley, but only after the latter had 'resolved ... to my full farewell of state imployments' – a resolution to which he adhered doggedly (ibid., pp. 12–13).

Essex's backing for Bodley, and the secret undermining of him by the Cecils, occurred during a renewed period of political tension which ultimately climaxed in Cecil's appointment as secretary. This event had profound effects in the business of intelligence. As secretary of state, Cecil was able to establish himself as the natural overseer of governmental intelligence gathering. He soon began to receive miscellaneous information sent by men 'as due to my place'.[250] He also played a greater role in co-ordinating intelligence gathered by other members of the council, such as the lord admiral and Lord Cobham.[251] Cecil's promotion gave him new confidence and encouraged foreign and domestic observers to treat him with greater respect. By contrast, Essex's prestige was rather dented by the elevation of the man widely recognised as his rival. Cecil's new confidence also put new pressure on Essex's intelligence endeavours in more direct ways. In February 1597, Anthony Bacon interpreted the recent lack of letters from Scotland as 'a notable effect of Mr Secretarye's aucthoretie and diligence at the entrie of his office (en crochetant les packetts sans espernier ou respecter les princes)'.[252] Even before this, Bacon had warned that Cecil might be trying to intercept Dr Hawkyns's dispatches, 'who belike is in love with Mr Dr Hawkins his stile'.[253]

Cecil's new competitiveness was also revealed in his extravagant expenditure on hiring new agents of his own. The catalyst for this rapid expansion was the state of the war. Despite the spectacular victory at Cadiz, England at the end of 1596 awaited a Spanish invasion fleet for the first time since 1588. As then, one response to this threat was a large and sudden increase in royal expenditure on intelligence. While Essex involved himself in readying the defending armies, Cecil launched a crash pro-gramme to hire spies who could report on Spanish naval activities. Although the Spanish fleet was destroyed by a storm, Cecil continued to expand his intelligence apparatus. In part, this was made possible by a

---

[250] PRO, SP 12/265, fol. 206ʳ.

[251] In 1596, the lord admiral recommended his agent Edmund Palmer to Cecil's patronage (PRO, SP 12/257, fol. 102ʳ). Thereafter, they ran Palmer jointly (PRO, SP 12/265, fol. 205ʳ), apparently oblivious to the impact of his work for Spain. Lord Cobham, as Cecil's father-in-law, had always been an important source of information for Cecil and Burghley (for example, HMCS, IV, pp. 305, 409, 529–30; ibid., VI, p. 424). This intelligence connection was reinforced by Cobham's irritation with Essex (see above) and by the desire of the Cecils to see Cobham's son retain his family's hold on the wardenship of the Cinque Ports (McKeen, II, p. 595).

[252] LPL, MS 655, fol. 137ʳ; LPL, MS 660, fol. 131ʳ.

[253] LPL, MS 659, fol. 21ʳ. See also LPL, MS 660, fol. 11ʳ. Bacon was probably correct in this claim. A fair number of documents which look very much like the weekly Italian reports sent home by Dr Hawkyns can be found in various Cecilian archives. See, for example, the reports from January and February 1597 in BL, Lansdowne MS 83, fols. 57ʳ–64ᵛ; LPL, Lansdowne MS 84, fols. 98ʳ–107ʳ.

revival of the official secretarial emolument for intelligence.[254] Although the precarious state of the royal budget meant that the amount was lower than in Walsingham's time, Cecil's receipt of this money indicated that he was now following the model of his predecessor in intelligence matters, not that of his father. Under the new secretary, a succession of new agents were hired to provide information from Spain itself.[255] Cecil also began to employ agents in other parts of Europe as well, often at great cost. Surveying these efforts, Anthony Bacon consoled Essex with the thought that they reaped 'all kinde of graine [and] game, how base soever'.[256]

Despite Bacon's scorn about the quality of Cecil's new contacts, it was patently obvious that Essex's intelligence-gathering was no longer without direct and strong competition from the secretary. Even the apparent return to friendship in 1597, which encouraged Essex to give Cecil access to reports from Dr Hawkyns,[257] could not disguise the shifting balance of intelligence supremacy in England. By the end of 1597, Cecil was spending over £900 a year on wages for only ten of his more than twenty agents in Spain, Portugal, France, Italy, Flanders, Sweden, Scotland and England. At least another £500 was spent that year on one-off expenses.[258] Despite Essex's undiminished ambitions of greatness at home and abroad, these figures underline a new reality in his relations with the Cecils and the other members of the privy council. By the end of 1597, if not some months before, Essex's pre-eminence among the queen's suppliers of intelligence was over.

---

[254] The sum of £800 per annum was allotted to Cecil by a privy seal of 27 September 1596, to be paid quarterly and spent 'in secretis et intimis negotiis Dominae Reginae' (PRO, E 403/1693, fol. 35ʳ). Cecil received the first two payments on 13 October and 27 December 1596 (PRO, E 403/2280, unfol., accounts of Edward Carey). These funds were later supplemented by an additional intelligence grant on 20 June 1599 (PRO, E 403/2655 (ii), fol. 254ʳ). Cecil was also given £250 for expenditure on some unspecified service in Scotland by a privy seal of 13 July 1597 (PRO, E 403/2280, unfol., accounts of Henry Killigrew).

[255] One example of Cecil's sense of urgency in this process was the constant pressure which he put upon George Gilpin from October 1596, first to recruit an agent for him from among the merchant community in the Low Countries and then to set the man forth for Spain. This can be tracked in PRO, SP 84/53, fols. 84ʳ–85ʳ, 109ʳ–110ʳ, 131ᵛ–132ʳ, 135ʳ, 154ʳ–155ʳ, 164ʳ–165ʳ, 184ʳ⁻ᵛ, 190ʳ.

[256] LPL, MS 656, fol. 118ᵛ. See also Bacon's comment about Cecil's extravagant favour to the clerk of the kitchen to a German prince (LPL, MS 655, fol. 156r).

[257] BL, Add. MS 4125, fols. 208ʳ, 214ʳ.

[258] These figures are based on PRO, SP 12/265, fols. 204ʳ–207ʳ (pr. L. Stone, *An Elizabethan: Sir Horatio Palavicino* (Oxford, 1956), pp. 325–30). Calculations have been based upon Stone's figure of 1 ducat being worth 5s 6d. It should also be noted that the number of agents given here does not include 'dyvers imployed with the privitie of Mr Wade' (PRO, SP 12/265, fol. 207ʳ). Another document from Cecil's secretariat indicates that he spent at least £1,700 on wages for spies between October 1596 and June 1598 (PRO, SP 12/272, fol. 5ʳ⁻ᵛ). Further evidence can be found in the payments recorded on the back of ciphers for individual agents in PRO, SP 106/1–3. Note that these volumes also include ciphers which once belonged to Walsingham and Phelippes.

6

'The shepheard of Albion's Arcadia'

Essex's political career broadened remarkably during the early 1590s. From being merely the queen's favourite and an ardent martialist, he made himself into an expert on foreign intelligence, proved himself as an industrious privy councillor and aspired to become an international statesman. However, despite the ever-expanding scope of his interests, Essex continued to be most deeply influenced by ambitions and concerns which were warlike in nature. Although he set himself to satisfy Elizabeth in 'matters of state' after his return from Rouen, and did so with striking success, Essex's 'ambition of warr' continued to embody the most heartfelt of his aspirations. His political dynamism and his work as a councillor, especially in military affairs, were profoundly influenced by his desire to become a great captain. This aspiration provided a consistent basis for all his political activities, especially through his deep commitment to waging war against Spain. It also shaped many of the ways in which he presented himself to the world.

Far more so than any of his contemporaries, Essex projected a public image of himself which was consciously – and conscientiously – created. Unlike Hatton, Burghley or Leicester, Essex constructed no great buildings to proclaim his glory and be a memorial to his name.[1] Rather than stone and brick, he sought to present the world with an image of himself as the embodiment of conspicuous virtue. This public persona portrayed Essex as soldierly, Protestant and specially favoured by the queen.

Essex's careful cultivation of his image was largely intended to assist in the advancement of his career. Especially early on, he sought to catch, and hold, the queen's attention by such means as spectacular appearances in the

---

[1] For example, compared to Leicester's extensive renovations there in the 1560s (and perhaps partly because of them), Essex made only minor alterations to Essex House in London. Apart from increasing the number of rooms available for secret consultations with his friends at the end of 1593, he made small changes to the building, such as having a shed built to house Anthony Bacon's coach in 1595 (LPL, MS 649, fol. 429ᵛ; Devereux MS 3, fol. 94ᵛ). See C. L. Kingsford, 'Essex House, formerly Leicester House and Exeter Inn', *Archaeologia* 73 (1923), pp. 1–54.

tilt-yard. By indulging in martial display, he also encouraged popular support for the war and for his own pre-eminent role in it. However, such open display was an inherently necessary part of Essex's dedication to the cult of honour. At the heart of this code was the idea that noble virtue should be both displayed and recognised publicly. In cultivating his public image, Essex was therefore constantly proclaiming his conformity to this code. Correspondingly, the popular acclaim which he received for his actions served to validate and reinforce these deeply held personal beliefs.

The most obvious means by which Essex sought to fashion a deliberate public image was through his participation in public spectacles. On some occasions, such as when he was entertained to dinner by the lord mayor of London[2] or when he joined the annual processions of knights of the garter,[3] Essex primarily sought to impress observers with the size and magnificence of his company, the traditional symbols of a great nobleman.[4] A rather more martial impression was intended when he arrayed his troop of soldiers before Elizabeth after the defeat of the Spanish Armada, in late August 1588. For this occasion, the climax to a week of parades by nobles' contingents, Essex made great efforts to ensure that his display was larger and more impressive than those which had preceded it. His two hundred light horsemen, sixty musketeers and sixty mounted harquebusiers all appeared in the Devereux colours of orange and white, some in velvet and silk. Even more notable was the conduct of Essex himself, who performed a mock battle for the onlookers. Beginning on horseback, he and his friend, the earl of Cumberland, continued a duel with swords on foot. However, when Elizabeth gave the signal for the battle to cease, the two eager combatants paid no heed. They continued to trade blows, oblivious even to their sovereign's indignant departure.[5] Clumsy as it was, this episode gives a telling insight into how Essex regarded these public occasions. For him, despite its overt purpose of honouring the queen, the parade was an golden opportunity to glorify himself.

Although he displayed an increasing degree of subtlety in doing so, Essex apparently displayed a similar willingness to upstage Elizabeth during his

---

[2] On 25 April 1593, Essex dined with the lord mayor accompanied by gentlemen and yeomen 'being in nomber CC men and upwardes' (Devereux MS 3, fol. 74[v]).

[3] I. H. Jeayes (ed.), *Letters of Philip Gawdy of West Harling, Norfolk, and of London to various members of his family 1579–1616* (Roxburghe Club, London, 1906), p. 81; H. S. Scott (ed.), 'The journal of Sir Roger Wilbraham, solicitor-general in Ireland and master of requests for the years 1593–1616', *Camden Miscellany* 10 (1902), p. 18. The garter ceremonies are a very important, but under-studied, subject: R. Strong, *The cult of Elizabeth: Elizabethan portraiture and pageantry* (London, 1977), ch. 6.

[4] Thus the cost of coats for Essex's attendants at the St George's Day parade in 1594, together with the summer liveries for his servants that year, amounted to no less than £300 – a bill which was still unpaid six years later (Cecil MS 179/128).

[5] *CSPSpan*, IV, *1587–1603*, p. 419.

many appearances in the tilt-yard. These are undoubtedly the most studied, and perhaps most important, of the public spectacles in which he partici-pated.[6] By the time Essex first began tilting before a public audience in 1586, the political value of creating a strong impression in the tilt-yard had long been recognised.[7] On every Accession Day, as well as on other less regular occasions, large crowds from the Court and the City flooded to see eager young courtiers test their martial skills and compete in conspicuous display.[8] Although he had once been a 'weake & tender' boy, Essex was a particularly energetic and accomplished jouster. At the Accession Day tilts of 1588, 1590, 1594 and 1596, Essex acted as a principal challenger, on the latter two occasions taking on all-comers by himself.[9] However, Essex's dominance of tournaments during the 1590s was based upon more than mere athleticism and knightly zeal. Essex also introduced a new sophistica-tion, even professionalism, into these occasions. Although he was never the queen's champion, Essex's position as master of the horse gave him a supervisory role over tournaments, which he exploited to its fullest potential.[10]

At their simplest level, the Accession Day tournaments allowed Essex to show himself to the world as a dashing young knight and the queen's particular favourite. All the magnificence of his appearance, and the elaborate praise of the speeches which accompanied it, were ostensibly in Elizabeth's honour. In turn, she recognised his efforts by bestowing gifts, such as her glove, as in 1594 and 1595,[11] which he wore as an open token of her admiration. Yet Essex also exploited these occasions to enhance his

6 Strong, *Cult of Elizabeth*, pp. 138ff; R. C. McCoy, '"A dangerous image": the earl of Essex and Elizabethan chivalry', *Journal of Medieval and Renaissance Studies* 18 (1983), pp. 316–23; also his *The rites of knighthood: the literature and politics of Elizabethan chivalry* (Berkeley, Los Angeles and London, 1989), pp. 79–86; A. R. Young, *Tudor and Jacobean tournaments* (London, 1987), esp. pp. 170–6.

7 See, for example, R. C. McCoy, 'From the Tower to the tiltyard: Robert Dudley's return to glory', *HJ* 27 (1984), 425–35.

8 A list of occasions on which tilts were held, together with sources of information about them, is printed in Young, *Tudor and Jacobean tournaments*, pp. 196ff. For comments on the audience and on the extravagant and costly spectacle, see G. von Bülow (ed.), 'Journey through England and Scotland made by Leopold von Wedel in the years 1584 and 1585', *TRHS*, n.s., 9 (1895), pp. 258–9.

9 Young, *Tudor and Jacobean tournaments*, pp. 37, 50; Strong, *Cult of Elizabeth*, p. 146. Essex broke fifty-seven staves in jousting against fifteen opponents in 1594. In 1596, he rode 108 courses against eighteen opponents and broke no less than ninety-seven staves in the process: R. Strong, 'Elizabethan jousting cheques in the possession of the College of Arms', in his *The Tudor and Stuart monarchy: pageantry, painting, iconography. II. Elizabethan* (Woodbridge, 1995), pp. 108–9.

10 Although he does not seem to recognise its significance, Young demonstrates the crucial role of the master of the horse by citing a letter written by the earl of Worcester, Essex's successor in the office, in 1602 (*Tudor and Jacobean tournaments*, p. 44).

11 Strong, *Cult of Elizabeth*, p. 156.

public reputation in other ways. He constantly sought to stand out from other competitors as a way of emphasising his pre-eminence in martial affairs. In 1590, he wore mourning garb to dramatise his own unhappy state and, in so doing, distracted attention away from the installation of his friend, Cumberland, as the successor to Sir Henry Lee as the queen's champion.[12] Essex's black costume may have been in memory of that late exemplar of 'perfect' knighthood, Sir Philip Sidney, or – more probably – in token of Elizabeth's recent anger over his marriage to Sidney's widow.[13] Essex also mounted increasingly elaborate entertainments to accompany his appearances in the tilt-yard. The set-piece which he presented in 1595 was probably the most sophisticated and politically significant display, but it was not unique. In the preceding year, he had paid for 'certain' scholars to come from Oxford to perform in his Accession Day entertainment.[14] He apparently made another stir with a speech declaimed before Elizabeth in 1596.[15]

Another feature of the tournament was the display of *imprese*, striking combinations of mottos and images which were intended to demonstrate the contestant's wit and imagination to all who were knowledgeable enough to decipher them.[16] In contrast to other elements of the tournament, *imprese* survived beyond the end of the competition, for the shields on which they were displayed were preserved on the walls of a long gallery at Whitehall.[17] Like Sidney before him,[18] Essex was a master at using *imprese*.

---

[12] Cumberland himself presented an elaborate pageant on this occasion, featuring Merlin and other Arthurian characters: A. R. Young, 'Tudor Arthurianism and the earl of Cumberland's tournament pageants', *Dalhousie Review* 67 (1987), pp. 180–3.

[13] See above, pp. 86–7.

[14] Devereux MS 3, fol. 91^r. From the time of their summons from Oxford, these scholars were given at least ten days to practise their parts (*ibid.*). Remarkably, Essex had also asked the visiting envoy from James VI to participate in his Accession Day presentation (LPL, MS 650, fol. 305^r).

[15] Rowland Whyte paid 2s 6d in order to send a copy of this speech to his master, Sir Robert Sidney (CKS, U 1475, A 38/5, accounts of Rowland Whyte, beginning 26 July 1596, unfol., entered in expenses for December 1596). This entertainment may also have been those 'my lorde's devises' of which Anthony Bacon was to take a 'perfect copy' (LPL, MS 660, fol. 207^r). This 'day of great triumph' is noted in John Stow, *A summarie of the chronicles of England* (London, 1598, STC no. 23328), p. 452.

[16] For a definition of *imprese*, see William Camden, *Remaines concerning Britaine: but especially England, and the inhabitants thereof* (2nd edn, London, 1614, STC no. 4522), p. 211. This topic is discussed in A. R. Young, 'The English tournament imprese', in P. M. Daly (ed.), *The English emblem and the Continental tradition* (New York, 1988), pp. 61–81 and A. R. Young, *The English tournament imprese* (New York, 1988), pp. 1–18.

[17] G. von Bülow (ed.), 'Diary of the journey of Philip Julius, duke of Stettin-Pomerania, through England in the year 1602', *TRHS*, 2nd ser., VI (1892), p. 23; G. W. Groos (ed.), *The diary of Baron Waldstein: a traveller in Elizabethan England* (London, 1981), pp. 51–3.

[18] R. W. Parker, 'The art of Sidney's heroic impresas', *English Literary Renaissance* 20 (1990), pp. 408–30.

He clearly relished the intellectual challenge of this rarefied art-form and the licence it provided to make statements which, in other circumstances, might have been regarded as outrageous. At the Accession Day tournament of 1595, Essex apparently used the device of a diamond and the legend *Dum formas minuis*, suggesting that – as in the cutting of a diamond – he could not be made to act against his own nature without being destroyed.[19] In light of Essex's arguments with Elizabeth and Burghley over war policy during the second half of 1595, this *impresa* strikes a remarkably defiant political stance for such a public event. On another occasion, according to a visiting German nobleman, Essex sounded a similar note. When baulked by Burghley in his urging that England must expand its war effort, he displayed an *impresa* showing a pen and a cannonball hanging in equal balance beneath a set of scales, with the inscription *Et tamen vincor*.[20] The clear message was that he has been defeated only because of Elizabeth unwillingness to recognise the superior weight of his arguments – and that this unnatural balancing act could not be sustained for long. Time and again, Essex succeeded in making these occasions almost as much a celebration of his own ideas and importance as of Elizabeth's.

The importance which Essex attached to his public displays in the tilt-yard can be seen in the time and money which he invested in them. Despite his busy schedule, Essex would spend up to a week honing his skills for the tournament.[21] In 1593, the costs of this practice period alone amounted to over £74.[22] In 1594, employment of the Oxford scholars cost Essex at least £13 2s 10d, a new silvered rapier and belt cost over £6 and white taffeta to fold around a gift of crystal for the queen cost 5s 6d.[23] The significant point about these figures is that they exclude the costs of the crystal itself and the remainder of the silvered costume which Essex wore for the occasion. They also exclude all the other costs involved in clothing the servants who accompanied him into the tilt-yard and in preparing and staging the entertainment itself. In 1584, a visiting German, Lupold von Wedel, claimed that contestants in the Accession Day tournament each spent several thousand pounds on outfitting themselves.[24] This estimate may be somewhat high but there is no doubt that Essex spent heavily to display himself appropriately on these occasions. Clearly, he viewed this as an essential investment for advancing and sustaining his reputation as Elizabeth's great chivalric favourite.

---

[19] 'While you form me, you deform me'. Young, *English tournament imprese*, p. 58.
[20] von Bülow, 'Diary of the duke of Stettin-Pomerania', pp. 23–5. The *impresa* means 'And nevertheless I am defeated'.
[21] LPL, MS 649, fol. 388ᵛ; LPL, MS 660, fol. 56ʳ.
[22] Devereux MS 3, fol. 74ᵛ.   [23] *Ibid.*, fols. 87ʳ, 91ʳ.
[24] von Bülow, 'Journey through England and Scotland made by Lupold von Wedel', p. 259.

2   Robert Devereux, 2nd earl of Essex, in 'sable sad'. Portrait by William Segar, 1590.

3   Frances, countess of Essex. Portrait by William Segar, 1590.

Given the cost and effort involved in these Accession Day celebrations, it is not surprising that Essex sometimes tried to create some permanent record of his athletic and artistic triumphs there. It seems likely that he commemorated his dramatic appearance at the 1590 celebrations by having his portrait painted by William Segar 'all in sable sad'.[25] As a herald and writer on matters of honour, Segar was a singularly appropriate choice

[25] See Plate 2. For discussion of this painting and its provenance, see D. Piper, 'The 1590 Lumley inventory: Hilliard, Segar and the earl of Essex' (in 2 parts), *Burlington Magazine* 99 (1957), pp. 231, 299–302 and Strong, *Cult of Elizabeth*, pp. 64, 66. As well as painting

of painter for this work.[26] Several years later, Essex employed the miniaturist Nicholas Hilliard to capture another tournament scene. Almost certainly, this was intended to represent his performance in 1595.[27] Significantly, the background of this image depicts an army camp, emphasising both the proven military experience which lay behind Essex's performance in the tilt-yard and the political course which he had been loudly urging upon the queen during that year.

Essex also showed a more general awareness of the value of portraiture. Considering the expertise in iconography which he demonstrated in his tournament *imprese*, this is perhaps not surprising. No scholar has yet made a comprehensive study of the portraits of Essex. [28] Nevertheless, the number of surviving images of Essex, and the provenance of some of them, suggests that he fairly often used paintings as a means of recognising special friendships.[29] Something of the importance which he attached to

this portrait, Segar also wrote a detailed description of the 1590 celebrations in his *Honor military and civill* (London, 1602, STC no. 22164), pp. 197–9.

[26] Segar was appointed Somerset herald in January 1589 (PRO, SO 3/1, fol. 177^r), a position which would have brought him into close contact with Essex. The two men probably first became acquainted when Segar joined Leicester's expedition to the Netherlands at the beginning of 1586 (*Leycester corr.*, p. 32; Stow, *Annales*, p. 717; BLO, Ashmolean MS 1131, fol. 82^r). Originally a client of Essex's friend, Sir Thomas Heneage, Segar may have painted a number of more conventional portraits of the earl (R. Strong, *The English icon: Elizabethan and Jacobean portraiture* (London and New York, 1969), pp. 17, 220, 222). It has also been suggested that Segar painted a portrait of the countess of Essex – see Plate 3 – about 1590 (Piper, 'Lumley inventory', p. 300; Strong, *English icon*, p. 222). This identification and dating seem quite plausible. The unusual placement of the subject's right hand behind her back may be a reference to the secrecy of her marriage to Essex or the queen's requirement that she live a semi-reclusive life distant from the Court. It is tempting to imagine that this portrait might be a kind of companion piece to the portrait of Essex 'all in sable sad'.

[27] See Plate 4. For discussion and reproductions of this miniature, see E. Auerbach, *Nicholas Hilliard* (London, 1961), pp. 125–6, pl. 98; R. Strong and V. J. Murrell, *Artists of the Tudor Court: the portrait miniature rediscovered 1520–1620* (London, 1983), pp. 136–7; Strong, *Cult of Elizabeth*, pp. 64–5, 67; Piper, 'Lumley inventory', pp. 302, 303; Young, *Tudor and Jacobean tournaments*, p. 140.

[28] For discussion of the portraiture of Essex, see Piper, 'Lumley inventory'; Strong, *Cult of Elizabeth*, pp. 61ff; R. Strong, *Tudor and Jacobean portraits* (2 vols., London, 1969), I, pp. 116–17.

[29] For example, E. M. Tenison seems to have traced portraits of Essex which he gave to Sir Henry Lee (Tenison, VIII, pl. 5), Sir Edward Littleton (*ibid.*, IX, pl. 4), and his own sister Dorothy (*ibid.*, X, pl. 4). Essex himself also probably gave the portrait of him which still hangs in the dining hall at Trinity College, Cambridge. Miniatures of Essex, which were probably also gifts, were owned by Fulke Greville and Carew Reynell (M. Edmond, *Hilliard and Oliver: the lives and works of two great miniaturists* (London, 1983), pp. 88, 109). Henry Wotton records that Giovanni Battista Basadonna, the unofficial Venetian agent in London, possessed a specially mounted portrait of Essex (L. P. Smith, *The life and letters of Sir Henry Wotton* (2 vols., Oxford, 1907), II, p. 494). Essex's own man in Venice, Dr Henry Hawkyns, also sought a portrait of the earl for the duke of Tuscany, perhaps at the latter's urging (LPL, MS 655, fol. 239^v; LPL, MS 659, fols. 372, 408, 410). For the widespread custom of exchanging and circulating portraits in early modern Europe, see

4   Robert Devereux as champion of the tilt-yard, wearing the Queen's glove on his arm. The portrait may celebrate Essex's role in the Accession Day tournament of 1595. Miniature by Nicholas Hilliard, c. 1595.

J. Peacock, 'The politics of portraiture', in K. Sharpe and P. Lake (eds.), *Culture and politics in early Stuart England* (Stanford, 1993), pp. 211–13. Peacock also emphasises the importance of the contexts in which portraits were actually displayed by their owners.

portraiture can be seen in his munificence towards Nicholas Hilliard, to whom he gave £140 to repair his collapsing house.[30] Significantly, Essex offered this extraordinary sum during 1595, the same year in which Hilliard apparently painted the tournament miniature.

Essex used paintings to commemorate many of the most important events in his career. Portraits were painted, for example, to immortalise his appointment as general of the Rouen expedition in 1591[31] and his capture of Cadiz in 1596.[32] With the salient exception of his portrait as the *Young man among the roses*, Essex consistently appears in his portraits in martial pose.[33] Yet even this quintessentially courtly image, which portrays a lovelorn Essex among the queen's climbing roses, bears a motto alluding to Pompey the Great.[34] Given that the miniature was seemingly painted in 1587 or 1588, this allusion seems especially pointed and personal. In addition to his later renown as Caesar's ally and rival, Pompey was famed for commanding his own army by the precocious age of twenty-three – the very age which Essex attained in November 1588. In this light, the obvious courtly and romantic connotations of the image are balanced by a more subtle complaint that royal favour prevents the young earl from emulating Pompey's feat.

Despite this youthful protest, many of Essex's portraits feature black and white, the colours of the queen, thereby representing his status as Elizabeth's servant and favourite. This is very clear, for example, in his famous Cadiz portrait. Here, he is powerfully depicted as a conqueror. As Cadiz burns in the background, Essex dominates the landscape, while his hands grasp his sword and general's baton. Yet this pose is counterpointed by his appearance dressed entirely in the queen's white, save for his armoured collar. Here is Essex the great captain – but still the queen's servant.

This great painting by Marcus Gheeraerts was a truly pivotal image for Essex.[35] Stylistically, it embodied a break with the neo-medieval art of

---

[30] R. C. Strong, 'Queen Elizabeth, the earl of Essex and Nicholas Hilliard', *Burlington Magazine* 101 (1959), pp. 145–9; Edmond, *Hilliard and Oliver*, ch. 10.

[31] This painting is owned by the earl of Jersey. It is reproduced in Strong, *Cult of Elizabeth*, p. 66 and Strong, *English icon*, p. 220.

[32] Reproduced here as Plate 5. Painted by Marcus Gheeraerts, the prime original of this very large portrait (211.2 x 127 cm, or 83.5 x 54 inches) is now at Woburn Abbey.

[33] See Plate 1. Strong argues at length for the identification of Hilliard's miniature with Essex in *Cult of Elizabeth*, ch. 2. In addition to the points made by Strong, the painting's French influences – unique in England in this period (*ibid.*, pp. 57–60) – should be emphasised. As argued above, Essex's concern with French affairs was becoming very pronounced during this period.

[34] The motto is 'Dat poenas laudata fides'. For discussion of it, see Strong, *Cult of Elizabeth*, pp. 77–8; Edmond, *Hilliard and Oliver*, p. 91.

[35] The precise dating of this painting (Plate 5) remains problematical. Some clue may be offered by the response to Dr Hawkyns's request for a portrait of Essex for the duke of Tuscany. On 24 October 1596, Anthony Bacon reported that Essex was simply too busy 'to

5   Robert Devereux, 2nd earl of Essex. Portrait by Marcus Gheeraerts the Younger,
    1596–7: the so-called 'Cadiz portrait'.

6   Robert Devereux, 2nd earl of Essex. Sketch from life by Isaac Oliver, preserved
as a miniature, 1596–7.

Segar and Hilliard in favour of the *avant garde* work of Gheeraerts and his
later-to-be brother-in-law, Isaac Oliver.[36] Gheeraerts and Oliver sought to
capture realism and a kind of romantic melancholy and, in contrast to
Hilliard, painted under a direct Italian influence.[37] Given Essex's bur-
geoning contacts with Italy in the mid-1590s, the latter quality may help to

---

sitt it owt' (LPL, MS 659, fol. 242[r]). Hawkyns was still waiting for a picture of Essex in
February 1597 (LPL, MS 655, fol. 239[v]). This suggests that either Essex was unwilling to
send Hawkyns a copy of the Cadiz portrait or that it was not actually painted until well
into 1597. It is possible that the painting could have been done immediately upon Essex's
return from Cadiz, but this seems very unlikely because of the competing demands on his
time during this period.

36   Oliver did not marry Sara Gheeraerts until February 1602 (Edmond, *Hilliard and Oliver*,
p. 138). However, it seems that a preliminary drawing of Essex by Oliver may have been
kept in Gheeraerts's studio (K. Hearn (ed.), *Dynasties: painting and drawing in Tudor and
Jacobean England, 1530–1630* (Catalogue for an exhibition at the Tate Gallery, London,
1995), pp. 178–9).

37   Strong, *English icon*, pp. 13–25, 269; Strong and Murrell, *Artists of the Tudor Court*, pp.
81, 103–7. Edmond, *Hilliard and Oliver*, chs. 9–11. Oliver had once been a student of
Hilliard but they were now rivals in style and in the quest for patronage.

explain his abandonment of Hilliard.[38] It may also be significant that both Segar and Hilliard were former image-makers for Leicester. Moving to Gheeraerts and Oliver severed another link between Essex and his late stepfather.

The Cadiz portrait and a related miniature of Essex's head by Oliver[39] are also important in other ways. Prior to these portraits, depictions of Essex showed a variety of hairstyles and changing facial features. With these portraits, however, Essex's visual image became essentially fixed – a somewhat gaunt face, dark eyes and a reddish spade-shaped beard, which he first grew while sailing to Spain. The beard, in particular, was a constant reminder of the Cadiz expedition and became a kind of trademark in the many subsequent images of Essex. The paintings of Gheeraerts and Oliver jointly created the definitive visual image of Essex, establishing a pattern which was duplicated and imitated in engravings as well as the many painted copies and variations of their work.[40] In this sense, the visual imagery of Essex in the second half of the 1590s was quite literally the face of Cadiz.

Essex consistently identified himself as a noble knight and as the queen's favourite through visual representations and the careful orchestration of his involvement in public spectacles. Whenever possible, Essex sought to reinforce this very stylised public image by indulging in calculatedly grand gestures. In November 1592, for example, he dramatically appeared in the

[38] Oliver apparently visited Venice during May 1596 (Edmond, *Hilliard and Oliver*, pp. 113–14; Strong and Murrell, *Artists of the Tudor Court*, p. 103). One might speculate whether he came into contact with Essex's agent there, Dr Hawkyns.

[39] See Plate 6. Oliver's original *ad vivum* sketch of Essex, or at least an early study that was intended to be the basis for his later images of the earl, is now held at the Yale Centre for British Art: L. Stainton and C. White, *Drawing in England from Hilliard to Hogarth* (London, 1987), p. 48.

[40] For discussion of the painted copies and variants of the images by Gheeraerts and Oliver, see Strong, *Tudor and Jacobean portraits*, I, pp. 116–17; Strong and Murrell, *Artists of the Tudor Court*, pp. 105–6. Strong suggests that both artists painted their original works with an eye to 'mass production'. An engraving by William Rogers in 1599 was directly influenced by these images. Roughly contemporary engravings of Essex in equestrian pose by Thomas Cockson and Robert Boissard are styled after other equestrian images but follow the facial pattern of Gheeraerts and Oliver. For all these engravings, see A. M. Hind, *Engraving in England in the sixteenth and seventeenth centuries* (3 vols., Cambridge, 1952–64), I, pp. 192, 245–6, 267–8, pl. 109, 126, 238. The sole major exception to the dominance of the Gheeraerts/Oliver pattern is a half-length portrait by Robert Peake showing Essex in garter robes and holding a staff of office (either as earl marshal or lieutenant of the order of the garter). This was probably painted in 1598 and shows him with slightly hooded eyes and longer and redder hair than that depicted by Gheeraerts and Oliver. Peake's portrait does not seem to have been copied but remained within the Devereux family until it was sold in 1991 (The Weiss Gallery, *Tudor & Stuart portraits 1530–1660* (priv. pr., London, 1986), pl. 13).

royal presence wearing a 'collor of esses, a thing unwonted & so unlooked for'.[41] In similar vein, Essex always endeavoured to respond to the many petitions for help which came to him from poor commoners by displaying the conspicuous liberality of a true aristocrat. 'My lord is noble & honorable', observed Edward Reynoldes, '& never sent strangers from hym discontented, in whome there was any merritt.'[42] Essex pointedly intervened to prevent a man losing his ears as punishment for having slandered him.[43]

This appreciation of the value of making public gestures sometimes helped to express the third great element in Essex's image, that of being the champion of Protestant godliness. After his return from Cadiz, for instance, Essex made a point of demonstrating his gratitude to God for his victory by 'not missing preaching nor prayers in the Courte'.[44] Perhaps appropriately, however, the very strongly Protestant nature of his public persona was most evident through the printed word.

Essex had a remarkable number of published works dedicated to him during the 1590s. One calculation suggests that the total was over sixty – more than for Elizabeth and almost three times as many dedications as Burghley or Lord Keeper Egerton received.[45] About half the books dedicated to Essex were of a primarily religious nature – no less than twenty separate works between 1592 and 1597 alone.[46] Although some of the authors were friends of Essex, the great majority of these dedications do not reflect his involvement in the work's publication, but simply the strength of his already-existing public reputation as a supporter of Protestantism. By their very publication, each of these dedications further reinforced and embellished this reputation. Nevertheless, Essex's own actions deliberately fostered his image as a Protestant champion, as some writers observed. Writing from Edinburgh, Alexander Hume was impressed by Essex's financial support for Dr Rainoldes's anti-Catholic lectures at

---

[41] LPL, MS 648, fol. 313ʳ. For the significance of the collar of esses, see D. Fletcher, 'The Lancastrian collar of esses: its origins and transformations down the centuries', in J. L. Gillespie (ed.), *The age of Richard II* (Stroud and New York, 1997), pp. 191–204. I am most grateful to Dr Fletcher for discussing this subject with me.

[42] LPL, MS 658, fol. 228ʳ.

[43] *APC*, XXVII, *1597*, pp. 112, 181–2.

[44] LPL, MS 659, fol. 9ʳ.

[45] A. Fox, 'The complaint of poetry for the death of liberality: the decline of literary patronage in the 1590s', in J. Guy (ed.), *The reign of Elizabeth I: Court and culture in the last decade* (Cambridge, 1995), p. 231. Fox provides a list of works dedicated to Essex, 1590–1600 (*ibid.*, pp. 245–8). Although unsatisfactory, there is a discussion of the works dedicated to Essex in G. L. Bird, 'The earl of Essex[,] patron of letters' (unpub. Ph.D. thesis, University of Utah, 1969).

[46] There were, in total, forty-two books of all kinds dedicated to Essex in this period.

Oxford.[47] William Hubbocke similarly praised Essex for supporting godly preaching among the 'captured enemies' in the Tower.[48] Later writers may also have been encouraged by the appearance of the Devereux arms at the front of Dr Nicholas Bownde's influential sabbatarian tract in 1595.[49] In this instance, at least, Essex manifestly saw the book before publication and decided to identify himself with it publicly.

Essex was widely regarded as a supporter of the godly and wished himself to be seen as such. As with the other salient characteristics of his public persona, this Protestant image embodied beliefs which were genuinely important to Essex: his faith and the personal and family identity which flowed from it. Yet, although he encouraged it and sought to profit by it, Essex had far less control over his reputation as a Protestant champion than over that of being the queen's knightly favourite. Although he consciously projected the latter image, the former was in many ways thrust upon him, as it had been since the death of Leicester. As the flood of dedications suggests, the godly constantly looked to Essex as the one privy councillor who might offer them political support and protection against the rising tide of Archbishop Whitgift's drive for religious conformity. Although Essex pulled back from political advocacy for the puritan cause even before his elevation to the council, the kind of private patronage cited by Hume and Hubbocke continued to encourage 'hope & expectation ... among her Majestie's most faithfull [i.e. most Protestant] subjects'.[50]

Despite the rather limited nature of his actions, the continuing expectations among the godly excited a steady stream of public praise for Essex which sought to sustain and galvanise his commitment to the Protestant cause. George Gyfford described the war with Spain as representing the 'final battles' foretold in the Book of Revelations and urged Essex to 'put on that fine white linnen and pure, ride upon that white horse among this blessed company, and follow this high captaine'.[51] In a previous dedication

---

[47] Alexander Hume, A rejoynder to Doctor Hil concerning the decense of Christ into hell ([Edinburgh, 1594], STC no. 13948), sig. A 3[vere 4][r–v].

[48] William Hubbocke, An apologie of infants in a sermon: proving by the revealed word of God, that children prevented by death of their baptisme, by God's election, may be saved (London, 1595, STC no. 13898), sig. A4[r]. Since Hubbocke styles himself here as preacher for the Tower, it may be assumed that he was in direct receipt of money from Essex when he dedicated the book to him. Essex certainly aided Hubbocke's suit for a prebend at Winchester during the following year (HMCS, VI, p. 317).

[49] Nicholas Bownde, The doctrine of the sabbath, plainely layde forth, and soundly proved ... (London, 1595, STC no. 3436). Essex's arms appear on sig. A1[v]. This is the only overtly religious book among the five works which bear the Devereux arms during these years.

[50] Josias Nichols, An order of houshold instruction ... (London, 1596, STC no. 18540), sig. A5[r–v].

[51] George Gyfford, Sermons upon the whole booke of the Revelation (London, 1596, STC no. 11866), sig. A5[v].

to Essex, Gyfford expressed the more common theme that 'God hath prepared your honour as a right worthy instrument' for His plans.[52] The primary purpose of these exhortations was to encourage Essex into more active support for the godly at home. However, these stirring appeals undoubtedly also fuelled his desire to win martial glory abroad and reinforced that powerful sense of his own public importance which underlay all of Essex's display and self-promotion. During the Cadiz expedition of 1596, Essex openly exalted in his crusading ancestors, whilst dismissing Spanish Catholicism as the worship of gods of wood and paint.[53] Although others hailed him as God's 'instrument', Essex himself took great pains to ensure that the world knew that he was the unswerving champion of 'God's cause' and the favourite of His lieutenant on earth.

As the steady flow of godly dedications suggests, Essex's diligent cultivation of his public image made a powerful impact. Essex's 1595 Accession Day entertainment was apparently well enough known to prompt an allusion at the Middle Temple Christmas revels more than two years later.[54] The skill shown in his tournament *imprese* was seen to warrant praise and exemplification even after his death.[55] There were also many signs that his actions had captured the public imagination. Ballads and other pamphlets were sold celebrating his comings and goings on campaign.[56] When news arrived of the victory at Cadiz, there was much 'gaping' among the printers 'for the coppy of my lord of Essex voyage'.[57] At times, it may be suspected that Essex or his friends deliberately encouraged such popular publications,[58] yet there can be no doubt that public interest in Essex – and the possibilities of commerical publishers turning a profit from it – were quite genuine.

---

[52] George Gyfford, *A treatise of true fortitude* (London, 1594, STC no. 11870), sig. A2ᵛ.

[53] J. S. Corbett, *The successors of Drake* (London, 1900), pp. 63, 106; 'Documentos relativos á la toma y saco de Cádiz por los ingleses en julio de 1596', in *Coleccion de documentos ineditos para la historia de Espana*, XXXVI (Madrid, 1860), pp. 285, 356–8.

[54] P. J. Finkelpearl, *John Marston of the Middle Temple: an Elizabethan dramatist in his social setting* (Cambridge, Mass., 1969), p. 53; M. Axton, *The queen's two bodies: drama and the Elizabethan succession* (London, 1977), p. 3.

[55] For example, see Camden, *Remaines*, pp. 219, 228; Henry Peacham, *Minerva Britannia or a garden of heroicall devises, furnished, and adorned with emblemes and impresas of sundry natures* (London, 1612, STC no. 19511), p. 114; C. H. Herford and P. Simpson (eds.), *Ben Jonson[: life and works]* (11 vols., Oxford, 1925–52), I, p. 148.

[56] E. Arber (ed.), *A transcript of the registers of the Company of Stationers of London, 1554–1640 AD* (5 vols., priv. pr., London, 1875–94), II, pp. 591, 594; *ibid.*, III, pp. 53, 71. See also F. J. Furnivall and W. R. Morfill (eds.), *Ballads from manuscripts* (2 vols., Ballad Society, London, 1868–73), II, pp. 195–252.

[57] Comments of Thomas Nash, cited in M. A. Shaaber, *Some forerunners of the newspaper in England 1476–1622* (Philadelphia, London and Oxford, 1929), p. 280.

[58] This is a subject which must remain a matter of speculation until adequate evidence can be found. Nevertheless, there are a number of publications during the 1590s which invite suspicion about behind-the-scenes support from Essex or his friends.

The combination of mercenary motives and real admiration for Essex was evident in the many dedications to him of non-religious works. Like the dedications of the godly, these always served in part to advance the personal objectives of their authors. When writers lauded Essex's nobility and greatness, they did so with half an eye to the exercise of one particular noble quality: liberality.[59] However, many of the praises heaped upon Essex were sincerely meant. When Matthew Sutcliffe wrote that 'God hath placed your lordship as it were on a high stage in this estate: never man had greater favour of the beholders, nor was more likely to obtain a singular applause of the people',[60] these words reflected his true feelings as well as gratitude for the support which Essex had given him. Again, such praise undoubtedly reinforced and validated Essex's belief in his own special public importance.

This was perhaps especially true of the comparisons which many writers made between Essex and Sir Philip Sidney.[61] The popularity of this theme suggests that the parallel was either widely recognised or known to be especially gratifying to Essex. In making this comparison, writers complimented Essex's public devotion to Sidney and urged him to make his own memory famous by continuing to cast his career in the same heroic Protestant mould. After his return from Portugal, George Peele applauded Essex's martial exploits there in a work deeply redolent of Sidney, *An eglogue gratulatorie ... to the ... shepheard of Albion's Arcadia.*[62] Although uninspiring in its verse, this work is significant as an approving statement of all the values to which Essex was seen to aspire: renown in battle and in virtue; pride in England and commitment to Protestantism; and a consciousness of his special status as the defender of his country from 'the grim wolfe' who threatened 'Elizae's gate'.[63] To Peele's mind at least, the very pursuit of these 'mightie thoughts' made it entirely proper, and

---

[59] See, for example, Thomas Churchyard, *A musicall consort of heavenly harmonie ... called Churchyard's charitie* (London, 1595, STC no. 5245), sig. A2ʳ–3ᵛ.
[60] Matthew Sutcliffe, *The practice, proceedings and lawes of armes* (London, 1593, STC no. 23468), sig. B2ʳ.
[61] Comparisons between Essex and Sidney include: John Philip, *The life and death of Sir Philip Sidney ...* (London 1587, STC no. 19871), sig. (A)2ʳ⁻ᵛ, B3ʳ; George Peele, 'Polyhymnia' (1590) in C. T. Prouty (ed.), *The life and works of George Peele* (3 vols., New Haven, 1952–70), I, pp. 235–6; Thomas Watson, *The first sett of Italian madrigalls Englished ...* (London, 1590, STC no. 25119), epistle dedicatory and madrigals nos. i, xix, xxiii, xxvii; William Gager, *Meleager* (Oxford, 1592, STC no. 11515), sig. A2ʳ⁻ᵛ; (Francesco Colonna), *Hypnerotomachia: the strife of love in a dreame* (London, 1592, STC no. 5577), sig. A1ᵛ, A2ʳ⁻ᵛ; Charles Fitz-Geffrey, *Sir Francis Drake his honorable life's commendation and his tragicall death's lamentation* (Oxford, 1596, STC no. 10943), sig. F1ʳ⁻ᵛ.
[62] Published in London, 1589 (STC no. 19534).
[63] *Ibid.*, sig. A3ᵛ.

even necessary, for Essex 'to royallize his fame'.[64] Clearly, this was advice which Essex took to heart.

Essex also demonstrated his commitment to war against Spain and the ideals of martial virtue by his close personal dealings with gentlemen soldiers. Probably a majority of his friends were men with whom he shared the special bond of going on campaign together. Significantly, Essex claimed that he rejoiced in the company of these men because of the qualities which made them uncourtier-like, even though most of them did in fact visit the Court at some time: 'I finde sweetenesse in their conversation, strong assistance in their imployment with mee, & happinesse in their friendshippe. I love them for their vertues' sake, for their greatnesse of minde: for little mindes though never so full of vertue, can be but little vertuous.'[65] For their part, a large proportion of military officers professed a special dependence upon Essex. They did so because of his increasing domination of the army and ordnance office and because they valued his influence at the Court, which many soldiers regarded as an alien and hostile environment.[66] Many captains also conceived a special admiration for Essex because he genuinely prized the profession of arms, and those who followed it. Not only did he display conspicuous favour to military men, but he showed himself to be a serious student of war.

Throughout his career, Essex endeavoured to make himself the pre-eminent patron of English soldiers. In this, he proved to be remarkably successful. As Gabriel Harvey noted, officers who wished to get ahead needed 'to devote themselves to sum valiant especial nobleman, or singular captayn of most famous vertu'.[67] Essex was the obvious choice for such devotion, because of his much-advertised personal virtue and his access to the crucial levers of military patronage. As royal favourite, he was able to approach Elizabeth when he needed to advance a suit, or to hinder that of another man. After February 1593, he was also able to capitalise on the privy council's growing control over all aspects of the war effort – appointment to military commands, pay, leave and contracts for supplies of every kind. Essex's own eagerness to intervene in such matters helped to reinforce, and even accelerate, this general trend towards centralisation in military administration.[68] When Essex summoned Captain John Aldrich

---

[64] *Ibid.*, sig. B1ʳ.   [65] *Apologie*, sig. B3ʳ.
[66] See, for example, Sheffield Central Library, Bacon Frank MS 2, no. 119; PRO, C 115, box M, bdle 15, no. 7364.
[67] G. C. Moore-Smith (ed.), *Gabriel Harvey's marginalia* (Stratford-upon-Avon, 1913), p. 190.
[68] Some aspects of this trend are discussed in L. Boynton, *The Elizabethan militia 1558–1638* (London and Toronto, 1967); C. G. Cruickshank, *Elizabeth's army* (2nd edn, Oxford, 1966); J. S. Nolan, 'The militarization of the Elizabethan state', *Journal of Military History*

home from the Netherlands in early 1595, Sir Francis Vere was delighted by the initiative: 'the choosyng owght of men in this manner wylbe a wonderfull encourraigment to make others follow the warres and desearve extraordynarily, for this is agaynst the ancient coustome, which was to make choyse of the neerest'.[69] Such actions made a powerful impression on officers eager to make their fortunes, and won Essex many hopeful followers.

By the time of Essex's appointment as master of the ordnance in 1597, Sir Robert Sidney felt able to boast that 'the managing of all matters of war, both by land and sea, are almost all in his lordship's hands'.[70] In reality, Sidney's claim was somewhat exaggerated, especially for appointments to military command. Perhaps because of the disastrous consequences of allowing Leicester to dominate military patronage in the Low Countries in the mid-1580s, no councillor was ever able to achieve such control again. The lucrative nature of commands and contracts for military supplies also meant that competition for them increased sharply in the 1590s. As a result, almost every captaincy and contract involved a struggle between rival candidates supported by different members of the council. Sometimes Elizabeth herself became involved in such matters. Nevertheless, Essex was recognised as having a powerful, and often decisive, influence in these contests. In December 1596, for example, when the council named Captain Coterill as muster-master for the Norfolk militia, Essex was able to ensure that Captain Herbert Bozom shared the council's endorsement.[71] Essex also had a powerful voice in the selection of officers for the army abroad, not only for the forces on the Continent, where his own interests were greatest, but also in Ireland.[72] Such was Essex's dominance and familiarity with these matters that, in August 1596, Sir Robert Cecil made a marginal note that the appointment of an officer in Ireland was to be delayed until Essex was consulted about other commands that the man might already hold.[73]

Essex was also able to exert himself in the dispensing of military patronage through his friendship with the queen's leading officers, many of whom were his clients. Apart from varying degrees of personal affection for

58 (1994), pp. 391–420; R. W. Stewart, 'The "Irish road": military supply and arms for Elizabeth's army during the O'Neill Rebellion in Ireland, 1598–1601', in M. C. Fissel (ed.), *War and government in Britain, 1598–1650* (Manchester and New York, 1991), pp. 16–37.

[69] Cecil MS 31/51 (pr. *HMCS*, V, pp. 156–7).   [70] *HMCS*, VII, p. 156.

[71] Essex backed Bozom as a favour to Anthony Bacon. For this suit, see LPL, 659, fols. 310ʳ, 311ʳ; LPL, MS 660, fols. 30ʳ, 115ʳ, 121ʳ, 176ʳ, 204ʳ, 207ʳ, 280ʳ.

[72] See, for example, *HMCS*, VI, pp. 570–1 (a copy of this list is BL, Lansdowne MS 78, fol. 138ʳ⁻ᵛ), 558; *ibid.*, VII, p. 269.

[73] PRO, SP 63/192, fol. 118ʳ.

him, these men came to depend upon Essex's special ability to win additional supplies for their commands and leave for themselves. Although they also cultivated links with other councillors, especially Burghley and Cecil, their power to appoint certain subordinate officers was most regularly taken advantage of by Essex. Essex won a promise from Sir Robert Sidney, for example, that Sir John Shelton would have the next captaincy which fell to Sidney's appointment.[74] Essex also cultivated Sir Francis Vere, Lord Burgh and even Sir Edward Norris, the governor of Ostend and brother of his rival, Sir John Norris.[75] In Ireland, Essex sought favour from Sir William Russell for 'divers of my servauntes & followers in that realme',[76] in return for having backed Russell's appointment as lord deputy.

Although he lacked the notorious thirst for vengeance of his stepfather, Essex's influence and prestige made him uniquely able to hinder officers who crossed him. Due to a misunderstanding, Sir Anthony Sherley briefly experienced something of the harm which could befall a soldier who was 'afflicted for the opinion of my lord of Essex his couldness towardes me': this 'yss nott only heavy to my minde but to my fortune ... I have founde since my cumming hyther my busines thwarted by the mayor & hindred by other devises, ass mutch ass mallice'.[77] Perhaps for precisely this reason, few captains dared be anything other than friendly with Essex. The great exception to this rule was Sir John Norris. After fighting as comrades during the Portugal expedition, Essex and Norris fell out during 1590 over who was to command the army which Elizabeth was sending to Brittany. When Norris was appointed, Essex felt that Norris had deliberately deceived him in order to win the post.[78] Thereafter, the tensions between them were never far below the surface.[79] By 1595, when Norris was sent to Munster (allegedly as a result of Essex's determination to ruin his career),[80] they were open rivals.[81] The story runs that Norris ultimately died of

---

[74] PRO, SP 84/54, fol. 5ʳ. Sidney, of course, was governor of Flushing and the former brother-in-law of Essex's wife.

[75] For Essex's relations with these men, see especially their correspondences with him printed in *HMCS*, V–VII.

[76] LPL, MS 656, fol. 240ʳ. [77] *Ibid.*, fol. 282ʳ. [78] See above, p. 95.

[79] For example, Essex's confidant, Sir Roger Williams, openly complained of Norris as a personal enemy (PRO, SP 78/22, fol. 233ᵛ; PRO, SP 78/24, fols. 112ʳ, 128ʳ, 132ʳ⁻ᵛ, 177ʳ, 219ʳ). In May 1590, Norris was also involved in a feud with another intimate of the earl, Sir Thomas Baskerville (BL, Harleian MS 4762, fol 53ʳ). For his part, Norris increasingly felt compelled to look to the Cecils for protection from Essex (PRO, SP 12/251, fols. 25ʳ, 201ʳ).

[80] Sir Robert Naunton, *Fragmenta regalia or observations on Queen Elizabeth, her times & favourites* (ed. J. S. Cerovski, Washington, London and Toronto, 1985), pp. 64, 76.

[81] *HMCS*, V, pp. 413–14; PRO, SP 63/186, fol. 211ʳ⁻ᵛ. In mid-1596, Norris was involved in the sequestration from command of Sir Richard Bingham, a rival in Ireland and follower of Essex (see below). Essex's hostility towards Norris was reflected in a paper on strategy

despair after Essex's friend Lord Burgh was appointed as lord deputy, for it 'broke the great heart of the general to see himself undervalued and undermined'.[82] True or not,[83] there is little doubt that Essex consistently criticised the only general whose stature rivalled his own. Essex could no more accept a rival for pre-eminence in war than he could endure competition for the queen's favour at Court.

The most dramatic evidence of the scale and significance of Essex's military following came at times when the queen dispatched forces abroad. On these occasions, Essex showed that he had a unique ability to officer Elizabeth's armies with friends and followers. This capability was testimony both to his influence over military affairs and to the number of captains who sought to associate themselves with him. Even though he lacked any military command at the time, Essex claimed that he named the infantry and cavalry commanders for the Portugal expedition and made '7 or 8 of my fast friendes colonels, and 20 at the least of my domestickes captaines: so as I might have authoritie and party enough when I would'.[84] Once Essex gained specific authority in military affairs, this pattern was repeated again and again. In 1591, although his choices were restricted by constraints imposed by Elizabeth, he was still able to place his friends in most of the available commands for the Rouen expedition.[85] In 1595, perhaps by virtue of being the venture's leading advocate on the council, Elizabeth allowed him to nominate virtually all the officers of the land force which accompanied the ill-fated expedition of Sir Francis Drake and Sir John Hawkins.[86]

Perhaps even more striking than the number of clients he appointed as officers were the many gentleman volunteers who accompanied each of the

which he began on his way home from Cadiz. Reviewing previous English attacks against Spain, Essex claimed that the Portugal expedition had failed because Norris 'shewed himself as ill a captayne in fayling of thatt place [Lisbon] as a cownsaylor of warr in going there' (Hulton MS (formerly BL, Loan 23), fol. 167ʳ).

82 Naunton, *Fragmenta regalia*, p. 76.

83 Although the rivalry between Essex and Norris was real enough, this account of Norris's career fails to recognise that his final move to Ireland was determined not by Essex, but by Burghley, Norris's chief patron. Norris's appointment reflected Burghley's determination that Ireland would replace France as the main theatre of war and was a move sideways, not a demotion. On the other hand, this made Norris's subsequent actions a direct challenge to Essex's policy that the Continent – and not Ireland – should be the primary theatre of war.

84 *Apologie*, sig. A3ʳ⁻ᵛ.

85 H. A. Lloyd, *The Rouen campaign 1590–1592: politics, warfare and the early-modern state* (Oxford, 1973), pp. 86–7; Tenison, VIII, pp. 338–9.

86 BL, Harleian MS 4762, fol. 12ʳ; K. R. Andrews, *The last voyage of Drake & Hawkins* (Hakluyt Society, 2nd ser., CXLII, 1972), pp. 16, 45–7. Essex had been known as 'a nominator of those that shall go [on] the Indian journey' at least as early as December 1594 (LPL, MS 650, fol. 344ʳ), when Elizabeth had displayed a earlier burst of enthusiasm for the idea of a Panama expedition.

armies which Essex formed. Lacking any formal appointment or pay, these men served with Essex in order to make conspicuous display of their martial ardour and in the hope of winning some profit from the venture. By virtue of their gentility and their high level of motivation, these men formed a disproportionately valuable addition to any army. 'I will awnswer upon my creditt', Essex asserted in 1591, 'thatt those gentlemen and adventurers thatt serve withowt pay shall do more service in any fight then the whole troupes besides.'[87] At the outset of the Rouen expedition, such volunteers swelled the size of Essex's own company of footmen by 61 men and raised the army's cavalry troop by 58, to 154.[88] The most spectacular instance of this phenomenon was undoubtedly the Cadiz expedition. When the army set out on that venture, '300 grene hedded youthes couvered with fethers, golde and sylver lace' accompanied the force, including the young John Donne.[89]

Essex's ability to draw large numbers of volunteers to the queen's standard increased the efficacy of her forces without any extra burden to her exchequer. This drawing power immensely strengthened Essex's own personal status, both as the general for a particular campaign and as Elizabeth's conciliar expert on land warfare. By surrounding himself with men who looked to him and upon whom he thought he could rely, Essex enhanced his ability to control an army in the field, giving him, as he termed it, 'partie and authoritie enough' for any necessity. Essex's personal links with officers and volunteers made it very difficult for Elizabeth to recall him once he took control of an army. When she tried to end his command in France, Essex and his advisers objected that his departure would raise the possibility of all the volunteers leaving with him.[90] Subsequent orders from the queen during that campaign tacitly reflected the force of this argument.[91] In 1596, similar considerations moved Burghley to oppose Elizabeth's desire to reduce the scope of the Cadiz expedition by denying Essex and the lord admiral permission to accompany it: 'a gret nombre of men of vallew that wold aventur of ther

---

[87] PRO, SP 78/25, fol. 366[r].
[88] Lloyd, *The Rouen campaign*, pp. 94–5.
[89] LPL, MS 659, fol. 1[r]. Anthony Bacon claimed in a letter to Dr Hawkyns that Essex was followed by 500 volunteers (LPL, MS 657, fol. 25[v]). A partial list of the volunteers on the Cadiz expedition is BLO, Rawlinson MS B 259, fol. 53[r–v]. For Donne's participation and consequent writings, see R. C. Bald, *John Donne: a life* (Oxford, 1970), ch. 5 and A. F. Marotti, *John Donne, coterie poet* (Madison, 1986), pp. 55–7, 97ff.
[90] PRO, SP 78/25, fols. 105[r], 366[r]; *Unton corr.*, p. 80. The latter reference stresses that Essex had in fact 'entertained a greate number of her Majestie's best captens *upon his owne purse*, who have no other charge, but come as voluntaries' (emphasis added).
[91] PRO, SP 78/26, fol. 153[r–v].

own charges to serve with these 2 lordes will not voluntarely serve under any other'.[92]

Although it gave him a peculiarly personal hold on the queen's armies, Essex's drawing power also saddled him with an enormous burden of expectation. As he knew only too well, going on campaign was an extremely expensive business and those who followed him ultimately expected some kind of material benefit for the great risk and expense to which they subjected themselves.[93] In consequence, Essex always sought to ensure that at least a proportion of these men received some reward. However, this raised a fundamental problem. After every expedition, Essex's reputation as the special patron of soldiers rode ever higher, and yet this image became ever harder to live up to. As a patron of soldiers, Essex became trapped in a vicious circle of his own devising.[94] Each success served to increase the numbers of hopeful soldiers who sought to win renown and reward with him when he next ventured on campaign. Such expectations inevitably affected Essex's stance on the council. As Elizabeth and Burghley became increasingly loath to maintain English troops on the Continent, Essex became ever more acutely aware that his followers among professional soldiers, in particular, depended upon his continuing staunch advocacy of anti-Spanish policies to secure their further employment. This pressure on Essex was powerfully demonstrated during the uncertain weeks which followed the return from Cadiz, when Essex House was 'continually hanted and barricaded with cavaliers' anxious about their future.[95]

The means by which Essex endeavoured to reward his soldier followers helped to drive this vicious circle. On occasions, Essex made gifts of money from his own purse,[96] but he simply could not afford to indulge in this

[92] PRO, SP 12/252, fol. 203ʳ (note that this memorandum has been incorrectly bound with documents relating to events in mid-1595. A copy of the paper, confirming its provenance, is BL, Cotton MS Otho E IX, fols. 318ᵛ–321ʳ). Despite Burghley's opposition, Elizabeth denied the generals permission to lead the expedition on 16 May. However, she ordered them to urge as many volunteers as possible to stay with the fleet (BL, Cotton MS Otho E IX, fol. 352ʳ⁻ᵛ). One hour later, she revoked this command (*ibid.*, fols. 352ᵛ–353ʳ).

[93] Robert Carey claimed that he spent £30 a week merely on food when he was a company commander under Essex in 1591 (F. H. Mares (ed.), *The memoirs of Robert Carey* (Oxford, 1972), p. 12).

[94] G. J. Hutson, 'The military following of Robert Devereux, 2nd earl of Essex, and the rising of 1601' (unpub. M.Litt. thesis, University of Oxford, 1987), pp. 23ff.

[95] LPL, MS 659, fol. 90ʳ. See also *ibid.*, fol. 88ʳ.

[96] Essex's steward claimed that he spent considerable, but unspecified, sums on 'gyftes to pore souldyers and men thatt had noe means and were owtt of intertaynementt' (Devereux MS 2, fol. 82ᵛ). He also subsidised the military activities, for example, of his cousin and childhood friend Sir Nicholas Clifford. Clifford received an £80 annuity from Essex's estates (Devereux MS 3, fol. 101ᵛ), but needed more than £50 more when he travelled to France in 1593 (*ibid.*, fol. 75ᵛ). When he went on the voyage to the Carribean with Drake and Hawkins in 1595, Essex gave him an additional £150 to set himself out (*ibid.*, fol. 83ᵛ).

practice too regularly. Instead, he depended upon the opportunities offered by war itself – by allowing his subordinates to gain from any available plunder and by knighting those who distinguished themselves in battle. Both of these means were hallowed by tradition and appropriate to the services rendered. Nevertheless, they repeatedly brought Essex into direct confrontation with Elizabeth. When large quantities of booty disappeared into soldiers' hands, as at Cadiz, and when Essex conducted mass dubbings at the end of a campaign, as he did at Rouen and Cadiz,[97] Elizabeth became infuriated. However justified these actions seemed to Essex, they stirred powerful feelings in the queen and helped to defeat his expectations that conspicuous military success would bring him greater political credit when he returned home from campaign.

At the heart of these tensions were the very different conceptions which Essex and Elizabeth harboured about soldiers and, indeed, about the whole nature of the war against Spain. Essex's attitude to the rewarding of soldiers was straightforward and consistent. In explaining the advantages won for the queen by the expedition to Cadiz, he asserted that 'her Majestie's men of warr, both soldiores and marriners, are made riche and fit to goe into anie action or service, aswell with more abilitie as with greater couradge'.[98] Essex placed great store in the material and psychological enabling of the queen's forces for future actions. His attitude towards bestowing knighthoods was similar. Writing from amidst the miseries of his disastrous Irish campaign in 1599, when he was particularly free with this distinction,[99] he claimed that 'yf I cold have found any other meanes to geve men of worth incouragemente or reward, or by any other circumstance cold have kept hope and spirite in this army, I had bene very sparing in bestowing this degree'.[100]

In contrast to Essex's desire to encourage martial endeavour, Elizabeth held a much less indulgent view of soldiers. In the Cadiz and Azores expeditions, her instructions made it quite clear that it was not the enrichment of her soldiers, but of her treasury, which was the priority. Any

Soldier friends also sometimes lent Essex money. Sir Thomas Baskerville, for example, loaned him £400 in June 1595 (*ibid.*, fol. 114[v]).

[97] Essex conferred twenty-eight knighthoods in Normandy (HEH, EL 1045, fol. 1[r]) and at least thirty-eight at Cadiz (PRO, SP 12/259, fol. 179[r]; BL, Sloane MS 226, fols. 23[v]–24[r]). By contrast, he made only nine knights on the Azores voyage (BL, Add. MS 5482, fol. 16[v]).

[98] LPL, MS 657, fol. 216[r]. A number of copies of this document ('The advantage Her Majestie hath gotten by that whiche hath passed at Caliz the 21st of June 1596') are extant in various manuscript collections, which suggests that it was circulated in order to bolster Essex's reputation. Copies include BL, Egerton MS 2877, fol. 177[r]; LPL, MS 657, fol. 220[r–v].

[99] He bestowed about eighty knighthoods in Ireland (BL, Add. MS 5482, fol. 18[r–v]).

[100] Hulton MS (formerly BL, Loan 23), fol. 119[r].

booty was supposed to be taken away from the fighting men to boost the finances of the crown.[101] The question of knighthoods was slightly more complex, but perhaps more significant. Although Elizabeth certainly recognised the need to reward soldiers, she was highly conscious of the social distinction which knighthoods would continue to carry after the war was over. She was well aware that men who already possessed this status were deeply hostile to any threat to their rank's social exclusiveness.[102] Knowing his 'love' of military men, Elizabeth was therefore initially unwilling to grant Essex the power to confer knighthoods on the Rouen expedition.[103] Although this decision was reversed, her instructions for this campaign, like those for the generals of other expeditions,[104] bound Essex primarily to weigh a man's family and wealth when honouring valour in battle in this way.[105]

Despite these instructions, on 8 October 1591 Essex made no fewer than 24 new knights.[106] According to Francis Bacon, Elizabeth responded to this news with a bitter sarcasm which made her concern about social status quite clear: 'my lord would have done well to have built his alms-house before he made his knights'.[107] However, Elizabeth's fury over Essex's action was also based upon other grounds. Perhaps above all, she saw it as a challenge to her personal authority as a sovereign. As Burghley wrote to Sir Henry Unton, Elizabeth viewed Essex's dubbing of the new knights as a direct act of disobedience to her instructions, while the knights themselves 'shee [held] not lawfull untill she shall make choice of the wourthiest, and them to make knights her selfe'.[108] To her mind, Essex had offended by ignoring his instructions and by usurping royal control over promotions to knightly status.

The circumstances surrounding this episode give some justification for

---

[101] BL, Cotton MS Otho E IX, fols. 346[r–v], 356[r]–362[v].

[102] *CSPIre, April 1599–February 1600*, p. 446. Cf. BL, Cotton MS Caligula E IX(i), fol. 201[v].

[103] *HMCS*, IV, p. 151.

[104] Cruickshank, *Elizabeth's army*, pp. 46–7. For a detailed discussion of the granting of knighthoods in Elizabeth's reign, see H. Leonard, 'Knights and knighthood in Tudor England' (unpub. Ph.D. thesis, University of London, 1970), pp. 111–28.

[105] PRO, SP 78/25, fol. 72[v]. The commission given to Essex and the lord admiral for the Cadiz expedition was perhaps even more insistent on this point: the generals might knight deserving men 'so as the same person have convenient living in possession or reversion to mainteine hym in such degree' (Devereux MSS, box 5, no. 80).

[106] Sir Thomas Coningsby, 'Journal of the siege of Rouen, 1591', ed. J. G. Nichols, *Camden Miscellany* 1 (1847), p. 27; HEH, EL 1045, fol. 1[r].

[107] J. Spedding, R. L. Ellis and D. D. Heath (eds.), *The works of Francis Bacon* (7 vols., London, 1857–9), VII, p. 125. In expressing her real concern about social status, Elizabeth's reaction was naturally far from unique: 'great mockery [is] made at my lord of Essex' 24 knightes' (PRO, SP 12/240, fol. 84[r]).

[108] *Unton corr.*, pp. 192–3.

Elizabeth's angry reaction. In his instructions, Essex was urged not to use 'the generality of your power in your commission' concerning knighthoods, but rather to report the names of deserving men to Elizabeth: 'we will our selves at your request upon your returne reward such persone with the dignity which their desertes shall deserve'.[109] In keeping with his generally careful observance of orders early on in the campaign, Essex initially respected this command.[110] However, on 8 October Essex made what he believed would be a permanent leave-taking from his army. Proclaiming to the assembled soldiers that 'he was verie sorrie that noe oportunitye was offered him to have ledd them into a place where they mighte have gayned honor', he then broke with his previous restraint on knighthoods.[111] This demonstrates Essex's general attitude towards bestowing knighthoods – clearly, he was conscious of the great weight of expectation among those who followed him, and he also believed that some of these men deserved 'notes of honor'.[112] Nevertheless, Essex was especially concerned to ensure that his army should see that it was himself – and not the queen – who had the special interests of soldiers at heart.

Elizabeth relied upon his liberality to soldiers in order to lessen her own costs in waging war, but she was sometimes drawn to fury by the means by which Essex sought to attach army officers to himself. At times, she may have been uneasy at the extent of this attachment. Elizabeth's anger over his making of knights may well have been heightened by an awareness of the special bond which the bestowing of that honour created between the parties involved.[113] Certainly, she always tried to restrict Essex's independence as a commander, issuing him with strict instructions and obliging him to heed the advice of subordinate officers. However, Elizabeth treated other generals in the same way and the subordinates whom Essex was required to consult were almost always men who were beholden to him. For all the anger that he caused her, Elizabeth also continued to appoint Essex to command her greatest expeditions – striking testimony to his success in establishing his indispensability to England's war effort.

---

[109] PRO, SP 78/25, fol. 72^v.
[110] Examples of such reports in his letters can be found in *ibid.*, fols. 287^r, 366^v. See also PRO, SP 78/26, fol. 113^v.
[111] Coningsby, 'Journal of the siege of Rouen', p. 27.
[112] *Ibid.* The same concern was evident in the brief speech which preceded the mass knightings by Essex and the lord admiral at Cadiz: 'they meant to knight some of them that had allreadie deserved it, and the rest in the hope they would deserve it' (BL, Add. MS 48152, fol. 189^r (pr. P. E. J. Hammer, 'New light on the Cadiz expedition of 1596', *Historical Research* 70 (1997), p. 198)). E. M. Tenison has endeavoured to argue that the men whom Essex knighted at Rouen and Cadiz were all worthy of the honour (Tenison, VIII, pp. 524–7; *ibid.*, IX, pp. 102–6).
[113] M. James, 'At a crossroads of the political culture: the Essex revolt, 1601', in his *Society, politics and culture: studies in early modern England* (Cambridge, 1986), pp. 428–9.

For his part, Essex's willingness to pre-empt Elizabeth over the making of knights did not represent any deliberate attempt to trench upon her authority. Essex acted in this way because he was desperate to be accepted by fighting men as one of them and, indeed, as pre-eminent among them. This was an essential part of that 'ambition of warr' which had fired Essex since his days in the Netherlands. Despite his success in remodelling himself as a politician, Essex continued to regard himself as fundamentally a soldier. In 1598, when he was accused of being a warmonger, he made his commitment to a martial career quite explicit: 'every man loveth those of his owne profession ... and I ... must reckon my selfe in the number of her [Majesty's] men of warre'.[114]

This self-identification as a man of war is crucial to understanding Essex's martial activities and, indeed, his whole career. Essex believed that he had a military vocation. In his mind, and in the opinion of many others, this was an age of conflict and God had specially chosen him to play a leading part in these struggles. Essex's association with soldiers was more than simply a logical concomitant to the notions of aristocratic virtue with which he had been brought up. His patronage of these men whom he 'loved', and his desire to be accepted as their leader, was a sign of his ambition to do nothing less than safeguard and shape the course of the military profession, a task which he regarded as crucial to his nation's future.

Essex had a distinctly elevated view of the importance of soldiers for the military and moral well-being of England. As a champion of martial virtue, he fervently believed that courageous soldiers merited special encouragement, regardless of restrictive guidelines imposed by Elizabeth. He also believed that the fortunes of such men must be shepherded to ensure that they remained financially able to serve in future actions. The vitality of the officer class was genuinely a matter of national urgency: 'they are England's best armour of defence and weapons of offence. If we may have peace, they have purchased it: if we must have warre, they must manadge it.'[115] For Essex, this was not only a political issue but a moral one, as his prediction about the impact on England of a hasty peace suggests. In his view, premature peace would allow the military power of Spain – 'the naturall roote of all [its] true confidence' – to swell, but England's soldiery would be ruined and 'our nation [would have] growen generally unwarlike'.[116]

This statement indicates that Essex subscribed to a commonplace of classical Roman thought – that in war lay the test of a nation's mettle, while a peace which was obtained without victory threatened the state with

---

[114] *Apologie*, sig. B3ʳ.   [115] *Ibid*.   [116] *Ibid*., sig. F3ʳ.

effete luxury.[117] Fulke Greville attributed very similar views to Sir Philip
Sidney: the nature of England was such that its people must either 'corrupt
with peace' or 'be kept from rust' by war abroad.[118] Sidney allegedly
believed that this foreign outlet was essential to the maintenance of social
order in England: 'if this multitude were not studiously husbanded and
disposed, they would rather diminish, than add, any strength to this
monarchie'.[119] Essex clearly held similar views.[120] Such sentiments would
help to explain why Essex was so consistently eager to act as the great
husbandman of men of war and to control the disposing of their appointments. In his view, meritorious soldiers were not only the physical
defenders of the realm and instruments for advancing the Protestant cause
abroad, but should be prized as guardians and exemplars of England's
national virility.

Essex's profound personal commitment to the profession of arms, and to
establishing his own dominance of it, was not only manifested in his
patronage of soldiers. Despite his own developing career as a councillor
and all the effort that he put into expanding his political role, his eagerness
to take the field himself remained unabated. Late in 1593, when he and the
lord admiral were delegated to supervise the reinforcement of Ostend,
Essex desperately hoped that he would have a chance to see action
again.[121] In 1594, he pressed hard to lead an army which was sent to
Brittany.[122] In 1595 he not only worked towards leading a new army to
France[123] but also apparently considered accompanying the expedition of
Drake and Hawkins.[124] Essex's success in winning command of the Cadiz
and Azores ventures in 1596 and 1597 must therefore be seen as the
culmination of a long and consistent effort to further his 'ambition of
warr'. Essex spent time on campaign, or made serious efforts to do so, in
every year between 1585 and 1597.

   Essex's personal commitment to the profession of arms was also evident
in his prodigious expenditure on war. Huge sums have already been cited

---

[117] Although his contemporaries would hardly need it, Essex makes the parallel with Roman
history explicit in *ibid.*, sig. E4[r].
[118] Sir Fulke Greville, *Life of Sir Philip Sidney* (ed. N. Smith, Oxford, 1907), p. 79.
[119] *Ibid.*, p. 112. See also pp. 79, 113.
[120] It is suggestive, for example, that Essex had a predilection for the metaphor of a man
rusting from lack of proper use – he used it at least twice in letters to Robert Naunton
(Ungerer, II, pp. 97, 124).
[121] A. H. Smith and G. M. Baker (eds.), *The papers of Nathaniel Bacon of Stiffkey*, III,
1586–1595 (Norfolk Record Society, LIII, 1987 and 1988), p. 259.
[122] LPL, MS 650, fol. 227[r–v]; PRO, SP 12/283A, fol. 154[r]; Jeayes, *Letters of Philip Gawdy*,
p. 82; *HMCS*, IV, p. 524; *HMC. Seventh report, appendix* (London, 1879), p. 652.
[123] *HMCS*, V, p. 390; Ungerer, I, pp. 353–4, 356–8.
[124] LPL, MS 651, fol. 169[r]; *HMCS*, V, pp. 77–8; Collins, *Sidney papers*, I, p. 343.

above for his early campaigns: £4,000 in the Netherlands, £3,500 for the Armada emergency in 1588, £7,000 in Portugal and £14,000 for the Rouen expedition, a total of £28,500.[125] By contrast, Essex's rental income by 1592 was still only about £2,500 a year,[126] with perhaps another £3,500 a year coming from the customs farm of sweet wines.[127] However, the picture is complicated by the fact that both of these sources of income were used to secure large loans and to meet outstanding debts.[128] In addition, Essex benefited from royal grants of land or leases, which he was able to sell off. By 1592, he and his accountants had managed to parlay grants worth £1,050 a year into one-off payments amounting to £38,500.[129] It was possible that Essex may just have been able to sustain his high expenditure on war – for the short term at least – but only by straining his resources to their absolute limit.

Essex was extremely conscious of the precariousness of his financial position. After his return from Rouen, he spent three days negotiating with pawnbrokers and money-lenders, men whom he viewed as 'the basest sort of people that are'.[130] Nevertheless, he continued to spend heavily on matters relating to war when he felt it was necessary. Although comprehensive figures are not available, his expenditure on the Cadiz expedition, for example, must have been truly astronomical. As part of his efforts to induce Elizabeth to agree to his leadership of that venture, he contracted to pay 2d a day for 1,000 of the 5,000 footmen who were to be sent on the voyage and to provide armour for 1,500.[131] Essex also provided the only cavalry to accompany the army, a company of 100 lancers.[132] Considering that he also attracted many volunteers to the queen's service, there can be

---

[125] These sums are all cited by Essex's steward, Gelly Meyrick, in a report on the state of the earl's finances (Devereux MS 2, fols. 82^r–83^v). The date of 1592 for this report is suggested by reference to such items as income from the grant of sweet wines for 'II yeres and a halfe'. It seems likely that it was composed to support Essex's pleas for financial assistance from Elizabeth in the months after his return from Rouen. As such, it is possible that Meyrick may have somewhat exaggerated the discrepancy between Essex's income and expenditure.

[126] *Ibid.*, fol. 82^v.

[127] F. C. Dietz, *English public finance 1558–1641* (New York and London, 1932), p. 316, n. 28.

[128] For explicit discussion of this practice in relation to the sweet wines grant, see *HMCS*, VII, p. 283. It should also be noted that these figures do not include any profits which Essex made from the offices which he held. Although Leicester had told him that the mastership of the horse was worth about £1,500 a year (the official salary was £666), I can find no obvious trace of this in Essex's surviving accounts.

[129] Devereux MS 2, fol. 82^r.   [130] Murdin, p. 656.

[131] BL, Cotton MS Otho E IX, fols. 317^v–318^r, 362^r; PRO, SP 12/256, fol. 210^{r-v}; PRO, SP 12/259, fol. 189^r. Slightly different details of his agreement are given by Cecil in PRO, SP 12/262, fol. 16^r. Payments to some of these men after the end of the campaign can be seen in Devereux MS 2, fols. 92ff.

[132] Alnwick, Northumberland MS 481, p. 8.

little doubt that Essex continued to live up to the claim which he had made at Rouen: 'I serve her [Majesty] good cheape for her.'[133] However, this was hardly the full extent of Essex's expenditure in the queen's service in 1596. At the end of April, he also paid out 10s a man to the two companies of soldiers who had returned from the disastrous expedition of Drake and Hawkins.[134] Moreover, when Elizabeth hesitated about whether to proceed with the Cadiz voyage, Essex maintained the whole army out of his own pocket while she made up her mind.[135] According to Anthony Standen, Essex put himself to the 'insuportable charges'[136] of paying 'halfe a crowne a man the weke the space of a whole monethe, and this to 10,000 men'.[137] This expenditure is all the more extraordinary because he also gave money towards Sir Anthony Sherley's private expedition against the Spanish in Africa during May.[138]

There can be no doubt about the extent to which Essex committed himself to the Cadiz expedition. As he himself protested, if it had been cancelled, he would have been more than merely bankrupt.[139] Essex staked every ounce of his credit on the success of the venture – not only that which he had with the money-lenders, but also his personal credit with the friends whom he pressured into assisting him 'as a great testimonie of their love'.[140] The priority which Essex accorded to war could hardly be more powerfully demonstrated. In spite of all the dedication and industry which he had displayed in making himself an effective politician, Essex was ultimately prepared to wager all his resources when he felt the state of the war demanded it. This was not a new sense of priorities. In 1591, when he was desperate to make a good impression as a general, Essex threatened to void the leases of any of his tenants who failed to contribute to his

---

[133] PRO, SP 78/25, fol. 300[r].   [134] BL, Cotton MS Otho E IX, fol. 335[r].

[135] *HMCS*, VI, pp. 164, 174–5. Essex disbursed at least £1,175 2s 6d to pay the army between 5 and 14 May 1596 (Devereux MS 2, fols. 87[r]–88[v]). Essex had briefly done the same during his previous command at Rouen. During the last two weeks of October 1591, when Elizabeth demanded that the army be recalled from France, Essex had paid all the troops himself (Lloyd, *The Rouen campaign*, p. 123 n. 93).

[136] LPL, MS 657, fol. 1[r].

[137] LPL, MS 659, fol. 1[r]. If Standen's claim is correct, Essex would have been paying out £1,250 a week.

[138] *Ibid.*, MS 657, fols. 5[r], 32[r–v]. This unfortunate venture is discussed in D. W. Davies, *Elizabethans errant: the strange fortunes of Sir Thomas Sherley and his three sons as well in the Dutch wars as in Muscovy, Morocco, Persia, Spain and the Indies* (Ithaca, New York, 1967), pp. 40ff.

[139] PRO, SP 12/257, fol. 10r; *HMCS*, VI, pp. 164, 175.

[140] Devereux MS 1, fol. 265[r]. Essex sent out letters on his own behalf to accompany the official orders for levying troops directed to deputy lieutenants and muster commissioners by the privy council (for example, BL, Stowe MS 150, fol. 86[r]; Longleat, Thynne MS 7, fol. 1[r]).

preparations.[141] When he sailed on the Azores voyage in 1597, his concern
with the expedition before all else was equally extreme. Essex's departure
on that journey coincided with the expiry of his grant of the sweet wines
revenues.[142] Although this grant was a linchpin for his finances and
although debts totalling £10,577 10s fell due within a few weeks,[143] Essex
was so anxious to hasten away to sea that he failed to ensure the grant's
renewal before he sailed.[144] Ironically, Essex only salvaged matters when a
storm shattered all his plans for the expedition and forced the fleet back to
port.[145]

Essex also demonstrated his identification with the profession of arms by
his behaviour as a military commander. Although the results of his
campaigns were decidedly mixed, his performance as a general was highly
regarded by his contemporaries.[146] Essex's own military instincts usually
proved to be sound but he readily accepted advice from his subordinate
officers – a characteristic which they clearly appreciated. Above all, his
exercise of military command was remarkable for its industry and attention
to detail. Acting as his own chief of staff, Essex's frenzied work during the
final weeks before the departure of an expedition led him to 'not onlie loose
my recreation of entertaining my freinds, but my very meate & sleepe'.[147]
As befitted a man dedicated to the profession of arms, Essex was renowned
as a strict disciplinarian. In showing himself to be 'severely true' to 'that

---

[141] FSL, L.a.260.
[142] PRO, C 54/1480, unfol., enrolment of indenture dated 12 October 1594.
[143] HMCS, VII, p. 283. Debts totalling another £3,280 10s were due during August, with
more to come at Michaelmas (ibid., pp. 375–6). Almost certainly, some of these debts
were contracted in order to subsidise the expedition. In late July, Essex boasted to Cecil
that he had spent only £1,800 of the queen's funds which had been sent to Plymouth
(PRO, SP 12/264, fol. 84^r). When he had to demobilise most of the soldiers who were
intended to accompany the expedition, he sought to keep the venture alive by offering to
Burghley that 'the dismission of the army ... may lye upon me', even though 'I assure your
lordship I have beggered myself' (BL, Lansdowne MS 84, fol. 141^r). Essex's financial
position was made all the more parlous by the recent payment of £4,000 to the earl of
Pembroke on 25 April (HMCD, II, pp. 272, 276).
[144] HMCS, VII, pp. 376; PRO, SP 12/264, fol. 100^{r-v}.
[145] LPL, MS 661, fol. 246r. Essex's grant was extended for a further three years by an
indenture dated 1 August, but enrolled 20 August, 1597 (PRO, C 54/1565, mm. 11^d–19^d).
[146] See, for example, the lord admiral's comments on Essex to Burghley after the victory at
Cadiz: '... I protest in my pore judgment [he is] a great soldior, for what he doth is in great
order and good discipline performed' (HMC. Calendar of the manuscripts of the Marquess
of Bath. II. (Harley Papers), (Dublin, 1907), p. 46). With the partial exception of J. S.
Corbett (Successors of Drake, pp. 10, 304, but cf. ibid., p. 24), modern writers have
traditionally portrayed Essex's generalship in a very poor light. Recent decades have begun
to see a somewhat more positive interpretation: Lloyd, The Rouen campaign, pp. 114–20,
156–8, 166–7; L. W. Henry, 'The earl of Essex and Ireland, 1599', BIHR 3 (1959),
pp. 1–23.
[147] LPL, MS 657, fol. 139^r.

implacable tyrant, Mars',[148] Essex's concern with discipline was grounded
not only upon precise observance of the rules of war, but also upon
personal experience of 'our desolate armyes'.[149] Memories of the feuding
among Leicester's officers in the Netherlands undoubtedly made him
anxious to try to forestall similar squabbling on the Cadiz expedition.[150]
His efforts could not prevent such quarrels from occurring among these
'greatest spiritts of our estate',[151] but his conduct certainly enhanced his
military reputation.[152] His insistence that civilians – even the 'tyrannical'
Spaniards – must be treated with respect also won him great plaudits.[153]

Closely allied to Essex's insistence on strict discipline was the high
priority which he placed upon preaching in his armies. In contrast to the
prevailing opinion that soldiers were the scum of society,[154] Essex claimed
that, with firm leadership, 'a campe ought to bee ... the best schoole to
make religion truely felt, and piety and honestie to be duly practised'.[155]
During the Rouen campaign, Essex was apparently mocked by Marshal
Biron for his concern with religious observance.[156] Essex's concern with
religion while in the field was perhaps most obvious during the Cadiz
expedition. Many of his letters during this period reflect an almost
apocalyptic tone, perhaps influenced by writings like those of George
Gyfford. Essex personally provided four chaplains for the army, rather than
the three he had agreed to find.[157] In addition, he initially refused to allow
the Portuguese prince Dom Cristobal to accompany the army because the
prince would not attend sermons with him.[158] By such actions, Essex
sought to impose strict religious standards upon his men – perhaps rather
unrealistically. However, these actions advertised to the army their general's
very personal commitment to the godly cause.

Essex made considerable efforts to cultivate a distinct image in the minds
of his troops. On campaign, this projection of a public persona was
especially important. Essex's self-promotion reinforced his claim to

---

[148] Greville, *Life of Sidney*, p. 202; *Apologie*, sig. B3ᵛ; Wotton, *Parallel*, p. 12. Cf. Lloyd, *The Rouen campaign*, p. 125.

[149] LPL, MS 657, fol. 208ʳ.   [150] *Ibid.*, fols. 89ʳ, 95ʳ, 139ʳ, 208ʳ.

[151] *Ibid.*, fol. 208ʳ.   [152] *Ibid.*, fol. 46ʳ.

[153] At Cadiz, Essex ensured a 'rare president of the worlde left to the memorie of posteritie' by preventing any of the women who left Cadiz after its capture being molested or searched for hidden jewels (BL, Add. MS 48152, fol. 188ᵛ). In the Azores, Essex assured the people of Flores and Cuervos full protection from his troops and made his men pay for everything they took, 'even to the value of a hen' (S. Purchas, *Hakluytus posthumus or Purchas his pilgrimes contayning a history of the world, in sea voyages and lande-travells by Englishmen and others* (London, 1625, Glasgow, 1905–7 edn in 20 vols.), XX, p. 69).

[154] See, for example, Cruickshank, *Elizabeth's army*, ch. 2.

[155] *Apologie*, sig. B3ᵛ.   [156] Camden, *Elizabeth*, p. 623.

[157] BLO, Rawlinson MS B 259, fol. 49ʳ; BL, Cotton MS Otho E IX, fol. 318ʳ.

[158] LPL, MS 661, fol. 150ᵛ. Essex had been asked to take the Portuguese prince on his next expedition in a death-bed letter from his father, Dom Antonio (Tenison, IX, p. 456).

pre-eminence among men of war and served the vital military function of boosting morale. As a general, Essex displayed an almost Napoleonic concern with the morale of his troops. His strict discipline was matched by a promptness in paying his men quite untypical of the age.[159] He also often showed conspicuous concern for officers and soldiers alike. During the Portugal expedition he 'commanded all his stuff to be cast out of his carriages and to be laden with sick men and gentlemen that fainted'.[160] Similar concern extended to chivalrous opponents. When he recognised a veteran of Zutphen among the Spanish prisoners taken at Cadiz, Essex personally paid the man's ransom in token of their shared experience.[161] Such generosity drew approbation from the enemy as well as his own men.

Essex often indulged in grand martial gestures to encourage his troops, such as the mass dubbing of knights[162] when he was first recalled from Rouen and after the capture of Cadiz. In Portugal and Rouen, he openly challenged enemy leaders to duels.[163] He also performed acts of spectacular, almost foolhardy, bravery. When amphibious landings were made against enemy troops waiting on the beach in Portugal and at Cadiz, Essex himself led the way. In the former instance, Essex and Sir Roger Williams jumped from their boat to face an aggressive enemy amidst 'huge billowes and most dangerous rockes that splytted diverse of our boates, and many of our men [were] cast awaye in landinge'.[164] When the siege of Lisbon was abandoned, he rode up and drove a lance into the city gates before departing.[165] At Cadiz, Essex himself boosted the first troops over the city walls[166] and then led the attack into the marketplace 'in his doublett and hose with his rapier drawen, upon whome theire played many shotte from

---

[159] Tenison, X, pp. 195–6.

[160] R. B. Wernham (ed.), *The expedition of Sir John Norris and Sir Francis Drake to Spain and Portugal, 1589* (Navy Records Society, CXXVII, 1988), pp. 238, 255.

[161] Tenison, X, p. 92. This was Gomez de Medina, who later praised the exceptional discipline of Essex's troops at Cadiz (Corbett, *Successors of Drake*, p. 104).

[162] See above, pp. 223–4.

[163] [Anthony Wingfield], *A true coppie of a discourse written by a gentleman, employed in the late voyage of Spaine and Portingale* (ed. A. B. Grosart, pr. for subscribers, 1881), pp. 84–5; BL, Stowe MS 159, fol. 371^r; J. X. Evans (ed.), *The works of Sir Roger Williams* (Oxford, 1972), pp. 13–14; [Pierre Cayet], *Chronologie novenaire, contenant l'histoire de la guerre, sous le regne du tres chrestien roy de France & de Navarre Henri IIII* (3 vols., Paris, 1608), vol. II, book 3, fols. 502^v–503^r; PRO, SP 78/26, fols. 194^r–195^r.

[164] BL, Stowe MS 159, fol. 370^r. See also BL, Harleian MS 167, fol. 114^v; BL, Add. MS 4102, fol. 15^v; PRO, SP 12/223, fol. 130^r; FSL, V.b.142, fol. 6^r. Essex subsequently approached the fort guarding Peniche and personally demanded its surrender: [Anon.], *A treatise paranetical, that is to say: an exhortation ... by a pilgrim Spaniard ...* (London, 1598, STC no. 19838), sig. E3$^{r–v}$.

[165] BL, Egerton MS 2598, fol. 22^r; HMC. *Ninth report, appendix i* (London, 1883), p. 278. Thus George Peele lauded Essex as he 'that brake his launce, with terror and renowne, against the gates of slaughtered Rhemus towne' (*An eglogue gratulatorie*, sig. B1^r).

[166] According to one observer, one of Essex's servants even stood on the earl's hands as he

the leades of the howses and windowes, which towched him not'.[167] During the Azores voyage, Essex was the first to land at Villa Franca and almost the last to leave.[168] Despite repeated explicit orders from the queen to the contrary, he consistently made sure that he was at the forefront of any battle.[169] As Marshal Biron noted in 1591, Essex's desire to prove himself in battle was such that he always wanted to be first in any fight.[170] The same compulsion was evident when he commanded warships at sea. During the naval battle in Cadiz harbour, Essex forced his ship's master to take his vessel closer to the enemy than any other ship.[171] The following year, Essex refused to turn back to harbour 'till my shipe was fallinge asunder, havinge a leake that we pomped 8[0] tunnes a day out of her, her mayne and fore mastes cracked, and most of her beames broken and rent, besides the opening of all her seames'.[172]

Essex was clearly exhilarated, even transformed, by the dangers of shot and shell. The thrill of the fight energised him, giving him a sense of almost superhuman invulnerability. The intoxicating rush of adrenalin perhaps helps to explain his compulsive desire to test himself on the battlefield. For a man brought up to consider himself a figure of destiny, each escape from such dangers must have reinforced his own perception of himself as an agent of God, especially when he survived so often when those around him died. Yet there was also an element of calculation in Essex's heroics. Many of his actions seem distinctly self-conscious, even stylised. During the Portugal expedition, he awaited a response to his challenge with great plumes tied to his helmet and a red scarf about his left arm, vowing that 'his rapier should bee longe ynough to encounter with the longest pike [which] should bee used against him'.[173] At Cadiz, he marked the decision

helped the man over the wall (BL, Add. MS 48152, fol. 187^v (pr. Hammer, 'New light' on the Cadiz expedition of 1596', *Historical Research* 70 (1997), pp. 182–202, at p. 195)).
[167] FSL, MS V.b.142, fol. 21^r.
[168] W. Dillingham (ed.), 'The commentaries of Sir Francis Vere, being divers pieces of service wherein he had command; written by himself, in way of commentary', in E. Arber (ed.), *An English garner: ingatherings from our history and literature* (8 vols., Westminster, 1895–6), VII, pp. 102, 106. Once again, the landing at Villa Franca was conducted in heavy surf. The re-embarkation of the army was undertaken in the expectation of an imminent attack from a superior enemy force, following a day of skirmishing. During the return to the ships, Essex twice almost sank his boat by overloading it with soldiers of the rearguard (Purchas, *Hakluytus posthumus*, XX, p. 118).
[169] PRO, SP 78/26, fols. 3^{r-v}, 152^{r-v}, 282^r, 290^{r-v}; *Unton corr.*, pp. 194, 231; BL, Cotton MS Otho E IX, fol. 345^v; *HMCS*, VII, p. 349.
[170] PRO, SP 78/25, fol. 362^r.
[171] BL, Add. MS 48152, fol. 186^v (pr. Hammer, 'New light', p. 192). The most comprehensive modern account of the battle at Cadiz is still Corbett, *Successors of Drake*, chs. 3–4.
[172] LPL, MS 661, fol. 246^r; *HMCS*, VII, p. 351.
[173] BL, Stowe MS 159, fol. 371^r.

to attack the Spanish fleet by casting his hat into the sea.[174] In the Azores, he showed a self-consciously Sidneian touch by refusing to wear armour when surveying a beach for amphibious assault because the men rowing him had no such protection.[175] These actions seem very much like a heightened form of the ritualised posturing which Essex performed in the tilt-yard, albeit with real blood and death. Undoubtedly, Essex's actions were performed with an awareness that he was participating in the grandest theatre possible – as Sir Walter Ralegh remarked of the battle at Cadiz: 'the best wilbe that ther was 16,000 witnesses'.[176]

As Ralegh's comment suggests, Essex was far from unique in indulging in acts of highly conspicuous courage. Indeed, he was surrounded by men who performed similar deeds. His challenges in Portugal and France were matched by those made by Sir John Norris[177] and Sir Henry Unton[178] respectively. Although the queen's ambassador to France, Unton sometimes endangered himself in battle in a similar manner to Essex.[179] Like Essex, these men were bent upon winning honour upon the battlefield in a manner recommended by Castiglione.[180] Essex's actions therefore cannot merely be seen as madcap bravery. They were deliberate acts to assert his pre-eminence by outdoing the deeds of others – leadership in the most literal sense.[181] Similarly, when things went wrong, Essex was always desperate to 'make yt knowne abroade' that he should not be reproached for any lack of personal courage or resolve.[182]

The problem for Essex was that this active style of military leadership

[174] Corbett, *Successors of Drake*, p. 75.
[175] Essex recalled Ralegh from undertaking this mission and made the reconaissance himself, 'unarmed altogether, but with his coller and sword, and without either shot or pyke to wayte on him'. When Ralegh urged him to wear armour or take a shield because he might come within range of enemy troops waiting on the shore, Essex replied 'that hee would none, because hee disdained to take any advantage of the watermen that rowed him'. (Purchas, *Hakluytus posthumus*, XX, p. 109). Essex's action seems to echo the story of Sidney disdaining to wear leg armour at Zutphen. The author of this account of the Azores expedition, Sir Arthur Gorges, does not draw this parallel but emphasises instead that Essex's boldness was an irresponsible way for a general to behave (*ibid.*, pp. 109–10).
[176] FSL, V.b.214, fol. 109ʳ. Cf. Birch, *Memoirs*, II, p. 364.
[177] Wingfield, *A true coppie*, pp. 84–5.
[178] BL, Cotton MS Caligula E VIII, fols. 231ʳ, 232ʳ.
[179] For example, *Unton corr.*, pp. 311–13.
[180] 'When the courtier finds himself involved in a skirmish or pitched battle, or something of that nature, he should arrange to withdraw discreetly from the main body and accomplish the bold and notable deeds he has to perform in as small a company as possible and in view of all the noblest and most eminent men of the army . . .' (Baldesar Castiglione, *The book of the courtier* (ed. G. Bull, Harmondsworth, 1967), p. 115).
[181] In the opinion of Sir Arthur Gorges, Essex was 'a man that did affect nothing in the world so much as Fame, and to be reputed matchlesse for magnanimitie, and undertaking, and could hardly indure any that should obscure his glory in that kinde, though otherwise he favoured them never so muche' (Purchas, *Hakluytus posthumus*, XX, p. 92).
[182] LPL, MS 661, fol. 246ʳ; *HMCS*, VII, p. 351.

did not sit comfortably with the status of being the queen's favourite. Nor did the highly individualistic nature of such behaviour accord with the notions of obedience and personal subservience which increasingly characterised expressions of service to Elizabeth. In this sense, the adherence of Essex and others to the dictates of Castiglione placed them at odds with the expectations of their own prince.[183] Essex recognised this problem but he could do nothing about it. Despite a profusion of royal commands, he could not temper his style of generalship because it reflected his own exuberance on the battlefield and embodied his own deep-seated conception of virtue: that he must always strive to be *primus inter pares* in every field of endeavour. This tension was perhaps all the more insidious because Essex was able to rationalise his behaviour by instancing the generalship of another prince – his early idol, Henri IV of France. During the Rouen campaign, Essex's eagerness for the fray and longstanding francophilia encouraged him to ignore Elizabeth's commands and legitimise his own actions by emulating 'la façon de la France', by which generals, including the king himself, were expected to lead from the front.[184] At Cadiz, Essex made this practice a matter of policy. According to his orders, colonels not only had to camp in the midst of their men but also lead their attacks and oversee their retreats in person.[185] Elizabeth expected this conduct from subordinate officers but she never ceased to criticise such boldness by Essex.

In addition to personal heroics and patronage, Essex proved his commitment to the profession of arms by showing himself to be a devoted student of war. Essex's appetite for information about military operations, like other foreign news, was insatiable. From the queen's commanders abroad,

---

[183] The tensions between individual honour and obedience to the state during this period are discussed in M. James, 'English politics and the concept of honour, 1485–1642' in his *Society, politics and culture: studies in early modern England* (Cambridge, 1986), pp. 308–415 and his 'At a crossroads of the political culture: the Essex revolt, 1601' in *ibid.*, pp. 416–65. See also K. B. Neuschel, *Word of honor: interpreting noble culture in sixteenth-century France* (Ithaca and London, 1989), esp. ch. 6, and E. Schalk, *From valor to pedigree: ideas of nobility in France in the sixteenth and seventeenth centuries* (Princeton, 1986).

[184] Philippe de Mornay, sieur du Plessis, *Mémoires et correspondance … édition complète …* (12 vols., Paris, 1824–5), V, p. 174. This style of leadership is well described by the Bohemian nobleman, Karel of Zerotin, who served as a volunteer at Rouen: 'The king takes me to the very front line, where bullets whizz past all the time, for this lord never stays still, sees to everything himself, goes everywhere, wants to know about everything, and exposes himself to every danger. His activity is admirable, and those who wish to obtain his favour have to do as he does, without sparing themselves' (D. Buisseret, *Henry IV* (London, 1984), pp. 38–9). Zerotin became acquainted with Essex at Rouen and his younger brother, Jan Divis, enjoyed the earl's hospitality during a visit to England in 1596.

[185] Cruickshank, *Elizabeth's army*, p. 53.

he expected – and received – the same frequent supply of information which he demanded from her ambassadors.[186] For the battle of Turnhout in January 1597, for example, he received two letters outlining Count Maurice's intentions and at least seven different accounts of the action itself.[187] Soon after his arrival in England, Anthony Standen was clearly taken aback when Essex delighted in telling him details of a recent engagement in France.[188]

Such intelligence kept Essex abreast of current developments abroad and provided fresh raw material for his intellectual pursuit of 'the art military'.[189] Like Sidney before him, Essex made a practice of studying, 'as it were, in the trade of our lives'.[190] One suggestive example of this process of deliberate self-education is a memorandum which Essex wrote after the Azores expedition in 1597. It is unclear whether this paper was intended solely for his own benefit or to be shown to Elizabeth. Either way, the document seems to exorcise his frustrations of the voyage by methodically explaining the importance of such things as naval carpentry and victuals for 'he thatt shall inable himself to commaund a fleete'.[191] The attention to detail and the ability to explain points clearly in this paper are especially striking.

Although these notes reflect recent practical experience, most of Essex's study in war centred on books, especially those on history and military science.[192] Among contemporary works of the latter kind, there was a considerable debate over the relative merits of ancient and modern military experience.[193] As in so many other things, in this debate Essex was a dedicated 'modernist'.

In fact, Essex was the dominant figure in a loose grouping of English

---

[186] See, for example, BL, Harleian MS 4762, fol. 121ʳ.

[187] HMCS, VII, pp. 9, 20, 24–5, 26, 28, 29–30, 31–2, 45–8. The reporting of this battle caused friction between Essex's followers, Sir Francis Vere and Sir Robert Sidney. Vere blamed Sidney for holding back his dispatch to the queen so that he could claim credit for reporting the victory and thereby exaggerate his own role in it. News of the battle was subsequently reported to correspondents on the Continent by friends of Essex (see, for example, Bayerische Staatsbibliothek, Munich, Clm 10364, no. 669, George Hungerford to Dr Joachim Camerarius, 19 January 1597).

[188] LPL, MS 649, fol. 229ᵛ.   [189] LPL, MS 657, fol. 208ʳ.

[190] J. M. Osborn, Young Philip Sidney, 1572–1577 (New Haven and London, 1972), p. 537, cited in L. Jardine and A. Grafton, '"Studied for action": how Gabriel Harvey read his Livy', Past and Present 129 (1990), p. 39.

[191] WRO, TD 69/6.2, item 74, undated holograph paper by Essex, incomplete.

[192] In this respect, Essex (like many of his contemporaries) obeyed the oft-stated injunction: 'a capten to be excellent must bee of good readinge' (marginal annotation in Alnwick MS 479, unfol., contemporary translation for the earl of Northumbumberland of Girolamo Franchetta's An idea of a booke for the governments of state and warr . . . , 'Policy of warr' discourse).

[193] See H. J. Webb, Elizabethan military science (Madison, Milwaukee and London, 1965), pp. 17–50.

The quest for greatness: 1593–1597

military reformers in the 1590s which included his soldier followers, Sir Roger Williams and Sir Francis Vere, and his aristocratic friends, Lord Willoughby and Lord Mountjoy. Willoughby commanded English troops in the Netherlands and France in the late 1580s but he spent much of the early 1590s travelling on the Continent. During these travels, he learned much about military practices overseas, some which he reported to Essex.[194] When Essex was angling for the post of master of the ordnance in late 1596, Willoughby supported his efforts by writing a series of papers about necessary reforms for the supply and distribution of munitions.[195] In return, Essex backed Willoughby's bid to succeed old Lord Hunsdon as governor of Berwick.[196] An equally eager student of war was Lord Mountjoy, who was 'grown by reading (whereunto he was much addicted) to the theory of a soldier'.[197] This study became all the more important when Elizabeth forbade him from again fighting abroad, in punishment for his repeated trips to serve under Sir John Norris without royal permission.[198] Even so, Mountjoy was appointed governor of Portsmouth in January 1594, and immediately began modernising the defences of this crucial base to bring them up to a minimum international standard.[199] Like Essex[200] and

[194] See, for example, HMCS, XIII, pp. 606–7; LPL, MS 654, fols. 218ʳ–219ᵛ.
[195] BL, Egerton MS 1943, fols. 77ʳ–79ᵛ, 85ʳ–86ʳ; HMCS, XIII, pp. 606–7; LPL, MS 659, fols. 352ʳ, 353ᵛ; HMCA, p. 336.
[196] HMCA, pp. 331–2, 336; LPL, MS 659, fol. 236ʳ. Willoughby finally suceeded in this suit, but not until March 1598 (TCP, XII [II], p. 679). For the importance of Berwick, see H. M. Wallace, 'Berwick in the reign of Queen Elizabeth', EHR 46 (1931), pp. 79–88. The governorship of Berwick is discussed in L. Stone, 'Office under Queen Elizabeth: the case of Lord Hunsdon and the lord chamberlainship in 1585', HJ 10 (1967), pp. 283–4.
[197] Sir Robert Naunton, Fragmenta regalia or observations on Queen Elizabeth, her times and favourites (ed. J. S. Cerovski, Washington, London and Toronto, 1985), p. 80.
[198] Ibid., pp. 80–1.
[199] C. Falls, Mountjoy: Elizabethan general (London, 1955), pp. 73ff; F. M. Jones, Mountjoy, 1563–1606: the last Elizabethan deputy (Dublin and London, 1958), pp. 29–33; H. M. Colvin (ed.), The history of the King's Works, IV, 1485–1660, part ii (London, 1982), pp. 526–7. Mountjoy's consultant engineer for this work was Paul Ive or Ivey (ibid., p. 413).
[200] In August 1595, Essex urged improvements to the defences at Plymouth, Falmouth and Milford Haven, giving Elizabeth a map of the latter location (LPL, MS 651, fol. 276ᵛ). The 'platt' of Milford Haven was passed to Burghley and is now at Hatfield House (CUL, MS Ee.iii.56, no. 58; Hatfield, CPM II.51, noted in R. A. Skelton and J. Summerson, A description of the maps and architectural plans in the collection made by William Cecil, First Baron Burghley, now at Hatfield House (Roxburghe Club, Oxford, 1971), p. 40). Although the privy council strongly supported Essex's plan and dispatched Paul Ivey to make a survey in early October (PRO, E 351/542, fol. 209ᵛ), the earl of Pembroke (as lord president of Wales) successfully lobbied the queen against taking any action (CUL, MS Ee.iii.56, nos. 58, 64). In 1597, Essex sought improvements to Pendennis Castle at Falmouth (HMCS, VII, p. 480). Although Ivey was again sent to survey the site (GL, MS 1752, pp. 294–5), the initiative fell foul of inertia and the queen's unwillingness to spend money (Colvin, King's works, IV, part ii, p. 600). Elizabeth was lucky that this indecisiveness did not bring disaster. In 1597, when a new Spanish fleet was being prepared for sea, Philip II and his minsters seriously considered Milford Haven as their fleet's target before

Willoughby,[201] he recognised that good fortifications were critically important in modern warfare.

Although relations between Mountjoy and Essex remained close throughout the 1590s, it was not until 1597 that they went on campaign together. Unfortunately, Mountjoy's appointment as commander of the army for the ill-fated Azores expedition infuriated Sir Francis Vere, who believed that his long-time command of the English troops in the Low Countries and close professional relations with Essex better qualified him for the post.[202] Vere certainly did much to professionalise the English forces under his command[203] and the products of his training formed the hard core of Essex's armies at Cadiz, the Azores and (later) in Ireland. Through their correspondence, Vere also provided Essex with valuable military advice in the mid-1590s. However, pride made Vere unbending over Mountjoy's appointment. Despite Essex's attempts to soothe his feelings, the bond between them was irreparably damaged. As a result, the drive to modernise England's army – already weakened by Essex's previous rivalry with Sir John Norris – was further diluted.

The best known and best documented relationship within this loose grouping around Essex was his long and close friendship with Sir Roger Williams. The personal bonds between Essex and Williams were very strong and the Welshman's influence on Essex's ideas of war was profound.[204] Something of this influence can be seen by a glance at Williams's *A briefe discourse of warre*, which he dedicated to Essex in 1590.[205] Although only a fragment of a projected larger work,[206] this book is

selecting Falmouth as the intended landing place (H. Kamen, *Philip of Spain* (New Haven and London, 1997), p. 308).

[201] Upon his arrival at Berwick, Willoughby suggested improvements to the defences there, even making a detailed sketch in his own hand for Burghley's consideration (Colvin, *King's works*, IV, part ii, p. 526). Once again, these suggestions brought no serious action.

[202] Dillingham, 'Commentaries of Vere', pp. 94–8; Falls, *Mountjoy*, pp. 81–2; Jones, *Mountjoy*, pp. 35–7.

[203] For the military career of Vere, see C. R. Markham, *'The fighting Veres': lives of Sir Francis Vere ... and of Sir Horace Vere ...* (London, 1888).

[204] See above, pp. 147–8. Williams was one of those men knighted by Leicester with Essex after the battle of Zutphen (BL, Add. MS 48014, fol. 163ʳ). They later fought together in Portugal and Normandy. For Williams's career, see *DNB*, XXI, pp. 441–5; *DWB*, p. 1069; Evans, *Works of Sir Roger Williams*, pp. i–lxxviii; A. C. Miller, 'Sir Roger Williams – a Welsh professional soldier', *Transactions of the Honourable Society of Cymmrodorion for 1971* (1972), pp. 86–118.

[205] London, 1590, *STC* no. 25732. It is printed in Evans, *Works of Sir Roger Williams*, pp. 1–51.

[206] In his dedication of the work to Essex, Williams claims that he had intended to present the earl with a larger book on 'the great actions' over the last twenty years in the Netherlands but a servant lost parts of the manuscript (Evans, *Works of Sir Roger Williams*, p. 3). Presumably, it was from those surviving sections of this larger work not incorporated into *A briefe discourse* that the antiquarian Peter Manwoode was able to publish *The actions*

essentially a manual for military leadership. Essex patently followed the book's advice and arguments, most of which concern the importance of imitating Spanish military practices.[207] Williams's stress on the central importance of the general ('all consists in the chiefe') and the qualities which he considers necessary for a general (conspicuous courage, consistency of purpose and liberality with his money) are good descriptions of the image which Essex tried to project when he was a commander.[208] For the Rouen campaign, Essex's emphasis on pikemen accorded with the views expressed by Williams.[209] Essex's later stated preference for a compact army of experienced men was also undoubtedly influenced by Williams's frequent insistence on the value of 'a few experimented souldiers'.[210]

With his large military following, his command of great armies, his work as a councillor, and his circle of like-minded officers, Essex was at the centre of efforts to reform and modernise England's war effort in the 1590s. Despite his eagerness to dominate military patronage, he was a keen enemy of actual corruption. For the Cadiz expedition, he abandoned the traditional practice of 'dead pays'.[211] In Star Chamber, he 'inveighed with great force' against abuses in the levy system and urged the death penalty for malefactors.[212] Elsewhere, he argued that specific military abuses should be treated as felonies and even drew up a draft parliamentary bill to this effect in his own hand.[213] Elizabeth herself recognised Essex's zeal for

of the Lowe Countries in 1618 (pr. *ibid.*, pp. 52–158). Manwoode perhaps obtained Williams's notes as a result of the dispersal of Essex's own papers after his fall in 1601. When he died in 1595, the arrangements which Williams had made for the disposal of his papers in his will of 1589 (Cecil MS 203/92 (pr. *HMCS*, XIII, p. 414)) had been overtaken by events. Williams probably left the contents of his desk to Essex, along with his jewels and cash (CKS, U 1475, C 12/41 (pr. Collins, *Sidney papers*, I, p. 377)).

207 Miller, 'Sir Roger Williams', p. 97. Williams himself served with the Spanish for four years, between 1574 and 1577 (Evans, *Works of Sir Roger Williams*, pp. 27–8). His enthusiasm for Spanish methods is a central feature of the work. When he refers to the 'great captaines', for example, he readily explains that 'I mean the Prince of Parma and his followers' (*ibid.*, p. 32).

208 *Ibid.*, p. 7.

209 PRO, SP 78/25, fol. 121ʳ; Lloyd, *The Rouen campaign*, p. 89. In practice, however, the proportion of pikemen in the army did not match Essex's expectations (*ibid.*, p. 94). Williams held the post of marshal of the field in Essex's army in Normandy (*APC*, XXI, 1591, pp. 318–19).

210 Evans, *Works of Sir Roger Williams*, p. 9. See also *ibid.*, pp. lxxxiii–lxxxiv, c–ci.

211 PRO, SP 12/256, fol. 210ʳ.

212 W. P. Bailsdon, *Les reportes del cases in Camera Stellata 1593 to 1609 from the original MS of John Hawarde of the Inner Temple* (priv. pr., 1894), p. 30. Before the departure of the Cadiz fleet, Essex publicly expelled an officer from the army for corrupt dealings with his men. A deserter and 'an arriver' were also hanged (FSL, V.b.142, fol. 20ʳ. Cf. BL, Harleian MS 167, fol. 112ʳ).

213 Essex's suggestion is argued in an undated holograph paper (WRO, TD 69/6.2, item 76). His draft bill (also undated and holograph) was intended for introduction in the House of

reform and appointed him master of the ordnance with specific directions to keep a tight rein on that notoriously corrupt organisation.[214]

Essex also sponsored more intellectual efforts at reform. Besides accepting the dedication of Williams's *A briefe discourse of warre*, he gave Matthew Sutcliffe 'first occasion, leisure and meanes to write' *The practice, proceedings and lawes of armes*.[215] Although he apparently served abroad with Essex, Sutcliffe was not a soldier but a civil lawyer, anti-puritan polemicist and chaplain to the queen.[216] Nevertheless, his book amplified Williams's arguments about the relevance of Spanish practices and the cardinal importance of a good general. It also emphasised the need for appropriate authority and rewards to be bestowed upon men of war – a theme to which Essex and his soldier friends returned endlessly.[217] Essex also patronised Alberico Gentili, the Italian-born regius professor of civil law at Oxford whose prolific and varied output included works on the laws of war which quickly became international standards.[218] Gentili dedicated to Essex his *De iure belli commentationes*, which were published in various forms between late 1588 and the end of 1589,[219] and subsequently formed

---

Lords, suggesting that he would sponsor it himself (Cecil MS 139/208 (pr. *HMCS*, XIV, p. 163)).

214 See above, p. 127.

215 Sutcliffe, *The practice, proceedings and lawes of armes*, sig. C1ʳ.

216 *DNB*, XIX, pp. 175–7; P. Lake, *Anglicans and puritans? Presbyterianism and English conformist thought from Whitgift to Hooker* (London, 1988), pp. 8, 111–13, 126–7, 129–30, 245; B. P. Levack, *The civil lawyers in England 1603–1641: a political study* (Oxford, 1973), pp. 89, 101, 272–3. Sutcliffe was a fellow at Trinity College, Cambridge, during the time of Essex's residence and quite possibly taught him mathematics (in which he was college lector). Sutcliffe claimed to have seen active service (probably as a military judge) in France, Italy, the Low Countries and Portugal (*The practice, proceedings and lawes of armes*, sig. C1ʳ).

217 For example, Sutcliffe argues: 'nothing is more hurtefull to the proceedings of warres then miserable niggardise ... For what courage can men have when there is no hope of rewarde? By this meanes all military discipline is disordered, souldiers famished, forward men impoverished, the honor of the military profession stained, and unworthy persons and greedy gulls that lie fatting and purchasing at home, enriched with the spoiles of their countrey' (*ibid.*, p. 42).

218 For Gentili, see *DNB*, VII, pp. 1003–6 and G. H. J. van der Molen, *Alberico Gentili and the development of international law: his life, work and times* (1937, Leyden, 1968 edn) chs. 2, 7. His ideas on international law, and especially the laws of war, are summarised in *ibid.*, ch. 5 and Alberico Gentili, *De iure belli libri tres* (2 vols., Oxford and London, 1933 edn), II, pp. 15a–51a. Gentili has previously been associated with Leicester, Sidney and Walsingham: van der Molen, *Gentili*, pp. 44, 46–7, 50, 127, 185 and E. Rosenberg, *Leicester: patron of letters* (New York, 1955), pp. 137, 286–93.

219 *De iure belli commentatio prima* (London, 1588, *STC* no. 11734.3), *De iure belli commentatio secunda* (London, 1589, *STC* no. 11734.7), *De iure belli commentationes duae* (London, 1589, *STC* no. 11735), *De iure belli commentatio tertia* (London, 1589, *STC* no. 11735.3), *De iure belli commentationes tres* (London, 1589, *STC* no. 11735.7). The dedication to the first commentary was dated October 1588, the second January 1589 and the third September 1589.

the basis of his monumental *De iure belli libri tres* of 1598.[220] These writings dealt with such vital topics as the legitimate grounds for war, rules of military conduct and mechanisms for re-establishing peace. In 1590, Gentili also dedicated to Essex *De iniustitia bellica Romanorum actio*, which dealt with similar matters.[221] Essex's support for Gentili in these ground-breaking intellectual endeavours was genuinely close and interested.[222] Not only did Essex stand as godfather to Gentili's son[223] but he lifted a quote featured in the professor's discussion 'Of necessary defence' to conclude his own *Apologie* of 1598.[224]

Essex also championed practical reforms to improve England's capacity to wage war. Initiatives of this kind included his sponsorship of Hugh Platt's experiments with rations designed to survive long sea voyages. When Drake and Hawkins set sail in 1595, Essex took the opportunity to send some of these victuals with them.[225] More fundamental reforms were embodied in Essex's attempts to encourage the use of smaller, but better trained, armies. Although consistent with the arguments of Sir Roger Williams, Essex's moves in this direction seem principally to have been driven by his original conception of the Cadiz expedition.[226] A small, well-disciplined army, he argued, could match the massed 'artificers and clownes' who composed the militia which defended Spain.[227] When his hopes were frustrated in 1596, he endeavoured to create such a force for what became the Azores voyage, only to be thwarted by storms, lack of

---

[220] Published in Hanau, Germany. This work was also dedicated to Essex. When a new edition was published there in 1612 (by which time Gentili and Essex were both dead), the dedication to Essex was retained but his honours were restated in terms of a male sovereign!: 'King's Counsellor, etc.' (Gentili, *De iure belli libri tres* (1933 edn), II, p. iii).

[221] Published in Oxford (*STC* no. 11734). The dedication to Essex is dated 24 December 1590 (sig. ¶3ʳ–4ᵛ).

[222] In his dedication to the *Commentatio secunda*, Gentili seems to suggest that Essex's secretary, Thomas Smith, had some active role in assisting him with the manuscript: 'with the same kindness with which you took the First from my own hand, so take this Second from the hand of my second self, Thomas Smith your secretary: a man not only of great excellence but I might almost say unequalled in writing Latin. For this is promised to you, is due to you . . .' (translation from Tenison, VII, p. 403).

[223] *DNB*, VII, p. 1007; van der Molen, *Gentili*, p. 55.

[224] 'Justum id bellum quibus necessarium est et pia arma quibus nulla nisi in armis spes est' (*Apologie*, sig. E1ᵛ). Cf. Gentili, *De iure belli libri tres* (1933 edn), I, p. 59.

[225] Andrews, *Last voyage of Drake and Hawkins*, p. 60. In the year before the Drake and Hawkins expedition, Platt dedicated *The jewell house of art and nature* (London, 1594, *STC* no. 19991) to Essex. Since this book was one of the few which featured Essex's coat of arms (*ibid.*, sig. A1ᵛ), it is clear that Platt enjoyed special favour from him. See also *DNB*, XV, pp. 1293–5.

[226] PRO, SP 12/259, fol. 42ʳ–ᵛ.

[227] Hulton MS (formerly BL, Loan 23), fol. 161ʳ. See also *ibid.*, fol. 160ᵛ: 'an army may consist aswell of too great a number as of too small . . .'.

supplies and sickness among the troops.[228] Even before that abortive exercise, however, Essex had also begun reforming England's own defence forces. Building on precedents set during the emergency of 1588, he broadened the use of military experts in the county militia ('superintendents') and organised the best of the soldiers into compact regiments, the quintessentially modernist troop unit.[229]

During 1598, Essex's proposals for the overhaul of England's manner of waging war became still more radical. Perhaps influenced by the *ad hoc* committees called to oversee national defence during the crises of 1596 and 1597, and almost certainly by thoughts of its Spanish equivalent, Essex argued that the realm required both a permanent council of war and a fixed annual budget for its operations of £100,000.[230] Bold as it was, this idea apparently made little impact, perhaps because England's war effort and royal finances were by then in such a state of disarray. Nevertheless, this suggestion exemplifies Essex's consistent efforts to encourage a modern, professional approach to war in England, emphasising the value of expert soldiers and the need to preserve, and benefit from, their experience. However, Essex did not urge this approach merely for the sake of modernity. Underlying all of his efforts at military reform lay a very clear practical purpose: by his reforms, Essex sought to fashion the instruments with which he could effectively confront Spanish power and effect his own plans for winning the war. These strategic conceptions represent the other half of his 'ambition of warr'.

During his military apprenticeship in the Netherlands, under the influence of Sidney and Leicester, Essex made plain his commitment to fighting for the 'Protestant cause' – the belief that the Protestant communities of northern Europe, and the religious truth which they represented, must be defended from the forces of the Counter-Reformation. From the start, Essex's views of war, and especially of his own part in it, were dominated not only by a nobleman's urge to win martial glory, but also by a crusader's religious zeal. The whole notion of the Protestant cause gave him a sense of mission on a truly international scale.

---

[228] L. W. Henry, 'The earl of Essex as strategist and military organiser', *EHR* 68 (1953), pp. 373ff.

[229] PRO, SP 12/262, fols. 227^{r-v}, 235^r-6^r; HEH, Hastings Correspondence, box 4, HA 4148. See also Corbett, *Successors of Drake*, pp. 162–4 and Boynton, *Elizabethan militia*, pp. 195–6.

[230] *Apologie*, sig. D3^v-4^r. For discussion of the Spanish council of war and its adoption of annual budgets after 1587, see I. A. A. Thompson, *War and government in Habsburg Spain 1560–1620* (London, 1976), pp. 38ff, 79–80 and his 'The Armada and administrative reform: the Spanish council of war in the reign of Philip II', *EHR* 82 (1967), pp. 698–725.

These ideas remained at the heart of Essex's ideas about international politics and strategy. Throughout his career, he was keenly aware that he was an actor upon the European stage: the word 'Christendom' is one which constantly appears in the writings of Essex and of those around him. Governing the role which he sought to play upon this stage was an abiding sense of public purpose, of being a man to whom God had given the unique potential to advance certain necessary political ends – a belief which harmonised with the praise by others of him as an instrument of God. After his bitter return from Cadiz, Essex consoled himself in a private letter to Anthony Bacon with the thought that 'to this worke ... yf I can butt cary one brick or one trowell full of morter, I shall live happily and dy cont[ent]edly'.[231] In similar vein, more than a mere intellectual conceit lay behind Essex's characterisation as the heroic figure of Aeneas in his correspondence with Antonio Perez during 1595.[232]

This analogy between Essex and Aeneas is very telling. Aeneas was particularly celebrated for his *pietas*, both towards the gods and towards his own ineluctable fate.[233] In broad terms, the quality of *pietas* was appropriate for Essex because of the importance of his religion. However, the connotations of performing a duty owed to fate is also very illuminating. The clear implication of this analogy is that, like Virgil's hero, Essex was ultimately fated – predestined, in Calvinist terms – to draw his country to a glorious new future. Yet Aeneas's triumph was only painfully achieved and the very resort to this analogy in late 1595 powerfully evokes a sense of Essex's own feeling of thwarted destiny at that time. This is underlined by allusions to Elizabeth as Juno.[234] By this analogy, Elizabeth's actions in 1595 seemed to Essex and Perez like those of Juno – spiteful and futile attempts to forestall a destiny which even a goddess of her power could not avoid.[235]

Essex, then, harboured a powerful personal sense of mission, which he was determined to pursue even in the face of hostility from Elizabeth. Thanks to his upbringing in the Protestant cause, Essex was conditioned to perceive this mission as leading a crusading alliance with the Dutch and Henri IV of France against Spanish 'tyranny'. Since the situation in the Netherlands was relatively stable by 1590, Essex's endeavours were

---

[231] LPL, MS 658, fol. 245ᵛ.
[232] Ungerer, I, pp. 329, 354, 367, 401–2. See also *ibid.*, II, pp. 365–6.
[233] In addition, it should be noted that Aeneas was also associated with the 'Brutus myth' of English history. According to this non-classical legend, England was seeded with the heroic blood of Troy by the arrival of Aeneas's great-grandson, Brutus.
[234] Ungerer, I, pp. 329, 354.
[235] It is also important to recognise that this characterisation of Elizabeth as Juno itself embodied a polar shift from the usual association of her with the figure of Venus, the mother of Aeneas (Strong, *Cult of Elizabeth*, pp. 47–54).

principally focused on France.[236] Essex dedicated himself to securing further English military assistance for Henri, becoming his 'greatest & onlye freind ... in England'.[237] Quite apart from his desire to support Protestants there[238] (of which he was regularly reminded by his friend Bouillon and others), Essex saw France as 'the theater and stage wheron the greatest actions are acted',[239] the place where the fate of Europe could be decided and the natural focus of his own martial ambition. Essex also had a very personal commitment to Henri IV himself, which had been cemented at Rouen. Essex not only admired the king and wished to emulate his military renown[240] but also clearly contrasted Henri's virile qualities with his own Juno-like sovereign.

Essex's profound commitment to European affairs – both visceral and intellectual – was quite different from the calculations of national interest which actually drove English policy. Essex's indulgent attitude towards the Dutch was out of step with the efforts by Elizabeth and Burghley to cut England's military expenditure in the Netherlands and secure the repayment of war debts. This pressure on the Dutch to pay became steadily more intense after 1594.[241] However, during the mid-1590s these negotiations never quite reached the state of crisis which characterised Anglo-French relations. Increasingly, it was only strategic considerations which moved Elizabeth and Burghley to continue support for France. Since she disliked and profoundly distrusted Henri, few observers were under any illusion about the nature of Elizabeth's continuing support for him: Henri still received grudging assistance because it was crucial for England's defence to prevent the Spanish from gaining control of the Channel coast. Burghley, who viewed the French – not the Spanish – as England's traditional foe,

---

[236] However, Essex assured Prince Maurice that he believed there was 'rein plus conioinct avecque le bien de l'Angleterre que la prosperite des provinces unis'. Essex professed himself similarly eager to ensure 'l'honneur, la grandeur et felicite du Comte Maurice' (Essex to Count Maurice of Orange, 26 December 1594, transcription from A. W. Thibaudeau (ed.), *Catalogue of the collection of autograph letters and historical documents formed between 1865 and 1882 by Alfred Morrison*, II (priv. pr., 1885), pl. 72, facing p. 96). Note that from September 1596, Maurice was styled Prince of Orange (*HMCS*, VI, p. 384).

[237] LPL, MS 660, fol. 49[r]. See also LPL, MS 661, fol. 74[r]; *CSPVen*, IX, 1592–1603, pp. 273–4; PRO, SP 81/7(ii), fols. 180[v]–181[r].

[238] For discussion of Essex's dealings with the Huguenots, see S. L. Adams, 'The Protestant cause: religious alliance with the West European Calvinist communities as a political issue in England 1585–1630' (unpub. D.Phil. thesis, University of Oxford, 1973), pp. 120ff. Essex's personal feelings towards the Huguenots were surely influenced by his boyhood companionship with the son of a former Huguenot leader, Count Montgomery.

[239] ULL, MS 187, fol. 14[r] (pr. P. E. J. Hammer, 'Essex and Europe: evidence from confidential instructions by the earl of Essex, 1595–6', *EHR* 111 (1996), p. 379).

[240] *Apologie*, sig. A3[v].

[241] W. T. MacCaffrey, *Elizabeth I: war and politics, 1588–1603* (Princeton, 1992), pp. 271ff.

was deeply suspicious of Henri, and other councillors began to share his doubts.[242] As Sir Thomas Wilkes expressed it in 1593, 'if the king of Spayne were dead, wee are like enoughe to care little for France'.[243]

The uneasy consensus between Essex, Elizabeth and Burghley about the need to support Henri came to an end in 1595. At the beginning of that year, Spanish troops were evicted from their last foothold on the shores opposite England.[244] With that success, Elizabeth was freed from the necessity of sending more aid to France, a point which she promptly made by rebuffing Henri's proposals for further combined action against the Spanish.[245] At the same time, Burghley and Cecil argued that the deteriorating situation in Ireland urgently required the transfer of more men and *matériel* there.[246] Given England's limited resources, this could only be at the expense of Essex's hopes for aid to France.[247] The shipping of veteran troops from Brittany to Ireland in early 1595, followed by the transfer of Sir John Norris to a new command in Ulster, was a portent of things to come.[248] Essex's advocacy of the French cause not only ran counter to Elizabeth's views of Henri IV but also conflicted with the Cecils' belief that Ireland must supplant France as the prime focus of the nation's war effort. As Essex told a French correspondent in March: 'je suis tout seul. J'ay l'esprit de Libra [Elizabeth] et tout son conseil opposite.'[249]

England's declining support for Henri IV began to cause Essex great

---

[242] LPL, MS 3200, fol. 11[r-v]; PRO, SP 81/7(ii), fol. 180[v]-181[r]; *CSPVen*, IX, *1592-1603*, p. 174; Murdin, p. 667.

[243] BL, Cotton MS Caligula E IX(i), fol. 182[v]. For reasons why Elizabeth was persuaded not to withdraw her support from Henri in 1593, for example, see PRO, SP 78/32, fol. 287[r-v].

[244] R. B. Wernham, *After the Armada: Elizabethan England and the struggle for Western Europe 1588-1595* (Oxford, 1984), ch. 24.

[245] BL, Stowe MS 166, fols. 193[r]-194[r].

[246] See especially W. D. Acres, 'The early career of Sir Robert Cecil c.1582-1597: some aspects of late Elizabethan secretarial administration' (unpub. Ph.D. thesis, University of Cambridge, 1992), ch. 4. A minor but significant sign of this concern was Burghley's use of Peter Proby to improve the system of posts to Ireland through Chester during early 1595: BL, Lansdowne MS 78, fols. 231[r-v], 233[r], 235[r], 236[r-v], 237[r-v]; BL, Lansdowne MS 100, fol. 239[r-v]. For Proby, see Acres, 'Early career of Cecil', p. 320.

[247] For the French ambassador's protest against this transfer of troops on 29 December 1594, see PRO, SP 78/34, fols. 320r-321[v].

[248] The transfer of 2,000 troops was agreed by 23 November 1594 but delays ensured that they did not arrive there until 18 March 1595 (Woburn Abbey, Russell MSS, HMC 12, Burghley to Sir William Russell, 24 November 1594; H. Morgan, *Tyrone's rebellion: the outbreak of the Nine Years War in Tudor Ireland* (Woodbridge, Suffolk, and Rochester, N.Y., 1993), pp. 177-8; C. Falls, *Elizabeth's Irish wars* (London, 1958), pp. 186-7). Norris himself arrived in Ireland on 4 May 1595.

[249] Essex continued: 'car mes compagnons ne preschent autre qu'avarice et securité. Ceste securité est nostre maladie, de la quelle si vous nous pourries gueryr vous fairies beaucoup et pour nous et our vous mesme' (Cecil MS 135/224 (pr. *HMCS*, XIII, p. 554)). This letter is a holograph draft and is undated, but internal evidence indicates that it was probably composed in mid-March 1595. The identity of the intended recipient is uncertain.

difficulties by the latter half of 1595. The discontinuance of English aid for Henri alarmed French Protestants, raising fears that the king might have to make up for this loss of support by giving genuine substance to his nominal conversion to Catholicism.[250] As Elizabeth's favourite and the great champion of French interests in England, Essex came under great pressure to make the queen change her mind.[251] Henri himself sent a series of envoys to England, each of whose missions Essex was expected to support,[252] but each of these envoys proved less successful than the last,[253] culminating in the disastrous visit by Mons. Loménie, whose aggressiveness brought Anglo-French relations to breaking-point.[254]

Essex's reaction to these developments was characteristically vigorous, but he became increasingly despondent. Despite his efforts to help the envoys, he complained to Perez about the 'inanes ... legationes' which Henri had sent.[255] When Loménie returned to France, he reported to Perez 'nimis vexatum et extra modum melancholicum fuisse *my lort* [ie Essex] pro mala expeditione et responso reginae'.[256] It also became apparent that the idea of Essex leading a new army to France, as he and the king had hoped, was now entirely unrealistic.[257] The fundamental problem lay in the price which Elizabeth set for her resumption of military support for Henri. This was nothing less than the return of Calais to English sovereignty. Despite the Spanish advance through Piccardy, this was a price which the French were never willing to pay. Although Essex earnestly pressed her to lay aside this condition, Elizabeth was so determined that she may even have threatened to make peace with Spain before she would forego this claim.[258] It is in these circumstances that Essex wrote to Perez

---

[250] See, for example, LPL, MS 652, fol. 166^v.
[251] See, for example, *ibid.*, fols. 256^v, 290^{r-v}, 291^r; PRO, SP 78/36, fol. 192^r.
[252] PRO, PRO 31/3, vol. 29, fols. 33ff; [J.] Berger de Xivrey (ed.), *Recueil des lettres missives de Henri IV* (9 vols., Paris, 1843–76), IV, pp. 422–4; Ungerer, I, pp. 341–4.
[253] PRO, SP 78/36, fols. 113^r–114^r.
[254] PRO, PRO 31/3/29, fols. 19^r–51^v; BL, Stowe MS 166, fols. 264^r, 276^r, 278^r; PRO, SP 78/36, fols. 52^r–54^r, 113^v–114^r; LPL, MS 652, fols. 183^r, 185^r. The impact of Loménie's mission is summarised in R. B. Wernham, *The return of the Armadas: the last years of the Elizabethan war against Spain, 1595–1603* (Oxford, 1994), pp. 38–42 and J. B. Black, *Elizabeth and Henry IV: being a short study in Anglo-French relations, 1589–1603* (Oxford, 1914), pp. 92–4.
[255] Ungerer, I, p. 354.
[256] *Ibid.*, p. 369. The italics indicate words in cipher in the original letter.
[257] *HMCS*, V, p. 390; Ungerer, I, pp. 353–4, 356–8.
[258] Ungerer, I, p. 354, n. 5. Rumours of Elizabeth's inclination to seek peace were certainly current in the Netherlands at this time. When the Dutch ambassador, Caron, approached Essex about the matter in early December, he exploded in fury and swore to oppose such a peace with all his might. When Essex took Caron to see Elizabeth on the following day, she emphatically denied any intention of abandoning the Dutch (S. P. Haak (ed.), *Johan van Oldenbarnevelt: bescheiden betreffende zijn staat-kundig beleid en zijn familie, 1570–1601* ('S-Gravenhage, 1934), pp. 320–1. The substance of this letter is summarised

quoting one of the most dramatic lines in the *Aeneid*, capturing the unreasonable hatred of Juno for Aeneas and his destiny: 'Flectere si nequeo superos, Acheronta movebo.'[259]

Essex's frustration and anger during the autumn of 1595 was profound. However, his sense of God's will being thwarted extended beyond the immediate fate of Henri and the Huguenots. Essex's broader concern was that, by pulling back from France, Elizabeth might be withdrawing England into an increasingly passive role in the war against Spain.[260] The growing insistence of Burghley and Cecil that English resources must be transferred to Ireland opened up the prospect that England's war effort could be turned away from the Continent altogether. This would cut off Essex's personal ambitions of martial glory. Even worse, this preoccupation with an internal enemy might open the way for peace with Spain, a possibility which Elizabeth's threat apparently confirmed. Even if she did not go this far, Henri intimated that Elizabeth's coolness might prompt him to make his own peace with Spain, leaving England isolated and exposed to the full weight of Spanish power.[261] For Essex, these scenarios were an appalling, indeed unbearable, prospect.

In Essex's eyes, the Spanish were 'an insolent, cruell and usurping nation that disturbed the common peace, aspired to the conquest of my countrey, and was a generall enemie to the libertie of Christendome'.[262] By their plots against Elizabeth, they had shown themselves to be both malicious and treacherous. By the sheer size of their dominions around the world, they displayed an apparently limitless appetite for subjecting others to their will. Moreover, Spain stood behind the repressive force of the Inquisition, 'vowing to compell all to worship the beast'.[263] With such an enemy, there could be no compromise, for 'yow twoo [Elizabeth and Philip] are like mightie champions entered into the lists to fight for the generall quarrels of Christendome, religion & liberty'.[264] For Essex, the war against Spain was not only necessary, but one that must be continued until Spain's ability

---

in J. L. Motley, *History of the United Netherlands; from the death of William the Silent to the Twelve Years' Truce, 1609* (4 vols., London, 1869 edn), III, pp. 356–7).

[259] Ungerer, I, p. 354. This line can be roughly translated: 'If I cannot bend the powers above to my will, I will let loose the hordes of hell.'

[260] *Ibid.*, pp. 353–4, 360.

[261] Henri laid the burden for avoiding this event squarely on Essex. According to Thomas Edmondes, 'they saie they cannot live in this state & therfore meane to come to the last issue with you to know [w]hatt you will doe in uttermost resolucion ...' (LPL, MS 652, fol. 291ʳ). Henri's threats had added credibility after he received absolution from the pope on 7 September 1595.

[262] *Apologie*, sig. A3r. Cf. Purchas, *Hakluytus posthumus*, XX, pp. 68–9.

[263] Hulton MS (formerly BL, Loan 23), fol. 159ʳ.

[264] PRO, SP 12/45, fol. 64ʳ. Another copy of this letter, bearing the date 12 August 1597, is Hulton MS (formerly BL, Loan 23), fols. 149ʳ–152ʳ.

to impose its ravening desires upon the world was removed. Aggressive self-defence was therefore an inadequate war policy. The nature of the task – even apart from such considerations as the lessons of history and the extent of Spanish wealth[265] – ultimately required that England and her allies must take the initiative to make Spain 'feede within his tether'.[266] Moreover, unless this task was fully accomplished, the suasions of 'our peace dreamers' merely offered Spain the prospect of regathering and increasing its strength, thereby imperilling both the realm of England and 'God's truth'.[267]

Essex's opinions were far from unique. His arguments against talk of peace, for example, were very similar to those that had been expressed by Leicester[268] and other supporters of the Protestant cause. Much of Essex's political significance lay precisely in the fact that his views were widely shared. Essex represented an important strand of political opinion in England, and he did so with great power because of the depth of his commitment. To those who thought as he did, the very force of Essex's conviction was magnetically compelling. Sir Robert Sidney was moved to declare that, 'though I were no way tyed unto yow for your owne particular favors, as long as yow have thesse ends yow now have, yow cannot seperate me from followinge yowr course'.[269] For all her disagreements with him, Elizabeth herself could do no less than respect his dedication.

While Essex despaired about England's growing estrangement from France during the autumn of 1595, new developments began to challenge his thinking. From the middle of the year, privy councillors became increasingly concerned about the strength of the Spanish navy and the possibility that another Armada might be launched against England or Ireland. Essex himself was worried by this prospect and redoubled his efforts to secure intelligence about the enemy's intentions, playing up the threat of a Spanish invasion in the process. In late July, a Spanish raid on Cornwall confirmed England's vulnerability and gave new credibility to Essex's warnings. Even the sceptical Cecils were soon persuaded.[270] By August, Elizabeth and her council were convinced by 'certain knowledge' that 'the preparations in Spaine' were 'farre greater then in the year 1588'.[271] Although this interpretation of Spanish actions was actually erroneous, the conviction that a new Armada was being prepared changed the political agenda at Court. Unlike the wrangling over aid to

---

[265] Hulton MS (formerly BL, Loan 23), fol. 162r; BL, Cotton MS Titus C VI, fol. 172[r–v].
[266] PRO, SP 12/45, fol. 64[r].
[267] Hulton MS (formerly BL, Loan 23), fols. 162[r], 159[r].
[268] BL, Cotton MS Galba D II, fols. 190[r]–191[v].
[269] LPL, MS 652, fol. 167[r].   [270] For all this, see above, pp. 188–90.
[271] Collins, *Sidney papers*, I, p. 342. Cf. GL, MS 1752, p. 39.

France, all agreed that the naval threat demanded a military response, which gave Essex's credentials as a military leader fresh relevance and weight. The prospect of a new Armada not only united Essex with Howard and Hunsdon – the other 'martial men' on the council – but also bridged the gap between him and the Cecils. Whereas large operations in Ireland and France were clearly rival strategies, naval action against Spain could be complementary to both. For the Cecils, eliminating the Spanish fleet seemed a far cheaper and less dangerous alternative to risking the arrival in Ireland of a Spanish army. Although Essex continued to argue for action against the Spanish forces in Piccardy, the political tide increasingly flowed in a quite different direction. Essex therefore had to complement his pleas on behalf of France with broader strategic thinking.

The first hint of this shift apparently came in September, when the council was split by a fierce argument about whether the intended expedition of Sir Francis Drake and Sir John Hawkins against Panama should still proceed.[272] Essex was the foremost supporter of this venture, in opposition to Burghley, who apparently feared that it would weaken the realm's defences. Although the expedition had been long in the planning, Essex now seems to have had a late change of mind about its objectives. Instead of Panama, he urged that the fleet should be sent to attack Spain itself.[273] Although the proposal failed, it is a sign of where Essex's thoughts were beginning to turn. Even so, this did not weaken his commitment to France. Indeed, Essex was so eager to encourage Elizabeth back into open and active alliance with Henri that he deliberately tried to force her hand over the issue. When the queen named his friend Sir Henry Unton as her new ambassador to France, Essex gave him secret instructions to exaggerate French concerns in order to push her into making concessions.[274]

However, even before Unton was nominated for France, plans were underway to counter the Spanish naval threat.[275] In company with a number of Dutch ships, the lord admiral was to lead a strike against the ports where the enemy forces were gathering, as Drake had done in 1587 and had been unsuccessfully attempted in 1588. Despite their growing

---

[272] Collins, *Sidney papers*, I, pp. 342–3; PRO, C 115, box M, bdle 18, no. 7510.
[273] Collins, *Sidney papers*, I, p. 343. For the aims and origins of the Panama expedition, see Andrews, *Last voyage of Drake and Hawkins*, ch. 1.
[274] LPL, MS 652, fol. 264^{r-v}; Ungerer, I, p. 404. Although dated 23 December in the copy which Anthony Bacon had made of them, these instructions may well have been delivered to Unton on 22 December. Having at last set out for France that morning, Unton was met at Gravesend about 11 a.m. by Edward Reynoldes, 'who came poste from my lord of Essex and brought me letters' (BRO, TA 13/3, fol. 2^{r}). For further comment about Essex's instructions to Unton, see also below, p. 331.
[275] Caron, the Dutch ambassador was requested to move the States to provide forces for this venture by late October 1595 (M. L. van Deventer, *Gedenkstukken van Johan van Oldenbarnevelt en zijn tijd* (3 vols., 'S-Gravenhage, 1860–5), II, p. 84).

disagreement over the matter of aid to France,[276] Essex, Burghley, Cecil and the lord admiral co-operated closely in this venture.[277] At some point during these preparations, it was realised that a sizeable army was needed to assist in attacks on enemy ports. When Essex was designated to lead this force,[278] his involvement soon expanded to the point where he became the venture's prime mover. This was a crucial event. After years of trying, Essex now had the prospect of returning to war again – if Elizabeth would actually let him go.

In the light of his recent anxieties about the nature of the queen's commitment to the war, the latter condition must have weighed heavily upon Essex's mind when he considered the task which awaited him. So, too, would the bitter arguments which had arisen with Elizabeth and Burghley over the Panama expedition and aid to France. By March 1596, as preparations were beginning to reach their climax, he also realised that his effort to force Elizabeth's hand by means of Unton's dispatches had failed. Faced with an impossible mission, Unton had neither impressed the French nor swayed the queen.[279] Indeed, the French were now becoming increasingly agitated about the impending strike against Spain. They feared that it signified England's final abandonment of France and the end of all hope of military support.[280] Essex began to look to the new expedition to do more than merely neutralise the Spanish naval threat. Now that he finally had the opportunity, he had to strike a blow which would pacify the French and have done with Elizabeth's unwillingness to press the war. What became the Cadiz expedition therefore embodied Essex's great gamble to force Elizabeth into waging an aggressive war against Spain.[281]

To ensure its success, Essex engaged all of his own resources and those of his friends in the voyage to Spain. When Calais was besieged during early April, he willingly diverted all his energies into the efforts to relieve it. However, when Elizabeth's vacillation prevented him saving the town from the Spanish, his dismay was so great that he felt only fresh glory could redeem his honour.[282] Accordingly, he wrote a letter imploring Elizabeth to

---

[276] CSPVen, IX, 1592–1603, p. 174. [277] Apologie, sig. A4ʳ.

[278] Essex was apparently invited to share in the leadership of the venture by the lord admiral himself (PRO, SP 12/259, fol. 40ʳ⁻ᵛ).

[279] LPL, MS 654, fol. 211ʳ; LPL, MS 655, fols. 176ʳ–177ʳ; BL, Cotton MS Caligula E VIII, fols. 162ʳ–170ʳ, 176ʳ; Ungerer, II, pp. 14–17.

[280] The French feared that the withdrawal of some English troops from the Low Countries to serve on this expedition would also prompt the Dutch to recall their troops serving in France (CSPVen, IX, 1592–1603, pp. 191–2; BL, Stowe MS 166, fol. 299ʳ). For Elizabeth's response to these complaints, see BL, Stowe MS 166, fols. 299ʳ–300ʳ.

[281] Essex's plans for the Cadiz expedition are further discussed below, pp. 250–1, 255–7.

[282] See, for example, PRO, SP 12/257, fol. 45ʳ. Essex's dismay was the all the greater because he had warned about a likely Spanish threat to a Channel port (he thought the target would be Ostend) at the end of 1595, but Cobham had encouraged Elizabeth and the

allow the Cadiz expedition to continue.[283] In part, the message was a reiteration of his familiar plea for bold endeavours: 'princes that ar once in warr, if theie doo littell, must suffer much'.[284] However, there was one important novelty. In arguing for the expedition, Essex explicitly advanced it as a greater priority than any new undertaking in France: 'in the Frenche [actions] you ar but an auxiliarie or coadjutor after the proportion of Switserland or pettie commonweales, [but] in this, lyke a princesse of power, you make the warr your self'.[285] Essex had recognised that serious support for Henri would have to wait until England's strategic outlook had changed.

Further surprises were revealed when the fleet finally set sail. The target itself, Cadiz, was apparently selected by the lord admiral[286] and only revealed to the subordinate officers after departure.[287] This extraordinary secrecy ensured that the Spanish were caught totally by surprise when the fleet reached Cadiz, in contrast to the débâcle of 1589.[288] Another secret was revealed soon after the fleet's departure: Essex's own intentions for the voyage. These were embodied in a letter to the privy council[289] which Essex insisted should not be delivered 'till the wind hath so served att least a weeke as yow may all judg us to be in Spayne'.[290] Although it again rehearsed his opinions about the need for aggressive action against Spain, the true significance of Essex's letter to the council lay in the special request which he made of them. Now that he had sailed, he asked them to win the queen's approval for the expedition to seize a base in Spain itself and to garrison it with 2,000–3,000 men, as 'a continuall diversion and to have lefte (as it were) a thorne sticking in his [Philip's] foote'.[291] The crucial point about this plan, and the reason why Essex had kept it secret until after he was safely at sea, was that it directly contradicted the formal

council to disregard this intelligence (D. McKeen, *A memory of honour: the life of William Brooke, Lord Cobham* (2 vols., Salzburg Studies in English Literature, CVIII, Salzburg, 1986), II, pp. 602–4).

283 BL, Cotton MS Titus C VI, fol. 172^{r-v}. This is a copy only, listed in the catalogue merely as a letter by an unknown captain. Its authorship, however, is quite obvious. Another copy, correctly identified as a letter by Essex, is FSL, V.b.214, fols. 60^v–61^r.

284 BL, Cotton MS Titus C VI, fol. 172^r.

285 *Ibid.*   286 *Apologie*, sig. A4^r.

287 LPL, MS 250, fol. 347^r.   288 BL, Sloane MS 226, fol. 7^r.

289 The original is PRO, SP 12/259, fols. 30^r–31^v. Essex finished the letter on 31 May and gave it to Fulke Greville, who sent it to Edward Reynoldes. According to endorsements on the original in the hand of a clerk and of Sir Robert Cecil, it was finally laid before the council on 13 June (*ibid.*, fols 31^v, 32^v).

290 WRO, TD 69/6.2, item 80, Essex to Edward Reynolds, 31 May (1596). Reynoldes was only to show the letter to Essex's most trustworthy friends, specifically including Anthony Bacon.

291 PRO, SP 12/259, fols. 41^v–43^v.

instructions under which the fleet had set out.[292] As Elizabeth intended it, the Cadiz expedition was to destroy Spain's fleet in its harbours and to seize as much plunder as possible, while carefully preserving its men and vessels for the defence of the realm. Once the Spanish ports had been cleared, the generals had promised to send the army home and begin a purely naval operation against the convoy which was soon due to arrive with treasure from the Americas.[293] Essex's proposal would have turned this venture on its head, transforming a pre-emptive strike into the establishment of a permanent foothold in Spain and drawing off the cream of England's troops and part of her fleet in order to sustain it.

Although Essex succeeded in capturing Cadiz, he failed to convince the lord admiral and the expedition's council of war to accept his radical plan. Flushed with success, the council of war initially agreed to the general idea of holding the city.[294] However, this early enthusiasm soon yielded to more sober thoughts about the implications. When Essex tried to have his way, a series of long arguments ensued. While the council was prepared to hold the city until they received the queen's resolution on the matter, they utterly rejected Essex's request that he command this temporary garrison.[295] In turn, Essex 'absolutely refused to give his consent that there should be any other governor left there then himself'.[296] In advancing this claim, Essex explained how he expected to make Elizabeth fall in with his scheme: 'hee did assure himselfe soe much of hir Majestie's favour towards him as shee would not suffer him to peruish in that defence'.[297] In other words, Essex's plan depended upon presenting the queen with a *fait accompli* which she would have to accept, and reinforce, to prevent him and his army from being overrun. However, neither the lord admiral nor the rest of the council of war were prepared to let Essex force Elizabeth's hand in this way. Seizing on the claim that the fleet lacked sufficient victuals to maintain a garrison,

---

[292] BL, Cotton MS Otho E IX, fols. 343^r–348^v. The most directly relevant section of these orders is that which governed attacks on towns. Attacks were prohibited against any town which was able to defend itself – precisely the kind of base which Essex's plan required – or if the riches had already been removed. Furthermore, even if these conditions were met, the commanders were required not to risk heavy casualties (*ibid.*, fol. 345^v). The latter restriction was given new emphasis by the disastrous results of the voyage of Drake and Hawkins. After the loss of both generals and many of their men, Elizabeth and the council were anxious that there should be no further weakening of the realm's defence forces.
[293] *Ibid.*, Cotton MS Galba D XII, fol. 48^v.
[294] Alnwick, Northumberland MS 481, p. 37; LPL, MS 250, fol. 354^v.
[295] LPL, MS 250, fol. 356^{r-v}; Alnwick, Northumberland MS 481, p. 40; PRO, SP 12/259, fol. 119^{r-v}; *Apologie*, sig. A4^v; Dillingham, 'Commentaries of Vere', p. 91; *HMCS*, VI, pp. 229, 250–1.
[296] Alnwick, Northumberland MS 481, p. 40. See also LPL, MS 250, fol. 356^v.
[297] Alnwick, Northumberland MS 481, p. 40. Sir George Carew also reported Essex as claiming that 'his presence would undowtedly assure present success' (LPL, MS 250, fol. 356^v).

they vetoed all proposals to hold the city. In the end, it was declared that it was 'a matter not warranted, neither by commission, nor instruction, to hold any such place'.[298] Cadiz was burnt and abandoned.[299]

Having been thwarted in his attempt to force Elizabeth into defending and reinforcing a base in Spain, Essex hastily endeavoured to extract the maximum possible benefit from the expedition. Like other men in the fleet, he rushed to claim his share of credit for the success by sending home an account of the victory. Unlike others, however, Essex did not restrict himself merely to dispatching a long letter, but sought secretly to publish a substantial account of the campaign under a false name. This was the notorious 'A true relacion of the action of Calez ...', which Henry Cuffe brought back to England at the end of July.[300] In the event, Elizabeth and the privy council were alerted to the scheme and its publication in London was forbidden, along with all other works about the expedition.[301] Nevertheless, the cunning and sheer brazenness of Essex's planning is remarkable:

conferre with Mr Grivill whether he can be contented to suffer the 2 first lettres of his name to be used in the inscription, which if he graunt, he must be entreated not to take notice of the author but to give out that indeede he receved it amongst other papers by the first messenger, bu[t] by the subscription (which may [be] D. T., or some other designed name as you shall thinke good) could not conjecture the writer ... if he be unwillinge, you may put R. B., which some noe doubt will interpret to be Mr Beale, but it skilles not.[302]

Such underhandedness is striking indeed. Yet the full sophistication of Essex's activities after the decision to abandon Cadiz only becomes apparent when it is recognised that the 'True relacion' was merely one component of a new, highly secret[303] strategy to force Elizabeth's hand over the conduct of the war.

---

[298] PRO, SP 12/259, fol. 119ᵛ. The lord admiral also raised the matter of their instructions, in an undated letter to Essex himself: 'to adventure you and the principal ships of this army, to the utter overthrow of all the whole journey, I cannot like it. My duty tieth me to my instructions, and I do pray your lordship to remember your promise to her Majesty' (*HMCS*, VI, p. 239).

[299] Characteristically, Essex was virtually the last man to leave the city (LPL, MS 250, fol. 357ᵛ).

[300] For identification and discussion of this document, see P. E. J. Hammer, 'Myth-making: politics, propaganda and the capture of Cadiz in 1596', *HJ* 40 (1997), pp. 633–5.

[301] For details of this episode, see LPL, MS 658, fols. 88ʳ⁻ᵛ, 135ʳ, 214ʳ, 234ʳ, 259ʳ–260ᵛ. The ban on Cadiz publications was still in force in early 1599: C. E. Armstrong, 'The "Voyage to Cadiz" in the second edition of Hakluyt's "Voyages"', *Papers of the Bibliographical Society of America* 49 (1955), pp. 254–62; D. B. Quinn (ed.), *The Hakluyt handbook* (2 vols., Hakluyt Society, 2nd ser., CXLIV–CXLV, London, 1974), II, pp. 490ff.

[302] LPL, MS 658, fol. 88ʳ⁻ᵛ. The reference to Beale is especially duplicitous because he and Essex were on poor terms after the earl's efforts to make Thomas Smith a clerk of the council during 1595.

[303] As a postscript to one of his letters to Reynoldes, Essex wrote that 'I exclude all menn [from knowledge of these plans] but Mr Anthony Bacon' (LPL, MS 658, fol. 136ʳ).

The 'True relacion' embodied an attempt by Essex to encourage support for the war against Spain, and to establish his own pre-eminence in it, by appealing over the heads of the queen and council to the wider literate population. Although these hopes were largely foiled by the printing ban,[304] Essex and his friends circumvented the prohibition by producing and circulating a variety of manuscript versions of the work.[305] This reduced the public impact of Essex's propaganda, but hit home in the town-houses and country estates of England's political élite. Manuscripts were also sent overseas for the earl's agents to translate and spread abroad.[306] A French version was clearly intended to bolster Essex's reputation there, justifying his decision to embark on the venture in spite of French protests.[307] Even before the ban on publications, Essex sought to supplement his literary propaganda with public festivities, approaching Archbishop Whitgift to proclaim 'a publike thanksgeving for this great

[304] However, Essex did sponsor the publication of a map of the battle at Cadiz which was drawn by Baptist Boazio and engraved by Thomas Cockson (*STC* no. 3171.5; E. Arber (ed.), *A transcript of the registers of the Company of Stationers of London, 1554–1640 AD* (5 vols., pr. priv., London, 1875–94), III, p. 77). For reproductions of the map, see A. M. Hind, *Engraving in England in the sixteenth and seventeenth centuries* (3 vols., Cambridge, 1952–64), I, pl. 133; Tenison, X, opposite p. 66.

[305] There is a tantalising comment by Sir Anthony Ashley which invites speculation about the mechanics of producing these manuscript copies. According to Ashley, Sir Gelly Meyrick sent one Best, a scrivener who lived within Temple Bar, to Plymouth 'about businesses of great importance and secrecy' in mid-September. Meyrick apparently often used Best 'in like causes that he wold not have knowen of' (Cecil MS 75/56 (pr. *HMCS*, VI, p. 584)). In the circumstances, it seems unlikely that Best's employment related to money-lending (in which scriveners were commonly involved), suggesting his task involved the urgent and discreet copying of documents. Since Ashley had himself surrendered the original fair copy of the 'True relacion' in London, it seems likely that a new version of the tract had to be reconstructed out of the rough drafts which remained with Essex's belongings at Plymouth, where he had disembarked. Since Essex had ridden post to Court, he must have left these notes behind. By the time the fate of the original fair copy was known, Cuffe would have arrived in London and Henry Wotton (Essex's other secretary who travelled to Cadiz) was probably not far behind him. Given the furore aroused by Ashley's revelations, it may have seemed unwise to risk bringing the precious notes to London or to send one of Essex's own men to take charge of them. In this light, it seems possible – although this must remain only speculation – that Best's task was to create a new fair copy of the 'True relacion', which served as the basis for the various documents which survive today.

[306] LPL, MS 658, fol. 259^v. Dr Hawkyns received a copy of it in Venice (LPL, MS 659, fol. 408^r). By early December, he had translated it into Italian and sent a copy to the historian, Cesare Campana (LPL, MS 660, fol. 254^r). Although it is not clear whether Sir Thomas Chaloner also took a copy with him when he went to establish himself at Florence at the end of 1596, James Guicciardini had certainly received a copy there by February 1597 (*HMCS*, VII, p. 95). Bacon probably also sent a copy to Robert Bruz in Scotland during October 1596 (LPL, MS 659, fol. 217^r).

[307] Mons. la Fontaine, the French *chargé d'affaires* in London, was to have drawn up an abstract to be sent to France (LPL, MS 658, fol. 135^r). Essex himself wanted to check over the French translation during September (LPL, MS 659, fols. 89^r, 90^r).

victory'.[308] Although Elizabeth restricted the celebrations to London,[309] on 8 August bonfires burned in the streets and the inhabitants spent the day 'drinking, banketting & other waies rejoycing'.[310] To ensure that this groundswell of enthusiasm for the war would have a practical military focus, Essex tried to force Elizabeth to keep the Cadiz army in being for further service,[311] preferably the recovery of Calais.[312] Accordingly, he instructed Edward Reynoldes to approach Caron and la Fontaine discreetly. Essex asked these men, on behalf of their governments, to press Elizabeth to retain all the Cadiz troops for an attack upon Calais. If that proved impossible, they were to ask her to keep the best 3,000 men for service elsewhere in France.[313] Both men duly approached the queen, although to little effect.[314] Essex also used one last lever against Elizabeth's lack of enthusiasm for an aggressive war, by calling upon his friends in the Corporation of London, and especially the lord mayor's remembrancer, Giles Fletcher.[315] Essex not only succeeded in inducing the City to urge

---

[308] LPL, MS 658, fol. 135ʳ.

[309] Whitgift readily agreed to Essex's request, but Elizabeth intervened after the affair of the 'True relacion' (*ibid.*, fol. 260ʳ). However, one of Whitgift's chaplains, Dr William Barlow, preached a notable sermon praising Essex at Paul's Cross (*ibid.*, fol. 260ʳ⁻ᵛ; M. MacLure, *Register of sermons preached at Paul's Cross 1534-1642* (revised and augmented by J. C. Boswell and P. Pauls, Centre for Reformation and Renaissance Studies, occasional publications, no. 6, Ottawa, 1989), pp. 72–3). Whitgift had earlier arranged for a special prayer 'for the prosperous success and victorious return of her Majestie's forces and navie' to be printed and sold for use in every parish church in the realm (BLO, Tanner MS 77, fol. 88ʳ⁻ᵛ).

[310] J. Stow, *A summarie of the chronicles of England* (London, 1598, STC no. 23328), p. 450. It would be interesting to know who footed the bill for this merriment – perhaps the City of London? Despite the official ban, there were some spontaneous celebrations elsewhere in the country, such as the ringing of bells at St Andrew's, Canterbury (C. Cotton, 'Churchwarden's accounts of the parish of St Andrew, Canterbury, from A.D. 1485 to A.D. 1625: Part IV. 1553/4–1596', *Archaeologia Cantiana* 35 (1921), p. 107).

[311] BL, Cotton MS Otho E IX, fol. 349ʳ.

[312] M. Oppenheim (ed.), *The naval tracts of Sir William Monson* (6 vols., Navy Records Society, XXII, London, 1902), I, p. 357.

[313] LPL, MS 657, fol 106ʳ; *ibid.*, fol. 136ʳ.

[314] Even before Reynoldes went to see him, Caron had already moved the queen about obtaining some of Essex's army to defend Hulst, but had found her extremely unwilling to countenance any proposal for using these troops (LPL, MS 657, fol. 112ʳ; van Deventer, *Gedenkstukken van Johan van Oldenbarnevelt*, II, pp. 125–8).

[315] LPL, MS 657, fol. 106r; LPL, MS 658, fol. 136ʳ. Giles Fletcher, brother of Richard, bishop of London, was 'intirelye devoted' to Essex (LPL, MS 658, fol. 202ʳ; LPL, MS 654, fol. 169ʳ. On Fletcher, see *Commons*, II, pp. 140–1). It is likely that Fletcher's advocacy of the Calais proposal to the mayor and aldermen was also supported by the corporation's recorder, John Croke (*Commons*, I, pp. 677–8). When Croke had stood for election as London's recorder in November 1595, Lord Mountjoy, a relative of Croke, had solicited Essex's assistance for him: 'alltho he bee a very honest man, I hope he will doo any injustice in the Cytye wee shall have occation att any tyme to desyre him, for whattsoever he be sworne unto, ungratitude amongst the Lacedemonians was punished withe deathe' (WRO, TD 69/6.2, item 59, Mountjoy to Essex, 4 November [1595]).

Elizabeth to recover Calais, but even to offer to 'contribute very largely to the uttermost of their ability' towards the costs of the venture.[316]

Despite all this extraordinary effort, Essex's plans again failed. Elizabeth was resolutely against any operation so bold as the recovery of Calais. The costs of the Cadiz expedition, despite being subsidised by Essex and (to a lesser extent) the lord admiral, were sufficent to turn her against any military operations in the immediate future. Moreover, the situation in Ireland was becoming desperate, consuming men and money more quickly than England could send them.[317] During Essex's absence, Elizabeth had finally agreed a new alliance with France, but the treaty's secret protocol declared that, because of the demands of Ireland, England would provide only half the number of troops promised in its public clauses.[318] Elizabeth had therefore finally given the commitment to France for which Essex had laboured so hard in 1595, but the task of giving it real substance still remained. It was symbolic of the new priorities that part of the Cadiz army was retained in the queen's pay and sent, not to the Continent, but to Ireland.[319]

During the voyage home from Cadiz, Essex began composing a document which sought to explain the strategy behind his unsuccessful attempt to hold the city.[320] Although this paper begins as an apologia for his actions at Cadiz,[321] its real significance lies in its later sections. Here Essex not only describes in great detail the strategy which lay behind his plans, but urges the desperate necessity of putting his ideas into effect in the near

---

[316] LPL, MS 658, fols. 202[r-v], 272[r].

[317] By the end of October 1596, all the money sent to Ireland in August had been spent and fresh demands for cash were piling up. Burghley despaired and wrote to Cecil that 'I cannot endure to bethinke myself of the perill' (CUL, MS Ee.iii.56, no. 103).

[318] For discussion of the Treaty of Greenwich, see Wernham, *Return of the Armadas*, ch. 5. A highly elaborate and richly decorated copy of the full treaty is BL, Add. Charter 74952. For diagrams of the oath-taking ceremony for the treaty on 29 August and the subsequent dinner, see BLO, Tanner MS 77, fol. 96[r-v].

[319] Sir John Norris had made an urgent request for 3,000 men from the Cadiz force in July (PRO, SP 63/191, fols. 239[r], 274[r]). Although Elizabeth refused to bear 'the chardge of new armies' in Ireland (LPL, MS 612, fol. 81[r]), she later relented and directed that 1,000 men from the Cadiz army be sent over (BL, Cotton MS Galba D XII, fol. 49[r-v]). No doubt, Essex was furious at having to surrender these troops to his rival.

[320] Hulton MS (formerly BL, Loan 23), fols. 154[r]-169[v]. Folio 155[v] is reproduced here as Plate 7. This unfinished paper is summmarised in Henry, 'Essex as strategist'. Essex wrote to Antonio Perez that he began this paper while sailing past Corunna, after all the other officers of the expedition had sailed off for home with all possible speed, leaving him to escort the slow ships in the fleet (WRO, TD 69/6.2, item 75, Essex to Perez, 16 September 1596 (pr. Ungerer, I, p. 446)). For further details of this document's provenance, see Henry, 'Essex as strategist', pp. 391–3.

[321] This part of the paper was circulated in manuscript form as 'Omissions of the Cales voyage', of which a number of copies exist: Hammer, 'Myth-making', p. 635, n.79.

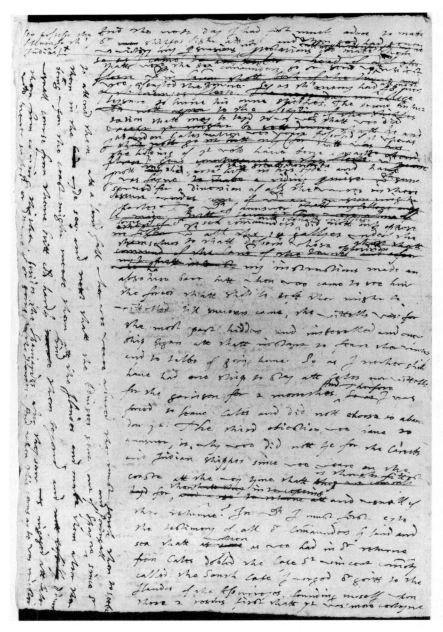

7 A page of Essex's unfinished discourse on military strategy, which he began writing during the voyage home from Cadiz, August 1596.

future.[322] Put simply, Essex suggests that England should seize Cadiz and Lisbon as permanent bases on the Iberian peninsula. Garrisoned with English troops, these ports would allow English ships to blockade the Spanish coastline. Deprived of treasure from the Indies and the Americas, and supplies from the Baltic, Spain would be strangled into submission. The aim of Essex's strategy was the complete destruction of Spanish power. The consequence was to be the establishment of an English hegemony upon the seas, and therefore upon the whole trade-dependent Continent as well: 'our souverayn shallbe trewly Regina maris and the trafike of th'Indyes and all thinges els thatt belong to one thatt commaunds the seas will be certaynly, and only, her's'.[323]

This plan embodied a fusion of ideas about the relative merits of land and sea power as instruments for waging war against Spain. Many men had previously argued that England must not only assault Spain itself but plant a permanent base there. Sir Roger Williams, for example, complained in 1589 that attacks against Spain are 'to little purpose unlesse we dwell & mainteyne a faccion in his cuntrye'.[324] However, unlike the Portugal expedition of that year, which sought to use Dom Antonio to create precisely such a 'faccion', Essex's design did not seek to conquer Spanish territory, merely to exercise control over its coastline from a secure port. Essex's army was primarily intended to ensure the effective use of his fleet by allowing its permanent presence off the Spanish coast. This permanence sharply differentiated Essex's scheme from the belief among sailors that naval operations alone could bring Spain to her knees – the 'idolatrie of Neptune'.[325] Like Williams, Essex completely rejected such ideas: without a secure Spanish base, these operations were merely 'idle wanderings upon the sea'.[326] In the light of events in 1597, Essex's comments about the tactic of lying in wait for Spanish treasure ships off the Azores are particularly telling: 'this is a fitter enterprise for some decayd private man then for a state, for yt savors of guerra di corsar'.[327]

Essex's desire to combine land and sea operations against Spain is significant because it reflects an ability to adapt to changing strategic and

---

[322] 'I protest I do not valew my lyfe att so high a rate as I shold do the ability to perswade this dessein as yt ought to be pursued' (Hulton MS (formerly BL, Loan 23), fol. 157[r-v]. See also *ibid.*, fol. 154[v]).

[323] *Ibid.*, fol. 167[v].

[324] Trinity College, Cambridge, MS R.5.18, fol. 64[v]. Williams is here specifically criticising naval attacks which 'inrich private navies & advance noe accion in generall'. For other statements by Williams about the need to deliver 'great blows' at the heart of Spanish power, see PRO, SP 78/24, fol. 78[v]; PRO, SP 78/31, fol. 23[r-v]; and BL, Lansdowne MS 58, fols. 162[r]–163[r].

[325] Wingfield, *A true coppie*, p. 103.

[326] Hulton MS (formerly BL, Loan 23), fol. 166[v].   [327] *Ibid.*, fol. 165[r].

political circumstances. Despite his involvement in the Portugal expedition, Essex had previously been associated mainly with those who advocated the primary importance of war on land. His military following was almost exclusively composed of soldiers, not sailors. His chief military advisers were land men, first Sir Roger Williams and then Sir Francis Vere.[328] There is very little evidence that he sponsored privateering ventures.[329] Essex clearly had some interest in naval matters but it was not until 1595 that this became politically significant.[330] During the first half of the year, there are even hints that he toyed with the idea of sailing to the Caribbean with Drake and Hawkins.[331] Essex was friendly with Drake from early on,[332] but he only began to attract expert seafarers like William Monson[333] and

---

[328] Vere's importance to Essex after Williams's death is apparent from his prominence in accounts of both the Cadiz and Azores voyages, even though he and Essex fell out at the start of the latter expedition. Vere also played an intimate role in the formulation of Essex's strategic thinking. He was clearly well aware of Essex's secret intentions for the Cadiz expedition and almost certainly helped to shape these ideas. Vere's involvement is suggested by Essex's decision to spend two days alone with him aboard the *Rainbow* during 18–19 May, sailing from Dover after the collapse of the operation to relieve Calais. Both men disembarked near Rye and galloped to Court, determined to make Elizabeth understand the necessity of continuing with the naval expedition against Spain (Dillingham, 'Commentaries of Vere', p. 81; LPL, MS 250, fols 344^v–345^r). This interlude assumes added significance for understanding Essex's Cadiz strategy when it is recognised that the unfinished paper on this subject which Essex began on the voyage home was apparently addressed to Vere. Although Henry claims that this paper was addressed 'to a hypothetical friend at Court' ('Essex as strategist', p. 363), Essex promises that 'I shall make yow able to defend both the reputation of your frend [i.e. Essex himself] and the counsell unto which yow persuaded the States' (Hulton MS (formerly BL, Loan 23), fol. 154^v). The latter function clearly identifies the addressee as Vere (PRO, SP 84/52, fols. 15^r, 71^r, 82^r–83^r, 87^r, 96^r–97^r, 98^{r-v}, 107^r–108^r, 113^{r-v}; BL, Cotton MS Galba D XII, fol. 13^r; HMCS, VI, pp. 67–8, 70, 86–8, 90–1). If the paper had been finished, it is conceivable that Essex intended Vere (as the recipient) to show it to Elizabeth.
[329] Piracy charges were brought against various servants of Essex in 1588 and 1589 and against some of his Carmarthenshire followers in 1590, but this does not indicate Essex's own involvement in such enterprises (BL, Add. MS 12506, fols. 239^r, 243^r, 249^r).
[330] In 1593, Essex bought (or was given) a pocket dial made of gilded brass (see Plate 8), which is now held in the British Museum (J. Bruce, 'Description of a pocket dial made in 1593 for Robert Devereux, earl of Essex', *Archaeologia* 40 (1866), pp. 343–56). This multi-function instrument includes a compass, a nocturnal and probably also a sundial, although the latter has now been lost. A nocturnal is designed to calculate the positions of stars and had a variety of specifically nautical uses (J. Williams, 'Note on the use of the nocturnal', *Archaelogia* 40 (1866), pp. 357–60). The pocket dial bears Essex's arms and personal motto, as well as other inscriptions. It was made by James Knyvyn, an instrument maker of London who had previously performed work for Gabriel Harvey, John Blagrave and Thomas Digges (Bruce, 'Pocket dial', pp. 347–49).
[331] Andrews, *Last voyage of Drake and Hawkins*, p. 16.
[332] Essex's father had been an early patron of Drake: J. Sugden, *Sir Francis Drake* (London, 1996 edn, orig. pub. 1990), pp. 80–8, 94–5, 109–10, 269, 275; J. Cummins, *Francis Drake* (London, 1995), p. 70.
[333] Monson became Essex's follower after breaking with his former patron, Cumberland, in mid-1595: Oppenheim, 'Naval tracts of Monson', I, pp. xiv–xv; R. T. Spence, *The*

8   The pocket dial of Robert Devereux, 2nd earl of Essex.

John Davis[334] to his patronage in late 1595 and early 1596. This was about
the time when he began increasing his intelligence operations in Spain and
encouraged Hugh Platt in developing new sea rations. These were clear
signs of Essex's growing commitment to his new combined arms strategy.

privateering earl: George Clifford, 3rd earl of Cumberland, 1558–1605 (Stroud, 1995),
    pp. 129, 151.
[334] Davis served as Essex's pilot in 1596 and 1597. His performance on the voyage home from
    the Azores later drew criticism from Sir Arthur Gorges (Purchas, *Hakluytus posthumus*,
    XX, p. 121). At the end of 1597, Essex sent Davis on a Dutch expedition to India (A. H.
    Markham (ed.), *The voyages and works of John Davis the navigator* (Hakluyt Society, 1st
    ser., LIX, London, 1880), pp. lxii–lxiii, 129–31; *Calendar of state papers, colonial series,
    East Indies, China and Japan, 1513–1616, preserved in Her Majesty's Public Record
    Office, and elsewhere* (ed. W. N. Sainsbury, London, 1862), p. 106).

Judging by the debt which his scheme owed to their plans for seizing Panama, Drake and Hawkins were probably the main influences behind Essex's new thinking.[335] Although ultimately reduced to being a large privateering venture, the original intention of their voyage was strikingly similar to Essex's Cadiz plan. Using its small army, the expedition was to capture Panama and hold it for six months, or even several years, as a base from which the fleet could interdict the flow of Spanish treasure from the Americas.[336] Panama itself had been seen as a logical target for many years. Drake and Hawkins had themselves tried to float the idea in 1592[337] and Essex's great hero, Sir Philip Sidney, had allegedly been planning something very similar with Drake in 1585.[338] Essex's Cadiz strategy therefore built upon a succession of earlier proposals,[339] but was novel both in applying these ideas to Spain itself and in the sheer scale of its conception.

Essex was also far from unique in combining powerful commitment to the international Protestant cause with support for a naval strategy which had a powerfully nationalist objective: to destroy Spanish power and replace it with an English maritime empire. Sidney had supported both a network of Continental alliances and an aggressive drive for English maritime hegemony,[340] whilst those who supported intervention in the Low Countries during the early 1580s had insisted that large-scale naval operations could complement and subsidise war on the Continent.[341] Essex shared this view of a broad conjunction between Continental and maritime strategies. For him, the logic of war demanded both kinds of endeavour. Essex saw no contradiction between Protestant internationalism and the means by which he would benefit his own country. He conceived it to be England's historic mission – as the leading Protestant nation – to champion the liberation of Christendom from the Spanish yoke, with his own role being that of a new Aeneas. In his Cadiz strategy, Essex envisaged clear benefits to England's Protestant allies, as well as to England itself. Not only

---

[335] Drake, of course, was famous for his raid on Cadiz in 1587 which 'singed the king of Spain's beard': N. A. M. Rodger, The safeguard of the sea: a naval history of Britain. I 660–1649 (London, 1997), pp. 251–3.

[336] Andrews, Last voyage of Drake and Hawkins, pp. 15–16.

[337] Ibid., pp. 12–14. Drake's ambition to seize Panama went back to at least 1571 (Rodger, Safeguard of the sea, pp. 242–3).

[338] Greville, Life of Sidney, pp. 109–20.

[339] See, for example, G. V. Scammell, 'The English in the Atlantic islands, c. 1450–1650', Mariner's Mirror 72 (1986), pp. 301–8.

[340] Fulke Greville claimed that Sidney's ultimate goal in 'planting upon the Main of America' was merely to establish 'an emporium for the confluence of al nations that love or profess any kinde of vertue or commerce' (Greville, Life of Sidney, pp. 118–19). However, this was clearly intended to be dominated by England.

[341] S. Adams, 'The lurch to war', History Today 38 (May 1988), pp. 24–5.

did he seek to drive Elizabeth into whole-hearted co-operation with the allies, but he hoped to force the withdrawal of Spanish troops from France and the Netherlands by shifting the main theatre of war to Spain itself.[342] As he claimed before the voyage to Cadiz, 'I am abowt to do more for the publike and for all our frendes then they can hope for.'[343]

Despite these arguments, Essex's naval strategy put genuine pressure on his various commitments to Henri IV and the French Protestants. While naval operations promoted closer co-operation with the Dutch and made them more attractive as allies for England,[344] the French saw such ventures as diverting English and Dutch aid away from France during a time of need. To Henri and his envoys, Essex's decision to press ahead with the Cadiz expedition seemed like desertion of their cause and they turned instead to the mediation of Cecil and even Henry Brooke, Essex's bitter enemy.[345] French criticism of the Cadiz expedition did Essex considerable harm, whilst the débâcle of Calais remained a lingering embarrassment.[346] The great irony about the French reaction is that Essex's articulation of his Cadiz strategy again demonstrated his extraordinary francophilia. In keeping with his understanding that compromise with Spain was impossible and that the war must be fought à outrance, Essex's strategy sought to cripple Spanish military power, leaving France as the dominant power on the Continent. This aim was emphatically not shared by the queen or Burghley. Remembering the fruitless wars of Elizabeth's predecessors, they remained wary of international aggrandisement and were unwilling to trust in the future good intentions of France. For Elizabeth and Burghley, the primary goals were to keep the queen's dominions safe and to ensure that no single power could threaten them by dominating Europe.[347] Elizabeth

---

[342] For the latter point, see Hulton MS (formerly BL, Loan 23), fol. 169ᵛ; PRO, SP 12/259, fols. 41ᵛ–42ʳ.

[343] WRO, TD 69/6.2, item 82, Essex to Edward Reynoldes, 10 May [1596]; copy is LPL, MS 657, fol. 140ʳ.

[344] Wernham, *Return of the Armadas*, pp. 78–81. Despite this improved co-operation, Burghley, in particular, remained anxious to reduce the queen's expenditure in the Low Countries and to extract repayments from the Dutch: CUL, MS Ee.III.56, no. 109.

[345] McKeen, *William Brooke, Lord Cobham*, II, pp. 661–2.

[346] Essex knew that some in France blamed him, rather than Elizabeth, for the loss of Calais to the Spanish (e.g. LPL, MS 657, fol. 87ʳ).

[347] R. B. Wernham, 'Elizabethan war aims and strategy', in S. T. Bindoff, J. Hurstfield and C. H. Williams (eds.), *Elizabethan government and society: essays presented to Sir John Neale* (London and Toronto, 1961), pp. 341ff; also his *The making of Elizabethan foreign policy, 1558–1603* (Berkeley, Los Angeles and London, 1980), pp. 82–4. In her speech to the 1593 parliament, Elizabeth claimed that, 'since the the beggininge [of her reign], she hathe refused good occasion to amplifie her kingdom' (H. S. Scott (ed.), 'The journal of Sir Roger Wilbraham solicitor-general in Ireland and master of requests, for the years 1593–1616', *Camden Miscellany* 10 (1902), p. 4). For Burghley's essentially dynastic view of international relations, in contrast to Essex's ideological perspective, see M. M. Leimon,

had spent her first decade in power clinging to friendship with Spain in order to balance the threat posed by a hostile France. Now, thirty years later, the same calculus applied. Even if they could bring Spain to its knees, neither Elizabeth or Burghley would have been willing to see Spain reduced to the point where it could not balance a resurgent France. Such fundamental differences over the ultimate purpose of the war explain why Elizabeth and Burghley disagreed so strongly with Essex about aid to Henri IV and the Panama voyage in 1595. They also suggest why Essex felt he had to foist his sweeping new strategy upon them at Cadiz.

After the failure of his grand scheme, Essex tried to repair the damage which Cadiz had done to his credibility in France by fêting Bouillon when he came to ratify the new Anglo-French treaty in late August and by overseeing the dispatch of English troops to Piccardy which that agreement required.[348] He also continued to urge Elizabeth to increase her support for Henri, although his enthusiasm for the French cause was clearly tempered by bitter experience. When Perez urged him again to throw his weight behind the pleas for assistance by the king, he agreed, but cautioned 'Decet regem virum agere et facere occasiones, quas non invenerit.'[349] Since Elizabeth refused to intervene further on the Continent without being guaranteed future sovereignty over Calais and Henri remained opposed to this idea,[350] the prospect of large-scale English intervention in northern France was now even less likely than it had been during 1595.[351]

'Sir Francis Walsingham and the Anjou marriage plan, 1574–1581' (unpub. Ph.D. thesis, University of Cambridge, 1989), p. 131.

348 Haak, *Oldenbarnevelt*, pp. 340–1. According to Anthony Bacon, Essex treated Bouillon and his train to 'the most magnificall noble banquett' at Essex House on Tuesday 31 August, spending 'at the least 1000 marks' (LPL, MS 659, fol. 160ʳ). Essex subsequently placed his cousin, Robert Vernon, in Bouillon's party for his journey on to the Low Countries (Hammer, 'Essex and Europe', p. 366). The 2,000 men sent to Piccardy under the terms of the August treaty were almost entirely officered by followers of Essex. According to the treaty, they were intended for garrison duty only.

349 'It is appropriate that the king, as a man, should set things in motion and create opportunities when he finds none to hand': Ungerer, I, p. 466. Significantly, Essex prefaced this comment with a recognition that England was more naturally inclined towards a naval war: 'habet Anglia naves, nautas, omnia ad bellum navale necessaria' (England has ships, seamen and everything necessary for war at sea). In a private letter to Bouillon, Essex made it clear that any hope of uniting their armies depended upon the duke and himself pressuring their sovereigns into 'a favourable decision' (Tenison, X, p. 177).

350 See, for example, Ungerer, I, pp. 482–3. In January 1597, Essex himself complained in exasperation to Perez about French demands for military assistance to recapture Calais when France would keep all the benefits of the venture (*ibid.*, p. 476).

351 Essex was constantly urged to make Elizabeth convert her token commitment in Picardy into a full-scale offensive operation in partnership with the French and Dutch: *ibid.*, pp. 92–3, 448–50; LPL, MS 659, fols. 289ʳ–290ᵛ; BL, Egerton MS 1943, fol. 79ʳ; PRO, SP 46/125, fol. 246ʳ⁻ᵛ; Inner Temple Library, Petyt MS 538, vol. 46, fols. 156ʳ-161ʳ. The idea of attacking Calais was also very keenly supported by Essex's friends resident in the Netherlands (*HMCS*, VII, pp. 1–2, 8–10, 34, 41, 74–5, 130, 139, 163, 164, 171–2,

Although French diplomacy parlayed the new Anglo-French treaty into a Triple Alliance embracing the Dutch in October,[352] operations in Flanders seemed increasingly irrelevant to England. Success at Cadiz had apparently provoked the very thing which that expedition had been intended to prevent: a new Armada. Thrown together in the months following the humiliation of Cadiz, the Spanish fleet was actually intended to seize Brest, although most observers believed that it was headed for Ireland.[353] The fleet was dispersed by an autumn gale off Cape Finisterre in mid-October. Thanks to poor intelligence, England remained in the grip of a national emergency until the end of November.[354] However, the Spanish fleet was only battered, not destroyed. Moreover, Spain's willingness to launch its attack during the 'close season' suggested that England must expect a better prepared, full-blown assault next year. This state of affairs virtually guaranteed that 1597 would see a replay of events in 1596, despite the inevitable doubts and hiccups. With England and France unable to agree upon a joint effort to recapture Calais, the possibility that this port might provide a haven for a new Armada almost compelled Elizabeth to authorise another naval strike against Spain in order to neutralise the threat at its source. The alternative – that the enemy fleet might be sent to reinforce the Irish rebels – seemed an equally alarming prospect. There was also a more positive reason for a new naval expedition. After the success at Cadiz, Elizabeth's longstanding ambition to capture the Spanish treasure fleet now seemed tantalisingly practicable. When Henri finally accepted the possibility that England might take custody of Calais after a joint action to recapture it, his overture was far too little and far too late.[355]

Despite his extraordinary behaviour during 1596, Elizabeth ultimately agreed to let Essex lead another expedition against Spain in 1597. Howard was clearly now too old for such strenuous military service and the only other senior aristocrat with significant naval experience, the earl of

---

191–2, 199–200, 205, 243–4, 248). Sir Francis Vere, in particular, seems to have been aggrieved that Essex did not succeed in bringing this latter scheme to fruition (*HMCS*, VII, p. 212).

[352] Wernham, *Return of the Armadas*, pp. 80–1.

[353] Kamen, *Philip of Spain*, pp. 307–8, 360 n. 47. Cf. P. Pierson, *Commander of the Armada: the seventh duke of Medina Sidonia* (New Haven and London, 1989), p. 215. The intention of landing in Ireland was deliberate disinformation, but it seemed highly credible because the rebel earl of Tyrone had made no secret of his overtures to Spain. During May he had received three separate Spanish military delegations (MacCaffrey, *War and politics*, p. 397; Morgan, *Tyrone's rebellion*, pp. 208–13).

[354] Wernham, *Return of the Armadas*, pp. 130–40.

[355] Henri's offer was embodied in the doomed missions of Fouquerolles in April 1597 and of de Reau a month later: Wernham, *Return of the Armadas*, pp. 151–3. Fouquerolles was allegedly so angry at Burghley's response to Henri's suggestions that he wanted to hit him: LPL, MS 656, fol. 344[r–v].

Cumberland, was deeply unpopular with England's Dutch allies. By contrast, Essex had been studiously cultivating Dutch leaders[356] and was eager to resurrect his plans of 1596. Court politics also came into play. The new friendship which developed between Essex, Cecil and Sir Walter Ralegh during the spring of 1597 removed any domestic opposition to Essex's appointment and put pressure on Elizabeth to grant him a freer hand than he had enjoyed in 1596.[357]

Essex initially put forward his plans for the new attack on Spain in mid-January 1597.[358] Apart from a powerful fleet, he demanded a compact, high-quality army – precisely in keeping with his proposals of 1596 and with his reorganisation of the county militia during the spring of 1597. During the next few months, Essex's involvement in the project apparently faded, as he became engrossed in the struggle over the wardenship of the Cinque Ports and in coming to grips with the militia and his new post as master of the ordnance. For a while, Essex also still hoped that he might yet be able to lead a full-scale army against Calais.[359] Nevertheless, by the beginning of May, his demands for the naval expedition had been accepted and he went to oversee the outfitting of his ship.[360] In contrast to the Cadiz expedition, Essex now had official sanction to put his combined-arms strategy into effect. His instructions required him to give priority to destroying the Spanish ships at Ferrol and specified the island of Terceira in the Azores as the place where he might establish a garrison.[361] However,

---

[356] Essex knighted several Dutchmen at Cadiz. After his return to England, Essex sent gifts in the form of chains to the leaders of the Dutch contingent, including Jan van Duyvenvoord, lord of Warmont and admiral of Holland (*HMCS*, VI, pp. 353–4). Essex was clearly the motivating force behind Elizabeth's personal letter of thanks to Duyvenvoord for his service on the Cadiz expedition (Motley, *History of the United Netherlands*, III, pp. 367–8). During the initial abortive attempt to sail for Spain in July 1597, Duyvenvoord's ship was the only one to stay with Essex during the storm (Corbett, *Successors of Drake*, p. 175). Essex also won the allegiance of another Dutch Cadiz knight, the young Count Lodowick (or Ludwig) of Nassau, son of Count John (*HMCS*, VI, pp. 383, 398, 464; *ibid.*, VII, pp. 141, 163, 208; GL, MS 1752, pp. 174–5).

[357] See below, pp. 381–2.

[358] PRO, SP 12/262, fol. 23ᵛ; LPL, MS 654, fols. 78ʳ, 283ʳ; *HMCS*, VII, p. 31. Cumberland outlined a less ambitious scheme about the same time (PRO, SP 12/262, fol. 23ʳ). Burghley noted that a conference was to be held to discuss these proposals at the end of January (*ibid.*, fol. 35ʳ). Further discussion apparently occurred in early February (LPL, MS 655, fols. 90ʳ, 98ʳ).

[359] *CSPVen*, IX, *1592–1603*, p. 274; BL, Add. MS 45359, fol. 5ʳ; LPL, MS 656, fol. 142ʳ. Vere tried to encourage these hopes by warning Essex against 'pety ymployments' which brought a high risk of failure. By contrast, the recapture of Calais 'hathe a gallant consequence' (Cecil MS 49/93 (pr. *HMCS*, VII, p. 139)). Perez also urged a similar line: PRO, SP 46/125, fol. 246ʳ.

[360] *HMCS*, VII, p. 11.

[361] The original of Essex's instructions, bearing the sign manual, is PRO, SP 12/263, fols. 147ʳ–150ᵛ. Terceira was chosen because the Spanish treasure fleets from the Americas sailed past the Azores – a powerful indication of Elizabeth's hunger for Spanish silver.

Essex's commission formally authorised him to seize and fortify *any* place within the king of Spain's dominions.[362] Moreover, regardless of the specificity of his instructions, Essex's own views were clear: 'when I hadde defeated that force [at Ferrol], I might goe after whether I listed, and doe almost what I listed; I meane in any places upon that coast'.[363] After the frustratingly incomplete nature of his triumph at Cadiz, the summer of 1597 seemed to offer the prospect of finally realising his grand military ambitions.

Heartfelt though they were, these hopes were crushed by the unseasonable weather of July. After all his careful preparation,[364] Essex's fleet was hit by a storm soon after it departed for Spain and was driven back to England in disarray.[365] According to Ralegh, Essex was 'dismayd by thes mischances yeven to death, although ther could not be more dun by any man upon the yearth, God havinge turned the heavens with that fury ageynst us, a matter beyound the poure or valure or witt of man to resiste'.[366] Although the fleet was not badly damaged, Essex's misfortunes did not end with the storm: Elizabeth angrily expostulated with him;[367] contrary winds penned his force in harbour, consuming his limited supplies; and sickness broke out among the troops. In the end, Essex felt compelled to reduce his army to a mere 1,000 veteran soldiers,[368] the very minimum required for an attack on Ferrol.[369]

With that decision went all hope of Essex carrying out his grand strategy against Spain. He was now reduced to leading the kind of venture which he had dismissed in the previous year as merely 'idle wanderings upon the sea'. In contrast to war on land, this was precisely the kind of warfare for which Essex lacked any suitable experience. Not surprisingly, the resultant voyage to the Azores proved a failure.[370] As Cecil had expected even before

---

Properly speaking, Essex was only to establish a garrison at Terceira if it would not require the provision of supplies from England.

[362] Devereux MSS, box 6, no. 87. This point was first noticed by L. W. Henry ('Essex as strategist', pp. 378–9), to whose whole analysis of the Azores expedition I am greatly indebted.

[363] *Apologie*, sig. B1ᵛ.   [364] *HMCS*, VII, p. 345.

[365] This is most famously described by John Donne in his poems 'The storme' and 'The calm' and (perhaps) in a letter to an unknown friend: E. Simpson *et al.* (eds.), *John Donne: selected prose* (Oxford, 1967), pp. 108–9.

[366] PRO, SP 12/264, fol. 56ʳ.   [367] *Ibid.*, fol. 19ʳ⁻ᵛ.

[368] Henry, 'Essex as strategist', pp. 381–5. Henry's criticism of Essex's actions in dismissing the bulk of his army, based upon dubious calculations about the number of effectives remaining on 14 August (*ibid.*, pp. 384–5), seems somewhat harsh.

[369] PRO, SP 12/45, fols. 65ᵛ–66ʳ; *Apologie*, sig. B2ʳ.

[370] For the Azores or 'Islands' expedition, see Corbett, *Successors of Drake*, ch. 8; Purchas, *Hakluytus posthumus*, XX, pp. 24–129; Oppenheim, 'Naval tracts of Monson', II, pp. 21–83; Dillingham, 'Commentaries of Vere', pp. 94–108; A. Haynes, 'The Islands voyage', *History Today* 25 (1975), pp. 689–96.

it departed,[371] Essex's fleet was unable to attack the Spanish at Ferrol.[372] Thwarted there, Essex made a desperate dash to the Azores to await the expected treasure ships. Since he had dismissed this tactic in 1596 as 'a fitter enterprise for some decayd private man then for a state', Essex had clearly given up all hope of military success. The best that he could aim for now was a political success: to capture enough booty to persuade Elizabeth to give him another opportunity in 1598. It was a desperate bid, and one that failed. Essex's ambiguous sailing orders led to confusion with Ralegh and even demands that he be court-martialled.[373] The treasure ships were missed by the heart-breaking margin of only a few hours.[374]

To make matters worse, the return of Essex's fleet coincided with the much-delayed sailing of the Spanish fleet which he had been unable to attack at Ferrol. Although often described as a new Armada, and believed to be such at the time, this Spanish fleet did not aim at a reprise of 1588.[375] Smaller than the *Gran Armada* of 1588[376] and lacking the large army which Parma had been intended to provide for that campaign, the Spanish fleet of 1597 – like that of 1596 – had far more limited objectives. Rather than a full-scale invasion, its task was to restore Spanish pride and demonstrate Spanish power by seizing a lodgement on English soil. If this served to provoke a Catholic rising in England, then so much the better. However, the Spanish naval expeditions of 1596 and 1597 were conceptually closer to England's raid on Cadiz than to the 'Enterprise of England' launched almost a decade before. In mid-October 1597, the Spanish fleet approached Cornwall at a time when the defensive measures which Essex had put in place during the spring had been abandoned and when his fleet

---

371 PRO, SP 63/200, fol. 187[v]; Cecil MS 54/75 (pr. *HMCS*, VII, pp. 361–2).
372 *Apologie*, sig. B2[r–v].
373 Corbett, *Successors of Drake*, pp. 198–200; Purchas, *Hakluytus posthumus*, X, pp. 92–6.
374 Corbett, *Successors of Drake*, pp. 202–4; PRO, SP 94/5, fol. 287[v].
375 This confusion has been greatly encouraged by the titles of R. B. Wernham's magisterial surveys of England's foreign relations in the 1590s: *After the Armada* and *Return of the Armadas*. Although the former is entirely legitimate, the latter is deceptive because it wrongly suggests that the Spanish fleets of 1596 and 1597 were comparable in scale and purpose with that of 1588. Although these later expeditions were *armadas* (in the literal sense of being fleets), they did not approach the size or scope of the *Gran Armada* of 1588. Wernham's misapprehension that the later fleets were true Armadas reflects contemporary English fears, but is contradicted by Spanish sources. I am indebted to Dr Pauline Croft for detailed discussion of this point.
376 *Pace* Wernham, *Return of the Armadas*, p. 184, The new Spanish fleet was further reduced in size because Philip II insisted that it sail from Ferrol before an additional 30 ships and 5,000 soldiers arrived from the south (*ibid.*). Despite this, the 1597 fleet was better prepared for its task than the 1588 Armada had been and enjoyed much more flexible instructions: A. J. Loomie, 'An Armada pilot's survey of the English coastline, October 1597', *Mariner's Mirror* 49 (1963), pp. 288–300; also his 'The Armadas and the Catholics of England', *Catholic Historical Review* 59 (1973), pp. 398–400.

was straggling home, worn out by months at sea.[377] By sheer good fortune, just as it was about to head for Falmouth, the Spanish fleet was caught by a storm and driven back to Spain.[378] Only the weather had prevented Spain from doing to England what Essex and Howard had done to Spain at Cadiz.

After the failure of his voyage to the Azores and the near-catastrophe that followed it, Essex had no new chance to execute his strategy against Spain. Philip II's failing health and two successive disasters ended Spain's enthusiasm for new naval expeditions against England. As matters in Ireland became ever more desperate, Essex's advocacy of overseas campaigns also seemed unaffordable and increasingly irrelevant to this looming disaster at home. Essex's grand conception of war against Spain therefore remained untested. No permanent base was ever planted in Spain and no permanent blockade of the Spanish coast was ever established. Yet, in a sense, his expansive strategic conception *had* been tried, and found wanting. Having at last won grudging political approval, the fate of his 1597 expedition demonstrated that, for all Essex's own clarity of thinking on the matter beforehand, the relative balance between sixteenth-century technology and the forces of nature made the implementation of his ideas entirely dependent upon good fortune. Even had he been able to seize a base in Spain, the shambles in the Azores suggests that Essex would have had great difficulty in maintaining an effective blockade of the Spanish coast. Unless he produced substantial booty, it might also be asked how long Elizabeth would have allowed him to continue the operation, regardless of its military efficacy.

Perhaps ultimately more significant than these doubts about the practicality of Essex's strategy were the consequences of its abandonment. From his adolescence, Essex had identified himself with martial achievement to an extraordinary extent. When frustrated during 1595, he went to remarkable lengths to remove the obstacles to performing what he conceived to be the predestined role of his nation and himself in the war. After the Azores voyage, all of this vast emotional, financial and political investment in war was threatened. With no return for their heavy expenditure on the voyage, many of Essex's soldier followers were faced with ruin, 'impairing' his reputation.[379] At Court, rumours spread that there would soon be new peace negotiations with Spain.[380] Most cutting of all, Essex returned to find that the lord admiral had been created earl of Nottingham. Not only

[377] The danger was so acute that Essex, who assumed command of the realm's defences, was directed by Elizabeth to send 'hourly' reports to Cecil (GL, MS 1752, pp. 264–5).
[378] Loomie, 'Armadas and Catholics', pp. 183–90.
[379] *HMCS*, VII, p. 392.
[380] WRO, TD 69/6.2, item 39, Lettice, countess of Leicester, to Essex, November 1597.

did this give him precedence over Essex but Nottingham's patent of creation gave the admiral all the credit for the victory at Cadiz.[381] Wounded and angry, Essex sought a very specific vindication of his martial honour by demanding that Elizabeth appoint him earl marshal. Even when Elizabeth finally agreed to this demand, Essex refused to accept the first draft of his patent: 'I am praised for too innocent virtues, where they are active virtues, and not negative, that should draw on a prince to bestow a marshal's office.'[382] Thwarted in his designs and confronted with the prospect of failure, Essex's towering sense of mission now began to drive him to pettiness and to dangerous provocation of his sovereign.

[381] Part of Essex's response to this claim on Nottingham's behalf can be seen in his behaviour on Accession Day. In keeping with his withdrawal from Court, he failed to appear at the annual tournament. Instead, Essex chose the Accession Day to have a very large psalter which had been captured at Cadiz presented on his behalf to the library of King's College, Cambridge (still extant there as MS 41). Chained to a desk for public display, this volume contained dedicatory verses in Latin which explained the book's provenance and lauded Essex as a greater hero than Hercules (G. W. Groos (ed.), *The diary of Baron Waldstein: a traveller in Elizabethan England* (London, 1981), pp. 105–7). This very pointed gesture was perhaps arranged by Dr Lionel Sharpe, one of Essex's chaplains and a senior fellow at King's (see below, p. 303).

[382] *HMCS*, VII, pp. 520, 527.

7

'My lord of Essex his men'

Essex made himself the 'great patron of the warrs'[1] and won a remarkable number of adherents among the queen's officers. However, this martial reputation came at a price. While Essex cultivated soldiers' affections and rewarded some of them highly, the concerns which they expressed about the conduct of the war and the prospects for their own future employment sharply limited his room for political manoeuvre. The same tendency can be observed among his many adherents outside the martial sphere, for Essex's actions and carefully cultivated reputation won him an extensive following across the realm. As with the officers, the claims which these followers could make upon Essex imposed constraints on his actions.

Like most well-used historical terms, 'following' and 'followers' are imprecise, but suggestive, words. A 'follower' of Essex was any person who openly associated his or her own interests with those of the earl. Essex's 'following' consisted of (primarily) men who were either his servants, clients (those linked to him by some significant patronage tie), relatives or close friends. Very often, individuals qualified as followers under more than one of these categories, and in such cases, the individual's personal commitment to Essex was especially strong. In political terms, Essex's following gave him much of his personal significance within the realm. Although Elizabeth's displays of conspicuous favour towards Essex marked him out as a special individual, it was the extent of his following which gave this relationship genuine political consequence. This fact again underlines the significance of Leicester's death in 1588. Before that time, Essex had some followers of his own but he was effectively part of Leicester's following and his status as a royal protégé was mainly significant for that reason. However, when Essex began to fill the vacuum left by his step-father's death and attracted significant numbers of followers in his own right, his political importance changed rapidly. As more and more men within the realm or in the army began to look to him to represent their

[1] Cecil MS 62/71 (pr. *HMCS*, VIII, p. 269).

269

interests, Essex's relationship with Elizabeth grew to have consequences far beyond the Court. This is perhaps another reason for his renewed aggressiveness in confronting rivals for royal favour – with growing numbers of men dependent upon his fortunes, the pressure of their expectations and the consequent swelling of his own sense of importance drove Essex to assert his pre-eminence among the younger generation at Court.

Essex's growing body of adherents created the illusion of power. However, sustaining a substantial following required a continuing hold on political influence and an appropriate power-base – those human and material resources which actually underpinned an important man's power and influence. A following and a power-base are by no means synonymous. Whereas a power-base embodied the actual means of power, a following was a manifestation of a great man's perceived political success. A following was normally much less restricted in geographical terms than a power-base. At a human level, the crux of the distinction is that a power-base existed where individuals had a distinct structural relationship with their leader, as between a tenant or servant and his master. A significant office, provided that tenure was secure and relations with subordinate officers were unaffected by rival jurisdictions, might also become a power-base over time. By contrast, a following, although it also included tenants and subordinate office-holders, depended upon a more personal relationship with its head and upon a sense of common interest. In political terms, this difference is crucial. While the former was a source of support and strength to its leader in a time of crisis, a following required cultivation and encouragement in order to survive and, in a crisis, tended to look for reassurance to the leader.

Essex's fundamental problem was that he had a large following – and correspondingly large expectations – but a relatively small power-base. Generally speaking, there were three components to the power-base of a great man in Elizabethan England: his family, his estates and his tenure of various offices. These elements not only encompassed an aristocrat's prime sources of income, but also his local or regional political muscle. In Essex's case, such local political influence was largely concentrated in four counties: Staffordshire and Herefordshire in the west midlands and the marches of Wales and Carmarthenshire and Pembrokeshire in south-west Wales. At least initially, this limited local influence represented Essex's political inheritance from his father.

Staffordshire was, as Essex wrote to Burghley in 1590, 'my own countrey'.[2] This was true not only in the sense that it had long been his family's native county, but also in the extent of his power there. The focal

---

[2] BL, Lansdowne MS 63, fol. 189^r.

point of Essex's influence in Staffordshire was the lordship of Chartley, the Devereux family's primary estate.[3] Essex was living at Chartley when his father died, before he went off to join Burghley's household and to Cambridge.[4] In conjunction with several other manors,[5] this estate gave Essex a substantial landed presence in the county and, with it, a considerable number of tenants and lease-holders. A range of greater and lesser gentlemen were also associated with these lands, some as servants to oversee their running and others as neighbours who were concerned to maintain harmonious dealings with the earl. Essex's supporters in the county included members of the Bagot, Littleton, Chetwynd, Trew, Okeover and Aston families. In some cases, these families had been associated with the Devereux for many decades. Essex's presence in the county was further reinforced by his mother's residence at Drayton Bassett, where she lived with her third husband, Sir Christopher Blount. This accumulation of landed influence also naturally extended into towns such as Lichfield,[6] Newcastle-under-Lyme,[7] Stafford,[8] and Tamworth.[9] Essex's connections with these boroughs were sufficiently powerful for him to be the natural nominator of many of their parliamentary representatives.[10]

In spite of his strong influence on the selection of burgesses at parliament time, the elections for the knights of the shire show that Essex was not all-powerful in Staffordshire. In 1593 and 1597, Essex expected to be able to dictate the choice of both knights and committed himself to doing so: 'I should thinke my credicte little in my owne cuntrie if I should not afford so smale a matter as this, esspeciallie [with] the men beinge so fitt.'[11] However, Essex failed to achieve this on either occasion.[12] Perhaps because

---

[3] On Chartley, see Sampson Erdswicke, *A survey of Staffordshire; containing the antiquities of that county* (ed. T. Harwood, London, 1844), pp. 55–6.

[4] BL, Lansdowne MS 25, fol. 96^r.

[5] Essex's lands in Staffordshire included the manors of Gayton, Huxton, Grenley, Frodeswall, Stowe Morton and Lee.

[6] At Lichfield, 'by the priviledge of the mannor', Essex (or his nominee) had the right to walk with the town bailiffs at an annual fair (FSL, L.a.462). For examples of Essex's dealings with Lichfield, see FSL, L.a.68, 254; BL, Harleian MS 6997, fol. 36^r; *VCH. Staffordshire*, XIV, p. 67. The Devereux family ultimately provided recorders for the borough of Lichfield for eight successive generations (*ibid.*, I, p. 249 n. 226).

[7] In May 1590, Essex procured the bill from the signet office for the incorporation of this borough (PRO, SO 3/1, fol. 239^v; *VCH, Staffordshire*, VIII, p. 26).

[8] Essex's influence upon this town was grounded upon the fact that it lay only half a dozen miles from Chartley (*Commons*, I, p. 243).

[9] Having been elected as steward of Tamworth as early as September 1578 (*HMCS*, II, pp. 207–8; BL, Lansdowne MS 27, fol. 16^r), Essex's hold on this office was made hereditary by the new charter of incorporation which the town obtained in the mid-1580s (FSL, L.a.509; H. Wood, *Tamworth borough records* (Tamworth, 1952), p. 3). Essex's servant Richard Broughton was also the town's recorder until his resignation in May 1598 (*ibid.*, p. 16).

[10] *Commons*, I, pp. 241–5.   [11] FSL, L.a.470.   [12] *Commons*, I, pp. 239–41.

he was away on campaign at the time, the 1597 election proved to be a particularly bitter defeat.[13] Nevertheless, Essex did have genuine power within the county. Using his knot of friends, servants and tenants there, and reinforced by his possession of various offices in the county, including that of *custos rotulorum*,[14] Essex was able to have John Robinson physically evicted when the latter seized lands held by his mother at Drayton Bassett.[15] After the death of the earl of Shrewsbury in November 1590, Essex acted as the effective lord lieutenant of the county,[16] although Elizabeth refused to give him a formal commission.[17] In combination with his tenantry and friends within the county, this *de facto* authority over local musters ensured that each of the armies which Essex led abroad had a core of men from his native county.[18]

In addition to his concentrated influence in Staffordshire, Essex had a scattering of estates and offices in other counties of the west midlands and Welsh marches.[19] The most important of these other interests lay in Herefordshire, where Essex's family held substantial lands[20] and where his friends included the ambitious and influential Sir Thomas Coningsby.[21]

13 WRO, TD 69/6.2, item 39, Lettice, countess of Leicester to Essex, November 1597. In a hotly disputed contest, Sir Christopher Blount, Essex's stepfather, was only elected into the junior place, while Sir Edward Littleton, Essex's friend and follower, was beaten out altogether.

14 Essex was appointed to this office upon the death of Thomas Trentham in May 1587. For the exercise of this function in Essex's name, see S. A. H. Burne, 'The Staffordshire quarter sessions rolls', which was printed in successive volumes of *Collections for a History of Staffordshire* between 1931 and 1933.

15 Essex moved against Robinson in November 1588 (FSL, L.a. 459) and again in January 1590 (FSL, L.a.461[i]; BL, Lansdowne MS 62, fol. 78ʳ). Despite this strong-arm approach, Robinson proved to be a continuing nuisance to the countess of Leicester. By January 1595, Essex was moved to deal with the lord keeper 'abowtes Robinson, for his commyttment' (BL, Add. MS 40630, fol. 40ʳ). For background to this dispute, see D. C. Peck, 'The earl of Leicester and the riot at Drayton Bassett, 1578', *N&Q* 225 (1980), pp. 131–5.

16 For example, FSL, L.a.22; *APC*, XXIV, 1592–3, p. 180.

17 LPL, MS 3199, p. 229; J. C. Sainty, 'Lieutenants of counties, 1585–1642', *Bulletin of the Institute of Historical Research*, supplement no. 8 (1970), p. 32.

18 FSL, L.a.208, 209, 216, 217, 260, 261, 465, 475; *Unton corr.*, p. 250.

19 For example, Essex owned the site and lands of the former abbey of Merevale in Warwickshire and Leicestershire (*VCH, Warwickshire*, IV, pp. 27, 144; *VCH, Leicestershire*, II, p. 210). In the following century, a coal mine on this estate was to become the single largest component of the income of his son, the third earl of Essex (V. F. Snow, *Essex the rebel: the life of Robert Devereux, third earl of Essex 1591–1646* (Lincoln, Nebraska, 1970), p. 199).

20 Significantly, Essex's junior titles included that of Viscount Hereford. His lands in the county included Weobley, Bodenham and Byford. He added the former episcopal manors of Ross Borough and Ross Foreign, as well as crown lands in Ross and Walford, by a combination of purchase and royal grant (PRO, C 54/1391, unfol., enrolment of indenture of 9 June 1591; W. H. Cooke, *Collections towards the history and antiquities of the county of Hereford. In continuation of Duncumb's history* (2 vols., London, 1892), I, pp. 104–5). Essex also had an iron works at Bishop's Wood (Devereux MS 3, fols. 73ᵛ, 103ᵛ).

21 Coningsby served as Essex's muster-master at Rouen. A substantial local landowner in his

After the death of Sir James Croft in September 1590, Essex made a major push to increase his influence in Herefordshire, aggressively seeking the high stewardships of Hereford[22] and Leominster.[23] Through a grant from Elizabeth and a deal with the earl of Shrewsbury, he was also able to control Wigmore Castle.[24] These offices, combined with the support of local agents like Coningsby and Anthony Pembridge,[25] made Essex the dominant figure in the county and combined with his interests in Staffordshire and elsewhere to create a distinct Devereux power-base in the Welsh marches. Nevertheless, his influence was not unchallenged and his followers in the county were frequently at odds with local rivals.[26] Other than at Leominster, he also had little success in trying to influence Herefordshire's parliamentary representation.[27]

In Wales, Essex had a solid power-base in the neighbouring counties of

own right, he acted as Essex's deputy at Leominster. He was a gentleman pensioner and had been a regular jouster in the 1570s. As a young man, he had toured Europe with Philip Sidney (*Commons*, I, pp. 638–40; W. J. Tighe, 'Country into Court, Court into country: John Scudamore of Holme Lacy (c.1542–1623) and his circles', in D. Hoak (ed.), *Tudor political culture* (Cambridge, 1995), pp. 165, 167 n. 38).

[22] Devereux MS 3, fol. 108^r. Essex's election as steward of Hereford actually required that the election to this office of Croft's son-in-law, John Scudamore, be overturned (BL, Add. MS 11053, fol. 30^r; Tighe, 'Country into Court, Court into country', pp. 167–9). When seeking renewed favour from Essex, a local correspondent pointedly reminded Gelly Meyrick of the sharp practices used by local adherents of Coningsby and the earl in defeating Scudamore: 'it is not unknown to you with what trouble it was to bring Hereford to my lord's devotion and then what plotes were layd to have a mayor to effect the same' (Devereux MS 1, fol. 296^r).

[23] *Commons*, I, p. 176; BL, Harleian MS 6997, fol. 48^r.

[24] In February 1594, by virtue of 'tam intimo amore', Shrewsbury assigned to Essex the offices of constable and gatekeeper for the castles of Wigmore and Radnor, which had been granted to him by the queen in 1589 in succession to his father (Devereux MSS, box 5, nos. 76, 77). Wigmore park, which 'doth adjoyne to the castle of Wigmore', was one of the parks granted to Essex in fee farm at the end of 1592 (BL, Lansdowne MS 69, fol. 177^r).

[25] *Commons*, III, pp. 196–7. It should also be noted that Pembridge was employed by Essex as a solicitor (with annuity of £20) from 1593 (FSL, L.a.251; Devereux MS 3, fol. 76^r). In addition to his legal work at Essex House during law term-time, Pembridge often supervised the courts held on his master's Herefordshire manors (e.g. *ibid.*, MS 1, fol. 161^r).

[26] For example, Pembridge was actually attacked by local gentlemen when he went about his business at Ross in 1590, even though he was not only Essex's agent but also the county's under-sheriff (*APC*, XX, *1590–1*, pp. 69–70, 82, 88–9, 104, 114–16). For discussion of the sharp divisions within the county, see W. J. Tighe, 'Herbert Croft's repulse', *BIHR* 58 (1985), pp. 106–9; also his 'Courtiers and politics in Elizabethan Herefordshire', *HJ* 32 (1989), pp. 257–79; and his 'Country into Court, Court into country', pp. 157–78.

[27] As steward of Leominster, Essex secured the return of Sir Francis Vere in 1593 and Thomas Crompton in 1597 (*Commons*, I, p. 176). His support may have aided Sir Thomas Coningsby to become senior knight of the shire in 1593, 1597 and 1601, but Herbert Croft was forced to turn to the earl of Shrewsbury to win the junior position in 1593 (*ibid.*, pp. 174–5). At Hereford, Essex's attempts to influence the choice of burgesses were apparently ineffectual (*ibid.*, pp. 175–6). As the bishop of Hereford explained to Robert Cecil (by then earl of Salisbury) in 1605, the town only chose local men: 'the late lord earle of Essex in his best fortunes and high stewardshipp of the said citye could not

Carmarthenshire and Pembrokeshire, in the south-west of the principality, and varying degrees of influence in the other counties of south Wales.[28] As in Staffordshire, Essex's dominant position in his Welsh heartland was based upon a combination of land holdings, family connections and local offices. In Carmarthenshire, the Devereux interest was powerfully symbolised by the tradition of public burials for family members at St Peter's Church in Carmarthen.[29] It is also striking that Essex succeeded to the constableship of Carmarthen Castle, along with various other offices previously held by his father in south Wales, in March 1577, when he was barely eleven years old.[30] Coming so young, this appointment was a clear recognition of the local importance of the Devereux and of Elizabeth's desire that it should continue. By 1586, at least four servants of Essex were members of the county's commission of the peace.[31]

Essex's position was equally powerful in Pembrokeshire, where his lands included the extensive estates of the former priory of Monkton. His influence in the county was further reinforced when his sister Dorothy unexpectedly married Sir Thomas Perrot, whose family were bitter local rivals of the Devereux.[32] However, this controversial marriage did not prove an unmitigated benefit. When Sir John Perrot was condemned for treason in 1592, the Perrot lands were forfeited to the crown, and Essex was drawn into a campaign, which continued throughout the decade, to recover as much property as possible for his sister.[33] Essex himself became

---

prevaile with them to nominate Sir Herbert Croft' (Cecil MS 191/7 (pr. *HMCS* XVII, p. 360)).

[28] For a general discussion of this, see H. A. Lloyd, *The gentry of south-west Wales 1540–1640* (Cardiff, 1968), pp. 112–18.

[29] E. J. Jones, 'The death and the burial of Walter Devereux, earl of Essex 1576', *The Carmarthen Antiquary* 1 (1941), p. 185.

[30] Devereux MSS, box 5, no. 67. Essex's father had made a special request before his death that Robert should succeed to these offices (J. Strype, *Annals of the Reformation and the establishment of religion, and other various occurrences in the Church of England* ... (4 vols., London, 1709–31), II, p. 465).

[31] P. Williams, *The council in the marches of Wales under Elizabeth I* (Cardiff, 1958), p. 282. Williams also lists another servant as a justice of the peace in Pembrokeshire and no less than five in neighbouring Cardiganshire.

[32] G. L. Craik, *The romance of the peerage* (4 vols., London, 1848–50), II, pp. 29–31; H. Morgan, 'The fall of Sir John Perrot', in J. Guy (ed.), *The reign of Elizabeth I: Court and culture in the last decade* (Cambridge, 1995), p. 113. Sir John Perrot had taken the opportunity of Earl Walter's death to 'vex and trouble' his heir by acting as the earl of Worcester's deputy as steward of the possessions of the diocese of St David's. On this pretext, he began holding local courts and sought to seize the manor of Llanfydd until he received payment of 1,000 marks – twenty-six years' worth of unpaid fees owing to the steward (Strype, *Annals*, III, part i, pp. 584–5). This malicious initiative was thwarted by an injunction, probably through the intervention of Essex's guardians (Devereux MS 5, fol. 24ʳ).

[33] Sir John Perrot's attainder imperilled Dorothy's jointure. Elizabeth promised Essex that his sister's rights would not be prejudiced and granted her £500 'of hir Majestie's ffree gift for

custos for Pembrokeshire,[34] albeit an absentee one who relied upon a deputy,[35] as in Staffordshire. Nevertheless, his uncle, George Devereux, maintained a strong and permanent family presence in Pembrokeshire by living at Llanfydd.[36] It was here that Essex first played the role of a local magnate. At Michaelmas 1584, he put on an impressive display of hospitality for the many gentlemen from the surrounding region who came to offer their respects and to pay over their rents in person.[37] It was also about this time that Essex headed the county's signatures to the Bond of Association[38] and paid a visit to the town of Haverfordwest.[39] Although such activities were ended by his removal to Court, Essex never lost interest in the affairs of this region, as the many interventions which he made on behalf of Pembrokeshire men in suits and legal cases show.[40]

hir releiffe' from the revenues received by the crown from the Perrot lands (PRO, E 403/2429, unfol., listed under payments upon extraordinary warrants, according to a privy seal of 3 December 1592). A special act of the 1593 parliament, which Essex helped to push through, also insulated Sir Thomas Perrot from the attainder of his father by ensuring his restoration in blood (D. Dean, *Law-making and society in late Elizabethan England: the parliament of England, 1584–1601* (Cambridge, 1996), p. 218). After Perrot's death in 1594, when Dorothy married the earl of Northumberland, Essex guaranteed her jointure with his own lands, redoubling his incentive to settle the business on favourable terms (*HMCS*, IV, pp. 261–2 (wrongly dated as 1592)). However, Perrot's death provided an opening for the new attorney-general, Edward Coke, to revive the seizure of the family lands. Thereafter, the whole matter became subject to complex and expensive litigation. A separate suit by James Perrot, one of Sir John's illegitimate children, was lost altogether in 1596, whilst a minor slip in the wording of a plea nearly proved disastrous for Essex and his sister (Devereux MS 1, fol. 269^r; Devereux MS 3, fols. 89^v, 90^r; PRO, E 163/15/31; BL, Harleian MS 6995, fol. 141^r; S. Thomas, 'The descent of the lordships of Laugharne and Eglwyscummin: Norman marcher lordships in south-west Carmarthenshire', *The Carmarthen Antiquary* 6 (1970), pp. 34–5, 36–7, 39–41). After this débâcle, the countess petitioned the queen over her misfortune (*HMCS*, XIV, p. 31). Things took a more positive turn in early 1597 after Essex renewed this suit with Burghley (LPL, MS 656, fol. 15^r; BL, Lansdowne MS 83, fol. 213^v; *HMCS*, IV, pp. 261–2). On 21 May 1597, Essex was granted a twenty-one-year lease of Carew and Tallaharne castles, both part of Perrot's sequestered estate (PRO, SP 38/5, unfol.; cf. PRO, C 66/1458, mm. 20–2). At some unspecified time, Essex was also appointed steward of the Perrot lands by a patent under the exchequer seal (Devereux MS 3, fol. 127^v). Despite these victories, the case rumbled on into the reign of James I.

[34] PRO, C 66/1421, m. 15^d; PRO, C 66/1435, m. 20^d; PRO, C 66/1468, mm. 15^d–16^d, etc.

[35] Naturally enough, Essex used George Devereux as his deputy for this office in Pembrokeshire (FSL, L.a.278).

[36] For Devereux, see *Commons*, II, pp. 34–5. He accompanied Essex on the Cadiz expedition in 1596 and was knighted there by the lord admiral (PRO, SP 12/259, fol. 179^r).

[37] Devereux MS 3, fols. 63^v, 67^r.

[38] PRO, SP 12/174, fol. 41^r.

[39] B. G. Charles (ed.), *Calendar of the records of the borough of Haverfordwest 1539–1660* (Board of Celtic Studies, University of Wales, History and Law Series, XXIV, Cardiff, 1967), pp. 195, 196.

[40] For example, BL, Harleian MS 6993, fols. 15^r, 109^r, 112^r, 116^r; BL, Harleian MS 6994, fols. 3^r, 15^r; BL, Harleian MS 6995, fol. 141^r; BL, Harleian MS 6996, fols. 93^r, 130^r, 218^r, 239^r; BL, Add. MS 12506, fol. 239^r.

Although his power-base lay in Carmarthenshire and Pembrokeshire, Essex also gained growing influence in other parts of Wales. In Breconshire, for example, partly as a result of his own lobbying at Court, another of Essex's uncles, Robert Knollys, became a deputy lieutenant.[41] Through his steward, Gelly Meyrick, Essex was also able to gain considerable influence in Radnorshire.[42] During the early and mid-1590s, Essex's influence also increasingly spread into north Wales and, in particular, into the eastern side of Denbighshire.[43] In large measure, this came about through contacts made during military service and through a conscious desire among some families in this area to secure Essex's backing in longstanding local disputes. However, although a number of these men became his servants, Essex's support in the north clearly represented an ardent following rather than a power-base, for Essex himself had few ties there as landlord, master or kinsman.

As the queen's favourite, Essex also received a succession of royal grants. These considerably boosted his income and made him the holder of many minor offices across the realm. However, such grants did not substantially extend his power-base beyond Staffordshire, Herefordshire and south-west Wales. In Berkshire, for example, Essex was granted the bulk of the forfeited estates of Sir Francis Englefield. Perhaps because these properties inherently composed a sustainable estate and lay close to the holdings of his maternal relatives, the prolific Knollys family, Essex retained as many of these lands as financial necessity allowed.[44] He even acquired leases to Englefield properties excluded from his grant.[45] Yet ownership of these estates did not give Essex any real power-base in Berkshire;[46] at best, it had

---

[41] BLO, Douce MS 393, fol. 41^r; *Commons*, II, pp. 416–17.

[42] *Commons*, I, p. 325. By Essex's means, Meyrick was appointed as a deputy lieutenant for Radnorshire, by a commission dated 6 October 1598 (PRO, C 231/1 fol. 56^v). Meyrick's power in the county was based upon kinship – especially his marriage into the Lewis family – and the purchase of a large estate, as well as Essex's position as constable and steward of Radnor castle (*Commons*, I, p. 325; Devereux MS 3, fol. 127^v). Meyrick also reinforced Essex's power in his natural territory of south-west Wales. Meyrick's daughter, Margaret, married the influential John Vaughan of Golden Grove, in Carmarthenshire. Vaughan's step-mother was Letitia, daughter of Sir John Perrot and sister of Essex's brother-in-law Sir Thomas Perrot (*DWB*, pp. 749, 995).

[43] A. H. Dodd, 'North Wales in the Essex revolt of 1601', *EHR* 59 (1944), pp. 348–70; also his 'The earl of Essex's faction in north Wales, c.1593–1601: supplementary notes', *The National Library of Wales Journal* 6 (1949–59), pp. 190–1.

[44] For the sale of Englefield lands by Essex, see PRO, C 54/1339, unfol., enrolment of an indenture of 12 July 1589; PRO, C 54/1407, mm. 26^d–27^d; PRO, C 66/1412, m. 25.

[45] PRO, C 66/1394, mm. 14–15; PRO, C 66/1397, mm. 42–3; PRO, C 66/1404, mm. 12–14; *VCH, Berkshire*, III, pp. 333, 434.

[46] Essex's influence was undoubtedly weakened by the continuing presence in the county of Francis Englefield Esq., who advanced his own claims to the rents and the loyalty of tenants in 1589 and 1592 (*APC*, XVII, *1588–9*, p. 144; *ibid.*, XXII, *1591–2*, p. 570). See also

an indirect effect, increasing the local influence of the Knollys family and of his friend, Sir Henry Unton, who helped to supervise these lands.[47]

As the examples of Herefordshire and north Wales suggest, Essex was aggressive in exploiting any local opportunities to expand his territorial influence. Given the scale of his political ambitions and the expectations which they encouraged among his followers, Essex needed to be forceful. He therefore eagerly accepted high stewardships wherever towns offered them to him, seemingly irrespective of the local politics involved.[48] These posts added to his prestige and gave him useful local patronage, especially at parliament time. They also increased the pool of men who might follow him when he went to war.[49] Nevertheless, Essex's power-base in the counties remained relatively small. Certainly, it did not compare with those of great regional magnates such as the earls of Shrewsbury, Pembroke, Northumberland or Derby. Yet Essex's power-base differed in more than merely size from those of such great local princelings. Unlike them, Essex did not base himself on his estates and make visits to the Court: after 1585, Essex based himself at Court and did not visit his distant heartland until 1599, when he passed through on his way to Ireland. Apart from those occasions when he travelled south or west for military reasons, Essex barely strayed further from Court during this time than Essex House in London or Wanstead in Essex.

One effect of this constrained existence can be seen in the flow of complaints and petitions from Essex's tenants. These came in from the distant counties to Essex House, the headquarters which administered his various interests across the realm, only to be referred back to local servants for enquiry or adjudication.[50] To his tenants, Essex must have seemed quite

G. de C. Parmiter, 'Plowden, Englefield and Sandford: II', *Recusant History* 14 (1977–8), pp. 16ff.

[47] Devereux MS 1, fol. 131^r.

[48] In addition to the local offices noted above, Essex's posts during the period of this study included those of high recorder of Maldon (where he succeeded Leicester) from November 1588 (Devereux MSS, box 5, no. 70), high steward of Dunwich from December 1595 (*HMC. Report on manuscripts in various collections* (London, 1914), VII p. 82), high steward of Ipswich and of the city of Oxford from August 1596 (Devereux MSS, box 6, nos. 83, 84) and supervisor of the musters for the tenants of the dean and chapter of Canterbury from March 1597 (*ibid.*, no. 86).

[49] While the value of such posts for influencing the return of members of parliament for boroughs has long been emphasised, the latter point about the military utility of local offices perhaps might bear some further investigation. Aside from his position at Canterbury, it is striking that Essex's appointment as hereditary steward of Tamworth in 1585 meant that 'we shall have no mustring thear but by my lorde's appoyntmente' (FSL, L.a.509). Before the Dissolution, the landed gentry were able to obtain military power through the possession of monastic stewardships (B. Coward, *The Stanleys Lords Stanley and earls of Derby 1385–1672: the origins, wealth and power of a landowning family* (Chetham Society, 3rd ser., XXX, Manchester, 1983), p. 96).

[50] For example, FSL, L.a.458, 463, 466, 467, 472.

literally a distant landlord. As a result, the role of his servants and friends out in the counties expanded to fill the gap left by his absence. Such men included friends such as Sir Edward Littleton[51] and Richard Bagot[52] in Staffordshire, and servants such as Anthony Pembridge, his old tutor Robert Wright, William Downhall, his gentleman of the horse,[53] Henry Lyndley, his comptroller and a former servant of Sir Philip Sidney,[54] Richard Broughton, the overseer of his estates during the period of his wardship,[55] and Charles Wednester, his auditor.[56] Above all, the man who benefited most from Essex's trust was his steward, Gelly Meyrick.[57] Through a combination of a strong personality, important family connections[58] and

---

[51] Appointed as a deputy lieutenant in July 1590 (APC, XIX, 1590, p. 349), Lyttleton had very extensive dealings with Essex's affairs in Staffordshire (for example, FSL, L.a.215, 409. 410, 462; Devereux MS 1, fol. 161ʳ; Devereux MSS, box 5, no. 79).

[52] A deputy lieutenant since 1585 (PRO, SP 12/179, fol. 106ʳ), Bagot and his family were vital supporters of the Devereux interest in Staffordshire. Something of the range of his work for Essex can be seen in those papers of the Bagot family which now comprise FSL, L.a.1–1049.

[53] Downhall was Essex's gentleman of the horse by 1596 (HMCS, VI, p. 200), in which capacity he naturally oversaw Essex's stock of horses (for example, ibid., VII, p. 27). Downhall may have previously been a servant of the earl of Leicester. A Mr Downhall was listed among Leicester's senior servants in the Netherlands (BL, Cotton MS Galba C VIII, fol. 98ʳ), as well as among those who composed Leicester's funeral procession (BLO, Ashmolean MS 818, fol. 38ʳ).

[54] Lyndley was listed as one of Essex's 'surveiors' in 1588, when he accompanied a number of the earl's other servants in making a circuit of his Herefordshire properties (FSL, L.a.251). Later, he was given 'the care of my [Essex's] poor store' (HMCS, VII, p. 275. Cf. Commons, II, pp. 478–9). Having prevailed upon the lord keeper to appoint Lyndley as a justice of the peace in Kent, Essex fought for his reinstatement in December 1595, when all servants were removed from commissions of the peace (BL, Harleian MS 286, fol. 25ʳ). As a servant of Sidney, Lyndley was not only a witness to his will, but also received an annuity of £40 from his estate (PRO, PROB 11/74, fols. 55ʳ, 56ʳ). This was still being paid in 1607 (CKS, U 1475, F 26/4).

[55] Commons, I, pp. 498–9. Broughton was a son-in-law of Richard Bagot and managed the Devereux estates during Essex's minority (Devereux MS 5, fol. 3ʳ⁻ᵛ). As noted below, Essex won Broughton a place on the council in the marches of Wales and a judgeship on the Anglesey circuit in 1594. Thereafter, his involvement in Essex's financial and estate matters seems to have decreased. As a judge, Broughton has been described as the only lawyer on the council of Wales in the latter part of Elizabeth's reign who was 'certainly . . . corrupt' (Williams, Council in the marches of Wales, pp. 284, 310).

[56] Wednester was paid an annual salary of £25 (Devereux MS 3, fols. 101ᵛ, 102ᵛ). As well as dealing in Essex's estate business in London (for example, ibid., fol. 74ᵛ), he also surveyed lands and held manor courts for his master (for example, Devereux MS 1, fols. 131ʳ, 161ʳ). Before becoming a servant of Essex, he had been auditor to the earl of Leicester (BLO, Ashmolean MS 818, fol. 38ʳ).

[57] As noted above, Meyrick entered Essex's service in October 1579, when Essex was still at Cambridge. He was knighted by Essex at Cadiz in 1596 and, ultimately, executed for his part in Essex's rising of 1601.

[58] For an extreme example of the importance of extended kinship relations in Meyrick's dealings in Wales, see Devereux MS 1, fol. 183ʳ. The son of Bishop Meyrick of Bangor, he married into the leading family in Radnorshire, while his daughter married the heir of Sir Walter Vaughan of Golden Grove, Carmarthenshire (see above, n. 42). Meyrick's brother

his well-known intimacy with Essex, Meyrick became a powerful and highly controversial figure in Wales.[59] One of his critics even claimed that he conducted himself there as if he were 'Lord Meryke'.[60]

It is perhaps a truism that political success in Elizabethan England was intimately related to influence at Court. Nevertheless, for Essex, whose landed power-base was modest in comparison to his lofty political ambitions, influence deriving from favour at Court was even more important than usual. As a royal favourite, Essex enjoyed a special bond with Elizabeth. However, the queen's moods could be fickle and Essex himself was frequently absent from the Court on campaign or other business. Sustained influence at Court therefore also required the solid foundations of office – itself a concrete sign of royal favour – and ties of kinship, especially among those who enjoyed easy access to the queen.

Essex gained his first courtly office when he was appointed master of the horse in 1587.[61] This brought him a healthy income and the potential for a certain amount of patronage in the royal stables,[62] and it also provided the formal underpinning for his domination of royal tournaments. Nevertheless, the main political effect of this post was to confirm Essex's status as Elizabeth's new favourite and Leicester's political heir apparent. Far more weighty in political terms was the mastership of the ordnance, which Essex gained in March 1597.[63] This formally confirmed Essex's equivalence with the lord admiral as the leading military man on the privy council. Although its patronage potential was sharply reduced by the number of positions already filled before his appointment,[64] the

Francis campaigned with Essex in Normandy and Rouen (PRO, SP 78/25, fol. 123[r]; Devereux MS 2, fol. 85[v]). Another brother, Henry, seems to have acted as Meyrick's personal secretary (Devereux MS 1, fol. 288[r]).

[59] HMCS, VIII, p. 423; Devereux MS 1, fol. 151[r]. See also D. Mathew, The Celtic peoples and Renaissance Europe: a study of the Celtic and Spanish influences on Elizabethan history (London and New York, 1933), pp. 341ff. Perhaps significantly, when Meyrick was finally granted a coat of arms in 1583, he chose a crest featuring two porcupines surmounted by a roaring lion, suggesting a powerful determination to defend his newly recognised social eminence (BL, Stowe MS 606, fol. 60[v]).

[60] HMCS, VIII, p. 423.   [61] See above, p. 60.

[62] For example, Essex appointed his old tutor and servant, Robert Wright, as clerk of the stables some time before May 1595 (BL, Add. MS 5750, fols. 142[v]–143[r]). In April 1591, he also appointed fourteen new grooms and two valets to replace a similar number of men who had been pensioned off (PRO, E 403/2276, unfol.; BL, Add. MS 22924, fol. 31[r]). By this time, the wage bill for the stables was at least £2,000 a year (PRO, SP 12/233, fols. 120[r]–121[v]). The mastership of the horse perhaps also increased his local influence in Staffordshire, because of the queen's stud there at Tutbury.

[63] See above, pp. 217, 238–9.

[64] LPL, MS 656, fols. 12[r], 15[r]. The signet office docquet book (PRO, SO 3/1) records that Essex's predecessor, the earl of Warwick, made some thirty-one placements as master of the ordnance between 1585 and his death in 1590. Thereafter, no single patron controlled the

office gave Essex a controlling role in military administration and a powerful voice in the formulation of strategy. In late December 1597, Essex also became earl marshal, the queen's arbiter of honour and overseer of the heralds. In other circumstances, this title might have made Essex the most important aristocrat in the realm. However, the manner in which Essex finally obtained this office diminished the prestige and influence which properly accompanied it.[65]

For much of his career, Essex seemed poorly endowed with royal offices for a man of his ambition. Although he became a privy councillor in 1593, the mastership of the horse remained his only royal office for a full decade. It was not until 1597, when he became master of the ordnance and earl marshal, that he received really weighty appointments. Nevertheless, this reckoning of offices is only part of the story. Leicester had been just a councillor and master of the horse for most of his career and yet his influence at Court was unparalleled. Leicester's career suggests that the key elements to substantial influence at Court were a firm hold on the royal favour, the creation of a network of courtly friends and followers over several decades, and a profusion of relatives in key posts who could support his initiatives or defend his interests in his absence. Essex undoubtedly enjoyed royal favour, but he failed to create a suitable network of courtly followers and found precious little support from family or friends.

During his meteoric rise to royal favour, Essex was able to trade upon Leicester's influence at Court and general disdain for Ralegh among 'the greatest'. However, Leicester's death, the eclipse of Ralegh and Essex's own political aggressiveness transformed this situation. As Essex's bold reinvention of himself as a budding statesman began to succeed, the importance of gaining support for his position from family and friends became all the greater and yet the limited ability of his intimates to play this role became all the more obvious. By her marriage to Leicester, Essex's mother won Elizabeth's extreme displeasure. Leicester's death and her subsequent remarriage to Sir Christopher Blount merely compounded matters, leaving the countess vulnerable to the queen's hostility and a political handicap to her son.[66] Essex's two older sisters had once been maids of honour but they

---

office and subordinate officers became entrenched in their own positions. Essex's attempts to make new appointments drew immediate and irritating opposition from these vested interests (R. Ashley, 'War in the Ordnance Office: the Essex connexion and Sir John Davis', *Historical Research* 67 (1994), pp. 337–45).

[65] For all this, see below, pp. 386ff.

[66] Apart from prompting stories that her liaison with Blount had begun before Leicester's death (Blount had been the earl's master of the horse), this marriage was scandalous in terms of social status and age: at the time, Blount was thirty-three and the countess of Leicester was in her late forties. Nevertheless, the countess of Leicester clearly needed a

both fell from grace and also became *persona non grata* with Elizabeth. Penelope, the elder of the two, although married to Lord Rich, maintained an openly adulterous relationship with Lord Mountjoy.[67] Dorothy forfeited royal favour by her dramatic marriage to Sir Thomas Perrot, which was conducted in complete defiance of her guardians and without Elizabeth's approval.[68] After Perrot's death in 1594, Dorothy married the earl of Northumberland.[69] This united the houses of Percy and Devereux and was perhaps Dorothy's only substantial contribution to her brother's political career. Unfortunately, the marriage was far from happy and Northumberland's bond with Essex was a rather equivocal one.[70] By contrast, Penelope was extremely active on Essex's behalf, despite her absence from Court. Men associated with Essex repeatedly praised her hospitality and intelligent

supportive and pliable husband because of Elizabeth's ill-will towards her and the threat which this posed to her finances. Essex was initially embarrassed by the match but it made Blount entirely dedicated to his cause (see, for example, WRO, TD 69/6.2, item 67, Sir Christopher Blount to Essex, n.d.).

[67] There are a number of books on Penelope Rich, née Devereux, none of them satisfactory. The most recent is S. Freedman, *Poor Penelope: Lady Penelope Rich. An Elizabethan woman* (Bourne End, Bucks, 1983). As a cousin of the queen, Penelope served as a maid of honour for a year or so before her marriage (*ibid.*, p. 36). Penelope was also a godchild of Elizabeth: M. Margetts, 'A christening date for Lady Penelope Rich', *N&Q* 239 (1993), pp. 153–4.

[68] For the extraordinary events surrounding this marriage in July 1583, see BL, Lansdowne MS 72, fols. 10^r–11^v. Elizabeth was especially angry because Dorothy was still a maid of honour (BL, Lansdowne MS 39, fol. 173^v). It may have been Dorothy's presence at Northaw, visiting the countess of Warwick, which sparked the explosion between Essex and Elizabeth in mid-1587 (see above).

[69] Perrot died in February 1594 but the precise date of Dorothy's remarriage is uncertain. An undated payment in Essex's accounts (£10 'to the players at Essex House at the marriag of therle of Northumberland') might suggest that it took place later in 1594 (Devereux MS 3, fol. 84^r). One story has it that Elizabeth herself organised this match to prevent any chance that Northumberland could be manoeuvred into marriage with Arabella Stuart (E. B. de Fonblanque, *Annals of the house of Percy* (2 vols. in 4 parts, London, 1887), II, part i, pp. 204–5). It seems more likely that Essex and Northumberland agreed the union for mutual political advantage.

[70] At first, Essex's relations with Northumberland were quite solid. In April 1595, Northumberland joined Lord Burgh and Lady Rich as godparents to Essex's son, Henry (W. B. Bannerman (ed.), *The registers of St Olave, Hart St, London, 1563–1700* (Harleian Society, XLVI, 1916), p. 17). In mid-1596, the two brothers-in-law were still sufficiently friendly for Essex to let Northumberland use his lodgings at Court while he was away on military service (LPL, MS 657, fol. 108^v). However, relations soon became more strained. In March 1597, Anthony Bacon secretly warned Essex that Northumberland was planning to embarrass him at Court over his continuing hostility towards Edward Coke, the attorney-general (LPL, MS 656, fol. 120^v). Coke had not only beaten Francis Bacon for the post of attorney-general, but spearheaded the crown's case over the Perrot lands. During the same month, an anonymous correspondent (possibly Bacon himself) informed the countess of Northumberland that her husband was conducting an adulterous affair at Court (*ibid.*, fol. 153^r). Shortly before this, Northumberland had been on the brink of a duel with Essex's friend, the earl of Southampton (LPL, MS 655, fol. 130^r).

conversation.[71] She also wrote many letters on her brother's behalf, including a considerable number to Sir Robert Cecil.[72]

Although Essex's mother and sisters could not aid him at Court, his mother's family, the Knollys, did provide important support there. By their connection with the Boleyns, the Knollys family were close relatives of Elizabeth. Essex's maternal grandfather, old Sir Francis Knollys, was the treasurer of the royal household.[73] Knollys kept a watchful eye on his grandson's early career but, by the time Essex joined the council, he was almost eighty and sidelined from political influence.[74] Nevertheless, when Knollys died in 1596, his eldest son, Sir William Knollys, was swiftly appointed comptroller of the household and replaced him at the council board.[75] Sir William was able to bolster Essex's position in Court and council, proving one of his few steadfast adherents in the years which followed, and two of Knollys' younger brothers, Francis and Robert, also actively supported Essex.[76] Their sisters provided further connections for Essex.[77] Potentially the most useful of these was Elizabeth Knollys, who was a long-serving lady of the privy chamber and married to Sir Thomas Leighton.[78] However, Lady Leighton does not seem to have been very

[71] See, for example, Ungerer, I, pp. 71, 79–92, 189, 190, 199–201, 232–3, 275–7; *ibid.*, II, pp. 238, 366; P. J. Blok, *Correspondance inedite de Robert Dudley, comte de Leycester, et de François et Jean Hotman* (Haarlem, 1911), p. 256.

[72] See, for example, *HMCS*, V, pp. 236, 239, 296; *ibid.*, VI, pp. 161, 307, 562.

[73] *Commons*, II, pp. 409–14; *DNB*, XI, pp. 278–8.

[74] An ardent opponent of the religious policies of Whitgift and Bancroft, Knollys suffered for supporting their critics too openly during the 1593 parliament (J. Guy, 'The Elizabethan establishment and the ecclesiastical polity' in his (ed.), *Court and culture* (Cambridge, 1995), pp. 136–7).

[75] *Commons*, II, pp. 417–19. Knollys was sworn as a privy councillor, together with Lord North, on 30 August 1596 (H. V. Jones, 'The journal of Levinus Munck', *EHR* 68 (1953), p. 236). Essex claimed – and his friends apparently accepted – that he 'brought in' both Knollys and North (LPL, MS 659, fol. 224^r; WRO, TD 69/6.2, item 75, Essex to Antonio Perez, 16 September 1596). In reality, Knollys principally owed his promotion to the fact that he was his father's son.

[76] *Commons*, II, pp. 408, 416–17.

[77] Anne Knollys married Thomas Lord De La Warr (*DNB*, XI, p. 278; *TCP*, IV, pp. 159–60). Their son and heir was associated with Essex in the late 1590s and was fined in the aftermath of the 1601 insurrection (*Commons*, III, p. 603). Catherine Knollys took as her second husband Sir Philip Butler (*DNB*, XI, p. 278), who accompanied Essex on his secret departure to join the Portugal expedition.

[78] Lady Elizabeth Leighton (wrongly named as Cecilia in *DNB*, XI, p. 278) was appointed as a gentlewoman of the privy chamber, with an annual salary of £33 6s 8d, on 5 January 1566 (BL, Lansdowne MS 59, fol. 43^r). She continued in this capacity until the queen's death. The only instance where she demonstrably aided Essex was before the incident between Essex and Elizabeth at Northaw (and perhaps afterwards) in 1587, described above. By the mid-1590s, she was increasingly eager to end her service at Court (*HMCD*, II, p. 271; P. Wright, 'A change of direction: the ramifications of a female household, 1558–1603', in D. Starkey (ed.), *The English Court from the Wars of the Roses to the Civil War* (London, 1987), p. 171).

active at Court on her nephew's behalf and she probably spent much of her time in Guernsey, where her husband was governor.[79]

Through his mother, Essex was also closely related to the queen's closest relatives, the Careys. Essex's maternal grandmother was Catherine Carey, Elizabeth's first cousin and gentlewoman of the bedchamber until her death in 1569.[80] Her brother was Lord Hunsdon, lord chamberlain from 1585 and one of the few councillors with military experience.[81] Although increasingly old and unwell, he worked with Essex in military matters and probably shared many of his great-nephew's views on the war. As governor of Berwick,[82] Hunsdon also retained a powerful interest in Scottish affairs. Among his Carey cousins, Essex was clearly friendly with Hunsdon's heir, Sir George Carey, who succeeded as 2nd Lord Hunsdon and replaced his father as captain of the gentlemen pensioners in 1596 and became lord chamberlain in 1597.[83] Essex was also supportive of Sir Edmund Carey.[84] He enjoyed even closer relations with Sir Robert Carey, Hunsdon's youngest son, who was a keen follower of Essex until he abandoned Court for life in the north in 1593.[85] Essex was also on good terms with

---

[79] *Commons*, II, pp. 458–9; A. J. Eagleston, 'Guernsey under Sir Thomas Leighton (1570–1610)', *La Société Guernsiaise: Report and Transactions* 13 (1937–45), pp. 72–108. This family connection, as well as Leighton's previous experience of campaigning in Normandy during the 1560s, made him a natural choice as Essex's official military adviser (and 'minder') during the Rouen campaign.

[80] *DNB*, XI, p. 278. She was buried in Westminster Abbey at royal expense.

[81] *TCP*, VI, pp. 627–9; *DNB*, III, pp. 977–9. He died on 23 July 1596 and, like his wife, was buried in Westminster Abbey at royal expense (BL, Lansdowne MS 82, fols. 123ʳ–125ʳ).

[82] L. Stone, 'Office under Queen Elizabeth: the case of Lord Hunsdon and the lord chamberlainship in 1585', *HJ* 10 (1967), pp. 279–85. The continuing Carey interest along the borders (Hunsdon's sons John and Robert retained key offices there after their father's death) may have aided Essex's contacts with Scotland. John Carey controlled Berwick – the crucial node of communication with Scotland – from his father's death until March 1598, when he was supplanted by Essex's friend Lord Willoughby (PRO, E 403/2453, fols. 300ʳ–301ʳ).

[83] *TCP*, VI, pp. 629–30; *DNB*, III, pp. 974–5. Like Essex and Cumberland, Sir George Carey had studied at Trinity College, Cambridge. He was appointed governor of the Isle of Wight in 1582 and spent much of his time there, before basing himself at Court from late 1596. He was sworn lord chamberlain and a privy councillor on 17 April 1597 (Jones, 'Journal of Munck', p. 237). For relations between them, see the warm tone of Essex's letter to Carey of October 1596: Gloucestershire Record Office, Berkeley Castle Muniments, MF 1161, fol. 85ʳ.

[84] Essex knew his cousin Edmund from their days in the Low Countries under Leicester, who knighted both of them. After he became steward of Grafton, Essex appointed Sir Edmund as keeper of the park. Grafton thereafter became Carey's main residence (*DNB*, III, p. 979; *HMCS*, VI, pp. 280–1).

[85] Hunsdon's youngest son, Robert Carey, was sent by Elizabeth to summon Essex back to Court after the incident at Northaw in 1587. Carey was mortified that Essex did not take him to Portugal in 1589 but accompanied him to Rouen, where Essex knighted him. After his marriage in 1593 (of which the queen disapproved), Carey went on to build a career on the marches towards Scotland, initially serving under his brother-in-law, Lord Scrope

Philadelphia Carey, who married Thomas Lord Scrope and served as a lady-in-waiting.[86] However, Lady Scrope's influence with Elizabeth was overshadowed by that of her older sister, Catherine Carey, who was married to Howard of Effingham, who was the lord admiral and (from October 1597) earl of Nottingham.[87]

Essex gained little tangible political benefit from his marriage to Frances Walsingham, the widow of Sir Philip Sidney, although the union was resonant with notions of the Protestant cause. The countess of Essex proved a supportive and – importantly, in the eyes of contemporaries – fertile wife.[88] However, she was apparently uncomfortable at Court and spent little time there. Her mother, Lady Walsingham, had some influence with Elizabeth as a result of the late secretary's long service, but her primary concern was to resolve the problem of debts to the crown which entangled her late husband's estate.[89] Nevertheless, Essex's marriage reinforced his connection with his late stepfather's kin, the extended Dudley–Sidney family. Anne, countess of Warwick, Leicester's sister-in-law, was perhaps especially important because her considerable influence with Elizabeth complemented his own hold on royal favour – she was prepared to use her influence to help Essex until at least the mid-1590s.[90] Essex was also close to Leicester's last surviving sister, Catherine, and her husband,

(*DNB*, III, pp. 984–5; *Commons*, I, pp. 550–1; F. H. Mares (ed.), *The memoirs of Robert Carey* (Oxford, 1972)).

[86] *DNB*, III, p. 979; *TCP*, XI, pp. 549–50. By October 1599, Lady Scrope was the only woman in the privy chamber prepared to 'stand firm' for him (*HMCD*, II, p. 400).

[87] *DNB*, III, p. 979; *ibid.*, X, p. 5; *TCP*, IX, 785–6. After her death in February 1603, the countess of Nottingham was described as having been Elizabeth's groom of the stool. This is probably a loose use of the term but it suggests her ascendancy in the privy chamber during the last years of the reign (Wright, 'Change of direction', pp. 149–50). Hunsdon's third daughter, Margaret, married Sir Edward Hoby, a close relative of the Cecils (*Commons*, II, p. 323).

[88] Children were a *sine qua non* for any kind of long-term dynastic aspirations. Although the countess of Essex conceived quite regularly, an alarming number of the children died as infants. She bore Robert Viscount Hereford in January 1591 (who succeeded as 3rd earl of Essex and lived until 1646), Walter in January 1592 (who died in February 1592), Penelope in late 1593 or early 1594 (who died in 1599), Henry in April 1595 (who died in May 1596), Frances in September 1599 (who lived until 1674) and Dorothy in December 1600 (who lived until 1636). The countess also had two still-births in December 1596 and in 1598 (Tenison, X, p. 161; *DNB*, V, pp. 889–90). This high mortality rate suggests that she may have spent much of her time in the country at Barn Elms, her father's old home, in an attempt to ensure a healthy environment for her children.

[89] C. Read, *Mr Secretary Walsingham and the policy of Queen Elizabeth* (3 vols., Oxford, 1925), III, pp. 442ff. Sir Francis Walsingham himself had a connection to an earlier generation of the Carey family – his stepfather was Sir John Carey, an uncle of Henry, 1st Lord Hunsdon (*ibid.*, I, pp. 13–14).

[90] For example, the countess of Warwick joined Essex in strongly backing Sir Robert Sidney for the wardenship of the Cinque Ports in early 1597 (see, *HMCD*, II, pp. 251ff). She and Essex also acted as intercessors at Court during 1595 for Lord Willoughby d'Eresby, who was then still abroad (*HMCA*, p. 330). Sir Robert Cecil apparently always regarded the

Henry, earl of Huntingdon. Although Huntingdon was rarely at Court because of his duties in the north, he was a relative of the Devereux and had been a guardian to Essex.[91] His death in December 1595 hit Essex very hard.[92] Like her husband, Catherine, countess of Huntingdon, was renowned as a godly guardian for aristocratic children, including Essex's own siblings.[93] In the wake of her husband's death and the bitter disputes with his successor over his debts, the countess spent more time at Court, winning considerable influence with Elizabeth during the last years of the reign.[94] Essex's marriage also tied him to Sir Robert Sidney[95] and the earl of Pembroke.[96] However, while Essex's relationship with Sidney was an extremely close one, that with Pembroke collapsed into sharp acrimony by late 1595.[97] Not all family ties were necessarily cordial.

Essex's success and personal charm also won him a number of aristocratic friends in the early 1590s, many of whom shared some family

countess as inclined towards Essex (D. J. H. Clifford (ed.), *The diaries of Lady Anne Clifford* (Stroud, 1990), p. 22).

[91] *TCP*, VI, pp. 656–7. For Huntingdon, see above, pp. 31–2.

[92] Essex allegedly 'tooke it so passionately that he tore his hear and all his buttons brake with the swelling of his stomach' (Sir John Harington, *A tract on the succession to the crowne (AD 1602)*, (ed. C. R. Markham, Roxburghe Club, London, 1880), p. 41). This sounds remarkably similar to Essex's behaviour at Rouen after the death of his brother Walter (see above, pp. 105–6).

[93] C. Cross, *The puritan earl: the life of Henry Hastings, third earl of Huntingdon, 1536–1595* (London and New York, 1966), ch. 2. The countess's other charges at Ashby de la Zouch included Thomas Sidney (younger brother of Philip, Robert and Mary), the earl of Rutland's sister, Edward 3rd earl of Bedford and a nephew of Sir Christopher Hatton (*ibid.*, pp. 57–9).

[94] *Ibid.*, pp. 270–3, 277–9. Elizabeth was perhaps never entirely trusting of the countess during the lifetime of her husband because Huntingdon had a distant claim upon the royal succession. In early 1563, Elizabeth had publicly humiliated the countess in order to disabuse her of any notion that her husband's blood might win her special favour (*ibid.*, pp. 142ff).

[95] For Sidney, see M. V. Hay, *The life of Robert Sidney, earl of Leicester, 1563–1626* (Washington, D.C., 1984).

[96] Pembroke was married to Mary Sidney, the sister of Sir Philip and Sir Robert Sidney (*TCP*, X, p. 412). For Mary, countess of Pembroke, see M. P. Hannay, *Philip's phoenix: Mary Sidney, countess of Pembroke* (New York and Oxford, 1990).

[97] In November 1595, Rowland Whyte reported 'unkindness' between Essex and Pembroke over the control of Norwood Park in Somerset (*HMCD*, II, pp. 188, 192, 196). By then, the two earls had already fallen out over plans to refortify Milford Haven (see above, p. 236). It is possible that the countess of Pembroke tried to engineer a *rapprochement* between them after Cadiz, penning a warm, but undated, letter to Essex in her own hand (Princeton University Library, Robert H. Taylor Collection, no. 49258). Hannay (*Philip's phoenix*, pp. 154–5) believes that the letter probably dates from this period and that Essex's 'safe arivall at Plimoth' refers to his return from Cadiz, but this is far from certain. Even if the dating is correct, the letter seems to have failed in its purpose. Tensions between Essex and Pembroke continued to mount, especially in Wales, where Pembroke was lord president: Williams, *Council in the marches of Wales*, pp. 287–8; Hannay, *Philip's phoenix*, pp. 74, 153–6.

connection with him. By the middle of the decade, these bonds had grown to place Essex at the centre of a substantial grouping of the English nobility. Through his sisters, he had strong personal ties with Northumberland, Rich[98] and Mountjoy,[99] although the earl was less a follower of Essex than the two barons. Essex was also close to the earls of Worcester,[100] Sussex,[101] Rutland[102] and Southampton,[103] and Lords Lumley,[104]

[98] For examples of Rich's dependency on Essex, see FSL, L.a.40; BL, Lansdowne MS 83, fols. 79[r], 80[v]; WRO, TD 69/6.2, items 51–3, Rich to Essex, respectively dated 23 December 1596, 16 April 1597, 11 September 1595.

[99] Mountjoy's adherence to Essex was frequently proclaimed in his letters to the earl: 'a harte most faythfully adicted unto youre lordshipp' (WRO, TD 69/6.2, item 55, Mountjoy to Essex, 5 August 1595); 'I am most youre lordshipp's, more then my owne' (*ibid.*, item 57, Mountjoy to Essex, 2 December 1596); 'I willbe ever all att youre lordshipp's commande-ment' (*ibid.*, item 59, Mountjoy to Essex, 4 November [1595]).

[100] Worcester's lands lay near to those of Essex in south Wales and he was related to Essex through his wife, Elizabeth Hastings, daughter of Francis, 2nd earl of Huntingdon. Essex deputed Worcester to act in his stead as master of the horse when he was away on campaign in 1596 (LPL, MS 657, fol. 108[v]) and 1597 (LPL, MS 661, fol. 247[r]: this is a copy of Cecil MS 98/91 (pr. *HMCS*, XIV, p. 106)). In November 1596, Worcester's two daughters were married at Essex House (LPL, MS 660, fol. 37[r]), an event which was celebrated in Spenser's *Prothalamion*. Worcester's elder son, William Lord Herbert, was knighted by Essex at Cadiz. After Herbert's death in January 1598 (*TCP*, XII, part 2, p. 856), plans were advanced for Worcester's second son, Henry (who now became the next Lord Herbert), to marry one of Essex's Knollys cousins, but the match ultimately fell through (WRO, TD 69/6.2, item 69, Sir Christopher Blount to Essex, 3 April 1598).

[101] Robert, 5th earl of Sussex, led a regiment under Essex at Cadiz and was knighted after the victory (PRO, SP 12/259, fol. 179[r]). Essex was a mourner at the funeral of his father, the 4th earl of Sussex, on 16 January 1594 (FSL, L.a.276). Sussex was related to Essex through Frances Sidney, aunt of Philip, Robert and Mary Sidney, who had married the 3rd earl of Sussex. The third earl had also been one of Essex's own guardians during his minority. In 1601, Sussex was suspected of involvement in Essex's rising and briefly committed to the custody of Sir John Stanhope (*TCP*, XII, part 1, p. 27).

[102] Essex's letters of advice to Rutland for his Continental tour of 1595–7 (see above, pp. 149ff) are the most obvious sign of the link between Rutland and Essex during this period. Rutland subsequently married Essex's step-daughter, Elizabeth (the daughter of Sir Philip Sidney) by 15 March 1599 (*TCP*, XI, p. 261).

[103] Southampton's association with Essex went back to at least 1591, when he offered to serve under Essex in Normandy and it was firmly established by the time Southampton came of age in 1594 (A. L. Rowse, *Shakespeare's Southampton: patron of Virginia* (London, 1965), pp. 57, 98ff.). Southampton was knighted by Essex during the Azores voyage (BL, Add. MS 5482, fol. 16[v]). Later in 1597, he and Worcester vouched that Essex's absence from the House of Lords was indeed due to ill health (*Journals of the House of Lords*, II (London, 1846), p. 198). In August 1598, much to the queen's fury, he secretly married Elizabeth Vernon, a maid of honour and a first cousin of Essex (*TCP*, XII, part 1, p. 130). The scion of a recusant family, his mother was a daughter of Anthony, 1st Viscount Montagu. On 2 May 1594, she took Sir Thomas Heneage, the vice-chamberlain, as her second husband. After his death in 1595, she married Sir William Hervey in 1598 (*ibid.*, p. 127).

[104] A former supporter of Leicester (BL, Cotton MS Galba D I, fol. 141[r]), Lumley's connection with Essex is suggested by his possession in 1590 of a portrait of Essex as master of the horse, painted by William Segar (D. Piper, 'The 1590 Lumley inventory: Hilliard, Segar and the earl of Essex', *Burlington Magazine* 99 (1957), p. 231). Essex also owned a

Eure,[105] Willoughby d'Eresby[106] and Lord Henry Howard.[107] As well, he 'brought up' the Irish Lord Bourke, the earl of Clanricarde's heir.[108] More

portrait of Lumley, which he removed from Wanstead after he sold that estate to Lord Mountjoy (FSL, G.b.4, unfol., inventory of goods removed from Wanstead to Essex House on 15 March 1599). Lumley's involvement in Essex's circle was further demonstrated by the visit which Sir Robert Sidney and Nicholas Clifford, both relatives and intimate friends of Essex, made to his house on 15 August 1593 (CKS, U 1475, A 38/2). Lumley was publicly named in 1596 as a supporter of Essex in John Harington's *Metamorphosis of Ajax*, together with Northumberland, Worcester and Viscount Montagu (E. S. Donno, *Sir John Harington's A new discourse of a stale subject, called the metamorphosis of Ajax* (London, 1962), pp. 223–4).

[105] Eure was in correspondence with Essex soon after being appointed warden of the middle march in October 1595 (Alnwick, Northumberland MSS, U.I, 2, rough book of accounts of William and Francis Wycliffe, payment of reward to Essex's man for bringing on letter from Eure to Northumberland, late 1595 or early 1596; LPL, MS 656, fols. 134ʳ, 352ʳ). During the early part of 1597, Eure was insistent about pushing forward negotiations for marrying his son William to a daughter of Lady Rich, Essex's closest unmarried female relative (LPL, MS 653, fol. 176ʳ; LPL, MS 655, fols. 118ʳ, 141ʳ; LPL, MS 656, fols. 131ʳ, 136ʳ, 375ʳ; LPL, MS 661, fols. 92ʳ, 93ʳ, 135ʳ, 139ʳ, 140ʳ). Eure's brother, who was intimately involved in these dealings, was knighted by Essex later that year in the Azores (BL, Add. MS 5482, fol. 16ᵛ). It is possible that these overtures were encouraged by the Carey family, who retained a powerful presence on the borders: in James's reign, Lord Eure married the widow of George, 2nd Lord Hunsdon (*TCP*, V, p. 182). Eure's son ultimately married Lucy Noel, but not until after Essex's death (*ibid.*). The connection between the Eures and Essex may also have been encouraged by the earl's reputation as a friend of Catholics. The Eure family leaned heavily towards recusancy, as did their Yorkshire neighbours, the Cholmeleys of Whitby. Richard Cholmeley was a servant of Essex and, like Sir William Eure, was implicated in the rising of 1601. In 1597, the Eures and Cholmeleys became engaged in a long feud with the godly Protestant Sir Thomas Hoby (the third husband of Walter Devereux's widow), who sought to have them prosecuted for recusancy (F. Heal, 'Reputation and honour in Court and country: Lady Elizabeth Russell and Sir Thomas Hoby', *TRHS*, 6th ser., 6 (1996), pp. 169–75).

[106] Willoughby's friendship with Essex began when they both served under Leicester in the Netherlands and was strengthened by their shared regard for Henri IV. After his bruising experiences as Leicester's successor in the Low Countries and general of an army sent to France in 1589, Willoughby spent much of the first half of the 1590s travelling on the Continent, only returning home in mid-1596 (he was at Stade awaiting passage for England on 9 June: PRO, SP 46/176, fol. 131ʳ). In the months after his return, he became a staunch partisan of Essex – disparaging Cecil's status as secretary (*HMCA*, p. 332), in almost daily contact with Anthony Bacon (LPL, MS 659, fol. 239ʳ) and passionately advocating Essex's appointment as master of the ordnance (for example, *ibid.*, fols. 289ʳ–290ᵛ).

[107] On Howard's association with Essex, see L. L. Peck, *Northampton: patronage and policy at the Court of James I* (London, 1982), pp. 13ff. In 1596, Howard was perhaps more of a Essex partisan than Peck suggests. In November that year, he described himself as a sponge from which Essex was able to wring the details of courtly intrigues against him (LPL, MS 660, fol. 107ʳ). In December, he ascribed to mere 'mallice' those who distinguished between 'the savegarde of our worthy person and the lyfe of your cuntry' (*ibid.*, fol. 275ʳ). Wotton described Howard as 'commonly *primae admissionis* [with Essex], by his bed-side in the morning' (Wotton, *Parallel*, p. 6). Howard wrote detailed political advice for Essex, which survives in DUL, Howard MS 2. By late 1599, however, Howard was reportedly 'held a newter' by Essex's circle (*HMCD*, II, p. 397).

[108] *HMCS*, VII, p. 345. Bourke had been schooled at Oxford by means of Sir Francis

loosely associated with Essex were friends such as earl of Cumberland,[109] Lord Burgh[110] and, until at least the middle of the decade, the earl of Shrewsbury.[111]

This glittering circle of friends was as impressive a grouping of noblemen as any seen in the sixteenth century. At a time when the succession was so uncertain, it held the potential to be enormously significant, even decisive, for the course of Elizabethan politics. However, this potential never came close to being realised. Many of these peers were young men who shared Essex's desire for martial glory and looked to him as the realm's military leader. Few of them ever received any significant rewards from Elizabeth or enjoyed any major office. With the council and positions of influence at Court monopolised by old men and with the queen constantly favouring an older generation,[112] these peers looked to Essex to blaze a trail which would lead to their own advancement. Some of these men bound themselves to Essex with a passion, but others – like the older and more worldly Lord Henry Howard – recognised that political success required the careful cultivation of a range of contacts, and subsequently distanced themselves from Essex in later years. The aristocratic bloc which centred around Essex only endured as long as he offered a pathway to honour and rewards from the crown, and there was always a tension between these aspirations.

The Elizabethan élite was also itself so interconnected by ties of blood and marriage that very few political relationships could ever be exclusive.

Walsingham. As earl of Clanricarde, he later married Essex's widow, as her third husband (*TCP*, III, pp. 230–1).

[109] Various connections between Essex and Cumberland have been noted above. They were also related: Cumberland's wife Margaret was the youngest daughter of Francis, 2nd earl of Bedford and sister of the formidable countess of Warwick. There was also a third Russell sister, Elizabeth, who was married to William, earl of Bath (*DNB*, XVII, p. 433; *TCP*, II, pp. 17–18; *ibid.*, III, p. 568). In 1593, Cumberland lent Essex £1,207 (Devereux MS 3, fol. 72r; R. T. Spence, *The privateering earl: George Clifford, 3rd earl of Cumberland, 1558–1605* (Stroud, 1995), p. 110).

[110] As governor of Brill (and hence dependent on support at Court from a range of mediators), Burgh was never a true Essex partisan. Nevertheless he had a strong bond with the earl through their shared opinions on the primacy of martial honour. This is powerfully evident in Burgh's correspondence with Essex in *HMCS*, V–VI. At some point, Burgh's notorious temper allegedly led him to try to stab Sir Walter Ralegh as he lay sleeping in his bedchamber (PRO, SP 9/55, item 12, no. 15).

[111] Essex and Shrewsbury shared influence in Staffordshire and were on good terms in the early 1590s. As Essex instructed his chief agent at Chartley in August 1592, 'Lett my lord of Shrewsburye's warrant [for hunting in the park] be as currant in Chartley as mine owne' (BL, RP 3195, holograph postscript). Shrewsbury allowed Essex to cement his hold on Wigmore and Radnor castles (see above, p. 273) and proved a useful ally during his confrontation with the earl of Derby over retainers in Lancashire in late 1593 and early 1594 (see below, p. 292). However, this co-operation later became somewhat strained because of Shrewsbury's close friendship with Sir Robert Cecil.

[112] L. L. Peck, 'Peers, patronage and the politics of history', in Guy (ed.), *Court and culture*, pp. 88–97.

The countesses of Warwick and Cumberland, for example, were connected to the Cecils and the Bacons through their sister-in-law, Elizabeth dowager Lady Russell;[113] Sir Robert Sidney was connected through his wife to the lord admiral;[114] Sir Robert Cecil claimed kinship by marriage with the Carey family;[115] through the remarriage of his sister-in-law, Margaret Dakins, Essex was himself connected to the Hoby brothers, their mother, dowager Lady Russell, and hence also to the Cecils and Bacons.[116] In this tangled web of human relationships, political dealings were necessarily complex. When serious political divisions began to emerge at Court in the mid-1590s, they were initially restrained by the many connections between those involved. However, as the conflict increased, the political élite was confronted by the problem of divided loyalties. This had never been an issue when upheaval at Court could be blamed on an outsider like Ralegh, but the growing tensions between Essex, the Cecils, Cobham and others tore at the heart of the courtly élite itself. Many who wished Essex well consequently declined to take his side openly.[117] Most of those who began to oppose him clearly regretted the necessity of doing so and earnestly hoped for a speedy compromise that would end the breach.

As politics became increasingly polarised in the mid-1590s, it became clear that Essex's active supporters at Court were relatively few and

---

[113] Elizabeth, fourth daughter of Sir Anthony Cooke of Gidea Hall, married Sir Thomas Hoby, by whom she had two sons, Edward and Thomas Posthumous. She subsequently married John Lord Russell, by whom she had two daughters. Russell was then heir to Francis, 2nd earl of Bedford, and a brother to the countesses of Warwick, Cumberland and Bath. After her husband's death in 1584, Elizabeth Cooke always signed herself as 'Elizabeth Russell dowager'. Elizabeth's own sisters included Mildred, the wife of Burghley and mother of Sir Robert Cecil, Ann, the widow of Sir Nicholas Bacon and mother of Anthony and Francis Bacon, and Katherine, wife of Sir Henry Killigrew (*DNB*, IV, p. 1002; *ibid.*, XVII, p. 433; *TCP*, II, p. 77; *Commons*, II, pp. 320–4). Like her sisters, Elizabeth Lady Russell was 'an intimidatingly learned and autocratic mother' (*Commons*, II, p. 323).

[114] Sidney married Barbara, daughter of John Gamage of Coity, Glamorganshire. The lord admiral, Charles, Lord Howard of Effingham (earl of Nottingham from October 1597), was the son of an earlier generation of the same family: his mother was Margaret, daughter of Sir Thomas Gamage of Coity (*TCP*, IX, p. 782; *Commons*, III, p. 384).

[115] Gloucestershire Record Office, Berkeley Castle Muniments, MF 1161, fol. 81ʳ. Cecil's first cousin Sir Edward Hoby was married to Margaret Carey, youngest daughter of Henry 1st Lord Hunsdon (*DNB*, III, p. 979; *Commons*, II, pp. 320–3).

[116] After the death of Walter Devereux near Rouen, his widow married Thomas Sidney, brother of Sir Philip, Sir Robert and Mary, countess of Pembroke. After his death in 1595, she married Cecil's cousin, Thomas Posthumous Hoby, on 9 August 1596 (*ibid.*, pp. 323–4).

[117] In the same vein, the countess of Huntingdon and others at Court were unwilling to lobby for Sir Robert Sidney during the struggle over the wardenship of the Cinque Ports in early 1597 because they perceived that Sir Robert Cecil was opposed to his suit (*HMCD*, II, p. 274).

uninfluential compared to the body of enemies which was beginning to line up against him.[118] This was not crucial when Essex himself had ready access to Elizabeth, but it became critical when he was absent from the Court – especially on military service, which was always prone to create circumstances that angered the queen. In August 1596, Essex's supporters at Court consisted of Worcester, Lord Henry Howard – who had a dubious past and enjoyed limited influence with Elizabeth – and two second-rank courtiers who had once been intimates of Sir Philip Sidney, namely Fulke Greville and Sir Edward Dyer.[119] From the end of that month, Sir William Knollys, newly appointed to the council, could also be added to this group of key supporters. These apart, Essex had to rely on good offices from courtiers who were well disposed towards him but whose willingness to assist him was compromised by competing ties with his enemies, such as the countess of Warwick, the chancellor of the exchequer, Sir John Fortescue,[120] and successive lord keepers, Sir John Puckering[121] and Sir Thomas Egerton.[122] Support from such figures depended upon circumstances and the calculation of whether a specific action might upset Essex's rivals or endanger their own standing with the queen.

By contrast, those most dedicated to Essex's cause, excluding his own servants, were probably men who existed, as it were, on the fringes of the Court. By the latter part of 1593, a recognisable group of such men was conspicuous among Essex's frequent attendants. Occasionally joined by

---

[118] The appearance of faction at Court is discussed below in Chapter 9.

[119] LPL, MS 658, fol. 279ʳ.

[120] *Commons*, II, pp. 148–51. Perhaps in the hope of reinforcing the connection between them, Essex used Fortescue to brief Elizabeth about intelligence received from Anthony Bacon's agents during his absence on the Cadiz expedition (LPL, MS 656, fol. 274ᵛ). However, as chancellor of the exchequer, Fortescue always had to preserve a close working relationship with Lord Treasurer Burghley.

[121] *Commons*, III, pp. 256–8. Essex had been able to count on Puckering because of the close association between them which dated back to Puckering's years as sole justice on the Carmarthen circuit. Many requests by Essex for favours survive among Puckering's papers (especially BL, Harleian MSS 6992–7).

[122] After being sworn as lord keeper on 6 May 1596, Egerton began receiving intelligence reports from Anthony Bacon, who sought to win his support for his brother's bid to succeed Egerton as master of the rolls and as an adherent of Essex. Friendly relations between Egerton and Essex extended to Essex's knighting of Egerton's eldest son on the Azores voyage in 1597 (BL, Add. MS 5482, fol. 16ᵛ). However, Bacon's gleeful talk in September 1596 of a 'worthy correspondency and noble conjunction betwixt Mars & Pallas, betwixt Justice & Valour' (LPL, MS 659, fol. 22ʳ) proved a false hope. In June 1596, Egerton wrote to the archbishop of York about a patronage matter that 'I am unwilling to contend with competitors or to hyndr your grace from pleasuringe any your good frendes who are better hable to stande you in stede then I can be' ((J. Raine, ed.), *The correspondence of Dr Matthew Hutton, archbishop of York ...* (Surtees Society, XVII, London, 1843), p. 110). This also seems to have been Egerton's attitude in politics: unwilling and unable to choose sides, he declined to do so.

visiting soldiers such as Sir Roger Williams and Sir Francis Aleyn,[123] this group centred around Francis Bacon and his house-bound brother Anthony, Anthony Standen and the exiled Spaniard Antonio Perez. These men were characterised not only by a profound attachment to Essex but also by a shared sense of bitterness about their failure to build the kind of careers which they believed their talents merited. Increasingly, they attributed this failure to the ill-will of Burghley, the grand old man of the Court. Talking and drinking together, they constantly compared notes on their unfavourable experiences of the lord treasurer and his son.[124] As a result, they became true Essexian partisans, ferociously loyal to (and dependent upon) the earl, and correspondingly hostile to the Cecils. In the latter respect, they almost certainly outran the feelings of their master and most of his other followers. Nevertheless, the transparency of their feelings magnified the tensions which arose between Essex and the Cecils.

In contrast to his limited power-base of local influence, royal offices and family connections, Essex's following was a far larger and more amorphous phenomenon. In addition to a hard core of servants and close adherents, it embraced many other well-wishers who claimed varying degrees of association with him. Many soldiers pledged themselves to Essex's interests, whilst the godly also often projected their hopes on to him. Judging by the number of recusants and suspected recusants about him, a good many Catholics likewise associated their interests with Essex.[125] Essex's military contacts, in particular, ensured that his following extended across the realm and beyond its borders. On special occasions, the number of followers whom Essex could bring together was very impressive. On military expeditions or great ceremonial occasions, his followers routinely numbered in the hundreds, many of them expensively clothed. Unlike his power-base,

[123] Knighted by Essex in October 1591 (HEH, EL 1045, fol. 1^r), Aleyn had served in the Low Countries and was a close friend of Anthony Bacon. Returning home from the wars in late 1593 in ill-health, his zeal towards 'my earle' (LPL, MS 648, fol. 217^v) was matched by enmity towards Burghley, whom he believed was opposing his renewed employment as a continuation of a vendetta which he had allegedly pursued against Aleyn's father (LPL, MS 650, fol. 50^{r-v}). Aleyn died on 26 March 1595 and was buried in Westminster Abbey (William Camden, *Reges, reginae, nobiles & alii in ecclesia collegiata B. Petri Westmonasterii sepulti, usque ad annum reparatae salutis 1600* (London, 1600, STC no. 4518), sig. I2^r).

[124] See, for example, LPL, MS 650, fols. 80^r–82^v, 226^v; LPL, MS 651, fols. 122^v, 159^r; LPL, MS 652, fol. 287^r.

[125] In addition to Lord Henry Howard, Worcester, Anthony Standen and Antonio Perez, Catholics (or suspected recusants) among Essex's following included Sir Christopher Blount (C. Devlin, *Hamlet's divinity and other essays* (London, 1963), pp. 116–17), Anthony Pembridge (*APC*, XX, *1590–1*, p. 116) and lesser men such as Swinburne, one of Essex's pages (C. Talbot, *Recusant records* (Catholic Record Society, LIII, Miscellanea, 1961 for 1960), p. 152).

Essex's following was suitably prince-like for an aristocrat of his lofty ambition.[126]

Men became followers of Essex for many reasons, but two basic motives can be singled out: the cause with which Essex identified himself so strongly – honour, godliness and bold national endeavour in war – and native self-interest. Both of these were present in differing degrees among Essex's followers. Among soldiers, Essex's martial stance was important in itself, but it also betokened the prospect of honour and employment. By contrast, for those who styled themselves as his followers out in the counties, and even for those who were his servants there, Essex's success in a particular campaign was a matter of great pride, but its primary importance was the extent to which his heightened national prestige might enable them to exert greater local influence in his name.

This powerful element of self-interest among Essex's followers indicates that caution is required in assessing his actions. Too often, modern commentators have simply assumed that Essex himself was necessarily the prime mover in events. Sometimes this was true. More often, however, Essex's conduct responded to initiatives made by his followers. Although Essex may have been eager to become steward of Hereford, he was only able to achieve this goal because certain men there had calculated that his appointment would advance their own interests at the expense of local rivals.[127] Similarly, when Essex became embroiled in a brief, but awkward, exchange with the earl of Derby during the winter of 1593–4, he did so because some of his retainers in Lancashire had deliberately provoked trouble. Former Stanley servants, these men apparently used the protection of the Devereux name to support a longstanding grudge against Ferdinando Stanley, who had recently succeeded as earl of Derby. Because these men wore his cloth, Essex was forced to intervene in this local squabble on their behalf. He only became aware of their previous history after the event.[128]

Essex was frequently forced into action on behalf of men who had deliberately sought his countenance as a means of ensuring his support in

---

[126] Thus, according to Anthony Bacon, before the Cadiz expedition departed, Essex was 'royallie accompanied at Plimouth' (LPL, MS 657, fol. 27^r).

[127] After the demise of Essex in 1601, his adherents in Hereford sought to retain their local ascendancy in other ways. Now discredited and desperate, they tried to induce the young 3rd earl of Pembroke to stand for the stewardship (PRO, C 115, box M, bdle 21, no. 7614). When this failed, they unsuccessfully sought to have their local rivals arrested on false writs of imprisonment for the recovery of debts (ibid., no. 7615).

[128] For this episode, see LPL, MS 3199, pp. 609, 633, 637, 645, 662, 669, 677–8, 681, 685–6, 687, 709; Sheffield Central Library, Bacon Frank MSS, vol. 2, no. 121. The event which triggered this affair was an unlicensed incursion by Essex's retainers into Derby's deer park at Lathom. Among Essex's accounts for 1593–4 is a bill of £4 10s for recognisances for nine gentlemen of Lancashire (Longleat, Devereux MSS, vol. 3, fol. 75^r). This is probably the group which trespassed upon Lathom park.

their local quarrels. This helps to explain why he so regularly signed letters
to law officers requesting special treatment for some individual facing legal
proceedings. However, association with Essex could be a path to advancement as well as a means of protection. As one Pembrokeshire correspondent observed, 'most of those that wears your honour's cloth in this
country is to have your honour's countenance and to be made sheriffs,
lieutenants, stewards, subsidy men, searchers, sergeants on the sea, mus-
termen – everything is fish that comes to their net'.[129] Many men were
anxious to wield such a profitable net.

As the sheer size of his following suggests, Essex was widely perceived as
a very valuable patron. Considering that he was a great man within the
realm who enjoyed frequent and easy access to the queen, and whom her
officials were always anxious to please, this was entirely understandable.
Essex was therefore often surrounded by a sea of would-be suitors begging
favours of every kind. Anthony Standen complained that, 'in Court, ytt is
harde negotiatinge wythe my lord for the multitudes that overwhelme
hym'.[130] Although Essex would not transact serious business in such
circumstances, curious results sometimes came from his rapid-fire response
to minor suits. One letter bearing his signature elicited an indignant
response from his mother. To this, he could only protest that 'I know nott
thatt my hand was sett to any lettre thatt did concerne ether your ladyship
or any towards you. Butt, amongst the infinite lettres which are offred to
us to signe, I might signe some such ere I knew whatt yt was.'[131] Adding to
the protean quality of Essex's patronage was the manner in which he
cheerfully pursued suits on behalf of third parties as a favour to close
friends. Many Norfolk and Hertfordshire suitors gained Essex's furtherance
through Anthony Bacon. Similar eagerness to please a friend explains why
Essex had retainers in Lancashire whose backgrounds he did not adequately know: 'he was by Sir Thomas [Gerard] preferred to me long before,
who is so much my frend as withowt question I sholde take any man upon
his worde'.[132] This exchanging of favours also entailed third parties
supporting suits for Essex. Such indirect patronage is difficult to track and

---

[129] *HMCS*, VIII, p. 423.   [130] LPL, MS 650, fol. 182[r].
[131] Hulton MS (formerly BL, Loan 23), fol. 52[r]. Cf. LPL, MS 652, fol. 118[r]. This problem of
having to sign letters in haste was not unique to Essex. Sir John Stanhope signed a letter to
Gelly Meyrick in September 1596 and added a holograph postscript stating that he could
not vouch for the contents of the letter (Devereux MS 1, fol. 273[r]).
[132] LPL, MS 3199, p. 633. Essex gave a similar response when August Jennings petitioned to
be made one of his retainers: 'yf any body thatt knowes him will geve testimony of his
fittnes I will receave him' (Devereux MS 2, fol. 310[v]). Essex's scrawled response is written
directly beneath a note by Edward Reynoldes on the outer page of the petition which
summarises the salient points of Jennings's plea. This strongly suggests that Essex was too
busy to read the petition itself (*ibid.*, fol. 309[r]).

some of Essex's actions on behalf of his followers will always remain obscure.[133]

Judging by the surviving and visible evidence, Essex had a mixed record of success as a patron. Although no patron could expect to get his way on every occasion, Essex's success rate seems to have varied sharply between suits involving the Court and the central machinery of government and those pertaining to the rest of the realm. In suits among the latter category, Essex was highly successful in advancing the interests of his followers. By his interventions on the council or with the lord keeper, many men were appointed to the kinds of local offices allegedly monopolised by his Pembrokeshire followers. Some of Essex's successes in this sphere were quite striking. In 1594, he won Richard Broughton a place on the council in the marches of Wales and a judgeship on the Anglesey circuit.[134] In 1598, he managed to have Gelly Meyrick appointed as a deputy lieutenant for Radnorshire, despite violent opposition from the earl of Pembroke, the lord president of Wales.[135]

By contrast, Essex was decidedly unsuccessful in seeking to advance ambitious followers to positions at Court or in the small central bureaucracy. Aside from winning a clerkship of the privy council for Thomas Smith, Essex won only a few minor posts for his followers at Court.[136] Moreover, he conspicuously failed in several highly public attempts to assist the preferment of Francis Bacon and Sir Robert Sidney. If he had survived his second embassy to France in 1596, Sir Henry Unton might perhaps have become treasurer of the queen's chamber with Essex's support, but events rendered this an unfulfilled possibility.[137] By any

---

[133] For example, Essex's part in the appointment of Lawrence Lyndley as lieutenant to Capt. Thompson in the Berwick garrison is revealed only because a rival tried to deny Lyndley the place. Hunsdon, who was governor of Berwick, made the appointment as a favour to Essex: PRO, WO 55/1939, fol. 127ʳ.

[134] Broughton had been the overseer of Essex's estate during his minority. Essex and Puckering initially tried to win him a place on the council in the marches of Wales in 1592, but failed. They had more success in 1594, when Broughton also became second justice on the Anglesey circuit. Pembroke apparently acquiesced to both endeavours (BL, Harleian MS 4293, fol. 39ᵛ; BL, Harleian MS 6997, fol. 203r; FSL, L.a.276, 277, 278; Williams, Council in the marches of Wales, p. 284). As noted above, Broughton proved to be a judge of highly dubious character.

[135] Williams, Council in the marches of Wales, pp. 124, 288. Pembroke unsuccessfully backed John Bradshaw for the post. Meyrick's appointment was all the more extraordinary, as Pembroke complained, because men who were servants of anyone other than the queen were supposed to be ineligible even for commissions of the peace.

[136] Wotton, Parallel, p. 10. One such success involved Essex's auditor, Charles Wednester, whom Essex helped to win a lucrative post in the exchequer as auditor of the prests (foreign accounts and first fruits): Commons, III, p. 592.

[137] Rowland Whyte reported that Elizabeth had reaffirmed a promise that Unton would have this post on his return just before Unton set out for France (Collins, Sidney papers, I, p. 382). Unton's high favour with Elizabeth at this time is evidenced by the fact that,

standards, Essex's record as an intercessor for posts around Court was remarkably poor.

This failure was a serious problem for Essex because it was at Court and in the central administration that the profits of place were greatest. The support of successful followers there would also have brought him the most obvious political benefit. However, the sheer attractiveness of such posts suggests one reason why Essex enjoyed little success in these suits: the appeal of a place in the household or related government department generated an enormous amount of competition. In seeking to win the appointment of one of his importunate followers to some county office, Essex had a number of advantages. There were usually very few candidates for the post, and fewer still who had a patron at Court who could match Essex's stature. In the areas of his power-base, he also had the benefit of seeming the natural nominator of local officers. None of these advantages obtained in suits for courtly or bureaucratic posts – candidates for these offices were many and were highly resourceful in cultivating support for their suits. Despite his position as master of the horse, and later master of the ordnance, there was also no real constituency of central government posts about which Essex could easily claim to hold an expert opinion. By contrast, Burghley's long tenure as lord treasurer and his renewed control of the secretaryship gave his recommendations for posts connected with these offices a special weight with Elizabeth.[138]

Although obtaining the favour of the relevant officer of state was a crucial step towards winning a suit at Court, gaining more important positions – and sometimes even relatively minor ones – required a suitor to win as many influential backers as possible. This was a natural response to the heightened competition of these so-called 'bottleneck years' of Elizabeth's reign.[139] The more support a man could muster for his suit, the greater likelihood he had of obtaining it. Essex's patronage was therefore often only one element in a suitor's campaign. Although Leonard Po's long

---

having taken his leave on 17 December 1595, he was summoned back to the royal presence on 21 December. Departing from that audience, 'I was called backe three severall tymes to kisse her Majestie's handes' (BRO, TA 13/3, fol. 2ʳ). For Essex's support for Unton in the contest to win the late Sir Thomas Heneage's offices, see *HMCS*, IV, pp. 68–9 (note that, despite the tentative dating assigned in the calendar, this letter clearly pertains to October 1595).

[138] Thus Henry Savile wrote to Sir Robert Cecil in April 1595 that 'the man that may do most good in this matter is your father, from whom one commendation in cold blood, and seeming to proceed of judgment, shall more prevail with the queen than all the affectionate speech that my lord of Essex can use' (*HMCS*, V, pp. 188–9).

[139] The term is that of Anthony Esler, who uses it with particular reference to the difficulties which a younger generation experienced during the 1590s in trying to assume an active role in public life from an older age cohort (A. Esler, *The aspiring mind of the Elizabethan younger generation* (Durham, N.C., 1966)).

quest to win a practitioner's licence from the Royal College of Physicians depended principally upon the advocacy of Essex, he also managed to gain the endorsement of the whole privy council in February 1592.[140] In May 1597, Sir William Cornwallis sought to gain Sir Robert Cecil's support for his suit to be confirmed as groom-porter, having already won the backing of Sir John Stanhope, Essex and the countess of Warwick.[141] Such tactics can be seen in action time and again. Until at least the mid-1590s, the ferocity of the competition for place at Court produced a striking plurality to the patronage there.

Essex's most spectacular endeavours as a patron, and his most public failures, came on behalf of two of his intimates, Francis Bacon and Sir Robert Sidney. As usual, these suits were initiated not by the earl, but by the ambition of his followers. Essex was only too eager to please his friends, but his affection for them blinded him to the fact that the offices which they sought were beyond their reach. Neither Elizabeth nor Burghley believed that Bacon could make a suitable attorney-general in 1593–4.[142] Sidney's hopes of displacing the Brooke family from the wardenship of the Cinque Ports four years later were equally forlorn.[143] Both suitors probably placed too much store in Essex's readiness to help them. In the case of Bacon, Essex's recent appointment to the council made him over-confident about his ability to sway the queen. By 1597, this excessive confidence had

---

[140] *HMC. Eighth report, appendix i* (London, 1881), p. 228. Po was finally granted his licence in July 1596 (*ibid.*).

[141] PRO, SP 12/263, fol. 105^{r-v}. Remarkably, this seems to be the same man who had pursued a vendetta against Essex in 1595 and 1596 (see below, pp. 320, 357–8). Cornwallis sought support from Essex and the others to counter support given to a rival candidate by Lord Buckhurst.

[142] Despite Essex's persistent belief that he would be able to bring Elizabeth around, it is clear that she thought Bacon too young (LPL, MS 649, fol. 190^r) and insufficiently learned to act as attorney-general: 'in lawe she rather thought yow could make shewe to the uttermoste of your knowledg then that yow wer deepe' (LPL, MS 650, fol. 197^r). Although he sometimes claimed that he was a firm advocate for Bacon, Burghley always doubted that Elizabeth would accept him. As a result, Burghley never consistently supported him in this suit. Bacon himself later sought to shift the blame for his failure away from his own perceived shortcomings. In 1604, he published a defence of his dealings with Essex, in which he quoted Essex as admitting: 'I know you are the least part of your owne matter, but you fare ill because you have chosen mee for your meane and dependance' (Sir Francis Bacon, *Sir Francis Bacon his apologie, in certaine imputations concerning the late earle of Essex* (London, 1604, STC no. 1111), p. 13). In fact, there is no evidence that Essex ever made any such admission. However, in one of his own letters to his brother, Bacon himself complained: '*my conceyte* is that I am the lest part of myne owne matter' (LPL, MS 650, fol. 44^v, emphasis added). Clearly, Francis Bacon tried to edit the historical record to bolster his own reputation.

[143] When Essex earnestly urged Elizabeth on Sidney's behalf, 'her answer was he is too young ... even now I pressed her again, and she answers she would not wrong the now Lord Cobham ... '. As a result, Essex felt the need to stand against Cobham himself (*HMCD*, II, p. 246).

long since gone, but his enthusiasm for Sidney's cause was reinforced by a desire to humiliate the new Lord Cobham. In neither case did Essex show the kind of cold-blooded calculation which Burghley tried to display when he dealt with important suits.

Essex's staunch, even excessive, advocacy of Bacon and Sidney demonstrates how thoroughly notions of friendship, trust and personal honour saturated his world-view. This is all the more striking because Essex received very explicit advice to the contrary from friends like Lord Henry Howard.[144] Essex was well aware of the tactics of patronage and the dangers of recklessly pursuing suits which would bring him little benefit, but he often chose to follow his heart instead of his head. Once committed, it became a point of honour to pursue the suit to its conclusion with all possible vigour: 'my affection leades me and my creditt tyes me to stand stiffely for him';[145] 'I told him I was sorry for the competition, but I must be very partial one way';[146] 'the attorneyship for ffrances ys that I must have, and in that will I spend all my power, might, autorytie and amytie, and with toothe and nayle deffende and procuer the same for hym agaynst whomesoever'.[147] For Essex, upholding one's family, friends and followers in their causes was a matter of political 'credit' and of personal honour. Once he accepted a man as an intimate, Essex also accepted the role of supporting his causes as a duty and expected that man to regard his own causes in the same light. This is why Essex felt able to trust men nominated by Sir Thomas Gerard 'withowt question . . . upon his worde'.

This sort of behaviour may have succeeded in matters of local patronage but, in important suits like those for Bacon and Sidney, it clashed headlong with the courtly world of dissimulation, tactical alliances and timely retreats. Despite emphasising 'friendship' rather than 'lordship' and operating from Court rather than in his own 'country', Essex's behaviour in these suits seems like old-fashioned aristocratic conduct of the sort which still persisted in regions distant from London. This is not surprising. The old evils of embracery and maintenance, which had been spawned by precisely such views, were still practised among his followers in Wales.[148] Essex himself spent his early years in Wales or near its borders, and always surrounded himself with Welshmen. Despite the humanist intellectual superstructure which he learned at Cambridge, the bedrock of Essex's ideas about nobility and appropriate behaviour clearly remained the notions of

---

[144] See, for example, DUL, Howard MS 2, fol. 63^{r-v}.
[145] BL, Harleian MS 6997, fol. 203^r. The man in question is Richard Broughton.
[146] *HMCS*, IV, pp. 68–9.   [147] LPL, MS 650, fol. 81^r.
[148] See, for example, *HMCS*, VIII, p. 423. As noted above, Essex's adherents in Hereford clearly also indulged in similar conduct.

personal honour and of supporting one's friends against local 'enemies' at all costs that he had imbibed during his childhood.[149]

Essex's views are perhaps most readily appreciated by contrast with those of a true politician like Burghley. In bestowing his countenance, as in recommending men's suits, prudence was Burghley's watch-word: 'be not willingly attended or served by kinsmen, friends or men entreated to stay, for they will expect much and do little'.[150] For Essex, such an attitude towards family and friends was quite alien. For Essex, to be his relative or friend was itself recommendation enough. For him, as in so many things, the most vital concern in helping his friends was not politic conduct, but what he perceived to be correct behaviour: adherence to the code of aristocratic honour.

As far as can be gauged without the survival of his check-roll, Essex's household had a composition very much like those of other noblemen of similar rank.[151] Judging by the discharging of twenty men in January 1597 from amongst those 'that attended hym in ordinary' at Court,[152] Essex's train of attendant servants was of considerable size. In keeping with his attitudes towards his family and followers, Essex's household reflected old-style notions of grand aristocratic hospitality.

Perhaps more unusual was the considerable number of foreigners who frequented Essex's household. In part, this reflected his role as the queen's host for visiting dignitaries, which led him to entertain Antonio Perez for two years, as well as numerous French, Portuguese, German and Italian visitors. However, foreigners also served in Essex's household. His wife's chief gentlewoman, Jane Daniel, was the daughter of a Dutch nobleman,[153]

---

[149] Here it is instructive to recall the self-assured young boy who received Edward Waterhouse when the latter brought orders from Burghley in November 1576. After reading Burghley's letter, Essex's first action was to consider 'his father's principall freendes in Wales' and carefully to compose individual letters to them (BL, Lansdowne MS 23, fol. 190ʳ). Significantly, Essex referred to 'my contryman Meryck' in 1579 (H. E. Malden (ed.), 'Devereux papers, with Richard Broughton's memoranda (1575–1601)', *Camden Miscellany*, n.s., 13 (1923), p. 21).

[150] L. B. Wright (ed.), *Advice to a son: precepts of Lord Burghley, Sir Walter Raleigh and Francis Osborne* (Ithaca, NY, 1962), p. 11.

[151] The structure of a nobleman's household was supposed to conform to certain conventions which varied according to his rank. See, for example, the notes made by the herald, Francis Thynne, in April 1590 (BL, Stowe MS 1047, fol. 316ᵛ). For a contemporary description of the various functions of the men in a nobleman's household, see S. D. Scott (ed.), '"A booke of orders and rules" of Anthony Viscount Montague in 1595', *Sussex Archaeological Collections, relating to the history and antiquities of the county* 7 (1854), pp. 173–212.

[152] *HMCD*, II, p. 233.

[153] PRO, SP 46/50(i), pp. 41, 49, 51. Jane Daniel was sufficiently trusted to have custody of the countess of Essex's jewels but later acted as an accomplice in her husband's attempt to blackmail the countess after Essex's death. For her husband and his chequered career, see

and one of Essex's pages was Balthasar van Weteren, whose brother attended upon Count Maurice of Nassau.[154] Foreign dignitaries sometimes tried to place acquaintances with Essex. In late 1598, the mayor of Boulogne asked Essex to take his younger brother as a page, while Dom Emmanuel requested that he take on one of his followers.[155] For his part, Essex provided an array of servants to accompany Perez when he returned to France in 1595.[156] Essex also sought to place his cousin, Robert Vernon, in the household of the duke of Bouillon, but Henri IV would not hear of this and insisted that Vernon stay with him instead.[157] As with Leicester before him, Essex's commitment to Continental affairs had a distinctly human face.

Another conspicuous group who flocked around Essex were university men. Given the expectation that Elizabethan gentlemen should be well-read and Essex's own lengthy sojourn at Cambridge, this is perhaps not surprising. For their part, academics have always been eager for patronage from the great and the good. However, Essex's involvement with scholars went well beyond conventional posturing. Although his claim that he was 'more inflamed with the love of knowledge then with love of fame' was somewhat exaggerated, Essex demonstrated 'bookishnesse from my very childhoode' and saw scholars as being equally natural companions for himself as soldiers.[158] They and their skills reflected his own enduring commitment to the humanist beliefs and practices which he imbibed at Cambridge and sustained thereafter. If notions of martial honour and personal loyalty appealed to Essex's heart, the ideas and companionship of intellectuals appealed to his head. Both were fundamentally important aspects of his character.

Essex employed a number of academics as close servants. Robert Wright,

---

G. Chesters, 'John Daniel of Daresbury, 1544–1610', *Transactions of the Historic Society of Lancashire and Cheshire* 118 (1967), pp. 1–17.

[154] Balthasar served Essex from 1595 until mid-1598, when Jan van Duyvenvoord requested his recall to the Low Countries (*HMCS*, VIII, p. 213).

[155] *Ibid.*, pp. 515, 390.

[156] Essex provided at least eight servants for Perez, including a bodyguard, secretary, a post, various minor servants and possibly a cook (Ungerer, II, pp. 1–11).

[157] Vernon's mother was Elizabeth Devereux, Essex's paternal aunt. Essex sent Vernon to France with Robert Naunton in January 1596. However, Henri's determination to keep him at Court stymied Essex's plans for him to learn about France and war under Bouillon (Ungerer, II, pp. 76–7, 97; *HMCS*, VI, pp. 46–7). Despite this, Vernon and Naunton travelled with Bouillon's train during his trip to England and the Low Countries to seal the Triple Alliance between August and November (Ungerer, II, p. 102; *HMCS*, VI, pp. 384, 498). Although he enjoyed close contact with Bouillon, Vernon stayed with the king until April 1598 (*HMCS*, VIII, p. 114; *ibid.*, XIV, pp. 25–6, 58). He and Naunton returned home by way of the Low Countries, arriving home by October 1598 (*HMCS*, VIII, pp. 346, 418).

[158] *Apologie*, sig. A1ᵛ.

his old tutor, remained with Essex until he was preferred to the post of the clerk of the queen's stables.[159] Thomas Smith, a fellow of Christ Church, Oxford, and university orator there, became Essex's secretary about 1585.[160] He was later joined by Edward Reynoldes, another Oxonian, who became Essex's 'confident' or personal secretary.[161] When Essex won Smith a place as clerk to the privy council in mid-1595, he replaced him with a full-blown secretariat. Henry Wotton had done well at Oxford and had spent several years abroad. His first-hand knowledge of Germany and Italy encouraged Essex to employ him even before Smith's advancement was certain.[162] Henry Cuffe was regius professor of Greek at Oxford and a fellow of Merton College. William Temple, the only Cambridge man in the group, was a fellow at King's and had been secretary to Sir Philip Sidney

[159] The precise date of Wright's preferment remains uncertain because so little of the paperwork from the royal stables for this period has survived. He was clearly acting as clerk of the stables by mid-1595 (BL, Add. MS 5750, fols. 142^v–143^r, 155^r). In the late 1580s and early 1590s, Wright was intimately involved in Essex's financial affairs and regularly acted as an assignee in property transactions for Essex. During this period, Wright was sometimes described as 'the earle's stuard' (e.g. W. A. Leighton, 'Early chronicles of Shrewsbury, 1372–1603', *Transactions of the Shropshire Archaeological and Natural History Society* 3 (1880), p. 326).

[160] For more detailed discussion of Smith and Essex's other secretaries, see P. E. J. Hammer, 'The uses of scholarship: the secretariat of Robert Devereux, 2nd earl of Essex, c.1585–1601', *EHR* 109 (1994), pp. 26–51. Smith was almost certainly recommended to Essex by Leicester, who was chancellor of Oxford and who had arranged for Smith's appointment as university orator after Arthur Atey left to become one of Leicester's own secretaries in 1582 (*ibid.*, p. 27 n. 3)

[161] Reynoldes may have entered Essex's service about 1588 as a result of contacts made during his previous work as secretary to Sir Amias Paulet, who acted as gaoler to Mary Queen of Scots at Essex's house at Chartley (*ibid.*, p. 28). However, it is also conceivable that Reynoldes came to Essex's attention through the mediation of Robert Wright. While a young fellow at All Souls, Reynoldes became friendly with Richard Madox, a more senior fellow in that college, whom Leicester sponsored on a voyage to the Moluccas in 1582. Madox was also a close friend of Wright, having been schoolboys at Shrewsbury together (E. S. Donno (ed.), *An Elizabethan in 1582: the diary of Richard Madox, fellow of All Souls* (Hakluyt Society, 2nd ser., CXLVII, 1976), pp. 76, 78, 91, 119).

[162] Wotton's experiences may have encouraged him to write a detailed survey of European states and their recent histories for Essex which was subsequently published as *The state of Christendom: or, a most exact and curious discovery of many passages, and hidden mysteries of the times* (London, 1657, Wing no. W 3654). Internal evidence shows that this was composed between February 1594 and February 1595 – precisely when Wotton returned to England and successfully sought employment with Essex. None of the surviving manuscripts of the work is in Wotton's hand, but this is true for all of Wotton's other prose works as well (P. Beal (ed.), *Index of English literary manuscripts. I, 1450–1625, Part ii: Douglas-Wyatt* (London and New York, 1980), pp. 562, 586–7, items WoH 296–301). Although the identity of the writer remains uncertain, Wotton seems the most probable author. Given its date and subject matter, it seems likely that 'The state of Christendom' was originally written as an elaborate show-case of the writer's knowledge and talents in order to secure employment from Essex. The dating and authorship of this work are discussed in Smith, *Life and letters of Wotton*, (2 vols., Oxford, 1907), II, pp. 455–9.

and William Davison. Both Cuffe and Temple enjoyed substantial reputations as scholars. Cuffe was well known for his exposition of classical texts, whilst Temple had won international renown as an exponent of Ramist logic.[163] By the end of 1595, Essex had a secretariat – Reynoldes, Wotton, Cuffe and Temple – which embodied a pooling of intellectual talent unmatched by any employer except Elizabeth herself. Together with the secret correspondences maintained by his friend Anthony Bacon, this secretariat equipped Essex with an administrative nexus which matched his ambitions as a statesman on the European stage.

Essex also enjoyed close dealings with many other academics. Although a Cambridge man, Essex had strong associations with Oxford because of his stepfather's long tenure as chancellor there. The rowdy behaviour of disappointed MAs when Elizabeth forced the university to elect Buckhurst as chancellor instead of Essex in December 1591 testified to the continuance of Leicesterian sentiments and Essex's own growing reputation at Oxford.[164] Although Essex had close dealings with individual scholars like Alberico Gentili and John Rainoldes,[165] he also had especially powerful connections with Christ Church[166] and Merton

---

[163] Hammer, 'Uses of scholarship', p. 31 n. 3. Essex had received instruction in Ramist logic at Cambridge, possibly from Temple himself. Essex had a Ramist tract dedicated to him as early as 1583: Richard Harvey, *Ephemeron, sive paean, in gratiam perpurgatae reformataque dialecticae* (London, 1583, STC no. 12912). Essex's use of Ramist logic can be seen in the way he sought to defend his conduct in Ireland in 1599 by framing his argument according to a dichotomous table, a quintessentially Ramist device (BL, Cotton MS Julius F VI, fol. 133ʳ: this is a copy endorsed 'ex autographo Roberti comitis Essexiae'). On Ramism, its strong association with Protestant thought and its general intellectual context, see L. Jardine, 'The place of dialectic teaching in sixteenth-century Cambridge', *Studies in the Renaissance* 21 (1974), pp. 31–62; W. J. Ong, 'Ramus: rhetoric and the pre-Newtonian mind', in A. S. Downer (ed.), *English Institute essays, 1952* (New York, 1954), pp. 138–70; J. M. Levine, *Humanism and history: origins of modern English historiography* (Ithaca, N.Y. and London, 1987), ch. 5.

[164] Oxford University Archives, NEP/Supra/Register L, fol. 252ʳ.

[165] In recognition of Essex's continuing support for his divinity lectures, Rainoldes dedicated to Essex his monumental *De Romanae ecclesiae idolatria* (Oxford, 1596, STC no. 20606), which has been described by one modern scholar as 'undoubtedly one of the great unknown Elizabethan books' (J. W. Binns, *Intellectual culture in Elizabethan and Jacobean England: the Latin writings of the age* (Leeds, 1990], p. 328). Essex maintained his contact with Rainoldes. In April 1600, while under house arrest, he repeatedly asked permission for Rainoldes to visit him (Cecil MSS 78/93, 79/5 (pr. *HMCS*, X, pp. 124, 127)). Like Gentili, Rainoldes had previously been a protégé of Leicester: E. Rosenberg, *Leicester: patron of letters* (New York, 1955), pp. 239–41.

[166] Dr William James, dean of Christ Church between 1584 and 1596, was a chaplain to Leicester. The college had played host to a string of students associated with the earl, including Philip and Robert Sidney, Robert Dudley (Leicester's illegitimate son), Baldwin Meetkerke (a Dutchman whose education Leicester paid for) and Essex's younger brother, Walter. Essex's chief contact with Christ Church was through his secretary, Thomas Smith. The following students and fellows can also be associated with Essex in some way:

College.[167] Henry Savile, the autocratic warden of Merton and probably the greatest scholar of his time,[168] became an intimate of Essex and gradually supplanted Thomas Smith as his chief agent at the university.[169] During the middle years of the decade, Essex mounted a long and acrimonious, but ultimately successful, campaign to make Savile provost of Eton.[170] The extent of Essex's growing web of contacts at Oxford can be gauged by the scholars who performed during the opening days of Elizabeth's visit to Oxford in September 1592: spearheaded by Savile and Smith, almost all of them already had an association with Essex or developed one soon afterwards.[171] Most of the honorary degrees conferred

William Gager, George Peele, Lord Richard Bourke (later earl of Clanricarde), Henry Danvers, Toby Matthew Jr, Robert Gentili and Abraham Colfe.

[167] Merton in this period was very much Henry Savile's college. Henry Cuffe was a protégé of Savile. Essex chose Merton for his cousin Robert Vernon in 1594 and later entrusted the education of his own son and heir to Savile (in his other capacity as provost of Eton). In August 1605, Essex's son (by then restored as 3rd earl of Essex) was created an Oxford MA through Merton. Other fellows and students of Merton associated with Essex include Thomas Bodley and Henry Neville.

[168] Savile exercised the queen in Greek and was well known to Burghley, who acted as his patron on several occasions. His friends included William Camden, Robert Cotton, and many other scholars in England and abroad. His intellectual interests and expertise encompassed the classics, mathematics and astronomy, medieval monastic histories, and editing biblical and patristic texts. He was knighted by James I and endowed the Savilian chairs of astronomy and geometry at Oxford. For Savile, see *DNB*, XVII, pp. 856–9; *Al. Oxon.*, IV, p. 1319; Wood, II, cols. 310–17; M. Feingold, *The mathematician's apprenticeship: science, universities and society in England, 1560–1640* (Cambridge, 1984), esp. pp. 124–31; J. R. Highfield, 'An autograph commonplace book of Sir Henry Savile', *Bodleian Library Record* 7 (1963), pp. 73–83; G. C. Brodrick, *Memorials of Merton College* (Oxford Historical Society, IV, 1885), pp. 60ff, 166–7. In 1595, Essex stood as godfather to Savile's son, sending Sir John Wingfield to the ceremony at Oxford as his proxy (Devereux MS 3, fol. 75ᵛ).

[169] Savile's reach also extended to Cambridge: when he wanted preferment for Dr Mountford's son at Cambridge in 1599, Essex wrote to Savile to enlist his assistance (PRO, SP 12/273, fol. 115ʳ).

[170] Although Savile was determined to win the post, Essex found the suit very difficult because Savile was not in holy orders and the fellows of Eton did not want him. Begun in 1594, the suit did not succeed until 1596 and required support from Burghley, Cecil and the countess of Warwick. See H. C. Maxwell Lyte, *A history of Eton College, 1440–1910* (4th edn, London, 1911), pp. 180–5.

[171] Elizabeth's visit to Oxford is described in an account by Philip Stringer (C. Plummer (ed.), *Elizabethan Oxford* (Oxford Historical Society, VIII, p. 1887), pp. 245–61; Nichols, *Progress*, III, pp. 149–60). In addition to Savile and Smith, the following men were named by Stringer as playing key roles in the ceremonies of the first two days, 22–3 September (Plummer, (ed.), *Elizabethan Oxford* pp. 250–4), and can be associated with Essex: Thomas Savile (Henry's brother), Ralph Winwood, Henry Cuffe, Francis Sidney, John Buckeridge and John Spenser. Essex himself was singled out for praise (together with Burghley, Hunsdon and Howard) in a speech by Thomas Savile on 25 September (*ibid.*, p. 256). A similar speech by Henry Savile three days earlier touched on the thesis 'Rei militaris et philosophiae studia in una republica vigere' and pushed the kind of bellicose

during the queen's visit also went to men who were close friends of Essex.[172]

Many of Essex's contacts in Cambridge, such as Andrew Downes, Richard Harvey and William Whitaker, dated back to the days when he was a student there. However, his chief liaison with Cambridge was probably Lionel Sharpe, one of his chaplains and a fellow of King's.[173] Sharpe played a crucial role in recruiting the young John Coke as an 'in-house' scholar for Essex's friend Fulke Greville,[174] and acted as Essex's intermediary over a fellowship at Eton in 1595.[175] Sharpe also seems to have been a powerful advocate for his master when Essex sought leases of college lands for his friends and followers.[176] After the crown and the church, college estates were the largest and most accessible source of land and money for men of influence. Like other councillors and leading courtiers,[177] Essex frequently sought leases and other forms of patronage from colleges, and often with success.[178] This was an important reason why Essex and other courtiers eagerly cultivated links with the universities.

---

anti-Spanish line espoused by Essex (*ibid.*, pp. 263–71; Nichols, *Progress*, III, pp. 161–7). The text of this speech was subsequently circulated in manuscript form.

[172] Among those who received honorary MAs on 27 September 1592 were the earls of Worcester, Cumberland and Pembroke (with whom Essex had not yet fallen out), Sir John Wingfield, Sir Thomas Coningsby, Sir William Knollys, Edward Darcy, Richard Bracken-bury, Anthony Ashley and the French ambassador, Beauvoir la Nocle (Wood, II, *Fasti*, cols. 260–1).

[173] For Sharpe, see *DNB*, XVII, pp. 1349–50.

[174] P. E. J. Hammer, 'The earl of Essex, Fulke Greville, and the employment of scholars', *Studies in Philology* 91 (1994), pp. 167–80.

[175] The fellowship became vacant after the death of Dr William Whitaker and was in the gift of the bishop of Winchester. The bishop had already promised the place to Essex but Burghley wrote in support of a rival candidate. Sharpe informed the bishop that Burghley and Essex 'hathe had conference' on the matter and agreed that Essex's man should have the fellowship (BL, Lansdowne MS 79, fol. 124ʳ).

[176] A biographical notice of Sharpe written in the 18th century bears a telling note: 'See King's College ledger books where I am inform'd Dr L. Sharpe appears to be too obsequious to his patron Robert earl of Essex in prejudice to our revenue' (College Archives, King's College, Cambridge, Allen's 'Skeleton Collegii Regis', vol. 2 (ad annum 1600), pp. 931–2). After Essex became chancellor of Cambridge in September 1598 (CUL, MS Mm.i.35, pp. 369–72), Sharpe became increasingly important as the university's liaison with Essex and the Court (*ibid.*, pp. 381ff).

[177] See, for example, the comments of Dr John Cowell, a fellow of King's College, Cambridge: *HMCS*, IV, pp. 611–12. Leicester, in particular, seems to have been adept at tapping into college estates (J. McConica (ed.), *The history of the University of Oxford. III. The collegiate university* (Oxford, 1986), pp. 430–1).

[178] For example, Essex won a lease of parsonages in Northumberland from Merton College, Oxford, which were assigned to Sir Robert Carey (Cecil MS 139/213 (pr. *HMCS*, XI, p. 570); PRO, SP 12/274, fols. 32ʳ–33ᵛ). A suit from Essex presumably explains why Christ Church granted a dubious lease of tithe corn from the rectories of Runcorn, Frodesham and Budworth to John Daniel of Daresbury (Christ Church, Oxford, MS XX.C.2, p. 723). Essex also succeeded in thwarting Sir John Perrot's intention of conveying parsonages in Carmarthenshire to his illegitimate son James by making them

Oxford and Cambridge also offered opportunities for prestige and display. This was perhaps most dramatically illustrated when Essex led a cavalcade of nobles and gentlemen to Cambridge for the BA Commencement at the end of February 1595.[179] The visitors were entertained with several plays at Trinity and Queens', and a series of academic disputations which involved the university's best young scholars. After the Commencement itself, a special congregation was held at which more than a dozen of Essex's guests were awarded honorary degrees.[180] The noblemen were so pleased by this honour that they left the ceremony in order to re-enter wearing the garb to which their new status entitled them.[181] The following morning, most of the party attended an important sermon by Dr Whitaker,[182] before giving substantial rewards to the university bedells.[183] The whole three-day visit was clearly stage-managed by Essex, right down to the disputation questions which he had sent up in advance.[184]

In return for such lavish spectacles and leases of college lands, university men sought political support for their colleges and the hope of advancement outside the university. Essex conspicuously gratified such aspirations,

over to one Oxford and one Cambridge college. Essex 'was a meane that theise colledges should surrender up theyr interest and trust committed unto them' so that the queen could grant a lease of these parsonages to his sister Dorothy (Cecil, MS 123/138 (pr. *HMCS*, XIX, p. 391)).

[179] The three days of ceremonies are described in CUL, MS Mm.i.43, pp. 529–34.

[180] MAs were awarded to: the earls of Shrewsbury and Rutland, Lords Cromwell, Sheffield and Compton, Sir Charles Cavendish, Sir Edward Wotton, Sir William Bowes, Sir Ferdinando Gorges, Sir Nicholas Clifford, Sir Conyers Clifford, Sir Clement Higham, Sir Thomas Read and Sir George Saville (*ibid.*, pp. 530–1). Another list of the honorands, 'found among the graces of 1594–5', is attached to the back cover of Cambridge University Archives, Grace Book E. This adds the names of Antonio Perez and Giovanni Battista Basadonna, omits Sir Clement Higham, and (erroneously) replaces the name of Sir George Saville with that of Mr Fulke Greville.

[181] 'Memorandum: That the nobell men came in sine habitu at the first, but being in the howse they desired to come in in ther habites, the which they presently dyd' (CUL, MS Mm.i.43, p. 531). This motion was clearly not anticipated by the university officials.

[182] Whitaker's sermon of 27 February 1595 was later printed at the end of his posthumous *Praelectiones ... in quibus tractatur controversia de conciliis* (Cambridge, 1600, STC no. 25367), sig. X6ʳ–Y5ᵛ. This source confirms that Sir George Saville was among the visitors and that Essex's party also included several friends who did not receive degrees during this visit: Lords Mountjoy, Burgh and Rich, and Sir Robert Sidney (*ibid.*, sig. X6ʳ; CUL, MS Mm.i.43, p. 529). Whitaker's sermon was not merely a social event but a highly public condemnation of anti-Calvinist theologians in Cambridge (P. Lake, *Moderate puritans and the Elizabethan church* (Cambridge, 1982), pp. 204–5).

[183] CUL, MS Mm.i.43, p. 531. On 1 March, Essex also made a very substantial donation to the fund for repairing the steeple of the university church, St Mary the Great: £10 10s. By contrast, the church received only 40s from Shrewsbury, 20s from Rutland, 40s from Rich, 20s from Compton, 20s from Sir Robert Sidney and 10s from Sir George Saville (J. E. Foster (ed.), *Churchwardens' accounts of St Mary the Great, Cambridge, from 1504 to 1635* (Cambridge Antiquarian Society, octavo ser., XXXV, 1905), p. 242).

[184] 'My Lord of Essex sent downe philosophy questions, written in his owne hand, the which wear disputed at severall tymes' (CUL, MS Mm.i.43, p. 530).

making a series of high-profile appointments which raised expectations in both universities. In addition to the men he employed as secretaries, Essex chose Dr Henry Hawkyns,[185] Robert Naunton[186] and Thomas Chaloner[187] as key agents overseas. His chaplains included well-known university men such as Lionel Sharpe, John Buckeridge[188] and William Alabaster.[189] After his visit to Cambridge in 1595, Essex chose two actors who had performed at Queens' College to participate in his Accession Day entertainment that year.[190] (Oxford scholars had featured in his show for the previous Accession Day.[191]) Essex also seemed a generous master to the men he picked out, as the rise of humble men like Robert Wright and Henry Cuffe testified. In contrast to the alleged coldness of Burghley and Cecil,[192] Essex

---

[185] Hawkyns was a fellow of Peterhouse, Cambridge. In 1586, he was granted leave to accompany Lord Zouche 'for conference in learning in the time of his aboad beyond the seas' (Peterhouse, Old Register, p. 323). Hawkyns subsequently studied civil law at several Italian and German universities. After his return in 1590, he won the patronage of Archbishop Whitgift and was employed in London 'in publick matters of state' (P. E. J. Hammer, 'Essex and Europe: evidence from confidential instructions by the earl of Essex, 1595–6', *EHR* 111 (1996) p. 361–2).

[186] Naunton migrated from Trinity College to Trinity Hall in 1592. He became university orator at Cambridge on 27 July 1594 and did not relinquish the post until 7 December 1611 (Cambridge University Archives, CUR 45, fol. 5^r; Ungerer, II, p. 109). Essex stifled an attempt to replace Naunton as orator during his long sojourn in France (CUL, MS Mm.i.35, pp. 373–4). As orator, Naunton was intimately involved in Essex's visit of February 1595 (CUL, MS Mm.i.43, p. 531). Since Naunton did not know Essex through their shared affiliation with Trinity College (Ungerer, II, p. 81), this visit apparently first brought them into contact. Naunton later married Essex's niece, Penelope Perrot, the daughter of Essex's sister Dorothy and Sir Thomas Perrot. For Naunton, see Hammer, 'Essex and Europe', pp. 365ff.

[187] A fellow of Magdalen College, Oxford, Chaloner had been the tutor to Leicester's illegitimate son, Robert Dudley (*DNB*, III, p. 1367; *Commons*, I, pp. 558–9; *Al. Oxon.*, I, p. 256).

[188] Buckeridge was a fellow of St John's College, Oxford, and ultimately became president of that college. He was the fourth (and last) replier to Thomas Smith in the disputation held before Elizabeth and her entourage at the university church, St Mary's, Oxford, on 23 September 1592 (Plummer, (ed.), *Elizabethan Oxford*, p. 253). For Buckeridge, see *DNB*, III, pp. 200–1; Wood, II, cols. 506–10, 881.

[189] Alabaster was a fellow of Trinity College, Cambridge, where he had matriculated several years after Essex's departure. He was the author of the much praised and extremely bloodthirsty Latin play, *Roxana*, which was first performed at Trinity about 1592 (Binns, *Intellectual culture*, pp. 122–3, 131–3). During Essex's 1595 visit, he led off a disputation on Thursday 26 February, defending three propositions which Essex had drafted. For Alabaster's turbulent life, see *DNB*, I, pp. 211–12; G. M. Story and H. Gardner (eds.), *The sonnets of William Alabaster* (London, 1959), pp. xi–xxiii; R. V. Caro, 'William Alabaster: rhetor, meditator, devotional poet' (2 parts), *Recusant History* 19 (1988), pp. 62–79, 155–70.

[190] George Meriton and George Montaigne, both fellows of Queens' College, Cambridge. The third academic involved in the entertainment was Toby Matthew Jr, a fellow of Christ Church, Oxford (A. H. Nelson (ed.), *Records of early English drama: Cambridge* (2 vols., Toronto, 1989), I, pp. 355–6; *ibid.*, II, p. 1228).

[191] Devereux MS 3, fol. 90^v.

[192] Younger scholars believed that Burghley and Cecil were deliberately unwilling to

sought to be a great patron of scholars, just as he was the great patron of soldiers.

Essex sought more than mere reputation through his patronage of scholars. In keeping with his humanist training, Essex believed that intellectual study was a purposive action which brought tangible benefits. Like Leicester and others before him,[193] Essex sought to harness the expertise of selected scholars for his own political benefit. Just as he sponsored the intellectual development or 'inablynge' of travellers to the Continent such as Hawkyns, Naunton and Vernon,[194] so he applied the same principle to himself at home. As a councillor, general and would-be statesman, Essex recognised that he needed to develop judgement and discernment beyond the bounds of his own experience and years. Accordingly, he hungered for news from his agents overseas: Hawkyns and other travellers were required to write detailed surveys of foreign states 'for your good and my instruction'.[195] He received detailed briefings from Antonio Perez, whose inside knowledge of the Spanish empire and European affairs provided Essex, Elizabeth and others with new insights into the world of their foe.[196] Essex also sought guidance from history, 'ffor rules and

encourage men of promise. A Bohemian nobleman who visited Oxford and Cambridge recorded a common criticism of Burghley: 'People say of him that "after climbing the ladder of success, he pulled it well out of everyone else's reach"' (G. W. Groos (ed.), *The diary of Baron Waldstein: a traveller in Elizabethan England* (London, 1981), p. 111). Similar feelings of disappointment can be seen in a jaundiced comment about the kind of men whom the Cecils employed as secretaries: 'base penn clarkes, that can do nothing but write as they are bidden, or some mecanicall dunce that cannot conceive his master's drifts and policies'. Allegedly, 'this was first brought [about] by the old lord threasurer, of whom it was written that he was like an aged tree that letts none growe which nere him planted bee, and it is well followed by his sonne at this day and by other that are eius farinae' (Thomas Wilson, 'The state of England, anno dom. 1600', ed. F. J. Fisher, *Camden Miscellany* 16 (1936), p. 42).

193 For some of Leicester's coterie of experts, see D. C. Peck (ed.), *Leicester's commonwealth: the copy of a letter written by a Master of Art of Cambridge (1584) and related documents* (Athens, Ohio and London, 1985), p. 116. Sir Walter Ralegh and the earl of Northumberland employed Thomas Harriot to instruct them in mathematics, navigation and other matters. Ralegh received specific instruction from Harriot in order to prepare for sea voyages in 1584 and 1595 (J. W. Shirley, *Thomas Harriot: a biography* (Oxford, 1983), p. 86; also his 'Sir Walter Ralegh and Thomas Harriot', in his (ed.), *Thomas Harriot: Renaissance scientist* (Oxford, 1974), pp. 17–18).

194 For the 'inablynge' of Hawkyns and others, see above, p. 194. Essex's hopes of instilling a desire for self-improvement in Vernon were not confined to his Continental tour. In 1596, Vernon wrote to thank Essex for his 'honorable disposition towardes mee eaven since the verie beginninge of my childenhoode untill nowe and those often honorable spiches and incorigments of mouthe delivered unto me & when I was at universitie by your honorable letters but espetially your lordshippes laste spiches unto mee att my departure outte of Ingland' (Cecil MS 174/41 (pr. *HMCS*, VI, p. 498)).

195 ULL, MS 187, fol. 10ᵛ (pr. Hammer, 'Essex and Europe', pp. 368, 375).

196 PRO, SP 12/245, fols. 59ʳ, 113ʳ; LPL, MS 649, fol. 426ʳ. Notes survive which outline three briefings by Perez for Elizabeth (Ungerer, I, pp. 94–8, 98–9, 103–8) and one for Burghley

patternes of pollecy are aswell learned out of olde Greeke and Romayne storyes, as out of of states which are at thys daye'.[197] Lord Henry Howard, himself a former Cambridge don,[198] wrote advices for Essex on political conduct studded with quotes and references from Thucydides and Livy.[199] With Cuffe[200] and Savile, Essex scrutinised ancient history for insight into war and politics. As the epistle to the reader which prefaced Savile's 1591 translation of Tacitus stated: 'in Galba, thou maiest learne that a good prince governed by evill ministers is as dangerous as if hee were evill himselfe … by Vitellius, that he that hath no vertue can never bee happy …'.[201] More subtly, this work yoked together Tacitean accounts of Roman history with notions of political 'virtue' derived from Machiavelli and

---

(ibid., pp. 100–2) in 1595. Perez claimed that he had been asked to brief the queen, 'writing such principall points of policy fitting her present estate as to his [i.e. Perez's] judgement should seem most convenient'. Elizabeth allegedly kept the papers in a cabinet and wore the key around her neck. After the accession of James I, Perez wanted a guarantee that these papers would remain secure or be burned (ibid., II, p. 234). Similar notes for briefings of Essex were probably destroyed, but his experience with Perez can be gauged in his advice to Robert Naunton: 'by conversinge sometymes with Signor Perez yow will fynde both delighte and profuite, ffor he is sweete of nature and ripe of judgemente, but yow will remember he is a Spaniarde and therfore punctilious, olde and infortunate, and therfore by accidente, thoughe not by nature, sometymes jelous and ympatiente, all of which a lyttle extraordinary respecte will healpe' (ULL, MS 187, fol. 12ᵛ (pr. Hammer, Essex and Europe', p. 377)).

[197] ULL, MS 187, fol. 13ᵛ (pr. Hammer, Essex and Europe', p. 378). The same point is spelled out in Essex's much-circulated letter of advice to the earl of Rutland: 'above all other books be conversant in the histories, for they will best instruct you in matter, moral, military and politic, by which, and in which, you must ripen your and settle your judgement' (Spedding, Bacon letters, II, p. 12). The special practical value of history was so widely accepted among Essex's contemporaries that Sir Philip Sidney felt the need specifically to argue against it in his apologia for poetry (Sir Philip Sidney, A defence of poetry (ed. J. A. van Dorsten, Oxford, 1966), pp. 35–8). According to Thomas Blundeville, Leicester also used 'to delyght moste in reading of hystories … not as many doe, to passe away the tyme, but to gather thereof such judgement and knowledge as you may therby be the more able, as well to direct your private actions, as to give counsell lyke a most prudent counseller in publyke causes' (H. G. Dick, 'Thomas Blundeville's The true order and methode of wryting and reading Hystories [1574]', Huntingdon Library Quarterly 3 (1940), pp. 154–5).

[198] Howard studied at King's College, before moving to Trinity Hall to study civil law in 1564. In the late 1560s, he held the post of reader in rhetoric and lectured on natural philosophy and civil law (Peck, Northampton, p. 8).

[199] DUL, Howard MS 2.

[200] For Cuffe's exposition of a passage of Lucan with Essex and of Aristotle's Politics with the earls of Southampton and Rutland, see Hammer, 'Uses of scholarship', pp. 49–50.

[201] [Henry Savile], The ende of Nero and beginninge of Galba. Fower bookes of the Histories of Cornelius Tacitus. The life of Agricola ([London], 1591, STC no. 23642), sig. A3ʳ. The manuscript of this work, cut up into mock page-proofs and bearing final amendments in the hands of Henry Savile and his brother Thomas, is BLO, MS Eng.hist.d.240. The manuscript bears the signature of Dr William James, vice-chancellor of Oxford, presumably authorising the book for printing (BLO, MS Eng.hist.d.240, fol. 13ᵛ). The address to the reader is not included in the manuscript, suggesting it was added at the last minute.

proponents of Huguenot resistance theory to impart lessons about the importance of military commanders making principled interventions in the political life of their state.[202] This was meat and drink to Essex, whose profound commitment to martial virtue and service to the nation tied in with an acute sense of his own significance. Although Savile's work was dedicated to Elizabeth, its contents clearly flowed from study with Essex. Some contemporaries believed that Essex himself composed the book's epistle to the reader.[203] Essex certainly wrote his own notes on Tacitus[204] and many of his closest associates were devotees of the Roman historian's themes and style.[205]

Although only fragments of evidence survive,[206] it is clear that Essex

[202] D. Womersley, 'Sir Henry Savile's translation and the political interpretation of Elizabethan texts', *Review of English Studies*, n.s., 42 (1991), pp. 313–42. Malcolm Smuts has observed that the period of Roman history covered in Savile's book – which involved the crisis of royal power and civil war between rival claimants to imperial status – was directly relevant to contemporary events in France, where Henri IV was still barely clinging to his throne. This is a significant point and, given Essex's earnest espousal of Henri's cause during this time, must indicate another reason for his keen interest in this work (M. Smuts, 'Court-centred politics and the uses of Roman historians, c.1590–1630', in K. Sharpe and P. Lake (eds.) *Culture and politics in early Stuart England*, (Stanford, 1993), pp. 27–8).

[203] C. H. Herford and P. Simpson (eds.) *Ben Jonson[: life and works]* (11 vols., Oxford, 1925–52), I, p. 142; Edmund Bolton, 'Hypercritica; or a rule of judgment for writing, or reading our historys . . . ' in, J. Haslewood (ed.), *Ancient critical essays upon English poets and poesy* (London, 1815), p. 254.

[204] Ironically, Essex's bitter enemy, Henry Lord Cobham, asked to borrow 'a paper boke of my lord of Essex notations of Cornelius Tacitus' from Robert Cotton in January 1603 (BL, Cotton MS Vespasian F XIII, fol. 290ʳ). The fate of these notes remains uncertain. Essex's purpose in compiling them is perhaps explained in the letter to Rutland: 'to help you to remember, you must use writing, or meditation, or both; by writing I mean making notes and abridgments of that which you would remember' (Spedding, *Bacon letters*, II, p. 13).

[205] Essex's secretaries Cuffe and Wotton were exponents of Tacitism, as were Savile, Antonio Perez, Arthur Atey, and Francis and Anthony Bacon (Ungerer, II, pp. 371ff.). Tacitism, or the study and emulation of Tacitus, has recently become the subject of a substantial body of scholarship, including P. Burke, 'Tacitism' in T. A. Dorey (ed.), *Tacitus* (London, 1969), pp. 149–71; A. T. Bradford, 'Stuart absolutism and the "utility" of Tacitus', *HLQ* 45 (1983), pp. 127–55; J. H. M. Salmon, 'Stoicism and Roman example: Seneca and Tacitus in Jacobean England', *Journal of the History of Ideas* l (1989), pp. 199–225; D. R. Woolf, *The idea of history in early Stuart England: ideology and the light of truth from the accession of James I to the Civil War* (Toronto, 1991), ch. 6; D. Womersley, 'Savile's translation and the political interpretation of Elizabethan texts'; also his 'Sir John Hayward's Tacitism', *Renaissance Studies* 6 (1992), pp. 46–59; Smuts, 'Court-centred politics and the uses of Roman historians', pp. 21–44.

[206] Before Essex's surrender in 1601, there was a 'great burning of his bookes and writings' (Ungerer, II, p. 234). According to Camden, many of Essex's papers were burnt 'lest (as he said) they should tell tales' (*Elizabeth*, p. 610). Sir Robert Cotton collected some of the papers which survived this holocaust, lending Cecil (by then earl of Salisbury) '[my] lord of Essex nottes and other memorialls' (BL, Harleian MS 6018, fol. 154ᵛ). Another of Cotton's notes also mentions 'heads and collections of pollycy of Earl [of] Essex and Cufe' (Cambridgeshire County Record Office, MS 588/Z1, fol. 163 (second foliation). I owe this reference to Dr Colin Tite: I have not seen the document myself).

pursued a vigorous, if unsystematic, programme of intellectual self-improvement. In occasional but intensive sessions, Essex studied key texts and explored subjects with experts: 'I have profited more by some expert man in half a day's conference than by myself in a month's study.'[207] Essex's friend, Lord Mountjoy, studied in a similar way[208] and Sir Philip Sidney had done the same.[209] Judging by the acquisition of an elaborate pocket dial, Essex probably began to study maritime navigation in 1593.[210] He discussed the merits of poetry with Henry Savile[211] and received lectures, probably of a religious nature, even on his sick-bed.[212] Essex's passion for history and its lessons extended beyond the classical world: he was interested in England's own history and probably discussed it with Savile and members of the Society of Antiquaries.[213] According to Richard

[207] Spedding, *Bacon letters*, II, p. 13. In his instructions to Naunton, Essex spelled out the approach required for getting the best out of such experts: 'with whome yow must use some arte to applye yourselfe to theire nature, and yealde them that kinde of respecte which they themselves woulde have, ffor when yow honor them muche, thoughe yow hurte them, you profuite your selfe with all men and with all natures, a meane betwixte suche a modestye as leave yow in darkenes and the importunety of continuall questioninge will be scornefull' (ULL, MS 187, fol. 15^r (pr. Hammer, 'Essex and Europe', p. 380)).

[208] According to Fynes Moryson, Mountjoy received a poor education at Oxford 'but in his youth at London, he so spent his vacant houres with schollers best able to direct him, as besides his reading in histories, skill in tongues, ... and so much knowledge (at least in cosmography and the mathematikes) as might serve his owne ends; he had taken such paines in the search of naturall phylosophy, as in divers arguments of that nature held by him with schollers, I have often heard him (not without marvelling at his memory and judgement) to remember of himselfe the most materiall points, the subtilest objections, and the soundest answers. But his chiefe delight was in the study of divinity ... ' (Fynes Moryson, *An itinerary containing his twelve yeeres travell through the twelve dominions of Germany, Bohmerland, Sweitzerland, Netherland, Denmarke, Poland, Italy, Turky, France, England, Scotland & Ireland* (4 vols., Glasgow, 1907–8 edn), II, p. 265).

[209] L. Jardine and A. Grafton, ' "Studied for action": how Gabriel Harvey read his Livy', *Past and Present* 129 (1990), pp. 36ff.

[210] See Plate 8. Even in the final weeks before his insurrection, Essex held meetings with William Barlowe and Edward Wright, experts in magnetism and mathematics (Cecil MS 75/105 (pr. *HMCS*, XI, p. 4)). Essex clearly had close contact with Barlowe long before this: Barlowe dedicated to Essex, 'my singuler good lord', *The navigators supply: conteining many things of principall importance belonging to navigation* (London, 1597, STC no. 1445), sig. A2^r–B3^r. This recent instruction may explain why Essex had the pocket dial with him after his fateful insurrection. He gave it to his chaplain, Abdias Assheton, on the morning of his execution (F. R. R[aines], 'The pocket-dial of the earl of Essex', *N&Q*, 4th ser., 9 (1872), pp. 9–10).

[211] J. Spedding, R. L. Ellis and D. D. Heath (eds.), *The works of Francis Bacon* (7 vols., London, 1857–9), VII, p. 134.

[212] *HMCS*, VII, p. 527.

[213] According to Gabriel Harvey, Essex 'much commendes Albion's England', whereas Lord Mountjoy 'makes the like account of Daniel's peece of the Chronicle [i.e. Holinshed's], touching the usurpation of Henrie of Bullingbrooke' (G. C. Moore-Smith, *Gabriel Harvey's marginalia* (Stratford-upon-Avon, 1913), p. 232). The book to which Harvey refers is William Warner's *Albions England: or a historicall map of the same island*, which was first published in 1586 and reissued in new editions in 1589, 1592, 1596 and 1597

Percyvall, who dedicated a Spanish dictionary and primer to him in 1591, Essex also spent 'much time, with happie successe, as well in the knowledge of the toongs, as of other commendable learnings beseeming your place and person'.[214] Perhaps encouraged by Percyvall, Essex added a smattering of Spanish to his knowledge of French, Latin, Greek and Italian.[215] A number of his friends did the same – his sister Penelope[216] and Anthony Bacon[217] became quite fluent in Spanish, while Sir Robert Sidney translated Spanish verse for his sister, the countess of Pembroke.[218]

Essex's taste for applying university-style learning to politics also extended to researching on specific topics. Sometimes such written advices were provided by friends – Antonio Perez[219] and Lord Willoughby[220] gave him papers on politics and military reform, while Savile's notes on the Roman army, which accompanied the 1591 translation of Tacitus, were also undoubtedly encouraged by Essex's martial interests.[221] Francis Bacon allegedly 'did nothing but advise and ruminate with myself to the best of my understanding, propositions and memorials of anything that might concern his lordship's honor, fortune or service'.[222] When he became earl

---

(STC nos. 25079–25082a). Savile was the leading academic among English antiquarians. He published the massive *Rerum Anglicorum scriptores post Bedam praecipui* (London, 1596, STC no. 21783), which featured scholarly editions of medieval English histories. By this date, Essex's interest in English history had already been recognised by dedications to him of Richard Harvey's *Philadelphus, or a defence of Brutus, and the Brutans history* (London, 1593, STC no. 12913) and Ralph Brooke's *A discoverie of certaine errours published in the much commended Britannia* (London, 1594, STC no. 3834). Several of Essex's friends were members of the Society of Antiquaries or involved in its activities, including his relative Henry Bourchier, Richard Broughton and his brother Hugh, Lancelot Andrewes and Savile (M. McKisack, *Medieval history in the Tudor age* (Oxford, 1971), pp. 157, 160; J. Evans, *A history of the Society of Antiquaries* (Oxford, 1956), pp. 11–13). In 1598, Bourchier bequeathed to Essex '[my] bookes of historyes, of Lattine, Frenche, Italion and Spanishe' (PRO, PROB 11/92, fol. 127ᵛ).

214 *Bibliotheca Hispanica: containing a grammar with a dictionarie in Spanish, English and Latine* ... (London, 1591, STC no. 19619), sig. A2ᵛ. Essex's arms appear at the front of this book, indicating that he had had contact with Percyvall in advance of its publication and wished to give the work his public endorsement.

215 Ungerer, I, pp. 77–8, 92–3; *ibid.*, II, p. 117. Essex's attitude towards learning Spanish was utilitarian. In his instructions to Robert Naunton, he wrote that 'to have Signor Perez willingly helpe yow in the Spanishe yow must pretende to studye the tonge as well, because it is hys, as for the excellencye of itselfe ... If you will use an amplificacion, yow maye saye yow learne Spanishe to understande Raphael Peregrino's [i.e. Perez's] booke as well as Bartas did Englishe to understande Sir Phillip Sydney's Arcadia' (ULL, MS 187, fol. 13ʳ⁻ᵛ (pr. Hammer, 'Essex and Europe', p. 378)). In other words, the real value of learning Spanish lay in allowing full access to the works written in that language.

216 Ungerer, I, pp. 79–80, 81 n.1, 82–3, 87–9.   217 *Ibid.*, II, pp. 258–9.

218 BL, Add. MS 58435, fol. 37ʳ.   219 Ungerer, I, pp. 92–3, 366, 406.

220 BL, Egerton MS 1943, fols. 77ʳ–79ᵛ, 85ʳ–86ʳ; LPL, MS 659, fols. 289ʳ–290ᵛ, 353ᵛ.

221 'A view of certaine militar matters, for the better understanding of the ancient Roman stories', in [Savile], *The ende of Nero*, sig. Ee1ʳ–Gg3ʳ.

222 Cited in L. Jardine and W. Sherman, 'Pragmatic readers: knowledge transactions and

marshal at the end of 1597, Essex requested briefing papers on the powers and prerogatives of his new office. Heralds searched old records for him,[223] whilst Lord Henry Howard 'laboured above my strengthe, not onlie in ryflinge all corners of my dustie cabinet about notes belonginge to an honor that dothe nowe concerne your self, but besides in swepinge downe the coppwebes everie other where, that I maie rightly judge, and yow maie truly understande, what is due to your authoritie'.[224] Essex's secretaries also provided him with research information. In 1595, Henry Wotton wrote a lengthy analysis based upon Perez's *Pedaços de historia ô relaciones*,[225] while William Temple was occupied in some task which required him to borrow a copy of 'the lawes of the borders' from Edward Reynoldes in February 1597.[226]

Although Wotton, in particular, had experience of extracting and excerpting 'state points',[227] it is probable that more mundane research was performed by scholars in Oxford and Cambridge. This is certainly the implication of a letter about research which was allegedly written by Essex

scholarly services in late Elizabethan England', in A. Fletcher and P. Roberts (eds.), *Religion, culture and society in early modern Britain* (Cambridge, 1994), p. 108.

[223] BLO, Ashmolean MS 862, pp. 63–6 is headed 'The summary of all that I & all others found concerning the office of earle marshall, when we were commanded by the earl of Essex, earle marshall, to make search into the recordes for the same, 1597.'

[224] BL, Harleian MS 286, fol. 268ʳ. Howard was searching through the papers of his late brother, the duke of Norfolk, who had been earl marshal before his execution in 1572. As a result of these exertions, Howard drew up a paper for Essex arguing that the earl marshal should oversee the actions of the heralds and must take action against the inflation of honours and false pedigrees which were circulating in the realm (Peck, *Northampton*, pp. 156–7. Cf. *ibid.*, pp. 117–19). Significantly, one of Essex's first actions as earl marshal was to issue a warrant on 31 December 1597 for the arrest of one William Dakyns, 'a notable dealer in arms and maker of false pedigrees' (M. Maclagan, 'Genealogy and heraldry in the sixteenth and seventeenth centuries', in L. Fox (ed.), *English historical scholarship in the sixteenth and seventeenth centuries* (London, 1956), p. 42).

[225] Ungerer, II, pp. 280–321. This analysis is discussed below at the end of the next chapter.

[226] As a result, when Essex also asked to look at the book, Reynoldes hastily had to borrow Anthony Bacon's copy (LPL, MS 655, fol. 65ʳ).

[227] Henry Wotton had offered to perform this kind of work for Lord Zouche during his stay at the Imperial Library in Vienna during 1590–1. As well as offering to excerpt for Zouche 'notable discourses on military matters' which were owned by the emperor, Wotton ventured that 'if in any other particular state-point you crave the like, no doubt, whatsoever the argument be, amongst 9,000 volumes (whereof the most part are manuscript) we shall find some author to please your honour' (Smith, *Life and letters of Wotton*, I, p. 255). At this time, Wotton was living with Hugo Blotius, the imperial librarian. Blotius was an old friend of Henry Savile, who had written Wotton a letter of introduction. Blotius, in turn, recommended Wotton to Lord Freidesham (Osterreichische Nationalbibliothek, Vienna, Cod. 9737, fols. 1ʳ–2ᵛ, 3ʳ⁻ᵛ, 4ʳ, 5ʳ, 8ʳ, 10ʳ⁻ᵛ, etc.). Wotton's letters from this period also reveal that he knew Henry Cuffe from his time at Oxford and had recommended him as a tutor for his own nephew (*ibid.*, fols. 4ʳ, 6ʳ). It was also during his time at Oxford that he began his close friendship with John Donne: T.-L. Pebworth and C. J. Summers, '"Thus friends absent speake": the exchange of verse letters between John Donne and Henry Wotton', *Modern Philology* 81 (1984), pp. 361–77.

to Fulke Greville.[228] This was apparently occasioned by Greville's decision to travel to Cambridge 'to get a scholler to your liking, to live with you, and 2 or 3 others to remaine in the universitie and gather for you'.[229] The contents of this letter are also significant because Essex – or the author(s) who composed the document in his name – discusses the best techniques for 'gathering'. Essex argues that collecting abridgements of individual books is much less valuable than compiling information from a wide range of sources according to specific subjects. Only the latter, he argues, can 'breed soundness of judgment, which is the true use of all learninge'.[230] For the same reason, the employer of scholars should 'gather the chiefest things and out of the chiefest books yourself' and form his own judgements about the material which his researchers gather: 'they should like labourers bring stone, timber, morter & other necessaries to your building, but yow should put them together and be the master workman yourself'.[231]

Although the letter to Greville is an idealised prescription for accumulating useful information, such research was genuinely important in Essex's political endeavours. This becomes clear from a petition to Elizabeth which Edward Reynoldes drafted on his master's behalf in 1599. Although Essex was then acting as a general and calling for additional military resources, Reynoldes cast the earl's services in a different light:

whose watchfullnes, studies and indefatigable indevors by the space of xi whole yeares I have seene & can justlie testifie, havinge never spared the facullties of his bodie or minde when question hath bene of your service. Wittnes so many excellent projectes & discourses which he hath written uppon all occasions presented; wittnes his severall successfull & happy imploymentes, prudentlie by Your Majesty invented and valiantlye by him executed, against that proude monarch to your great glorie & everlastinge fame & to your divertinge of imminent dangers threatened to your state.[232]

The priority which Reynoldes here accords to Essex's 'projectes &

---

[228] This document survives in two copies: BLO, Tanner MS 79, fols. 29^r–30^v and PRO, SP 14/ 59, fols. 4^r–5^v. The latter is in the hand of Essex's personal secretary, Edward Reynoldes. The letter is printed in Spedding, *Bacon letters*, II, pp. 21–6 and discussed in V. F. Snow, 'Francis Bacon's advice to Fulke Greville on research techniques', *HLQ* 33 (1959–60), pp. 369–78. The attribution of this letter to Francis Bacon is rejected as too simplistic in Hammer, 'Essex, Greville and the employment of scholars', pp. 169ff. The latter article argues that this document was composed by Essex or, more likely, on his behalf (probably as some kind of joint effort), between January and October 1600, in the hope of aiding his political rehabilitation. It is also argued that the premise of this letter – Greville's desire to employ scholars at Cambridge – genuinely reflects the manner in which John Coke was recruited by Greville from Trinity College about 1590.

[229] BLO, Tanner MS 79, fol. 29^r (pr. Spedding, *Bacon letters*, II, p. 21).

[230] BLO, Tanner MS 79, fol. 29^v (pr. Spedding, *Bacon letters*, II, p. 23).

[231] BLO, Tanner MS 79, fol. 30^v (pr. Spedding, *Bacon letters*, II, p. 26).

[232] BL, Add. MS 4125, fol. 352^r. It is unclear whether Reynoldes ever presented this letter to the queen.

discourses' over his military 'imploymentes' is quite startling, but there is ample evidence that Essex sought to advance his political views by the pen quite as much as by heroics and verbal persuasion. According to the Dutch ambassador, Essex swayed Elizabeth against peace talks with Spain 'with many good reasons and discourses'.[233] Many of his surviving letters are powerfully written arguments in favour of actions which he wished to be pursued.[234] When England faced an invasion threat in August 1595 and when a Spanish fleet actually set sail in October 1596, Essex responded to both occasions by writing detailed and carefully argued papers about appropriate countermeasures.[235] During 1596 and 1597, he wrote a series of long letters and papers expounding his views on strategy and defending his own conduct. The bitter experience of the Azores voyage, in particular, may explain why Essex began writing a treatise for 'he thatt shall inable himself to commaund a fleete'.[236] Essex was also associated with propagandistic documents which had a more 'literary' quality, such as the letter of advice to the earl of Rutland, the 1595 Accession Day entertainment, the 'True relacion' of Cadiz, his own *Apologie* of 1598 and the letter to Fulke Greville about research techniques.

Modern scholars have traditionally played down Essex's facility with the pen and ascribed the authorship of his more literary works to friends such as Francis Bacon. There is logic to this tendency because some draft fragments of Essex's 1595 Accession Day entertainment survive in Bacon's hand[237] and parts of the letter to Rutland seem suspiciously similar to Bacon's later works.[238] However, the undoubted involvement of Francis Bacon in composing works for Essex should not obscure the fact that Essex and others were also involved in producing these documents. Moreover, the

---

[233] 'Veel goede redenen en discoursen geseyt' ('with many good reasons and discourses') (in S. P. Haak (ed.), *Johan van Oldenbarnevelt: bescheiden betreffende zijn staat-kundig beleid en zijn familie, 1570–1601* ('S-Gravenhage, 1934), p. 321). This letter is dated 13 [i.e. 3 Old Style] December 1595.

[234] Hence, according to the testimony of a servant of Burghley, Essex 'was a great lover of learning, and well learned himself, as might well appear by diverse letters and discourses which he wrote with great elegancy & judgment' (BL, Add. MS 22925, fol. 42^r (pr. John Clapham, *Elizabeth of England: certain observations concerning the life and reign of Queen Elizabeth* (eds E. P. and C. Read, Philadelphia, 1951), p. 94)). Wotton also claimed that Essex's writings 'are beyond example' (*Parallel*, p. 8).

[235] LPL, MS 651, fol. 276^{r-v}; PRO, SP 9/52, no. 23.

[236] WRO, TD 69/6.2, item 74, undated holograph paper by Essex, incomplete.

[237] The manuscript evidence for this entertainment is discussed in detail in P. E. J. Hammer, 'Upstaging the queen: the earl of Essex, Francis Bacon and the Accession Day celebrations of 1595', in D. Bevington and P. Holbrook (eds.), *The politics of the Stuart Court masque* (Cambridge, 1998), pp. 41–66.

[238] Spedding, *Bacon letters*, II, pp. 6–15. Spedding also describes the letter to Greville as 'so very Baconian in matter and manner, that I see no reason why every word of it (the opening and closing paragraphs excepted) might not have been written by Bacon himself in his own person' (*ibid.*, p. 21).

precise percentage of Bacon's authorship or of Essex's is ultimately irrelevant because these were corporate works written on Essex's behalf and in his name. This was spelled out by Henry Cuffe, when informing Edward Reynoldes about the 'True relacion' of Cadiz:

You shall receve a discourse ... penned very truly according to his lordship's large enstructions, by which besides my owne knowledge he enformed me of sundry particulers of moment in the processe therof. And after I had penned it as plainely as I might, alteringe little or nothinge of his owne drawght, I cawsed his lordship to peruse it once againe and to adde extremam manum, which he hathe donne, as you may perceve by the enterlyneinge.[239]

Essex was entirely capable of writing such documents himself and may sometimes have done so. He also possessed sufficient literary ability to write poetry which was well regarded by his contemporaries.[240] Nevertheless, the many demands upon his time and the possibilities offered by utilising specialists such as Bacon and Cuffe often probably restricted him to setting guidelines and editing the resultant texts. In this context, the uncompleted state of Essex's long apologia written on the return from Cadiz and his notes on naval command is significant: aboard ship, he had time to write at length but, once he returned to the hurly-burly of politics, he had no time to finish documents which could not be passed on to friends and servants for completion.

'Projectes & discourses' were an important weapon in Essex's political arsenal. Although Elizabeth insisted on brevity in verbal reports, she also liked reading documents which she could ponder at her leisure – provided they were well written.[241] Essex's papers catered to this taste and demonstrated cool and reasoned 'judgement' to complement the charm and passion which characterised his quotidian dealings with her. In this sense, these writings were an integral part of his long campaign to convince Elizabeth his policies were sound and that he should succeed Burghley as her chief adviser. Essex also hoped that the cold, hard logic of his papers would overcome Elizabeth's instinctive opposition to entanglement in Europe. In this endeavour, the news gathered by intelligencers and the analyses and arguments supplied by intellectuals provided vital political ammunition which Essex eagerly deployed. However, Elizabeth's misgivings continued to thwart Essex and by late 1595 he began to resort to a

---

[239] LPL, MS 658, fol. 88[r].

[240] S. W. May, 'The poems of Edward De Vere, seventeenth earl of Oxford, and Robert Devereux, second earl of Essex', *Studies in Philology* 77, Texts and Studies issue (1980), pp. 43–64. According to Henry Wotton, Essex had a penchant for evaporating his humours by writing verse (*Parallel*, p. 3).

[241] Hence Elizabeth sought to test Essex's aptitude and resources for gathering intelligence after his appointment to the privy council by demanding that he draft instructions for an agent notionally being sent to Rheims and Rome (LPL, MS 653, fol. 189[r]).

new strategy. In parallel with the confidential papers which he gave to the queen, Essex started to write or commission semi-public documents such as the letter to Rutland or the text of his Accession Day entertainment, which were circulated in manuscript among friends at Court and beyond. The aim of these more literary documents was to portray Essex in the best possible light and build political momentum behind him, thereby increasing pressure on Elizabeth to recognise his talents and give him greater influence in government. A similar approach was attempted with the 'True relacion' of Cadiz. This was the classic tactic of political 'outs', retailing an alternative policy agenda in a manner which was difficult to track or suppress. By circulating documents in manuscript, Essex and his adherents were able to circumvent the censorship of printed works and to target their audience more precisely than would have been possible with books or broadsides. It is remarkable testimony to Essex's frustration and the scale of his political ambition that he should have adopted this strategy when he remained at the very centre of politics.

Although Essex continued to believe that he would triumph and that Elizabeth would one day be forced to accept his views on Europe and the war, his circulation of partisan tracts and penchant for intellectualising politics had potentially awkward consequences for the future. As the affair of the 'True relacion' demonstrated, Essex's willingness to propagandise on his own behalf risked alienating the queen and his fellow councillors. Essex's studies offered political insights[242] but they also risked raising dangerous political questions. In 1595, Henry Wotton wrote a detailed analysis of Perez's *Pedaços* but it trespassed upon matters of royal sovereignty and remained highly confidential.[243] Analysing politics in terms of classical history and 'virtue' also risked distorting perceptions of Elizabeth's Court according to the morally loaded accounts of Tacitus or Livy. Case studies of tyranny and the politics of murder, deceit and the hounding of virtue could assume a new and unpleasant perspective if Essex and his friends ceased to believe that their views might one day triumph. At the end of 1597, such thoughts remained inchoate but the shocks which Essex received over the preceding eighteen months and the relentless efforts which he made to vindicate his martial virtue raised the prospect of a future eerily reminiscent of Tacitus's accounts of Germanicus or Agricola.

---

[242] Essex can sometimes be seen making direct use of his studies. In one instance, he claimed that Tacitus's account of Tiberius offered guidance for interpreting the likely actions of the duke of Montpensier (Ungerer, I, p. 466). On another occasion, he assured Lady Bacon that 'Plutarke taught me long since to make profit of my enemies' (LPL, MS 660, fol. 281r).
[243] Ungerer, II, ch. 9.

8

'Your Majestie's creture and vassall'

Essex's endeavour to deduce the 'rules and patternes of pollecy' by studying history reflected his innate 'bookishnesse' and the need to prove himself a man of judgement. However, it also suggested an uncertainty, even an unease, about political life. In his study of princes past, Essex revealed not only a penchant for intellectualising politics but also a need for reassurance and guidance about his own prince and fellow courtiers. This is not surprising because, for all his grand schemes to play a leading role on the international stage, Essex's world centred upon the English Court. Only there could he win Elizabeth over and realise his political aims. The Court was also perforce his habitual place of residence, where he attended upon the queen, participated in privy council business, and cut a figure of style and importance. Yet this little world was also a hot-house environment, where jealousies and back-biting flourished. Moreover, Essex had far less experience of Court than his older conciliar colleagues. Even Cecil enjoyed a political apprenticeship under his father which was far more intensive than Essex's brief spells at Court with Leicester.

Guidance and reassurance became increasingly important for Essex when he sought to transform himself from being merely the queen's young favourite. Slowly and painfully, he forced Elizabeth to recognise him as a soldier, a councillor and a politician. In doing so, he refashioned his position at Court and added new complexity to his relationship with Elizabeth. As simply a favourite, Essex was frustrated by his lack of sustained influence on royal policy. Yet a favourite also enjoyed a special status which was distinct from, and in some senses above, that of the queen's councillors. By becoming a councillor himself, Essex lost this distinct status. Looking back on events, Henry Wotton ventured that 'my lord of E[ssex], after being made a councillor, lost the queen's favour, for before she made him controller of her council, showing them through him her power'.[1]

---

[1] L. P. Smith, *The life and letters of Sir Henry Wotton* (2 vols., Oxford, 1907), II, p. 493 (notes from Wotton's commonplace book).

Although hardly satisfactory as an analysis of Essex's career, Wotton's comment contains a nugget of truth in its emphasis upon the change which occurred when Essex became a member of the privy council. In his personal dealings with Elizabeth, Essex remained her favourite but, in affairs of state, he became only one among a number of sometimes competing advisers. As Essex's role on the council grew, the trust and intimacy which formed the basis of Elizabeth's relationship with her favourite were increasingly tempered by the recognition that he was an ambitious and resourceful competitor for political influence. Essex's aggressive actions as a politician gradually and inevitably eroded his unique status as royal favourite. This is why Francis Bacon suggested in October 1596 that Essex should yield the place of favourite to some other pleasing, but pliable, candidate – just as Leicester and Hatton had done in assisting the rise of Essex himself.[2]

Despite the risks which it entailed, Essex's reinvention of himself also brought unique opportunities to enhance his political prospects. As both favourite and councillor, Essex could claim to serve Elizabeth more completely than other councillors. This dual status clearly encouraged him to believe that he had a greater hold on her than his colleagues and convinced him that he could eventually bring her to accept his views on war and Europe. At a practical level, Essex's promotion strengthened his existing rights of private access to Elizabeth. As a privy councillor and master of the horse, Essex had not just the right, but a redoubled duty, to attend upon her.[3] At times, he found this an onerous burden, since it restricted him (except for the periods when he was given leave of absence) from moving more than the distance of a rapid gallop from Court. In a typical instance, Essex had no time for more than a flying visit to confer with Anthony Bacon in London, before having to ride back to attend upon Elizabeth at her midday meal.[4] Sometimes he was not able to leave the Court at all. In June 1593, he lamented the impossibility of visiting the sick Francis Bacon because he was the only leading member of the royal household who remained with the queen.[5]

This almost constant responsibility to be present at Court brought its own benefits and burdens for Essex. Above all, Essex benefited from his special intimacy with Elizabeth and enjoyed the signs of familiarity and affection which went with it. These signs were keenly noted by observers at

---

[2] Spedding, *Bacon letters*, II, p. 45.

[3] LPL, MS 660, fol. 9^r. Regarding the attendance of privy councillors, it is significant that Burghley described them as 'her Majesti's counsell *about her person* for her publique affayres' (PRO, SP 12/255, fol. 149^r; emphasis added).

[4] LPL, MS 653, fol. 184^r.

[5] *Ibid.*, fol. 220^r (although undated, the dating of this letter is clear from its reference to the return of Anthony Standen). For a similar case of Essex, alone of the leading courtiers, being present to attend upon the queen, see LPL, MS 650, fol. 358^r.

Court as cynosural proof that he remained the royal favourite. When Essex returned to Court in December 1593, after a spell away, it was pointedly reported that Elizabeth welcomed him back with '*a payre of busses*'.[6] At other times, she visited him when he lay sick in bed[7] and even on his ship as he prepared to sail for Spain.[8] At the Twelfth Night celebrations at the beginning of 1594, she had him stand beside her high throne during proceedings and 'often devised [with him] in swete and favourable maner'.[9] For his part, even after he became a councillor, Essex continued to play the role of the queen's special companion by such activities as composing sonnets to be sung to her.[10] However, not all of these verses were necessarily complimentary – sometimes these songs embodied a refined form of protest against what Essex conceived to be Elizabeth's ill-treatment of him.[11] As well as its benefits, intimacy with the queen brought its own pressures.

Essex sometimes found this habitual intimacy and the general frustrations of courtly life too much for him. All courtiers experienced bouts of disillusionment but Essex, when his emotions had built up 'like a gathering of clouds', would 'brake forth into certayne suddaine recesses',[12] as if physically sloughing off the pressures upon him. While such action was normally limited to shutting himself in his chamber,[13] occasionally he abandoned the Court altogether. In late November 1593, he simply vanished from Court, only to reappear early one morning three days later. Not surprisingly, one of his supporters was moved to comment that these 'startes of his instealinge maner mutche trowblethe hys folowers and

---

[6] LPL, MS, 649, fol. 425[r]. The italics indicate that these words were in cipher in the original.

[7] For example, LPL, MS 652, fols. 222[r], 219[r]; LPL, MS 655, fols. 64[r], 66[r], 72[r].

[8] BLO, Rawlinson MS A 173, fol. 11[r].   [9] LPL, MS 649, fol. 10[r].

[10] Wotton refers to Essex's writing of sonnets to be sung to the queen 'by one Hales, in whose voyce shee tooke some pleasure' (*Parallel*, p. 3). Essex's reputation in this regard also won praise from musicians who sought his patronage. John Mundy, for example, described the earl in 1594 as the tenth Muse (*Songs and psalmes composed into 3 4 and 5 partes, for the use and delight of such as either love or learne musicke* (London, 1594, STC no. 18284), unpag. dedication), while Thomas Watson lauded him as a potential Apollo and asked 'Ecquis enim vestrae nescit conamina Musae, metraque ad Aoniam saepe canenda lyram?' (*The first sett of Italian madrigalls Englished* ... (London, 1590, STC no. 25119), dedicatory verse). In 1593, Essex gave at least £16 as gifts to various of the queen's musicians (Devereux MS 3, fol. 75[v]). For Essex's poetry, see S. W. May, 'The poems of Edward de Vere, seventeenth earl of Oxford and of Robert Devereux, second earl of Essex', *Studies in Philology* 77, special fifth issue (1980) esp. pp. 14–22, 43–64 and 84–115. For Robert Hales, see D. Poulton, 'The favourite singer of Queen Elizabeth I', *The Consort*, no. 14 (1957), 24–7.

[11] Essex sometimes used John Dowland to set his verses to music. For discussion of this and the plaintive nature of some of Essex's songs, see D. Poulton, *John Dowland* (2nd edn, Berkeley and Los Angeles, 1982), pp. 226–9, 262–3, 285–6.

[12] Wotton, *Parallel*, p. 3.   [13] For example, LPL, MS 650, fols. 25[r], 26[r].

wellwillers'.[14] Reprimanding him for his lack of duty, Elizabeth left Essex 'extreamly shaken up' for this 'ranginge abrode'.[15]

The obverse side of the familiarity and affection in the peculiarly personal relationship which existed between a favourite and his sovereign was seen in displays of royal anger. As has already been observed with Essex's departure for Portugal, his secret marriage and his conduct at Rouen, Elizabeth could be roused to particular fury against him, especially as his behaviour on these occasions had an impact upon matters of state. Occasional reprimands about the performance of his duties also had an obvious official importance. However, more purely personal incidents also added tensions to Essex's relations with Elizabeth. In particular, his dealings at Court were troubled by his reputation as a philanderer.[16] For Essex, this reputation was especially awkward because, whenever such talk came to her knowledge, it reminded Elizabeth that she was not the centre of Essex's emotions, as she had been for Hatton and (despite his own affairs) for Leicester. Moreover, the women involved were the queen's own attendants and their families were well connected and likely to react angrily to scandal.[17] Elizabeth took such matters very seriously. When she learned in

---

[14] LPL, MS 649, fol. 378ʳ.   [15] *Ibid.*, fol. 376ᵛ.

[16] According to one contemporary, 'to fleshly wantonnes he [i.e. Essex] was much inclined' (BL, Add. MS 22925, fol. 42ʳ (pr. John Clapham, *Elizabeth of England: certain observations concerning the life and reign of Queen Elizabeth* (eds. E. P. and C. Read, Philadelphia, 1951), p. 94)). Lady Bacon also made dark, but fleeting, allusions to Essex's 'carnal concupiscence' in letters to her son Anthony. Like other sensitive matters in her letters to him, these comments are written in Greek characters (LPL, MS 651, fol. 108ʳ; LPL, MS 658, fol. 167ʳ). E. M. Tenison tries to rebut such 'hoary scandals' (X, pp. 320–4) but her argument about Essex's innocence is unconvincing. At the other extreme, the recent claim by Alan Haynes that Essex 'was having affairs with four maids of honour simultaneously' seems to be based upon a wild misconstruing of the evidence (*Sex in Elizabethan England* (Stroud, 1997), p. 43).

[17] Although there were rumours in late 1596 and again late in 1597 that he was having an adulterous affair with the young countess of Derby (see below), most of the evidence of Essex's amorous liaisons suggest little more than excessive flirting. In April 1597, Elizabeth Brydges and Elizabeth Russell had their ears boxed by the queen for an assignation in the privy gardens which probably involved Essex (*HMCD*, II, p. 265). According to a report of Rowland Whyte in February 1598, Essex 'is againe fallen in love with his fairest B' (*ibid.*, p. 322), which suggests a well-known previous attachment to one of these women ('B' could stand for Bess Russell or, more likely, Bess Brydges). Elizabeth Brydges was the elder daughter of Giles, 3rd Lord Chandos, and was aged nineteen in 1597. She later made a disastrous marriage to Sir John Kennedy (Tenison, X, pp. 325–6). Elizabeth Russell was the daughter of the late John Lord Russell and Lady Elizabeth Russell (née Cooke), making her a first cousin of Sir Robert Cecil and of Anthony and Francis Bacon. On 16 June 1600, she married Worcester's son and heir, Henry Lord Herbert (*TCP*, XII, part 2, p. 858). Another maid of honour, Lady Mary Howard, also received a stern warning about her behaviour towards an unnamed earl in 1597 (J. Arnold, *Queen Elizabeth's wardrobe unlock'd: the inventories of the wardrobe of robes prepared in July 1600 ...* (London, 1988), p. 104). The object of Mary Howard's affections might have been Essex or (more likely) Southampton.

May 1595 that Elizabeth Southwell had borne Essex a son back in 1591,[18] he was cast into a tempestuous sea.[19] Elizabeth was incensed. Not only had Essex managed to conceal his misdemeanour for four years, but she had imprisoned an innocent man to boot.

Some courtiers believed that Essex's hold on Elizabeth had finally been broken and urged the earl of Southampton to make a bid for royal favour.[20] However, Southampton would not turn against his friend and the storm eventually subsided. Even so, the threat of further such revelations, whether true or imaginary, continued to haunt Essex. In large measure, this was due to the intense atmosphere of the Court, where personal jealousy and bitterness towards the queen's favourite were no less endemic than desire for his support in a suit. This had been one element in the general hostility towards Ralegh, from which Essex himself had profited during his rise to favour. Now Essex came to be the subject of hostile gossip and bids to score points against him with the queen. As he complained to Lady Bacon, 'I live in a place where I am howerly conspired against and practised uppon.'[21] Only a few months after the furore over the birth of his illegitimate child, it was reported that 'Sir William Cornwalles doth often trouble her Majestie's eares with tales of my lord of Essex, who is thought to be an observer of all his doings.'[22] After the Cadiz expedition, when tensions at Court became palpable, rumours of Essex's sexual incontinence again began to circulate.[23] One such story drove the strait-laced Lady Ann Bacon to write and berate him for 'infaminge a noble man's wyffe and so nere aboute her Majestie'.[24] Essex indignantly asserted his innocence of the

---

18 LPL, MS 651, fol. 122ʳ. For Elizabeth Southwell, see above, pp. 95–6.
19 Hence Antonio Perez asked Essex 'quid de isto tempestuoso mari? quid de Junone [Elizabeth], quae Aeolum [Burghely] et ventos contra te convocat et commovet?' (Ungerer, I, p. 329. Note that my interpretation of this letter differs from the gloss given by Ungerer.) According to Anthony Standen, Lady Scudamore and the queen's physician, Dr Gifford, were 'also in the chase' over this matter (LPL, MS 651, fol. 122ʳ). Elizabeth's anger against Essex was perhaps sharpened by the fact that his wife had given birth to a legitimate son, Henry, less than a month before (HMCD, II, p. 158; W. B. Bannerman (ed.), The registers of St Olave, Hart Street, London, 1563–1700 (Harleian society, xlvi, 1916), p. 17).
20 Collins, Sidney papers, I, pp. 348–9. Essex was reportedly coming back into favour by 24 May (LPL, MS 651, fol. 159ʳ), but Southampton was encouraged to pursue royal favour as late as September, suggesting that Essex's relationship with Elizabeth came under serious pressure in 1595.
21 Essex continues: 'What they cannot make the world beleve, that they perswade the queen unto, and what they cannot make probable to the queen, that they give out to the worlde. They have allmost all the howse [i.e. household] to serve them for instruments' (LPL, MS 660, fol. 281ʳ). See also Essex's comments to Sir Henry Unton of July 1595 about 'this crew of sycophants, spies and delators' (HMCS, V, p. 280).
22 Collins, Sidney papers, I, p. 348.
23 Essex himself complained to Antonio Perez in September 1596 that 'si zelotypia status excitari non possit, lasciviae tamen nunquam depellet' (Ungerer, I, p. 445).
24 LPL, MS 660, fol. 149ʳ⁻ᵛ. The woman involved – 'a partie more nere to me then gratious to

charge, but his reply also suggested how far he had previously left himself open to such accusations: 'since my departure from England towardes Spaine, I have bene free from taxation of incontinentcy withe anie woman that lives'.[25] Such restraint did not last. In late 1597, the story spread 'that he laye with my lady of Darbe before he went [to the Azores], as his enymes witnesse'. Not surprisingly, the news left him 'in noe greate grace' with the queen.[26]

In the end, such tales of Essex's philandering never decisively threatened Elizabeth's affection for him. Like Leicester before him, his status as a favourite had already survived even the revelation of a clandestine marriage. Nevertheless, the temporary pall which these stories cast certainly caused Essex harm. Such disfavour briefly undercut his ability to deal with Elizabeth in matters of state and killed his prospects of winning fresh royal grants until she was ready to forgive him. This latter point was important. With his finances stretched to the limit, Essex depended upon royal favour to stay afloat, both through direct royal grants and through the heightened ability to roll over loans which his association with the queen gave him.[27]

her stocke', whose 'unwiflike and unshamfast demeanour ... hathe alredie made her antient noble husband to undoe his howse by sellinge as one out of comforte' – was clearly Elizabeth de Vere, who had married William, 6th earl of Derby, at Greenwich Palace on 26 January 1595 (C. Read, *Lord Burghley and Queen Elizabeth* (London, 1960), p. 502). Lady Bacon's use of the term 'antient' refers to Derby's lineage, not his age. Elizabeth de Vere was the daughter of the earl of Oxford and his wife Anne (née Cecil), making her Burghley's grand-daughter and Lady Bacon's great-niece. Although the couple soon had a daughter, also named Elizabeth, the marriage initially proved to be a disaster. A passing reference by Anthony Standen to rumours about Essex and 'the newe coyned countes' suggests that Lady Derby may have been involved with Essex as early as May 1595 (LPL, MS 651, fol. 122ʳ). This may have been one of the 'divers injuries and wrongs' which her father, the earl of Oxford, complained he had received from Essex by October 1595 (*HMCS*, V, pp. 426–7). The countess was clearly more interested in the delights of Court than in her husband and, by July 1596, Burghley was upset that she was even ignoring her child (PRO, SP 12/259, fol. 140ᵛ). Derby himself was frustrated that she did not behave like a dutiful wife, but he could do little to change her behaviour: 'it is said he lovethe her and greatlie as withe greefe laborethe to winne her' (LPL, MS 660, fol. 149ʳ).
25 LPL, MS 660, fol. 281ʳ. *Pace* Tenison (IX, p. 165), this comment indicates that Essex had not indulged in 'incontinentcy' since before his departure on the Cadiz expedition – implying that he *had* done so before this time. Lady Bacon's response to Essex's reply is LPL, MS 660, fol. 151ʳ.
26 Cecil MS 55/45 (pr. *HMCS*, VII, p. 392). Despite Essex's protestations to Lady Bacon in December 1596, this report suggests that his liaison with the countess of Derby continued, and became more serious, after the countess's return to Court in mid-April 1597 (*HMCD*, II, p. 268). Presumably in the hope of avoiding a scandal, she was forced to leave London and move to her husband's house at Knowsley in Lancashire during July (*HMCS*, VII, pp. 327, 339). By then, Derby's 'humer of ffrendsey' had begun to threaten a 'violent course' against his wife (Cecil MS 54/14 (pr. *HMCS*, VII, p. 339)).
27 In this regard, it should be noted that the size of Essex's debts did not simply reflect massive expenditure on his part (and also by his late father, whose debts to the queen still remained unpaid). In an age in which all aristocrats lived on credit, such hefty debts represented a gauge of how creditworthy Essex seemed to lenders. On this point, see G. R. Batho (ed.),

Since his expenditure and ambitions both grew apace after his appointment to the privy council, this material dependence upon the queen increased, rather than diminished, over the years. Essex also increasingly needed to extract the fruits of patronage from Elizabeth in order to satisfy the swelling number of his own followers.

Essex was enormously successful in securing royal grants for himself. One estimate claims that he managed to take almost half of what Elizabeth gave away in the latter years of her reign.[28] Perhaps more impressive is a list of some of the grants which she made to Essex: the stewardship of the honour of Grafton, formerly held by Hatton, in September 1593;[29] a grant worth £4,000 in July 1594;[30] renewal of his lease of the farm of sweet wines in 1594 and 1597;[31] and a cash grant of £7,000 from the sale of a cargo of cochineal in February 1598.[32] Each of these grants reflected Essex's signal favour with Elizabeth. However, there was also a political purpose behind her largesse. As well as displaying her princely liberality ('de gratia nostra speciali ... '), these grants were given as a reward for Essex's efforts in her service ('pro bono & laudabili servicio') and as recompense for his expenditure.[33] The scale and value of these rewards were not simply a measure of Elizabeth's affection for him, but also a means by which she financially enabled him to continue serving her as a councillor and a general.

Elizabeth made these hefty grants to Essex even though she had few illusions about the force of his ambitions, or even about the lengths to which he would go to achieve them. During the Rouen campaign, she believed that Essex and Henri IV actually conspired together in order to

The household papers of Henry Percy, ninth earl of Northumberland (1564–1632) (Camden Society, 3rd ser., XCIII, 1962), pp. xlvii–lvi; S. Doran, 'The finances of an Elizabethan nobleman and royal servant: a case study of Thomas Radcliffe, 3rd earl of Sussex', *Historical Research* 61 (1988), p. 287.

28 L. Stone, *The crisis of the aristocracy 1558–1641* (Oxford, 1965), p. 473. Precisely how Stone produced this fraction is unclear. Although it apparently derives from an appendix (App. xix.C.1 (*ibid.*, p. 775)), the meaning of this table is rather opaque. Some contemporary sources also give an overall figure for the queen's largesse to Essex of £300,000 (for example, Sir John Harington, *A tract on the succession to the crown (AD 1602)*) (ed. C. R. Markham, Roxburghe Club, London, 1880), pp. 79–80). However, this figure is based upon a misunderstanding of charges brought against Essex for his government in Ireland (*HMC. Calendar of the manuscripts of the Most Honourable the Marquess of Bath preserved at Longleat, Wiltshire* (5 vols., London, 1904–80), V, p. 270).

29 PRO, C 66/1400, mm. 5–7.   30 LPL, MS 650, fol. 227ᵛ.

31 PRO, C 54/1480, unfol., enrolment of indenture of 12 October 1593; LPL, MS 661, fol. 246ʳ.

32 BLO, Ashmolean MS 1729, fols. 25ʳ⁻ᵛ, 27ʳ.

33 Perhaps the most obvious examples of this are the grants made by the queen to Essex (in the legal guise of his servants Gelly Meyrick and Henry Lyndley) in order to help meet the costs of entertaining Antonio Perez (Ungerer, I, p. 223).

manipulate her for their own martial ends.[34] When Essex again returned to war in 1596, she complained of his 'wilfulnes and rashnes, alleaginge that yow would not be ruled, and that she would brydle and staie yow'.[35] Essex's departures on campaign, when Elizabeth's power over him was peculiarly weak, were not the only times that she berated his ambition. According to Francis Bacon, on one occasion when Essex pressed her about filling major offices of state, she 'answered nothing to the matter, but rose up on the sudden and said I am sure my office will not long be void'.[36] Clearly, Elizabeth had a fair understanding of the existence and nature of Essex's secret contacts with James VI.

Although she was sometimes profoundly suspicious of his conduct (and often rightly so), Elizabeth recognised that Essex also deserved and needed her support. In this regard, her reported comments on giving him a large grant in 1594 are instructive.[37] Essex's forwardness in her service, she said, were 'to be liked and highly commended'. Indeed, she valued Essex so highly that she refused to let him risk his life 'in anie lesse accion then that which should import her crowne and seate'. Finally, she gave him a gentle warning: 'looke to thy selfe, good Essex, and be wyse to help thy selfe without givinge thy ennemies advantage, and my hande shalbe redier to help then any other'. Despite her mistrust of his actions on campaign, Elizabeth knew that Essex's zealous pursuit of his 'ambition of warr' made him vulnerable in the rough and tumble of courtly politics and, sometimes at least, sought to encourage him accordingly.

Although Elizabeth was willing to support and reward Essex more generously than any other subject, she was far less eager to approve his suits on behalf of his followers. This posed a problem for Essex, who believed that liberality and whole-hearted support for his 'friends' were matters of honour. He sought to make amends for his lack of success as an advocate by passing on to his followers much of the material benefit which he derived from the queen's liberality.[38] This was perhaps what Elizabeth intended and expected when she made her grants. Nevertheless, Essex took the trickle-down system of patronage to new extremes by such spectacular gestures as his gift of land at Twickenham to Francis Bacon[39] or his

---

[34] *Unton corr.*, p. 208.
[35] LPL, MS 657, fol. 109ᵛ. These comments were made to Bouillon and there must be some suspicion that Elizabeth deliberately exaggerated her anger at Essex in order to deflect Henri IV's criticism about the Cadiz expedition away from herself.
[36] J. Spedding, R. L. Ellis and D. D. Heath (eds.), *The works of Francis Bacon* (7 vols., London, 1857–9), VII, p. 167.
[37] LPL, MS 650, fol. 227ʳ⁻ᵛ.
[38] BL, Add. MS 22925, fol. 42ʳ (pr. Clapham, *Elizabeth of England*, p. 94).
[39] Bacon apparently sold this land for £1,800 (Spedding, *Bacon letters*, I, pp. 371–2; Tenison, IX, p. 349).

promise to Sir Francis Aleyn in 1594 that 'I will divide one howse with you, yf you will live with me, or setle you in one yf I had but 2 in the world, for while I have any fortune, Sir Francis Allen shall have part of it.'[40] Despite such fine sentiments, Essex's failure as a patron at the highest level undermined any claim to the kind of 'domesticall greatnesse' which had been desired for him by his civilian followers since Leicester's death.

The example of Leicester suggested to many of Essex's well-wishers that he, too, should aspire to great political influence within the realm by making his status as favourite both the keystone and focus of his political activities. This opinion was epitomised in a letter which Francis Bacon wrote to Essex in October 1596: 'win the queen: if this be not the beginning, of any other course I see no end'.[41] In other words, if Essex did not make sure that Elizabeth loved and trusted him, any political activity which he undertook was worse than merely useless. It would, indeed, be a positive liability. Unless Essex assured himself of special royal favour, Bacon wondered 'whether there can be a more dangerous image ... represented to any monarch living ... ' than his combination of militarism, ambition and pursuit of popular acclaim?[42] Bacon's comments on the offices which Essex should seek indicate the thoroughly domestic nature of the political career which he envisaged for him. Instead of a military office like master of the ordnance, Essex should aim for the post of lord privy seal, which would give him heightened precedence within the realm, super-intendence over the queen's secretariat, and wealth and influence through the post's 'affinity' with the court of wards.[43]

As many historians have observed, this advice seems wise in the light of later events, but it was also totally at odds with Essex's career and personality. Leaving aside its obsessive emphasis on dissimulation as a means to political success, Bacon's letter is perhaps most interesting for the questions it raises about the nature of Essex's relationship with Elizabeth. Did Essex ever really seek any kind of 'domesticall greatnesse' like that proposed by Bacon? How unrealistic was the advice which Bacon allegedly offered to him? How, in fact, did Essex view his special favour with the queen?

[40] LPL, MS 650, fol. 309ʳ.
[41] Spedding, *Bacon letters*, II, p. 40. Although extremely well known, this document must be treated with considerable caution. Jonathan Marwil questioned whether Essex ever actually saw this letter (*The trials of counsel: Francis Bacon in 1621* (Detroit, 1976), pp. 83 n. 41, 71 n. 18). In the light of Essex's thwarted attempt to follow Bacon's advice by suggesting Lord Willoughby as master of ordnance, it seems likely that Essex did in fact receive the letter. However, Marwil also notes (correctly) that Bacon's analysis reduces Essex's position to a virtual caricature and 'represents a fundamentally solipsistic view of Essex's situation' (*ibid.*, p. 83).
[42] Spedding, *Bacon letters*, II, p. 43.   [43] *Ibid.*

Although these issues are all inter-related, some kind of direct answer can be given to the first question. That answer must be, by and large, in the negative. Essex did not really make a sustained, direct effort to use his status as favourite to build the kind of domestic power-base described by Bacon and envisaged for him by his followers since the death of Leicester. When Essex supported Bacon so vigorously in his efforts to win a place among the queen's legal counsel, he did so because Bacon was his friend and because his own pride became involved in the matter. Essex was essentially responding to Bacon's own desires, rather than using him to further his own courtly ambitions. There was, however, a more ambiguous character to his later support for the preferment of Sir Robert Sidney.[44] Sidney himself was desperate to win the wardenship of the Cinque Ports in early 1597[45] and Essex agreed to support him as a friend and because he believed that the realm needed a military man to oversee what was now a front-line command. Out of deference to the incumbent, old Lord Cobham, Essex refrained from lobbying very hard for Sidney until Cobham was dead. Once Cobham was dead, it soon became clear that Elizabeth would not appoint Sidney ahead of the new Lord Cobham, Essex's bitter foe Henry Brooke. This accentuated the profoundly *ad hominem* nature of Essex's support for Sidney: by backing Sidney and even threatening to stand for the wardenship himself, Essex was able to use the suit as a stick to beat Henry Brooke.[46] Although he callously kept Sidney in expectation for several months, Essex quickly recognised that the new Lord Cobham would win the day and tried to humiliate him by denying him the wardenship for as long as possible. Perhaps out of guilt for abusing Sidney's trust in this extremely messy political confrontation, Essex subsequently tried to win Sidney a peerage and the office of vice-chamberlain. Both endeavours soon petered out when Elizabeth proved unwilling to provoke Cobham and his friends by advancing Sidney.[47]

[44] A conventional account of this affair is M. V. Hay, *The life of Robert Sidney earl of Leicester (1563–1626)* (Washington, London and Toronto, 1984), pp. 152ff. A more sophisticated and convincing analysis is D. McKeen, *A memory of honour: the life of William Brooke Lord Cobham* (2 vols., Salzburg Studies in English Literature, CVIII, Salzburg, 1986), II, pp. 668–74. I have been much influenced by McKeen's account.

[45] For Sidney's restlessness in his tiresome command at Flushing during 1596 and 1597, see Hay, *The life of Robert Sidney*, pp. 153, 156.

[46] Essex's initial tactic was to seek Elizabeth's approval for Sidney by emphasising the need for a warden with military experience and by belittling Brooke's credentials (Collins, *Sidney papers*, II, p. 29–31; *HMCD*, II, p. 246; PRO, SP 12/256, fol. 172^r (a copy of this letter is *HMCD*, II, p. 242)). When Elizabeth refused to snub Brooke by appointing a mere knight like Sidney to a post held for so long by successive Lords Cobham, Essex put himself forward for the wardenship, as an earl, rather than let Cobham win it by default (*HMCD*, II, pp. 246, 247, 248). In addition to the mutual antipathy between Essex and Henry Brooke, there was a sharp rivalry between the Brooke and Sidney families for pre-eminence in Kent going back at least a generation.

[47] Hay, *The life of Robert Sidney*, pp. 157–60.

Judging by these *causes célèbres*, Essex's advocacy at Court for the promotion of his supporters became increasingly partisan, in the sense that it was intended to spite his rivals as much as to advance his friends. Yet such actions can hardly be said to embody a genuine attempt to attain a 'domesticall greatnesse'. Indeed, they suggest the reverse. Essex's clumsy support for Sidney and opposition to Cobham, like his other extreme behaviour in 1596 and 1597, reflected the fact that he had previously neglected to create an appropriate domestic power-base. This was not because Essex was heedless of Leicester's example: 'he was not so ill a grammarian in Court', as Henry Wotton put it.[48] Rather, Essex's actions were constrained by two factors: his belief that events on the Continent made other matters seem of secondary importance, and Burghley's overwhelming dominance of government and patronage. While Burghley remained alive, no other councillor could even pretend to 'domesticall greatnesse'. From this perspective, there was some sense in Essex's belief that he could gain political influence at home through his endeavours in foreign and military affairs. This belief was bolstered by Essex's whole conception of service to, and reward from, the crown. As a result, Essex made little effort to use his position as favourite to win a specifically 'domesticall' kind of 'greatnesse'. Inevitably, this political naivety later cost him dear. When the Court started to dissolve into those who were for or against him, Essex began to feel insecure and to thrash about partly because he was frustrated by his lack of friends able to assist him there.

The fact that Essex was forced 'to stand alone like a substantive'[49] – or at least that he failed to pause sufficiently in the pursuit of his grander ambitions to forge useful alliances at Court – helps to explain both the nature and lack of success of his advocacy of Bacon and Sidney. Although all courtly offices were the subject of ferocious competition, the various suits of Bacon and Sidney were especially disadvantaged for two general reasons: because both men damaged their credibility by initially seeking to win places which were beyond their grasp and because of Essex's heavy-handed advocacy. In supporting Bacon, in particular, the essential thrust of Essex's advocacy was that Elizabeth should appoint him to the desired post because Bacon was his special friend and he was prepared to vouch for Bacon's suitability. Essex felt that his endorsement should itself be a sufficient qualification for office in Elizabeth's eyes. Learning from his failures with Bacon, he made a stronger case for Sidney, arguing the special relevance of his military and administrative experience. Nevertheless, when Sidney's suit faced defeat, Essex again deliberately cast the matter in very personal terms: 'I will protest unto the queen against him [Lord Cobham]

---

[48] *Parallel*, p. 10.   [49] *Ibid.*

and avow thatt I will thinke yt is the reward of his slanders and practise against me.'[50] Unable to compete with the number, subtlety and quality of those who lobbied for rival candidates, Essex played the only card which he thought might stave off defeat – making the success of his suit an expression of his own degree of favour with the queen.

In trying to make these suits into test-cases for the strength of his special relationship with Elizabeth, Essex resorted to the fundamentally personal tactics of a favourite, using a kind of emotional blackmail. This was precisely how he won many of his grants from the queen. In September 1594, for example, it was noted that, 'my lord of Essex did of late absent himself 10 dayes from the Court and hath bin in an exceeding fitt of mellancholy. But that humor is well diverted with an other promise of an other 50[li] in parckes.'[51] However, by using such tactics on behalf of Bacon and Sidney, Essex was conflating matters of state with relations between the queen and her favourite, for both men sought politically important offices – successively attorney-general, solicitor-general and master of the rolls in Bacon's case and warden of the Cinque Ports in Sidney's. Favour and influence always played an important part in matters of state but, for Elizabeth, these attempts to dictate key appointments were altogether too blatant. Essex's total lack of success in these suits underscores the point. It was one thing for Elizabeth to indulge Essex when he was merely her favourite – that, after all, was what was expected of a favourite – but it was quite another for her to allow personal affection to govern her decisions in affairs of state.

Since he pursued these different suits over long periods of time, the question naturally arises of whether Essex himself ever understood this distinction. Quite possibly, he did not. Despite these traumatic, but infrequent, rebuffs, this aspect of his relations with Elizabeth may have been obscured by the kind of daily intimacy sketched above, by his success in obtaining grants for himself using similar tactics, and by the seriousness with which she treated his views in matters of state. Of course, an alternative explanation is also possible: Essex may have deliberately tried to blur this very distinction which Elizabeth so desperately sought to maintain. Although it is impossible to give a conclusive answer one way or the other, the balance of probability lies with the former explanation. Essex showed considerable sophistication in his dealings with Elizabeth, but he also displayed genuine naivety in his appreciation of how Court politics actually worked. Both of these phenomena can be observed in the tactics which he employed in his pursuit of royal grants.

---

[50] PRO, SP 12/256, fol. 172[r].   [51] PRO, C 115, box M, bdle 20, no. 7587.

Once simple persuasion for a suit failed, Essex resorted to continual repetition of his request. As he explained to Sir Henry Unton, 'ther is not so much gotten of the queene by earnestnes as by often soliciting, accordinge to the proverbe, *saepe cadendo*'.[52] In practice, this frequent repetition verged on an attempt to browbeat Elizabeth. William Camden described Essex's actions as 'an obstinate kind of extorting (as it were) of favours from her'.[53] Francis Bacon later claimed that he always urged Essex against this behaviour because it was inherently corrosive of the very grace and favour which it played upon.[54] No doubt, it also contributed to the growing hostility towards Essex and his methods among other leading courtiers. Yet Essex's record shows that he was remarkably successful in his dealings with Elizabeth, a fact which reinforced his belief in the efficacy of his robust approach. Bacon later lamented that 'I well remember, when by violent courses at any time he had got his will, he wold aske me: now sir, whose principles be true?'[55]

Whether the product of his own mind or quoting Essex directly, Bacon's use of the word 'principles' in this context is significant, for it suggests a deliberateness in Essex's methods of obtaining grants. This connotation is entirely appropriate. Despite the undeniable crudeness of his overall strategy of wringing favours from Elizabeth, Essex demonstrated real calculation and tenacity in the tactics by which he sought to implement this strategy. This can perhaps best be seen in some of Essex's dealings on behalf of Bacon himself. Firstly, like all courtiers, Essex realised that the timing and preparation of his interventions with the queen were crucial. In one illuminating letter to Bacon, he analysed her mood and concluded: 'I finde nothinge to distaste us, for she doth not contradict confidently, which they that knowe the minde of women say is a signe of yeldinge. I will to morowe take more tyme to deale withe her and will sweten her withe all the arte I have.'[56] However, only days before this, Essex had had a sharp exchange with Elizabeth about Bacon's capabilities. The most striking fact about this disagreement was that it represented a quite deliberate tactic on Essex's part. On the following day, as he explained to the anxious Bacon, he would

---

[52] *Unton corr.*, p. 317. Essex used the same expression, '*saepe cadendo*', in a letter to Francis Bacon eighteen months later, in August 1593 (LPL, MS 649, fol. 253^r). This suggests that the phrase may have been a kind of maxim for him in his dealings with the queen.
[53] Camden, *Elizabeth*, p. 624.
[54] *Sir Francis Bacon his apologie, in certaine imputations concerning the late earle of Essex* (London, 1604, *STC* no. 1111), p. 16. Essex's conduct was also directly counter to the central piece of advice which Edward Dyer once gave to Hatton: he must never let the queen 'imagine that yow goe about to imprison her fancie and to wrappe her grace within your disposition ... [for] that will breed despyght and hatred in her towards yow' (FSL, V.b.214, fol. 109^v).
[55] Sir Francis Bacon, *Sir Francis Bacon his apologie*.   [56] LPL, MS 650, fol. 147^r.

ride away from the Court 'of purpose, and on Thursdaie I will wryght an expostulatinge lettre to her. That night, or upon Fridaie morning, I wilbe here againe and followe the same course, stirringe a discontentment in her.'[57] There was a real self-consciousness about many of Essex's dealings with the queen.

This is not to suggest that all of Essex's many stormy exchanges with Elizabeth were similarly scripted. Essex was constantly under enormous pressure, both from his own high expectations and from the hopes of those around him. Inevitably, the frustrations inherent in bearing this constant burden sometimes boiled over, as his 'sudden recesses' showed. Moreover, in his advocacy of suits, Essex was peculiarly able to control the circumstances of his approaches to the queen. On other occasions, this was not the case. Once his exchange with Elizabeth departed from his prepared mental script, Essex ran the risk of betraying his true feelings about her, as he did most explicitly in the grief-ridden, hectoring and yet also desperate letters which he wrote to her during his command in Normandy, and again in the last years of his career.[58]

Essex's feelings towards Elizabeth were decidedly ambivalent. This is perhaps not surprising because, although she represented the defining identity of the realm and embodied all that he had been taught to revere and obey, Elizabeth also often inhibited his efforts at public service. On the one hand, there was undoubtedly a strong vein of respect and affection in his praise for Elizabeth. These feelings should not be underestimated. Nevertheless, Essex clearly had growing difficulty with her indecisiveness and her unwillingness to allow him fully to pursue his conception of how the war should be fought. That he went to great lengths to make himself an expert in such matters merely made this all the more galling. As he lamented about her irresolution over his all-important Cadiz expedition: 'the queene wrangles with our action for no cause butt because yt is in hande'.[59] To be fair, all of Elizabeth's ministers found her prevarication and inconsistency a trial at times;[60] nevertheless, for Essex, who was decidedly a man of action and who habitually overstretched his own resources in

[57] Ibid., fol. 148ʳ.
[58] For examples of Essex's letters to Elizabeth, see Hulton MS (formerly BL, Loan 23), fols. 10ʳ–49ʳ, 58ʳ–133ʳ (these are printed in Devereux, Lives, and summarised in HMC. Twelfth report, appendix, part ix: The manuscripts of the duke of Beaufort, K.G., the earl of Donoughmore, and others (London, 1891), pp. 166ff); BL, Cotton MS Titus C VI, fols. 173ff; BL, Royal MS 17.B.l, fol. 17ʳ⁻ᵛ; FSL, V.b.214, fols. 106ʳ⁻ᵛ, 202ʳ.
[59] WRO, TD 69/6.2, item 82 (Essex to Edward Reynoldes, 10 May [1596]); copy is LPL, MS 657, fol. 140ʳ.
[60] See, for example, Walsingham's complaint to Burghley in September 1587 that 'she hathe no power to doe thinges in season' (BL, Harleian MS 6994, fol. 98ʳ) and Burghley's own dismay over her indecision about the relief of Calais in April 1596 (HMCS, VI, p. 141).

order to advance the war effort, the frustrations of dealing with Elizabeth could be acute.

Like most others who also felt themselves hindered by Elizabeth, Essex felt there was a simple explanation for his difficulties with her. As he told the French envoy de Maisse, he and his colleagues 'laboured under two things at this Court, delay and inconstancy, which proceeded chiefly from the sex of the queen'.[61] Essex was similarly blunt in letters to his sister Lady Rich: 'the tyme wherein wee live [is] more unconstant then women's thoughtes, more miserable then old age and breedeth both people and occasions like to itself, that is, violent, desperate and fantasticall'.[62] His poems constantly recited similar themes:

> Forget my name since you have scornd my love,
> And woman-like doe not to late lamente.[63]

For Essex, the fact his sovereign was a woman, and an ageing woman at that, created profound and unsettling difficulties. Despite his constant intimacy with her over more than a decade, it is doubtful whether he ever felt that he really understood Elizabeth. In this regard, his comment to Bacon about 'they that knowe the minde of women' is telling. Despite his confident adherence to his 'principles' for wringing favour from her, Essex wrote to Antonio Perez in October 1595 that Elizabeth was a sphinx whose riddles he could not unravel.[64]

Essex's fundamental mistrustfulness about the consequences on decision-making of the queen's sex determined his manner of dealing with her. When she did not respond positively to his flattery or a straightforward request, he clearly believed that it was necessary to force her to see sense.

---

61 [André Hurault, sieur] de Maisse, *A journal of all that was accomplished by Monsieur de Maisse ambassador to England from Henri IV to Queen Elizabeth anno domini 1597* (eds. G. B. Harrison and R. A. Jones, London, 1931), p. 115.

62 A. Freeman, 'Essex to Stella: two letters from the earl of Essex to Penelope Rich', *English Literary Renaissance* 3 (1973), pp. 248–50, letter II. Essex pursued the same idea in another letter to his sister: 'To hope for that which I have not is a vaine expectation, to delighte in that which I have is a deceaving pleasure, to wish the returne of that which is gone from me is womanish unconstancy' (*ibid.*, letter I).

63 May, 'Poems of Oxford and Essex', p. 46, ll. 8–9 of Essex poem no. 5 ('To plead my faith where faith hath noe reward ... '). The plaintive nature of Essex's surviving poetry can be partly explained by the conventions of courtly love, on which it plays. However, the aggrieved tone of a suitor bemused and unfairly scorned by his mistress seems to be more insistent than can be explained simply by literary convention.

64 Ungerer, I, pp. 360–1. Perez's playful reply is *ibid.*, pp. 367–8. For further comment by Essex about the riddling nature of the queen's responses to his requests, see Murdin, pp. 655–6. The characterisation of Elizabeth as Juno in his correspondence with Antonio Perez (mentioned above) also clearly reflects deep uncertainty about the queen. From Aeneas's point of view (i.e. Essex's), Juno is not only a powerful force who needs to be placated, but also embodies an essentially irrational female hostility to a future order that is both inevitable and necessary.

According to Bacon, Essex 'had a setled opinion that the queene could be brought to nothing but by a kind of necessitie and authority'.[65] Essex's response to a negative response from his female sovereign was to attempt a reassuring assertion of his own domineering masculinity. On one occasion, perhaps in the late summer of 1595, Essex did follow Bacon's advice and adopted a more humble tone, renewing 'a treaty with her Majestie of obsequious kindness'. However, he felt bitter at the results of this new approach, complaining that 'she had taken advantage of it'.[66] As a result, Essex became even more convinced about the need to adopt an assertive manner when trying to press Elizabeth. When he was bent on pushing a suit, this resulted in the kind of calculated 'extorting ... of favours' already observed. Essex could also be equally unscrupulous and high-handed in larger matters, although he recognised the need for extreme circumspection when crossing Elizabeth in issues of policy: 'I must, like the waterman, rowe one waie and looke an other.'[67]

Seeing himself as a latter-day Aeneas, whose righteous efforts to bring down the Spanish enemy were being thwarted by the Juno-like opposition of Elizabeth, Essex was prepared to indulge in underhand means to advance his views on war and foreign policy, especially during the crucial years of 1595 and 1596. At the end of 1595, he gave secret directions to Sir Henry Unton, when the latter went as ambassador to France, which embodied an explicit attempt to outflank the queen's opposition to further military aid to Henri IV.[68] If necessary, Unton was instructed to encourage the French king 'to cast out words that eyther *the queen* is caried to some secret treatye with *the king of Spain*, the hope of which makes *the queen* abandon him, or elce some of her ministers ar corrupted to seele her eyes & gnaw with their envious teeth the cordes of amitye' between them.[69] This was a quite outrageous transgression of his position as a member of the privy council. Yet Essex undertook a series of even more ambitious endeavours to force Elizabeth's hand over the scale and direction of the war effort in 1596. From his perspective, one of the principal aims of the whole Cadiz venture was to present her with a *fait accompli* of such magnitude that she could not avoid falling into line with his military strategy. When

---

[65] Bacon, *Apologie*, p. 16.
[66] Spedding, II, *Bacon letters*, p. 40. The dating of this episode to late summer 1595 is suggested by the queen's presence at Nonsuch during that period (E. K. Chambers, *The Elizabethan stage* (4 vols., Oxford, 1923), IV, App. A, p. 109) and the existence of a conciliatory letter from Essex to Elizabeth which may perhaps have been written in support of this initiative (*HMCS*, XIII, pp. 549–50).
[67] LPL, MS 658, fol. 136^r.
[68] LPL, MS 652, fol. 264^{r–v}. Hence Perez wrote to Essex of Unton as 'orator vester' (LPL, MS 653, fol. 150^r).
[69] LPL, MS 652, fol. 264^v. The words in italics are in cipher in the original.

that plan proved impractical, he sought to extract as much political advantage as possible from the victory by using furtive means to massage domestic public opinion about the war, to inflate his own reputation, and to press Elizabeth to keep part of the Cadiz army in being.

Despite the brazenness of the tactics which he used to manipulate her, Essex always saw himself as profoundly loyal to Elizabeth. When taxed by Burghley in the aftermath of his machinations over Cadiz, he replied emphatically: 'I pray your lordship beleive that I have no ambition but her Majestie's gratious favour & the reputation of well serving her.'[70] This reply was not simply an exercise in casuistry. Despite his vast frustrations with Elizabeth in person and her female 'delay and inconstancy', Essex dedicated himself absolutely to working for what he perceived as her own greater good – for the larger physical and moral community which she embodied. As he remarked on one occasion, 'I know I shall never do her service butt against her will.'[71]

In making this distinction between the queen's public and private persons, Essex demonstrated an attitude towards royal service which was quite in keeping with the behaviour of Elizabeth's generals and admirals, who usually ignored her instructions when it suited them.[72] Nevertheless, this attitude was quite different from that of his conciliar colleagues, most notably Burghley and Cecil. This fundamental divergence in outlook between Essex and the Cecils was an important ingredient in the growing tensions between them in the middle years of the decade. As he grew older and more feeble, Burghley increasingly looked to the person of the queen as the only guarantee of stability in those turbulent times.[73] Burghley also emphasised an elevated, indivisible conception of divinely ordained monarchy when training his son in the ways of statecraft. Thus he instructed Robert of his response when Elizabeth acted contrary to his advice:

I will not chang my opinion by affirmyng the contrary, for that war to offend God,

---

[70] LPL, MS 659, fol. 196r.

[71] WRO, TD 69/6.2, item 82 ; copy is LPL, MS 657, fol. 140r.

[72] See, for example, R. B. Wernham, *After the Armada: Elizabethan England and the struggle for Western Europe* (Oxford, 1984), pp. 107, 159, 522; also his *The expedition of Sir John Norris and Sir Francis Drake to Spain and Portugal* (Navy Records Soc., CXXVII, 1988), pp. xxx–xxxi, xxxvii–lix, xlii ff, liv–lvi, lxv–lxvi; C. Haigh, *Elizabeth I* (London and New York, 1988), pp. 125ff. Perhaps significantly, Sir Francis Walsingham also had similar views: 'the two generalls ar wysse and men of corage: they will venter rather to hazard her Majeste's dyslyke rather then to overthrowghe the actyon' (PRO, SP 12/224, fol. 9r).

[73] This is apparent in some of Burghley's marginal annotations on various state papers. On a document describing the woes of Scotland, for example, he wrote: 'a miserable state that may cause us to bless ours and our governes' (PRO, SP 52/50, no. 67). On another paper which reported Catholic claims that he sought to make himself master of the queen and to control the succession, he scrawled: 'it war better for Cecill hymself to dy first' (PRO, SP 85/1[ii], fol. 150v).

to whom I am sworn first, but as a servant I will obey her Majeste's commaund-ment, and no wise contrary the same, presuming that, she being Gode's cheff minister heare, it shall be Gode's will to have hir commandmentes obeyed.[74]

By contrast, Essex's conception of 'well serving' the queen made him willing to risk her wrath for the sake of what he regarded as the greater loyalty that he owed her. In practical terms, this meant that he was prepared to defy and manipulate Elizabeth in order to commit her to a crusade against Spain which he believed was necessary and would vastly increase her power and prestige.

However, if he was willing to act boldly in what he conceived to be her best interests, Essex also expected that Elizabeth would display special gratitude to him when she finally recognised – as he imagined – the wisdom of his ways. This was a belief encouraged by the whole ethos of the cult of knightly honour. By this view, his noble virtues would be revealed to the world not only in his deeds against the Spanish but also in his constancy of purpose. In turn, this active expression of virtue would constitute 'merit', a personal worth inherently deserving of public acclaim and reward from the sovereign.[75] At times when Elizabeth remained averse to his pleadings, this could be a consoling belief. Shortly before he sailed to Cadiz, Essex wrote to her in response to her 'unkind dealing' at a time when he was about to do her 'exceeding great service': 'howsoever it pleaseth you to punish me at my going oute, I knowe your just and royall hart will ryght me at my returne, and then I will bury my sorrowes in the joy I shall receave'.[76] It is also telling that during the campaign season of 1597 – when the success of his political and martial aspirations hung in the balance – Essex consistently signed his letters to Elizabeth as her humble 'vassall', rather than her faithful 'servant'.[77] By invoking his status as her vassal, Essex not only stressed his duty of service to Elizabeth but reminded her that rewards for brave subjects were the very foundation of the social order.[78]

---

[74] CUL, MS Ee.iii.56, no. 85. Burghley repeated this injunction in his very last letter to Robert: 'serve God by servyng of the quene, for all other service is in dede bondage to the devill' (*ibid.*, no. 138).

[75] It is interesting that a forward Protestant such as Essex should describe the state which placed an obligation on the queen to reward the good works of her servants with a word which was so redolent of Catholic theology. Although his religious beliefs were clearly opposed to the tenets of Catholicism, it seems that Essex's cultural values were still powerfully influenced by traditional notions. As noted above, for example, Essex and many other internationally minded Protestants frequently described Europe by invoking the essentially Romanist concept of 'Christendom'.

[76] Cecil MS 40/66 (pr. *HMCS*, VI, p. 171).

[77] Devereux, *Lives*, I, pp. 414, 415, 416, 420, 427, 433, 434, 447, 448, 454. For Essex's previous preference for signing himself as Elizabeth's 'most humble servant', especially in his letters from Normandy in 1591–2, see *ibid.*, pp. 207, 219, 237, 241, 242, 244, 245, 247, 250, 256.

[78] The etymology of the 'vassal' – of which Essex would have been well aware – was spelled

This conception of the nature of his service to the queen is crucial to understanding Essex's career. It provides the moral underpinning for the enormous drive and scale of his work for Elizabeth, with its characteristic mixture of personal ambition and professions of extreme loyalty to his sovereign. It also captures something of the great and principled consistency in Essex's actions, for it represents a deep adherence to the advice urged upon him in the funeral sermon for his father: 'throw the helve after the hatchet, and leave your ruynes to be repayred by your prince'.[79] On the other hand, this expectation that Elizabeth would ultimately repair his ruins, and more, was fundamentally naive and loaded with obvious potential for disillusionment. This was especially so because Essex's conceptions about virtue and reward did not fit well with the realities of politics.

Something of the difficulties underlying these expectations can be seen by exploring the implications of Essex's claim that 'the greatnesse of her Majestie's favour must growe out of the greatnesse of her servantes' merite'.[80] In this formulation of his credo, designed for public consumption, Essex emphasised a necessary relationship between virtuous service on the part of royal servants and reward on the part of the queen: while the former must earn reward, preferably in war, the latter is expected to respond to merit by bestowing reward. Although apparently simple, this understanding of royal service and the political efficacy of merit had profound implications for Essex's behaviour at Court, and even for his loyalty to Elizabeth.

At first glance, Essex's conduct at Court might seem contradictory, even schizophrenic. On the one hand, he could behave as a paragon of courtly accomplishment – renowned for his skills in the tilt-yard, lauded for his speech and poetry, admired for his theatrical sense of display, and favoured above all other courtiers by the queen.[81] Yet Essex also stood aloof from,

---

out by Robert Dallington: 'The feif is the thing, by acceptation wherof, they that hold it are bound in oath and fidelitie to their lordes: and therefore are called vassals, of (wesses) the olde Gaule word which signifieth valiant, for to such were feifs given ...' Dallington also explains: 'the word feif hath his etymologie of (foy) faith, signifying lands given by the king to his nobilitie or men of desert with *hault et basse justice*, with an acknowledgement of fealtie and homage, and service of the king in his warres at their owne charge ... ' (*The view of Fraunce* (London, 1604, STC no. 6202), sig. K4ʳ⁻ᵛ, K3ᵛ). These definitions catch the mix of aristocratic, martial, historical, moral and political connotations which Essex consciously evoked by his choice of the word 'vassal'. Dallington attended upon the earl of Rutland during his trip to Italy in 1596 and his account of France is based upon travel there on the way home in 1598: K. J. Holtgen, 'Sir Robert Dallington (1561–1637): author, traveller and pioneer of taste', *Huntington Library Quarterly* 47 (1984), pp. 158–9.

[79] See above, p. 22.   [80] *Apologie*, sig. A3ᵛ.
[81] See, for example, R. Heffner, 'Essex, the perfect courtier', [*A Journal of*] *English Literary History* 1 (1934), pp. 7–36.

and even opposed to, much of the characteristic behaviour of the Court. In particular, he sought to affect a very straightforward, and even blunt, manner which made him seem, as his contemporaries subsequently noted, 'not a man made for the Court'.[82] Essex always eschewed the kind of dissimulation suggested to him by Francis Bacon and other advisers,[83] even though he certainly was prepared to use calculated and underhand means to manipulate Elizabeth in other ways. Despite being the royal favourite, Essex deliberately distanced himself from the courtier-like behaviour associated with the great favourites before him, seeking 'to fly and avoid ... the resemblance or imitation of my lord of Leicester and my lord chancellor Hatton'.[84]

In all this, Essex's dedication to winning honour by the pursuit of virtue, and his conception that this quest must inevitably win him royal favour, are vitally important. Indeed, the apparent contradiction in his behaviour at Court instead assumes a general consistency. For, while courtly accomplishments were recognised as evidence of personal virtue, the indirectness and flattery endemic to Court were seen by Essex as antithetical to virtue.[85] This is clear in his abhorrence of sycophancy, which he saw as profoundly inimical to merit. Flattery not only suggested a counterfeit form of honour, but – as he knew from reading Tacitus's biography of Agricola[86] – provided

---

[82] Camden, *Elizabeth*, p. 624. See also Clapham, *Elizabeth of England*, pp. 94–5 and Wotton, *Parallel*, pp. 1, 9. The French ambassador, de Maisse, also commented on Essex's aloofness ('independence') from the ordinary pettiness of the Court (de Maisse, *Journal*, p. 19).

[83] Lord Henry Howard likewise encouraged Essex to adopt a more calculating approach to his words and actions (DUL, Howard MS 2). Henry Cuffe may also have counselled Essex to use dissimulation. According to Camden, Cuffe 'was wont to complain to me [that the earl] ... carried his love and his hatred always in his brow, and could not hide it' (Camden, *Elizabeth*, p. 624).

[84] Spedding, II, *Bacon letters*, p. 42.

[85] See, for example, *HMCS*, V, p. 280. A similar attitude was expressed by many self-confessed 'martial men', despite (or, perhaps, because of) the fact that many of these men sometimes attended at Court. Essex's friend, Lord Willoughby, is alleged to have proclaimed 'that he was none of the *reptilia* [of Court], intimating that he could not creep and crouch' (Sir Robert Naunton, *Fragmenta regalia or observations on Queen Elizabeth, her times & favourites* (ed. J. S. Cerovski, Washington, London and Toronto, 1985), pp. 61–2).

[86] The danger posed by sycophancy at Court was spelled out at great length by Savile in his notes on the story of Agricola: 'the most capitall kinde of enemies, commenders. To hurt or disgrace by way of commendation, albeit it seemeth a strange position at the first sight, yet may be, & daily is, both easily & diversly performed. For example: to commende a man to his prince for those qualities wherein the prince himselfe either by his place ought to excell, or otherwise upon some speciall fancy affecteth to excell, & principally if he finde any weaknes that way in himselfe, is one of the most suttle, ready & pernicios means to worke a great man in disgrace with his prince ... above all other kindes of commendations, that toucheth most nearly & worketh most danger where the quality commended breedeth not only love but admiration also generally among the meane people: as militar renowne, patronage of justice against al oppressions & wrongs, magnificence & other heroical

a ready means to poison the mind of a prince against virtuous men. Being a 'sycophant' was one of the most heartfelt of the charges of 'baseness' which Essex made against his bitter enemy, Henry Brooke, during the struggle over the wardenship of the Cinque Ports.[87] In order to distinguish himself from such conduct, and believing that the active display of virtue must bring recognition and reward, Essex combined his exhibition of courtly accomplishments with a directness of manner which was quite uncourtier-like and yet which, in his mind, connoted a kind of blunt honesty.[88] From this perspective, Essex's sometimes domineering manner with Elizabeth takes on a new light. Not only could Essex justify his attempts to manipulate or bully her by the 'goodness' of the ends to which he sought to sway her, but the very crudeness of his strategy was itself intended to suggest an honourable artlessness.

Essex's conduct at Court and his manner of dealing with Elizabeth were fundamentally conditioned by his notions of virtuous behaviour. Essex's resort to 'violent courses' was therefore a far more 'principled' perception of courtly conduct than Francis Bacon realised, dooming his efforts to change this behaviour to failure from the start. Although he understood Bacon's advice, Essex's attitudes were based upon assumptions which were so fundamental to his world-view that he could not accept it. However, Bacon was in many ways correct about the problems inherent in Essex's approach to courtly life. His tendency to use coercion when he sought something important from Elizabeth inevitably undermined his personal relationship with her, especially after he became a councillor as well as a favourite. As the political stakes were raised, Essex was also constrained to adopt ever more 'violent' means to put pressure on Elizabeth.[89] The

---

vertues properly belonging to, or chiefly beseeming, the prince's person. And this being general to al in some measure, no prince in the world havinge his minde so well armed against this cunning but that some breach may be made at some seasons into it ... Many other kindes might be reckened of this sort of sophistrie, as to commende a man publickely, where it can doe no good (beside that it maketh the party secure of all danger from thence) and secretely dispraise him, where it should doe the most harme ... ' ([Henry Saville], *The ende of Nero and beginninge of Galba. Fower bookes of the Histories of Cornelius Tacitus. The life of Agricola* ([London], 1591, *STC* no. 23642), sig. Dd4^v–Dd5^v (pp. 46–8 of second pagination)).

87 *HMCD*, II, pp. 238, 246, 251; PRO, SP 12/256, fol. 172^r. Cf. Wotton, *Parallel*, p. 9. The attitude of Essex and his circle towards the new Lord Cobham is strongly expressed in a letter of Anthony Bacon to Dr Henry Hawkyns, reflecting on Cobham's final success in winning the wardenship of the Cinque Ports: 'the generall hatred & contempt of whose former course of lyfe & humours, I feare me, will hardlie be worne out or covered by the robes of an honorable baron' (LPL, MS 656, fol. 72^r).

88 According to John Clapham, 'so farre was hee [i.e. Essex] from soothing and simulation that he would not use it, even at those times when it might have most avayled him' (BL, Add. MS 22925, fol. 42^v (pr. Clapham, *Elizabeth of England*, p. 95)).

89 Cf. Bacon, *Apologie*, pp. 16–17.

insistent advocacy with which he vainly supported the suits of Francis
Bacon therefore gave way to the undisguised venting of his spleen towards
Cobham over the Cinque Ports issue. By the end of 1597, Essex was even
prepared to withdraw himself from the queen's business and to plunge
Court and council alike into disarray in order to win the office of earl
marshal.[90]

As well as profoundly influencing his behaviour at Court, Essex's
conception of royal service and the rewarding of merit necessarily raises
again the question of his loyalty to Elizabeth. At the heart of this
conception lay an ideal of reciprocity between the sovereign and her
virtuous servant. This was an essentially moral understanding of public
action and laden with potential problems, not least because the whole
notion of reciprocity was decidedly vulnerable to pressures created by both
parties to this imagined accord. For a start, Elizabeth's desire and ability to
reward her subjects were subject to the inevitable vagaries of political
circumstance. Yet when she failed to respond to merit, for whatever reason,
Essex's conception of service and reward came under strain. At the same
time, in his own case at least, this problem was vastly accentuated by the
sheer energy and ambition which characterised his royal service. Since
Essex's whole career was dedicated to forever loading the scales with new
acts of meritorious conduct, how could Elizabeth continue to balance his
expectations with suitable rewards? From this, in turn, springs a question
which opens up the matter of his loyalty: how far was Essex able to sustain
his sense of loyalty to Elizabeth when his fundamental conception of royal
service and reward was undermined by her failure to reward him appropriately?

Until at least the end of 1597, Essex remained resolutely loyal to
Elizabeth, albeit in a way which sometimes allowed him to seek to
manipulate or bully her for what he conceived to be her own greater good.
Despite occasional tensions between them and the growing force of
political considerations, Essex's ingrained sense of loyalty to his lawful
sovereign coincided with, and reinforced, the more directly personal loyalty
of a favourite towards his 'mistress'. If Elizabeth remained unwilling to
recognise the merit of his advice or service, Essex still comforted himself
with the belief that she must do so eventually. Nevertheless, the shattering
criticism which he received for his efforts at Cadiz and the Azores made
this conviction increasingly hard to maintain. There were also a few straws
in the wind which pointed towards the kind of ambiguous loyalty and
fractured trust which characterised relations between Essex and Elizabeth
at the end of the decade. The philosophical raw materials, for example,

[90] See below, pp. 386ff.

were already at hand. The system of values expressed in the knightly honour cult – in spite of its ceremonial focus upon the sovereign – posited a conception of moral legitimacy which was actually independent of the idea of a divinely appointed monarchy.[91] In the mind of Essex, and many others like him, this moral legitimacy necessarily had a political authority. Thus, on occasions when he was involved in a dispute with Elizabeth, Essex consistently justified his resistance to her on the grounds of honour.[92]

Far more controversial ideas about the relationship between loyalty and honour were also aired in Essex's circle. In 1595, his secretary Henry Wotton wrote a paper about some of the issues raised by a new edition of Antonio Perez's autobiographical *Pedaços de historia ô relaçiones*.[93] The aim of this exercise was to demonstrate that Elizabeth could, and indeed should, declare war upon the king of Spain on behalf of the people of Aragon. This was perfectly in tune with Essex's staunchly anti-Spanish opinions. However, the true significance of this paper lies in the dangerous ground which Wotton traversed in order to reach this conclusion. In particular, Wotton gave explicit support to the idea of limited monarchy: 'in violating the latter [the laws of nature], they [princes] remember not their maker on earth; for the people and peers of the realm are their makers next unto God'.[94] This was directly at odds with the official Elizabethan dogma of obedience to the divinely ordained prince as a duty to the Lord. Equally significant is the role which the nobility plays in Wotton's argument. According to him, the concept of nobles disciplining their sovereign, should he or she be seen to err greatly in some way, is as 'common and ordinary' as lesser officers taking their superiors to task for gross negligence.[95] Similar ideas were commonplace among Huguenot political theorists and Essex (like Wotton) would have been very familiar with them

---

[91] M. James, 'English politics and the concept of honour' in his *Society, politics and culture: studies in early modern England* (Cambridge, 1986), pp. 308–415; also his 'At the crossroads of the political culture: the Essex revolt, 1601', in *ibid.*, pp. 416–65; R. C. McCoy, '"A dangerous image": the earl of Essex and Elizabethan chivalry', *Journal of Medieval and Renaissance Studies* 18 (1983), pp. 313–29; also McCoy, *The rites of knighthood: the literature and politics of Elizabethan chivalry* (Berkeley, Los Angeles and London, 1989).

[92] See, for example, his behaviour during his argument with Elizabeth at Northaw in July 1587 (BLO, Tanner MS 76, fol. 29^{r-v}; BL, Tanner MS 77, fol. 178^r), his response to the traumatic criticism which he recieved from the queen during the early part of the Rouen campaign in 1591 (Hulton MS (formerly BL, Loan 23), fols. 25^r, 28^r, 34^r) and his steadfast refusal to attend Court after his return from the Azores without having his honour upheld and rewarded by the queen (*HMCD*, II, pp. 302, 305; de Maisse, *Journal*, pp. 18, 28, 48–9, 64, 67–8, 70–1, 75, 90).

[93] This paper is printed in Ungerer, II, pp. 280–321. In the first instance, this analysis was presumably intended for Essex himself.

[94] *Ibid.*, p. 304.   [95] *Ibid.*, pp. 307–8, 313.

in that context.[96] However, Wotton's argument was particularly dangerous because he explicitly related it back to England. In order to dramatise the plight of Aragon, Wotton implies a potential local relevance for this claim by comparing Philip's infringement of the rights of the Aragonese nobility to the idea of a prince removing the right of trial by one's peers from the English nobility.[97] Perhaps not surprisingly, Wotton's paper was not published until some sixty years after it was written.[98]

Dangerous ideas about the nature of loyalty to a sovereign, and of a sovereign's responsibilities in return for such loyalty, were therefore pondered within Essex's intellectual circle as early as 1595. Essex did not necessarily encourage this line of questioning or agree with these ideas at the time, but he must have been fully cognisant of them. However, when Essex did publicly criticise the orthodox doctrine of monarchy, as he did in mid-1598 ('Cannott princes erre? Cannott subjectes receive wrong?'[99]), it is clear that he did so with a full understanding of what he was doing. There is thus more justice in Francis Bacon's use of that criticism as evidence against Essex during his trial of 1600 than has usually been recognised.[100] However, Essex did not feel the need to make such a profession of his doubts before mid-1598.

By the end of 1597, Essex's position as favourite, like his relations with many of the leading figures at Court, was clearly dissolving. His extraordinary campaign against the promotion of the lord admiral, and for his own elevation to the post of earl marshal, severely dented the image of zealous concern for the queen's business which he had fostered through years of hard work. By his absence from Court, he engaged in a direct test of wills with Elizabeth. Yet a fundamental core of loyalty still remained during this crisis, albeit at times a tenuous one. Covering his withdrawal

---

[96] See L. F. Parmalee, *Good newes from Fraunce: French anti-League propaganda in late Elizabethan England* (Rochester, N.Y., 1996), esp. ch. 4, and the various other works cited therein.

[97] Ungerer, II, p. 310.

[98] It was finally published as an appendix at the end of Wotton's *The state of Christendom* in 1657.

[99] Essex's profession continues: 'Is an earthly power or aucthoritye infinite? Pardon me, pardon me, my lord, I can never subscribe to these principles' (HEH, EL 1612, p. 64). This quotation is from only one of the very many copies which survive of Essex's exchange of letters with Lord Keeper Egerton. The ubiquity of such copies among manuscript collections strongly argues that Essex had them widely circulated as a semi-public statement of his position. Copies of these letters are frequently bound with an account of Essex's own trial in 1601, suggesting that these documents together constituted a package which was seen as having special moral or political value by those who lived under the Stuarts. On the subject of dating these letters, see G. B. Harrison, *The life and death of Robert Devereux earl of Essex* (London, 1937), p. 342.

[100] For Bacon's use of this letter against Essex, see Fynes Morison, *An itinerary containing his ten yeeres travell . . .* (4 vols., Glasgow, 1907–8 edn), II, p. 316.

from public business by the fig-leaf of ill-health, Essex turned to Elizabeth to uphold his honour and strengthen him against his courtly 'enemies'. For all the nakedness of the pressures which he was applying to her, Essex still looked to Elizabeth as the rewarder of merit. It was only in 1598, when his whole political and personal *raison d'être* was challenged by the prospect of peace with Spain, that Essex ventured to criticise her directly.[101] However, the crossing of that Rubicon is a subject which properly belongs outside the scope of this study. At the end of 1597, despite his frequent anguish about Elizabeth's treatment of him, Essex still had hope of winning her over and reordering English policy according to his martial agenda.

[101] This was most famously expressed by the incident, probably at the beginning of July 1598,when Elizabeth struck Essex in a council meeting and the earl, in turn, tried to draw his sword on her (Camden, *Elizabeth*, pp. 555–6). See also Essex's bitter letter to Elizabeth remonstrating that she had 'nott only broken all lawes of affection, butt [had] done [so] against the honour of your sex' (Hulton MS (formerly BL, Loan 23), fol. 113^{r-v}).

9

'Yf we lyved not in a cunning world ... '

After the queen, Essex's most important relationship at Court was with Burghley, the old lord treasurer. This was a complex and difficult relationship. Burghley had been Essex's most influential guardian and had continued to treat him as a protégé, despite the earl's close association with Leicester. However, after Essex's return from Rouen, first an awkwardness and then a kind of rivalry developed between them. Although they differed sharply in temperament, and later also in policy, the real bone of contention between them was the question of who would have the prime influence on Elizabeth's government after Burghley's inevitable demise. Essex increasingly sought this role for himself, while Burghley was equally resolute in advancing and protecting the interests of his younger son, Sir Robert Cecil. Once Essex endeavoured to make himself into a politician, conflict between former guardian and former ward became virtually inevitable.

Reduced to this bare outline, the course and nature of Essex's relations with the Cecils would seem very simple. In reality, matters were far less straightforward. On both sides, there remained mixed feelings and uncertainties about the nature of their relations with each other. For several years, despite the obviousness of the clash between them, there was a more or less sustained effort to defend a *modus vivendi* which allowed them to co-operate closely in managing government business. Essex's relationship with Burghley also had a different character to his dealings with Cecil. For their part, Burghley and Cecil started with different perceptions of Essex, although a more singularly 'Cecilian' view of Essex might be said to have emerged during the course of the 1590s.[1]

---

[1] This view is perhaps best expressed in the distinctly Cecilian accounts of Elizabeth's reign later written by William Camden and John Clapham. In gratitude for their favour towards him, Camden proclaimed himself 'bound for ever Ceciliano nomini, wherunto I have allwayes [been], and will continewe, devoted' (BL, Add. MS 36294, fol. 24^r). Clapham was an intimate servant of Burghley, whose will he witnessed and by whom he was left an annuity of £6 13s 4d (PRO, PROB 11/92, fol. 245^r). Both writers portray Essex in a similar light: that he was politically unwise and dangerous, but was not inherently evil, odious (as they saw Leicester) or lacking in many laudable qualities. Broadly speaking, these views

As Essex's former guardian and Elizabeth's chief minister, Burghley possessed a certain moral and political superiority over Essex, which the earl himself respected. For his part, the lord treasurer recognised that his former ward had a special weight in political affairs, because of his nobility and much-advertised personal qualities, and because he was the queen's favourite.[2] At times, especially during 1593, this mutual regard came close to being lost. Nevertheless, despite the cross words and daggered thoughts which sometimes passed between them, this mutual respect seems to have endured. Even at the end of 1597, when the picture he paints of the English Court is that of sharp division, the French envoy de Maisse noted of Burghley and Essex that 'they have great respect for each other and render strange charities to each other'.[3] When Burghley finally died in 1598, there is little reason to doubt that Essex's grief was truly heartfelt.[4]

Robert Cecil's position relative to Essex was initially that of very considerable inferiority. Cecil's advancement depended entirely upon his father winning him promotion to a place where he could try to gain the queen's respect through his own feverish industry.[5] Together with a self-consciousness about his unprepossessing personal appearance, this encouraged Cecil to present a deliberately self-effacing image to the world.[6] With Essex, whom he had known since childhood, Cecil's feelings of personal insecurity were probably fairly acute. Essex's often arrogant sense of his own nobility and his physical presence – quickly growing from a 'weake & tender' boy into a tireless jouster and ornament of the Court – must have seemed daunting in the light of his own stooped figure and his status as the

---

probably embody a distillation of opinions expressed to them by Burghley or Cecil, albeit with the vital added ingredient of hindsight.

[2] The importance which Burghley attached to Essex's aristocratic status is suggested by his well-known fascination with family pedigrees. Burghley's attitude towards Essex also exhibits some parallels with his indulgent and deferential behaviour towards the young duke of Norfolk in the 1560s: C. Read, *Mr Secretary Cecil and Queen Elizabeth* (London, 1955), pp. 331–2.

[3] [André Hurault, sieur] de Maisse, *A journal of all that was accomplished by Monsieur de Maisse ambassador to England from Henri IV to Queen Elizabeth anno domini 1597* (eds. G. B. Harrison and R. A. Jones, London, 1931), p. 114.

[4] N. E. McClure (ed.), *The letters of John Chamberlain* (2 vols., American Philosophical Society, Memoirs, XII, 1939), I, p. 41.

[5] From the start, Cecil had to endure the queen's mocking of his physical appearance. In February 1588, when Elizabeth wrote to him 'under her sporting name of pygmy', the young Cecil was clearly cut to the quick. Unable to complain to Elizabeth herself, he wrote to John Stanhope that 'I mislike not the name only because she gives it' (P. M. Handover, *The second Cecil: the rise to power, 1563–1604, of Sir Robert Cecil, later first earl of Salisbury* (London, 1959]), p. 57).

[6] See, for example, *HMCS*, IV, p. 535. Even after he was well established on the council, Cecil continued to affect this self-deprecating image, in part (although not entirely) because it was politically useful. See, for example, his reply to a request by Thomas Bodley in April 1596 (PRO, SP 84/52, fol. 132[r]).

younger son of a newly ennobled baron.[7] Cecil and Essex were quite friendly during their adolescence and early adulthood – a friendship which Burghley deliberately encouraged – but Cecil must have realised that this relationship was lubricated by Essex's feeling of easy superiority and by deference on his own part.

Like his father, Cecil clearly expected that Essex would be a dominant figure in the political landscape for decades to come. When tensions first arose between his father and Essex in 1591, Cecil was placed in an awkward position. On the one hand, he was his father's son, and a son who was true to contemporary ideals of filial duty at that. Thus he was always anxious to obtain the office of secretary of state, which would secure his own future influence and reinforce his father's political position, even though this was anathema to Essex. On the other hand, Cecil also knew – even more acutely than his father – that he would have to accommodate himself to Essex's continued presence on the political stage for long years ahead. Cecil therefore not only sought to avoid open competition with Essex as far as possible, but also to follow any difficulties with Essex by seeking to re-establish an appearance of friendly relations between them.

As with much else in his career, the Rouen command and its aftermath proved to be a watershed in Essex's relations with the Cecils. While in Rouen, he had looked to Burghley as both Elizabeth's chief co-ordinator of the campaign and his own chief defender at Court.[8] By contrast, the more familiar tone of his letters to Cecil suggests that Essex viewed him as a friend and as an informal route for information to his father.[9] However, the painful experiences of the Rouen campaign eroded Essex's trust in Burghley. As Sir Henry Unton warned Cecil, Essex 'suspecteth my lord your father hath not so much favored him in his absence as he expected'.[10] By the start of 1592, Burghley's own position had also changed. With Hatton's death in November 1591, he gained an unprecedented dominance over government and policy. Hatton's death also meant that Essex lost a powerful protector and that Burghley could no longer rely on Hatton to push for Cecil's advancement. Henceforth, Burghley would have to manage Cecil's preferment himself.

Essex's feelings of resentment on his return from France did not prevent

---

[7] In December 1595, Cecil was reported to have referred to Essex as 'long slang' (CKS, U 1475, C12/41 (pr. *HMCD*, II, p. 198)). Although derisive, this comment suggests Cecil's constant awareness of Essex's greater height and physical presence.

[8] See, for example, PRO, SP 78/25, fols. 170^r, 256^r, 275^{r-v}, 287^r, 299^r–300^r, 338^r, 365^r–6^v; PRO, SP 78/26, fols. 48^r–49^v, 69^r–71^r, 113^r–16^r, 157^{r-v}, 271^r, 273^r, 278^r, 328^r–30^r.

[9] See, for example, BL, Add. MS 6177, fol. 14^r; PRO, SP 78/25, fol. 338^r. Sir Roger Williams also stated that Cecil proved himself to be 'most kind unto the earle of Essex' businesse' when the latter was in France (PRO, SP 78/27, fol. 139^r).

[10] *Unton corr.*, p. 264.

him from working with Burghley in matters where he needed the great man's help. During the early months of 1592, together with Cecil, they co-operated closely over further assistance to Henri IV.[11] Essex also sought to mobilise Burghley's support to prevent Sir John Perrot – his sister's father-in-law, a privy councillor and former lord deputy of Ireland – from being tried for treason.[12] However, Perrot's case would have done little to ease tensions left over from Rouen. Despite Essex's protestations, Perrot's trial went ahead.[13] Moreover, Essex must have come to realise that Burghley's support for Perrot was distinctly half-hearted. Although it is unclear when the penny dropped, Essex must have finally recognised that Burghley was playing hard-ball politics at its most brutal. Although posing as Perrot's friend, Burghley was ruthless enough to throw his colleague to the wolves and to obtain Elizabeth's acquiescence to Perrot's condemnation in a farcical show-trial. By doing so, Burghley protected the reputation of his client and relative, Sir William Fitzwilliam, who was Perrot's successor in Ireland. Burghley also concealed his own part in Irish affairs from scrutiny and ensured that the English regime there was dominated by men loyal to Cecilian interests.[14] Although Essex was never very close to Sir John Perrot, this episode must have been an object lesson in the reality of Burghley's power and a warning not to meddle too closely in Irish matters. It was also another reminder of Essex's own inability to influence key matters of government business while he still lacked a place on the council.

As the Perrot affair was coming to a head, Essex was also concerned with money. After his return from Rouen, Essex expected reward – or at least recompense – from Elizabeth in return for his all labours and expenditure in her service. The pursuit of his martial ambitions in France had cost Essex

---

[11] BL, Cotton MS Caligula E VIII, fol. 176^r; PRO, SP 12/241, fol. 98^r; *Unton corr.*, pp. 277ff.

[12] PRO, SP 12/242, fol. 7^r. For Essex's earlier efforts to assist Perrot, see PRO, SP 12/238, fol. 118^r; PRO, SP 15/32, fol. 10^r; FSL, L.a.264.

[13] Perrot's trial began on 27 April 1592. Although Elizabeth stayed proceedings on no less than six occasions, Perrot was found guilty on 16 June and sentenced to death. The execution was never carried out and Perrot died in the Tower in September. The delays, the failure to carry out the sentence, and the speedy restoration in blood of Sir Thomas Perrot by an act of the 1593 parliament suggest a kind of political *quid pro quo* by which Elizabeth agreed to allow Perrot's condemnation, whilst his enemies accepted that his destruction would be political and not extend to his life or lands. In this process, Perrot's innocence of treason seems to have been irrelevant. To satisfy the need for blood and to make the charges against Perrot seem genuine, an Irish lord, Brian O'Rourke, was tried and executed in London for allegedly related treasons at the end of 1591 (H. Morgan, 'Extradition and treason-trial of a Gaelic lord: the case of Brian O'Rourke', *Irish Jurist* 22 (1987), pp. 285–301).

[14] For all this, see H. Morgan, 'The fall of Sir John Perrot', in J. Guy (ed.), *The reign of Elizabeth I: Court and culture in the last decade* (Cambridge, 1995), pp. 109–25. Morgan argues that Burghley was forced into this manoeuvre after Fitzwilliam's own clumsy attempt to smear Perrot threatened to backfire and bring down Fitzwilliam himself.

very dearly indeed. However, when he pushed Elizabeth for a grant to lighten his debts, he met with a cool response. She instructed Essex to make his suit through Cecil, now the most junior member of the council.[15] Although Elizabeth may have chosen this tactic as a means of encouraging co-operation between Essex and Cecil, Essex regarded it as an insulting response to his appeal. When his increasingly desperate pleas for relief[16] were met with inconclusive replies from Elizabeth, Essex had renewed cause to become, 'of all other, the most discontented person of the Court'.[17] Cecil was merely an intermediary in this process but, for a while, he became the immediate target of Essex's frustrations: 'your friend, if I have cause'.[18] Such letters would hardly have endeared Essex to Cecil's protective father.

In spite of these strains, Essex and the Cecils were apparently on good terms again by the end of 1592. In October, Essex sent 'my best thankes' to Burghley for his assistance in negotiating a grant from the queen which finally provided some help with his debts.[19] At this point, Essex's main response to the Rouen experience – his new resolution to enter into 'matters of state' – had not yet made a real impact upon his dealings with the Cecils. That finally came in 1593, when Essex was appointed to the privy council. Essex's promotion encouraged him to push himself forward

---

[15] Murdin, p. 656.

[16] In March 1592, Essex's servants Thomas Crompton, Robert Wright and Gelly Meyrick sold a manor in Devon, undoubtedly to help meet the earl's debts (PRO, C 66/1392, m. 29). By July, Essex was himself forced to spend three days dealing with money-lenders and pawnbrokers (Murdin, p. 656). Despite these distasteful dealings and a later grant from the queen (noted below in note 19), he had to sell lands later in the year to Peter Osborne (PRO, C 66/1383, m. 39; PRO, SP 38/2, fol. 73^r) and to Sir Thomas Sherley (ibid., fol. 122^r). In June, he also explored the possibility of selling his Irish lands in County Monaghan (ibid., SP 63/165, fol. 15^r). However, these lands were instead leased out to the unscrupulous John Talbot by December (PRO, SP 63/168, fols. 126^r, 209^r; APC, XXIII, 1592, pp. 376–7).

[17] A. G. Petti (ed.), The letters and despatches of Richard Verstegan (c.1550–1640) (Catholic Record Society, LII, 1959), p. 59.

[18] Murdin, p. 655. Essex's extant letters to Cecil concerning this episode are printed in ibid., pp. 655–7.

[19] BL, Lansdowne MS 71, fol. 192^r. This grant, in the form of a fee farm of royal parks, seems to have been some months in the making. Sir Thomas Heneage mentioned its imminence in August (Longleat, Talbot MS 2, fol. 104^r), as did Burghley, who noted that Essex was to receive a fee farm worth £300 a year, but at double the existing (ie old and unrealistic) rent (Murdin, p. 799). By November, however, it was agreed that Essex would pay the current rent of £52 13s 8d on the specified parks until the existing leases expired. Only then would he begin to pay the new rent. He was also to have the very lucrative right to remove all the timber from the parks, for which he was to enter a £1,000 bond (ibid., p. 800; BL, Lansdowne MS 69, fol. 177^r). One further change was that the grant was no longer to be made directly to Essex himself, as at first intended (PRO, SP 12/242, fol. 232^r; PRO, SP 46/19, fols. 66^v–67^r), but to Thomas Crompton, Robert Wright and Gelly Meyrick on his behalf (BL, Lansdowne MS 69, fol. 177^r).

as the future successor to Burghley as Elizabeth's chief minister.[20] In 1593 and early 1594, Essex became nakedly aggressive in his relations with the Cecils, impelled by a combination of enthusiasm and political naivety. Both Cecils bristled in return. Essex's new confidence and sense of urgency was epitomised in a letter to Sir Henry Unton: 'their chief hour glass [i.e. Burghley] hath little sand left in it and doth run out still'.[21]

Although Burghley and his son may not immediately have been cognisant of his efforts to reopen contacts with James VI, they were all too aware of some of Essex's other activities in these months. During 1593, Essex's heavy investment in foreign intelligence began to pay off, giving his voice greater weight in the queen's counsels. Sometimes Essex used his foreign dispatches to score points against the lord treasurer, even on occasion racing to be first to report an item of news to Elizabeth. Such direct, needling competition was inevitable as Essex endeavoured to measure himself against Burghley and to convince Elizabeth of his fitness to take over from him in matters of state. This desire for comparison with the lord treasurer also implicitly asserted Essex's sense of superiority over Cecil.

In the eyes of Essex and those around him, Cecil still seemed merely his father's apprentice. Essex and his friends joked about 'the father and the son' as if they were an indivisible unit, without which Cecil would have no importance.[22] When they did speak of Cecil by himself, despite his ever-growing involvement in government,[23] it was usually with a tone of arrogant mockery. Anthony Bacon cruelly described one outburst of anger by Cecil as 'like a little pot soon hott'.[24] Their expectation was that, as soon as Burghley died, Essex would simply brush Cecil's hunched form out of the way. For Essex and his followers alike, the chief concern in his relations with the Cecils lay not in the possible future importance of Sir Robert, but in dealing with the immediate and imposing presence of the old lord treasurer.

Essex's relations with both Cecils in 1593 were also strained by two specific initiatives which he drove forward. The first of these was his noisy campaign to bully Elizabeth into appointing Francis Bacon as attorney-general, which he began in the middle of the year. This cut right across Burghley's own ideas of how such major offices of state should be filled, quite apart from his views on how to deal with the queen. Uncomfortable

[20] See above, pp. 144ff.
[21] *HMCS*, IV, p. 116. On the correct date of this letter (8 June 1593), see C. Read, *Lord Burghley and Queen Elizabeth* (London, 1960), p. 586, n. 22.
[22] See, for example, LPL, MS 649, fol. 429ʳ. For Essex's own use of the expression, see LPL, MS 651, fol. 159ʳ.
[23] In early December 1593, for example, Cecil was ordered by Elizabeth to take charge of her diplomatic correspondence while his father was sick (BL, Stowe MS 166, fol. 80ʳ).
[24] LPL, MS 650, fol. 226ᵛ.

with Essex's approach and aware of the unlikelihood that Elizabeth would ever choose Bacon, Burghley soon began to drift from half-hearted support for Bacon towards backing Sir Edward Coke, Bacon's rival and the more obvious choice. As a result, although he kept urging him to help Bacon, Essex's impatience with the lord treasurer began to grow palpable.

The second issue which damaged relations between Essex and the Cecils in 1593 was the fate of Anthony Standen, the spy who returned to England during June.[25] Standen's case initially posed a far more direct challenge to Essex's relationship with Burghley and his son than Bacon's suit. Standen had been an agent of the lord treasurer, but Essex precipitately took him into his own protection after his arrival in England. Not surprisingly, Burghley and Cecil thereafter showed themselves to be unhelpful and even hostile towards Standen,[26] who in turn became bitterly resentful towards them.[27] Despite this antagonism, all parties sought to maintain a veneer of civility in their public dealings with each other. Without this pretence, the peace of the queen's Court and the co-operation necessary for her government would both have been imperilled – as would any hope of future employment for Standen himself. In his continuing efforts to mollify the lord treasurer, Standen put on his best smile for a man whom he privately wrote of as an enemy to his advancement, and who he knew was himself trying to conceal his own antagonism towards Standen.[28] Essex's feelings were less easily hidden but he also recognised the limits imposed by the need for all to live and work together. Although Standen became a frequent attendant in his apartments at Court, Essex declined to allow him lodging at Essex House[29] and left his immediate financial support to Anthony Bacon.[30]

During 1593, relations between Essex and the Cecils deteriorated to the point where each side began to believe that the other might now be hostile. Nevertheless, as Essex's tacit distancing of himself from Standen suggests, these difficulties between them were not all-encompassing. At a private level, Essex sold Cliffe Park to Burghley in November,[31] while Burghley

---

25 See above, p. 173.

26 See, for example, LPL, MS 650, fols. 132^r–133^r, 226^{r-v}. Cf. LPL, MS 649, fol. 429^{r-v}; LPL, MS 653, fol. 240^r.

27 See, for example, LPL, MS 649, fols. 372^r, 386^{r-v}, 379^r, 429r; LPL, MS 650, fols. 80^r–82^v.

28 See, for example, LPL, MS 650, fols. 80^r–82^v, 132^v.

29 LPL, MS 653, fol. 216^r. Standen was undoubtedly angling for a room in Essex House during December 1593 (LPL, MS 649, fol. 429^v) but, in the event, he had to make do with the offer of 'a restinge place' at Francis Bacon's house of Twickenham Lodge (LPL, MS 650, fol. 82^v).

30 Anthony Bacon paid out sums to Standen totalling £123 17s 8d between 1594 and 1596 (LPL, MS 661, fol. 41^r). For his part, Essex secured Standen a lease from the bishop of London (LPL, MS 658, fol. 143^v; LPL, MS 660, fol. 117^r).

31 PRO, C 54/1464, unfol., enrolment of indenture made on 22 November 1593. Burghley

pointedly instructed Cecil to support Essex over the suit of a Frenchman who sought to buy English ordnance during December.[32] In the public sphere, Essex, Burghley and Cecil continued to work closely together in conciliar business.[33] Although very real tensions threatened to poison relations between them, a shared sense of restraint and political necessity held both sides back from openly disavowing their association of so many years' standing.

These characteristics were also evident during 1594. During the early part of that year, the problems of 1593 continued to fester, bringing relations to a new pitch of unease. In January, Burghley and Cecil initially poured cold water on Essex's charges against Dr Lopez.[34] When Elizabeth consequently rebuked him, Essex's anger and sense of humiliation were profound.[35] Although the Cecils soon changed their views about Lopez, other difficulties remained. In February, rumours again began to circulate that Cecil would be given a share of the office of secretary of state.[36] This idea was always abhorrent to Essex. Initially, he had opposed it because Cecil's appointment would have been at the expense of William Davison. However, as Essex became more determined to make himself into a statesman, the real reason for his opposition was a fear that this appointment would allow Cecil to stake a claim to Burghley's mantle, which Essex was bent on winning for himself. Once the post of secretary of state was filled, its occupant would inevitably gain a hold on government business which could only expand once Burghley died. On the other hand, the longer the office remained unfilled, the more uncertain Cecil's claim to be his father's legatee would become. Essex therefore threw his weight against Cecil's appointment,[37] even though securing it was the Cecils' most cherished aim.[38]

Another element in the difficulties between Essex and the Cecils early in 1594 was Francis Bacon's continuing suit to become attorney-general. By February, despite all that Essex did to sustain it, this suit had lost most of its credibility and momentum. When the opportunity presented itself at the start of that month, Cecil urged Essex to abandon the suit as a lost cause.

had held the keepership of this park (located in Northamptonshire) since 1564, while the fee farm of the park itself was one of those granted to Essex in November 1592. According to the enrolment, Burghley was to pay the (surely erroneous) sum of £4,040 for the land. Essex's accounts only note receipt of £500 (Devereux MS 3, fol. 73^r). In October 1592, the old rent of Cliffe Park, part of 'the auncient inheritaunce of the crowne', was noted at 26s 8d (BL, Lansdowne MS 69, fol. 177^r).

[32] CUL, MS Ee.iii.56, no. 12. [33] See, for example, LPL, MS 653, fol. 234^r.
[34] See above, pp. 138, 160–2. [35] LPL, MS 650. fols. 25^r–26^v.
[36] *Ibid.*, fol. 80^r; BL, Cotton, MS Caligula E IX(i), fol. 177^v.
[37] LPL, MS 650, fol. 80^r.
[38] See, for example, Cecil's own nervous comments about this to Lady Ann Bacon during January (*ibid.*, fol. 33^r).

This initiative prompted a sharp exchange which brought important aspects of their relationship out into the open.[39] The incident took place in a coach as Essex and Cecil travelled back to Court after interrogating Dr Lopez together in the Tower. The setting for this exchange is significant. Not only was the venue very private but Cecil's *démarche* came as he and Essex were returning from another session which demonstrated the extent to which he and his father had buried their differences with Essex over the guilt of Lopez. Although the only account of the episode is a thoroughly partisan one, it seems that Cecil's intention in this conversation was to push Essex away from a position in which he would publicly lose face by backing a losing candidate. Cecil offered a compromise by suggesting that Francis Bacon might be able to win the lesser post of solicitor-general. Essex, however, refused to countenance such an idea. Characteristically, he adopted a lofty moral tone. Rather than distance himself from Bacon, he trenchantly declared that his support for Bacon was utterly unequivocal.

Essex's reaction to Cecil's compromise was in keeping with his views of virtuous behaviour at Court. Faced with the suggestion that he make a tactical withdrawal in his campaign to win preferment for Bacon, he reacted by reaffirming his belief that he must 'stand stiffly' for his friends. If this response was politically maladroit and led him to browbeat Cecil, it was also – in his own eyes – virtuous. It also clearly reflected his attitude towards Cecil. When Cecil suggested that Bacon's candidacy for the solicitorship 'mought be . . . of easier disgestion to her Majestie', Essex did not mince words in his reply: 'disgest me no disgestions! . . . the attorney-ship for ffrances ys that I must have'. Essex did not merely refuse Cecil's proffered olive branch, but beat him about the ears with it. Essex was thoroughly frustrated over Bacon's lack of success and vented his feelings at Cecil. However, the extreme bluntness of Essex's language is also indicative of his estimation of Cecil: Essex felt able to be so blunt, not only because their conversation was in private, but because he still assumed a natural superiority towards him. Something of this attitude continued to be evident even after Cecil finally won the secretaryship. In the weeks following his return from Cadiz, Essex wrote to Anthony Bacon that 'this day I was more braved by your little cosin then ever I was by any man in my lyfe'.[40] Essex's tone is a mixture of annoyance, disdain, and surprise.

[39] This episode is described in a letter from Anthony Standen to Anthony Bacon of 3 February 1594 (*ibid.*, fols. 80^r–82^v). Standen recounts the story as he heard it from Essex himself, but adds a number of sarcastic comments about Cecil in the margin ('a kynde cousin'; 'a stowte resolution').

[40] LPL, MS 659, fol. 142^r. Bacon himself quoted this phrase in a letter to Dr Henry Hawkyns a few days later (*ibid.*, fol. 161^r). On another occasion late in 1596, Essex described Burghley as 'piger pardus' but Cecil as 'asellus agilis' (*ibid.*, fol. 349^r).

For Cecil, who had taken the initiative to try and defuse the tensions with Essex, this incident must have been deeply galling. Nevertheless, the intention of Cecil's action is significant. Although this particular initiative brought no positive result, it underlined the discomfort which both Cecils felt – and Sir Robert in particular – over their tense relations with Essex. During the middle of 1594, the Cecils therefore renewed their efforts to re-establish a *modus vivendi* with Essex. External events helped to encourage this process. In addition to their close co-operation during the investigation of Dr Lopez,[41] Essex and the Cecils shared a mutual concern with the situation in Brittany.[42] For his part, Essex was undoubtedly chastened by the way that Elizabeth rebuffed him over Bacon. The confident expectations which he had held as a new councillor now sat less easily with him.

By Easter 1594, Cecil was noted to be courting Essex's favour 'with grete owtwarde observations'.[43] To that end, like his father, Cecil showed himself to be supportive of Francis Bacon's new suit to become solicitor-general.[44] Cecil also helped Sir Nicholas Clifford, a follower and relative of Essex who had incurred royal anger for accepting a knighthood from Henri IV.[45] By May, Essex was thanking Cecil for his 'offers of kindness and profession of affection'.[46] A few weeks later, a letter from Cecil seemed to show that they had recovered the kind of frank familiarity which they had shared during the Rouen campaign: 'my good lord, yow shall not need to make ceremony with me for opening of any lettres, publick or private'.[47]

Despite this apparent renewal of their old association, Essex's relationship with Cecil and his father was now quite different from 1591. The very fact that Cecil courted, and won, Essex's good will demonstrated that Cecil's own importance as a political actor had grown greatly. Moreover, Cecil showed himself to be more readily accommodating to Essex than Burghley, who seems to have remained rather aloof from his son's wooing of the earl. In July, it was even reported that 'sum housholde wordes have past between my lord tresorer and my lord of Essex, nott suar fitt to be

---

[41] See, for example, *HMCS*, IV, pp. 483, 486, 487; Hulton MS (formerly BL, Loan 23), fol. 55^{r-v}.

[42] R. B. Wernham, *After the Armada: Elizabethan England and the struggle for Western Europe* (Oxford, 1984), pp. 526ff.

[43] LPL, MS 650, fol. 358^r.

[44] See, for example, LPL, MS 649, fol. 92^r; LPL, MS 650, fol. 197^r; BL, Harleian MS 6996, fol. 101^r.

[45] *HMCS*, IV, pp. 492–3, 498, 518, 519, 523, 526. For the queen's fury at Clifford and Sir Anthony Sherley, see BL, Harleian MS 6996, fols. 82^r, 84^{r-v}, 85^r; BL, Cotton MS Caligula E IX(i), fol. 201^v; I. H. Jeayes (ed.), *Letters of Philip Gawdy of West Harling, Norfolk, and of London to various members of his family 1579–1616* (Roxburghe Club, London, 1906), p. 82.

[46] *HMCS*, IV, p. 524.   [47] PRO, SP 12/249, fol. 5^r.

written'. This outburst was swiftly 'compounded',[48] but it was apparently not until August that 'the good reconcilement' between the two men was finally certain.[49]

By late 1594, an equilibrium had been re-established at Court between Essex and the Cecils. Characterised by a mutual desire to avoid open or direct competition, this manner of coexistence was to endure – albeit under mounting strain – well into 1596 and, in some senses, perhaps even longer. After the urgent tensions of 1593, both sides now set themselves for the long haul. Essex endeavoured to promote himself as a genuine statesman, particularly overseas. By contrast, Burghley, who was increasingly hampered by his pains, became more and more the grand old man of the council. As a result, he left an increasing amount of routine administration to his son. More than ever, therefore, observers tended to describe both the Court and government policies as resting on a balance between Essex, on the one hand, and the Cecils, on the other, and particularly between the earl and Burghley. The German envoy, von Buchenbach, who visited the Court in April 1595, was told that 'great jealousy and no little envy' obtained between Essex and Burghley, 'wherefore what the one was at pains to promote, the other thwarted with all his might'.[50]

By and large, this contemporary analysis is accurate. A genuine rivalry patently did exist between Essex and the Cecils. Despite their *rapprochement*, neither side could forget the anxieties of 1593. More importantly, new tensions were added to their relations by the swelling ambitions of Essex and the growing urgency of Cecil's desire to win the secretaryship. In early May 1595, Burghley and Cecil clearly made a major effort to secure this appointment. On 20 May, the dowager countess of Shrewsbury actually wrote to Cecil to congratulate him on his promotion.[51] Reports received in Scotland and Flanders show that equally premature claims had also been made there.[52] It can hardly be a coincidence that this was

---

[48] BL, Add. MS 11042, fol. 87ᵛ. Elizabeth may have had this incident in mind when she warned Essex on the evening of 25 July: 'looke to thy selfe good Essex and be wyse to help thy self without givinge thy ennemies advantage and my hande shalbe redier to help then any other' (LPL, MS 650, fol. 227ᵛ). Elizabeth was very aware of the tensions between Essex and the Cecils and her comments here were undoubtedly intended to calm the waters. The word 'ennemies', which was often used loosely, should not be taken to suggest that Elizabeth believed the problems at her Court were irreconcilable. Assuming that she actually used the word (this letter is only Anthony Standen's account of what Essex had told him about the conversation), Elizabeth probably did so to indicate her understanding and sympathy for Essex's position.

[49] *HMCS*, IV, p. 587.

[50] V. von Klarwill (ed.), *Queen Elizabeth I and some foreigners, being a series of hitherto unpublished letters from the archives of the Hapsburg family* (trans. T. H. Nash, London, 1928), p. 362.

[51] *HMCS*, V, p. 213.

[52] LPL, MS 651, fol. 86ʳ; Petti, *Verstegan letters*, p. 242.

precisely the time when Essex was embarrassed by the revelation of his illegitimate son.[53] Nevertheless, despite Elizabeth's anger towards him over that indiscretion, Essex managed to stave off Cecil's appointment, as he did 'to the uttermost of his power ... above a yeare'.[54]

The matter of the secretaryship remained a fundamental focus of rivalry between Essex and the Cecils throughout this period. In September 1595, Anthony Standen wrote to Anthony Bacon that Cecil still 'heves harde to b[e] secretary'.[55] The emotion which both sides invested in this contest also affected some suitors at Court, as von Buchenbach had been warned. One of the casualties was Thomas Bodley, the queen's ambassador in the Netherlands. When Essex praised Bodley to Elizabeth 'with some prodigall speeches of my sufficiency for a secretary, with speaches of disgrace against Sir Robert Cecill',[56] he immediately became *persona non grata* with the Cecils. Cecil later told Bodley:

that his [Essex's] daily provocations were so bitter and sharpe against him and his comparisons so odious when he putt us in ballance as he thought he had great reason to use his best meanes to putt any man out of hope of raising his fortunes whome the earle with suche violence to his extreame prejudice had endeavored to dignifie him.[57]

The bluntness of Essex's lobbying and the extreme sensitivity of the matter in question drove Cecil to lash out secretly against those who seemed to imperil his own advancement.[58]

A powerful mutual antagonism prevailed between Essex and the Cecils over the issue of the secretaryship, which observers at Court eagerly noted. Despite this, the reconciliation of 1594 still retained some considerable force, at least in matters of outward show. When von Buchenbach approached Essex, for example, the earl sent back a message 'that I should

---

[53] It is also probably no coincidence that Burghley and Cecil both incurred Elizabeth's displeasure at the very time that Essex began to return to favour (LPL, MS 651, fol. 159ʳ). Although the evidence is only suggestive, it seems likely that Elizabeth turned against the Cecils when she began to feel less angry at Essex and realised how crudely they had sought to take advantage of his embarrassment – and of her own reaction to it.

[54] BL, Egerton MS 2026, fol. 32ʳ.   [55] LPL, MS 652, fol. 51ʳ.

[56] BL, Cotton MS Titus C VII, fol. 173ᵛ. It is not clear when Essex commended Bodley to the queen as a secretary of state. Bodley was back in England during 1595 – between 9 May (*HMCS*, V, p. 202) and the end of July (PRO, SP 84/50, fol. 167ʳ⁻ᵛ; PRO, SP 84/51, fol. 55ʳ) – but he received a very bad reception from Elizabeth (LPL, MS 651, fol. 141ʳ) and was briefly in fear of losing his post as ambassador to Sir Robert Sidney (*ibid.*, fols. 223ʳ, 231ʳ). Bodley returned to England permanently at the end of April 1596 (PRO, SP 84/52, fol. 161ʳ). Relations between Bodley and Cecil subsequently improved in later years.

[57] BL, Cotton MS Titus C VII, fol. 174ʳ.

[58] As a highly conspicuous client of Essex, Francis Bacon may perhaps have been another victim of Cecil's understandable insecurity. By 1596, Anthony Bacon was moved explicitly to ask Essex not to seek help for his brother (now bidding to become master of the rolls) from either Burghley or Cecil (LPL, MS 657, fol. 22ᵛ).

not neglect to go to the lord treasurer and to follow his counsel'.[59] In September 1595, when a servant of Essex was brought before him for violent behaviour, Burghley was anxious that his son inform Essex what had really happened, 'lest the same showld be otherwise reported to my lord of Essex then the trewthe was'.[60] During October, when they apparently agreed 'so kindly' about the need to help Lord Burgh in the Netherlands,[61] Cecil was 'troubled to think' that there might be any possibility of awkwardness with Essex because of the competing claims of Sir Henry Unton and John Stanhope for the office of vice-chamberlain. Rather than encourage strife, 'he thought plainly that neither of you both should carry it'.[62] In the same month, Cecil also warned Sir John Norris not to seek his help in a quarrel with Essex: 'yf there were growen any drynes [between Norris and 'so great a person'], I could not from yourself take any notice of such alteracion'.[63]

These deliberate courtesies demonstrate the wariness with which each side now regarded the other. After the apparent attempt to take advantage of Essex's disfavour with the queen (a clumsy ploy which would hint at desperation on the Cecils' part[64]), the larger rivalry between them over future political dominance in England, which the issue of the secretaryship encapsulated, took on a new edge.[65] Essex's response came at the Accession Day tournament in November, when he used a public occasion intended for glorifying the queen to spell out his own political credentials.[66] Essex's display must have seemed like sheer effrontery to the Cecils and the ambiguous nature of its characters – the hermit and the statesman appeared

[59] von Klarwill, *Elizabeth and some foreigners*, p. 362.
[60] CUL, MS Ee.iii.56, no. 59.   [61] PRO, SP 84/51, fol. 211^r.
[62] *HMCS*, IV, pp. 68–9. Note that this letter has been misdated by the editor(s) but clearly relates to October 1595. Although friendly with Essex, Stanhope was a distant relative of the Cecils. There was also a bond of affection between the Cecil and Stanhope families which stemmed from Burghley's friendship with Stanhope's father, Sir Michael Stanhope, in the Edwardian period. Both men were followers of the duke of Somerset but, whereas Burghley survived the duke's final fall in 1552, Stanhope followed Somerset to the block (*Commons*, III, p. 436). Unton was seen as Essex's man.
[63] Cecil MS 35/63 (pr. *HMCS*, V, pp. 413–14).
[64] Greater urgency was undoubtedly given to the question of Cecil's advancement by his father's increasing intimations of mortality. At the end of April 1595, Burghley's pains were so bad that he could not write to Cecil 'with myne owne hand in any sort' (CUL, MS Ee.iii.56, no. 45; *HMCS*, V, pp. 191–2). On 12 May, Burghley was again bedridden, 'wherby he knoweth not he can come to the Court' (*ibid.*, p. 203). In September, when he achieved 'my period of lxxiiii ye[ar]s', he wondered whether he would survive to see the next spring (CUL, MS Ee.iii.56, no. 58).
[65] Hence Essex now quite deliberately cast Burghley in the blackest possible light – 'he who rules there is begun to be loathed at by the best and greatest sort there' – in his secret correspondence with James VI: G. P. V. Akrigg (ed.), *Letters of James VI & I* (Berkeley, Los Angeles and London, 1984), pp. 142–3. See above, pp. 168ff.
[66] See above, pp. 144ff.

to many observers to be caricatures of Burghley and Cecil, rather than abstract exemplars of contemplation and politics – would have rubbed salt into their wounds. To make matters worse, Essex and the Cecils were now increasingly at odds about how Elizabeth should respond to the prospect of another Spanish naval offensive and further aid to France.[67] Sometimes these differences over strategy caused 'great distemper of humures on both sides'.[68] Yet, despite these centrifugal forces pulling them apart, an uneasy equilibrium still remained. Although he and Essex crossed swords in council late in 1595 over the question of further military aid to France,[69] Burghley pointedly agreed not to oppose the earl's candidate for a fellowship at Eton in December.[70]

The tensions between Essex and the Cecils were undoubtedly exacerbated, but ultimately perhaps also contained, by the many dangers which seemed to confront Elizabeth and her council in late 1595. During summer, there had been disturbances in London, culminating in a riot on Tower Hill at the end of June.[71] To Burghley and Elizabeth, this must have seemed clear evidence that the nation's war effort could not be sustained at its current level for much longer, let alone increased. Burghley knew that the queen's finances were in a terrible mess, but he could not reveal the full truth to his sovereign or colleagues without exposing his own inability, or unwillingness, to stem the massive corruption and waste.[72] In October,

---

[67] See above, pp. 244ff.   [68] Collins, *Sidney papers*, I, p. 343.

[69] *CSPVen*, IX, *1592–1603*, p. 174.

[70] BL, Lansdowne MS 79, fol. 124ʳ. Burghley had written to the bishop of Winchester in support of a candidate for the fellowship but withdrew his backing for the man after conferring with Essex.

[71] R. B. Manning, *Village revolts: social protest and popular disturbances in England, 1509–1640* (Oxford, 1988), pp. 208–10.

[72] The finances of Elizabeth's government are an under-explored subject and much of the work which has been done on this topic remains unpublished. Nevertheless, some points need to be made here. Firstly, Burghley (who had been lord treasurer since 1572) dominated all matters of finance – Sir John Fortescue, the chancellor of the exchequer, was a subordinate figure. Whereas warrants for payment had previously required the signature of at least three councillors, Burghley authorised many by himself in the 1590s (J. Guy, 'The 1590s: the second reign of Elizabeth I?' in Guy (ed.), *Court and culture*, p. 14). Burghley also knew about a series of financial scandals and covered them up or took action only when he had no choice. Tellers of the exchequer regularly used the queen's money for their own purposes and some cases – such as that of Richard Stoneley – cost the crown tens of thousands of pounds. Since this kind of peculation had attracted criticism as far back as the 1560s (C. Coleman, 'Artifice or accident? The reorganisation of the exchequer of receipt, c.1554–1572', in C. Coleman and D. Starkey (eds.), *Revolution reassessed: revisions in the history of Tudor government and administration* (Oxford, 1986), pp. 191–7), Burghley's failure to deal with the problem was a major failing. Richard Stoneley's dealings were first investigated in the 1570s, but it was not until December 1588 that Burghley finally forbade him to handle the queen's money and another ten years after that before Stoneley was actually dismissed (J. Guy, *Tudor England* (Oxford, 1988), pp. 394–5). George Goring, receiver-general of the court of wards (of which Burghley was master), also saddled the

Doleman's book embarrassed Essex and stirred up the matter of the succession, prompting the arrest of the earl of Hertford.[73] In November, the lieutenant of the Tower, Sir Michael Blount, was prosecuted and dismissed from his office for planning to hold the Tower after the queen's death on Hertford's behalf.[74] Elizabeth had been sick in 1594[75] and many regarded it as ominous that her life had now entered its climacteric sixty-third year. Death hung over the Court. Sir Thomas Heneage, the vice-chamberlain, was felled by a stroke in October, thrusting more work upon Hunsdon, the lord chamberlain, who was himself visibly failing.[76] Outside the inner circle of power, death also claimed the veteran soldiers Sir Roger Williams and Sir Thomas Morgan and created a political vacuum in the north with the passing of Huntingdon.[77] The old order was under assault from all sides. Yet despite this, or perhaps because of it, the tensions between Essex and the Cecils remained contained. As before, Burghley and Cecil were perhaps more accommodating towards Essex than he was towards them, but Essex was also content not to rock the boat too much. For Essex, these last months of 1595 were a time of deep frustration and of

crown with heavy debts in 1594 (*ibid.*, p. 395), whilst Richard Young's debt of over £10,000 on the London customs in December 1594 shocked Burghley so deeply that he was unable to write for some days (CUL, MS Ee.iii.56, no. 35). Burghley must also have been aware of the even larger misappropriation of funds by Sir Thomas Sherley in the Low Countries and by other officials in Ireland, where Cecil clients dominated after the fall of Sir John Perrot. At the least, the frequency and scale of such corruption reflects very poorly on his ability as a financial administrator.

[73] See above, p. 177. Doleman's tract focused renewed attention on the claim to the throne of the house of Seymour (C. Breight 'Realpolitik and Elizabethan ceremony: the Earl of Hertford's entertainment of Elizabeth at Elvetham, 1591', *Renaissance Quarterly* 45 (1992), pp. 38ff). Hertford and his sons were arrested at the end of October (*HMCD*, II, pp. 177, 183). Hertford was only released from the Tower into the custody of the archbishop of Canterbury at the beginning of January 1596 (BL, Harleian MS 6997, fols. 156ʳ, 158ʳ; PRO, SO 3/1, fol. 567ʳ).

[74] R. B. Manning, 'The prosecution of Sir Michael Blount, lieutenant of the Tower, 1595', *BIHR* 57 (1984), pp. 216–24. Blount's clumsy planning was revealed when he began stockpiling supplies at the Tower early in November. His actions were reported to the privy council by the London authorities, whom Blount had antagonised by actively hindering the efforts of the lord mayor during the Tower Hill riot of 29 June.

[75] Elizabeth's ill health in 1594 directly encouraged Blount's plan to control the Tower (*ibid.*, pp. 216, 219).

[76] According to Hunsdon, who was himself suffering badly from gout (*HMCD*, II, p. 175), Heneage looked 'verie gastly' and was impaired in his speech (Cecil MS 172/78 (pr. *HMCS*, V, p. 425)). He finally died on 17 October, although the news seems to have not reached the Court until the 19th (*HMCD*, II, p. 175). He was buried in St Paul's on 20 November (*Commons*, II, p. 293; *DNB*, IX, p. 409).

[77] Williams died on 12 December and Morgan ten days later, both in London. Huntingdon died at York on 14 December. After Huntingdon's death, no new president of the council of the north was appointed until Cecil's older brother, Thomas 2nd Lord Burghley, was given the post in August 1599 (R. R. Reid, *The king's council in the north* (London, 1921), pp. 229–31).

waiting upon a change of fortune in the new year, when his manuscript propaganda and secret dealings over France began to make an impact and when the Spanish threat would demand military action. In the meantime, the *modus vivendi* between Essex and the Cecils limped along, fractured by mistrust on both sides but not yet broken beyond all repair.

Viewed in the larger context of the Court and of the various patronage networks which reached out across the realm, the growing rivalry between Essex and the Cecils had a disturbing impact upon national politics. Bit by bit, the nation's political élite became divided by this rivalry, and the divisions between the two sides became increasingly bitter. As contemporaries and subsequent commentators have universally recognised, the tensions between Essex and the Cecils ultimately escalated into a factional struggle *par excellence*. Nevertheless, the process by which this escalation occurred has not been studied in any detail. There is also a strong tendency among those writing with the benefit of hindsight to assume that rivalry and factionalism are synonymous, or that one necessarily leads to the other. Certainly, there is a serious lack of precision in our understanding of the 1590s. This greatly weakens our comprehension of political life in Elizabeth's last decade, but it also has a larger significance. Because of the quality and accessibility of evidence about faction in the late 1590s, perceptions of events in these years have had a powerful impact upon the historical interpretation of English politics throughout the early modern era. Not surprisingly, the model of faction which arose from this crude understanding of faction in the 1590s has proved highly unstable when subjected to close scrutiny by scholars studying other periods,[78] since the model itself was based upon false premises.

The word 'faction' is a problematical term. Like the word 'puritan', it was originally a term of disapprobation: forming a 'faction', or being 'factious', were charges which those in the sixteenth-century applied to men other than themselves. The word 'faction' also shares at least one other common characteristic with the term 'puritan'. Both words are so instantly evocative of their general, although not their specific, meaning that they have been much used and abused by modern historians. This has prompted a degree of soul-searching in recent years about how the term 'faction' should properly be employed. Much of this debate has revolved around the confusion caused by the loose use of the term, which suggests

---

[78] See, for example, G. Walker, *Persuasive fictions: faction, faith and political culture in the reign of Henry VIII* (Aldershot, 1996), esp. pp. 1–23, and S. Gunn, 'The structures of politics in early Tudor England', *TRHS*, 6th ser., 5 (1995), pp. 59–90. The influence of Elizabethan historiography on perceptions of early Tudor faction is explicitly acknowledged in *ibid.*, pp. 60–1.

the necessity of adopting a tighter definition of 'faction'.[79] Accordingly, it is argued here that a courtly faction consisted of a body of men who felt themselves personally bound to one particular great man *and* who also saw themselves as necessarily opposed to other men who had a similar bond to a different leader. A faction was therefore quite different from a following. Whereas the latter was the normal manifestation of the patronage system in operation, the appearance of factions was analogous to the onset of wartime conditions at Court: it was as if an enemy army suddenly became visible and both sides responded by throwing up barricades against each other and by scheming to drive the other side from the field of battle. Unlike a following, a faction depended upon a rigid identification of those who were friends or enemies and looked, not simply towards securing the choicest fruits of patronage, but towards winning clear political dominance over its rival.

Applying this definition to politics in the mid-1590s suggests that true factionalism still remained absent by the end of 1595. In the latter months of 1593 – when Francis Bacon's suit for the attorney-generalship began to falter – a hard core of Essexian partisans began to emerge who were devout in their commitment to the earl and who felt deeply embittered towards the Cecils.[80] This was the group which Anthony Standen had in mind when he wrote that he was 'hartely sory to heare us made a ffootebale in the worlde'.[81] This was also the group who had the closest dealings with the exiled Spaniard Antonio Perez, whose profound personal insecurities undoubtedly did much to nurse the resentments among Essex's circle.[82] However, despite the hostility of these men towards Burghley and his son, it is very difficult to identify any similar group of Cecil partisans, even by 1595. Some individual courtiers allegedly sought to undermine Essex, but only Henry Brooke (later Lord Cobham) and Sir William Cornwallis are noted by name. Both of these men certainly had kinship connections to the Cecils,[83] but it would be stretching the evidence too far to claim that their

---

[79] For comment on this debate, see P. E. J. Hammer, 'Patronage at Court, faction and the earl of Essex', in Guy (ed.), *Court and culture*, pp. 65–8. A contrary view is argued in R. Shephard, 'Court factions in early modern England', *Journal of Modern History* 64 (1992), pp. 721–45.

[80] See above, pp. 290–1.   [81] LPL, MS 651, fol. 122ᵛ. This letter is dated May 1595.

[82] Perez's almost pathological resentments are evident throughout Ungerer's collection of the correspondence of his exile. Perez's extreme personal antipathy towards Sir Robert Cecil, for example, led him to call Cecil by such epithets as 'microgibbus' and 'Robertus diabolus' (Ungerer, I, pp. 336, 388; *ibid.*, II, p. 191). Since he viewed Thomas Edmondes as rival to himself as a purveyor of information to Essex, Perez also became obsessed with the idea that Edmondes was a secret follower of Cecil and enemy of the earl (*ibid.*, I, pp. 369–70, 388. Cf. *ibid.*, I, p. 392 and n. 9).

[83] Brooke was the brother of Cecil's wife, Elizabeth née Brooke (*Commons*, I, pp. 495, 571), while Cornwallis 'traded heavily' on the fact that his sister-in-law was married to Sir

actions were driven by thoughts of faction. Between Brooke and Essex, at least, there existed a notoriously personal animosity.[84] Cornwallis, who enjoyed fewer prospects than Brooke, also probably hoped to lever himself forward at Essex's expense.

A sense of factional allegiance also remained absent from the pursuit of patronage. Until at least the end of 1595, patronage links at Court were strikingly pluralist in their nature. As Essex and Burghley increasingly came to be seen as the two leading – and rival – figures of influence at Court, common sense suggested that suitors try to seek support from both of them, and preferably from other important men and women as well. This became a frequent phenomenon. Jane Yetswiert, for example, the widow of a clerk of the signet, sought the good lordship of Burghley in May 1595 to 'let my contenders knowe that I have a protector',[85] even though she had already gained the active support of Essex.[86] Sir Robert Sidney, like the queen's other official representatives abroad, habitually called upon both the Cecils and Essex to move Elizabeth for his requests.[87]

Although further examples could be given, the point is clear enough. The desire of suitors to win support from both Essex and the Cecils – and their ability to gain it – underlines the fact that they were widely perceived as rivals. At the same time, this also undermines the idea that true Devereux and Cecil factions already really existed at Court. Sharp lines of demarcation between friend and foe were not yet in evidence,[88] except perhaps in the minds of embittered partisans of Essex such as Anthony Standen.

Thomas Cecil. By the mid-1590s, however, when he was dogging Essex at Court, Cornwallis's fortunes seem to have fallen pretty low, in spite of his Cecil connection (*ibid.*, p. 659).

[84] The original motivation for this feud is uncertain. Essex got on well with Brooke's younger brothers, William and George, and his cousin Calisthenes. William was knighted by Essex at Rouen and enjoyed a command under him during the Azores expedition of 1597 (D. McKeen, *A memory of honour: the life of William Brooke, Lord Cobham* (2 vols., Salzburg Studies in English Literature, CVIII, Salzburg, 1986), II, p. 436, 655). However, Essex viewed Henry Brooke as a man who made no account of honour and who sought to build his career solely by capitalising on his family connections and currying favour with Elizabeth by criticising others. Brooke had a fiery temper, performed only the most perfunctory military service in 1588, never jousted, remained unmarried until 1601, and made no impact on his contemporaries until he became recognised as an exponent of money-grubbing backstairs politics in the mid-1590s (*ibid.*, I, p. 176; *ibid.*, II, pp. 433–7, 655ff). On all of these grounds, he must have seemed to Essex the very antithesis of what any aristocrat should aspire to be.

[85] BL, Harleian MS 6997, fol. 18[r].   [86] *Ibid.*, fol. 16[r].

[87] See, for example, *HMCD*, II, p. 153; PRO, SP 84/51, fol. 112[r]; PRO, SP 84/53, fols. 76[r]–77[r], 92[r], 166[r]; PRO, SP 84/54, fols. 39[r–v], 113[r]. Despite these appeals to Burghley and Cecil, Sidney obviously still relied on Essex as his prime supporter at Court (LPL, MS 652, fol. 166[r]; *HMCD*, II, pp. 144, 156).

[88] This point can be further underscored by noting two minor instances during January 1596. Despite Anthony Bacon's apparent objections, Essex was quite happy for Cecil to convey letters to Elizabeth (possibly containing intelligence) from a Scottish merchant (LPL, MS

Nevertheless, even Standen felt able to appeal to Burghley when he thought it might do him some good.[89] This is not to say that the tensions between Essex and the Cecils over the secretaryship did not make themselves felt among their followers. Undoubtedly, a fair amount of anger was vented by both sides in private.[90] But, despite this, the desire to maintain a *modus vivendi* persisted.

One final qualification needs to be added to this argument about patronage and faction. Although sharp lines of demarcation were not yet evident, there was nevertheless much talk of 'friends' and 'enemies' at Court. This talk was not an expression of nascent factionalism, but the way in which sixteenth-century suitors explained failure or delay in their quests for a grant. Instead of impersonal explanations such as the imbalance between the number of suitors and the number of appropriate places available, Tudor courtiers characteristically saw their problems as stemming from specific human agents, whether this was strictly accurate or not. It was a commonplace that the Court was, as Sir George Carey described it in 1585, 'daungerouslie poisoned with the secrett stinges of smilinge enemies'.[91] When Nicholas Trott sought to win the place of secretary to the council in the north in early 1595, 'I made account of many adverse parties and of th'ordinarie proceding of the Court, that is, from inquisition into my life to likely suspition and from thence to plain fiction.' Even so, Trott was shocked by 'this impudent slaunder work' by which a rival sought to disqualify him from obtaining the post.[92] In 1595, it was still the rough and tumble of the struggle for place, not faction, which spawned loose talk of friends and enemies.

Before considering how such terms began to acquire a more explicitly political meaning during 1596 and 1597, it is necessary to touch upon the implications of factionalism for Elizabeth. Commentators who wrote about Elizabeth's reign in the seventeenth century were often eager to emphasise that she had maintained her authority in her Court by deliberately balancing 'factions' there.[93] By this, they meant that she had prevented any

---

654, fol. 190ʳ). Essex also freely suggested that George Gilpin, Bodley's deputy in the Low Countries, should turn to Cecil for help with his suit (*ibid.*, fol. 251ʳ).

89 See, for example, Standen's approach to Burghley in April 1595 to renew his remarkably ambitious suit to replace William Dethicke as garter king of arms (BL, Lansdowne MS 79, fol. 188r; copy is LPL, MS 652, fol. 320ʳ). In 1596, Standen also pointedly sent Burghley an account of the capture of Cadiz (BL, Harleian MS 6845, fols. 101ʳ–102ʳ).

90 Since most of this must have occurred in conversation, little evidence of it has survived. Around Essex, it is apparent in the correspondence between Anthony Standen and Anthony Bacon and in the poisonous comments which Antonio Perez makes about Cecil in some of his letters from France (see, for example, Ungerer, I, pp. 336, 388). No corresponding material seems to survive for Burghley or Cecil and their intimates.

91 PRO, C 115, box M, bdle 15, no. 7364.   92 LPL, MS 651, fol. 134ʳ.

93 The *locus classicus* for this view is Sir Robert Naunton, *Fragmenta regalia or observations*

one of her courtiers from becoming too powerful and had deliberately harnessed the natural rivalries among leading courtiers to benefit her own royal service. Although these writers had their own peculiar reasons for over-emphasising this analysis,[94] there is some evidence to support it.

When Essex began his political career, Elizabeth was already well into her fifties. By the time Essex became a councillor, she was almost sixty. Although the years were beginning to weary her, Elizabeth was not a passive participant in the affairs of the Court which surrounded her. She dealt with the business of government every day, often at some length. Nevertheless, in the world of the Court itself, Elizabeth's role seems to have been an intermittently reactive one. When she felt it necessary, or when she simply felt the urge to do so, she intervened in the relations between her courtiers. Sometimes she acted to settle quarrels, as she did several times with Essex and Ralegh in the late 1580s, with mixed success. Her directive that Essex should apply for recompense for the Rouen campaign through Sir Robert Cecil was another example of her political engineering. However, Elizabeth sometimes deliberately sought to foment divisions at Court, when she felt that the pressures upon her over a particular issue were likely to become too powerful. As a woman prince among proud men, Elizabeth was always conscious of this danger. When Burghley seemed to be lining up with Essex by backing Francis Bacon's suits for high legal office, she demanded that both councillors name some alternative candidate. She complained that the conjunction of their support 'did make menn give a more favorable testemonie [of Bacon] then els they would doe, thinkinge thereby they pleased us [Burghley and Essex]'.[95] In this light, Sir Roger Williams's interview with Elizabeth in December 1593 takes on a new significance: '*Syr* Ro[ger] speakethe boldely *to the queen*, of whome he hathe understood that the *lord treasurer is your brother's sole* obstacle, [although he is pretending to be] a good and kind parent in the meane tyme'.[96] Such a comment to Williams, a known intimate of Essex, can only have been calculatedly mischievous.

Elizabeth's practice of queenship depended upon preserving the decorum of her Court and, above all, her own sense of control and superiority over courtiers. Her actions often sought to remove the disruption caused by quarrels, but sometimes it also suited her to exacerbate the inevitable

on Queen Elizabeth, her times & favourites (ed. J. S. Cerovski, Washington, London and Toronto, 1985), pp. 40–1.
[94] See especially S. Adams, 'Favourites and factions at the Elizabethan Court', in R. G. Asch and A. M. Birke (eds.), *Princes, patronage and the nobility: the Court at the beginning of the modern age, c.1450–1650* (London, 1991), pp. 280ff.
[95] LPL, MS 650, fol. 197r. For repetition of the same argument, see also *ibid.*, fols. 33r, 45r, 148r; LPL, MS 653, fol. 75v.
[96] LPL, MS 649, fol. 426r. Italics indicate that the words are in cipher in the original.

tensions which existed at Court. However, this is very far from fostering faction. Indeed, if quarrels were troublesome to courtly decorum, Elizabeth would have known only too well that the existence of factions was profoundly inimical to it. This is implicit in the definition of faction given above: since it necessarily involved a struggle for the exclusion of rivals from political influence, the onset of factionalism patently also indicated a failure by the sovereign to maintain order at Court. During 1596 and 1597, when faction came into open bloom, Elizabeth's grip on her Court slackened. Once lost, this grip could never truly be regained.

During the first half of 1596, the wary balance between Essex and the Cecils still persisted. Nevertheless, after the sharp disagreements of the previous autumn over strategy, there were some fears among Essex's circle that the Cecils might work against the earl's great new expedition. At the beginning of March, Edward Reynoldes reported to Anthony Bacon that Essex was 'so much troubled with the crosses & traverses which he findeth in the intended journey'.[97] When Bacon sought assistance in a wardship case, which would require approval from Burghley as master of the court of wards, Essex replied 'that he could not nowe for an earledome undertake the getting of a ward'.[98] However, by mid-March, Essex, Burghley and Cecil were all apparently united in their efforts to urge Elizabeth to proceed with the expedition.[99] Although he was ordered by Elizabeth to ensure that Essex and the lord admiral would not have too free a hand as its joint commanders,[100] Burghley was sufficiently committed to a strike against Spain to support Essex's pleas that the venture go ahead even after the disastrous news of the deaths of Drake and Hawkins.[101]

In pushing forward the Cadiz expedition, Essex and the Cecils were united, superficially at least, by a common sense of purpose and military necessity. Yet, despite this, the Cadiz expedition turned out to be decisive in the collapse of Essex's relationship with the Cecils, and in the outbreak of factionalism which accompanied it. The expedition proved to be a turning-point because the venture had a remarkable polarising effect on English politics and because Essex sought to hijack the whole campaign for his own

[97] LPL, MS 656, fol. 67ʳ.   [98] *Ibid.*, fol. 69ʳ.
[99] For Burghley's expression of concern to Cecil about 'the uncertenty for resolution' in this matter, see CUL, MS Ee.iii.56, no. 85.
[100] PRO, SP 12/256, fols. 200ʳ–201ʳ; CUL, MS Ee.iii.56, no. 87.
[101] Burghley's holograph notes *pro et contra* about the wisdom of proceeding with the expedition after the loss of Drake and Hawkins, see PRO, SP 12/252, fols. 202ʳ–203ʳ (this paper has been incorrectly placed with documents of 1595). In May, with 'the queen daylye in change of humors about my lorde's voyage', Edward Reynoldes reported that 'the wisest [i.e. Burghley] was fayn to use his wisest reasons & argumentes to appease & satisfye her' (LPL, MS 657, fol. 46ʳ).

ends. Both phenomena served to shatter the *modus vivendi* between Essex and the Cecils. Both phenomena were also beyond Elizabeth's power to control once events were under way.

The ability of the Cadiz expedition to focus discontent and to polarise men's attitudes towards each other became apparent even before it left England. Well before the fleet raised anchor, quarrels broke out among the officers, including the generals themselves. Despite their previous record of co-operation, Lord Admiral Howard could not forget that this expedition had originally been of his making, before Essex entirely transformed it by adding a large army to the fleet. During the abortive relief of Calais, Howard's resentment at the way Essex dominated that operation brought him to the point of resignation, 'for I am yoused but as the druge'.[102] A few days later, while the Calais force was being broken up, Howard became so infuriated with Essex's manner of acting as his superior that he cut the earl's signature out of a letter they had jointly written to Burghley.[103] However, after this explosion, both generals began to treat each other with a wary civility, anxious to maintain their own *modus vivendi* for the duration of their impending voyage to Spain.

Apart from the need to wage a vitally important campaign together, Essex and Howard recognised that they had to mend their ways for the sake of discipline during the expedition. As Essex admitted, it was 'a purgatory ... to governe this unweldy body and to keepe theese sharpe humors from distempering the whole body'.[104] Although Essex went to great lengths to maintain order in the army, he could do no more than suppress the kind of rivalry which immediately arose between Sir Francis Vere and Sir Walter Ralegh.[105] For Ralegh, this voyage offered a long-awaited chance at rehabilitation after four years in the political wilderness. Vere, however, had the pride of a man whose cousin was the 17th earl of Oxford and who was accustomed to commanding English troops in the Netherlands. He believed it was intolerable that a failed courtier like Ralegh should claim precedence over him. For others, Ralegh's appointment as rear-admiral also raised dark suspicions about his intentions,

---

[102] Cecil MS 40/6 (pr. *HMCS*, VI, p. 144). Essex asked Cecil not to let the queen see Howard's protest, 'for yt is too passionate and may breake all our actions yf she take him att his word' (PRO, SP 12/257, fol. 44ʳ). Clearly, she did, however, for she sent the lord admiral a reprimand which he grudgingly accepted, 'but shall ever think myself more worth than I have done' (*HMCS*, VI, p. 146).

[103] PRO, SP 12/257, fol. 50ʳ⁻ᵛ.   [104] LPL, MS 657, fol. 89ʳ.

[105] On this quarrel, see, for example, *ibid.*, fols. 3ʳ⁻ᵛ, 5ᵛ, 6ʳ; BL, Harleian MS 7021, fol. 322ᵛ; W. Dillingham (ed.), 'The commentaries of Sir Francis Vere, being divers pieces of service, wherein he had command: written by himself, in way of commentary', in E. Arber (ed.), *An English garner: ingatherings from our history and literature* (8 vols., Westminster, 1895–6), VII, p. 81.

especially as he seemed to dally about joining up with the fleet.[106] Reynoldes speculated to Essex that, if he and the lord admiral were withdrawn from expedition by the queen, 'it wilbe turned into some Guiana voyage, and then your lordship shall easelie discover the plot'.[107]

Reynoldes's notion of a 'plot' against Essex suggests that the earl's remaining supporters at Court had chronic feelings of insecurity even before the fleet set sail. They may have had some grounds for concern. Ralegh, like Henry Brooke (who was also causing anxiety to Reynoldes[108]), was known as both a devious man and an intimate of Cecil.[109] Recent events also made Essex's departure seem potentially very inopportune. Sir John Wolley, the Latin secretary, died at the end of February[110] and Lord Keeper Puckering died on 30 April.[111] The appointment of new privy councillors could hardly be delayed much longer.[112] At the end of March, the bishop of St David's delivered a sermon at Court which focused upon Elizabeth's own apparently imminent demise.[113] The bishop was promptly imprisoned for his temerity,[114] but his comments reflected a widespread sense of unease. Elizabeth herself broke down in tears during the ceremony

---

[106] See, for example, LPL, MS 657, fols. 1ʳ, 11ʳ, 17ᵛ. Cf. *ibid.*, MS 659, fol. 1ʳ. Ralegh emphatically denied delaying his arrival for any ulterior motive (*HMCS*, VI, p. 169).

[107] LPL, MS 657, fol. 110ʳ. During the previous year, Ralegh had led an expedition to Guiana and travelled up the Orinoco River in an attempt to find the fabled realm of El Dorado. He subsequently publicised his endeavours in *The discoverie of the large, rich and bewtiful empyre of Guiana* (London, 1596, *STC* no. 20636).

[108] LPL, MS 657, fol. 110ʳ.

[109] Ralegh's attachment to Cecil from the time of their co-operation in dealing with the prize goods from the *Madre de Dios* in late 1592 is apparent in his letters to Cecil printed in *HMCS*. After his return from Guiana in November 1595, Ralegh dedicated his account of the voyage to Cecil and the lord admiral (one manuscript copy is LPL, MS 250, fols. 315ʳ–337ᵛ: this has some annotations which look like Cecil's hand). Cecil also personally examined Ralegh's journal of the voyage (CUL, MS Ee.iii.56, no. 62). Suspicions of Ralegh's devious nature seem well merited. See, for example, the copies of his letters in PRO, SP 9/55 (12), especially nos. 2, 3, 5, 9, 13.

[110] *Commons*, III, pp. 644–5; *DNB*, XXI, pp. 787–8.

[111] W. J. Jones, *The Elizabethan court of chancery* (Oxford, 1967), p. 79. His tenure as lord keeper is discussed in *ibid.*, p. 44ff.

[112] Some other more minor (but administratively important) offices were filled during the spring – by men known to be followers of the Cecils (W. D. Acres, 'The early political career of Sir Robert Cecil, c.1582–1597: some aspects of late Elizabethan secretarial administration' (unpub. Ph.D. thesis, University of Cambridge, 1992), p. 340).

[113] The bishop, Dr Anthony Rudd, later published his sermon: *A sermon preached at Richmond before Queene Elizabeth of famous memorie, upon the 28 of March 1596* (London, 1603, *STC* no. 21432). Rudd took as his text Psalms 90.12: 'Teach us so to number our dayes that we may applie our hearts unto our wisedome.' Rudd subsequently claimed that his sermon was about old age in general, not about the queen, but his excuses were rather disingenuous: 'O Lord, I am now entred into the climactericall yeare of mine age ...' (*HMCS*, VI, p. 139; Rudd, *A sermon preached at Richmond*, pp. 51–2).

[114] *HMCS*, VI, pp. 139–40. Although Essex had procured the queen's assent for Rudd's appointment as bishop of St David's in May 1594 (PRO, SO3/1, fol. 467ʳ), it seems unlikely that Essex had any part in prompting his bold sermon.

appointing Sir Thomas Egerton as Puckering's successor on 6 May, exclaiming that he would be the last lord keeper of her reign.[115] In this uncertain time, Essex's friends feared that 'enemies' such as Brooke and Ralegh would exploit his absence from Court to do him harm.[116] Whether or not there was any real substance behind these fears – Ralegh, after all, was away on campaign as well – the impact of these ideas was genuine enough. Essex's courtly followers became convinced of the hostile intentions of men like Brooke and Ralegh, and began to adopt a siege mentality. These feelings were transmitted to Essex himself through anxious letters and must also have soon become evident to the men whom the Essexians now regarded as enemies. In time, this interpretation of events became a self-fulfilling prophecy.

While the Court remained uneasily balanced, Essex, Howard, Ralegh and the expedition's soldiers and sailors remained at Plymouth for a month, fretfully awaiting a fair wind and Elizabeth's approval to proceed.[117] Like the Court, the expeditionary force was a hot-bed of worry and discontent. Put simply, there was a fundamental divergence of interests between the soldiers who looked forward to battles on Spanish soil, like Essex and Vere, and the sailors, like Howard and Ralegh, who hoped to capture rich Spanish cargo ships. Exacerbating this problem was the fact that the army and sea captains formed two more or less distinct communities.[118] As far as Reynoldes was concerned, the latter simply represented 'the sea faction'.[119] This division was vastly accentuated over the course of

---

[115] The story of Elizabeth's tears and Burghley's feeble attempt at optimism – '"God forbid, madam", said the lord treasurer, "I hope you shall bury four or five more"' – was recorded by Stephen Powle (BLO, Tanner MS 168, fol. 92ʳ (pr. Jones, *Elizabethan court of chancery*, pp. 81–2)).

[116] As noted above, Essex's principal 'friends' at Court during this time were the earl of Worcester, Lord Henry Howard, Fulke Greville and Sir Edward Dyer. Other Essexians around or near the Court included the Bacon brothers and servants such as Reynoldes and William Downhall.

[117] Essex was at Plymouth by 1 May. Howard had arrived before this but Ralegh was in London until 3 May and did not leave Dover until the 13th. He reached Plymouth soon after the 19th. Once the queen's permission had been granted, the generals moved aboard ship on the 24th and the army was embarked between the 28th and 30th. The fleet tried to set sail on 31 May but they were quickly driven back to the English coast. It was not until 3 June that a change of wind enabled the fleet to sail for Spain.

[118] This was graphically demonstrated on the eve of the attack, on 20 June, when the army officers gathered on Essex's ship and the naval officers on the lord admiral's, leaving Ralegh to shuttle back and forth in an attempt to agree a single plan for the assault (Dillingham, 'Commentaries of Vere', p. 82). Jealousy between the two groups also explains why Ralegh later vetoed Sir Edward Conway's plan for soldiers in long boats to seize the merchantmen anchored in Cadiz Bay. As a result, the Spanish had time to burn these ships, leaving the English sailors empty-handed (J. S. Corbett (ed.), 'Relation of the voyage to Cadiz, 1596; by Sir William Slyngsbie', *Naval Miscellany* 1 (Navy Records Society, London, 1902), p. 79).

[119] LPL, MS 658, fol. 9ʳ.

the campaign. Quite apart from the jockeying for the places of greatest honour before and during the battle at Cadiz, there was much rancour over the spoils of the victory there. With the city captured, but the merchant ships burnt, the sailors felt bitter that the soldiers were able to gain almost all the available booty. When the fleet finally returned home in August, it was the soldiers' turn to be driven to despair, when Elizabeth tried to recoup her investment in the campaign by seizing as many of their prize goods as could be found. As charge and counter-charge were made about who had gained what from the expedition, many of the land captains turned to Essex, their patron, for help. Literally surrounded by the clamour of these men,[120] Essex must have felt that all his friends and followers were under siege. The manner of their pleas also perhaps influenced his perceptions, for soldiers 'are commonly of blunt and too rough counsels'.[121]

In addition to the anxieties of Essex's courtly followers and the quarrelling between soldiers and sailors, the Cadiz expedition provoked one further incendiary contribution to English politics. This came from France, where Henri IV and his Court viewed Essex's new venture with horror, fearing the diversion of resources abroad and the absence of Essex himself. Given Essex's long record of championing the French cause, the French at first believed that the expedition must be a Machiavellian ploy by Burghley, whom they saw as hostile both to themselves and the earl.[122] Accordingly, Henri sought to forestall the expedition by mobilising Essex's friends Bouillon and Perez to urge him against it.[123] When Essex had a brief meeting with Bouillon at Dover in April, the duke sought to convince him that the enterprise was 'un dessain de ses ennemis pour l'eslonger [i.e. l'éloigner] de sa maistresse et le jetter au hasard'.[124] French anxieties about

---

[120] LPL, MS 659, fols. 88^r, 90^r.   [121] Naunton, *Fragmenta regalia*, p. 77.

[122] *CSPVen*, IX, *1592–1603*, pp. 191–2. French suspicions about this were perhaps especially acute because it had been hoped in March 1596 that Essex would lead an English delegation to a conference at Abbeville to discuss the long-mooted league between England and France. 'Praeterea', Perez added, 'rex ardenter avet te videre. Immo nil sperat, nil tu speres, nisi adfueris' (Ungerer, I, pp. 437–8).

[123] Henri IV may also have tried to use Anthony Bacon to influence Essex not to go on the voyage ([J.] Berger de Xivrey (ed.), *Recueil des letters missives de Henri IV* (9 vols., Paris, 1843–76), IV, p. 562). For the diplomatic pressure which the king applied to stop this venture, see the instructions on this matter given to Sieur de Sancy, Bouillon's fellow envoy to England (BL, Add. MS 5456, fols. 174^r–191^r).

[124] 'A design on the part of his enemies to separate him from his mistress and expose him to danger'. PRO, PRO 31/3, vol. 29, fol. 58^r. See also the account of this meeting given by Thuanus (cited in Birch, *Memoirs*, I, pp. 466–7. Cf. LPL, MS 250, fol. 344^v; *HMCS*, VI, p. 146). Because his meeting with Essex at Dover was so brief, Bouillon clearly attempted to continue his suasions by correspondence. In mid-May, he promised to send Essex 'lettres of some great importance, whiche he desired might falle into no other menn's fingeres, bycause he ment to deale freelie withe your lordship in them' (LPL, MS 657, fol. 109^r). Bouillon also sent Essex one final warning 'that your ruin is hoped and worked for'

the expedition, and their partisan and relatively crude understanding of the rivalry between Essex and the Cecils, therefore led Bouillon to urge a conspiracy theory upon the earl. When the duke and his entourage arrived at the English Court, this view rapidly gained wider currency, reinforcing the fears of Essex's supporters and perturbing the Cecils.

Despite the urgency of Bouillon's pleading, his warning initially made little impression on Essex. This was not because Essex trusted the Cecils: after his experience in 1595, he had learned enough to make sure that he had 'a faithfull promise' from Elizabeth that she would not appoint Cecil as secretary while he was away.[125] However, Essex had his own reasons for confidence about the venture. After long acquaintance with frustration, he had formed his own secret plans to hijack the expedition for his own ends. Thus he rejected Bouillon's renewed complaints by protesting that 'I am about to do more for the publike and for all our frendes then they can hope for.'[126] Presumably by being more explicit about his plans, Essex even managed to convince Antonio Perez to support the expedition, in spite of Henri's directions for him to work against the venture.

Ironically, this little success itself had explosive consequences. Apart from crippling his career in France, Perez's disobedience exacerbated the tensions at Court. Treated as a pariah by Bouillon and Sancy, Perez began to suffer as English courtiers followed the French lead.[127] It did not help that Perez's arrival in England also coincided with news of the disasters which had befallen Drake and Hawkins.[128] Perez's arguments about Spanish vulnerability and the need for aggressive action had helped to encourage this expedition, and he now reaped the blame for its failure. With his protector Essex absent, all the bitterness which Perez had earned during his previous stay in England was now openly turned against him. As Anthony Bacon warned Dr Hawkyns, Perez 'findes the queen's majestie extremelie incenst against him by the 2 fathers & the 2 sonnes, to witt, the lord treasurer & the Lord Cobham, Sir Robert Cecill & Henrie Brooke, who have so slandered & pepered him' that he became determined to leave England as soon as he could.[129]

With this persecution of Perez, factionalism began to become apparent at

    when he left England after concluding his negotiations at the end of May (*HMCS*, XIII, pp. 573–4).

125 BL, Egerton MS 2026, fol. 32[r].
126 WRO, TD 69/6.2, item 82; Bacon's copy is LPL, MS 657, fol. 140[r].
127 For all this, see Ungerer, I, pp. 305–9. For Naunton's description of Perez's problems in France even before he returned to England, see LPL, MS 651, fols. 43[r]–46[r].
128 News of the catastrophe first reached Court on 25 April (H. V. Jones, 'The journal of Levinus Munck', *EHR* 68 (1953), p. 236). Perez had arrived in England on 16 April and reached Greenwich two days later (Ungerer, I, pp. 305–6).
129 LPL, MS 656, fol. 274[r].

Court. The Essexians, already feeling under siege, could now see an open attack upon a man well known as an intimate of their lord and could identify his assailants. This, too, was reported to Essex by letter, not least because the aggrieved Perez made the lives of Essexians like Anthony Bacon an absolute misery.[130] Simply by the pressure of events, then, the Cadiz expedition had served to focus all the tensions which were already latent in English politics and crystallised them into sharp divisions. It is perhaps conceivable that these divisions might have been repaired once the expedition was finished. What made this impossible, however, was the manner in which Essex sought to use the Cadiz venture for his own advantage.

As already explained, Essex attempted to use the Cadiz expedition to foist upon Elizabeth his own conception of how the war against Spain should be waged.[131] What he had hitherto been unable to achieve at Court, he now sought to win by a feat of arms abroad. Like much else in his career, the breadth of vision and the daring of this initiative were quite remarkable. If he had succeeded in making Cadiz a permanent English base, it would have been extremely difficult for Elizabeth to abandon it and consequently the whole trend of English policy would have been changed: instead of shifting resources from France to Ireland, Elizabeth would have been forced to commit her resources to Spain itself. At home, this plan would also have resulted in a dramatic reduction – or even the elimination – of Cecilian influence in foreign and military affairs. With their special interest in Ireland and concern for limiting the cost of war, the notion of a permanent bridgehead on the Iberian peninsula was anathema to the Cecils. However, Essex's victory and the new strategy which it represented would have forced them to make a choice. They would either have had to fall into line with this strategy and accept Essex as the guiding light in its implementation, or fall by the wayside. Either way, Essex's domination of the council would have been the result.

The boldness of Essex's initiative also shows the extent to which he now believed that he must do Elizabeth necessary service – as he saw it – even though it was against her will and without her knowledge. Since Elizabeth and Burghley had failed to heed his advice during the preceding autumn, he would vindicate himself and prove his commitment to the queen's best interests by action. This determination to put an end to shilly-shallying was undoubtedly reinforced by Elizabeth's disastrous tergiversations over the relief of Calais, which drove even Burghley to despair.[132] Faced with

[130] *Ibid.*, fol. 267[r–v]; LPL, MS 657, fols. 6[r], 11[r], 12[r], 17[r], 18[v], 108[r].
[131] See above, pp. 250ff.
[132] CUL, MS Ee.iii.56. nos. 85, 89, 90; BL, Lansdowne MS 82, fol. 2[r].

another delay in his efforts to save the town, Essex protested to Cecil that, 'before God, I wold redeeme the infamy of yt with many ownces of my blood, yf the bargayne cold be made'.[133] News of the deaths of Drake and Hawkins, and of his own young son Henry, would also have stiffened Essex's sense of duty to a cause larger than himself.[134] The final impetus to go through with this bold plan, regardless of warnings from the French, must have come on 16 May, when Elizabeth decided to prevent Essex and the lord admiral from leading the expedition to Spain,[135] only to change her mind again an hour later.[136] Essex realised that, if he did not strike now, Elizabeth's obvious inability to stick to a decision might not give him the opportunity again: 'as they say, I will ether against the heate go thorough with yt or, of a general, become a monke upon an ower's warning'.[137]

The letter outlining Essex's plans which Reynoldes delivered to the council on 13 June[138] was a carefully conceived political bombshell. Surprisingly – or, perhaps, not surprisingly – surviving evidence does not record any explicit reaction to the letter's arrival by either the councillors or Elizabeth.[139] However, given the circumstances, it seems legitimate to speculate that this document encouraged Elizabeth's decision to break her recent promise to Essex not to appoint Cecil as secretary of state in his absence. On 5 July, Elizabeth formally made this appointment.[140] When the news came to Essex at sea, he was beside himself with fury, 'which discontent hee could not conceale, being thereupon exceedinglie dejected in countenance and bitterly passionate in speech'.[141]

Such rage was understandable. After his long struggle to prevent it, Cecil's appointment as secretary came as a severe political defeat for Essex. Cecil had now gained a post which seemed to guarantee him a role of pivotal importance when his father died. In the eyes of foreigners, Essex's

---

133 PRO, SP 12/257, fol. 45[r].

134 Henry Devereux was buried at All Hallows, Barking, on 7 May (Tenison, X, p. 11).

135 BL, Cotton MS Otho E IX, fol. 352[r–v].   136 *Ibid.*, fols. 352[v]–353[r].

137 WRO, TD 69/6.2, item 82; copy is LPL, MS 657, fol. 140[r]. Essex's all-or-nothing approach can also be seen in his letter to Cecil of 14 May: 'wee are as yow know over head and eares [i.e. in debt] and we must make this our master's prize. Yow are to help us now or to forsake us forever, for yt is the last tyme thatt I will have neede of frendes' (Cecil MS 40/78 (pr. *HMCS*, VI, p. 176)).

138 See above, p. 250.

139 The only indication of a response to Essex's letter appears in the underlinings and marginal notes on the original (PRO, SP 12/259, fols. 30[r]–31[v]), the latter mainly in Burghley's hand. Although the notes themselves are not very illuminating, one of the heaviest underlinings is significant: the phrase 'I [have] forgotten those reverend formes which I shoulde have used' is underscored twice (*ibid.*, fol. 30[v]).

140 *APC*, XXVI, 1596–7, p. 7. One of Cecil's secretaries, Levinus Munck, records the date as 6 July (BL, Harleian MS 36, fol. 384[v]. Cf. Jones, 'Journal of Munck', p. 236). The original patent for Cecil's appointment is dated a week later, 13 July (Cecil MSS, Deeds 219/20).

141 BL, Egerton MS 2026, fol. 32[r].

failure to prevent Cecil's success dealt a major blow to his international prestige. Cecil's success was all the more unpalatable to Essex because, by then, his own plans to hold Cadiz had collapsed. Rather than changing the course of the war (and with it the whole balance of political influence at home), Essex discovered that he had merely won a victory abroad at the cost of allowing his domestic rivals to buttress their position.

It is often implied that Cecil's appointment as secretary finally secured his political future and spelled doom for Essex's hopes of winning decisive influence on royal policy. In fact, Cecil's position remained somewhat uncertain and Essex, despite the bitter blow which this appointment represented, still had all to play for. Now that he had the title of secretary of state, Cecil had the urgent task of cementing himself in the office and making himself indispensable to Elizabeth while he could still benefit from his ageing father's influence. Cecil's promotion did not mark the end of his long struggle for security so much as a new phase in his desperate race against time. Unless he could prove his worth beyond all doubt before Burghley died, Cecil clearly feared that Essex would still be able to sideline him, or shackle him with a pliable colleague. Essex undoubtedly made similar calculations.

Cecil's efforts to consolidate his position soon seemed to give genuine substance to Bouillon's warnings to Essex. Within days of Cecil's appointment, Essex's maverick follower in Ireland, Sir Richard Bingham, was sequestered from his governorship of Connaught.[142] In London, Thomas Wright, the Jesuit who had surrendered himself into Essex's protection, was suddenly ordered into more stringent custody.[143] Anthony Bacon soon

[142] The queen's letter to this effect was dated 16 July (Jones, 'Journal of Munck', p. 236). Bingham had been waiting in Dublin since early May for a response to accusations reported against him by Sir John Norris (CSPIre, July 1596–December 1597, p. 37). On the same day that Cecil was appointed secretary, the investigation of these charges was delegated to Norris and Sir Geoffrey Fenton, both of whom were clients of the Cecils and enemies of Bingham (APC, XXVI, 1596–7, pp. 9–10). News of this decision and his subsequent sequestration prompted Bingham to flee to England. Upon his arrival, he was imprisoned in the Fleet (HMCD, II, p. 225; PRO, C 115, box M, bdle 17, no. 7436). Although he was severely reprimanded by Elizabeth and suspended from his post, Bingham benefited from Essex's return. On 10 November, Essex and Cecil jointly signed a letter authorising his removal from the Fleet to his own lodgings in Westminster (APC, XXVI, 1596–7, pp. 305–6). On 2 December, Bingham was sent back to Ireland in the company of Sir Conyers Clifford, Essex's follower, who was charged with acting as 'chief commissioner for the province of Connaught' while local grievances against Bingham were investigated (ibid., pp. 341–2, 421; CSPIre, July 1596–December 1597, p. 211). Bingham suffered little harm from these local grievances but he did not recover the governorship of Connaught until Essex was dispatched to Ireland as lord lieutenant in 1599 (DNB, II, pp. 514–15).

[143] In July, Anthony Bacon wrote to Cecil requesting that Wright be released from the requirement that he lodge with the dean of Westminster. This request was rejected. Instead, Wright received an order from Burghley on about 20 July which forbade him from

began complaining that letters to him from abroad were being inter-cepted.[144] Emboldened by his promotion and Essex's absence, Cecil felt free to exercise his new authority on matters which had irritated him but in which he had previously never dared to intervene. The appointment of Cecil's father-in-law, Lord Cobham, as lord chamberlain on 8 August was another ominous sign for Essex's followers.[145] At Oxford, Lord Buckhurst completed his riposte to Essex's powerful influence at the university by overseeing the appointment of Dr Thomas Ravis as vice-chancellor.[146] Even foreign merchants, it seemed, took their cue from the success of Essex's rivals. Giovanni Battista Basadonna, the Venetian agent in London and a crucial prop of the earl's intelligence operations in Italy, suddenly found himself the victim of rival merchants, who sought to destroy his credit.[147] In the eyes of his adherents, Essex's absence had given their enemies free rein on every front and the longer he stayed away, the worse things would become. In mid-August, Edward Reynoldes was greatly relieved when he wrote to his master that 'your lordship's more spedie retorne then some expected hath much crossed their desseins, for their meaninge was to have holden yow longer in this imploiment bycause they would have more time to worke and effecte their purposes for officers and councillores'.[148] The day before, Anthony Bacon had warned Essex of 'a plott' to induce him to leave the realm again by 'plausable offers' of a new military command.[149] By September, Essex himself was convinced that

even leaving the dean's house during the day. Bacon was stunned by this order, for which he felt there was no justification. Bacon wrote to Essex about Wright's treatment and Wright himself protested his confinement both before and after Essex's return from Cadiz. However, Wright had received no relief by 20 November 1596 (Birch, *Memoirs*, II, pp. 70–2, 101, 162, 197).

144 LPL, MS 659, fol. 21ʳ; LPL, MS 660, fol. 11ʳ.

145 McKeen, *Life of William Brooke*, II, ch. 23. The confrontation between the new lord chamberlain and Edward Jones, a friend of the Bacon brothers and aspirant to a place on Essex's secretariat, indicates the tone of personal animosity which was taking hold at Court. Jones had married a rich widow but Burghley awarded the lucrative wardship of the woman's son to Cobham. Jones was dismayed at this decision. When Cobham saw Jones at Court, the lord chamberlain publicly humiliated him by berating him as a 'sawcy fellowe'. Jones subsequently wrote a letter of complaint to Cobham but seems to have received no answer (*ibid.*, pp. 652–3).

146 Ravis was elected vice-chancellor on 17 July (Wood, II, *Fasti*, col. 272). Buckhurst had deliberately taken advantage of Essex's absence to push through Ravis's election as dean of Christ Church at the end of May (HMCS, VI, pp. 194–5, 197). For Ravis, see *DNB*, XVI, pp. 762–3.

147 Basadonna's principal enemies were the Florentine Filippo Corsino and Juan de Ribera, a Spaniard who was protected by Cobham (Ungerer, II, pp. 175–6). Basadonna's credit sank so low that he was close to leaving England at the end of August. Essex's timely return saved him from his creditors (Birch, II, p. 118).

148 LPL, MS 657, fol. 106ᵛ.

149 LPL, MS 658, fol. 279ʳ.

such ideas were indeed a deliberate ploy by his enemies: 'relegetur ideo specie imperii . . . '.[150] The conspiracy theory had become accepted fact.

With the appointment of Cecil as secretary and Cobham as lord chamberlain, the growth of factionalism at Court gained a powerful momentum. Followers of Cecil were seemingly encouraged to be more open about their feelings towards Essex, while Essexians felt ever more under siege. As Anthony Bacon was warned by his mother after Cecil's triumph, 'all were scant sownd before betwixt *the earl* & him. Frendes had ned to wake [ie walk] more warely in his diebus . . . [for] the father & sonne are joyned in power & pollicy'.[151] In these circumstances, Essexians could only keep their heads down and await the return of their lord, trusting that the glory of his victory would be sufficient to overcome the dominance of their newly strengthened adversaries.

Essex's return raised the tensions at Court to a new pitch. Both sides were now on edge. Having intercepted the 'True relacion' of Cadiz, the Cecils must have been alarmed at the aggressive and potentially dangerous way in which Essex had sought to make political capital out of his victory, even after his attempt to hold Cadiz itself had been thwarted. They could see that Essex's plea from Cadiz for Burghley to 'pleade for me till I returne'[152] had not inhibited him from plotting to undermine their political influence. They could also see – if they had not already done so – how greatly Essex's conception of loyal service to the queen varied from their own. Other councillors undoubtedly shared their alarm at such behaviour. For his part, Essex complained that his enemies sought to deprive him of the credit for his victory – a truly heartfelt accusation for a man so dedicated to winning martial renown. On the one hand, they advanced Ralegh as the hero of the sailors,[153] while, on the other, they played upon Elizabeth's concern about money in order to shift the focus of debate away from Essex's martial accomplishments: 'et ni mereri videar, reus sum factus . . . oeconomicae magis quam imperatoriae virtutes requiruntur'.[154]

Although he had steeled himself against an unfavourable reception at his

---

[150] 'He might therefore be banished under the pretence of giving him military command . . . '. Essex's holograph draft of this letter, endorsed 16 September 1596, is WRO, TD 69/6.2, item 75 (pr. Ungerer, I, p. 446). This phrase has a distinctly Tacitean flavour.

[151] LPL, MS 658, fol. 28^r. The words in italics are written in Greek letters in the original.

[152] BL, Lansdowne MS 82, fol. 24^r.

[153] LPL, MS 658, fol. 259^r. In response to news of the victory, the privy council ordered an account of the battle at Cadiz to be drawn up from Anthony Ashley's notes (*ibid.*). It is significant that Cecil amended the first draft of this paper to accentuate the role of Ralegh (PRO, SP 12/259, fols. 226^r–227^r).

[154] 'And instead of being seen as worthy of reward, I have been the subject of accusations . . . the virtues being prized are those of the bean-counter rather than the general'. WRO, TD 69/6.2, item 75 (pr. Ungerer, I, p. 445).

return – recalling how Norris and Drake had been treated in 1589[155] –
Essex was cut to the quick by Elizabeth's initial coldness and by the
bluntness of the inquisition into the expedition's finances.[156] Elizabeth had
been led to expect great riches from the victory at Cadiz[157] and was furious
when so little money reached her coffers and so much was pilfered by her
soldiers. Undoubtedly, Burghley and Cecil did their subtle best to encourage
her fury, placing the chief blame for the poor return on Essex rather than
the lord admiral. Henry Brooke and Sir William Cornwallis also added
their quota of venom, renewing their private vendettas of the previous
year.[158] The personal tone of this criticism infuriated Essex, but he could
not have been surprised by the nature of the enquiry. From the start, he
knew that he and the lord admiral would be held accountable for the
financial success of the expedition. However, this scrutiny now proved
extremely uncomfortable. For the first time since he joined the council,
Essex had to account for his actions to his colleagues and various of the
queen's bureaucrats. This proved deeply wounding to his martial and
aristocratic pride. Not only were the Cecils able to embarrass him
politically with this financial inquisition, but the 'base' nature of the whole
penny-pinching exercise besmirched his honour.[159]

The attack on Essex's probity encouraged new bitterness among his
followers, who feared the political consequences of this criticism. The new
tone was reflected in Francis Davison's comments written from Italy: 'if my
lord breake their neckes, as nature hath broke their backes, they may
comforte their fall with the noblenes of the aucthor'.[160] Anthony Bacon
reflected a different kind of violence when he told Dr Hawkyns that 'our
earle, God be thanked, though he be continuallie baited like a beare of
Paris garden with bande doges, yett he shakes them of lustely and, God

---

[155] LPL, MS 658, fol. 158ʳ. On another occasion, he described his commission as like 'a jaile
delivery' (*ibid.*, fol. 153ʳ).

[156] BL, Cotton MS Otho E IX, fols. 363ʳ–364ᵛ, 368ʳ–371ᵛ. One sign of the very forthright
nature of the inquest which followed Essex's return was Elizabeth's summoning of a secret
meeting of the council within the privy chamber on 19 August (LPL, MS 658, fol. 228ʳ).
The icy tone of this reception contrasted sharply with the letter of congratulations which
Elizabeth sent to the generals when she first heard the news of their victory (BL, Cotton
MS Otho E IX, fol. 366ʳ⁻ᵛ).

[157] These expectations had been greatly encouraged by the first report brought back from the
fleet by Sir Anthony Ashley and Sir Robert Cross: 'the spoiles worth in the towne half that
[which] is in London. The common souldiers disdayning bagges of peper, sugar, wine and
such grosse commodities by the space of five or sixe dayes, with their armes full of silk and
cloth of gold, in as ample a manner as if they had been in Cheapside. ...' (Corpus Christi
College, Oxford, MS 297, fol. 24ʳ⁻ᵛ).

[158] Birch, II, p. 96.   [159] Ungerer, I, p. 445.

[160] LPL, MS 660, fol. 235ʳ. Davison's main target here is clearly Sir Robert Cecil, whom he
also terms Essex's 'arch enemy, id est, his enemy made like an arch' (*ibid.*).

willing, will tire them all'.[161] For many Essexians, the nature of this 'baiting' was especially hurtful. By attacking Essex over the booty obtained by his soldiers and the potential profits lost to the queen by failing to capture either of the Spanish treasure fleets, it seemed that Elizabeth was being led to disregard the victory at Cadiz and to impugn the whole field of martial honour. This criticism of Essex threatened to expose fundamentally divergent views about war and honour of the kind which had already fuelled the private arguments over strategy between Essex, Elizabeth and Burghley. Pointed contrasts were drawn between the bold spirit of men who ventured their lives in the service of their country and indoor men whose boldness extended only to the scale of their peculation from the queen's coffers. Essex himself believed that the superior attitude of the Cecils and their assistants about alleged misappropriation of royal funds was rank hypocrisy: 'Ceciliani enim quidam, fungi homines, qui non modo quaestoris officium sed quaestuarias omnes artes norunt.'[162] Lord Willoughby was equally scathing about these accusations, condemning those penny-pinchers who criticised fighting men as corrupt: 'howsoever you deck him, he will prove a harpy and contrary to sound judgment & weale publicques'.[163]

The financial inquisition into the Cadiz expedition spawned anger and mutterings of counter-accusations which had the potential to mobilise men of 'virtue' in an open campaign against the corruption which they believed was imperilling England's ability to wage war. Given Burghley's long stewardship of the royal finances, the chief target of such criticism would have been obvious. Such criticism would also have been justified. Burghley's financial administration was characterised by a profound conservatism, sometimes verging on inertia, which inhibited the efficient use of crown resources, exacerbated the steady decline in the rate of tax collection and allowed internecine warfare among officials in the exchequer.[164] Many of

---

[161] LPL, MS 658, fol. 161^r.

[162] 'There are certainly some Cecilian men, mushroom men, who are not only well acquainted with the office of a paymaster but also with the tricks of a paymaster.' WRO, TD 69/6.2, item 75 (pr. Ungerer, I, p. 445). Essex was also upset that Burghley and Cecil explicitly blamed him in the queen's presence for the low quantity of prize goods recovered from the fleet after its return, even though this task had been deputed to various friends and associates of the Cecils (LPL, MS 659, fol. 142^r).

[163] BL, Egerton MS 1943, fol. 78^v (Anthony Bacon's copy of this document is LPL, MS 659, fol. 290^r). For Willoughby's criticism of Cecil, and praise of Essex, at this time, see also *HMCA*, p. 332.

[164] See, for example, R. W. Hoyle (ed.), *The estates of the English crown, 1558–1640* (Cambridge, 1992), pp. 44, 419–20, 423–4; R. Schofield, 'Taxation and the political limits of the Tudor state', in C. Cross, D. Loades and J. J. Scarisbrick (eds.), *Law and government under the Tudors* (Cambridge, 1988), pp. 239–40, 255; G. R. Elton, 'The Elizabethan exchequer: war in the receipt', in his, *Studies in Tudor and Stuart politics and government* (4 vols., Cambridge, 1974–92), I, pp. 355–88.

these problems would have been apparent to Essex and his friends, who clearly recognised the need for financial reform and resented the fact that they spent their blood and money to sustain England's war effort while others indulged in 'expencefull vanities'.[165] However, 'old Saturnus'[166] was a dangerous target to attack. Moreover, the stakes were very high because the whole regime seemed increasingly insecure. In June, a veteran captain, Sir John Smythe, had made an extraordinary attack during musters at Colchester on the government's right to levy men for service overseas and had called Burghley a traitor for his handling of the war effort. Smythe was connected to the earl of Hertford and his outburst included a call to support the Seymour family's claim to the succession.[167] The summer had also brought the realm its third bad harvest in a row, sending grain prices soaring and making the government fearful of a popular rising.[168] In the event, the only stir came in November in Oxfordshire, where wild plans for violent protest drew no support from the local people. Even so, the privy council revealed its anxiety by twisting the law to execute the ringleaders for high treason.[169]

By early September, the financial charges against Essex had lost their sting. New intelligence vindicated Essex's claims about the Spanish silver fleet and cast Ralegh's conduct in a poor light.[170] Elizabeth herself was also

---

[165]   *Apologie*, sig. D3ʳ.   [166]   *HMCD*, II, p. 122.

[167]   PRO, SP 12/259; *APC*, XXV, *1595–6*, pp. 450–1, 459–60, 475, 480, 501–2; Sir John Smythe, *Certain discourses military* (ed. J. R. Hale, Ithaca, N.Y., 1964), pp. lxxxiv–xciv; *DNB*, XVIII, pp. 474–6. At the time of his outburst at Colchester, Smythe was accompanied by Thomas Seymour, Hertford's second son. Smythe escaped treason charges by claiming that he had been drunk during the incident and because Burghley insisted that the slanders against himself should not be investigated (*APC*, XXV, *1595–6*, p. 507). Nevertheless, Smythe was immediately sent to the Tower and was not released to house arrest until January 1598 (PRO, SP 12/266, no. 4). He remained confined to the proximity of his home until the end of the reign. Smythe had achieved some notoriety at the start of the decade for his rivalry with Sir Roger Williams over the value of the longbow in contemporary warfare and for his belated criticism of Leicester's generalship in the Low Countries.

[168]   As George Abbott (later archbishop of Canterbury under James I) exclaimed in a sermon of December 1596: 'Behold what a famine God hath brought into our land ... One yeare there hath been hunger, the second year there was a dearth, and a third, which is this year, there is great cleannesse of teeth ... our yeares are turned upside downe; our sommers are no sommers; our harvests are no harvests; our seed-times are no seed-times' (cited in D. M. Palliser, *The age of Elizabeth: England under the later Tudors, 1547–1603* (2nd edn, London, 1992), p. 58).

[169]   J. Walter, 'A "rising of the people"? The Oxfordshire Rising of 1596', *Past & Present* 107 (1985), pp. 90–143; Manning, *Village revolts*, pp. 221–9.

[170]   LPL, MS 659, fol. 160ʳ⁻ᵛ. During the return home from Cadiz, Essex and Lord Thomas Howard had offered to take part of the fleet and lie in wait for the Spanish treasure ships. Ralegh had argued strongly against this and had carried the day (M. Oppenheim (ed.), *The naval tracts of Sir William Monson* I (Navy Records Society, XXII, London, 1902), pp. 355–6). Intelligence now belatedly proved that the claims of Essex and Howard had been correct.

eager to end the factional bitterness which was wracking her Court. At the end of August, she pointedly paired Essex and the lord admiral to assist her washing at the banquet which sealed the treaty with France.[171] Some weeks later, she joined Essex and Burghley with Egerton to assist her when she touched for scrofula.[172] To balance the promotions of Cecil and Cobham, Elizabeth appointed Lord North and Sir William Knollys to fill gaps in the council and household left by the deaths of Heneage and old Sir Francis Knollys.[173] Neither of the new councillors was really Essex's man,[174] but their appointment suggested that the ascendancy of his rivals was over. This made it easier for Essex to make a gesture of reconciliation by entertaining Cecil, the lord admiral and other noblemen at a lavish feast on 6 September.[175] Burghley and Cecil made one last unsuccessful effort to discredit his financial management before Elizabeth on the following day.[176] Nevertheless, Burghley, in particular, seems to have been anxious to rebuild the shattered *modus vivendi*. Since Cecil was now established as secretary and the realm was facing danger from all sides, the lord treasurer clearly felt that it was time to smooth relations with the ambitious earl and to put aside the disputes which threatened the effective running of government.

Ironically, Burghley's overtures to Essex began with another outburst of bitterness. Using the good offices of Elizabeth, dowager Lady Russell, he made an approach to Anthony Bacon, Lady Russell's nephew, at the beginning of September.[177] According to Bacon, Burghley's approach consisted of a sharp complaint that he was not siding with his kin, the

---

[171] BLO, Tanner MS 77, fol. 96ᵛ. Cobham (Cecil's father-in-law), Northumberland (Essex's brother-in-law) and Cumberland were also involved in Elizabeth's washing.

[172] *CSPVen*, IX, *1592–1603*, p. 238. For these touching ceremonies, see C. Levin, '"Would I could give you help and succour": Elizabeth I and the politics of touch', *Albion* 21 (1989), pp. 191–205.

[173] Roger Lord North was sworn as treasurer of the household and Sir William Knollys as comptroller on 30 August 1596. They were also sworn as councillors on the same day (Jones, 'Journal of Munck', p. 236). Sir Francis Knollys, the treasurer of the household, had died on 19 July, four days before Hunsdon, the lord chamberlain. North took Knollys' office and Cobham replaced Hunsdon. Sir William Knollys initially sought his father's office, but lost out to North. Instead, he became the effective replacement for Heneage. However, Knollys preferred to take the office of comptroller of the household (which had been vacant since the death of Sir James Croft in 1589) rather than Heneage's post of vice-chamberlain (*Commons*, II, p. 418).

[174] A close friend of Leicester, North had been waiting (and lobbying) for a place on the council for several years. Now in his mid-sixties, he was probably closer to Burghley than Essex, but was friendly with both. Like Essex, he had been made a knight banneret after Zutphen (*TCP*, IX, pp. 652–4; *DNB*, XIV, pp. 614–18). Sir William Knollys proved to be a vital supporter for Essex, but he clearly gained his seat at council board because he was his father's son (and hence a cousin of the queen), not because he was Essex's uncle.

[175] LPL, MS 659, fol. 9ʳ.   [176] *Ibid.*, fol. 142ʳ.

[177] Bacon's account of his visit from Lady Russell (LPL, MS 659, fols. 23ʳ–26ᵛ), which he wrote for Essex, can be dated to Saturday 11 September (*ibid.*, fols. 11ʳ, 21ʳ, 138ʳ). The conversation itself took before 8 September, as the sequence of subsequent correspondence

Cecils. Burghley may have hoped that reminding Bacon of the ties of blood would pave the way for a reconciliation, but Lady Russell's indignant tone and Bacon's own accumulated anger towards the lord treasurer had the opposite effect. In this case at least, factional allegiances were becoming too powerful to be restrained by appeals to family unity. Bacon and Burghley began an acrimonious exchange of views, with Lady Russell as the go-between.[178] Finally, on 22 September, Burghley wrote directly to Essex, again using Lady Russell as the intermediary. Burghley protested that he was his friend and had won the queen's displeasure by arguing that Essex should be granted the profits of ransoms from Cadiz.[179] Essex quickly responded in kind,[180] 'challenginge goodwill for goodwill', as Burghley termed it in his own subsequent letter.[181] Clearly, neither of them wished to be on bad terms with the other. By late September, a fragile veneer of amity had been pasted over the bitter divisions between them.

This façade of restored friendship was perilously thin. A mutual wariness still prevailed between Essex and Cecil. Moreover, the political aims of Essex and the Cecils remained profoundly divergent. While Burghley agonised over the state of the queen's finances and Cecil sought to consolidate his position as secretary, Essex lobbied for action in France and for a reorganisation of the realm's military administration, with himself as master of the ordnance or earl marshal. The latter prospect appalled Francis Bacon, who wrote a stinging letter to Essex at the start of October: 'I cannot sufficiently wonder at your lordship's course.' Bacon urged Essex to pull back from military affairs and to delegate control of the ordnance to a friend like Lord Willoughby. Instead, Essex should seek to become lord privy seal, which – significantly – 'hath a kind of superintendance over the secretary'.[182] Although much of Bacon's advice was unpalatable to him, Essex did approach Willoughby about the mastership of the ordnance. Willoughby not only declined to seek the post but argued that Essex alone had the political clout to carry through the necessary reforms.[183] Although

---

shows. Bacon only committed the story to paper because Essex was too busy to speak to him about it in person (*ibid.*, fol. 142[r]).

[178] The correspondence is: 8 September, Lady Russell to Bacon (*ibid.*, fols. 104[r]–105[r]; Bacon's copy is 162[r–v]); 9 September, Bacon to Lady Russell (*ibid.*, fol. 187[r]; a partial draft is *ibid.*, fol. 199[r]. Essex gave his approval to this letter the day before it was sent (*ibid.*, fol. 142[r])); 9 September, Lady Russell to Bacon (*ibid.*, fol. 106[r]). On 14 September Essex secretly went to speak with Bacon about these recent events (*ibid.*, fol 136[r], 138[r]).

[179] *Ibid.*, fol. 201[r] (pr. Devereux, *Lives*, I, pp. 389–90).

[180] *Ibid.*, fol. 196[r] (pr. Devereux, *Lives*, I, p. 391).   [181] *Ibid.*, fol. 133[r].

[182] By drawing attention to this power, Bacon was clearly hinting that Essex could use the post to 'superintend' Cecil. For Bacon's letter, see above, pp. 317, 324ff, 336.

[183] LPL, MS 659, fol. 236[r]. Willoughby opined: 'none but a Hercules can cutt of Hidra's heades of ignoraunce, or an Alexander unloose a Gorgon's knott of ill customes and abuses crept yn' (BL, Egerton MS 1943, fol. 86[r]).

Willoughby cast his argument in terms of overcoming obstruction from within the ordnance office, it seems clear that he also envisaged potential opposition stemming from Burghley and believed only Essex could counter this interference.[184] These arguments about military reform and partisan politics killed Bacon's programme stone dead. At precisely the same time, Essex's sense of rivalry with the Cecils also led him to join Archbishop Whitgift in nominating Richard Bancroft as bishop of London. Out of gratitude for Whitgift's support over the summer and because Burghley and Cecil opposed Bancroft's nomination, Essex helped to ensure that a notorious persecutor of radical Protestants won a post where the new bishop might be able to do the puritans great harm.[185] Given Essex's enduring status as the darling of the puritans, this action is a telling sign of his desire to thwart the Cecils. Political tensions were beginning to produce strange bedfellows.

In the last week of October, urgent intelligence from abroad finally forced Essex and the Cecils to put aside their feelings of mistrust. News that Philip II was determined to launch a new fleet against England, regardless of the autumn weather, sparked a full-scale military emergency which lasted a month.[186] Co-operation and trust between the secretary of state and Essex (who acted as a commander-in-chief of the queen's forces) was now vital, and both men recognised this. When a temporary council of war was established on 3 November, Essex took a conciliatory line by suggesting that the first meeting should be held at Burghley's house and by nominating Ralegh and Sir George Carew as members.[187] This respectful tone continued after the crisis had passed. At the end of November, Essex

---

[184] The potential for clashing with Burghley is clearly evident in Willoughby's reasoning to Anthony Bacon: 'if he [i.e. Essex] have it [i.e. the mastership of the ordnance], he shall have one eye to se into the disbursinge of the queen's treasure at warres, wherof he may judge the better of the rest and to a man of his place to have an insight and dealings therein is of no small importance' (LPL, MS 659, fol. 236ʳ).

[185] LPL, MS 659, fol. 241ʳ. The efforts of the Cecils 'to putt him [i.e. Bancroft] by' mark a continuation of Burghley's long-running opposition to Whitgift's tough line on religious conformity in the Church. Bancroft's nomination was highly significant because he was not only the archbishop's right-hand man but he had preached the sermon which had launched the anti-presbyterian campaign of 1589–92. Anthony Bacon's comment that Essex 'seconding the archbishopp ... upon very honorable conditions' suggests that Essex extracted some sort of promise that Bancroft would go easy on puritans in London who were under his protection. In the following year, Essex certainly won Bancroft's agreement not to persecute Stephen Egerton, even though the latter was 'of the presbiteriall faction' (Cecil MS 85/138 (pr. HMCS, XI, p. 154)). As Bacon predicted, the Cecils could do no more than delay Bancroft's appointment: he was elected on 21 April 1597 and consecrated on 8 May (DNB, I, p. 1030; E. B. Fryde, D. E. Greenway et al. (eds.), Handbook of British chronology (3rd edn, London, 1986), p. 259).

[186] See above, p. 263.

[187] HMCS, VI, p. 469. Burghley was president of this committee. Carew was a friend of Cecil and had been in charge of the ordnance during the Cadiz expedition.

carefully informed Cecil of his recent dealings with the French ambassador 'because if there be not some good care taken there may be some mal entendu'.[188] By mid-December, Cecil was eager for an open *rapprochement*. As before, Anthony Bacon was the man approached, but this time the intermediary was Sir George Carew. Some time before 11 December, Carew went to visit Bacon and protested that Cecil was now truly bent upon friendship with Essex and Bacon.[189] To give some substance to the claim, Cecil was careful to be helpful to Bacon's mother when they met a few days later.[190] Finally, on 31 December, Carew called upon Bacon again and talked for two hours. Afterwards, aside from Carew's own professions of duty to Essex,[191] Bacon was able to report that 'Mr Secretary of late hath professed very seriouslye an absolute *amnesia* of all misconceites passed, with earnest prostestation' that Bacon had but to call upon his aid to receive it.[192] These were generous sentiments, but both sides knew that rebuilding a semblance of trust now depended upon actions, not words alone.

By the start of 1597, an equilibrium had been re-established at Court. Essex and the Cecils were superficially courteous to each other and even friendly, albeit in a self-conscious manner. While Cecil promised to help Anthony Bacon, he also asked Essex to support the suit of one of his father's body servants.[193] More importantly, Essex and Cecil began to consider how they could pursue their own political objectives without coming into conflict. However, despite these surface appearances, the new accommodation did little more than paper over the deep cracks which had appeared at Court. In September 1596, one leading Essexian had opined that '*Cecil's* doings are so well known unto hym [Essex] that their is no hope of reconcilement.'[194] Although this prediction proved awry, the thoughts which had encouraged it could not be forgotten. Outward appearances now belied men's inner thoughts. As Thomas Lake wrote at the start of November: 'the factions [are] never more malicious, yet well smothed outward'.[195]

As the winter dragged on into 1597, courtiers continued to categorise

---

[188] *Ibid.*, p. 493.   [189] LPL, MS 660, fol. 134[r–v].

[190] *Ibid.*, fol. 129[r]. Anthony Bacon himself privately scoffed at the idea that Cecil would have 'the patience to read so scribled a hand' as his mother's (*ibid.*, fol. 147[r]). He was probably right – Lady Bacon's writing is execrable.

[191] *Ibid.*, fol. 127[r–v].

[192] *Ibid.*, fol. 124[r]. The word in italics is in Greek letters in the original.

[193] PRO, SP 12/262, fol. 55[r].

[194] HMCD, II, p. 218. The word in italics is in cipher in the original.

[195] *Ibid.*, p. 227.

each other as friends or enemies[196] and waited for some event to break the calm. Tension began to take its toll. When his wife died in childbirth on 24 January, Cecil was stricken with grief.[197] Cecil's father-in-law, Lord Cobham, also entered a terminal decline, encouraging Essex and Sir Robert Sidney to hope that Elizabeth would replace him with a more soldierly warden of the Cinque Ports.[198] However, Essex was also feeling the strain. In mid-January, he apparently made another of his 'suddaine recesses' from Court, a clear sign that he felt under stress.[199] A month later, much to the consternation of his friends and servants,[200] he announced his intention to leave Court to visit his Welsh estates.[201] Instead, however, he fell sick.[202] For nearly two weeks, and then again intermittently thereafter, he barely stirred from his chamber at Court.[203]

Some contemporaries believed that these periods of withdrawal were deliberate ploys by Essex to pressure Elizabeth over the wardenship of the Cinque Ports and his plans for a new expedition against Spain in the summer.[204] Modern historians have tended to adopt a similar view.[205] There is clearly some force to this argument – when he felt that the occasion warranted it, Essex had little compunction about seeking to manipulate Elizabeth. It is also undeniable that Essex's withdrawal during February and March 1597 brought tangible reward. When he threatened to leave for Wales, after being told that Cobham would have the Cinque Ports, Elizabeth offered him the mastership of the ordnance – allegedly because she could not face his further absence from Court.[206] However, the timing of Elizabeth's offer may have equally been influenced by a growing sense of

---

[196] For a few Essexian examples of the factional mind-set, see LPL, MS 654, fol. 283[r]; LPL, MS 660, fols. 145[r], 180[r]; Ungerer, I, p. 463.

[197] McKeen, *Life of William Brooke*, II, pp. 666–8. By the queen's command, Lady Cecil was buried with the pomp reserved for a baroness.

[198] *Ibid.*, pp. 668ff. Cobham lingered on until 6 March 1597. He was succeeded as lord chamberlain and as a privy councillor by George, 2nd Lord Hunsdon, on 17 April (*HMCD*, II, p. 267; Jones, 'Journal of Munck', p. 237). Hunsdon thus succeeded to an office which had been held by his late father until the preceding July.

[199] LPL, MS 654, fol. 151[r]. Anthony Bacon claimed that 'during your absence my heart was not mine owne'.

[200] Above all, his friends feared that the trip 'will geve tyme, oportunity and advantage to the cunning plotters & practizers of this Court, who wourk at all tymes & prevayle too much' with the queen (LPL, MS 656, fol. 20[r]. See also *ibid.*, fols. 14[r], 143[r]; *HMCD*, II, p. 231).

[201] *HMCD*, p. 233.   [202] *Ibid.*

[203] *Ibid.*, pp. 239, 240; LPL, MS 656, fol. 71[r].

[204] Henri IV, for example, heard 'dominum comitem 20 dies a curia abfuisse male contentum' (Ungerer, I, p. 480). Rowland Whyte also had his doubts about how sick Essex really was (*HMCD*, II, pp. 236, 265).

[205] For example, G. B. Harrison, *The life and death of Robert Devereux earl of Essex* (London, 1937), pp. 137–8.

[206] *Ibid.*, p. 248. This occurred on Thursday 10 March. However, it took another eight days, and some wrangling, before Elizabeth finally signed Essex's patent (*ibid.*, pp. 251, 252).

crisis in military administration, which culminated in the bankruptcy of Sir Thomas Sherley, the treasurer at wars for English troops on the Continent.[207] Essex's actions during this period were also not entirely calculated. Indeed, it seems that the accumulated effects of his physical and mental exertions over the previous year now caught up with him. At the beginning of March, Edward Reynoldes noted that 'his lordship seemeth not so myndfull of those ordinary busines as he hath bene'.[208] A fortnight later, after he had received his patent as master of the ordnance, Essex was again sick and talking of a trip to Wales, heedless of Elizabeth's desires. This drove Reynoldes to despair: 'trewly, I feare that his lordship is weeryed and skorneth the practizes and dissembling courses of the place, and therefore desireth to solace hym self and by degrees to discontinewe & so to retire from among them'.[209] Wearied with the double-dealing of Court and the burden of always arguing his case alone, it seems that Essex's commitment to politics finally wavered. After all the great hopes and bitter disappointments of 1596, his aversion to the back-biting and dishonesty of courtiers made him question whether he should continue to pursue his grand schemes.

Such doubts were not surprising. For the first time since the Rouen campaign – itself a painfully salutary experience – the Cadiz expedition represented Essex's full-blooded attempt to make political profit out of military endeavour, and it had failed. Unlike at Rouen, he now had the prospect of a second chance at success, thanks to the continuance of the Spanish naval threat. Yet Essex now also had to face the fact that the Court had become a factional battleground, where each side feared the other would take any opportunity to ruin them. He had to reckon 'how carefully mine enemies lie in wait to carp at all my actions, and how many things are therefore censured to be done ill because they are done by me'.[210] For Essex, such an environment was extremely hard to endure. Success there

---

[207] The crisis began with William Beecher, a contractor for supplies to the queen's forces, who went bankrupt in December 1596. Beecher's fall left Sherley financially exposed and encouraged Beecher to curry favour at Court by reporting Sherley's peculation. Sherley 'broke credit' on 8 March 1597 (*HMCD*, II, p. 247). The privy council finally began a detailed scrutiny of Sherley's accounts on the same day that Elizabeth nominated Essex as master of the ordnance (*ibid.*, p. 252). It was soon apparent that the accounts were a shambles and that corruption had been occurring on a grand scale for many years. Sherley (protected by the Cecils) and Beecher (probably encouraged by Essex) traded accusations and almost came to blows when appearing before the council in April. A final determination was not reached until August, when it was decided that Beecher had paid some £15,000 to Sherley in kick-backs to obtain military contracts since 1589, that Beecher owed Sherley £18,000, and that Sherley owed the queen £23,000! For all this, see D. W. Davies, *Elizabethans errant: the strange fortunes of Sir Thomas Shirley and his sons* (Ithaca, N.Y., 1967), pp. 41–6 and F. C. Dietz, *English public finance 1558–1641* (New York and London, 1932), pp. 452–4.

[208] LPL, MS 656, fol. 24^r.   [209] *Ibid.*, fol. 20^r.   [210] *HMCS*, VII, p. 10.

depended upon dissimulation and flattery, the very kinds of 'baseness' which he most detested. Moreover, his insistence upon the primacy of honour made him all too prone to fury and anguish over the slings and arrows cast by his rivals, which he knew made him all the more vulnerable to their schemes. The prospect of escape from this hostile and stressful world must have seemed very appealing to Essex in early 1597, particularly when it became obvious that his arch-enemy Henry Brooke would become the new warden of the Cinque Ports. However, Essex believed that he had a duty – indeed, a destiny – which he could not shirk. Although his confidence may have wavered briefly, he knew that he could not abandon the struggle to set Elizabeth and the realm upon what he believed to be the right path to the future. Once this moment of doubt was over, Essex returned to the fray with a new determination to realise his strategic and political ambitions.

In contrast to the complexities of 1596, the main thrust of politics in 1597 was relatively simple. Following the renewed professions of friendship expressed between Essex and the Cecils at the end of 1596, a superficial kind of trust between them began to grow over the early months of 1597. In early March, Ralegh started to act as 'the mediator' between Essex and Cecil.[211] Despite the ructions over the wardenship of the Cinque Ports, these contacts continued to develop until they formed the basis of an understanding about how they could each pursue their divergent political ambitions without causing the kind of violent cleavage which had been witnessed in the previous year. A deal was apparently struck whereby Cecil and his father would support Essex's appointment as sole commander of another great expedition, in which Ralegh was again to participate, while Cecil would become chancellor of the duchy of Lancaster.[212] The Cecils presumably also withdrew any objections which they might have had to Essex becoming master of the ordnance. Ralegh would also return to his old post as captain of the queen's guard.[213] The final terms of this agreement were settled after a dinner at Essex House on 18 April.[214]

As a result of this mutual gratification, relations between Essex, the

---

[211] HMCD, II, p. 243. For subsequent contact between Essex, Ralegh and Cecil, see ibid., pp. 259, 268, 271.

[212] Ibid., 268. This appointment was being mooted in early March 1597 (ibid., p. 248) but was only made by Elizabeth on 7 October, when Essex was abroad (BL, Harleian MS 36, fol. 385 (pr. Jones, 'Journal of Munck', p. 237)). At the time of his appointment, Cecil 'professeth intire correspondence to my lord [of Essex], and useth very respectivelie his lordship's freendes & cheife servauntes in his absence' (BL, Harleian MS 286, fol. 262^r).

[213] With the backing of Essex and Cecil, Ralegh was readmitted by Elizabeth as the captain of her guard on 1 July 1597 (HMCD, II, pp. 285–6; LPL, MS 3203, fol. 35^r).

[214] 'After dinner, they were very private all 3 for two howres, where the treaty of a peace was confirmed' (Collins, Sidney papers, II, p. 42. Cf. HMCD, II, p. 268).

Cecils and Ralegh were almost effusively friendly during the middle of the year, until the final departure of what became the Azores expedition. Ralegh passed on jokes from Cecil to Essex[215] and Cecil himself went to visit the fleet at the end of June.[216] When he wrote to Cecil, Essex signed himself 'your fast and affectionat frend', protesting that 'this paper is nott sufficient to answer your many kind and trew offices'.[217] Burghley and the lord admiral exchanged elaborate courtesies with Essex, the lord treasurer even writing to console Essex over the fleet's dispersal by a storm in July when Burghley could only see in one eye.[218] Essex and the lord admiral also received significant new royal grants.[219] With all this show of concern and bonhomie, Essex perhaps came to seem a little too trusting of his new-found allies. Sir William Knollys, Essex's uncle, felt the need to warn him: 'yf we lyved not in a cunning world, I shold assure my self that Mr Secretarye wear whollye youres, as seming to rejoyce at everye thing that maye succeede well with you, and to be greved at the contrarye'.[220]

However, despite appearances, Essex remained well aware that he lived in a cunning world. Despite Cecil's plea to Lord Burgh to view Essex and himself 'not as paralels',[221] they remained rivals. Essex could not be unaware that the basis of an anti-Essex coalition was forming at Court during 1597. Although the hostility of the Cecils and the lord admiral was temporarily suspended, he would have heard that Sir John Stanhope, once a good friend, had reluctantly decided to side with his Cecil relatives in March[222] and that Lord Buckhurst declared himself an ally of his bitter

---

[215] PRO, SP 12/264, fol. 12[r].

[216] WRO, TD 69/6.2, item 45 (Sir William Knollys to Essex, [late June 1597]); Hulton MS (formerly BL, Loan 23), fol. 64[r].

[217] PRO, SP 12/264, fol. 11[r]. These 'kind and trew offices' included Cecil's support for a suit by Edward Reynolds and repeated professions of good will to Anthony Bacon (Cecil MS 53/99–100 (pr. *HMCS*, VIII, pp. 332–3); BL, Add. MS 4125, fols. 227[r], 319[r], 322[r], 342[r], 344[r]). For his part, Essex passed on to Cecil edited versions of intelligence reports which he received from Venice (BL, Add. MS 4125, fols. 208[r], 214[r]).

[218] PRO, SP 12/264, fols. 66[r], 67[r].

[219] In June, Essex was given a lease of Carew Castle in Carmarthenshire and Tallaharne Castle in Pembrokeshire (PRO, C 66/1458, mm. 20–2; PRO, SP 38/5, unfol., entry of 31 May 1597). Both castles had previously been part of the Perrot estate and this grant should be seen as a positive response to the suit which Essex had made to Burghley on behalf of the countess of Northumberland earlier in the year (see above). Essex had apparently been seeking the lease of these castles for three years, but it was only now that Burghley withdrew his opposition to the deal (Collins, *Sidney papers*, II, p. 54). On 15 June, Howard was appointed chief justice of courts in royal forests south of the Trent, an office previously held by Leicester and Hunsdon (PRO, C 66/1458, mm. 31–2; PRO, E 403/2453, fols. 256[v]–257[r]). Given its timing, it seems likely that Howard's grant was some kind of compensation for accepting that Essex should have sole command of the Azores fleet.

[220] WRO, TD 69/6.2, item 45.   [221] PRO, SP 63/200, fol. 187[v].

[222] *HMCD*, II, pp. 251, 254, 259. Cf. PRO, SP 78/25, fol. 390[v]. In 1595, Stanhope and his brothers had been sufficiently close to Essex to offer Nicholas Williamson a place in the

enemy, Cobham, in August.[223] He could no longer even hope for support from a former comrade like Lord North, who sought to make a marriage alliance with the Cecils in June.[224] Essex was also painfully aware how his erstwhile allies could take advantage of his absence on campaign.[225] Nevertheless, like Cecil and Ralegh, he was eager to maintain the illusion of friendship because it enabled him to achieve his own ends.

If they had not come to an arrangement, Essex and the Cecils would each inevitably have sought to thwart any move attempted by the other. Neither side would gained any advantage from this situation and the acrimony could only have increased. A deal, however, allowed each side the chance to achieve at least some material success. By pushing for what became the Azores command, Essex gambled that he could outweigh the benefits which he allowed his rivals by achieving in 1597 what he had failed to do in 1596. To the dismay of many of his friends,[226] he was in effect playing for double or nothing. Cecil, on the other hand, gambled that Essex's expedition would not be successful enough to endanger his own position. However, Cecil was able to play with loaded dice. By supporting Essex's military strategy and aiding his preparations, he could claim a share of credit for any victory. If the expedition proved a failure, Cecil knew that his rival would lose face, or worse. Either way, he would still receive a lucrative office which controlled considerable patronage across the realm. Once the initial departure of the fleet was thwarted by storms and the army was reduced to a token force, Cecil's position became even stronger. As he confided to Lord Burgh, 'these weake watery hopes ... do but faintly nourish that noble earl['s] harte's comfort'.[227] For Elizabeth, acquiescence to these designs brought a more peaceful Court and council, but it was an ominous sign for the future that grants in her gift were so readily divided up as spoils among the courtly rivals.[228]

---

earl's service if he provided damaging information against the earl of Shrewsbury (*HMCS*, 5, p. 227). For the bitter local rivalry between the Stanhopes and Shrewsbury, see W. T. MacCaffrey, 'Talbot and Stanhope: an episode in Elizabethan politics', *BIHR* 33 (1960), pp. 73–85.

[223] PRO, SP 12/264, fol. 103ʳ. Buckhurst was especially anxious about Essex's influence at Oxford, which he felt was detrimental to his own status as chancellor of the university (*HMCS*, VI, pp. 195, 197).

[224] BL, Lansdowne MS 84, fol. 129ʳ.

[225] Friends also repeatedly gave him warnings of this danger (e.g. *HMCS*, VII, p. 244).

[226] See, for example, Cecil MS 49/93–4 (pr. *HMCS*, VII, p. 139); LPL, MS 654, fol. 78ʳ; *HMCD*, II, p. 231; Sir Francis Bacon, *Sir Francis Bacon his apologie, in certain imputations concerning the late earle of Essex* (London, 1604, STC no. 1111), p. 19; BL, Egerton MS 2026, fol. 32ᵛ.

[227] Cecil MS 54/75 (pr. *HMCS*, VII, pp. 361–2). Cecil clearly thought that Essex should have abandoned the whole expedition in July after violent storms thwarted the first attempt to sail for Spain and disease forced the demobilisation of most of the army.

[228] Elizabeth was most unhappy about permitting Essex's new expedition to Spain. In mid-

In the end, Essex's great gamble failed completely, although not for want of trying.[229] In consequence, Essex's position at Court – and, indeed, his whole career – was badly undermined. During the expedition, as in 1596, bitter squabbles broke out between the officers, culminating in an attempt to court-martial Ralegh.[230] Factionalism had again burst into the open. Above all, however, Essex failed to meet the cardinal requirement of all politicians who advocate militarist policies: although he remained undefeated, he failed to deliver victory in battle. Without this victory, Essex's prestige sagged and, more importantly, his expensive strategic policies lost their appeal. With Ireland absorbing resources at an alarming rate[231] and the realm enduring yet another disastrous harvest – the mid-1590s saw the worst run of harvests in the whole century – the time for foreign campaigns was over. As if to underline the final collapse of Essex's hopes, an envoy from the king of Denmark arrived in London at the start of September to discuss the prospect of brokering new peace talks between England and Spain.[232] The grand designs which he had been constructing since at least 1595 had come to nought.

In these circumstances, Essex's return from the Azores was inevitably a cold and bitter one.[233] To make matters worse, the fleet's return coincided with the arrival off Falmouth of the Spanish fleet and, despite desperate efforts to put ships back to sea, only a storm prevented the Spanish from seizing the port, just as Essex had done at Cadiz a year before.[234] Essex had little time for chagrin because he was immediately summoned to Dover to reinforce the English garrison at Ostend, which was threatened with a

---

May, she berated the council – and Burghley, in particular – for moving ahead so quickly with preparations for the voyage. Despite urgings 'by some of the lords [of the council]', she ordered a halt (Collins, *Sidney papers*, II, p. 52). However, the combined efforts of her leading councillors soon overcame Elizabeth's opposition.

229 See above, pp. 232, 265–6.

230 S. Purchas, *Hakluytus posthumus or Purchas his pilgrimes contayning a history of the world, in sea voyages and lande-travells by Englishmen and others* (London, 1625, Glasgow, 1905–7 edn in 20 vols.), XX, pp. 2–6.

231 As Burghley confided to Cecil at the start of October: 'I se noe towardlines of anie good end there but a perpetuall charge heare to the realm in levienge still more men withowt accompt what is becomm of the former nombers' (CUL, MS Ee.iii.56, no. 127).

232 BLO, Tanner, MS 77, fol. 118ʳ. The envoy had his first audience with Elizabeth at Theobalds on 7 September (Jones, 'Journal of Munck', p. 237). He and his entourage were lodged in London in the houses of Alderman Houghton and Customer Smith (*APC*, XXVII, *1597*, pp. 363–4).

233 *HMCD*, II, p. 302. Anticipating the inevitable criticism, Essex and his leading officers composed a belligerent defence of the expedition: 'so wee having failed of nothing that God gave us meanes to doe … deserve not now to be measured by the event … as for others, that have set warme at home and descant upon us, wee know they lacked strength to performe more, and beleeve they lacke courage to adventure so much' (Purchas, *Hakluytus posthumus*, XX, p. 33).

234 See above, pp. 266–7.

siege.[235] Only when this danger had passed did Essex return to London,[236] painfully aware of the magnitude of his failure. At Court, he found that his rivals had consolidated their strength and multiplied in number, while his own position had deteriorated sharply. Cobham had finally received his inevitable appointment as warden of the Cinque Ports in late September.[237] Lord Burgh's unexpected death in October marked the end of any genuine co-operation between Essex and the Cecils over the government of Ireland.[238] Essex also found himself haunted by reverberations of his affair with Burghley's grand-daughter, the countess of Derby. This rash act of passion infuriated many at Court, including Elizabeth, and added a very personal dimension to the suspicion of Essex among the countess's relatives.[239] However, Essex's return confronted him with something even worse. Whether through the insensitivity of Elizabeth or the deliberate provocation of his enemies, Essex was pitched into direct conflict with the

[235] The alarm over Ostend began on 23 October and was gearing up to become a full-scale emergency when new intelligence ended the crisis on 3 November (*APC*, XXVIII, *1597–8*, pp. 48–52, 81–9). Essex had been given a commission to oversee the relief of Ostend on 31 October (GL, MS 1752, p. 268; Devereux MS 3, fol. 132ʳ).

[236] He was in London, but keeping to his house, by 5 November (*HMCD*, II, p. 302).

[237] PRO, SP 38/5, unfol., entry of 27 September 1597.

[238] Burgh died on 14 October (*TCP*, II, p. 424) but the news did not reach the Court until 26 October (*HMCD*, II, p. 299). No new lord deputy was appointed until Essex himself was nominated as lord lieutenant of Ireland at the end of 1598.

[239] As noted in the previous chapter, the affair between Essex and Elizabeth, countess of Derby, must have occurred between her return to Court in late April and Essex's departure to begin preparing the Azores expedition in late June. In July, the countess was sent to her husband's house at Knowsley in Lancashire, possibly to avoid scandal. However, despite an attempt to prevent Burghley hearing the worst about his grand-daughter (Cecil MSS 54/14, 21 (pr. *HMCS*, VII, pp. 339, 344)), the story could not be contained. On 9 August, Derby received letters in Lancashire from Cobham, Lady Ralegh and the countess of Warwick – clearly all of them giving news of his wife's infidelity – which drove him into 'suche a storme as is wonderfull' (Cecil MS 54/14 (pr. *HMCS*, VII, p. 339)). The earl's servants joined the countess in persuading Derby not to ride to Court immediately. Nevertheless, he went to Greenwich soon afterwards. There Derby was forced to write a declaration disavowing any belief that his wife had been 'dishonest of her body' and challenging any gainsayer to a duel to the death. This declaration was signed on 20 August in the presence of Burghley, the lord admiral and Cecil (Cecil MS 179/140 (pr. *HMCS*, XIV, p. 20)). Despite this attempt to suppress the story, Thomas Audley's letter to Edward Smith in December suggests that the tale had been revived after Essex's return from to London in early November (Cecil MS 55/45 (pr. *HMCS*, VII, p. 392)). The countess of Derby herself remained in Lancashire over the summer and was still there when her infant daughter Elizabeth died shortly before 25 October at Pymmes, one of Burghley's houses in Middlesex (T. Lewis, 'The Cecils and their Edmonton, 1561–1600', in J. Burnby (ed.), *Elizabethan times in Tottenham, Edmonton and Enfield* (Edmonton Historical Society, Occasional Paper no. 56, 1995), p. 31. I am grateful to Ms Helen Payne for alerting me to this reference). For Burghley, who had doted on this great-grandchild, the coincidence of this tragedy and renewed rumours surrounding the child's mother must have been especially painful. Although she remained in Lancashire over the winter, the countess had separated herself from her husband by mid-1598 (*HMCS*, VII, pp. 344, 362, 430; *ibid.*, VIII, p. 281).

lord admiral, who was created earl of Nottingham by Elizabeth on 23 October, while Essex was still absent.[240] This promotion gave the lord admiral precedence over Essex for the new parliament which was then gathering at Westminster. Even more wounding to Essex was Nottingham's patent of creation, which gave him all the credit for the victory at Cadiz.[241] The great triumph which had been played down during the previous autumn had now been stolen outright from Essex. This was nothing less than a direct and public assault upon his honour.

Essex's response to this challenge was utterly extraordinary, and yet also consonant with other incidents in his career. After about a week at Court, he left and claimed to be sick for over a fortnight.[242] It soon became clear that this illness was merely a fig-leaf to cover naked political extortion. Essex bluntly refused to return to Court or to carry out the duties of his various offices until Elizabeth agreed to appoint him as earl marshal and changed the wording of Nottingham's patent.[243] When Nottingham refused to surrender his patent, Essex offered to vindicate himself by means of a duel with the lord admiral or one of his sons.[244] Elizabeth sent Ralegh to mediate between the two earls,[245] but the real crisis remained between the queen and her favourite. By standing upon his honour in this fashion, Essex locked himself into an open test of wills with his sovereign, to the great despair of his followers.[246] Although he eventually abandoned the tactic of boycotting the Court, Essex still refused to beg redress from Elizabeth and remained completely aloof from his responsibilities as a councillor.[247] Even after she finally agreed to make him earl marshal,[248] he haggled over the terms of his patent and refused to attend council business until his patent was signed and proclaimed.[249]

---

[240] *HMCD*, II, 298.

[241] Nottingham's patent is PRO, SP 13, case G, no. 8.

[242] de Maisse, *Journal*, p. 5. See also *HMCS*, VII, p. 479; PRO, SP 12/265, fols. 10^r, 16^{r-v}.

[243] de Maisse, *Journal*, pp. 6, 15, 28. Despite subsequent promises, Essex did not succeeed in having Nottingham's patent amended.

[244] *Ibid.*, p. 28; *HMCD*, II, p. 305.

[245] *HMCD*, II, p. 305. After the first few weeks, Nottingham became more conciliatory towards Essex. However, Essex's appointment as earl marshal prompted him to leave Court and claim ill health. The breach between the two earls was outwardly smoothed over by the time parliament reconvened on 11 January (R. W. Kenny, *Elizabeth's admiral: the political career of Charles Howard, earl of Nottingham, 1536–1624* (Baltimore, 1970), pp. 211–12).

[246] de Maisse, *Journal*, pp. 28, 67–8; PRO, SP 12/265, fols. 10^r, 16^{r-v}. Burghley also sent Essex a series of concerned letters (PRO, SP 12/265, fols. 9^r, 26^r, 36^r).

[247] de Maisse, *Journal*, pp. 48–9.   [248] *Ibid.*, p. 75.

[249] *Ibid.*, p. 97. The patent was finally signed and proclaimed on the evening of 28 December 1597 (*ibid.*, pp. 100–1; Jones, 'Journal of Munck', p. 237). Before then, Essex had rejected the wording initially proposed by Cecil (*HMCS*, VII, p. 520) and had suggested his own alternatives (*ibid.*, p. 527). At Essex's request, Cecil had tried to push the patent through before Christmas (HEH, EL 1408).

Essex's actions during this crisis were politically disastrous. At a time when many of his followers were being hounded by creditors because of the debts which they had run up in the expectation that the Azores voyage would bring them profit, Essex marginalised himself for weeks and crippled his ability to give them succour. Essex's conduct towards the lord admiral also poisoned his relations with the whole sprawling Howard family.[250] However, none of these consequences could outweigh Essex's concern for his own honour. Feeling his martial honour besmirched, and his pre-eminence among the aristocrats on the council challenged, he felt impelled to browbeat Elizabeth until she publicly acknowledged his 'merit' by naming him as earl marshal. As he protested to Cecil, 'I retch att nothing to which I lay nott a trew clayme.'[251] If anything, the perilous nature of this quest made Essex believe that his actions were all the more virtuous. As his defiant personal motto proclaimed, the envy of others was the natural companion of virtue – and hence true virtue must be pursued regardless of the risks which this entailed. Essex's resolute determination to become earl marshal is also significant.[252] This post not only gave him precedence over

[250] Although Lord Henry Howard does not seem to have been very close to Nottingham (L. L. Peck, *Northampton: patronage and policy at the Court of James I* (London, 1982), pp. 19, 26–7), Essex's behaviour clearly put Lord Thomas Howard in a difficult position. 'Good Thomas', as Essex frequently described him in letters, served on the Cadiz and Azores expeditions and enjoyed warm relations with both Essex and Nottingham. He became very sick in late 1597 and was expected to die when he was hurriedly created Baron Howard de Walden on 5 December (*TCP*, VI, p. 590; *ibid.*, XII[I], p. 463 note d; *DNB*, X, pp. 71–3). Thomas was the nephew of Lord Henry Howard, but Nottingham belonged to an even older generation of the Howard family: Nottingham's father was the younger son of Thomas, 1st duke of Norfolk, while Lord Henry Howard was the younger son of this duke's grandson and Lord Thomas Howard was the younger son of his great-grandson. The feud between Essex and Nottingham also confirmed the hostility towards Essex of Nottingham's wife, who was a dominant figure in the privy chamber. Since the new countess of Nottingham was one of Essex's Carey cousins, this quarrel between the earls was destructive of family unity. This feud also reinforced the enmity between Essex and Frances Howard, dowager countess of Kildare. The second of the lord admiral's three daughters, Lady Kildare, may have been the woman whom Essex 'used to terme the spyder of the Court'. It has been suggested that she hated Essex because of his affair with Elizabeth Southwell, half-sister of Sir Robert Southwell, who was married to her older sister Frances. Lady Kildare married Cobham in 1601 (Wotton, *Parallel*, p. 9; McKeen, *Life of William Brooke*, II, p. 437).

[251] Cecil MS 57/121 (pr. *HMCS*, VII, p. 527).

[252] This office clearly had a special importance for Essex. Aside from his own desire for public vindication of his honour, Essex must have recalled that his father had held the post of earl marshal of Ireland (PRO, C 66/1149, m. 16; FSL, L.a.237). Earl Walter had originally wanted this to be an hereditary office, rather than for life (PRO, SP 12/45, fol. 45^v), and had vainly hoped that his son might be granted it after his death (BL, Harleian MS 6992, fol. 54^v). It is possible that Essex may actually have kept his father's staff of office about him. After Earl Walter's death, the staff was initially entrusted to the safe-keeping of Walter Bagot of Blithefield, an old Devereux follower in Staffordshire (Devereux MS 5, fol. 22^v).

the lord admiral but it made him the realm's chief guardian of honour. In Essex's mind, this meant that the office was really that of an earl *martial*.[253]

Perhaps surprisingly, Essex's shocking behaviour over the last two months of 1597 did not spell the end of his ability to work and affect a superficial friendship with Burghley and Cecil. Once he was appointed earl marshal, Essex again became a remarkably co-operative and energetic member of the Court and council. In February and March, he even acted as secretary of state when Cecil went on a diplomatic mission to France. However, factional bitterness had become even more entrenched during his spell on the political sidelines.[254] The divisions which had emerged into the open during 1596 were now clearly permanent. Essex's conduct also had other damaging effects on political life. His absence from the Court and council was deeply disruptive: 'here is such a doe about yt as yt troubles this place and all other proceedinges'.[255] Ironically, this is powerful testimony to Essex's success in gradually making himself essential to Elizabeth's government. Yet the blatant manner in which he ignored his responsibilities undermined this success. For the sake of vindicating himself against the lord admiral and winning the post of earl marshal, Essex did irreparable harm to the reputation which he had established so painfully over the years as a conscientious – indeed, invaluable – royal servant. At the same time, the crudeness of his tactics must have weakened his grasp on royal favour. Essex's success in winning the office of earl marshal proved to be his last great triumph at Court. This was a decidedly pyrrhic victory.

[253] Hence Essex complained about the initial draft of his patent, 'wher I am praysed for to innocent vertues when they are active vertues, and nott negative, thatt shold draw on a prince to bestow a marshall's office' (Cecil MS 57/109 (pr. *HMCS*, VII, p. 520)). The final phrase suggests that Essex saw his promotion as similar to the title of marshal which the king of France bestowed upon his most senior generals.

[254] See, for example, PRO, SP 12/265, fol. 16^{r-v}; de Maisse, *Journal*, p. 49.

[255] *HMCD*, II, p. 305. For disruption to the council, see de Maisse, *Journal*, pp. 18, 27, 28, 49, 64, 67, 70–1, 73, 97.

CONCLUSION

'A greater worke then ever any gentleman'

By the end of 1597, the heart of the Elizabethan regime was torn by fierce and increasingly unmanageable political rivalries. Elizabeth's Court and council had sometimes experienced genuinely sharp tensions earlier in the reign, as in the 1560s or over her intended marriage to the duke of Anjou in 1579–80. The question of intervention in the Low Countries had also generated great passions in the late 1570s and the first half of the 1580s. However, these earlier outbursts of political tension had ultimately been contained, as the issues which sparked them – Elizabeth's desire to take a husband or some crisis abroad – ran their course and faded away. Painful as they were, these political spasms helped to ensure that the Elizabethan regime remained flexible. Each successive crisis encouraged the expression of a variety of opinions and a reshuffling of political alliances. Experience also demonstrated that, once these periods of intense disagreement were over, political life returned to normal. Suitors expected answers to their requests, government business demanded co-operation, and the queen's peace of mind required amity among her intimates. Over the years, Leicester, Hatton and Burghley, in particular, recognised that the issues which sometimes divided them were less enduring than the experiences and fears which they shared. Despite the differences between them, the potential for factional rivalry was contained by a recognition that each of the leading councillors had a special bond with Elizabeth and by a sense of collegiality around the council board. External factors reinforced this sense of mutual respect. By the 1580s, virtually all members of the Elizabeth's inner circle were worried about Spanish aggression and feared the consequences of Mary Queen of Scots renewing her claim to the English throne. Once open war began in 1585, there was even less room for personal rivalries, especially when Spain began preparing an Armada. When Leicester tried, and failed, to lock Elizabeth into partnership with the Dutch by unilaterally accepting the office of governor-general in 1586, and when Elizabeth hesitated over executing Mary Queen of Scots in early 1587, the council acted in unison to protect Leicester and destroy Mary.

This world of co-operation and mutual respect steadily disappeared during the mid-1590s. By 1597, political decisions and key matters of patronage were increasingly decided by bargaining between the earl of Essex and a group of his rivals, headed by Burghley and Cecil. Despite a façade of courtesy, even bonhomie, relations between these two groups were now openly adversarial. Where no agreement was possible, as over the appointment of a new lord president of the north to replace the earl of Huntingdon or a successor to Lord Burgh in Ireland, offices simply remained unfilled. The advanced age of many key officers and Elizabeth's own unwillingness to introduce fresh blood had already made her government sclerotic. This political polarisation now threatened to choke off the last vestiges of flexibility. The new divisiveness also increasingly marginalised Elizabeth herself, leaving her to contend with rivals who refused to be reconciled with each other except on their own terms. Essex's withdrawal from royal service over the last two months of 1597 demonstrated how severely this rivalry could disrupt government. In the end, Elizabeth had to bribe Essex to return by accepting his demand to be appointed earl marshal. For the majority of courtiers who still remained outside this rivalry between Essex and his adversaries, the hardening of attitudes now made it increasingly difficult to maintain friendly relations with both sides. The time was fast approaching when the men and women of the Court would have to choose which side to support, or consider what it might mean to remain neutral.

This dramatic change in the political climate was the result of the coming together of a whole series of problems. The regime's Protestant consensus was severely shaken by the anti-presbyterian campaign launched in 1589. This set Whitgift and Hatton against Burghley and ended up destroying the political career of old Sir Francis Knollys. Even after the campaign had passed its peak, Burghley and Whitgift remained on poor terms, each prone to see malice in the other's actions. Yet this campaign was only possible because of the earlier deaths of key puritan supporters on the council (Leicester and Mildmay, for instance), the backlash provoked by the scurrilous attacks on the church in the Marprelate tracts, and the declining relevance of Protestant radicalism to the war against Spain. The anti-presbyterian campaign dented the political pattern which had been established over the previous twenty years. Nevertheless, it was not a guide to the factionalism which lay ahead. For a while at least, Essex, Ralegh and Burghley lined up against Whitgift, while Buckhurst, later one of the anti-Essex alliance, supported Whitgift against Burghley. Like other crises earlier in the reign, this episode generated considerable passion and anguish, but it did not create permanent political divisions for the future.

If recent arguments about the fall of Sir John Perrot are correct, the early

1590s witnessed a dramatic intrusion of factionalism from Ireland into the Court. Politics in Ireland were more bitter and openly corrupt than their metropolitan equivalent. They were also nakedly partisan. The death of Perrot's patron, Sir Francis Walsingham, opened the way for his enemies in Ireland to attack him. Burghley's willingness to connive in this process – and even to take a more active role – saw Perrot tried and convicted for treason. That Elizabeth could be badgered into approving this farce, despite her repeated efforts to halt proceedings, was a foretaste of what would happen when open factionalism emerged several years later. However, Perrot's fate did not galvanise opinion and encourage the formation of a party to defend him. Perrot had few friends at Court, and many enemies. Although Essex tried to help him, he was too politically naive to recognise Burghley's double game and lacked sufficient influence to challenge senior members of the council. By the time Perrot came to trial, Hatton was dead and Burghley was left unchallenged as Elizabeth's single dominant minister. If Perrot's case left any lasting impression at Court, it was the influence of 'old Saturnus' and the ruthlessness which lay behind his professions of selfless service to the crown. In Ireland, the fall of Perrot opened the way for even greater corruption and the dominance of Cecilian influence on the administration there.

More directly related to the polarisation of politics in the mid-1590s were the twin problems of the succession and the conduct of the war. The succession issue during the period covered by this study was not simply the question of when Elizabeth would die and who would succeed her, although this was a constant source of worry which loaded every political action with added significance. The problems of an ageing regime and of political renewal also embraced the queen's leading ministers: who would succeed Leicester and Hatton as her favourites, and who would succeed Burghley as the driving force of her administration? In effect, there were three separate, but intimately linked, succession problems. The jostling to lay claim to become the next royal favourite continued throughout the 1580s. The earl of Oxford and Sir Philip Sidney failed in their bids for favour, but Essex and Ralegh battled it out during the latter years of the decade. Although the choice of a favourite was peculiarly a matter for Elizabeth, the leading courtiers clearly took a hand in this struggle, backing Essex against the outsider Ralegh. Burghley and Hatton were similarly active in trying to control the transfer of power to a younger generation of councillors. Frustrating Essex's youthful ambition and shielding him from outbursts of royal anger, they sought to ease him into power with Sir Robert Cecil. However, the death of Hatton destroyed these plans, leaving Burghley alone in a position of unparalleled influence – and determined to ensure the success of his son. Burghley's dominance of politics was now so great that it was almost impossible for Essex's ambitions to avoid bringing him into direct conflict with the lord treasurer and his son. Whichever way he turned, Essex would collide with vested Cecil interests. Burghley's example also introduced a new degree of concentration into politics. Although his accumulation of offices and influence was unprecedented, it now became the standard against which any serious aspirant to political power would be measured: what Burghley had achieved over forty years of service, Essex or Cecil would also need to attain in order to meet the new expectations of what it meant to be politically dominant.

In 1585, when England was poised on the brink of war, Burghley was accused of seeking to establish, by stealth, a *regnum Cecilianum*, a Cecilian stranglehold on power. Despite Burghley's innate monopolistic leanings, this charge can be dismissed as wild exaggeration, part of the ferment of political claim and counter-claim when vital issues were at stake. Leicester was charged with similar ambitions by his critics. After Hatton's death, to say that there was a *regnum Cecilianum* would still have been an exaggeration, but an increasing number of observers began to believe in its existence. Despite his remarkable industry, Burghley was too old and infirm to dominate the queen's affairs entirely, even if he had wished to do so. However, Burghley had friends and clients in many key government posts. He also made sure that his views weighed heavily in most of the major decisions, routinely exerting his influence with his conciliar colleagues and tailoring his advice to Elizabeth to achieve the desired result. Burghley's influence was not ubiquitous, but was readily apparent where it mattered: 'olde Saturnus is a melancholy and wayward planett, but yett predominant here'.[1]

Burghley's obvious decrepitude gave a special urgency to the competition between Essex and Cecil to establish themselves as heir-apparent to Burghley's power and authority. Neither Burghley nor Elizabeth, it seemed, could last long. This impatience can be seen in Essex's claim to James VI in 1589 that Elizabeth could not survive 'above a yere or ii'.[2] In 1593, after his appointment to the privy council, he was equally certain of Burghley's imminent demise: 'their chief hour glass hath little sand left in it and doth run out still'.[3] Cecil harboured the same thoughts – or, in his case, fears – but did not express them so openly. By 1595, when Burghley was increasingly crippled by pains, Cecil's need to win the secretaryship of state seemed extremely urgent.

By themselves, these various succession problems would have ensured

---

[1] *HMCD*, II, pp. 122–3. The discussion of this subject in N. Mears, '*Regnum Cecilianum*? A Cecilian perspective of the Court', in J. Guy (ed.), *The reign of Elizabeth I: Court and culture in the last decade* (Cambridge, 1995), pp. 46–64, is ultimately unconvincing.
[2] Cecil MS 18/51 (pr. *HMCS*, III, pp. 435–6).   [3] *HMCS*, IV, p. 116

serious rivalry between Essex and the Cecils. However, the conduct of the war made such tensions potentially explosive and added a dangerous element of ideology. For Essex and many others who shared his views, the war against Spain was a crusade which involved religion and a sense of national destiny. For Burghley, as for Elizabeth, it was a necessary evil. England had to be defended and national honour had to be protected, but the primary aim was avoiding defeat and expense, not achieving victory. Burghley was more willing than Elizabeth to endorse military action when it seemed necessary. However, he had mixed feelings about Essex's glorification of war and martial values. Endowed with an outsider's reverence for aristocrats of long lineage, Burghley was glad to see youthful noblemen like Essex live up to the martials ideals of their rank. Yet he certainly did not wish these personal ideals to influence government policy.[4] His son Cecil probably shared very similar views.

The war had its most divisive effects on English politics when circumstances allowed Elizabeth room to consider her options and choose from a variety of alternative actions. When the threat of war was at its most insistent, such as during the Armada campaign of 1588 or when new Spanish fleets set sail in 1596 and 1597, the danger served to unify the regime and stifle rivalry. When Henri IV of France came close to losing his throne between 1589 and 1592, averting his defeat became the 'common cause' of all members of the privy council. When Elizabeth sought to draw back from France, they cajoled her into staying the course. By 1595, however, Henri's cause seemed less urgent and the consensus was broken. Essex's constant pleading for new aid to France now seemed like further evidence of his excessively close relationship with the French king. For his part, Essex believed that Elizabeth's eagerness to save money and Burghley's urgings about the needs of Ireland were short-sighted and threatened a humiliating retreat from 'the stage of Christendome'.

The defeat of Spanish forces in Brittany at the end of 1594 brought a pause in the war and provided an opportunity to advance rival strategies – Essex's continuation and expansion of England's Continental commitment

---

[4] Burghley's fundamental suspicion about the consequences of excessive martial influence on government are revealed in notes which he wrote during the political crisis over the Anjou match. Considering 'the perills that may happen to the queen's Majesty if she lyve unmarryed', he reflects upon the pitfalls of the following two 'remedyes': '1. The provision of treasur, to maynteane force ether abrode to dyvert offences, or at home to withstand invasions, or rebellions. And how tresor can be had but with greff of people by subsidyes, it is easy to se'; and '2. The enhablyng of men of warr, which being encreased may per[hap?]se torn to the prejudyce of the queen, in divertyng ther forces to the contrary intent.' In consequence, he decides: '3. The best remedy is to govern the realme to content God in causyng the people to serve him, and to content the people with justyce and favorable government, which is not to exact frequent paymentes, nor to molest them with innovations' (Cecil MS 148/30).

and Burghley's wary defence coupled with the transfer of resources to Ireland. Since the realm's resources could not stretch to cover both options, one of these policies had to be rejected. To make matters worse, these rival policies encapsulated rival values and the continuing struggle over the succession to Burghley's authority. Essex's option marked a continuation of the Protestant cause which had first galvanised Englishmen to take up arms with the Dutch. It embodied England's commitment to Europe, to leadership of the Protestant states, to waging war on the largest scale on the grandest possible stage, and to a crusade against Spanish 'tyranny'. This was the war of Essex's dreams, the path to a fame which would outshine even Sir Philip Sidney. The consequence of adopting this policy would have been virtuous employment for Essex's military followers and, ultimately, reward from Elizabeth in the form of domestic political dominance. Although he shifted his strategic focus from France to Spain during the course of 1595, the nature of the war which he envisaged, and its consequent rewards, remained essentially unchanged. By contrast, the Cecilian emphasis on Ireland threatened to destroy these hopes for ever and to direct England's money and soldiers into a war on the periphery of Europe, where most of the chief beneficiaries would be men who looked to the Cecils for patronage and advancement. This would be a dirty war, fought without chivalry in 'bogland',[5] and reeking of corruption and personal gain. It is not surprising, then, that Essex came to believe that the fate of the realm, as well as his own political future, was at stake in this struggle over military strategy.

The strategic and ideological split over the conduct of the war drove Essex to actions of breathtaking boldness in his efforts to outbid the Cecils and win over Elizabeth to his cause. Essex's willingness to promote himself and his policies led him to circulate partisan manuscripts, to attempt to pressurise Elizabeth through intelligence reports and ambassadorial dispatches, and even to appropriate the queen's Accession Day celebrations for his own polemical purposes. In 1596, he almost succeeded in subverting the Cadiz expedition to meet his strategic and political needs. This venture crystallised the political tensions which had become evident during 1595 and openly encouraged notions of conspiracy and factional enmities. Events in 1597 confirmed these developments, demonstrating that professions of friendship could no longer bridge the gulf of mistrust which had opened up. If factionalism at Court was nascent in 1595, it became overt in 1596 and deeply rooted by 1597.

If 'the motor of political strife'[6] was largely fuelled by Essex's actions, his

---

[5] This is Burghley's private term for Ireland. He also sometimes described the Irish as 'the Boglish'.
[6] J. Guy, 'The 1590s: the second reign of Elizabeth I?', in his *Court and culture*, p. 6.

behaviour was driven by inexorable political logic just as much as his own vast ambition. Essex initially believed that Elizabeth could be argued into adopting his expansive war policies, especially if he could counter Burghley's voice of caution. Events in 1595 conclusively proved that Elizabeth could not be swayed by words alone. Essex now realised that he could only succeed by giving Elizabeth no choice in the matter. Urging Unton to slant his ambassadorial reports was an obvious, limited first step. However, as the pressures on him mounted, Essex was impelled towards a correspondingly larger solution which would solve all his problems at a single blow: diverting the Cadiz expedition to his own ends. He would have done the same again in 159 if his plans had not been ruined by storms and sickness in his army. Throughout, Essex remained committed to a clear agenda and, each time he was baulked, he chose to raise the political stakes rather than accept defeat, each step making it harder to hold back – the enmeshing logic of escalation.

In contrast to Burghley, whose response to events involved short-term expedients and muddling through, Essex followed the logic of his ideas to develop long-term plans. While urging Elizabeth to accept his scheme, he prepared for the accession of James VI of Scotland, the heir-presumptive, calculating that Elizabeth could not live much longer and that a king would give him the support which the queen denied him. Essex had no reason to suspect that James would prove an even more irenic sovereign than Elizabeth. Essex also prepared for the future in other ways. Realising that his plans would require a permanent military administration and an overhaul of the realm's financial machinery, he recruited and 'enabled' promising men who could staff this new bureaucracy. Useful friendships were fostered among the French and the Dutch, as well as quasi-diplomatic contacts with potential allies in Italy and Germany. Individually, these initiatives demonstrated Essex's commitment to the queen's service but, taken together, they suggest the outlines of a serious plan to reshape her government according to the needs of European war. The more thought and energy Essex invested in these plans, the more imperative it seemed that he should be able to implement them soon, regardless of opposition from his rivals or the queen.

While Essex refined his plans and escalated his pressure on her, Elizabeth proved remarkably unable to stop him or stem the tide of political polarisation. The state of the war meant that she could not dispense with either Essex or his rivals, nor even effectively discipline them. In wartime, any female ruler – even a prince as capable and dogged as Elizabeth – became dependent on men and was forced to yield to expert military advice. Time and again, Elizabeth's generals took advantage of these circumstances to ignore her commands and pursue their own objectives.

Despite her expressions of anger, the exigencies of war provided an unanswerable excuse for ambitious men to establish a degree of autonomy from the dictates of their female sovereign. To make matters worse, Elizabeth's advancing age encouraged expectations of her impending demise and further weakened her authority.

For Essex and a hard core of his followers, the struggle to control the queen – for that was what it became – was about place and policy. Essex needed Elizabeth's approval for his aggressive war plans and control of suitable offices to implement it. Patronage was a secondary matter, the inevitable corollary of these primary goals. Many of his followers, however, took a less ideological view of political life and regarded patronage as the main objective. Their attachment to Essex was based largely upon admiration of the earl and calculations of the benefits which he might bring them. For followers of this sort, commitment to Essex entailed material advancement and the thwarting of rivals rather than principle. This was also true of the loose coalition of councillors and courtiers which began to organise itself against Essex during the middle years of the decade.

Although the rivalry between Essex and the Cecils was obvious even by 1593, no overt Cecil faction appeared to counter this challenge. The professions of both Cecils about being first and foremost the queen's loyal servant were incompatible with open factional allegiance. Until 1597, or even later, the Cecils also hoped that they could find a lasting compromise with Essex. Throughout these years of rivalry, they consistently sought to renew a *modus vivendi* with him. They believed that Essex would play a dominant role in English politics for long years to come and that building a relationship with him that could endure through the turbulence of Elizabeth's death and the founding of a new dynasty was critically important for the future both of the realm – and of Sir Robert Cecil. This task assumed even greater urgency if the Cecils were aware – as they must have been – of Essex's close dealings with James VI. As Essex became ever more desperate to push through his war policy and more brazen in his efforts to exert pressure on Elizabeth, these hopes of political compromise came under severe strain. Not only did Essex's actions increase the stakes over Cecil's bid to become secretary of state, but his efforts to do Elizabeth service 'against her will' offended Cecilian notions of loyalty and duty.

Essex's heavy-handed behaviour also offended others at Court. Buckhurst was upset by his influence at Oxford and the lord admiral turned from friend to enemy as he felt himself shunted aside by Essex's drive to control the war effort. Henry Brooke, later Lord Cobham, developed a personal hatred of Essex, which was entirely reciprocated. Sir Walter Ralegh, once a bitter enemy of Essex, seems to have preserved a degree of friendship with him, but the experiences of the Azores voyage and his political dependence upon Cecil left no doubt where his loyalties would lie when the time came to choose sides.[7] Influential women also turned against Essex, including the lord admiral's wife and his daughter, the countess of Kildare. In the hot-house world of the Court, jealousies over Essex's philandering added personal venom to political rivalries. As the ranks of his adversaries grew and became more open in their hostility towards him, Essex also saw old supporters die. Hunsdon, Sir Francis Knollys and Sir Thomas Heneage were replaced on the council by lesser men and left gaps in the queen's affections which allowed Howard and Buckhurst to step up in political importance. Many courtiers also seem to have maintained their good will towards Essex but became unwilling to give him active support because his adversaries were also their friends and relatives. The broad support of 'the greatest' which had helped to protect Essex during his climb to power completely dissolved during the mid-1590s.

Essex himself was the chief force which served to bind his enemies together. Although Burghley and Cecil were his most direct political rivals, the grouping of his adversaries which had emerged by 1597 was essentially an anti-Essex coalition, not a Cecil faction. Ties between the enemies of Essex began to increase. Significantly, these new connections were often financial, emphasising the extent to which they joined together for mutual benefit. Over the winter of 1595–6, Cecil joined the lord admiral in building a ship – appropriately, named the *Truelove* – which they subsequently used for privateering. In 1598, Cecil and Buckhurst jointly purchased a monopoly for the manufacture of starch. They also joined the earl of Shrewsbury in funding prospecting along the Scottish border.[8]

In his rivalry with Essex, Burghley consistently cast himself as the selfless servant of the queen's will and the purveyor of honest and seasoned counsel. His long years of faithful service gave him a special place in Elizabeth's affections. Although they often made him sour, the aches and

[7] Ralegh assiduously cultivated of Cecil's support after his expulsion from Court in 1592, but their friendship does not seem to have been very deep. In his will of July 1597, Ralegh bequeathed some fine porcelain to Cecil, but only if his son Walter did not live to inherit them instead. Other than this, 'my right honorable good frinde Sir Roberte Cecill' received nothing from Ralegh: A. M. C. Latham, 'Sir Walter Ralegh's will', *Review of English Studies*, n.s., 22 (1971), p. 134.

[8] L. Stone, *Family and fortune: studies in aristocratic finances in the 16th and 17th centuries* (Oxford, 1973), pp. 6–7. The building of the *Truelove* with the lord admiral was only the first of several naval and mercantile ventures between them. In 1597, they sought to maximise their return from the ship's involvement in the Azores expedition by fraudulently claiming double rations for the crew (*ibid.*, pp. 7–8; also Stone, 'The fruits of office: the case of Robert Cecil, first earl of Salisbury, 1596–1612', in F. J. Fisher (ed.), *Essays in the economic and social history of Tudor and Stuart England* (Cambridge, 1961), pp. 92–4).

pains of his declining health also reinforced her respect for him.[9] However, Burghley was no passive victim of Essex's thrusting ambition. Despite his fury at any mention of a *regnum Cecilianum*, he had displayed strong monopolistic tendencies for many years.[10] The crippled careers of Sir Henry Unton, Anthony Standen, Thomas Bodley and Sir William Russell also proved that the old lord treasurer could strike out at those who showed ingratitude or threatened his ambitions for his son. Burghley was responsible for introducing a new brutality into high politics by his subtle destruction of Perrot – a ruthlessness which Cecil emulated in his prosecution of Richard Hesketh in 1593 and Essex reprised in his campaign against Dr Lopez in 1594. However, for all his dominance of patronage and government administration, Burghley was also burdened by vulnerabilities which made him bristle when they were exposed. Until Cecil was appointed secretary of state in 1596, all his hopes for ensuring his own political succession remained uncertain. As lord treasurer over three decades, he was responsible for failing to prevent large-scale peculation among the queen's financial officers. In Ireland, his clients presided over massive corruption and growing administrative chaos. Burghley's constant anxieties about the spiralling costs of the war were not simply motivated by concern for the commonwealth, but also by a personal fear that the whole system might collapse and expose his own shortcomings. Although it was impolitic to express his opinion too openly, Essex clearly believed that clients and friends of the Cecils were tainted by corruption and excessive profiteering from the war.

Burghley himself seems to have been relatively restrained in the profits which he made from his portfolio of offices. Others, including Sir Robert Cecil, exploited their opportunities far more ruthlessly. If they had had the chance, many of Essex's own followers would doubtless have done the same. Essex himself had few scruples in exploiting the possessions of the

---

[9] One contemporary (probably his secretary Michael Hickes) observed the impact of ill health on Burghley in the 1590s: 'in 30 years together he was seldom seen angry or moved with joy in prosperity or sorrow in adversity, his temper ever noted as one of his greatest virtues until within 3 or 4 years before his death, when age, the mother of morosity, and continuance of sickness altered even the course of his nature, with pains in his body, griefs and cares in his mind, crosses in council, and oppression with multitude of business for his country, which, not succeeding nor sorting to his desires, so distempered his mind as bereaved him of his wonted mildness, altered his natural disposition, and gave way to age's imperfections' (A. G. R. Smith (ed.), *The anonymous life of William Cecil, Lord Burghley* (Lewiston, Queenston and Lampeter, 1988), pp. 103–4). For Elizabeth's concern to ensure Burghley's comfort, see, for example, 'A briefe view of the state of the Church of England', in T. Park (ed.), *Nugae antiquae: being a miscellaneous collection of original papers ... by Sir John Harington, knt* (2 vols., London, 1804), II, p. 182.

[10] S. Adams, 'Eliza enthroned? The Court and its politics', in C. Haigh (ed.), *The reign of Elizabeth I* (Basingstoke and London, 1984), p. 63.

diocese of Oxford for his own financial benefit.[11] However, for Essex, the ends were more important than the means. He believed that his own financial dealings and exploitation – and probably also Burghley's private gain – were legitimate because it supported his endeavours on behalf of the state, whereas those who merely lined their pockets for their own private benefit were enemies of the public good. In the emotionally and politically loaded vocabulary of virtue, the former denoted 'industrie' and 'the publike use for which wee are all borne', while the latter meant 'idlenes' and moral decay.

Notions of virtuous behaviour were vitally important to Essex. They gave his life meaning and allowed him to justify his innate sense of ambition. They also made Essex himself the final, incendiary element in the complex process which encouraged open factionalism in Elizabethan politics during the 1590s. Essex's pursuit of virtue conditioned him to see politics in moral and ideological terms. In a time of war, when martial values enjoyed a new urgency and vitality, this belief in virtue seemed all the more compelling, both to Essex himself and to the many Englishmen who regarded his accomplishments with respect and admiration. When the course of the war created uncertainty over strategy in the middle of the decade, Essex's beliefs about virtuous conduct encouraged him to respond to this debate in an increasingly aggressive manner. In his eyes, the debate over war policy concerned not only the future direction of the war and England's relationship with her allies, but also his own destiny and the kind of country that England should become. Ideology had always been inherent in Essex's political conduct, but now it came to the fore. His actions – relentless self-promotion and increasingly overt efforts to apply pressure to Elizabeth – ensured that it began to infect the whole political scene.

Essex's style as a politician was always direct and based on an appeal for others to follow where he led. As in a military operation, he prepared the ground as well as he could but, when it came to the crunch, he was prepared to act boldly, believing that others would be galvanised by his example. In this sense, his landing at Peniche or in the first boat at Cadiz was emblematic not only of his style of generalship but also of his whole approach to politics and life. Essex based his career on leading from the front and urging others to follow his lead by the force of his own commitment and his willingness to take risks. To Essex, this was an expression of virtue but, to those who disagreed with his views, such behaviour seemed profoundly confrontational.

Essex's commitment to martial values and the pursuit of virtue can be

---

[11] R. Lacey, *Robert, earl of Essex: an Elizabethan Icarus* (London, 1970), p. 75.

traced to his childhood in the marches of Wales, where he learned about 'enemies' and ties of blood and friendship. These lessons were reinforced and placed in a broader context at Cambridge, where he was drilled in classical scholarship and humanist notions of service. Wales and Cambridge shaped Essex at a very profound level but, throughout his career, there was clearly a tension between the modes of behaviour which these influences encouraged in him: the calculating and intellectual Essex, carefully weighing the appropriate tactics to win some grant from the queen or analysing the latest intelligence reports, and the emotional Essex, who was stirred to rash actions by ties of honour and comradeship.

Essex's concern with virtue was all the greater because he grew up in the shadow of war. He was taught that a great struggle was at hand for the fate of Europe and that any man of honour must seek to prove his worth in this conflict. The example of Sir Philip Sidney, his cousin by marriage, solidified this linkage between war, virtue and faith, and inspired Essex to emulate and excel him. Although he married Sidney's widow and brought up his child, Essex did not measure himself against the real Sidney who met a slow and miserable end. Instead, Essex competed with the mythologised version, the pattern of a perfect Protestant knight who had defeated death by the exemplary display of virtue during his own lifetime. Like this imaginary Sidney, Essex lived his life as self-consciously as if it were a work of art, and sought to make himself indisputably the leader of his generation by excelling all of his contemporaries in accomplishments and zeal.

Essex's appeal to the myth of Sidney not only emphasised virtue and self-sacrifice in war, but also youth and the potential of a rising generation of soldiers. In a regime which was increasingly conservative and senescent, Essex stood out as the only military man who succeeded in winning significant offices and genuinely influencing the course of policy. Despite his laudable qualities, this was something which Sidney had conspicuously failed to do. At a time when courtly offices were being filled by men of advanced years and the queen seemed unable to treat virile young aristocrats with the seriousness which they expected, Essex became the natural focus for gentlemen of military age. Like Sidney in the Low Countries, he seemed to be blazing a path which others of his generation might follow to honour and profit. For many, his rivalry with the Cecils was a struggle against the dead hand of a generation which should have long since relaxed its grip on power. Although almost the same age as Essex, Sir Robert Cecil seemed like an old man in a younger body. Once Essex supplanted the Cecils, many believed, youth would finally have its day and Sidneian virtue would replace Cecilian caution as the touchstone of English government. In the meantime, Elizabeth's regime became ever more sclerotic and younger aristocrats became ever more resentful towards her and her aged ministers.

Until at least the mid-1590s, many observers also expected Essex to become another Leicester and some of his followers tried to shape his actions according to this mould. However, Essex could never have been another Leicester. Whereas his stepfather had used his favour with Elizabeth to build up enormous political influence over a period of three decades, Essex sought to make an impact in a few short years. Moreover, while Leicester had established himself at the same time as Burghley built up his position, Essex had to match himself against a lord treasurer who enjoyed an unprecedented concentration of influence and offices. Even if Essex had wanted to match Leicester's 'domesticall greatnesse', Burghley's dominance made this impossible. While Burghley remained alive, Essex could only position himself to take advantage of his eventual death and seek to exploit the one area of patronage which Burghley did not dominate: military command. This elementary political calculation reinforced Essex's own 'ambition of warr'. It also helped to accentuate the differences between Essex and his stepfather. In order to demonstrate his pursuit of virtue, Essex consistently distanced himself from the courtly skills of Leicester, affecting a soldierly bluntness which sometimes jarred with the expectations of Elizabeth and his fellow courtiers.

The periods which Essex spent with Leicester at Court were relatively brief and hardly amounted to a political apprenticeship. It was not until 1592 that Essex began to see life at Court as more than a temporary and undesirable diversion from the battlefield. For the first time, he now began to study politics and sought to remake himself as a credible politician. Since he had already become established as the queen's sole favourite, Essex had to make this transition in the full glare of public attention. As ever, the larger goal behind this endeavour was martial – after Rouen, he recognised that genuine influence over strategy and foreign policy was a *sine qua non* for successful military operations abroad. As ever, Essex could not be satisfied with merely winning political credibility, and he set himself the task of becoming a true statesman on the international stage.

Essex had to undertake this task without an obvious mentor, except perhaps Elizabeth herself, who variously praised and chided his early efforts as a councillor. However, with characteristic 'industrie', Essex set about 'inablynge' himself for royal service and his own political advantage. Studying with scholars like Henry Savile, he sought to divine the 'rules and patternes of pollecy' from classical history. He also benefited from the diverse talents of Francis Bacon, who took full advantage of Essex's hunger for advice in the early 1590s to inflate his own sense of self-importance: 'no other faute hathe the erle but he muste contynewally be puld by the eare as a boye that learneth ut, re, ma, fa'.[12] Bacon later became deeply disillusioned with the earl when he recognised that he was not as politically malleable as he had believed. Bacon's older brother Anthony was even more important to Essex, providing vital contacts in Scotland and building an intelligence system which soon spanned the Continent. In politics, knowledge is power. This increasing intelligence provided insights which complemented the lessons learned from ancient history and allowed him to confront Elizabeth with arguments and information which supported his contentions about the conduct of the war. This material made Essex's political views not merely credible, but increasingly persuasive. By the end of 1595, he had scotched any talk of seeking peace and convinced Elizabeth and his fellow councillors that England faced a renewed threat from Spain which could only be dealt with by a pre-emptive naval strike.

Although it crystallised the many tensions which were now plaguing English politics, the resultant expedition to Cadiz also demonstrated why Essex was so important to Elizabeth and her realm in the 1590s. When danger loomed and the military resources of the nation needed to be mobilised, Essex played a part which no other councillor could match. As the 'great patron of the warrs', he was both a talisman and a magnet for all those men who wished to test their fortunes as a soldier. During these years, England sustained a war effort greater than it had done for half a century. Waging war on many fronts, Elizabeth's government managed to avoid defeat and frequently embarrassed their enemy. Despite suffering from the worst run of harvests in the century, the government managed to continue the war without serious disturbances at home and won increasing respect abroad. This remarkable achievement was attributable to Essex just as much as to Burghley and Howard. Stretching himself to the limit, and beyond, he made an entirely disproportionate contribution to the nation's war effort. Like some latter-day Valerius,[13] he consistently sought to follow the advice which he had been offered as a child: 'rather throw the helve after the hatchet, and leave your ruynes to be repayred by your prince then any thing to degenerate from honorable liberalitie'.[14]

If any single document captures Essex's unswerving commitment to the war effort and the tensions which this provoked, it is his letter to Cecil from Plymouth on 7 May 1596. Anxiously waiting for confirmation that

---

[12] LPL, MS 650, fol. 81ᵛ. The words here are written by Anthony Standen, but they very clearly reflect the feelings of Francis Bacon, with whom Standen has been discussing Essex's support for Bacon's bid to become attorney-general. Cf. PRO, SP 12/238, fol. 206ʳ.

[13] 'There will ever be found some Valerii that so the state may stand and flourish, care not though they leave not the wherewith all to bury themselves, though other[s] bury their money not caring what case they leave the state' (*Apologie*, sig. D3ᵛ).

[14] See above, p. 22.

the Cadiz expedition will proceed, he writes 'somwhatt freely' of his hopes and fears, seeking to cajole his fellow councillors into action on his behalf. This letter expresses in his own voice what made Essex such a dynamic contributor to Elizabeth's government and also a source of such political friction:

I have undertaken and hitherto proceeded with a greater worke then ever any gentleman of my degree and meanes did undergoe. I have asked her Majestie no mony to levy, no autority to presse, nor no allowance to cary the troupes from the places of ther levyes to this rendevous. Butt heere I have our full numbers and heere I keepe them without spending our sea vittells or asking allowance or meanes from her Majestie. I am myself, I protest, ingaged more then my state is worth; my frendes, servants and followers have allso sett up ther restes. My care to bring a chaos into order and to governe every man's particular unquiett humors possesseth my tyme both of recreation and of rest sometymes. And yett I am so farr from receving thankes, as her Majestie keepeth the same forme with me as she wold with him thatt thorough his fault or misfortune had lost her troupes. I meane no one word of comfort or favor by lettre, message or any meanes whattsoever. When I looke out of myself upon all the world, I see no man thus delt withall and when I looke into myself and examin whatt thatt capitall fault shold be thatt I had committed, I find nothing except yt be a fault to strive to do her Majestie more service then she cares for. Well, I will nether amuse her nor justify myself. Butt to yow thatt are my fellowes, I will say thatt as I leave and cast of al care of myself to care for her Majestie's state and publike service, yow do wrong me and betray her service yf yow do nott putt her Majestie in mind how much she is bound in honor and justice to be protectres of me against all the world butt myne owne actions, in which whattsoever come I will never aske pardon for wante of fayth nor, yf I be not intangled by new directions or skanted of the meanes allotted to us, pleade excuse for want of fortune. Butt yf they come to us thatt are behind and every man joyne to do his best, I will aunswer the successe with my lyfe, for I know our cause is good, our meanes sufficient, and our way certayne.[15]

These lines epitomise the vast energy, ability and self-sacrifice of Essex. However, the letter also displays a querulous tone, hurt by Elizabeth's lack of gratitude for his great efforts and quick to strike the lofty moral pose of an injured man of virtue. Both aspects were entirely characteristic of Essex. However, during 1596 and 1597, the querulous tone increasingly began to submerge his positive attributes, culminating in the decidedly hollow triumph of being appointed earl marshal.

Essex was very far from being 'a playboy of the western world'. If anything, his problem was that he took politics too seriously because he framed his actions according to principle. Although he showed considerable resilience and tactical flexibility, he did not understand – or would not accept – that politics is ultimately the art of the possible. Yet, for a man to whom politics so obviously did not come naturally, Essex was remarkably

[15] Cecil MS 40/67 (pr. *HMCS*, VI, p. 172).

successful in reinventing himself as more than a mere ornament of Court. This was not simply the result of royal caprice, the indulgence of an ageing queen anxious to please her youthful protégé. As he proved in many spheres of activity, he was a man of great ability and dogged commitment. More than anything else, Essex built his career on war. In many ways, he was the great political beneficiary of England's long conflict with Spain. As a general, a patron of soldiers and a military administrator, he quickly made himself indispensable to the nation's war effort. However, Essex's 'ambition of warr' was also his greatest vulnerability, as Francis Bacon belatedly recognised. The more effort and emotion which Essex invested in advancing his view of war policy, the less able he was to accept anything short of success – and the greater was the cost if he should fail. When events seemed to threaten his vision of the war in 1595, he felt driven to defend what he regarded as sacred matters of principle by actions which became increasingly overt and extreme. Over the course of the following two years, these actions ratcheted up the pressures against him and helped to polarise Elizabethan politics. While England remained at war, Elizabeth could do little to restrain Essex and his growing band of enemies could do little more than thwart him. Nevertheless, these checks drove Essex to ever more radical behaviour, as he struggled to impose his vision of war on a queen and a council which was increasingly unreceptive to his views. This placed him in an extremely precarious position if he should ever cease to be indispensable to the war effort. In the years after 1597, this was precisely what happened and it cost Essex all that he had achieved in the preceding years, and more. However, the disintegration of Essex's career is another story in its own right.

BIBLIOGRAPHY OF PRIMARY SOURCES

MANUSCRIPTS

ALNWICK CASTLE, NORTHUMBERLAND

Papers of the duke of Northumberland

(**Note:** These papers are available on microfilm as BL, M 280–M 416, subject to granting of the owner's approval for consultation.)

Accounts

U.I,2 Accounts, 1589–99.

Manuscripts

MS 479 A contemporary translation for the earl of Northumberland of Girolamo Franchetta's *An idea of a booke for the governments of state and warr* ....
MS 481 Account of the Cadiz expedition by Sir William Slingsby.

BAYERISCHE STAATSBIBLIOTHEK, MUNICH, GERMANY

Clm 10364 Correspondence of Dr Joachim Camerarius of Nuremberg.

BERKSHIRE RECORD OFFICE, READING

TA 13/2 Photostatic copy of (incomplete) diary of Sir Henry Unton during his first embassy to France, 23 July–1 October 1591 (original MS held in Alderman Library, University of Virginia).
TA 13/3 Photostatic copy of Unton's diary during his second embassy to France, 17 December 1595–6 March 1596.

BODLEIAN LIBRARY, OXFORD

Additional Manuscripts

D 109

Ashmolean Manuscripts

818, fol. 38^r Description of the funeral procession of Robert Dudley, earl of
  Leicester.
840
862
1113
1115
1131
1729

Bodleian Manuscripts

966

Douce Manuscripts

171, fols 1^r–13^r, 20A^r–25^v Accounts relating to Essex's minority, 1577–81.
393

Dugdale Manuscripts

32

English Historical Manuscripts

c.61
c.121
c.477
d.240 Manuscript page-proofs of Henry Savile's *The ende of Nero* (1591).

Misc. Manuscripts

Don.c.188 Letter from Essex to Penelope Lady Rich, undated.
Top.Oxon.e.5

Rawlinson Manuscripts

A 173
B 259
D 1175

Tanner Manuscripts

76, 78, 79, 82, 338

University of Oxford Archives

NEP/Supra/Registers KK, L Registers of congregation and convocation, 1564–95.

BRITISH LIBRARY

Additional Charters

74952 Formal copy of public and secret treaties concluded between England and France, May 1596.

Additional Manuscripts

4102
4125 Papers of Anthony Bacon (originals).
5455 Instructions to French ambassadors, 1562–92, copies.
5456 Instructions to French ambassadors, 1593 onwards, copies.
5482 Lists of knights, sixteenth century.
5750–1 Original warrants for the queen's household, temp. Elizabeth.
5845
6177
8159 Roll of gifts exchanged with queen at New Year 1587.
11042 Correspondence of the Scudamore family, Herefordshire.
11053 Correspondence of the Scudamore family, Herefordshire.
11335 Annals of the city of Chester.
12097 Papers of Sir Julius Caesar.
12506 Papers of Sir Julius Caesar.
12510
12511
19401 Papers relating to Scotland, temp. Eliz.
22583 Poems of William Gager.
22924
22925 John Clapham's 'Elizabeth of England'.
30352 'Musae Boreales', by Richard Eedes.
32092
32117
33207
33769 Presentation copy for Essex of John Norden's 'An exact discription of the county of Essex', 1594.
35841
36294 Drafts of letters etc. by William Camden.
36768 Register of the Order of the Garter, 1 Mary–19 James I, copy.
37232
39828 Tresham MS.
40630
48014 Yelverton MSS (papers of Robert Beale).
48027 Yelverton MSS (papers of Robert Beale).
48029 Yelverton MSS (papers of Robert Beale).
48129 Yelverton MSS (papers of Robert Beale).
48152 Yelverton MSS (papers of Robert Beale).
58435 Holograph poems of Sir Robert Sidney.
64081 A 'fantasticall lettre' by Essex for his sister, Penelope, undated.

Cotton Charters

iii.10 Letter of Robert Cecil to Essex, 26 January 1588.

Cotton Manuscripts

Julius F VI
Caligula E VII
Caligula E VIII
Caligula E IX
Galba C VIII
Galba C XI
Galba D I
Galba D II
Galba D XI
Galba D XII
Otho E IX
Vitellius C XVII
Vespasian C XIII
Vespasian F XIII
Titus B VI
Titus B VII
Titus C VI
Titus C VII
Appendix, vol. 39

Egerton Manuscripts

6 French diplomatic papers, temp. Eliz.
8 French diplomatic papers, temp. Eliz.
1943 Papers of Peregrine Lord Willoughby.
2026
2262
2598 Papers of William Asheby, ambassador to Scotland, July 1588–January 1590.
2623
2877
3052 Roll of gifts exchanged with the queen at New Year 1584.

Hargrave Manuscripts

225

Harleian Manuscripts

36
61
167–8
285–8
290
296

305
787
1629
1813
2125 Annals of the city of Chester.
4293
4762 Papers of Sir Thomas Baskerville.
6063
6845
6992–7 Papers chiefly relating to Lord Keeper Puckering, 1575–96.
7002
7021
7031 Copies of documents relating to the University of Cambridge.

Harleian Rolls

D.35.1 Inventory of the possessions of the late earl of Leicester, made by order of the Prerogative Court of Canterbury, 1589.

Lansdowne Charters

17 Roll of gifts exchanged with the queen at New Year 1589.

Lansdowne Manuscripts

17, 23, 25, 27–8, 30,
31, 34, 36, 39, 45, 53,
58–63, 68–9, 71–2,
78–9, 82–4, 96, 99–100
102, 103, 108–9, 115, 158, 238

Reserved Photocopies

RP 445 Letter of Essex to [Richard] Bagot, March 1590.
RP 2895 Mock charter from queen to Burghley, dated 10 May 1591.

Royal Manuscripts

17.B.l
18.C.xxi Papers relating to the Armada crisis, 1588. Copies.

Sloane Manuscripts

226 Account by Dr Roger Marbecke of the Cadiz expedition, 1596.
814 Jewels of the queen delivered to Katherine Howard, 1572–87.
871
1697, fol. 54 Horoscope for Robert Devereux, 2nd earl of Essex.

Stowe Manuscripts

145
150
166 Papers of Thomas Edmondes, 1592–6.
606 Pedigrees.
774 Household book of Roger, Lord North, 1580s.
1047 Precedent book of Francis Thynne, Lancaster Herald.

CAMBRIDGE UNIVERSITY LIBRARY

Manuscripts

Dd.xi.76 Meditations on God's salvation of England from the Spanish Armada, 1588, composed by Oliver Pigge.
Ee.iii.56 Private letters from Lord Burghley to Sir Robert Cecil, 1593–8.
Hh.vi.10 Report of a disputation among London ministers concerning the intended expedition to Portugal, held November 1588.
Mm.i.35 Copies of MSS relating to University of Cambridge.
Mm.i.43 Copies of MSS relating to University of Cambridge.
Mm.2.22 Copies of MSS relating to University of Cambridge.

University of Cambridge Archives

Collect.Admin.5 Copies of documents relating to public ceremonies at Cambridge.
CUR 45 Documents relating to the office of university orator, 1568–1820.
Grace Books D, E
MS Lett.9 Original letters, temp. Elizabeth.

CANTERBURY CATHEDRAL LIBRARY, CANTERBURY

Diary of Arthur Throckmorton (3 vols.)
(**Note:** At the time of consultation, this diary had not been assigned a call number.)

CENTRE FOR KENTISH STUDIES, MAIDSTONE, KENT

De L'Isle Manuscripts, papers of the Sidney family

(U 1475/–)
A 38/2 Expenses of Sir Robert Sidney, 1593–4.
A 38/5 Accounts of Rowland Whyte, beginning 26 July 1596.
C 12/26, 41 Letters from Rowland Whyte to Sir Robert Sidney, dated 22 November and 13 December 1595.
F 26/4 Miscellaneous papers relating to Sir Philip Sidney.
F 26/11 Patent of Charles IX of France creating Sir Philip Sidney a gentleman of his chamber.
(**Note:** Some of the accounts are available on microfilm in the British Library as M 772.)

Papers relating to the Foulis family in the possession of Viscount De L'Isle
(U 1886/–)
C 3 Privy seal dated 22 June 1594 for Burghley to pay £4000 to David Foulis on behalf of James VI.
O 2 Receipt by David Foulis for the above sum, 1 July 1594.

CHRIST CHURCH, OXFORD

Evelyn MS 258b Disbursement book of Robert, earl of Leicester, 1584–6.
MS XX.C.2 Estate ledgers, 1540–87.

COLLEGE OF ARMS, LONDON

Vincent MS 90, p. 311 Funeral certificate for Sir Roger Williams, December 1595.
Vincent MS 188, fol. 10^v Bill relating to the funeral of Sir Roger Williams, December 1595.

CORPUS CHRISTI COLLEGE, OXFORD

MS 297, fols. 23^r–24^v Report by Sir Anthony Ashley and Sir Robert Cross of the capture of Cadiz, 1596.

DURHAM UNIVERSITY LIBRARY, DURHAM

Howard MS 2 Political notes by Lord Henry Howard for Robert, earl of Essex, undated.

FOLGER SHAKESPEARE LIBRARY, WASHINGTON D.C., USA

G.b.4 Inventories etc. relating Essex, drawn together after the sequestering of his estates, 1601.
(Note that only part of this manuscript is foliated and citations in the footnotes vary accordingly.)
L.a.1–1076 Papers of the Bagot family of Blithefield, Staffs.
V.b.142
V.b.214 A commonplace book compiled by an unknown follower of Essex, possibly a member of the Scott or Knatchbull families of Kent.
Z.d.16 List of gifts exchanged with the queen at New Year 1585.
Z.e.3 Drawing of funeral procession for Sir Christopher Hatton, 1591.

GLOUCESTERSHIRE RECORD OFFICE

MF 1161 Berkeley Castle MSS, Select Letters, vol. 2.

GUILDHALL LIBRARY, LONDON

MS 1752 Letter-book, Signet Office, 1595–9.

HAROLD B. LEE LIBRARY, BRIGHAM YOUNG UNIVERSITY, PROVO,
UTAH, USA

Beale-Walsingham Papers

Nos. 23–48 Misc. papers of Robert Beale and Sir Francis Walsingham, including thirteen letters from Thomas Wilkes, 1586–8.

HATFIELD HOUSE, HATFIELD, HERTFORDSHIRE

Cecil Papers

Accounts

4/21 Income received by Essex from his estates upon his release from wardship, 1586–8.
133/17 Leicester's receipts for the sweet wines grant, 1587–8.

Bills

2/10 Miscellaneous bills relating to expenditure on Theobalds, 1570s.

Deeds

117/4 Burghley's will, copy.
219/20 Original patent for Sir Robert Cecil's appointment as secretary of state, 13 July 1596.

Legal

22/2 Indenture between Essex and queen of 7 August 1590 concerning Keyston Manor, Hunts.

Manuscripts

MSS 14, 18, 20, 25,
31, 35, 37, 40–1, 45,
47, 49, 53–5, 57, 62,
75, 78–9, 85, 98–9,
135, 139, 168, 174,
179, 191, 203, 226.
(**Note:** The Cecil Manuscripts, although not the other papers, must initially be consulted on microfilm, as BL, M 485.)

HENRY E. HUNTINGTON LIBRARY, SAN MARINO, CALIFORNIA, USA

Ellesmere Manuscripts

EL 1045
EL 1205a
EL 1408
EL 1612

Huntingdon Correspondence

Boxes 3, 4 Letters relating to the 3rd and 4th earls of Huntingdon.

INNER TEMPLE LIBRARY

Petyt Manuscripts

538, vols. 46–7

JESUIT PROVINCIAL ARCHIVES, FARM ST CHURCH, LONDON

Stonyhurst College, MS Anglia A I Documents relating to Elizabethan Catholics. (**Note:** This manuscript is held here in copy form only.)
MS 46/12/3 Transcripts and translations by Fr Leo Hicks of manuscripts relating to Robert Persons, 1589–96.

KING'S COLLEGE, CAMBRIDGE

MS 41 Psalter seized on the Cadiz expedition, presented to the college by Essex in November 1597.

College Archives

Allen's 'Skeleton Collegii Regis', vol. 2 Notes on fellows of King's to the year 1600.

LAMBETH PALACE LIBRARY

MS 178
MS 250 Volume of papers relating to foreign voyages.
MSS 605, 612, 614, 617 Carew manuscripts.
MSS 647–62 Papers of Anthony Bacon.
MSS 701, 707 Shrewsbury manuscripts.
MS 930 Papers of Francis Bacon
MS 936 Papers of Francis Bacon
MS 2004
MSS 3199, 3200, 3201 Talbot papers (formerly vols. H, I and K respectively at the College of Arms).

LONGLEAT, WILTSHIRE

Devereux Manuscripts

MS 1 Correspondence relating to estate matters.
MS 2 Papers, mainly financial.
MS 3 Accounts.
MS 5 Papers relating to the minority of Essex.
Boxes 5, 6 Commissions and legal instruments, 1577–1603.

Dudley Manuscripts
MSS 2, 3
Box 3, no. 56 Leicester's superseded will of 30 January 1582.

Talbot Manuscripts
MS 2

Thynne Manuscripts
MSS 6, 7, 40

ÖSTERREICHISCHE NATIONALBIBLIOTHEK, VIENNA, AUSTRIA
Cod. 9737 Correspondence of Henry Wotton.

PETERHOUSE, CAMBRIDGE
Old Register

PRINCETON UNIVERSITY LIBRARY, PRINCETON, NEW JERSEY, USA
Robert H. Taylor Collection
No. 48470 Essex to Richard Bagot, 20 August 1588.
No. 49258 Mary, countess of Pembroke, to Essex, n.d.

PRIVATE COLLECTION, MANUSCRIPT
Hulton MS (formerly BL, Loan 23)
This volume was withdrawn from the British Library in July 1990, after it had been consulted there by the author. A microfilm copy of the MS can still be consulted at the BL, with the owner's prior consent, as BL, M 2001. The volume was unsuccessfully offered for sale at Sotheby's in December 1992. While the future ownership of the manuscript remains uncertain, the Hulton Family Trust is unwilling to allow access to the original. The most recent information received by the author suggests that the volume has unfortunately now been broken into two separate lots to encourage its sale. One part comprises various holograph letters of Robert, 2nd earl of Essex, to Queen Elizabeth, while the other consists of various longer holographs by Essex. Some minor items contained in the original volume which were not written by Essex have already been sold as separate items to the Folger Shakespeare Library in Washington D.C.

PUBLIC RECORD OFFICE
C 54 Chancery, close rolls.
C 66 Chancery, patent rolls.
C 115, box M Chancery masters' exhibits, deeds of the duchess of Norfolk (Papers of the Scudamore family of Herefordshire).

C 231/1 Chancery, entry book of clerk of the crown, July 1595–March 1603.
E 101/107/33 Fragmentary accounts relating to the queen's stables, temp. Eliz.
E 163/15/31 Exchequer, miscellanea, file relating to legal proceedings over the lands of Sir John Perrot.
E 163/16/15 Exchequer, miscellanea, file relating to the debts of the late earl of Leicester, compiled 1603.
E 351/242 Exchequer, pipe office, declared accounts of Sir Thomas Heneage, treasurer for the army during the Armada crisis of 1588.
E 351/542–3 Exchequer, pipe office, declared accounts of the treasurer of the household, 1579–96, 1596–1603.
E 401/1847, 1858 Exchequer of receipt, tellers' views of receipts, 1590, 1596.
E 403/1693 Exchequer of receipt, issue books (pells), 1597–8.
E 403/2276, 2277, 2280 Exchequer of receipt, tellers' views of payments, 1590–1, 1596–7.
E 403/2363 Exchequer of receipt, register of payments of fees and annuities, 1600–1.
E 403/2426–7, 2429 Exchequer of receipt, payment books for privy purse, wardrobe, ambassadors etc., 1588–9, 1589–90, 1592–3.
E 403/2453 Exchequer of receipt, auditors' patent books, 1574–1603.
E 403/2655–6 Exchequer of receipt, privy seals dormant, 1st series, 1597–9, 1597–8.
E 407/55 Exchequer of receipt, miscellanea, expenses of Star Chamber, 1581–1637.
KB 8 King's Bench, Baga de secretis (records of treason trials).
MPF/76 Maps and Plans, coloured map of County Monaghan, December 1590.
PC 2/20 Register of the privy council, 1592–3.
PRO 31/3/29 Transcripts by M. Armand Baschet and others of manuscripts relating to Great Britain and Ireland from the National Archives, Paris.
PROB 11 Wills proved in the Prerogative Court of Canterbury.
SO 3/1 Signet Office docquet book, 1585–March 1597.
SP 9 State papers, domestic: Williamson collection, pamphlets, miscellaneous.
SP 12 State papers, domestic, Elizabeth I.
SP 13 State papers, domestic, Elizabeth I (cases).
SP 14 State papers, domestic, James I.
SP 15 State papers, domestic, addenda, Edward VI to James I.
SP 38 Signet Office: docquets.
SP 40 State papers, domestic, warrant books.
SP 45 State papers, domestic, various.
SP 46 State papers, domestic, supplementary.
SP 52 State papers, Scotland, series I, Elizabeth I.
SP 59 State papers, Scotland, border papers.
SP 63 State papers, Ireland, Elizabeth I to George III.
SP 77 State papers, foreign, Flanders.
SP 78 State papers, foreign, France.
SP 81 State papers, foreign, Germany (States).
SP 84 State papers, foreign, Holland.
SP 85 State papers, foreign, Italian States and Rome.
SP 94 State papers, foreign, Spain.
SP 97 State papers, foreign, Turkey.
SP 99 State papers, foreign, Venice.

SP 106 State papers, foreign, ciphers.
WO 55/1939 War Office, miscellanea, letterbook of Sir Henry Witherington, knight marshal of Berwick, 1582–92.

SHEFFIELD CENTRAL LIBRARY

Bacon Frank Manuscripts (BFM)
Vols. 2, 5 Papers relating to the Talbots, earls of Shrewsbury.

SOCIETY OF ANTIQUARIES, BURLINGTON HOUSE, LONDON

MS 444A Volume of misc. letters by historical figures.

TRINITY COLLEGE, CAMBRIDGE

College Archives
Upper Commons Book, 1580–5

College Manuscripts
MS R.5.18

UNIVERSITY COLLEGE, LONDON

Ogden MS 7/41 Copies, letters from (Sir) Robert Cecil to Sir Christopher Hatton, 1590–1, and of letters of Francis Bacon.

UNIVERSITY OF EDINBURGH LIBRARY

Laing Manuscripts
Division iii, no. 193 Commonplace book of Anthony Bacon, early 1580s.

UNIVERSITY OF LONDON LIBRARY

MS 187, fols. 9^v–15^r Secret instructions by Essex for Dr Henry Hawkyns, Anthony Ersfield and Robert Naunton, 1595–6.

WARWICK COUNTY RECORD OFFICE, WARWICK

TD 69/6.2 A volume of holograph letters and papers relating to the earl of Essex, owned by the earl of Aylesford.

WOBURN ABBEY, WOBURN, BEDFORDSHIRE

Russell MSS
HMC 12 Correspondence of Sir William Russell, 1594.
HMC 13 Journal of Sir William Russell, June 1594–May 1597.

PRINTED

Academiae Cantabrigensis lachrymae, London, 1587. (*STC* no. 447).

Acts of the privy council of England, n.s., X, XIV–XXXII, ed. J. R. Dasent, London, 1897–1907.

Adams, S. (ed.), *Household accounts and disbursement books of Robert Dudley, earl of Leicester, 1558–1561, 1584–1586*, Camden Society, 5th ser., VI, Cambridge, 1996.

Akrigg, G. P. V. (ed.), *Letters of James VI & I*, Berkeley, Los Angeles and London, 1984.

Andrews, K. R., *The last voyage of Drake & Hawkins*, Hakluyt Society, 2nd ser., CXLII, 1972.

Anon., *A select collection of interesting autograph letters of celebrated persons, English and foreign ... engraved in exact facsimile of the originals*, Stuttgart, 1849.

Anon., *A treatise paranetical, that is to say: an exhortation ... by a pilgrim Spaniard ...*, London, 1598 (*STC* no. 19838).

Anon., *Ephemeris expditionis Norreysii & Draki in Lusitaniam*, London, 1589 (*STC* no. 18653).

Arber, E. (ed.), *A transcript of the registers of the Company of Stationers of London, 1554–1640 AD*, 5 vols., priv. pr., London, 1875–94.

Arnold, J., *Queen Elizabeth's wardrobe unlock'd: the inventories of the wardrobe of robes prepared in July 1600 ...*, London, 1988.

Bacon, Sir Francis, *Sir Francis Bacon his apologie, in certaine imputations concerning the late earle of Essex*, London, 1604 (*STC* no. 1111).

Bailsdon, W. P., *Les reportes del cases in Camera Stellata 1593 to 1609 from the original MS of John Hawarde of the Inner Temple*, priv. pr., 1894.

Baker, T., *History of the College of St John the Evangelist, Cambridge*, ed. J. E. B. Major, 2 vols., Cambridge, 1869.

Bannerman, W. B. (ed.), *The registers of St Olave, Hart Street, London, 1563–1700*, Harleian Society, XLVI, London, 1916.

Barlowe, William, *The navigators supply: conteining many things of principall importance belonging to navigation*, London, 1597 (*STC* no. 1445).

Batho, G. R. (ed.), *The household papers of Henry Percy, ninth earl of Northumberland (1564–1632)*, Camden Society, 3rd ser., XCIII, 1962.

Beal, P. (ed.), *Index of English literary manuscripts. Vol. I, 1450–1625*, 2 parts, London and New York, 1980.

Birch, T., *Memoirs of the reign of Queen Elizabeth, from the year 1581 till her death, from the original papers of ... Anthony Bacon*, 2 vols., London, 1754.

Blandie, William, *The five bookes of the famous, learned and eloquent man, Hieronimus Osorius, contayninge a discourse of civill, and Christian nobilitie ...*, London, 1576 (*STC* no. 18886).

Blok, P. J., *Correspondance inedite de Robert Dudley, comte de Leycester, et de François et Jean Hotman*, Haarlem, 1911.

[Bodley, Sir Thomas], *The life of Thomas Bodley ... written by himselfe*, Oxford, 1647 (Wing no. B 3392).

Bolton, Edmund, 'Hypercritica; or a rule of judgment for writing, or reading our historys ... ', in J. Haslewood (ed.), *Ancient critical essays upon English poets and poesy*, London, 1815.

Bond, E. A. (ed.), *Russia at the end of the sixteenth century*, Hakluyt Society, 1st ser., XX, London, 1856.

Bownde, Nicholas, *The doctrine of the sabbath, plainely layde forth, and soundly proved* . . . , London, 1595 (*STC* no. 3436).

Brodrick, G. C., *Memorials of Merton College*, Oxford Historical Society, IV, 1885.

Brooke, Ralph, *A discoverie of certaine errours published in the much commended Britannia*, London, 1594 (*STC* no. 3834).

Broughton, Hugh, *Moses his sights on Sinai*, n.pl., 1592 (*STC* no. 3873).

Bruce, J. (ed.), *Correspondence of James VI of Scotland with Sir Robert Cecil and others in England, during the reign of Queen Elizabeth* . . . , Camden Society, LXXVIII, 1861.

Correspondence of Robert Dudley, earl of Leycester, during his government of the Low Countries, in the years 1585 and 1586, Camden Society, XXVII, 1844.

Burke, J. and Burke, J. B., *A genealogical and heraldic history of the extinct and dormant baronetcies of England, Ireland and Scotland*, 2nd edn, London, 1844.

Burne, S. A. H., 'The Staffordshire quarter sessions rolls', 1581–97, *Collections for a history of Staffordshire*, 1931 for 1929, 1932 for 1930 and 1933 for 1932 volumes.

Butler, G. G., *The Edmondes papers*, Roxburghe Club, Westminster, 1913.

Cabala, sive scrinia sacra: mysteries of state and government in letters of illustrious persons and great ministers of state, 2nd edn, London, 1691 (Wing no. C 186).

Calendar of letters and state papers, relating to English affairs, preserved principally in the archives of Simancas, III–IV, ed. M. A. S. Hume, London, 1896–9.

Calendar of state papers and muniments, relating to English affairs, existing in the archives and collections of Venice, and in other libraries of northern Italy, VIII–IX, ed. H. F. Brown, London, 1894–7.

Calendar of state papers, colonial series, East Indies, China and Japan, 1513–1616, preserved in Her Majesty's Public Record Office, and elsewhere, ed. W. N. Sainsbury, London, 1862.

Calendar of state papers, domestic series, of the reign of Elizabeth, preserved in Her Majesty's Public Record Office, 1581–1603, eds. R. Lemon and M. A. E. Lemon, London, 1865–70.

Calendar of state papers, foreign series. of the reign of Elizabeth, XVIII–XXIII, eds. S. C. Lomas, A. B. Hinds and R. B. Wernham, London, 1914–50.

Calendar of state papers relating to Ireland, of the reign of Elizabeth, III–VI, VIII, eds. H. C. Hamilton and E. G. Atkinson, London, 1880–1900.

Calendar of the state papers relating to Scotland and Mary, Queen of Scots, 1547–1603, preserved in the Public Record Office and elsewhere in England, III–XII, eds. W. K. Boyd, H. W. Meikle, A. I. Cameron and M. S. Giuseppi, Edinburgh and Glasgow, 1910–52.

Calendar of the Wynn (of Gwydir) papers, 1515–1690, in the National Library of Wales and elsewhere, Aberystwyth, Cardiff and London, 1926.

Camden, William, *Reges, reginae, nobiles & alii in ecclesia collegiata B. Petri Westmonasterii sepulti, usque ad annum reparatae salutis 1600*, London, 1600 (*STC* no. 4518).

Remaines concerning Britaine: but especially England, and the inhabitants thereof, 2nd edn, London, 1614 (*STC* no. 4522).

The history of the most renowned and victorious Princess Elizabeth, late queen of England, 4th edn, London, 1688 (Wing no. C 363).

Cameron, A. I. (ed.), *The Warrender papers*, 2 vols., Scottish History Society, 3rd ser., XIX, 1931–2.

Caraman, P., *John Gerard: the autobiography of an Elizabethan*, 2nd edn, London, New York and Toronto, 1956.

Castiglione, Baldesar, *The book of the courtier*, ed. G. Bull, Harmondsworth, 1967.

[Cayet, Pierre], *Chronologie novenaire, contenant l'histoire de la guerre, sous le regne du tres chrestien roy de France & de Navarre Henri IIII*, 3 vols., Paris, 1608.

Chappell, W. (ed.), *The Roxburghe ballads*, 2nd edn, The Ballad Society, 8 vols., 1877–95.

Charles, B. G. (ed.), *Calendar of the records of the borough of Haverfordwest 1539–1660*, Board of Celtic Studies, University of Wales, History and Law Series, XXIV, Cardiff, 1967.

Churchyard, Thomas, *A musicall consort of heavenly harmonie . . . called Churchyard's charitie*, London, 1595 (*STC* no. 5245).

Churchyards challenge, London, 1593 (*STC* no. 5220).

Clapham, John, *Elizabeth of England: certain observations concerning the life and reign of Queen Elizabeth*, eds. E. P. Read and C. Read, Philadelphia, 1951.

Clifford, D. J. H. (ed.), *The diaries of Lady Anne Clifford*, Stroud, 1990.

C[okayne], G. E., *The complete peerage of England Ireland Great Britain and the United Kingdom extant extinct or dormant*, eds. V. Gibbs *et al.*, 13 vols. in 14, London, 1910–59.

Collins, A., *Letters and memorials of state . . . [of the Sidney family] . . . from the originals at Penshurst Place in Kent*, 2 vols., London, 1746.

[Colonna, Francesco], *Hypnerotomachia: the strife of love in a dreame*, London, 1592 (*STC* no. 5577).

Coningsby, Sir Thomas, 'Journal of the siege of Rouen, 1591' (ed. J. G. Nichols), *Camden Miscellany* 1 (1847).

Cooke, W. H., *Collections towards the history and antiquities of the county of Hereford. In continuation of Duncumb's history*, 2 vols., London, 1892.

Corbett, J. S. (ed.), 'Relation of the voyage to Cadiz, 1596; by Sir William Slyngsbie', *Naval miscellany* 1, Navy Records Society, London, 1902.

Crino, A. M., 'Avvisi di Londra di Petruccio Ubaldini, fiorentino, relativi agli anni 1579–1594, con notizie sulla guerra di Flandra', *Archivio Storico Italiano* 127 (1969), pp. 461–581.

Croft, P., *The Spanish Company*, London, Record Society, IX, 1973.

Dallington, Robert, *The view of France*, London, 1604 (*STC* no. 6202).

Davies, Richard, *A funerall sermon preached the xxvi day of November in the yeare of Our Lord MDLXXVI in the parishe church of Caermerthyn . . . at the buriall of the right honourable Walter earle of Essex and Ewe . . .* , London, 1577 (*STC* no. 6364).

De Maisse, [André Hurault, seigneur de,] *A journal of all that was accomplished by Monsieur de Maisse ambassador in England from Henri IV to Queen Elizabeth anno domini 1597*, eds. G. B. Harrison and R. A. Jones, London, 1931.

[Devereux, Robert, 2nd earl of Essex], *An apologie of the earle of Essex, against those which jealously, and maliciously, tax him to be the hinderer of the peace and quiet of his country*, London, 1603 (*STC* no. 6788).

Devereux, W. B., *Lives and letters of the Devereux, earls of Essex, in the reigns of Elizabeth, James I, and Charles I, 1540–1646*, 2 vols., London, 1853.

Dictionary of literary biography, continuing series, Detroit, 1978–.

Dictionary of national biography, eds. L. Stephen and S. Lee, 22 vols., London, 1885–1900, 1908–9 edn.

Dictionary of Welsh biography down to 1940, produced under the auspices of the Honourable Society of Cymmrodorion, London, 1959.

Dillingham, W. (ed.), 'The commentaries of Sir Francis Vere, being divers pieces of service, wherein he had command; written by himself, in way of commentary', in E. Arber, *An English garner: ingatherings from our history and literature*, 8 vols., Westminster, 1895–6.

'Documentos relativos á la toma y saco de Cádiz por los ingleses en julio de 1596', in *Colección de documentos ineditos para la historia de Espana*, 36 (Madrid, 1860), pp. 205–467.

Doleman, R., *A conference about the next succession to the crowne of Ingland*, n.pl., 1594 (*STC* no. 19398).

Donno, E. S. (ed.), *An Elizabethan in 1582: the diary of Richard Madox, fellow of All Souls*, Hakluyt Society, 2nd ser., CXLVII, 1976.

Sir John Harington's A new discourse on a stale subject, called the metamorphosis of Ajax, London, 1962.

Edwards, E., *The life and letters of Sir Walter Ralegh*, 2 vols., London, 1868.

[Egerton, Francis H., 8th earl of Bridgewater], *The life of Thomas Egerton lord chancellor of England*, Paris, [1816].

Erdswicke, Sampson, *A survey of Staffordshire; containing the antiquities of that county*, ed. T. Harwood, London, 1844.

Evans, J. X. (ed.), *The works of Sir Roger Williams*, Oxford, 1972.

Ferne, John, *The blazon of gentrie: devided into two partes ...* , London, 1586 (*STC* no. 10824).

Fisher, G. W., *Annals of Shrewsbury School*, London, 1899.

Fitz-Geffrey, Charles, *Sir Francis Drake his honorable life's commendation and tragicall death's lamentation*, Oxford, 1596 (*STC* no. 10943).

Foster, C. W. (ed.), *Lincoln episcopal records in the time of Thomas Cooper, bishop of Lincoln AD 1571 to AD 1584*, Canterbury and York Society, XI, 1913.

Foster, J. (ed.), *Alumni Oxonienses: the members of the University of Oxford, 1500–1714*, 4 vols., Oxford, 1891–2.

Churchwardens' accounts of St Mary the Great, Cambridge, from 1504 to 1635, Cambridge Antiquarian Society, octavo series, XXXV, 1905.

Freeman, A., 'Essex to Stella: two letters from the earl of Essex to Penelope Rich', *English Literary Renaissance* 3 (1973), pp. 248–50.

Furnivall, F. J. and Morvill, W. R. (eds.), *Ballads from manuscripts*, 2 vols., The Ballad Society, London, 1868–73.

Gager, William, *Meleager*, Oxford, 1592 (*STC* no. 11515).

Gaskell, P., 'Books bought by Whitgift's pupils in the 1570s', *Transactions of the Cambridge Bibliographical Society* 7 (1977–80), pp. 284–93.

Gentili, Alberico, *De iniustitia bellica Romanorum actio*, Oxford, 1590 (*STC* no. 11734).

De iure belli commentatio prima, London, 1588 (*STC* no. 11734.3).

De iure belli commentatio secunda, London, 1589 (*STC* no. 11734.7).

De iure belli commentationes duae, London, 1589 (*STC* no. 11735).

De iure belli commentatio tertia, London, 1589 (*STC* no. 11735.3).

De iure belli libri tres, 2 vols., Oxford and London, 1933 edn.

Goodman, Godfrey, *The Court of King James the First*, ed. J. Brewer, 2 vols., London, 1839.

Greenlaw, E., Osgood, C. G., Padelford, F. M., *et al.* (eds.), *The works of Edmund Spenser: a variorum edition*, 10 vols., Baltimore, 1932–57.

Greville, Sir Fulke, *Life of Sir Philip Sidney*, ed. N. Smith, Oxford, 1907.

Groos, G. W. (ed.), *The diary of Baron Waldstein: a traveller in Elizabethan England*, London, 1981.

Gyfford, George, *A treatise of true fortitude*, London, 1594 (*STC* no. 11870).

Sermons upon the whole booke of the Revelation, London, 1596 (*STC* no. 11866).

Haak, S. P. (ed.), *Johan van Oldenbarnevelt: bescheiden betreffende zijn staatkundig beleid en zijn familie, 1570–1601*, 'S-Gravenhage, 1934.

Halliwell, J. O. (ed.), *The private diary of Dr John Dee, and the catalogue of his library of manuscripts*, Camden Society, XIX, 1842.

Ham, R. E., 'The autobiography of Sir James Croft', *BIHR* 50 (1977), pp. 48–57.

Hammer, P. E. J., 'Essex and Europe: evidence from confidential instructions by the earl of Essex, 1595–6', *EHR* 111 (1996), pp. 357–81.

'New light on the Cadiz expedition of 1596', *Historical Research* 70 (1997), pp. 182–202.

Harington, Sir John, *A tract on the succession to the crowne (AD 1602)*, ed. C. R. Markham, Roxburghe Club, London, 1880.

Harvey, Richard, *Ephemeron, sive paean, in gratiam perpurgatae reformataeque dialecticae*, London, 1583 (*STC* no. 12912).

Philadelphus, or a defence of Brutus, and the Brutans history, London, 1593 (*STC* no. 12913).

A theologicall discourse of the Lamb of God and his enemies ..., London, 1590 (*STC* no. 12915).

Hasler, P. W. (ed.), *The history of parliament. The House of Commons 1558–1603*, 3 vols., London, 1981.

Herford, C. H. and Simpson, P. (eds.), *Ben Jonson[: life and works]*, 11 vols., Oxford, 1925–52.

Heywood, T. (ed.), *Cardinal Allen's defence of Sir William Stanley's surrender of Deventer, January 29, 1586–7*, Chetham Society, XXV, 1851.

HMC. A calendar of the manuscripts of the Most Hon. the marquis of Salisbury, KG, &c, preserved at Hatfield House, Hertfordshire, II–VII, XIII–XIV, XXIII, London, 1888–1973.

HMC. Calendar of the manuscripts of the Most Honourable the Marquess of Bath preserved at Longleat, Wiltshire, 5 vols., London, 1904–80.

HMC. Eighth report, appendix i, London, 1881.

HMC. Eleventh report, appendix iii, London, 1887.

HMC. Fifteenth report, appendix v, London, 1897.

HMC. Fifth report, London, 1876.

HMC. Ninth report, appendix i, London, 1883.

HMC. Report on manuscripts in various collections, VII, London, 1914.

HMC. Report on the manuscripts of the earl of Ancaster, preserved at Grimsthorpe, Dublin, 1907.

HMC. Report on the manuscripts of Lord De L'Isle and Dudley preserved at Penshurst Place, I–II, London, 1925–34.

HMC. Seventh report, appendix, London, 1879.

HMC. Supplementary report on the manuscripts of the earl of Mar & Kellie preserved at Alloa House, Clacmannanshire, London, 1930.

HMC. Twelfth report, appendix, part iv. The manuscripts of His Grace the duke of Rutland, GCB, preserved at Belvoir Castle, I, London, 1888.

HMC. Twelfth report, appendix ix, London, 1891.

Holinshed, Raphael, *The chronicles of England, Scotlande and Irelande*, 3 vols., London, 1587 (*STC* no. 13569).

Holinshed, [Raphael], *Chronicles of England, Scotland and Ireland*, 6 vols., London, 1807–8 edn.

[Holland, Henry], *A treatise against witchcraft* ... , Cambridge, 1590 (*STC* no. 13590).

Horne, D. H., *The life and minor works of George Peele*, New Haven and London, 1952.

Hubbocke, William, *An apologie of infants in a sermon: proving by the revealed word of God, that children prevented by death of their baptisme, by God's election, may be saved*, London, 1595 (*STC* no. 13898).

Hughes, C., 'Nicholas Faunt's discourse touching the office of principal secretary of estate, &c 1592', *EHR* 20 (1905), pp. 499–508.

Hume, Alexander, *A rejoynder to Doctor Hil concerning the decense of Christ into hell*, Edinburgh, 1594 (*STC* no. 13948).

Humphrey, Lawrence, *The nobles, or of nobilitye: the original nature, dutyes, right and Christian institucion thereof*, London, 1563 (*STC* no. 13964).

Inderwicke, F. A. (ed.), *A calendar of the Inner Temple records*, 5 vols., London, 1896–1936.

Jeayes, I. H. (ed.), *Letters of Philip Gawdy of West Harling, Norfolk, and of London to various members of his family 1579–1616*, Roxburghe Club, London, 1906.

Jones, H. V.,'The journal of Levinus Munck', *EHR* 68 (1953), pp. 234–58.

Journal of the House of Lords, II, London, 1846.

Knox, T. F. (ed.), *Records of the English Catholics under the penal laws. Chiefly from the archives of the see of Westminster. II. The letters and memorials of William Cardinal Allen (1532–1594)*, London, 1882.

Laing, D., *Original letters of Mr John Colville 1582–1603. To which is added his palinode, 1600*, Bannatyne Club, CIV, Edinburgh, 1858.

Larke, John, *The boke of noblenes, that showeth how many sortes & kyndes there is* ... , London, n.d. [*c.* 1550?] (*STC* no. 3325).

Law, T. G. (ed.), 'Documents illustrating Catholic policy in the reign of James VI, 1596–1598', *Miscellany of the Scottish History Society* 1 (1893), pp. 3–70.

Legh, Gerard, *The accedens of armory*, London, 1562 (*STC* no. 15392).

Le Laboureur, J. (ed.), *Les memoires de Messire Michel de Castelneau, seigneur de Mauvissiere*, 3 vols., Brussels, 1731.

Lewknor, Lewis, *The estate of English fugitives under the king of Spaine and his ministers*, London, 1595 and 1596 edns (*STC* nos. 15564–5).

List and analysis of state papers, foreign series, Elizabeth I, preserved in the Public Record Office, ed. R. B. Wernham, 6 vols., London, 1964–94.

Lysias (ed. by Andrew Downes), *Eratosthenes, hoc est, brevis et luculenta defensio Lysiae pro caede Eratosthenis*, Cambridge, 1593 (*STC* no. 17121).

MacGregor, A. (ed.), *The late king's goods: collections, possessions and patronage of Charles I in the light of the Commonwealth sale inventories*, London and Oxford, 1989.

M[aidment], J. (ed.), *Letters and papers during the reign of King James the Sixth. Chiefly from the manuscript collections of Sir James Balfour of Denmyln*, Abbotsford Club, Edinburgh, 1838.

Malden, H. E., 'Devereux papers, with Richard Broughton's miscellanea (1575–1601)', *Camden Miscellany*, n.s., XIII (1923).

Mares, F. H. (ed.), *The memoirs of Robert Carey*, Oxford, 1972.

Markham, A. H. (ed.), *The voyages and works of John Davis the navigator*, Hakluyt Society, 1st ser., LIX, London, 1880.

May, S. W., 'The poems of Edward de Vere, seventeenth earl of Oxford, and of Robert Devereux, second earl of Essex', *Studies in Philology* 77, special fifth no. (1980).

McClure, N. E. (ed.), *The letters and epigrams of Sir John Harington together with 'The prayse of private lyfe'*, Philadelphia, 1930.

The letters of John Chamberlain, 2 vols., American Philosophical Society, Memoirs, XII, 1939.

Meads, D. M. (ed.), *The diary of Lady Margaret Hoby*, London, 1930.

Merson, A. L., *The third book of remembrance of Southampton 1514–1602*, III, *1573–1589*, Southampton Records Series, VIII, 1965.

Moffet, Thomas, *Healths improvement*, London, 1655 (Wing no. M 2382).

Nobilis or a view of the life and death of a Sidney, ed. V. B. Heltzel and H. H. Hudson, San Marino, 1940.

Moore-Smith, G. C., *Gabriel Harvey's marginalia*, Stratford-upon-Avon, 1913.

Moresin, Thomas, *Papatus, seu depravatae religionis origo et incrementum ...* , Edinburgh, 1594 (*STC* no. 18102).

Morison, Fynes, *An itinerary containing his ten yeeres travell ...* , 4 vols., Glasgow, 1907–8 edn.

Morris, J. (ed.), *The letter-books of Sir Amias Poulet keeper of Mary Queen of Scots*, London, 1874.

Mundy, John, *Songs and psalmes composed into 3 4 or 5 partes, for the use and delight of such as either love or learne musicke*, London, 1594 (*STC* no. 18284).

Murdin, W., *A collection of state papers relating to affairs in the reign of Queen Elizabeth, from the year 1571 to 1596 ...* , London, 1759.

Naunton, Sir Robert, *Fragmenta regalia or observations on Queen Elizabeth, her times & favourites*, ed. J. S. Cerovski, Washington, London, and Toronto, 1985.

Nelson, A. H. (ed.), *Records of early English drama: Cambridge*, 2 vols., Toronto, 1989.

Nenna, Giovanni Battista, *Nennio or a treatise of nobility*, trans. William Jones, London, 1595, ed. A. Shalvi, Jerusalem and London, 1967 edn.

Nichols, J. G., *The progresses and public processions of Queen Elizabeth*, 3 vols., London, 1823.

Nichols, J. G. (ed.), *The Unton inventories*, Berkshire Ashmolean Society, London, 1841.

Nichols, Josias, *An order of houshold instruction ...* , London, 1596 (*STC* no. 18540).

Oppenheim, M. (ed.), *The naval commentaries of Sir William Monson*, I, Navy Records Society, XXII, London, 1902.

[Overall, W. H. and Overall, H. C. (eds.)], *Analytical index to the series of records known as the Remembrancia preserved among the archives of the City of London. AD 1579–1664*, London, 1878.

424 *Bibliography*

Park, T. (ed.), *Nugae antiquae: being a miscellaneous collection of original papers* ... *by Sir John Harington Knt*, 2 vols., London, 1804.

Paule, Sir George, *The life of the most reverend and religious prelate John Whitgift lord archbishop of Canterbury*, London, 1612 (*STC* no. 19484).

Peacham, Henry, *Minerva Britannia or a garden of heroicall devises, furnished, and adorned with emblemes and impresas of sundry natures*, London, 1612 (*STC* no. 19511).

Peck, D. C. (ed.), *Leicester's commonwealth: the copy of a letter written by a Master of Art of Cambridge [1584] and related documents*, Athens, Ohio and London, 1985.

' "News from heaven and hell": a defamatory narrative of the earl of Leicester', *English Literary Renaissance* 8 (1978), pp. 141–58.

Peel, A. (ed.), *The notebook of John Penry 1593*, Camden Society, 3rd ser., LXVII, 1944.

Peele, George, *An eglogue gratulatorie* ... *to the* ... *shepheard of Albion's Arcadia*, London, 1589 (*STC* no. 19534).

Percyvall, Richard, *Bibliotheca Hispanica: containing a grammar with a dictionarie in Spanish, English and Latine* ... , London, 1591 (*STC* no. 19619).

Petti, A. G. (ed.), 'Roman Catholicism in Elizabethan and Jacobean Staffordshire: documents from the Bagot Papers', *Collections for a history of Staffordshire*, 4th ser., IX, 1979.

The letters and despatches of Richard Verstegan (c. 1550–1640), Catholic Record Society, LII, 1959.

Philip, John, *The life and death of Sir Philip Sidney* ... , London, 1587 (*STC* no. 19871).

Phillips, John, *The perfect path to paradice* ... , London, 1586 (*STC* no. 19872).

Platt, Hugh, *The jewell house of art and nature*, London, 1594 (*STC* no. 19991).

Plessis, Philippe de Mornay, sieur du, *Memoires et correspondance pour servir l'histoire de la Reformation* ... *Édition complète* ... , 12 vols., Paris, 1824–5.

Plummer, C. (ed.), *Elizabethan Oxford*, Oxford Historical Society, VIII, 1887.

Pollen, J. H., 'Tower bills 1595–1681, with Gatehouse certificates, 1592–1604', *Catholic Record Society Miscellanea* 4 (1907), pp. 217–46.

Poole, R., 'A journal of the siege of Rouen in 1591', *EHR* 17 (1902), pp. 527–37.

Powel, Griffin, *Analysis analyticorum posteriorum sive librorum Aristotelis demonstratione* ... , Oxford, 1594 (*STC* no. 20157).

Profitable instructions: describing what speciall observations are to be taken by travellers in all nations. By Robert, late earle of Essex. Sir Philip Sidney. and Secretary Davison, London, 1633 (*STC* no. 6789).

Prouty, C. T. (ed.), *The life and works of George Peele*, 3 vols., New Haven, 1952–70.

Purchas, S., *Hakluytus posthumus or Purchas his pilgrimes contayning a history of the world, in sea voyages and lande-travells by Englishmen and others*, London, 1625, Glasgow, 1905–7 edn in 20 vols.

[Raine, J.], *The correspondence of Dr Mathew Hutton, archbishop of York* ... , Surtees Society, XVII, London, 1843.

[Rainoldes, John], *De Romanae ecclesiae idolatria* ... , Oxford, 1596 (*STC* no. 20606).

[Ralegh, Sir Walter], *A report of the truth of the fight about the Iles of the Acores*, London, 1591 (*STC* no. 20651).

The discoverie of the large, rich and bewtiful empyre of Guiana, London, 1596 (*STC* no. 20636).

Renold, P. (ed.), *The Wisbech stirs (1595–1598)*, Catholic Record Society, LI, 1958.

Ringler, W. A., *The poems of Sir Philip Sidney*, Oxford, 1962.

Rouse Ball, W. W. and J. A. Venn, *Admissions to Trinity College, Cambridge. II. 1546–1700*, London, 1913.

Rudd, Anthony, *A sermon preached at Richmond before Queene Elizabeth of famous memorie, upon the 28 of March 1596*, London, 1603 (*STC* no. 21432).

Rye, W. B., *England as seen by foreigners in the days of Elizabeth and James the First. Comprising translations of the journals of the two dukes of Wirtermberg in 1592 and 1610 ...*, London, 1865.

Rye, W. (ed.), *The visitacion of Norfolk made and taken [in] ... 1563 ... and also ... 1613 ...*, Harleian Society, XXXII, London, 1891.

Rylands, W. H. (ed.), *The four visitations of Berkshire made and taken [in] ... 1532 ... 1566 ... 1623 and ... 1665–66*, 2 vols., Harleian Society, LVI–LVII, London, 1907–8.

Savile, Henry, *Rerum Anglicorum scriptores post Bedam praecipui*, London, 1596 (*STC* no. 21783).

The ende of Nero and beginninge of Galba. Fower bookes of the Histories of Cornelius Tacitus. The life of Agricola, [London], 1591 (*STC* no. 23642).

Saviolo, Vincentio, *Vincentio Saviolo his practise. In two bookes. The first entreating of the use of the rapier and dagger. The second, of honor and honorable quarrels*, London, 1595 (*STC* no. 21788).

Scott, H. S. (ed.), 'The journal of Sir Roger Wilbraham solicitor-general in Ireland and master of requests for the years 1593–1616', *Camden Miscellany*, X 1902.

Scott, S. D. (ed.), '" A booke of orders and rules": of Anthony Viscount Montague in 1595', *Sussex Archaeological Collections, relating to the history and antiquities of the county* 7 (1854), pp. 173–212.

Segar, William, *Honor military and civill*, London, 1602 (*STC* no. 22164).

Short-title catalogue of books printed in England, Scotland and Ireland, and of English books printed abroad 1475–1640, eds. A. W. Pollard and G. R. Redgrave, revised by W. A. Jackson, F. S. Ferguson and K. F. Pantzer, 3 vols., London, 1976–91.

Short title catalogue of books printed in England, Scotland, Ireland, Wales and British America, and of English books printed in other countries, 1641–1700, ed. D. Wing, 3 vols., 1945–51, 2nd edn, New York, 1972–88.

Sidney, Sir Philip, *A defence of poetry*, ed. J. A. van Dorsten, Oxford, 1966.

Simpson, E. *et al.* (eds.), *John Donne: selected prose*, Oxford, 1967.

Skelton, R. A. and Summerson, J., *A description of the maps and architectural plans in the collection made by William Cecil, First Baron Burghley, now at Hatfield House*, Roxburghe Club, Oxford, 1971.

Smith, A. H. and Baker, G. M. (eds.), *The papers of Nathaniel Bacon of Stiffkey*, III, *1586–1595*, Norfolk Record Society, LIII, 1987 and 1988.

Smith, L. P., *The life and letters of Sir Henry Wotton*, 2 vols., Oxford, 1907.

Smith, W. J. (ed.), *Calendar of Salusbury correspondence 1553–circa 1700 ...*, Board of Celtic Studies, University of Wales, History and Law Series, XIV, Cardiff, 1954.

Sotheby's of London, sale catalogues issued by:
Sale of 12 and 13 June 1911 (the library of Henry and Alfred H. Huth), lot 62: letter from Sir Francis Drake to Essex, 16 February 1588.

Sale of 25 April 1912, lot 46, transcript on pp. 13–14: letter from Essex to Jean Hotman, 30 June [1590].

Sale of 21 July 1916, p. 24, lot 136: letter from Essex to Sir John Spencer, 30 July 1588.

Sale of 14 December 1992, whole catalogue: sale of the Hulton Papers.

Spedding, J. (ed.), *The letters and life of Francis Bacon, including all his occasional works*, 7 vols., London, 1861–74.

Spedding, J., Ellis, R. L. and Heath, D. D. (eds.), *The works of Francis Bacon*, 7 vols., London, 1857–9.

Stern, V. F., *Gabriel Harvey: his life, marginalia and library*, Oxford, 1979.

Stevenson, R. J. (ed.), *Correspondence of Sir Henry Unton, knt, ambassador from Queen Elizabeth to Henry IV king of France, in the years MDXCI and MDXCII*, Roxburghe Club, London, 1847.

Story, G. M. and Gardner, H. (eds.), *The sonnets of William Alabaster*, London, 1959.

Stow, John, *The annales of England, faithfully collected out of the most autenticall authors, records and other monuments of antiquitie, from the first inhabitation untill this present yeere 1601*, London, 1601 (*STC* no. 23336).

A summarie of the chronicles of England, London, 1598 (*STC* no. 23328).

Stoye, J. W., 'An early letter from John Chamberlain', *EHR* 62 (1947), pp. 522–32.

Strype, J., *Annals of the Reformation and the establishment of religion, and other various occurrences in the Church of England . . .* , 4 vols., London, 1709–31.

Sullivan, E. (ed.), *The civile conversation of M. Steeven Guazzo: the first three books translated by George Pettie, anno 1581, and the fourth by Barth[o-lomew] Young, anno 1586*, 2 vols., London and New York, 1925.

Sutcliffe, Matthew, *de Catholica orthodoxa et vera Christi ecclesia*, London, 1592 (*STC* no. 23455).

The practice, procedings and lawes of armes . . . , London, 1593 (*STC* no. 23468).

Talbot, C., *Recusant records*, Catholic Record Society, LIII, Miscellanea, 1961 for 1960.

Tenison, E. M., *Elizabethan England: being the history of this country 'in relation to all foreign princes'*, 12 vols. in 13, pr. for subscribers, Leamington Spa, 1933–61.

Thibaudeau, A. W. (ed.), *Catalogue of the collection of autograph letters and historical documents formed between 1865 and 1882 by Alfred Morrison*, II, priv. pr., 1885.

Tomkys, John, *A sermon preached the 26 day of May 1584 in S. Maries Church in Shreswesbury*, London, 1586 (*STC* no. 24110).

Ungerer, G., *A Spaniard in Elizabethan England: the correspondence of Antonio Perez's exile*, 2 vols., London, 1974–6.

van Deventer, M. L., *Gedenkstukken van Oldenbarnevelt en zijn tijd*, 3 vols., 'S Gravenhage, 1860–5.

Venn, J. and Venn, J. A., *Alumni Cantabrigienses: a biographical list of all known students, graduates and holders of office at the University of Cambridge from the earliest times to 1900. Part I. From the earliest times to 1751*, 4 vols., Cambridge, 1922–7.

Victoria history of the counties of England, The, continuing series, London and elsewhere, 1900–.

von Bulow, G. (ed.), 'Diary of the journey of Philip Julius, duke of Stettin-

Pomerania, through England in the year 1602', *Transactions of the Royal Historical Society*, 2nd ser., 6 (1892), pp. 1–67.

'Journey through England and Scotland made by Leopold von Wedel in the years 1584 and 1585', *Transactions of the Royal Historical Society*, n.s., 9 (1895), pp. 223–70.

von Klarwill, V. (ed.), *Queen Elizabeth and some foreigners, being a series of hitherto unpublished letters from the archives of the Hapsburg family*, trans. T. H. Nash, London, 1928.

The Fugger letters, second series, being a further selection from the Fugger papers specially relating to Queen Elizabeth and matters relating to England during the years 1568–1605, trans. L. S. Byrne, London, 1926.

Watson, Thomas, *The first sett of Italian madrigalls Englished* . . . , London, 1590 (*STC* no. 25119).

Wernham, R. B., *The expedition of Sir John Norris and Sir Francis Drake to Spain and Portugal, 1589*, Navy Records Society, CXXVII, 1988.

Whitaker, William, *Praelectiones* . . . *in quibus tractatur controversia de conciliis*, Cambridge, 1600 (*STC* no. 25367).

Willet, Andrew, *Synopsis papismi* . . . , London, 1592 (*STC* no. 25696).

Sacrorum emblamatum centuria una . . . , Cambridge, [1592] (*STC* no. 25695).

Williams, Sir Roger, *A briefe discourse of warre*, London, 1590 (*STC* no. 25732).

Wilson, Thomas, 'The state of England, anno dom. 1600', ed. F. J. Fisher, *Camden Miscellany*, XVI (1936).

[Wingfield, Anthony], *A true coppie of a discourse written by a gentleman, employed in the late voyage of Spaine and Portingale*, London, 1589 (*STC* no. 6790).

Wood, A. A., *Athenae Oxonienses: an exact history of all the writers and bishops who have had their education in the University of Oxford. To which are added the fasti, or annals, of the said university*, ed. P. Bliss, 4 vols., Oxford, 1891–2.

Wotton, Sir Henry, *A parallel betweene Robert, late earle of Essex, and George late duke of Buckingham*, London, 1641 (Wing no. W 3647).

Reliquiae Wottonianae, or a collection of lives, letters [and] poems with characters of sundry persons, 4th edn, London, 1685 (Wing no. W 3651).

The state of Christendom: or, a most exact and curious discovery of many passages, and hidden mysteries of the times, London, 1657.

Wright, L. B. (ed.), *Advice to a son: precepts of Lord Burghley, Sir Walter Raleigh and Francis Osborne*, Ithaca, N.Y., 1962.

Wright, T., *Queen Elizabeth and her times*, 2 vols., London, 1838.

Xivrey, [J.] Berger de (ed.), *Recueil des letters missives de Henri IV*, III–IV, Paris, 1846–8.

INDEX

['Sir' in parentheses indicates that the person received the title during the period 1585–97]

Drake, Sir Francis 45, 62, 74–5, 82, 189, 260, 366, 368, 372
  and Essex 82–3, 258, 260
  see also military operations
Draper (or Diapar), Robert 159–60
Drayton Bassett 33, 271, 272
du Plessis 108, 143
Dudley, Ambrose, earl of Warwick (d. 1590) 33, 35, 61, 100, 123, 279
Dudley, Anne (née Russell), countess of Warwick 66, 85, 91, 130, 281, 284, 288, 289, 290, 296, 302, 385
Dudley, Lettice (née Knollys), countess of Leicester, widow of Walter, 1st earl of Essex, mother of 2nd earl 13, 15–16, 33, 46, 55, 96, 130, 131, 271, 272, 280–1
Dudley, Robert (illeg. son of Leicester) 35, 130, 148,
Dudley, Robert, earl of Leicester (d. 1588) 2, 14, 25, 27, 32, 39, 42–3, 44, 45–6, 48, 50–1, 53, 63, 70, 71, 74, 81, 88, 92, 94, 100, 104, 107, 114, 133, 136, 141, 148, 167, 169, 170, 184, 199, 206, 211, 213, 217, 218, 237, 247, 286, 299, 303, 307, 374, 375, 382, 389, 390, 391, 392
  politics:
  appointed lord steward (June 1587) 60–1
  character assassinations of 33, 36–7
  death of 76
  and expedition to Low Countries (1585–6) 37, 46ff.
  and expedition to Low Countries (1587) 61, 70
  marriage of (1578) 33, 35
  reputation of 64
  wills of 52, 70
  relationships with others:
  Burghley 34, 37–8, 39–40, 42–6, 48, 49–50, 58, 59–60, 67, 88
  Elizabeth 33, 39, 42–3, 46, 49–50, 57–8, 60–1
  Essex 4, 15, 16, 17, 32ff., 58ff., 66, 70ff., 76ff., 83, 88–91, 130–1, 141, 170, 199, 211, 230, 269, 278, 279, 280, 287, 300, 301, 306, 316, 317, 324ff., 335, 341, 401
  Hatton 43, 49, 57–8, 67
  Ralegh 63, 64–5
  Walsingham 39–40, 42–6, 49–50, 58, 67
Dudley, Robert, Lord Denbigh (d. 1584) 35, 59
Dudley, (Sir) Robert (illeg. son of Leicester) 35–6, 301, 305
duelling 64, 84
Dunwich 277
Durham 32

Duyvenvoord, Jan van 264, 299
Dyer, (Sir) Edward 61, 62, 102, 190, 290, 328, 364

Edinburgh 91, 173, 212
Edmondes, (Sir) Thomas 181, 195–6, 246, 357
Edward VI 2
Eedes, Richard 32
Egerton, (Sir) Thomas 182, 212, 290, 339, 364, 375
Egerton, Stephen 377
Elizabeth I, queen of England
  and Court 57–8, 59–60, 60–1, 84–5, 96, 100–1, 170, 317–18, 319–20, 360–1, 375, 383
  as Cynthia 68
  and Europe 128–9, 221, 243ff.
  and faction 1ff., 263–4, 359–61, 374–5, 383, 389, 390, 391, 395ff.
  and favourites 56–8, 67, 76, 84–6, 89–90, 100–1, 146, 391
  and gender 40, 329ff.
  and government 40–1, 43, 44, 46, 49–50, 59–60, 67, 71, 75, 85, 98, 101, 102–3, 104–6, 117, 118–19, 152, 155, 162, 165ff., 186, 193, 217, 219, 236–7, 255, 295, 314–15, 327, 329–30, 332, 344, 359–61, 361–2, 353–4, 365, 367–8, 372, 383–4, 390, 391, 400–1
  as Juno 242–3, 246, 320
  mortality of 57, 92, 355, 363–4, 392, 395
  and peace talks 65, 70, 71, 75, 138, 162, 245–6, 384, 402
  and Scotland 165ff., 193
  visit to Oxford (1592) 302–3, 305
  war aims of 39–41, 44, 45–6, 48, 75, 102–3, 243–4, 248–9, 251, 255, 261–2, 263–4, 354, 361, 367–8, 372–3, 393
  relationships with others:
  Burghley 58, 59–60, 67, 100, 105, 144, 220, 329, 332–3, 352–3, 360, 364, 367, 384, 398
  Cecil 100, 332–3, 342, 352–3, 360
  Essex 54, 55ff., 71, 72, 74, 77, 83ff., 92, 95, 98, 103ff., 111ff., 117, 129, 132, 138, 140–1, 145, 146, 148, 152, 161, 166, 173–4, 180–1, 186, 187, 188, 192, 200–1, 203, 208, 220, 221ff., 227–8, 233–4, 238–9, 242ff., 247, 248ff., 251, 252, 254, 261–2, 265, 266, 267–8, 269–70, 274–5, 277, 279, 282, 295, 296–7, 312–13, 314–15, 316ff., 341, 346, 350, 351–2, 366, 367–8, 372–3, 374–5, 379–81, 386ff., 392ff., 402ff.

Cambridge Studies in Early Modern British History

Titles in the series

* Also published as a paperback